DICTIONARY OF TERRORISM

Terrorism is one of the primary concerns of the modern world and is increasingly becoming a major factor in all international relations in the twenty-first century. This revised and updated second edition of a major reference work in the area contains definitions and descriptions of all aspects of terrorism and political violence, including:

- Individual terrorists (e.g. Abu Nidal, Yasser Arafat, Carlos, Osama Bin Laden, Unabomber)
- Terrorist organisations (e.g. Al-Qaeda, FARC, Hizbullah, IRA, Shining Path)
- Terrorist incidents (e.g. Bali bombing, Oklahoma bombing, September 11, Omagh bombing)
- Countries affected by terrorism (e.g. Colombia, Iraq, Israel, Northern Ireland)
- Types of terrorism (e.g. bio-terrorism, cyber-terrorism, eco-terrorism)
- Measures against terrorism (e.g. CIA, counter-terrorism, Europol, FBI)
- Forms of political violence (e.g. civil war, ethnic conflict, kidnapping)
- History of terrorism (e.g. terrorism in the 1960s, twenty-first-century terrorism)
- Psychology of terrorism (e.g. terrorist beliefs, terrorist types)

With a select bibliography for each reference and a detailed cross-referencing system throughout, the revised edition is an excellent resource for academics, students and policy-makers alike.

John Richard Thackrah commenced his study of terrorism at the Institute for the Study of Conflict in London. Afterwards he created courses on Terrorism and Political Ideology at the Police Staff College, Bramshill. He has written books on twentieth-century history and politics including articles and books on terrorism and conflict.

DICTIONARY OF TERRORISM

Second edition

John Richard Thackrah

Routledge
Taylor & Francis Group

LONDON AND NEW YORK

First published 2004
by Routledge
11 New Fetter Lane, London EC4P 4EE

Simultaneously published in the USA and Canada
by Routledge
29 West 35th Street, New York, NY 10001

Routledge is an imprint of the Taylor & Francis Group

© 2004 John Richard Thackrah

Typeset in Baskerville by Taylor & Francis Books Ltd
Printed and bound in Great Britain by
TJ International Ltd, Padstow, Cornwall

British Library Cataloguing in Publication Data
A catalogue record for this book is available from the British Library

Library of Congress Cataloging in Publication Data
Thackrah, John Richard
Dictionary of Terrorism/John Richard Thackrah
p. cm
Revised and updated ed. of: Encyclopaedia of Terrorism and Political
Violence. 1987.
Includes bibliographical references and index.
1. Terrorism–Dictionaries. I. Thackrah, John Richard. Encyclopaedia of
Terrorism and Political Violence. II. Title
HV6431.T56 2004

ISBN 0–415–29820–2 (hbk)
ISBN 0–415–29821–0 (pbk)

Contents

Preface and Acknowledgements

This work explains the aims and purpose of terrorism and many issues in achieving a broad-based strategy against terrorism. What we all fear as a global community is that terrorists seek to force, through the use of fear, the adoption of measures of a police state. One has to bear in mind, in devising such policy and tactics, the crisis management capability; the involvement of the state in countering state sponsored terrorism; the balance between media coverage and any censorship; the use of the military; the policy of negotiating, if at all, with terrorists, and their legal status and international response. Some of the root causes of the problem of terrorism seem too intractable for many countries to face; for example, the challenges of poverty, bribery and corruption, and the absence of a binding definition of terrorism in international law. The economic gap between the global North and South continues to widen; and the growth of the Third World gives rise to economic hopelessness.

There are many differing approaches to educating people about terrorism: dissertations, analytical and comparative studies, and appraisals of the political and economic responses to terroristic violence. To help us understand the subject there are training and information manuals, research monographs, databases, bibliographies, encyclopaedias and dictionaries. In this dictionary I have chosen examples, ideas, groups, people and events that epitomise the whole issue, given the constraints on the length of the work. It is a sad reflection that many tomes are needed to give a full and comprehensive analysis of a phenomenon that has been with us in varied forms, terms and guises throughout history.

As the book goes to print at the dawn of the twenty-first century, the world has witnessed a new type of transnational terrorist, skilled in the use of transnational communications and financial returns as a means of co-ordinating the activities of dispersed followers who have made no promises to any state and have no territorial desires. Governments are very concerned that they are being increasingly bypassed by terrorists.

The first edition was referred to as an encyclopaedia, but the changes made in this second edition have moved the author to change the title to that of dictionary, especially as there are so many different definitions and an ever increasing variation of terminology of different types of terrorism. The work can be viewed as a constant reference and bulky topics such as September 11, 2001 and the different aspects of terrorism can be viewed under the headings **September 11** and **Terror and Terrorism**. Detailed cross-referencing takes the reader to various parts of the book. After most entries there are References and Further Reading, and at the back of the book a selection of website addresses from where further information can be gleaned. Cross-referencing proves that terrorism crosses many academic boundaries, and this is enhanced by a conceptual map which helps apply a mental/philosophical appraisal across the topics of the entries. Some entries have been updated since May 2003 at proof stage.

This work will be of use to those involved in academia, the military, government, business and law enforcement. A single entry cannot inform the reader of all there is to know about its subject matter because it is related to other entries. To know something about hostages, one has to be aware of the people and countries involved, the victims, psychological facts, finances and motivation. As the detailed cross-referencing implies many entries could have been listed with almost equal relevance under other entries. The reader can find beyond a basic definition or description a more detailed explanation, so that the person can proceed directly in their reading without having to stop and search among textbooks, commentaries, biographies, monographs or eyewitness accounts.

Inevitably the production of a work of this nature could not have been possible without the help and assistance of many and my thanks are due to Craig Fowlie and Zoe Botterill, respectively Senior Editor and Editorial Assistant, Politics, International Relations and Asian Studies, and Simon Bailey and Alex Meloy, Production Editors at Routledge, and also Alan Whitworth of Culva House Publications, Whitby, for placing the entire work in a computerised form, checking the draft manuscript for inconsistencies and making various useful suggestions. The Chief Librarians and staff at the National Police Library, Bramshill, Hook, Hampshire; the Royal Military Academy, Sandhurst; the Prince Consort Library, Aldershot; University of St Andrews Library; Brotherton Library, University of Leeds; University of York Library and Whitby Library have been helpful with their patience, advice, courtesy and assistance.

I am grateful to the academics who pioneered the teaching of terrorism in the carousel course; for senior officers at the Police Staff College, Bramshill in the 1980s, where the author was a civilian tutor (1977–1989), namely Professor P. Wilkinson, University of St Andrew's; the late Professor Dr R. Clutterbuck, Exeter University; Professor J. Potter, RMA Sandhurst and visiting Professor, Exeter University; Dr D. Carlton, University of Warwick; Dr K. G. Robertson, University of Reading and Dr F. E. C. Gregory, University of Southampton.

Thanks are due to the police who attended the many courses created by myself on this subject; and the many hundreds of authors of books and articles that provided me with inspiration to teach, research and write about the varied and diverse topic of terrorism. I apologise for any omission of thanks.

Other experts notably Christopher Dobson, Ronald Payne, Brian Crozier and Peter Janke inspired me to develop further interest in the subject.

Finally, I am grateful for the constant encouragement of my friends and parents, without whose support this work would not have been possible.

John Richard Thackrah,
Whitby, North Yorkshire, May 2003

Introduction

This dictionary has been prepared with the following issues in mind. The general public have to be made aware of the main issues surrounding one of the most intractable global problems at the start of the twenty-first century. Currently courses are organised for the police and the military as part of a postgraduate programme in politics and international relations. Since September 11, however, an increase in interest in the subject has been shown and bookshelves in high street book outlets contain considerably more titles on terrorism. People want to be made aware why terrorists so misunderstand society and why this uncertainty is reciprocated by democracies all over the globe. In other words, terrorists face just as many problems as the democratic society which they are hoping to destroy. Uncertain conflicts litter the world terrorist thought, with the terrorists' vision of the future appearing more and more bizarre and incoherent as each year progresses. When one analyses the nature of the impact and the problems, the history of terrorism can be written in a more meaningful way, and primarily an insight can be gained in organisational behaviour and operational postures.

Courses in terrorism can have several educational goals – to define and distinguish between the state as a terror agent and acts of non-state terrorist groups. Particular conceptual frameworks for analysing terror can be applied to each terror group studied. One can distinguish the controversies surrounding the use of terror and the role of the media in world society, the development of international law, the safety of hostages and the preservation of civil liberties in a democratic society. One can articulate and define a personal value position on how to reconcile values such as freedom and justice or the preservation of life and security in the world including terror and political violence.

Exercises on the problem can aim at finding, organising and presenting information based on sources likely to be consulted in the future if they are to become informed global citizens. Simulation and gaming can teach problem-solving skills, conflict theory, bargaining and negotiation. Conflict management is a crucial area – covering concepts, conflict sources and dynamics, thought traditions, coping with conflicts, assumptions of conflict settlement and conflict resolution.

Events over the past three years have shown the importance of understanding proposals for government and international responses to terror. A national level response would include anti-terror measures, police as intelligence agents, the army's role, mobilising the public and special powers of detention. International levels of response would examine the 'political' offences loophole, intelligence and police co-operation, bilateral co-operation, extradition problems, guidelines for responses by democracies, and the avoidance of over-reaction.

Topics on a course can cover democracy and coping with terrorism; an analytical framework of study and control of agitational terror; a typology of terror; international terror weapons; conceptualising terror; a general strategy for analysis; quantitive research; models of terror as an ongoing process; profiles and terrorism and the role of the police and the military.

Educational objectives and terrorism have to be clearly ascertained. Students have to be provided with concepts and skills which will increase their ability to be independent thinkers. They should be able to apply a framework for analysing terrorism to each terror group studied. One can discuss controversies surrounding the use of terrorism and the role of media in society – the development of international law, the safety of hostages and preservation of civil liberties. Students can articulate and defend a personal value position on how to reconcile values such as freedom and justice or the preservation of life and security in a world of increasing terrorism and political violence.

Simulation exercises of terrorist situations which have occurred can be extremely useful. Lessons can be learnt. Response patterns and negotiating positions have to be viewed in the broader context of government policy-making. Problems shown up by simulation can be examined with a view to solution – are policy-makers prepared for a potential crisis or not? Communications breakdown, working at cross purposes and the impact of critical disorganisation are regular difficulties. Terrorist tactics and strategies change and this can strain the capabilities of the authorities to respond effectively.

Hostage negotiation exercises are vital in order to be able to respond quickly and effectively to an emergency. They have to be conducted by specially trained personnel skilled in intervening in crisis situations. Hostage negotiation is a subtle means of outmanoeuvring an opponent or a tactical prelude to all out confrontation. Possible mistakes hopefully can be rectified at the exercise stage – such as losing patience, precipitate action and making value judgements about the hostage taker. Successful intervention in a hostage situation requires the use of a dynamic blend of appropriate tactical responses and a negotiating technique developed by behavioural scientists.

Simulation and hostage negotiation exercises can stimulate discussion on the problem of deviating from previous policy when negotiating with terrorists; moral issues raised by various policy options; and the impact of various policies on the domestic and international environment.

Debriefing exercises are a necessity above all in getting each participant to prepare a check list of factors designed to pinpoint differences in attitudes and perceptions. However, these exercises can create scepticism about their value – in particular, the distance of the scenario and student actors from the 'reality' they portray.

If simulations are judged critically it is on the basis of structure, mode of operation and format. A structure can yield two kinds of simulations: technical simulations covering physical conditions and behavioural simulations which simulate human behaviour as exemplified by war games. Behavioural simulations can be played by people, computers and different combinations of men and machines. Human simulations can be done by games, simulation games and gaming simulations for training and educational purposes. Men-machine simulations can be played by human beings and results achieved by computers. The format can cover three kinds of simulation free form – minimal rules and only general scenarios; rigid format with strict and clearly defined rules; and a mixed format combining free moves in one phase as part of a simulation and rigid constraints in other phases or parts.

Counter-terrorism simulations can involve three small teams: terrorists, hostages and government. Teams can formulate policies and government officials deal with the problem. Terrorists decide whether to negotiate, accept offers of government officials, execute threats or give the government more time to respond. More sophisticated simulation includes senior policy-makers and crisis management teams.

Simulations can be useful for training policy-makers and officials in a direct response to terror, research, planning and the education of the public groups and individuals directly involved in dealing with terrorism – reporters, diplomats and military officers.

Projects can help in educating people about dealing with terrorism – work can be done on a particular group; on a portrayal of differing terrorist leaders at work; a revolutionary planning group to demonstrate deterioration in law and order; the conduct of an anti-terrorist counter-insurgency operation and the forming of legislation; and the compilation of a list of revolutionary events to examine the phases of subversion.

Scenarios also have to be developed, with the conduct of simulations to be agreed and debriefing and evaluation. Simulations have links with role playing and parties concerned are represented by teams and most players have specific roles. The Middle East conflict can be studied in this way.

To distinguish between state and non-state terrorism, one could develop a detailed exercise in distinct parts, based on acts of terrorism committed in any one calendar year. One can choose five acts of terrorism committed by national governments and non-state actors and decide who declared such acts to be 'terrorist'. For each act one can look at the most identifiable cause of terror, the justification 'terrorists' provided for their act and the response of the other political actors to the terror act. Are there identifiable linkages between 'state terrorism' and 'group terrorism' in the acts examined? If so, in what ways are the events related?

The bibliography of terrorism is a vast topic, and for the purposes of this dictionary some of the chief texts, articles and research papers have been utilised and referred to after each entry. In undertaking research from the huge numbers of works, researchers follow the general principles of utility, value, currency and variety. All types of bibliographies have been useful in compiling this dictionary – those that are specific to one aspect of study, comprehensive ones, annotated volumes, and those which divide works into reference and general. One has to bear in mind that bibliographic resources have to constantly evolve as the tactics of terrorism are in constant evolution and the counter-terrorism forces have to keep abreast of the changes.

As this dictionary shows from the thousand plus references utilised, the will to use terrorism to achieve various perceived goals has not diminished.

Any omissions of fact or theory are entirely the author's responsibility. To make such a dictionary is certainly not dull work. It needs such a dictionary to remind one that the eyes are the windows of the soul in examining the complex thoughts and the evils committed by politically violent terrorists around the world.

References

Henderson, A. (2001) *Global Terrorism: The Complete Reference Guide*, New York: Checkmark Books.

Hoffman, B. (1998) *Inside Terrorism*, New York: Columbia University Press.

Huntington, S. P. (1996) *The Clash of Civilisations and the Remaking of the World Order*, London: Touchstone Books.

Lakos, A. (1986) *International Terrorism: A Bibliography*, Boulder, CO: Westview Press.

Lakos, A. (1991) *Terrorism 1980–1990: A Bibliography*, Boulder, CO: Westview Press.

Laqueur, W. (1987) *The Age of Terrorism*, Boston: Little, Brown & Co.

Schmid, A. P. (1983) *Political Terrorism: A Research Guide to Concepts, Theories, Data Bases and Literature*, New Brunswick, CT: Transaction Publications.

Thackrah, J. R. (1989) 'Educational Objectives and Terrorism'. Unpublished MS.

Further Reading

Anderson, S. and Sloan, S. (1995) *Historical Dictionary of Terrorism*, Metuchen, NJ: Scarecrow Press.

Bader, E. J. and Baird-Windle, P. (2001) *Targets of Hatred: Anti Abortion Terrorism*, New York: Palgrave.

Bobbitt, P. (2002) *The Shield of Achilles: War, Peace and the Course of History*, London: Allen Lane, Penguin Books.

Combs, C. and Slann, M. (2002) *Encyclopaedia of Terror*, New York: Facts on File.

Crelinsten, R. D. (ed.) (1977) *Research Strategies for the Study of International Political Terrorism*, Montreal: International Centre for Comparative Criminology.

Crenshaw, M. and Pimlott, J. (eds) (1997) *Encyclopaedia of World Terrorism*, Armunk, New York: M. E. Sharpe.

Ehrenfeld, R. (1990) *Narco-Terrorism*, New York: Basic Books.

Fanon, F. (1963) *The Wretched of the Earth*, New York: Grove Press.

Flood, S. (ed.) (1991) *International Terrorism: Policy Implications*, Chicago: University of Chicago Office of International Criminal Justice.

Follain, J. (1998) *Jackal: The Complete Story of the Legendary Terrorist, Carlos the Jackal*, New York: Arcade.

Heyman, E. S. and Mickolus, E. (1980) 'Responding to Terrorism: Basic and Applied Research' in Sloan, S. and Schultz, R. H. (eds) (1980) *Responding to the Terrorist Threat: Prevention and Control*, New York: Pergamon.

Howard, L. (1992) *Terrorism: Roots, Impact, Responses*, New York: Praeger.

Lavery, R. (1981) 'Anti-Terrorism Games Can Save Money, Lives' *JVT Journal*, vol. 2, no. 12, pp. 3–6.

Marcuse, H. (1964) *One Dimensional Man*, Boston, MA: Beacon Press.

Martin, G. (2003) *Understanding Terrorism: Challenges, Perspectives and Issues*, Thousand Oaks, CA, London, New Delhi: Sage Publications.

Rashid, A. (2001) *Taliban: Militant Islam, Oil and Fundamentalism in Central Asia*, New Haven, CT, Yale: Nota Bene.

Rosie, G. (1987) *The Directory of International Terrorism*, New York: Paragon House.

Russett, B., Starr, H. and Kinsella, D. (2000) *World Politics: The Menu for Choice*, Boston/New York: Bedford, St Martin's.

Schechterman, B. and Slann, M. (eds) (1999) *Violence and Terrorism*, Guilford, CT: Dushkin and McGraw-Hill.

Silke, A. (2001) 'The Devil You Know: Continuing Problems with Research on Terrorism', *Terrorism and Political Violence*, vol. 13, no. 4 (winter), pp. i–ix.

Simonsen, C. E. and Spindlove, J. R. (2000) *Terrorism Today: The Past, the Players, the Future*, Englewood Cliffs, NJ: Prentice Hall.

Soan, S. (1961) *Simulating Terrorism*, Norman, OK: University of Oklahoma Press.

Sun Tzu (1963) *The Art of War*, New York: Oxford University Press.

White, J. R. (2002) *Terrorism 2002 Update*, USA/UK: Thompson, Wadsworth.

Wilkinson, P. (2002) *Terrorism versus Democracy: The Liberal State Response*, London and Portland, OR: Frank Cass.

Abbreviations and Acronyms

AD	Action Directe (France)
AIS	Armée Islamique du Salut (Algeria)
ALF	Animal Liberation Front (UK)
ANAPO	National Popular Alliance Party (Colombia)
ANC	African National Congress (South Africa)
ANO	Abu Nidal Organisation
ARDE	Alianza Revolucionária Democratica (Nicaragua)
ARM	Animal Rights Militia
ASALA	Armenian Secret Army for the Liberation of Armenia
ASG	Abu Sayyaf Group
ATE	Anti-terrorism ETA
AZAPO	Azanian People's Organisation (South Africa)
BLA	Black Liberation Army (USA)
BSO	Black September Organisation (Middle East)
CCC	Cellules Communistes Combattantes (Belgium)
CE	Council of Europe
CGUP	Guatemalan Committee of Patriotic Unity
CIA	Central Intelligence Agency (USA)
CIGN	Groupe d'Intervention Gendarmerie National
CIRT	Critical Incident Response Team (USA)
CLODO	Committee to Liquidate or Neutralise Computers (France)
DFLP	Democratic Front for the Liberation of Palestine
DLF	Dhofar Liberation Front (Oman)
DRIL	Iberian Revolutionary Directorate of Liberation (Spain)

Dw-Sol	Revolutionary Left (Turkey)
Dw-Yol	Revolutionary Way (Turkey)
EAM	National Liberation Front (Greece)
EGP	Guerrilla Army of the Poor (Guatemala)
ELAS	Greek National Liberation Army (military wing of EAM)
ELF	Eritrean Liberation Front
ELN	National Liberation Army (Colombia)
EM	Death Squad (Guatemala)
EOKA	Ethniki Organosis Kipriakou Agonos (National Organisation of Cypriot Struggle)
EPLF	Eritrean People's Liberation Front
EROS	Ealam Revolutionary Organisation of Students (Sri Lanka)
ERP	Egercito Revolucionario Popular (Argentina and El Salvador)
ESA	Secret Anti-Communist Army (Guatemala)
ETA	Euskadi ta Askatasuna (Euskadi and Freedom) (Spain and France)
ETAM	ETA Military
ETAP-M	ETA Political-Military
EU	European Union
EUROPOL	European Police Office
EZU	Emiliano Zapata Unit
FAN	Armed Forces of the North (Chad)
FANE	Federation of National and European Action (France)
FAPLA	Angolan People's Liberation Armed Forces
FARC	Revolutionary Armed Forces of Colombia
FARN	Fuerzas Armadas de la Resistencia Nacional (El Salvador)

FBI	Federal Bureau of Investigation (USA)		ICAO	International Civil Aviation Organisation
FDN	Fuerzas Democraticas Nicaraguenses (Nicaragua)		IG	Al Gama'at al Islamaya, Islamic Group (Middle East)
FDR	Frente Democratico Revolucionario (El Salvador)		IHRC	Inter-American Human Rights Commission
FDR	Democratic Front against Repression (Guatemala)		IMF	International Monetary Fund
FEMA	Federal Emergency Management Agency (USA)		IMRO	Internal Macedonian Revolutionary Organisation
FIS	Islamic Salvation Front (Algeria)		INLA	Irish National Liberation Army
FLN	Front de Libération Nationale (Algeria)		INTERPOL	International Criminal Police Organisation
FLQ	Front de Libération du Québec		IRA	Irish Republican Army
FMLN	Frente Farabundo Marti de Liberacion Nacional		IT	information technology
			ITERATE	International Terrorism: Attributes of Terrorist Events
FNE	European Nationalist Alliance (France)		IZL	Irgun Zvai Leumi (National Military Organisation) (Middle East)
FNLA	Frente Nacional de Libertação de Angola		JDL	Jewish Defence League (USA)
FPL-FM	Fuerzas Populares de Liberación – Farabundo Marti (El Salvador)		JVP	Janatha Vimukti Peramuna (Sri Lanka)
FRAP	Frente Revolucionario Antifascista y Patriótico (Spain)		KAU	Kenya African Union
			KKK	Ku Klux Klan
FRC	Fatah Revolutionary Council		KNDO	Karen National Defence Organisation (Burma)
FRELIMO	Frente de Libertação de Moçambique (Mozambique)		LTTE	Liberation Tigers of Tamil Ealam (Sri Lanka)
FRETILIN	Frente Revolucionária Timorense de Libertação e Independência (East Timor)		LVF	Loyalist Volunteer Force
			M-19	National Liberation (April 19) Movement (Colombia)
FROLINAT	Chad National Liberation Front		MACP	Military Aid to the Civil Power
FRP	Federal Response Plan (USA)		MCP	Malayan Communist Party
FTO	Foreign Terrorist Organisation		MIL	Iberian Liberation Movement (Spain)
GARI	Gruppo de Accion Revolucionária Internacionalista (Spain)		MK	Umkhonto We Sizwe (Spear of the Nation) (military wing of ANC)
GEO	Grupo Especial de Operaciones (Spain)		MNLF	Moro National Liberation Front (Philippines)
GIA	Group Islamique Armée (Algeria)		MNR	Movimiento Nacional Revolucionario (El Salvador)
GPP	Guerra Popular Prologanda (Spain)			
GRAE	Revolutionary Government of Angola in Exile		MPAIAC	Movement for Self-Determination and Independence of the Canaries Archipelago
GRAPO	Grupo de Resistencia Anti-Fascista Primero de octubre (Spain)		MPLA	Movimento Popular de Libertação de Angola
GSG	Grenzschutzgruppe		MRLA	Malayan Races Liberation Army
GUNT	Transitional Government of National Unity (Chad)		MRTA	Tupac Amaru Revolutionary Movement (Peru)
HAMAS	Harakat Al-Muqawoma Al-Islamiyya		NAP	National Action Party
HUA	Harakat ul-Ansar *now* Harakat ul-Mujahidin (Pakistan)		NAR	Armed Revolutionary Nuclei (Italy)

NATO	North Atlantic Treaty Organisation	RAF	Red Army Faction (Rote Armee Fraktion) (West Germany)
NF	National Front		
NFN	New Nazi Front (France)	RAND	Influential US Think Tank and Research Organisation (based in California)
NICRA	Northern Ireland Civil Rights Association		
NORAID	Irish Northern Aid Committee	RSPCA	Royal Society for Prevention of Cruelty to Animals
NPA	New People's Army (Philippines)		
NPD	National Democratic Party (Germany)	RISCT	Research Institute for Study of Conflict and Terrorism
NUSAS	National Union of South African Students	RUC	Royal Ulster Constabulary
		RZ	Revolutionary Cells (West Germany)
OAS	Organisation Armée Secrète (Algeria)	SACP	South African Communist Party
		SAM	surface-to-air missile
OPEC	Organisation of Petroleum Exporting Countries	SAS	Special Air Service
		SASO	South African Student Organization
ORPA	Revolutionary Organisation of the People in Arms (Guatemala)	SDS	Students for a Democratic Society (USA)
PAIG	Partido Africano da Independência da Guiné e Cabo Verde (Guinea-Bissau)	SL	Sendero Luminoso
		SLA	Symbionese Liberation Army (USA)
		SPLA	Sudanese People's Liberation Army
PCS	Partido Comunista Salvadoreño	SNLF	Sandinist National Liberation Front (Nicaragua)
PDC	Christian Democrat Party (El Salvador)		
		SSD/Pda	Volkssozialistische Bewegung Deutschland/Partei der arbeit
PFLO	Popular Front for the Liberation of Oman		
		SWAPO	South West Africa People's Organisation
PFLOAG	Popular Front for the Liberation of Oman and the Arabian Gulf		
		SWAT	Special Weapons and Tactics (USA)
PFLP	Popular Front for the Liberation of Palestine	TELO	Tamil Ealam Liberation Organisation (Sri Lanka)
PFLP-GC	Popular Front for the Liberation of Palestine – General Command	TRAC	Terrorism Research Analytical Center of National Security Division of FBI
PIJ	Palestine Islamic Jihad		
PIRA	Provisional IRA	TREVI	Informal Group of European Countries to Fight Terrorism
PKK	Kurdistan Workers Party		
PLA	Palestine Liberation Army	TUF	Tamil United Front (Sri Lanka)
PLA	Popular Liberation Army (Lebanon)	TULF	Tamil United Liberation Front (Sri Lanka)
PLF	Palestine Liberation Front		
PLF	Popular Liberation Force (Eritrea)	UDA	Ulster Defence Association
PLO	Palestine Liberation Organisation	UDF	United Democratic Front (South Africa)
PNC	Partido de Conciliaçion Nacional (El Salvador)		
		UDT	Timor Democratic Union
POLISARIO	Popular Front for the Liberation of Saquiet el Hamra and Rio de Oro (North West Africa)	UFF	Ulster Freedom Fighters
		UN	United Nations
		UNITA	Unido Nacional pare a Independencia Total de Angola
POW	prisoners of war		
PREPAK	People's Revolutionary Party of Kungleipak (India)	UNO	Union Nacional Opositora (El Salvador)
PSF	Popular Struggle Front (Palestinian)	URNG	Guatemalan National Revolutionary Unity

UVF	Ulster Volunteer Force	ZANU	Zimbabwe African National Union
WMD	Weapons of Mass Destruction	ZAPU	Zimbabwe African People's Union
ZANLA	Zimbabwe African National Liberation Army		

Conceptual Map

Activities

Animal Rights
Assassination
Extortion/Product Pollution
Hostage-taking
Kidnapping
Mafia/Organised Crime
Narco-Terrorism
Piracy
Super-Terror

Concepts

Civil War
Freedom Fighters
Guerrilla Warfare
Insurgency
Insurrection
Political Violence
Psychology
Revolution
Rights
Terrorism
Zionism

Counter-Terrorism

Counter-Insurgency
European Union
Extradition
Government
International Criminal Court
Media
Police–Army Co-operation
United Nations

Events

Achille Lauro
Lockerbie
Munich Olympics 1972
September 11
Teheran Embassy Siege
World Trade Center 1993, 2002

Future

Cyber-Terror
Mega-Terrorism
Technology
Weapons of Mass Destruction (WMD)

Groups

Aum Shinrikyo Cult
Basques
Children
Hizbullah
IRA
Neo-Nazis
Palestine Liberation Organisation (PLO)
Rogue States
Sandinistas
Tupamaros/Japanese Red Army
Women

Ideals

Beliefs of Terrorist
Dynamics Terrorist
Fear and Terror
Messianic Terror
Motivation

Political Disobedience
Religious-based
Rights Terrorists
Stockholm Syndrome

Individuals

Abu Nidal
Arafat, Yasser

Carlos
Debray, Regis
Fanon, Franz
Guevara, Che
Osama Bin Laden
Marighella, Carlos
Marx, Karl
Rabin, Yitzak
Ramzi, Yousef
Victims

Glossary

Action Directe	Direct Action
adwam	Aggression
al Gihud	Striving (Egypt)
Aliyah	Jewish immigration into Palestine
Al-Jama'a	al-Islamiyyah
al Muqatilah bi-Libya	Libyan Islamic Fighting Group (Libya)
an-Nidal	Struggle (used by Lebanon Groups)
al-Fida	Sacrifice (Palestine)
al Qaeda	the Base
al Saiqa	The Thunderbolt (Palestine) – Organisation set up by Syria to govern the PLO
Asbat al-Ansar	the Partisans' league (Lebanon extremist-based Sunni Group
assassini	Drug Users (derived from 'hashshashin')
Aum Shinrikyo	Supreme Truth
Brigate Rosse	Red Brigade (Italy)
Epanastatiki Organosi	Revolutionary Organisation (Greece)
Euzkradita Azatasuna	Basque Fatherland and Liberty
fatah	the Victory
fatwa	Islamic religious ruling
fedayean	warriors
Forcas Populares	Popular Forces (April 25) (Portugal)
Ghazu	Invasion
glasnost	transparency
GRAPO	Grupo de Resistencia Antifascista Primero de octubre
Hajj	Holy Pilgrimage to Mecca
Hamas	Zeal or Enthusiasm
Harakat ul-jihad-i-Islami	Movement of Islamic Holy War (Afghanistan)
Harakat ul-Mujahidin	Movement of Holy Warriors

Hizbullah	the Party of God
Imam	faith
intifada	Shuddering
Irgun Zvai Leumi	National Military Organisation (Israel)
Jihad	Struggle for defence of Islam
Lashkar-e-Tayyiba	Army of the Righteous (Pakistan)
madrasa	Islamic religious school
Mahdi	the Chosen One (in Sunni Theology)
Mujaheddin	Holy Warrior
perestroika	restructuring
Posse Comitatus	Power of the Country
Resistencia Nacional Mocambicana	Mozambique National Resistance
Revolutionaere Zellen	Revolutionary Cells (Germany)
Rote Armee Fraktion	Red Army Faction (Germany)
salam	Arab-Israeli Peace
Sendero Luminoso	Shining Path (Peru)
shahada	Creed
Shahid	hero
sharia	Muslim Law
shari'ah	Islamic Law
sha'a	follow
shi'ah	Religious sect (another word for Shi'ite)
shuhada	Martyrs (Lebanon)
Sinn Fein	We Ourselves
sulh	Reconciliation (by Palestine with Israel)
Terra Lliure	Free Land (Catalan)
towhid	a divinely integrated classless society (Iran)
umma	Universal Islamic Community

Abu Nidal

b. 1937; d. 2002

Sabri Khalil al Banna was born in Jaffa, in Palestine. His family later moved to the West Bank and he went to **Egypt** to study engineering and became involved with the revolutionary Ba'ath Party of Jordan in 1955. After the failed coup against King Hussein in 1957 al Banna found work in **Saudi Arabia**. He joined a Fatah cell and was expelled from the country in 1967. In 1969 by now calling himself Abu Nidal he was sent to Khartoum to open a Fatah office. In 1970 he was posted to Baghdad as the representative of the **Palestine Liberation Organisation** (PLO) and built up links with Iraqi Intelligence. He broke from Yasser **Arafat** and in 1974 from al Fatah when its officials accused him of plotting to assassinate their leaders and sentenced him to death in his absence. In response, he formed the Fatah Revolutionary Council as the true force of leadership for the Palestinians. He built up the organisation with considerable Iraqi help. In 1980 he moved to **Syria** where he was mainly engaged in attacks on the PLO and Jordanian targets at Syria's behest.

It was reported in June 1984 that Mr Sabri Khalil al Banna leader of the Revolutionary Council of Fatah (a Palestinian splinter organisation which was commonly referred to as the Abu Nidal Group after Mr al Banna's code name), had left Damascus for Baghdad for treatment of a heart condition, and that the Group's activities had been curtailed. Mr al Banna had been expelled from Baghdad in November 1983, and his readmission

to Iraq was seen as being conditional on the cessation of the group's operations. Al Banna was again expelled from Iraq in November 1984, and relocated the headquarters of the group in Damascus.

The Abu Nidal Group had claimed responsibility for the attempted assassination in June 1982 of Mr Shlomo Argov, the then Israeli Ambassador to the UK, and also for the assassination of the moderate Palestinian leader, Dr Issam Ali Sartawi, in April 1983. The Group had also been associated with terrorist activity in France and had recently supported the Syrian-backed rebellion by units of the PLO opposed to Yasser Arafat.

In almost simultaneous actions in December 1985 by Arab gunmen at the international airports of Rome and Vienna, 20 people were killed, including four of the seven gunmen involved. Responsibility for the incidents was widely attributed to the Palestinian Abu Nidal Group, acting with the support of **Libya**. The four gunmen who participated in the Rome operation had statements on them signed by the 'Palestinian Martyrs'; and the Arab Guerrilla Cells also claimed responsibility, stating that they, 'hereby declare the birth of a revolutionary and **suicide** group'.

A day after the atrocity a telephone caller to a Spanish radio station claimed responsibility for the attacks on behalf of the 'Abu Nidal Commando'. A US Presidential spokesman claimed all the evidence pointed to the Abu Nidal Group. On the same day, Israeli officials began to refer specifically to the Abu Nidal Group as the culprit. It had apparently erroneously been reported that he had died in late 1984. The PLO itself had consistently condemned the activities of the group, and in his absence Abu Nidal had been sentenced to death by the organisation. Unconfirmed reports from Arab diplomatic sources suggested that Abu Nidal might have been expelled from Syria to Libya following the June 1985 TWA **Beirut Hijack**, as part of a secret agreement between Syria and the **USA**. A week later Arafat claimed that the Syrian and Libyan Intelligence Services were sponsoring terrorism in an effort to discredit the PLO, and he described Abu Nidal as a 'tool of Syrian and Libyan intelligence'. Israel tacitly acknowledged that the attacks were not the work of mainstream PLO but affirmed that militant breakaway factions such as the Abu Nidal group were ultimately part of the same movement.

A joint meeting of Italian and Austrian security officials held on 1 January 1986 reportedly concluded that all seven gunmen involved in the December attacks were members of the Abu Nidal Group and had been trained in Lebanon. One of the surviving gunmen had apparently confessed that the name 'Palestinian Martyrs' was a front for the Abu Nidal Group. It was subsequently reported that the gunmen had travelled to Europe via Damascus and Yugoslavia. The US Administration produced a Report on 2 January listing sixty incidents, which it claimed had involved the Abu Nidal Group over the past two years. The Report also asserted that the Libyan regime was actively supporting the Group, a claim which Colonel **Gadaffi** denied. On 5 January 1986 he refuted allegations that Libya provided training camps or assistance of any kind to Abu Nidal, who, he said, did not live in Libya, although he admitted having met with him during 1985. He added that as head of state he did not regard the airport attacks as 'legal', but said that it was the duty and strategy of Palestinian guerrillas 'to liberate Palestine by all means'. At this time, due to a failure to locate any Abu Nidal power bases, the military option was not being seriously considered by US forces.

On 13 January 1986, an Abu Nidal newspaper published what it claimed was an interview with Abu Nidal, during which he admitted that his Group had carried out airport attacks, which he described as 'absolutely legitimate'. He praised Gadaffi as an 'honest man', and claimed to have visited the USA several times using forged passports, and to have recently undergone cosmetic surgery to avoid recognition.

On 20 January, the *New York Times* published an interview with Ahmed **Jabril**, leader of the radical PLO group, the Popular Front for the Liberation of Palestine – General Command (PFLP-GC), which enjoyed close ties with Libya. Mr Jabril affirmed that the Abu Nidal Group was responsible for the airport attacks, and added that the Group received considerable material assistance from Iran where Abu Nidal himself spent most of his time. He claimed that the Group also received assistance from revolutionary organisations around the world as well as from conservative Arab states, and that it required relatively little money to carry out its activities.

A Rome Public Prosecutor issued an arrest warrant for Abu Nidal on 23 January 1986. By the early-1980s he had established ties with Colonel Gadaffi. Many of his men had installed themselves in camps in the Libyan Desert from where they continued their battle against Fatah. His efforts to regain control of the Fatah Revolutionary Council in 1987 precipitated a bloody internal feud that led to 50 deaths. In his later years Abu Nidal became paranoid and saw his organisation torn apart by infighting.

Rumours immediately emerged on his death in August 2002 that he had been murdered on the orders of Saddam Hussein for refusing to help in the training of **al Qaeda** fighters who had moved to Northern Iraq after fleeing **Afghanistan**. Saddam had also wanted Nidal to carry out attacks against the USA and its allies. Saddam's Intelligence Chiefs ordered the assassination, which was carried out by Iraqi security forces. There is still an unsubstantiated claim that Abu Nidal was behind the **Lockerbie** aeroplane bombing. Abu Bakr, a former spokesman for Nidal's Revolutionary Council said Nidal had told him his Group was responsible for Lockerbie.

Many believe that Iraqi Intelligence did not kill Abu Nidal as he was their guest. Abu Nidal killed Yasser Arafat's number two man in the PLO based in Tunis, Salah Khalaf, also known as Abu Iyad. It took time for Iyad's supporters to exact their revenge, but this they did when they knew Nidal was in Baghdad seeking treatment for his cancer. Indeed, Abu Nidal's family who live on the West

Bank, were told that the assassination was the long-awaited revenge of the PLO for the death of Abu Iyad.

See also: Anti-Semitic Terrorism; PLO.

References

Melman, Y. (1987) *The Master Terrorist: The True Story Behind Abu Nidal*, London: Sidgwick & Jackson.

Miller, A. (1987) 'Portrait of Abu Nidal' in Laqueur, W. (ed.) *The Terrorism Reader*, New York: Meridian, pp. 309–314.

Seale, P. (1992) *Abu Nidal: A Gun for Hire*, New York: Random House.

Further Reading

Abu Nidal (1986) 'The Palestinian Goal Justifies Terrorism' in Szumski, B. (ed.) *Terrorism: Opposing Viewpoints*, St Paul, MN: Greenhaven Press, pp. 113–118.

Editorial (2002) 'Who Killed Abu Nidal?' *Jane's Foreign Report*, no. 2702, pp 1–2.

UK Foreign and Commonwealth Office 'Abu Nidal Group and State Terrorism' in Alexander, Y. (ed.) (1987) *The 1988 Annual on Terrorism*, Dordrecht: Martinus Nijhoff, pp 283–297.

Achille Lauro Hijack

The Italian cruise liner *Achille Lauro* was hijacked on 7 October 1985 en route between the two Egyptian ports of Alexandria and Port Said by four Palestinian guerrillas who, it later transpired, were members of the Tunis-based faction of the Palestinian Liberation Front (PLF) – a constituent part of the **Palestine Liberation Organisation** (PLO). Under the hijacker's directions, the ship with 180 passengers and 331 crew on board (approximately 600 passengers having disembarked at Alexandria) circled in the Eastern Mediterranean. During the period of the hijacking the guerrillas demanded the release of 50 Palestinian prisoners and threatened to kill the passengers. Only one of the passengers, a disabled Jewish American named Mr Klinghoffer, was murdered – he was shot and subsequently thrown overboard.

After lengthy negotiations over two days with Egyptian and Italian officials and two PLO members including the PLF Leader Abul Abbas, the hijackers surrendered reportedly in return for free passage out of Egypt.

The identity and affiliations of those responsible for the *Achille Lauro* hijack remained unclear for some time. The Israelis believed the action was a deliberate attempt by Yasser **Arafat** and the PLO to prevent further progress towards peace negotiations. The operation was widely denounced in Arab and Palestinian circles, with both the mainstream PLO and the anti-Arafat Damascus-based groups condemning it. The hijackers themselves said they were members of the PLF, although Mr Arafat denied that members of any PLO group were involved, and the Damascus-based PLF under Talat Yacoub disclaimed responsibility. It was only after the surrender of the hijackers that it became clear that the operation had been mounted by the Tunis-based breakaway wing of the PLF, led by Abbas.

The PLF itself had originally been created by Yacoub as a breakaway from the Popular Front for the Liberation of Palestine – General Command (PFLP-GC) of Ahmed **Jabril**. Abbas had joined the PLF on its formation but had led a breakaway pro-Arafat loyalist faction, which had subsequently based itself in Tunis when the main PLF had held its seventh congress in Tunis, and passed a resolution opposing the Arafat-Hussein reconciliation. In Tunis, Abu Abbas promised that the PLF would continue the struggle, trying to achieve PLO unity and legitimate leadership.

After the hijacking was over, Abbas confirmed earlier reports that the hijackers had been under orders to use the liner only as a means of transport to the Israeli port of Ashdod (where it had been scheduled to call), and had not intended to take it over. They had been precipitated into the hijack when they were discovered in a cabin cleaning their weapons. A senior PLO official said that the guerrillas were under written orders from Abu Abbas to carry out a suicide mission in **Israel** and that they had changed their minds out of cowardice and decided to hijack the ship; thus the PLF would be punished for the action.

After Mr Klinghoffer's death had been revealed President Mubarak of **Egypt** stated that the hijackers had left Egyptian territory, and were probably in the hands of the PLO. The PLO in Tunis denied that it was holding them, and said that they were still awaiting the arrival of the guerrillas, whom they intended to put on trial. President Reagan called on the PLO to hand over the hijackers to an appropriate sovereign state for trial.

On the night of 10 October, an Egyptian plane en route to Tunis with the hijackers, Abbas and a (unnamed) PLO official on board was intercepted by four American fighter planes and forced to land at a NATO base in Sicily, where the Palestinians were taken into custody by the Italian authorities. Abbas later flew to Rome. The Italian government refused an American request for the hijackers and for Abbas to be handed over to US authorities. This policy of appeasement of the terrorists caused dissent within the Italian government. On 12 October Abu Abbas flew to Yugoslavia, where the Yugoslavian authorities rejected a US request that he be arrested. The **USA** administration subsequently publicly criticised the Italian decision to allow Abbas to leave the country.

The US action in intercepting the Egyptian aircraft was praised by Israel and the UK and criticised by many Arab states. It provoked further anti-American demonstrations throughout the Arab world. The trial of the hijackers, together with a Syrian alleged to be their accomplice, on charges of illegal possession of arms and explosives took place in Genoa; they were convicted and received sentences of between four and nine years in jail.

In April 2003 Abu Abbas was arrested in Baghdad by American troops during the War with Iraq. He had been living quietly in that country since the *Achille Lauro* incident. Whilst he was no longer on the American and Israeli Governments 'Most Wanted' list of terrorists, the Italian government are to seek his extradition.

Abbas, born in a Palestinian refugee camp, had for many years been active in Palestinian extreme activities; and had even attempted, albeit unsuccessfully, to raid Israel with hot air balloons and hang-gliders.

See also: Maritime Security.

References

Gooding, G. V. (1987) *Fighting Terrorism in the 1980s: The Interception of the Achille Lauro Hijackers*, Yale, Journal of International Law, vol. 12, no. 1 (winter), pp. 158–179.

Further Reading

Cassese, A. (1989) *Terrorism, Politics and Law: The Achille Lauro Affair*, Oxford: Policy Press.

Paust, J. (1987) 'Extradition and United States Prosecution of the Achille Lauro Hostage Takers – Navigating the Hazards', *Vanderbilt Journal of Transnational Law*, vol. 20, no.2 (March}, pp. 235–257.

Afghanistan and the Guerrilla Movement

Even prior to the **Soviet** invasion in 1979, the secularisation of Afghan politics and the reliance on Russian advisors alienated many Afghans and gave renewed credence to Islamic-inspired rationalism.

The Russians after their blitzkrieg-style attack did little to calm the religious and monarchist opposition in the country. The armed resistance of the Mujaheddin (holy warriors) was restricted to roving bands. The Russians pumped much cash into the country to keep the government in power. The Russians relied on unwieldy mechanised columns against elected guerrilla areas. There was the disdain of regular soldiers for bandit operations, as has recently been witnessed in Chechnya. The assertion of airborne night squads against guerrilla camps and suspected ambushes was not a total success. Helicopters were used in a limited way to cut off the retreat of Mujaheddin. The Russians it appears from subsequent events only came into Afghanistan to shore up the incumbent regime, 'blood' some of their vast military manpower and test some vital new military technology (Ellis, 1995).

The world first became aware of the varied groups and strengths of the Afghan guerrilla movements after the Soviet invasion in 1979.

This was rigorously opposed by a variety of Islamic and tribal movements and alliances. In spite of the strength of arms of the invading force, the guerrillas, or Mujaheddin, succeeded in conducting protracted warfare with very heavy casualties on either side. External support for the rebels has come from Pakistan, the USA and many Western European nations. By 1986 the Mujaheddin controlled well over three-quarters of the country, including some of the towns. Soviet troops suffered considerably at their hands and there were large-scale desertions from the Afghan armed forces to the Mujaheddin.

The Mujaheddin alliances varied in number and extent. The initial overall organisation of several guerrilla factions was the Islamic Alliance for the Liberation of Afghanistan created in 1980 and dissolved in 1981. The dissolution was due to deep divisions between moderate factions, consisting of the Afghan National Liberation Front, and the National Islamic Front for Afghanistan, and the fundamentalist Moslem factions such as the Islamic Afghan Association and the Islamic Party. Another Mujaheddin alliance consisted of a merger of six guerrilla factions that first appeared in 1981 under the title of the Islamic Unity of the Mujaheddin of Afghanistan.

Mujaheddin organisations were as split and divided as the alliances. For example, the Islamic Party had two factions. One of these, led by Gulbuddin Hekmatyar, was the most well-armed and organised Peshawar-based guerrilla faction, which emphasised its own variety of strict Sunni interpretation of Islam and was run in the style of an Islamic warlord. The other was led by Younes Khales, and was a group mainly supported by Pathan tribesmen who had split from Hekmatyar's party. It was more traditionalist than fundamentalist. There was also a group totally opposed to the Islamic Party, called Against Oppression and Tyranny, which expressed opposition to Pathan domination, especially in areas inhabited by ethnic minorities such as the Tadzhiks in Badakshan province in North East Afghanistan, who were Shia Muslims, distinct from the Sunni Muslim majority in Afghanistan. Two minor organisations were the Islamic Movement Organisation of Afghanistan, which sought the establishment of an Islamic Republic of Afghanistan on the model of that of Iran; and the Militant Front of Combatants of Afghanistan, a socialist front solely based inside Afghanistan (unlike other resistance movements

which were represented in Pakistan). Rather unusually, there was a group of pro-Chinese communists opposed to the Soviet-backed regime in Kabul and also to the presence of Soviet military forces in Afghanistan.

See also: September 11: Attacks.

References

Ellis, J. (1995) *From the Barrel of a Gun*, London: Greenhill Books and PA, Mechanicsburg: Stackpole Books.

Further Reading

Combs, C. C. (2003) *Terrorism in the 21st Century*, Third Edition, New Jersey: Prentice Hall.

Ustinov, G. (1986) 'Afghan Rebels are Terrorists' in B. Szumski (ed.) *Terrorism Opposing Viewpoints*, St Paul, MN: Greenhaven Press.

Wheeler, J. (1986) 'Afghan Rebels are Freedom Fighters' in B. Szumski (ed.) *Terrorism Opposing Viewpoints*, St Paul, MN: Greenhaven Press.

Agca, Mehmet Ali

b. 1958

A Turkish citizen, Mehmet Ali Agca tried to assassinate Pope John Paul II in May 1981 in St Peter's Square in the Vatican City. Agca had been involved in a sophisticated programme of promoting destabilisation and terrorism in **Turkey** and elsewhere, with the ultimate aim of serving the political purposes of the **Soviet Union** and Warsaw Pact countries. Agca admitted that his goal was to fight against the Western democracies and destroy them. The reason for the terrorist activity was ideological.

In the summer of 1980 Agca had been brought to **Syria** by Teslim Tore, the head of Turkey's pro-communist People's Liberation Army. Here he was trained in the use of weapons, explosives, Cold War concepts, how to carry out *coups d'état*, and revolutionary history. He met Bulgarian agents in Damascus, the capital of Syria (Bulgaria was seen as a country which could help Agca and his followers achieve their aims) and received money from them to deliver to two Leftist labour groups in Turkey. The money was to be used to fund subversive activities. Working under the direct tutelage of Abuzer Ugurlu, a reputed Turkish Mafia godfather in Istanbul, Agca and his accomplices established an organisation with the specific political aims of undermining capitalism and of severing Turkey's ties with the West.

Agca developed a wide range of associations with a Turkish terrorist organisation known as the Grey Wolves – both as a 'cover' and in order to draw Right-wing terrorists into supporting anti-Western goals. He never became a Grey Wolf himself and did not join the outlawed National Action Party (NAP) with which the Grey Wolves were associated (both are Rightist groups led by Colonel Alpaslan Turkes). In spite of widespread Leftist allegations that Agca had killed Abdi Ipecki, a liberal Istanbul newspaper editor, in 1979, at the instigation of the NAP, no link could be found. Ugurlu was in continual contact with Bulgarian agents working out of the Bulgarian Consulate in Istanbul. His alleged Mafia operations involved the supply of arms to various factions throughout Turkey's political spectrum and to both Right and Left groups in Iran via Turkey. Along with Teslim Tore, one of Agca's closest associates in every phase of his activities was Oral Celik, a childhood friend who was also involved with the Bulgarians. Celik and Tore worked to place Turkey in the Soviet orbit. The Turkish government reopened its case against Agca in early-1983, after the Italians had arrested Sergei Ivanov Antonov, a Bulgarian airline official living in Rome, and published the purported Bulgarian connection.

The Turkish investigation included detailed probing into the reputed Mafia operations of Ugurlu, who was extradited from Germany to Turkey in March 1981 and was reported to have Bulgarian drug- and arms-smuggling connections going back to the 1960s. Only after some considerable time was a link suspected between Agca and Ugurlu, the Turkish Mafia godfather.

Agca issued a threat against the Pope's life on his escape from prison in November 1979. Agca's explanation of the threat could help pinpoint when the plot to kill the Pope began to take shape. There is no reliable evidence that he was motivated by religion or Islamic fundamentalism in particular.

It is clear that Agca had close relations with the Bulgarians starting as early as 1978. Historical and circumstantial evidence all tend to point in the same direction towards Moscow to explain the plot against the Pope. There is a strong probability that the Kremlin leadership and the KGB were the architects of the plot to kill John Paul II.

See also: Turkey.

References

Henze, P. (1983) 'The Plot to Kill the Pope: A Survey', *Journal of East and West Studies*, vol. 27 nos. 118/119, pp. 2–21.

Further Reading

Friedlander, R. A. (1983) *An Infantry of Mirrors: Mehmet Ali Agca and the Plot to Kill the Pope*, Gaithersburg, MD: International Association of Chiefs of Police.
Sterling, C. (1985) 'The Great Bulgarian Cover-Up', *The New Republic*, vol. 129 no. 21, pp. 16–21.

Al-Aqsa Martyrs Brigade

The Al-Aqsa Martyrs Brigade was created at the start of the Intifada in the early-1990s to attack Israeli targets in Palestine, with the long-term aim of creating an independent Palestinian state. Suicide bombings and shootings are carried out against Israeli personnel. The Brigade operates almost entirely out of the West Bank. The activists in the group are affiliated to Al Fatah (Griset and Mahan, 2003: 326). It is a martyrdom society of fighters drawn from Al Fatah and is a secular PLO affiliated brigade.

References

Griset, P. L. and Mahan, S. (2003) *Terrorism in Perspective*. Thousand Oaks, CA, London and New Delhi: Sage Publications.

Algeria

The Algerian Civil War of the mid-1950s is often viewed as a model of **guerrilla warfare**. Over 1.5 million Algerians were killed or disappeared during the eight-year conflict of national liberation from November 1954 to May 1962. The war was fought with great cruelty on both sides. A third of the economic infrastructure of the country was destroyed during the war in the countryside and the vicious battles waged in the cities between the Front de Liberation Nationale (FLN), a militant nationalist and originally moderate Socialist movement founded in 1954, and the Organisation Armee Secrete (OAS). Over a million Europeans fled, immediately after the commencement of hostilities or during the last summer of the war in 1962, which meant the loss of many professional workers.

The French had ruled Algeria harshly for more than a century before the War of Liberation. French cruelty toward, and degradation of, the native population, was compounded by the fact that military governors ruled the country for much of the nineteenth century, often using it as a testing ground of the army's prestige and as a vehicle for their own careers. The Colons, European settlers in Algeria many of whom were not themselves French, were constantly at odds with the military regime pressing for ever more exploitative policies toward the native; and most of the Muslims refused to convert to Christianity or to assimilate fully the French culture, thus increasing the already lively disdain for them on the part of the metropolitan French, as well as of the Colons. These polarisations within Algerian society, which were accompanied by the expropriation of the best lands and retributive taxes, grew only more extreme when, during and after the First World War, the native labour force became deeply entangled in the French economy, the army and the factories and plantations of the Colons. The generation of stored resentment explain in part the savagery of the war and the harshness of the post-revolutionary regimes. Such an example of savagery occurred at the village of Melouza in 1957, where all the males were executed by the FLN for rebelling against FLN terrorism, supporting a rival nationalist group and also for co-operating with the French army. The FLN managed to persuade most Muslims in Algeria that it was the French who had committed the murders in order to discredit the FLN.

The revolutionary theorist, Frantz **Fanon**, saw in his adopted country the need for violence as a cleansing force that unified the people, and he advocated terrorism as a tool for freeing the natives from feelings of inferiority, and from despair and inaction. The FLN leader, Ouzegane, who suggested that terrorism fulfilled other functions internally, namely relieving the tension caused by inaction and controlling impatience among militants, supported Fanon in his views.

The insurgency, which bedevilled the country in the 1990s, developed as a result of the cancellation of elections in January 1992. When the first round of the elections suggested the Muslim Front Islamique du Salut (FIS) was likely to be the clear winner in round two, the military stepped in and democracy was replaced with a High Council of State.

Since 1992 over 75,000 people have died in Algeria as two Muslim military groups, the Armée Islamique du Salut (AIS) and the more extreme Group Islamique Armée (GIA), have brought bombings to the cities and massacres to the villages.

The West is concerned that any further move towards **Islam** in Algeria could pose serious questions for security in Europe as many thousands of Algerians live in France and are able to travel around Europe. Algeria is a fluid society balanced precariously between its historical French influenced cultural links and modern Arab concepts. The young are very disillusioned and are a fertile recruiting ground for militants.

See also: Fanon.

Reference

Slone, M. (1997) *The Agony of Algeria*, London: Hurst & Co.

Further Reading

Alleg, Henri (1990) 'Political Violence in Algeria' in Darby, J., Dodge, N. and Hepburn, A. C. (eds) *Political Violence: Ireland in a Comparative Perspective*, Ottawa: Ottawa University Press, pp. 103–130.
Crenshaw Hutchinson, M. (1978) *Revolutionary*

Terrorism: The FLN in Algeria 1945–62, Stanford: Hoover Institution.

Harris, P. (1997) 'Algerian Election Puts Democracy Against Terrorism', *Jane's Intelligence Review*, vol. 9, no. 9, pp. 422–425.

Al Jazeera

This Qatar-based television station has been active as a voice for pro-Islamic solidarity and rationalisation across the Muslim world. There are 35 million viewers worldwide and an even larger audience are available due to the media. Since late 2001, the station has been providing other stations with much of its material.

It has been operating since 1998 but really came into its own with the Palestinian Intifada in September 2000. Al Jazeera's daily coverage of scenes of brutality against Palestinians inflamed Arab viewers and embarrassed pro-Western regimes. **Osama Bin Laden** has appeared provocatively on Al Jazeera's TV screens, most interestingly in November 2002, when indeed, many people believed he had been killed in Afghanistan. To the Western world, Al Jazeera has provided a view of life in the Muslim world previously unseen. Islam is neither monolithic nor immutable – indeed, one-fifth of humanity is Muslim. Bin Laden represents Islam for Americans, but he does not speak for a majority of Muslims. In September 2003, Bin Laden appeared on TV and rumours circulated that he was in Pakistan.

See also: Afghanistan and the Guerrilla Movement; September 11: Attacks.

Reference

Jacquard, R. (2002) *In the Name of Osama Bin Laden*, Louisiana: Duke University Press.

Al Jihad

The word *Jihad* literally means 'striving' and is often translated as 'Holy War'. Maintaining the purity of religious existence is thought to be a matter of jihad. The Muslim concept of struggle – jihad – has been employed for centuries in Islamic theories of both personal salvation and political redemption. To the Ayatollahs in **Iran** the notion of fighting was basic to human existence and on a level with religious commitment. Moderate observers believe that jihad has social and economic dimensions, as well as the more widely known military and political roles.

In **Egypt**, *al Gihud*, as it is known, has managed to infiltrate its armed and teaching cells into many levels of society. In 1981, along with another Islamic group, Al-Gama'a al-Islamiyya, they assassinated the country's President, Anwar Sadat, at a military parade. This brought about distrust between civilians and the military and led to a renewed period of Islamic terrorist activity in the 1980s and 1990s, including the targeting of tourists at Luxor in 1997.

Bin Laden has argued that jihad, the Islamic concept of struggle has been going on since the 1920s. In contemporary Arabic there is a clear distinction between struggle that is legitimate jihad, and that which is aggressive, i.e.. adwan (aggression) and ghazu (invasion).

The Arabic term jihad is equivalent to self-control and self-exertion to undertake a variety of activities in furtherance of the will of God. Since Islam addresses the individual Muslim directly, there is a strong sense of obligation to comply with what is believed to be Sharia, regardless of the policy of the State and this can be jihad. The proponents of jihad as an aggressive war are more likely to be supported by the majority of Muslims in a world where military force and self-help prevails over the rule of law in international relations. After **September 11**, in rejecting an open call to jihad issued by the Taliban and its supporters, some Islamic nations acted out of interest, others out of principle, but most out of a combination of both. Muslim leaders who distanced themselves from Bin Laden believe the notion of jihad is best understood in terms of spiritual rather than physical struggle. The mistake of Jihad is to confuse religion with a love of death and this perhaps accounts for its unacceptability in many parts of the non-Islamic world. Bin Laden's alliance is the World Islamic Front for the Jihad against Jews and Crusaders is viewed as an attack on globalisation.

See also: Al Qaeda; Osama Bin Laden.

References

Juergensmeyer, M. (2000) *Terror in the Mind of God: The Global Rise of Religious Violence*, Berkeley and London: University of California Press.

Al Qaeda

In 1989 **Osama Bin Laden** set up Al Qaeda (the Base) in Peshawar in **Pakistan** as a service centre for Arab Afghans and their families and to promote Wahabbism – a strict form of the Muslim faith practised in **Saudi Arabia** – among the Afghans.

In 1985 Bin Laden had amassed millions of pounds from his family and company wealth and from donations from wealthy Arab Gulf merchant families, to organise Al Qaeda recruitment centres in Saudi Arabia, Egypt and Pakistan, through which he recruited, enlisted and sheltered Arab volunteers. They have been internationally active since that date.

One of the founding members of Al Qaeda was Mahmoud Salim, who after his arrest in Germany in 2000 was identified as a financial adviser and weapons procurer for Bin Laden.

After the Soviets left Afghanistan Bin Laden began to retrain his troops in the Al Qaeda organisation and moved away from anti-aircraft and anti-tank tactics used against the Soviets to urban **guerrilla warfare**, sabotage and terrorism aimed at destabilising the societies and governments that were to become his targets. For many years Bin Laden had been generous with financing for weapons, transport and incomes for families of the fighters against the Soviets. Bin Laden established a good relationship with a charismatic Palestinian Abdullah Azzam who became one of the inspirers of the Hamas Movement, rejecting Arafat's mainstream **Palestine Liberation Organisation** (PLO) and the smaller Palestinian groups as too Marxist and not sufficiently Islamic.

The workforce of companies owned by Bin Laden included thousands of militant Arabs and other veterans of the Afghan jihad. He paid for many to go to the Sudan in 1993–94 who were now under threat from crack-downs on them in Pakistan,

Egypt and **Algeria**. A branch of the Al Qaeda network was created in the Sudan. Later, this information was to influence President Clinton's decision to launch US cruise missile attacks on Sudan and Afghanistan, but to little effect as some missiles went astray and others hit the wrong targets.

In 1993 Bin Laden allegedly agreed to an Al Qaeda plan to consider buying a complete nuclear missile or highly enriched uranium from the former Soviet Union in the glorified pursuit of an Islamic bomb. This plan, however, came to nothing, as there were no missiles for sale. Consideration was then given by Al Qaeda to develop a nuclear suitcase bomb, which would be developed by the Chechen **Mafia** with cash given by the Al Qaeda group. We now know that Al Qaeda was developing links with Saddam Hussein in Iraq to construct weapons of mass destruction, especially of a biological content.

The Afghan Arab organisation was directed from its camps in Afghanistan after Bin Laden's forced departure from the Sudan in 1996. It next turned its attention to massive assaults on US personnel and property abroad. Two American embassies were destroyed in Kenya and Tanzania in August 1998 and two years later a suicide bomber in Aden harbour in Yemen attacked the *USS Cole*. Twenty Americans and 300 Africans were killed in total.

In 1996 the organisation was behind the bombing of a US military housing complex in Dharan in Saudi Arabia when nineteen American servicemen were killed.

A close ally of Bin Laden, Khalid Al-Fauwaz, working in London, was given some command of Al Qaeda.

The moulding together of the Al Qaeda organisation helped to secure Bin Laden a large personal following throughout the Muslim world, as it proved that he could unify disparate groups of Islamic Militants.

In Afghanistan, from 1996 Bin Laden also gained increasing status, and was sheltered by the Taliban government in that country. The Taliban were professional in managing the Afghan drugs trade and Bin Laden and Al Qaeda benefited.

By the end of the 1990s the **FBI** and CIA had publicly identified it as Bin Laden's main vehicle for international terrorist operations during that decade and indeed, can claim it to be Bin Laden's terrorist organisation. He had laid the groundwork in preparing a terrorist army for war. Bin Laden's ideas and membership of Al Qaeda soon spread via Yemen and Albania into the rest of Europe, Africa and the Middle East – many finance and accounts departments supporting Al Qaeda were created in several European capitals.

The group opposes all nations and institutions, which do not adhere to the Islamic way of life and beliefs. It adheres to the 1998 fatwa or religious ruling stating that Muslims should kill Americans wherever they are in the world. Furthermore, all Muslim governments corrupted by Western influence must be overthrown by force.

To assist it carry out such ideology and objectives it has a command and control structure which includes a Majlis al Shura (a Consultancy Council) to approve all terrorist operations. It also has a business committee, a religious committee, a media committee and a travel office.

Al Qaeda's financial source of support comes from Bin Laden's personal fortune estimated at circa $300 million obtained from his father's construction company and also from agricultural, leather and investment companies and export industries in the Sudan linked with agricultural products. Sinisterly, these companies provide cover for the procurement of operatives, weapons and chemicals and the transportation of operatives. Money has also been received from Islamic clergy and the Dubai Islamic Bank. As with other terrorist groups operations are also financed by robberies and the commercial activities of business personnel. It is a growing international group with links in over 55 countries.

Initially Al Qaeda's base was Palestine, and then it relocated to the Sudan and finally settled in Afghanistan (the Tora Bora ex-military base and other sites). Here it grew as a training centre and a loose network of cells and sleepers were developed in more than 40 countries after the September 11 attacks. Radical Islamic groups with links to Al Qaeda – such as Abu Sayyaf in the Philippines – began to challenge states through terrorist activity. The war in Afghanistan in late 2001 led to many Al Qaeda members fleeing especially to some parts of Central Asia (some were alleged to be involved in the Chechen war for independence from Russia)

and to the Yemen. Its tactics have a common theme with other groups, and include bombing, hijacking, kidnapping, assassination and suicide attacks. The group has been linked to the production of the chemical VX in Sudan and the biological agent ricin, and in trying to obtain enriched uranium.

Old-style revolutionary parties were hierarchical and had some clear organisational structure. In the new world of global social movements the network pattern of association is emerging as the most effective mode of operation. The information revolution favours the role of network forms of organisation, and this has obviously helped to redefine conflict.

The strength of Al Qaeda lies in its ability as a flexible network of relationships to appeal to a widely diverse sentiment within which people can be recruited. The appeal of the message of Bin Laden's militant religious movement rests on its call to fight for a religious vision of the future. Bin Laden and Al Qaeda represent extremes that can merge in the new age of desecularised modernity and social movement of protest and revolution (Voll, 2001).

Al Qaeda's hidden target is globalisation as well as liberalism. Training manuals instruct its jihad warriors to assume every appearance of normality in order to evade detection within Western civil society. Terror can be war as well as crime. Bin Laden operated onshore and offshore, yet the US government was unable to stop September 11 – and they were not helped by federal criminal agencies not disclosing investigative information to them. Al Qaeda killed innocent non-combatants in an attempt to spread terror, and their attacks on military targets were illegal as they were carried out in civilian disguise. They have been part of a conspiracy to commit war crimes. Al Qaeda has failed to observe the 'Rules of War', or to wear identifying insignia, or to carry arms openly (Wedgwood, 2002).

The intelligence services of both Israel and the UK warned the Americans that there would be a major attack on the United Sates. In July 2001 Mossad, the Israel Secret Service, warned of an attack being imminent. In 1999, MI6 received an indication that Bin Laden's followers were planning attacks in which civilian aircraft could be used in 'unconventional ways'. Information did not specify targets. In 1998, Al Qaeda was plotting fresh attacks according to MI6, some concerning American interests in Europe.

Yemen is the ancestral home of Osama Bin Laden and there are hundreds of Al Qaeda fighters hiding throughout the country. Allied forces, mainly American and French, are based in Djibouti awaiting orders to go into the Yemen. Here they can also target Somalia, but the main priority is Yemen, specifically its border with Saudi Arabia, a lawless region suspected of harbouring those responsible for attacking the *USS Cole*.

Al Qaeda activities from September 2001 to September 2002 include the targeting of American embassies in Albania, Austria, Bosnia, Cambodia, France, Indonesia, Italy, Jordan, Philippines, Singapore, Vietnam and Yemen. The NATO headquarters in Belgium was targeted. In Singapore a list of 200 American-owned companies was recovered from the terrorists and if these had been attacked significant collateral damage would have been done.

See also: September 11.

References

Bergen, P. L. (2001) *Holy War: Inside the Secret World of Osama Bin Laden*, New York: Free Press.

Voll, J. O. (2001) 'Bin Laden and the New Age of Global Terrorism', *Middle East Policy*, vol. VIII, no. 4, pp. 1–4.

Wedgwood, R. (2002) 'The Laws Response to September 11', *Ethics and International Affairs*, vol. 16, no. 1, pp. 6–13.

Further Reading

Alexander, Y. and Sweetman, M. (2001) *Osama Bin Laden's Al Qaeda: Profile of a Terrorist Network*, Ardsley, NY: Transnational Publishers.

'Al Qaeda's Captured Men', *Sunday Times* 30 June 2002.

Carter, A. *et al.* (1998) 'Catastrophic Terrorism: Tackling the New Danger', *Foreign Affairs*, vol. 77 (November/December), pp. 80–92.

'The Hunt for Al Qaeda One Year On', *Guardian*, 4 September 2002.

Jaquard, R. (2002) *In the Name of Osama Bin Laden*, Durham, NC: Duke University Press.

Ruthven, M. (2002) 'The Eleventh of September and the Sudanese Mahdiya in the Context of Ibn Khaldun's Theory of Islam History', *International Affairs*, vol. 76, no. 2, pp. 339–51.

Smith, P. J. (2002) 'Transnational Terrorism and the Al Qaeda Model: Confronting New Realities', *Parameters*, US Army War College Quarterly, vol. XXXII, no. 2.

Williams, P. L. (2002) *Al Qaeda Brotherhood of Terror*, London: Alpha Pearson Education.

Angolan Civil War 1974–1976

By 1964 the wind of change had blown across most of black Africa, but Angola – the heartland of Portugal's African empire – appeared to be firmly under Portuguese control. In Leopoldville (now Kinshasa), capital of what was then the Congo (now Zaire) were the headquarters of what at that time appeared to be the chief Angolan liberation movement, the Revolutionary Government of Angola in Exile (GRAE). GRAE was run by Holden Roberto, whose brother-in-law was Joseph Mobutu, was at that period Commander-in-Chief of the Congolese Army and soon to be the country's autocratic ruler.

Many members of the Portuguese Colonial Army and Portuguese settlers were killed in the early-1960s by Roberto's followers in the Bakongo tribe, who in turn suffered at the hands of the army.

Roberto had formed the first (outlawed) political parties in the Portuguese colony of Angola, and in 1962 had proclaimed the GRAE, with himself as its head. His advantage was that the Bakongo were a vigorous people who had tasted freedom and power in one part of their territories – Joseph Kasavubu, the Congo's first president, was a Bakongo – and were ready to struggle for it elsewhere. Kasavubu's disadvantage was that he represented only the Bakongo and they were limited to the north of Angola. Only about one in ten of the six million Angolans were Bakongo. It was inevitable that other leaders should spring up elsewhere in that vast country to represent the other tribal or ethnic groups.

Jonas Savimbi defected from the GRAE in 1964, where he had been a close associate of Roberto, but was always playing second fiddle. He went to the

south of Angola, to his own people, the Ovim-
bundu, who were three times as numerous as the
Bakongo in Angola; two years later he founded the
Unido Nacional para a Independencia Total de
Angola (UNITA). With the rival claim of UNITA it
became hard for Roberto to maintain the fiction
that he was leading a united government-in-exile.
The GRAE gradually faded away, to be replaced
by the more militant and military Frente Nacional
de Libertação de Angola (FNLA), also led by
Roberto.

Another liberation movement on the Angolan
scene was a somewhat more sophisticated group,
the Movimento Popular de Libertação de Angola
(MPLA). Founded in 1956, the MPLA was an
urban movement, its greatest strength lying in the
capital of the country, the port of Luanda, where
half a million people (including 150,000 Portuguese
lived). It was a party of intellectuals and theorists,
and very much influenced by Marxism. There were
many pure blacks in its ranks – led by a poet,
Agostinho Neto. But there were many pure
Portuguese in the party too, as well as *mestizos*
(Angolans of mixed Portuguese-African blood) free
from tribal links and loyalties.

Until 1974 the Portuguese hung on, but
maintaining an army in Angola was a drain on
Portugal's resources. The FNLA was largely
inactive and UNITA operated mainly in areas
run by Portugal's white allies.

On 25 April 1974 the whole situation changed
and in an almost bloodless revolution, the autocratic regime in Portugal was overthrown by the
Armed Forces Movement and the anti-fascist 'Junta
of National Salvation' took control of Portugal.
Two months later Portugal offered independence to
Angola, Mozambique and Guinea. Of the three,
Angola proved a problem, and it was impossible to
bring the warring factions together in a transitional
government.

The Portuguese Army had declined from its
original position as a strong military force, and lost
the will to fight – many of its soldiers supported the
MPLA. The longer-established Portuguese, the
settlers, artisans, tradesmen, and rich minority of
plantation owners, right-wing by both inclination
and tradition, tended to support anyone who
opposed the MPLA.

The USA immediately gave direct and indirect

support to the rival movements – Roberto's FNLA
and, in the south, Savimbi's UNITA, to prevent at
all cost another Western ex-colony being taken over
by a pro-Soviet movement.

China gave support to the FNLA for anti-Soviet
reasons; and in mid-1975, **Cuba** became involved,
with Soviet support, through a commando assault
by sea on the UNITA-held port of Lobito and
nearby railhead of Benguela. UNITA was pushed
back into the interior. The Cuban leader, Fidel
Castro, proceeded to pour in troops and money.

South Africa reacted by sending helicopters
and troops across the border to protect the
hydroelectric works at Ruacana. Fierce fighting
raged in Luanda, where with Cuban help and
Soviet arms, the MPLA attacked and destroyed the
FNLA headquarters in the capital. The MPLA
consolidated their hold and UNITA moved inland.
Thousands of whites and *mestizos* fled the country;
coffee, sisal and cotton crops went unpicked and the
diamond industry collapsed. But the MPLA had
perhaps reacted too soon, for Zaire gave more aid
to the FNLA and South Africa gave more
committed support to UNITA, and achieved
success in the south. In the north, however, an
FNLA move on the capital led to disaster. In the
same month, November 1975, the MPLA proclaimed independence with Neto as President of
the Democratic Republic in Luando, while UNITA
proclaimed independence at Nova Lisboa; and the
FNLA proclaimed independence in Ambriz with
Holden Roberto as President of the Democratic
Republic. Despite South Africa-backed columns
and CIA intervention, Zaire still posed problems
for the MPLA.

In despair Roberto decided with CIA approval
to switch tack, as he was concerned by the poor
fighting qualities of the Zairean forces, and hired
sympathisers from Britain and the **USA**. These
men showed great courage and ability in attacking
advancing Cuban and MPLA columns head on.
Their leader, Colonel Callan, a mercenary, maintained discipline ultimately through executions; as
a consequence, morale soon collapsed and Callan
himself was captured. UNITA, under Savimbi,
also suffered, and after a defeat at the hands of the
MPLA the remnant retreated to the bush. By
1976 Roberto was safe in Kinshasa, but with all
hopes destroyed; the Americans halted their

operations and South Africa withdrew from the Ruacana Dam.

The **civil war** was in effect over and President Nero ruled the country. The captured mercenaries were put on trial and, amid a blaze of publicity, Callan and three others were executed. It was a triumph for the MPLA, for Castro and for the Russians; and a body blow not merely to Portuguese pride, but to **South Africa**, the CIA and the West in general.

In 1985 a big MPLA offensive was conducted with the aid of 15,000 Cuban troops. The US resumed aid to UNITA and South Africa intervened on a large-scale. Both sides agreed to demobilise to prepare for national elections in 1990; but UNITA and MPLA, both without their respective supporters, started fighting, yet the government remained in control despite UNITA controlling 70 per cent of the country (Ellis, 1995).

Jonas Savimbi died in 2002 when he was surprised in his last redoubt 500 miles south east of Luanda, the capital. He died while firing at advancing government forces. The international community now believe the time is right for talks to start to begin to an end Africa's longest running Civil War. In the immense mineral-rich state 500,000 lives have been taken and millions of poverty-stricken people displaced. The Left-wing government called on UNITA to cease fighting, but they said they would continue to fight. In recent years Western governments, especially the USA, have shown interest in the oil deposits.

Reference

Ellis, J. (1995) *From the Barrel of a Gun*, London: Greenhill Books and Mechanicsburg, PA: Stackpole Books.

Further Reading

Alberts, D. J. (1980) 'Armed Struggle in Angola', in O'Neill, B. E., Heaton, W. R. and Alberts, D. J. (eds) *Insurgency in the Modern World*, Boulder, CO: Westview Press, pp. 235–268.
Sidler, P. (1985) 'Angola, Namibia and their Guerrillas', *Swiss Review of World Affairs*, vol. 34, no. 10, pp. 8–11.

Animal Rights

Increasingly, individuals and groups have expressed fears about the predicament of animals, especially those used in experiments. Groups can be concerned with general animal welfare, such as the Royal Society for the Prevention of Cruelty to Animals (RSPCA), or with animal rights, such as the Animal Liberation Front (ALF). The three main sectors within the animal rights groups are the established societies with huge funds that act within the law, the local animal rights groups existing in most towns, districts and universities, and extremist movements which are semi-clandestine and break the law. The leaders have motivation and ability – some are motivated genuinely for animal rights reasons; others, however, are politically motivated and use animal rights as a means to an end; and, lastly, others are bored and frustrated and wish to make an impact on society. For this last group of people violence can become an addiction. Small demonstrations can act as diversions for sinister activities by a larger group who desire to inflict economic damage on animal abusers.

Many of the groups have their own system of funding, often a newspaper or magazine, and are worth thousands, and in some cases, millions of pounds. In some groups there has been a radical challenge to seize control, and to become increasingly political.

The animal rights movement first developed on a wide-scale in Western Europe and Scandinavia, and then spread to Britain and the **United States**.

Ultimately, members of some of these groups are willing to undertake widespread destruction and killing to try and achieve their aims. Some have sympathies with anarchists, and undertake widespread civil disobedience.

The development of animal liberation groups in Britain represented a new and ugly extremist dimension in the operation of 'issue groups', prompting police to consider the establishment of a special squad to counter the increasingly violent activities of the groups. Extremist elements within the animal rights movement are actually indulging in acts of terrorism. Animal rights activists have used violence as a policy with the expressed intent of coercing the government to enact specific legislation. Claims of poisoned sweets or other consumer bombs, the destruction of property, or even aggressive slogans painted on walls engender fear. Some members of the ALF do wish to change government policy by violent, undemocratic and illegal means. The Front believes in coercive intimidation, of which law-breaking has been an unavoidable consequence. Animal welfare is a popular cause, and there are few who are so inhumane as not to espouse its general aims. But the extremist animal rights movement provides an avenue for those who seek to disrupt the stability of the nation. The Front is structured in a network of cells, each independent and in contact only by a liaison representative. It is secretive and conspiratorial. The style of dress worn during raids – hoods, camouflage smocks or overalls – and the use of pick handles and other hazardous items point to an emulation of urban guerrillas. Terror tactics are employed – breaking and entering in a violent manner and the flouting of the law. ALF propaganda is disseminated by recognised terrorist groups. The outrages committed by extremist behaviour bring media attention and perhaps encourage recruiting.

The reality is that frustration evoked by perceived public apathy or revulsion can prompt the militant fringe to opt for a campaign of excesses, attacks and raids that can result in death. Future possibilities are varied. Amateur animal rights supporters wishing to become dedicated to the cause, or individuals who do not have formal association with the movement, could carry out illegal acts similar to those undertaken by the ALF membership. An individual could also act rashly merely on the basis that 'righteousness' of the cause condones it.

Letter bomb production, contamination threats and car bombs characterised the period between 1982 and 1988. During this time the Animal Rights Militia (ARM) appeared – a group willing to use violence against people in the name of animal rights. They attacked the homes of scientists' and then turned their attention to attacking laboratories carrying out animal experimentation (Monaghan, 1997).

Product contamination signified a change in tactics from the mid-1980s. The public felt threatened. In 1988 Mars bars were allegedly adulterated with rat poison – the Mars Company losing £6 million as a result of what turned out to be a hoax. Bombs were used; especially incendiary devices and they were employed in the fur departments of Debenham stores in the summer of 1987. In the mid-1990s ARM claimed to have targeted shops selling leather goods, a fishing tackle shop, a high street chemist and charity shops.

At its height in the late-1990s, ALF claimed 5,000 adherents contributing money. Companies have taken increased security measures and some individuals have foiled kidnap and death threats to themselves and their families for supporting the use of animals in medical research.

From the use of 'sabbing' in the early-1960s – namely a variety of tactics used to prevent foxhunters from catching their quarry – over the following two decades and more there has been a marked escalation in the violence of the actions used by ALF. For example, raids on laboratories were replaced by letter bombs and product contamination. Their targets have always been a wide range of institutions and individuals who either use animals or animal products or sell products for use with animals. Basic criminal damage – graffiti and breaking windows – occurs regularly. An unusual form of attack is known as 'Animal Liberation Investigation' which entails entering a research establishment or animal breeding facility during the day without causing damage, but stealing papers, files and computer disks to study and returning them later, arguing that this is not a crime. They also break into laboratories, farms or animal breeding centres and remove the animals kept there, and in particular attacks in the Cambridge area have been common. Car bombs were used in the late-1980s on vehicles of people associated with laboratory animal experimentation.

ALF activity in Europe is more loosely organised, but can be just as effective. The police in the UK keep checks on activists through the Animal Rights National Index.

In the 1990s there was a decrease in ALF activity in the UK; but an increase in similar activity in the USA. Many of the American activists have visited their British counterparts to learn about new tactics – but so far their level of violence has not overtaken the British levels.

Within the Animal Liberation Front, activists choose their own targets and method of carrying out attacks. Lately, they have received support increasingly from national organisations concerned with anti-vivisection.

The *Prevention of Terrorism Acts* do not cover the activities of violent animal right activists, as there is no perceived threat to the realm from these 'issue' groups. Individuals and businesses using animals whether for profit or scientific advancement have had to respond to the potential threat that the ALF pose. The latest tactic has moved from breaking and entering premises to sending poster tube bombs containing hypodermic needles and the planting of car bombs.

References

Collins, J. G. (1990) 'Terrorism and Animal Rights', *Science*, vol. 249, no. 4967, p. 345.

Garner, R. (1993) *Animals, Politics and Morality*, Manchester: Manchester University Press.

Matfield, Dr M. (1997) 'The Animal Liberation Front: When Animal Rights Becomes Terrorism' in *Terrorism: A Global Survey*, London, Jane's Information Group, pp. 29–34.

Monaghan, R. (1997) 'Animal Rights and Violent Protest', *Terrorism & Political Violence*, vol. 9, no. 4 (winter), pp. 106–116.

Smith, G. Davidson (1984) 'Issue Group Terrorism: Animal Rights Militancy in Britain', *TVI Journal*, vol. 5, no. 4, pp. 44–47.

Further Reading

Monaghan, R. (1999) 'Terrorism in the Name of Animal Rights', *Terrorism and Political Violence*, vol. 11, no. 4, pp. 159–168.

Mulgannon, T. (1985) 'The Animal Liberation Front', *TVI Journal*, vol. 5, no. 4, pp. 39–43.

Singer, P. (1991) *Animal Liberation*, London: Thorsons.

Smith, G. Davidson (1985) 'Political Violence in Animal Liberation', *Contemporary Review*, vol. 247, no. 1434, pp. 26–31.

Wardlaw, G. (1990) *Political Terrorism*, (2nd edn), New York and Cambridge: Cambridge University Press.

Anti-Semitic Terrorism in Europe

From being a particular problem associated with the creation of the Israel state and attacks on Jews in that country, Palestine and other Arab countries, anti-Semitic terrorism has spread to include a wide range of Jewish targets in Europe. Seventeen West European countries have been affected, with the highest proportion of attacks occurring in Britain, France and West Germany. Most of the attacks have been targeted against Israeli facilities or citizens and the rest against local Jewish community institutions, or Jewish individuals. Well over a quarter of all attacks against Jews and Israelis in Europe involved people rather than property, and such attacks were obviously intended to cause casualties. Perpetrators connected with Palestinian terrorist organisations, have carried out the greatest numbers of attacks.

Jewish communities in Europe tend to keep log books of anti-Semitic events and rely on the direct reporting of local organisations and private persons who may have received threatening telephone calls, abusive letters or whose property might have been painted with anti-Semitic graffiti, swastikas, and the like.

Jewish public awareness of the necessity to report every single anti-Semitic occurrence may differ from country to country; and many smaller incidents can remain unreported. The high number of reported general anti-Semitic incidents in the UK is probably due to a combination of a particular community awareness as well as professional and conscientious attitude towards establishing a proper record of incidents. For instance, the daubing of synagogues and the desecration of cemeteries deeply affects the feelings of Jews. Unrelated spontaneous acts of simple prejudice, violent as they may be, are still of a different class from premeditated terrorist atrocities requiring the acquisition of a weapon or the handling of explosive charges.

Only rarely in these anti-Semitic attacks have the perpetrators been apprehended on the spot. Armed attacks have almost always lasted less than four minutes, and the perpetrators have been able to use the public confusion in the wake of the attack to escape. The radical non-mainline Palestinian groups who oppose the ban on international terrorism issued by Yasser Arafat have carried out most of the more serious attacks. These include operatives of **Abu Nidal**, the Lebanese Armed Revolutionary Faction, the Black June Group, and 15 May, who have increased their level of activity against Jewish targets. Whether some of the less conspicuous attacks, such as arson attempts on synagogues and Jewish-owned shops, which are often accompanied by night-time Nazi-type daubing, are necessarily of Right-wing origin is only speculative. Theories have also circulated about the activities of the French group Action Directe, to the effect that hardcore factions may indulge in deadly terrorism against Israeli or Jewish targets, whereas a more moderate faction would decide to hit only at 'economic' targets such as trade and banking agencies.

Fears existed in the 1980s and 1990s over globalisation winning over nationalism leading to a loss of national identity amid a growing influx of immigrants. During the early-1990s for example, German **Neo-Nazis** who had begun fighting Leftist, switched their focus to beating up immigrants, tourists and Jews.

In France, the National Front (NF) gained much support during the period 1980–90 based on an anti-immigration platform. Attacks were made on Jewish cemeteries and synagogues, leading many Jews to consider fleeing France. Austria saw a rapid rise of extreme right-wing sentiments in 1999, which declined equally rapidly by 2002 amid global concerns.

Right-wing terrorism did not gain as much ground in the 1990s as left-wing groups had in the previous decade.

See also: Neo-Nazi Terrorism.

Reference

Hill, R. (1988) *The Other Face of Terror: Inside Europe's Neo-Nazi Network*, London: Grafton.

Further Reading

Harris, G. (1990) *The Dark Side of Europe: The Extreme Right Today*, Edinburgh: Edinburgh University Press.

Von Beyne, K. (ed.) (1988) *Right-Wing Extremism in Western Europe*, London: Frank Cass.

April 19 Movement (M-19)

Formed in **Colombia** in 1974, the M-19 group took its name from the date on which ex-President General Rojas Pinilla, the leader of the National Popular Alliance, had been defeated in the 1970 presidential elections. The M-19 claimed to be the armed wing of the ANAPO – the National Popular Alliance Party– although the latter rejected this claim. While ANAPO was a hierarchically organised party standing for 'Colombian Socialism' on a Christian Socialist basis, by the end of the 1970s the M-19 came to be regarded as left-wing and Marxist, and its leaders declared as its aim the achievement of a democratic and ultimately socialist state by political means. Initial operations included thefts and **kidnapping** and it was reported to have declared war in 1978 on the government of President Ayala, which had introduced increased penalties for acts of violence such as armed **rebellion**, kidnapping and bombing. Seizure of weapons was a common feature of the M-19's activities.

Major M-19 operations in 1980 included the temporary occupation of the embassy of the Dominican Republic in Bogotá from February to April, when M-19 guerrillas seized 57 hostages, including the ambassadors of 14 countries – among them those of Israel, Mexico and the **USA** – as well as the Papal Nuncio. The demands originally made by the kidnappers for the release of the hostages were in protracted negotiations involving, among other intermediaries, the Inter-American Human Rights Commission (IHRC) of the Organisation of American States, and were eventually reduced to payment of a ransom of $10,000,000 and the release of 28 political detainees. The guerrillas accepted assurances that trials of M-19 suspects would be monitored by IHRC observers, and left by air for Havana on 27 April, taking with them the 12 remaining hostages (who were later released in **Cuba**). All other hostages had been freed in stages during the negotiations and one of the guerrillas was killed in a shooting incident at the beginning of the siege. The ransom eventually paid amounted to $2,500,000.

Later, the M-19 continued to engage in numerous acts of violence, including bomb attacks, hijackings and even the interruption of TV broadcasts in 1980, and increased violence in Bogotá. Two amnesties announced by the government against the guerrillas were rejected, because such an amnesty did not include those who had carried out murders and kidnappings. Recommendations by a Peace Commission set up by the government that the government should enter into direct negotiations with M-19 leaders were rejected by the government (owing to opposition by the armed forces and certain political sectors), and when they rejected another of the Commission's recommendations (to suspend sentences imposed on guerrillas), five of the Commission members resigned.

In 1982 a further amnesty appeared to have more success, because it covered those convicted of sedition, conspiracy and rebellion. The political command of M-19 had talks with the Interior Minister with a view to obtaining a 'social justice guarantee' before M-19 laid down its arms. Kidnappings still continue to the present day, including the kidnap of a banker's daughter in 1983, and more spectacularly in 1985, the holding in the Supreme Court in Bogotá of judges involved in justice trials against M-19 members. This resulted in the army storming the law building and the deaths of fifty persons, including the leader of M-19 and the Chief Justice of Colombia.

See also: Colombia.

Further Reading

TVI Report Profiles (1989): April 19 Movement (M-19), *TVI Report*, vol. 9, no. 1, pp. 1–4.

Arafat, Yasser

b. 1929

Leader of the Palestinian peoples, his real name is Mohammed Abed Ar'ouf Arafat. In the 1950s he was one of the founders of the al Fatah and in 1968 he became President of the **Palestine Liberation Organisation** (PLO). Al Fatah (victory) also known as the Palestine National Liberation Movement was established in the late-1950s and began

guerrilla warfare and terrorism against Israel in the mid-1960s.

For over a decade Arafat and his comrades refused to recognise the state of Israel and that it was there to stay. There was equal prevarication over the renunciation of territories by the PLO. Yet dissidents within the PLO accused Arafat of incompetence and weakness when in the 1980s he opened negotiations with King Hussein and President Mubarak, both of whom supported an American plan in that decade which involved recognising Israel. Arafat's bitterest enemy was **Abu Nidal** and Al Fatah had sentenced him to death and Nidal tried to have Arafat assassinated. Ahmed **Jabril**, the head of PFLP-General Command was a fierce rival of Arafat, as he was linked with a Palestinian organisation set up by Syrians to rule the PLO, namely Al Saiqa (the Thunderbolt). In the 1980s after Israelis had driven Arafat and the PLO out of Lebanon, a dissident leader, Abu Mussa, allied himself with the Syrians and challenged Arafat in the PLO camps in the Bekaa Valley and Northern Lebanon. It was part of President Assad's rivalry with Arafat: the Syrian president was determined to control all the players in Lebanon, and Arafat was the last to oppose him. On 14 December 1988 Arafat formally recognised Israel's right to exist and renounced the policy of terrorism (a week later a bomb destroyed a jumbo jet over **Lockerbie**).

Arafat was forced to move away and set up his new Al Fatah headquarters in Tunis. He remained the most prominent leader of the Palestinians and several moderate faction men were assassinated. His bodyguard increased and he was afraid of both Israelis and his Arab rivals. Later, the **Hamas** leader, Ahmed Yassin had praises heaped upon him by Arafat, as Yassin remained an important and honoured figure in Gaza. Arafat paid frequent visits to the **Soviet Union** – the Soviet view being that he was a leader of a political movement, and a statesman recognised by many members of the **United Nations** Council.

Arafat was committed to the basis of a Palestinian state, and despite various oppositions from within his own ranks, he took part in secret negotiations with the Israelis in 1993, brokered by the Norwegians. The Declaration of Principles signed in Washington in September 1993 provided no more than the outlines of a political settlement. The peace process, however, found considerable opposition among Palestinian and Israeli people. In order to see a positive outcome the Nobel Peace Prize was awarded jointly to Arafat and the Israeli Prime Minister, Yitzhak **Rabin**, and to the Israeli Foreign Minister, Shimon Peres.

Subsequent years saw Arafat's position undermined by his inability to counter the rapid rise of Islamic Fundamentalism and support for it in some quarters of the Palestinian government. He was one of the first Arab leaders to denounce the horrific events of **September 11**. He had paid a heavy price for his support of Saddam Hussein after the invasion of Kuwait in 1990. Moderate Palestinians and Arafat distanced themselves from **Osama Bin Laden**. Since September 11 the rapid rise of Hamas suicide bombings in **Israel** and the inability seemingly of Arafat to stop them, has led to a concerted campaign by Ariol Sharon the Israeli Prime Minister against Arafat, including the bombing of his headquarters at Ramallah on the West Bank.

References

Gowers, A. and Walker, T. (1990) *Behind the Myth: Yasser Arafat and the Palestinian Revolution*, London: W. H. Allen.

O'Ballance, E. (1984) 'Arafat and the PLO', *Journal of the Royal United Services Institute for Defence Studies*, vol. 129, no. 1, pp. 49–52.

Further Reading

Brogan, Patrick (1992) *World Conflicts: Why and Where They Are Happening*, London: Bloomsbury.

Kelman, H. C. (1983) *Understanding Arafat*, Tel Aviv: The International Centre for Peace in the Middle East.

Mishal, S. (1986) *The PLO and Arafat: Between Gun and Olive Branch*, New Haven, CT: Yale University Press.

Army–Police Co-operation

In a liberal democracy when the subject of co-operation against terrorism is broached in army and **police** circles, the usual response is that an armed policeman is not a soldier and a soldier is not an armed policeman. Any response to terrorism must be acceptable to the government of the day, but it is also important that the response is acceptable to the public and the police, since the police function in a democracy rests on the consent of the citizens to be policed.

Effective police work against terrorism depends on intelligence, and intelligence depends on public co-operation. In Britain, the government has the power to requisition troops when a threat to order has developed beyond the capacity of the police to deal with it. In general, the police role is one of keeping the peace by the use of traditional procedures and legal machinery, whereby in a democratic society lawlessness is contained and processes are controlled by methods acceptable to the public as a whole. Conversely, the soldier is the embodiment of the ultimate sanction of force necessary to every government for protection from external attack or dealing with domestic extremist activities. The army does not act, as a police force does, on behalf of the community as a whole, but on the orders of its political masters to whom it is accountable through its command structure. In Britain, military aid to the police is restricted to very small numbers of troops, strictly limited in purpose and short-lived in duration. There is a consensus view that Army-Police emergency measures should be kept to a minimum, as there are dangers of doing the terrorists' work for them by alienating the host community, escalating the conflict and eroding democracy in the cause of security. The military can never come to the aid of civil power without the permission of the government of the day. Modern democratic governments prefer to rely on the police to handle disorder because it reduces the chances of politicisation of the military. An army is not fitted or trained to sustain a police role at least not as a permanent function in conjunction with military duties.

There has traditionally been a dichotomy between civil and military relations. Free societies have faced the eternal balancing task of harmonising liberty and national security. Preserving such a balance has been complicated by the fact that the one institution indispensable to the nation's security, the military, exercises a power not necessarily in harmony with an open democratic society. Ulster shows that it is hard to deny that since the government in a democracy should have the monopoly of armed power, the military should be regarded as the backup to maintain the rule of law.

Democratic countries prove that a soldier can do nothing useful to combat terrorism, suppress insurrection and assist or substitute for the police unless he is given the necessary legal powers to do so. The army is conscious of its constitutional subordination to the law, and will do nothing that is not authorised lawfully to do. If a soldier has to substitute for a policeman, he has to be given the powers to make this substitution effective.

There are differences between civil police forces and the armed services – in approach, and purpose, and accountability. There is a difference between counter-revolutionary warfare and keeping the peace. The military are necessary to prevent the overthrow of lawful government by force, for only they are suited by equipment and training to suppress force by force. Police officers keep the peace using old, complex, and sensitive procedures whereby in a democratic society lawlessness is contained and excesses controlled by the avoidance of arbitrary force. In the West, such force can only be used with the approval of courts and public opinion. There are advantages to the state in having several police forces, which increasingly are more heavily armed, in particular that they enable most disorders to be contained without calling out the regular army.

Throughout the democracies, people reject the idea of a military-style police force (a third force) but believe small numbers of troops have to be involved in any plan for military where loss of life might be minimised in situations involving terrorists or political fanatics.

Populations in democracies clamour for the maintenance of a balance between civil liberties and efficient policing, and to draw distinctions between the right to protest and actions to undermine the government of the day. Mutual understanding in democracies between the police and army is improved only by army acceptance that there can be no quick solution to the troubles, as has been experienced in Kenya, Cyprus and **Northern Ireland**.

An army built up in a staunchly democratic society has a direct idea of its role in countering terrorism, and must tread the fine balance between over-reaction and pusillanimity. It would be hard for the civil power to become over-dependent upon the army's presence, especially with all the constraints imposed by a democratic way of life.

States need constitutional organisation and policing laws that make mastery of terrorism possible. Modern governments prefer to rely on the police to handle disorder because it reduces the chances of disagreement with the military about their role.

See also: Counter-insurgency.

References

Bryett, K. (1987) *The Effects of Political Terrorism on the Police of Great Britain and Northern Ireland since 1969*, Ph.D Dissertation. Aberdeen: University of Aberdeen.
Clutterbuck, R. (1983) *Terrorism in an Unstable World*, New York: Routledge.
Thackrah, J. R. (1983) 'Army-Police Collaboration against Terrorism', *Police Journal*, vol. 56, no. 1, pp. 41–52.
Wilkinson, P. (2002) *Terrorism versus Democracy: The Liberal State Response*, London and Portland, OR: Frank Cass.

Asbat Al-Ansar

Also known as the Partisans' League, this is a Lebanon-based **Sunni** extremist group, composed primarily of Palestinians, which is associated with **Osama Bin Laden**. They avowedly believe in violence against civilian targets to achieve political ends. It began in the early-1990s and has attacked public buildings and international targets within **Lebanon**. Three hundred fighters are active and many come from refugee camps. Funding in part comes from the **Al Qaeda** network (Griset and Mahan, 2003: 327).

See also: Al Qaeda; Osama Bin Laden.

Reference

Griset, P. L. and Mahan, S. (2003) *Terrorism in Perspective*, Thousand Oaks, CA, London and New Delhi: Sage Publications.

Assassins

As a political weapon, terrorism was first exclusively used during the twelfth and thirteenth centuries by a secret medieval dissident Islamic religious order, popularly known as the 'Assassins'.

The term itself is derived from the Arabic and translates literally as 'hashish-eater', or 'one addicted to hashish'. This group of sectarian Muslim fanatics, who often acted under the influence of intoxicating drugs, was employed by its spiritual leaders to spread terror in the form of violence and murder among prominent Christians and other religious enemies. These zealots were, in effect, the first armed terrorist groups, and their fearsome activities entered European folklore by way of the returning crusaders and the writings of Marco Polo. Ultimately, the Mongol invaders destroyed them, but their use of murder as a political instrument provided a grim inheritance for the modern world.

Assassin is now a common noun in most European languages, and from the time of their enigmatic founder, the legendary 'Old Man of the Mountain', they were the first group to make planned, systematic, and long-term use of murder as a political weapon – and their ideals and activities had many adherents.

They were able to turn their reputation to good account. Under threat of assassination they exacted payments from both Muslim and Christian rulers in the Levant in the thirteenth century. The end of the power of the Assassins came under the double assault of the Mongol invaders and of the Mameluke Sultan of **Egypt**.

The Ismaili Assassins did not invent assassination; they merely lent their name. Murder as such is as old as the human race. It is significant that in all their murders, in both Persia and **Syria**, the Assassins always used a dagger, never poison, and never missiles (arrows, spears), though there must have been occasions when these would have been easier and safer. The Assassin was almost always caught, and usually made no attempt to escape; there was even a suggestion among the group that to survive a 'mission' was shameful.

It was the loyalty of the Assassins, who risked and even courted death for their master, that attracted the attention of Europe and made their name a byword for faith and self-sacrifice before it became a synonym for murderer. The victims of Assassins belong to two main groups – the first being made up of princes, officers and ministers, the second of *qadis* and other religious dignitaries.

Concerning the place of the Assassins in the history of **Islam**, four things may be said with reasonable assurance. First, their movement, whatever its motivation may have been, was regarded as a profound threat to the existing order, whether political, social and religious: the second is that they are no isolated phenomenon, but one of a long series of Messianic movements, at once popular and obscure, impelled by deep-rooted anxieties, and occasionally exploding in outbreaks of revolutionary violence. There was a reshaping and redirecting of the vague desires, wild beliefs and aimless rage of the discontented into an ideology and an organisation which, in cohesion, discipline and purposive violence, have no parallel in earlier or later times. Ultimately the most significant point was their final total failure. They did not overthrow the existing order; they did not even succeed in holding a single city of any size. Yet the under-current of Messianic hope and revolutionary violence, which had impelled them, flowed on and their ideals and methods found many imitators. For these idealists the great changes of our times have provided new cause for anger, new dreams of fulfilment and new tools of attack.

Assassination can be described as murder for political ends by the disinterested agent of a revolutionary cause. Throughout history – ever since it was first employed in Persia in 1092 – it has been justified or even urged as a revolutionary means by a number of respectable and considerable authorities.

During the century before 1870 there were more than a score of revolutionary assassinations in **Europe**, but the high point in political, usually revolutionary, assassination began about 1865 and notable victims included three American Presidents – Lincoln, Garfield and McKinley, and a British Secretary for Ireland. Assassinations tended to be used by revolutionaries chiefly when no other means of over-throwing the establishment seemed open to them; it was favoured by Anarchists and Nihilists, but in general repudiated by Socialists and Communists.

Over the past decades there has been a large increase in assassinations and attempted assassinations. International terrorist groups have engaged in numerous types of acts to increase public awareness of their causes, and above all, they have been willing to assassinate government leaders for blatant political purposes.

In March 2003 the Serbian Prime Minister, Zoran Djingic was shot dead by an unknown sniper near government buildings in Belgrade. He had taken a hard line in wanting Serbians accused of war crimes to appear before the International War Crimes Tribunal in The Hague, The Netherlands. Djingic was probably the victim of a criminal gang involved in prostitution and drug trafficking, and it is alleged his government was getting near to breaking up the network.

In general, developed countries have tended to experience lower levels of political unrest and assassination than less developed countries. Most of the assassination incidents in the 1960s and 1970s occurred in nations that are primarily agricultural. The **USA** and France appear as notable exceptions to the rule.

See also: Cults.

References

Snitch, J. H. (1982) 'Terrorism and Political Assassinations: A Transnational Assessment 1968–80', *Annals of the American Academy of Political & Social Science*, vol. 463, pp. 54–68.

Sterling, C. (1985) *The Time of the Assassins*, New York: Holt, Rinehart & Winston.

Further Reading

Clarke, James W. (1982) *American Assassins: The Darker Side of Politics*, Princeton, NJ: Princeton University Press.

Little, P. W. (1989) 'Abduction and Assassination Reconsidered', *TVI Report*, vol. 8, no. 3, pp. 16–19.

Aviation Security

Over the past fifteen years aviation terrorism has increased with attacks on civil aviation targets of all kinds, including airports and airline offices. The most notable infamous events have been **Lockerbie** and **September 11**. Attacks on aeroplanes cause worldwide publicity, especially if hostage taking is involved which might lead to the release of terrorists from prison and the payment of ransoms.

Although improved aviation security measures in certain countries have deterred and prevented many attacks, nevertheless terrorists have shown that there are serious weaknesses.

The long standing *Montreal Convention 1971* with supplements in 1988 and 1994 is directed at a variety of forms of destruction or sabotage that would compromise the safety or operation of civil aviation systems. The *Hague Convention* for the suppression of unlawful seizure of aircraft (**hijacking**) dates from 1970.

Despite highly-respected international agreements there are weaknesses in aviation security. Ten years after **Lockerbie**, most countries have failed to introduce regulations to require the screening of all hold-luggage on international flights. Costs have perhaps caused some of the weaknesses – for instance, the aviation industry has opposed the proposal for positive passenger-baggage reconciliation on the grounds of cost and because of their fear that it would disrupt their service.

Some airlines have poorer security than others and as a consequence, are more prone to terrorist attacks.

September 11 showed how governments have to meet future security threats at airports, by devising updated security measures. These can include an explosive detection system for personal and carry-on luggage which will restrict the size and amount of hand-held luggage; searching all planes deemed 'high-risk' and to ensure the security of pilots throughout the flight. Other measures could include the accessing of criminal records to check the background of staff and passengers and fingerprints to screen baggage, passenger and airport workers who have access to luggage and aircraft and to ensure all airports have a security chief and set national standards for training security workers who would undergo annual updating and testing. Bomb-proof containers could be utilised to hold baggage and cargo.

See also: Lockerbie; September 11.

References

Wilkinson, P. (ed.) (1993) *Technology and Terrorism*, London: Frank Cass.

— (ed.) (1998) 'Enhancing Global Aviation Security', *Terrorism and Political Violence*, vol. 10, no. 3.

Further Reading

Gazzini, T. (1996) *Sanctions against Air Terrorism – Legal Obligations of States*, London: Research Institute for Study of Terrorism.

Koniak, J. (1983) 'Access to Airport Security', *Security Management*, vol. 32, no. 11 (November), pp. 145–75.

Taillon, J. P. de B. (2002) *Hijacking and Hostages: Government Responses to Terrorism*, Westport, CT and London: Praeger.

Walker, C. (1990) 'The World Has Changed after Lockerbie', *Jane's Airport Review*, June, pp. 6–8.

B

Bali, Indonesia

In October 2002 more than 180 people were killed and over 300 injured in a bombing outside a packed tourist bar in Bali. Over thirty of the dead were British and most of the remainder Australian. A chief suspect in the attack confessed on live television in February 2003 to his role as a bomb-maker. Ali Imron said that he was proud of his work. He admitted he had links with the militant Muslim cleric, Abu Bakar Bashir, the alleged leader of Jemaah Islamiya. Another 29 suspected members have been arrested. **Al Qaeda** and local Islamic groups were blamed. One of these is the main Indonesian terror group Jamaah Islamiya, led by the academic cleric Abu Bakar Bashir. The group wishes to create an Islamic super-state comprising of Malaysia, Indonesia and the Southern **Philippines**. In December 2001 they plotted to blow up targets of Western interest in Singapore. They are a threat to Western tourists and expatriates in the region. The other group is Lashkar Jihad led by Ja'far Umar Thalib, whose goal is to expel Christians from the region. They have tried to expel Christians from the Moluccas and have killed more than 6,000 people and forced around a million to leave their homes. Thalib fought alongside **Osama Bin Laden** in **Afghanistan** and he supported the **September 11** attacks. Membership numbers over 10,000 and they are active in SE Asia. They are a real danger to all Christians in the country.

They developed plans in 1997 to target American interests in Singapore, and most members were trained in Al Qaeda training camps in Afghanistan and the Jemaah Islamiya have received funding from Al Qaeda. Currently there are about 600 members (Griset and Mahan, 2003: 354).

See also: September 11.

References

Griset, P. L. and Mahan, S. (2003) *Terrorism in Perspective*, Thousand Oaks, CA, London and New Delhi: Sage Publications.
'The Threat from Islamic Terrorist Groups', *Independent*, 15 October 2002, p. 17.

Basque Nationalism

Political violence is a continual aspect of Spain's historical development. Francoism itself emerged as a result of the **Civil War** in Spain (1936–39). Francoism was in its turn soon attacked by the Communist guerrilla fighters of the *maquis*. Sporadic actions either of an anarchist character or of groups like DRIL (Iberian Revolutionary Directorate of Liberation) were also points of violent resistance to the dictatorship of General Franco. But it was in 1959 that Euskadi ta Askatasuna (ETA), or Basque Fatherland and Freedom, which would become the fatal protagonist of terrorism during the political transition, first began its activities on a small scale. The French equivalent is Iparretarrak, formed in 1973. Although it became violent in 1976, its acts of terrorism have been few and far between. Emerging from a generational changeover in Basque nationalism and carrying out a radical redefining of this nationalism, ETA planted their first bomb in July 1961. Both men and material were limited; but in May 1962 it celebrated its first assembly where it defined itself as the Basque revolutionary movement of national liberation created in patriotic resistance. It considered the armed struggle as the only possible action against Francoist repression.

In the view of ETA, the recourse to violence and terrorism had ideological justification. By 1970 the repressive policies of the state had caused ravage among the militants, which together with a lack of cohesion internally, provoked a situation of hopelessness. However, the power of Francoism shown at the Burgos trial made ETA rise from its ashes. This trial, in late-1970, tried sixteen Basque nationalists accused of banditry, military rebellion and terrorism. Owing to the internal situation of the Franco regime, the national and international repercussions of the event were extraordinary. Francoism fuelled support for ETA's protector, while quite a large part of Spanish public opinion felt sympathy towards the clandestine operations in the false conviction that it was a group of youths carrying out a stronger resistance against an ominous dictator. However, ETA was fighting against Spain and not just Franco, and this was highlighted by their greatest success in terms of publicity and propaganda: namely the murder of the Spanish Prime Minister, Admiral Carrero Blanco, in 1973.

Nevertheless, although the armed struggle was still not questioned in ETA, the growing autonomy and importance of the military sector became unendurable for the pro-worker sector of the group. By late-1974 the break between ETA political military (ETAP-M) and military ETA (ETAM) became definitive. For the latter the armed struggle was the exclusive method, whereas for the former this was combined with other types of political action.

At this time FRAP (Frente Revolucionario Anti-fascista y Patriótico), a left-wing Maoist group especially active in the 1970s, proclaimed its existence. It had come from the Communist Party of Spain (Marxist-Leninist). Anarchist-inspired and short-lived organisations arose, such as the MIL (Iberian Liberation Movement), one of whose members was condemned to death and executed. Other extreme right groups also emerged in Spain: Warriors of Christ the King, ATE (Anti-terrorism ETA), Triple A, and the Spanish Basque Battalion.

Political violence in the Basque country appears more and more connected not with movements proposing social-political change but with an organisation which pretends to be more and more openly military. The definitive separation between the two factions of ETA came about when the party supported by the military branch decided to present itself at the first general election in the post-Franco era in 1977. Some of the extreme militants at this time created a new terrorist group, Los Comandos Autonomos Anti-capitalistas. Other groups, such as MPAIAC (Movement for Self-Determination and Independence of the Canaries Archipelago) and GRAPO (Grupo de Resistencia Anti-Fascista Primero de Octubre), and the extreme right all added to the domestic problems. The gangster-like activity of the last mentioned revealed a plan for political destabilisation, which reached its maximum point with the murder of five lawyers, specialists in labour cases, in Madrid. By 1977, with FRAP virtually broken up, GRAPO emerged strongly, with its declared objective to prevent the perpetuation of Franco.

With the onset of democracy, Spanish society became bent on conciliatory moderation. Violence became more and more associated with intransigence. With the foundations for Spanish political life set up, a new period of consolidation began. As the political transformations accelerated, terrorism became more FRAP-oriented. The Basque groups benefited from a broadening of the machinery for economic extortion and from other changes in methods of operation. The deaths of an army general and of senior police chiefs in 1978 began a strategy of provocation directed against the army and aimed at feeding the temptations of the hotheads in certain sectors of the army bureaucracy.

Throughout, the terrorism of ETA has been inseparable from the Basque question. From Basque nationalism, ETA extracted a delegitimising vision of the State, and the hostile attitude necessary for the will to fight. There would be no neutral non-belligerents, only patriots and traitors.

In practice the main difference between terrorism that is essentially nationalistic, and other versions is found in the degree of support from the population; active support, passive support or ambiguous neutrality. Thus one had the Statute of

Autonomy accepted by political-military ETA and rejected by military ETA.

In 1993 ETA suffered serious set-backs. Co-operation between French and Spanish security forces led to the arrest of some of its leaders and the discovery in south west France, of the organisation's main weapons deposit. Nevertheless the Basque nationalist sentiment is still strong, despite crack-down attempts by the Spanish authorities. In 1998, for example, ETA declared a ceasefire but by 2000 the group was again undertaking large-scale attacks. Furthermore in the 1990s ETA and the Provisional IRA began a long-standing cooperation.

The political coalition Herri Batasuna (Peoples Unity; created in 1979), increasingly undertook initiatives in the late-1980s and 1990s. The initiatives were linked with greater regularity being detected in speeches by ETA members wanting to negotiate and to inspire, due to sound reactions against violence and increased police efficiency. Deaths and destruction declined as genuine attempts were made to endorse democratic princi-ples and proceedings. In 2002 Batasuna was disbanded, in an attempt by the Madrid govern-ment to achieve a lasting ceasefire.

References

Janke, P. (1981) 'Spanish Separation: ETA's Threat of Basque Democracy', *Conflict Studies*, no. 123, London: Institute for Study of Conflict.
— (1986) 'Spanish Separatism: ETA's Threat to Basque Democracy' in W. Gutteridge (ed.) *Contemporary Terrorism*, New York: Facts on File.
Reinares, F. (ed.) (1987) 'The Dynamics of Terror-ism during the Transition to Democracy in Spain', in P. Wilkinson and A. M. Stewart (eds) *Contemporary Research on Terrorism*, Aberdeen: Aberdeen University Press.
— (1988) 'Nationalism and Violence in Basque Politics', *Conflict*, vol. 8, nos. 2/3, pp. 141–156.
— (2000) *European Democracies against Terrorism: Governmental Responses and Intergovernmental Co-operation*, Ashgate: Dartmouth Publishing.

Further Reading

Clark, R. P. (1990) 'Negotiating with ETA: Obstacles to Peace in the Basque Country

1975–1988', *The Basque Series*, Reno, NV: Uni-versity of Nevada Press.
Moxon-Browne, E. (1988) 'Terrorism and the Spanish State: The Violent Bid for Basque Autonomy' in H. H. Tucker (ed.) *Combating the Terrorists*, New York: Facts on File, pp. 155–172.
Reinares, F. (1996) 'The Political Conditioning of Collective Violence: Regime, Change and In-surgent Terrorism' in Spain'. *Research on Democracy and Society*, vol. 3, JAI Press, pp. 297–326.
Zulaika, J. and Douglas, W. A. (1986) *Terror and Taboo: The Follies, Fables and Faces of Terrorism*, New York: Routledge.

Beirut Hijack

The hijacking of a US TransWorld Airline 727 jumbo jet en route from Athens to Rome by two Lebanese **Shi'ite** Muslims on 14 June 1985, and the subsequent murder of one American passenger and the detention of others by Shi'ite militiamen in Beirut pre-occupied the **USA** administration until the release of the last 39 hostages on 30 June.

The crisis was seen as paralleling that which had confronted President Carter between 1979–81 when 52 US hostages were held for 444 days in Teheran, **Iran**, before their release on 20 January 1981, the date of Reagan's inauguration as President. As on that occasion, the crisis proved a subject of consuming interest for the US **media**; the administration, despite a deliberate intention to avoid creating the appearance of being unable to give effective attention to other issues, was forced largely to abandon other matters while it lasted. Nevertheless the early resolution of the Beirut crisis ensured that Reagan did not experience the loss of authority which Carter had suffered as a conse-quence of the **Teheran Embassy** affair and which had been seen as a principal factor in his electoral defeat in November 1980.

A notable feature of the crisis was the role played by the American TV networks. These were criticised by some, including a number of eminent journalists, for having entered into a 'symbiotic relationship' with the Shi'ite militiamen, exchan-ging access to the prisoners for publicity (which was seen as the lifeblood of terrorist activity), and broadcasting unedited interviews with prisoners who were being held at gunpoint, in which the prisoners appeared to express gratitude to their guards for good treatment and to extend sympathy for their cause. Television journalists did not tax the militiamen with questions deemed likely to inflame the situation, and there were rumours, denied by the networks, that payment had been made to guards to obtain interviews with the hostages.

See also: Lebanon; Media; Teheran Embassy Siege.

Beliefs *see* Psychology of Terrorism: Beliefs of Terrorists

Bin Laden *see* Osama Bin Laden

Bio-Terrorism

This is perhaps the ultimate in warfare and has been described as the next threat. The three main types of weapons of mass destruction (WMD) are biological agents, nuclear bombs and chemical weapons. For chemical weapons the raw materials are powerful nerve toxins, which are easy to obtain, but are not well suited to inflicting widespread damage. To kill a sizeable number of people with sarin one would need a large number of small adapted aircraft such as crop dusters.

For a nuclear weapons attack, a terrorist would need to get hold of a fissionable substance such as enriched uranium – but even if it could be obtained from new states of the former **Soviet Union** for instance, it would take 70 Kg of uranium plus hundreds of kilos of casing and machinery to make a weapon. The greater fear could be an attack on a nuclear power plant with conventional explosives.

For biological weapons possible agents include anthrax and smallpox and both are potentially lethal. During the **Cold War** both sides developed anthrax as a biological weapon and today quite a few nations have biological weapon programmes. Water supplies can be affected by contaminating reservoirs. In recent times the world became aware of the possible development of bio-warfare in 1988 when the forces of Saddam Hussein used cyanide bombs in an attack on the Kurdish held village of

Halabja. This sent shockwaves throughout many nations.

It is said that the Romans first tried biological warfare, catapulting diseased meat into forts and cities during a siege. Chemical warfare – usually gas – was first used on any scale during the First World War.

There are differences: biological attacks attempt to infect the target population with live bacteria in the hope that victims will increase the spread by infecting others; and chemical attacks use 'dead' toxic agents such as mustard gas which depends on inhalation or contact. Chemical and biological weapons are relatively cheap and easy to produce but nuclear weapons are expensive and difficult to obtain.

The panic effect on the population would be considerable; however, both weapons are unpredictable. Counter-measures can be developed, the shelf-life of many agents is short and the methods of delivery have to be large-scale. A terrorist can easily make use of anthrax, plague and smallpox. These can be countered by vaccines and antibiotics as the recent anthrax scares in the **USA** and **UK** post-**September 11** events have shown. However, such scares in March 2003 are reputed to be more of a criminal and in some cases, hoax element, rather than outright terrorist acts. Stocks of anthrax in some of the former states of the Soviet Union, Kazakhstan and Uzbekistan were secretly buried in early-2003 to avoid falling into terrorist hands.

Toward the end of 2002 and the beginning of 2003 it was suggested by medical experts that any terrorist attack was likely to be low key with the spread of an infection such as salmonella or e-coli. Hospitals around the world are quickening up their planned responses to any bio-terror attack. Panic in this area of potential warfare is clear. The most worrying aspect is that biological weapons could be linked to the **Al Qaeda** network – some of the hijackers involved in the events of September 11 had rented property in Florida. Plague by post causes perhaps the greatest panic of all. Scientists are perhaps more likely to make anthrax than terrorist groups. A tiny amount only can kill and inhalation is easy – but the disease is not contagious and if caught early enough is treatable.

Iraq, it is alleged, has an advanced biological warfare testing programme and the fear in the West is that Iraqi fundamentalists could help Al Qaeda.

No evidence of this was found in 2003 before, during or after the war.

Bio-technology is lethally fascinating to potential super-terrorists as it has endless possibilities. Super-terrorism is the use of chemical or biological agents to bring about a major disaster with death tolls in thousands.

The events of September 11 have demonstrated any disaster is plausible, especially bio-terrorism, and forced people to think the unthinkable. Biological weapons attacks cover a wide area like a nuclear weapon, but are much cheaper.

A doomsday scenario would be any attempt to weaponise Ebola with smallpox. In the twenty-first century experts believe that biological weapons will be the poor man's nuclear bomb – contrary to all international legal conventions.

A cyber-terrorist can remotely access the processing control systems of any business. Computerised bombs can be placed on an industrial complex especially a chemical or petroleum site. Banks, international financial transactions and stock exchanges can be targeted resulting in a loss of confidence in the economic system. Transport control systems can be attacked causing accidents to occur. Gas and electricity supplies can be disrupted. Our day to day existence can be disrupted by such terrorists.

Since September 11 both Europe and the USA have given enormous attention to possible terrorist use of chemical and biological weapons to incur mass casualties. The spate of anthrax cases and scares especially in America have made people feel very uneasy.

A new watershed in terrorist violence would be reached and crossed if an effective delivery system was found to utilise the agent. A new culture of death as we saw with September 11 is developing based around marginalisation in society and techno-rage to revenge for real or imaginary wrongs.

The new terrorists are more motivated in being uninhibited by the need to spare innocents.

There are several key threat factors: The actor; the size of the organisation whether hierarchical or a network; intentions in terms of casualties sought; willingness to experiment and accept failure; and capabilities including financial, scientific, technical and operational.

The 'what' factor will bring success for the terrorist in terms of mass casualties; but only if such issues as the availability, ease of handling, fragility, ease of dissemination, susceptibility to the elements are taken into account. An understanding of the targets is vital to achieve the end result, for example, open air versus enclosed spaces.

The operational requirements of an attack would be a constraining factor. Building an effective dissemination device is particularly challenging and requires many technical hurdles to be overcome. Few terrorists have the necessary combination of size, resources, skills and organisation to achieve mass casualties with biological weapons. It is doubtful even if the **Al Qaeda** group has the requisite scientific and technical expertise.

Two weeks after September 11 anthrax was used for the first time, sent in letters to New York news teams. Anthrax has numerous advantages over other biological agents. It is cheap, portable, and less detectable and can be used as a biological weapon. Anthrax is more effective when inhaled rather than absorbed through the skin, as it causes flu like symptoms and organs tend to break down in the body. Freeze dried bacteria can be put into a deadly spray-like powder and tests were conducted in the 1950s with spraying from planes. Anthrax is not contagious.

Research on biological weapons was started in the USA in 1942 in university laboratories, military factories and private companies under contract. The Russians experimented early on in the **Cold War** when so-called 'superbugs' where created, and during the crisis over **Cuba** in 1962 a biological attack was planned by the Americans but never carried out. In 1969 President Nixon renounced germ weapons. Three years later the Biological Weapons Convention was signed by both superpowers, to end weapons production. **Russia** used the Treaty to develop germ warfare plants (many in states bordering **Afghanistan**).

Biological weapon attacks can take place over a wide area and are much cheaper than nuclear weapons. Experiments almost of a Domesday variety have occurred with bacteria causing Legionnaires disease, Ebola and smallpox. The collapse of the Soviet Union in 1989 left many unemployed qualified biological weapons experts looking for work, and quite a few have gained employment in the so-called rogue states.

It is very hard to check in any country whether or not bio-weapons are being produced – both good and bad technology can be involved. For example, fomenters used for producing bio-germs can be used for food storage. In 2000, the Americans built their own special bio-warfare laboratory.

Osama Bin Laden has the biological weapons but a primitive delivery system and a camp in Afghanistan was used for animal testing with an anthrax germ. Observers believe in the twenty-first century that biological weapons will be the poor man's nuclear bomb. Over 1,300 sites around the world stock anthrax. It has been alleged that **Iraq** had an advanced biological warfare testing programme and that in the late-1990s they hid material from the **United Nations** inspectors.

The fear, following the Tokyo underground attack in **Japan** in 1995, is that tube networks in capital cities could be threatened as bacteria is pushed and pulled along the system. Biological sensors in some cities have been placed at strategic centres in the underground. Rapid recognition of illness caused by a biological attack is vital. Proactive measures have been taken for instance, emergency medical supply packs at strategic areas around the USA. A contagious disease attack in a city would stop people moving and entering and the city would be isolated. September 11 has made any disaster plausible including bio-terror and forced people to think the unthinkable.

In the twentieth century the use of biological and chemical weapons has progressed in a series of major developments.

The use of chlorine and other gases in the First World War was soon surpassed by the use of nerve gases and experimentation with disease agents such as anthrax in the Second World War.

In the post-war era the **United States** used chemical agents to destroy plants in Vietnam.

All these developments were themselves surpassed by the current stage – characterised by the use of advanced biotechnology and genetic engineering to produce agents that are far more potent, less detectible and easier to spread (Levinson, 2002).

Depending on the target there is no way to effectively monitor, control or prevent the use of biological weapons. At the time of writing research is underway to develop technology to detect and destroy biological agents before they cause any harm.

See also: Weapons.

References

Buck, K. A. (1989) 'Super-terrorism – Biological Chemical and Nuclear', *Terrorism*, vol. 12, no. 6, pp. 433–434.

Cole, L. A. (1997) *The Eleventh Plague: The Politics of Biological and Chemical Warfare*, New York: W. H. Freeman.

Cornish, Dr P. (1997) 'Sabotage by Sarin: The Threat of Terrorism and Weapons of Mass Destruction', *Intersec*, vol. 7, no. 9, pp. 193–195.

Levinson, D. (ed.) (2002) 'Terrorism' in *Encyclopaedia of Crime and Punishment*, London: Sage.

Moodie, M. (2001) 'Response to Bio-terror', *The World Today* (November), pp. 5–6.

Further Reading

Cole, C. A. (1996) 'The Spectre of Biological Weapons', *Scientific American*, vol. 275, pp. 60–65.

Mylroie, L. (2001) *The First World Trade Center Attack and Saddam Hussein's War against America*, Washington, DC: AEI Press.

Black June and Black September

These are both hard-line Palestinian groups. The Black June group took its name from the intervention of **Syria** during the **civil war** in **Lebanon** in June 1976, after which the Palestinian-backed Lebanese Muslim leftists were defeated by the combined forces of the Syrians and the Lebanese Christians. In September 1976, three members of the group were tried and hanged for an attack on a hotel in Damascus with the object of enforcing the release of a number of persons arrested on charges of having committed acts of violence. The leader of the group was killed by Syrian troops and four persons held hostage also lost their lives in the attack.

Black September, under the leadership of Abu Daoud, took its name from the month in which the forces of Al Fatah were defeated by Jordanian troops in 1970. It broke away from Al Fatah because it disagreed with the latter's emphasis on the need for political action as a 'national liberation movement'. The Black September group belonged to a minority group of 'avenging' Palestinians, members of which committed individual acts of violence. It was held responsible for the killing of the Jordanian Prime Minister Wasfi Tell in Cairo in November 1971 – in revenge for the killing of its former leader, Abu Ali Iyad, in July of that year. Other acts of violence attributed to Black September include the hijacking of a Sabena airliner at Lod (Israel) in May 1972; the murder of eleven Israeli athletes at the **Olympic Games** in Munich on 5 September 1972; the seizure of the Israeli Embassy in Bangkok in March 1973; and the murder in Khartoum of the US Ambassador and the Belgian Charge d'Affaires at the Saudi Arabian Embassy in March 1973. In August 1973 two members of the group made an attack at Athens airport, killing five people and injuring 55 others – they were sentenced to life imprisonment.

Abu Daoud, the group's leader, was among the 1,000 political prisoners released by King Hussein of Jordan under an amnesty in 1973, most of them having been held since the 1970–1971 Jordanian action against Palestinian guerrillas. In January 1977, Abu Daoud was arrested in Paris while attending a funeral. Within days a French court released him after German authorities had not immediately made their request for his extradition on charges of his involvement in the attack on the Israeli athletes at Munich in 1972, and as Israel was considered to have no right to ask for his extradition.

The Black September-June organisation was described as a merger of the Black September and Black June organisations, and the **Abu Nidal** Group led by Sabri Khalil al Banna (Abu Nidal). It claimed responsibility for killing the United Arab Emirates Foreign Minister in October 1977 in Abu Dhabi, instead of the Syrian Foreign Minister who was then visiting Abu Dhabi. The **assassin**, who was said to have been supported by the Iraqi regime, was condemned to death and executed. Yasser **Arafat** was quick to condemn the attack as was the Al Fatah Central Committee.

See also: Abu Nidal; Olympic Games Attack; PLO.

Reference

Livingstone, N. C. and Halevy, D. (1990) *Inside the PLO: Covert Units, Secret Funds and the War against Israel and the United States*, New York: William Morrow.

Black Terrorism

In the late-1960s and early-1970s Black militants were active in the **United States**, especially in urban areas. Two of the main groups were separatist Black religious **cults** such as the Nation of **Islam** and black nationalists such as the Black Panthers. Black nationalists carried out a guerrilla war against the police and factional feuding occurred. Black separatist cults murdered randomly selected whites, as well as dissidents (those who have abandoned their religion). Blacks felt frustrated and alienated and yearned for civil rights and racial equality. The extent of black political power in three cities in particular – San Francisco, New Orleans and New York – was linked to the rate of violence. Civil rights initiatives fell short of what blacks wanted and their frustration led to widespread rioting and the emergence of violence-prone black nationalist and separatist groups.

Reference

Miller, A. H. and Schaen, E. (2000) 'Democracy and the Black Riots: Rethinking the Meaning of Political Violence in Democracy', *Terrorism and Political Violence*, vol. 12, nos. 3/4, pp. 345–360.

Further Reading

Hewitt, C. (2000) 'The Political Context of Terrorism in America: Ignoring Extremists or Pandering to Them?', *Terrorism and Political Violence*, vol. 12, nos. 3/4, pp. 325–344.

Businesses Targeted by Terrorists

Many terrorist attacks are directed against private companies because of the types of businesses in which they are engaged, for example, companies that are part of the 'military industrial complex'. Financial institutions are a key target especially those involved in government-based work often against terrorists themselves. Targets also include companies involved in advanced technologies such as communications or computers, particularly as they may apply to weapon systems. Targets with repercussions for the public and much favoured by terrorists are public utility companies, which cause maximum disruption when put out of action. Companies with operations in politically sensitive countries are key ideological targets. Those companies, who due to changes in the political climate may find themselves on the 'wrong side' of emotional political issues, are particularly vulnerable. Ultimately, and indeed more frequently, in recent years, transnational corporations, which because of their size or history of business domination have become symbolic of America, are ones which megaterrorists are keen to attack.

Shopping centres and malls have become tempting targets for many terrorists because of the numbers of people confined in one area and the number of 'brand-name' department stores, and of course, it is easy to hide bombs or other devices in such places.

Security guards – unarmed – are being employed by many major department stores to combat any potential threat of violence; and increasing use is being made of close-circuit TV monitoring. Bag, car and body searches or plain questioning are options for guards to take in the event of an incident.

What terrorists hope to achieve with regard to the very vulnerable target of attacking shoppers, are devastation involving carnage, the effects of disruption and loss of trade and forcing changes in shopping habits; from city centres to out of town, or even to force people not to shop out of sheer fear of the consequences. At Warrington, in Cheshire, in 1993 a bomb was placed in a litter-bin, in a busy shopping street leading to the deaths of three people including two children. Security bins have, as a result of such acts, increasingly been developed for use in many inner urban areas.

Threats of an extreme nature can be made to business operations, as the world witnessed on September 11. Suicide attacks can be made with firearms and explosive attacks on groups at entry to buildings; and chemical, biological and radiological materials can be released in buildings and on roads, planes, buses, trains and tunnels. Chemical, biological and radiological attacks can take place using materials ranging from anthrax and sarin to Caesium-137 and Uranium-235. **Cyber-terrorism** can undermine public and market confidence and E-commerce. Ultimately an attack on the critical infrastructure such as water, power transmission buildings and transport can lead to terror in the population.

Action can be taken proactively against such attacks. Banks can make global continuity plans, and promote net banking. Chemical industries can have a closer monitoring of high volume movements or storage that could be extreme weapons. Electricity and gas distribution and oil and gas industries can be sensitive to attack. Key points have to be protected. In the insurance field, the development of new financial instruments for companies as risk financing and the support for enhanced internal continuity practices needs to be planned. An urgent need is perceived for a separation of extreme events causation from other loss categories to preserve the general insurance market (Briggs, 2002: 36).

Survival tactics to be used by businesses can include risk-financing resources, protection of decision-makers and the protection of critical company infrastructure, personnel and families.

Many insurance schemes now include terrorism in their policies. It is defined as any act or acts including but not limited to (a) the use or threat of force and/or violence and/or (b) harm or damage to life or to property (or the threat of such harm or damage) including but not limited, to harm or damage by nuclear and/or chemical and/or biological and/or radioactive means, caused by any person(s) or group(s) of persons, or so claimed, in whole or in part, for political, religious, ideological or similar purposes. Any action taken in controlling, preventing, suppressing or in any way relating to the above.

See also: Commercial Interests; Cyber-terrorism; Extortion.

References

Beck, A. and Willis, A. (1997) *Terrorist Threat to Safe Shopping*, Leicester University: Scarman Centre Papers for Public Order, Paper no. 193.

Bolz, F., Dudonis, K. J. and Schulz, D. P. (1990) *Counter-terrorism Handbook*, New York: Elsevier.

Briggs, R. (ed.) (2002) *The Unlikely Counter-Terrorists*, London: Foreign Office Policy Centre.

Jenkins, B. M. (1985) *Terrorism and Personal Protection*, Stoneham, MA: Butterworth.

Further Reading

Clutterbuck, R. (1994) 'The Channel Tunnel Security Threats and Safety Measures', *Conflict Studies*, no. 269. London: RISCT.

Combs, C. C. and Slann, M. (2002) *Encyclopaedia of Terrorism*, New York: Facts on File.

Jenkins, B. M., Purnell, S. W. and Wainstein, E. S. (1985) 'The Effects of Terrorism on Business' in B. M. Jenkins (ed.) *Terrorism and Personal Protection*, Stoneham, MA: Butterworth.

Nelson, J. (2002) *The Business of Peace*, London: International Alert, Council on Economic Priorities, Prince of Wales Business Leaders Forum, 2000.

Ryan, C. (1991) 'Tourism, Terrorism and Violence: The Risks of Wider World Travel', *Conflict Studies*, no. 214, London: RISCT.

Stewart, B. (ed.) (1986) 'International Terrorism: The Threat to Industry', Arlington, VA: SRI International.

C

Carlos (Ilyich Ramirez Sanchez)

b. 1949

Carlos, real name Ilyich Ramirez Sanchez, is a Venezuelen **assassin**, who has been described as the world's first truly transitional terrorist (or autonomous non-state actor) and millionaire. He spent some time at the Lumumba University in Moscow (used as a selection course for Third World students chosen for training as leaders of 'liberation armies'), before being expelled. However, he maintained close connections with the KGB, and with the German Baader-Meinhof Group. The exposure of Carlos and the international ramifications of his network convinced many people throughout the world that the upsurge of bombing and assassination and the taking of hostages for political gain was no ephemeral affair, and no short-term aberration. In the early-1970s he operated in London on behalf of the Popular Front for the Liberation of Palestine. A series of errors, due to misrouting of information, prevented his arrest in London and enabled him to carry out his spectacular series of terrorist crimes, culminating in the kidnapping of **OPEC** oil ministers in Vienna in 1975. He is rumoured to have received a bonus from Gadaffi of nearly $2,000,000 for this operation, and other reports suggest that he took a cut of the $5,000,000 ransom paid by Saudi Arabia and Iran for the release of their ministers. Carlos has received support or approval, either covertly or overtly, from many groups, individuals, organisations and governments. He regularly operated out of France and became the Popular Front for the Liberation of Palestine's chief hitman there. He was dubbed the superstar of violence, and married a woman terrorist Magdalena Kaupp. Reputedly he now runs the Palestinian terrorist organisation known as the International Faction of Revolutionary Cells. It is derived from the German Revolutionary Cell organisation that was divided into two sometimes competing sections, one of which operated inside Germany and the other internationally. Ultimately, Carlos's future lies in receiving finance and support for these terrorist ventures.

In 1994 Carlos was finally apprehended by the French secret service in Khartoum in the Sudan, and in 1997, he was tried and convicted in France for his terrorist attacks. He alleged at his trial that he was driven to violent activity due to repressive states and an unresponsive internal order. He was a vain individual who craved publicity and attention, yet always stated that he was a normal family man. There is no evidence that Carlos would have sanctioned or participated in mega-terror attacks such as **September 11**. Carlos in his younger days saw himself as lean, hungry and unspoiled by the temptations of high living (as perhaps many other 'terrorists' see themselves) but when the former playboy grew fat and spent much of his time in nightclubs, his terrorist days were over.

He has been described as a peripatetic and an individual in his actions and has become one of the world's first transnational terrorists. He spent much of his latter days as an active terrorist in Eastern Europe working with local secret services against political enemies. Carlos moved to Damascus, Yemen and eventually ended in the Sudan, where a financial deal was done with France for his arrest.

His girlfriend testified about the international nature of the groups' operations, showing who had paid them and how passports and safe houses had been provided. There were warrants out for his arrest in many parts of the world. Even though he had been of use to **Libya**, he was eventually refused entry to that country.

He was fearless and never admitted that he had done wrong – Carlos even complained to the European Courts of Justice that he had been kidnapped and taken in chains to France. He had a genuine conviction that he was the victim.

See also: OPEC Siege, Vienna 1975.

References

Hoffman, B. (1998) *Inside Terrorism*, London: Victor Gollancz.

Yallop, D. (1993) *To the Ends of the Earth: The Hunt for the Jackal*, London: Jonathan Cape.

Further Reading

Laqueur, W. (2001) *The New Terrorism: Fanaticism and the Arms of Mass Destruction*, London: Phoenix Press.

Yallop, D. (1993) *Tracking the Jackal: The Search for Carlos, the World's Most Wanted Man*, New York: Random House.

Central Asia and Caucasus

Most of the states that are in this region were formerly constituent republics of the **Soviet Union** such as Kazakhstan and Uzbekistan and they border onto areas of traditional instability such as **Afghanistan**, **Iran** and **Nepal**.

Attitudes to human life are different and inter-ethnic and inter-religious conflicts are common-place. The new generation of terrorists are indeed, driven by a mixture of nationalist and religious hate, rather than solely political ideals. Propaganda and financial effort are not in short supply. Rival groups represent competing interests fuelled by gangsterism, which places criminals of national minority against another. Organised crime had become more and more linked to terrorism. For instance there are tensions between America and Azerbaijan; Georgia and Abkhasia and Ossetia and Ingushetia as well as the more publicised **Chechnya/Dagestan** and **Chechnya /Russia** clashes.

Central Asia is rich in natural resources but in Tadzhikistan there is conflict between regional clans and new elites, each of which wants power and riches. Outside intervention could inflame the situation, and internal conflicts are proving hard to resolve as are linguistic conflicts and the struggle for autonomy i.e. Kashmir-Tibet and these in turn are adjacent to the Hindu-Muslim struggle.

Drug-trafficking is an intractable problem, and in the last few years, drug routes northwards from Iran and **Pakistan** into Central Asia have been opening up. There is evidence that a drug route into Tajikistan was being used to smuggle uranium and other dangerous contraband toward Pakistan. Drugs are even harder to control because of the endemic corruption between political and military elites who are supposedly trying to stem the narcotics trade.

When the Taliban came to power in Afghanistan in 1994 there were fears that they would sweep northwards into Tajikistan intensifying endemic civil unrest there and elsewhere, which in turn had been born in Afghanistan. The main ingredient of this crime was the drug culture. **Al Qaeda** was built on the Muslim Brotherhood and drawing in its committed followers, its structures and its experience, the Central Asia family of Brotherhood stretched from **Turkey** across Muslim Central Asia into Xingjiang in **China**. From Afghanistan Al Qaeda was able to recruit several hundred Soviet Central Asians – Uzbeks, Kazakhs, Kyrghyz, Tajik and Turkmen – into its ranks. Islamic movements reasserted themselves here. Al Qaeda supported the Tajik Islamists' struggle to topple the Russian-backed Communist government. The threat by some Muslim groups, such as the Muslim Union of Uzbekistan was used by Central Asian States to secure more funding from Western donors.

In the aftermath of the defeat of the Taliban it is feared that some Al Qaeda fighters may have retreated to Central Asia to team up with Al Qaeda-trained associate members; who have built a pro-Islamic network linking the key Islamist groups in the region. Many Central Asian nations had provided assistance to the Northern Alliance to keep the Taliban pinned down in a guerrilla struggle during their years in power.

References

Panico, C. (1995) 'Conflicts in the Caucasus: Russia's War in Chechnya', *Conflict Studies*, no. 281 (July), London: RISCT.

Hyman, A. (1994) 'Power and Politics in Central Asia's New Republics', *Conflict Studies*, no. 273 (August), London: RISCT.

Further Reading

Gunaratna, R. (2002) *Inside Al Qaeda: Global Network of Terror*, London: Hurst & Co.

Channel Tunnel

The Channel Tunnel which connects England and France (after centuries of debate and seven years in the making), was finally opened to the public in May 1994. The purpose of any terrorist attack on the Tunnel would be to attract publicity. The likeliest tactics would be to cause a bomb to explode in a train, to halt traffic by hoax or sabotage or to stop a train in the tunnel by **hijacking** it or taking hostages.

Counter-terrorist units would wish to detect terrorists using the Tunnel to transport themselves or their equipment to Britain for future operations or to escape arrest after carrying out attacks in Britain or the Continent. Frustrated asylum seekers or illegal immigrants could be persuaded by terrorist groups to smuggle explosives into the Tunnel. Bombs in tunnels can kill or maim many people as large numbers are confined in a small space, and gas as proved by the Aum Shinrikyo **cult** in **Japan** can be lethal.

Drug smuggling is a relatively easy activity to undertake via the Tunnel, made easier by the relaxation of customs control in France. Good intelligence can be the main enemy against the drug dealers.

Organised crime is burgeoning in Europe and criminal gangs are closely involved also with other threats to security – terrorism, illegal immigration and drug trafficking. They can effectively utilise the Tunnel for their operations in the **UK**. Above all, the Tunnel is vulnerable to a total blockage for a long period of time, which would have an effect on trade and commerce.

See also: Narco-Terrorism; Organised Crime.

Reference

Clutterbuck, R. (1994) 'The Channel Tunnel: Security Threats and Safety Measures', *Conflict Studies*, no.269, London: RISCT.

Further Reading

Crighton, G. S. and Leblond, L. (1989) *Tunnel Design*, London: Telford.

Chechnya

In 1991 Chechnya declared its independence from the Russian Soviet Federative Socialist Republic. Three years later the Russians moved against the rebel Chechen state to depose the leader and bring it back into the fold. Bloody fighting has continued there ever since, and Russian repression met with increasing Chechen resistance. They are indigenous Caucasian mountain people, and practice **Sunni** Islam; and are mainly farmers. The Chechen Pan National Congress President, Dzhokhar Dudayev particularly stood by the rhetoric, 'Chechen independence or death'. Parliamentary opposition led to warlordism in the mid-1990s, which was armed opposition supported by **Russia**. Uprisings occurred in the Grozny urban centres, especially Central Grozny. The abysmal state of the Russian military forced it to conduct operations, which were costly to the civilian population – both sides suffered terrible loses. As the war moved into the Caucasian Mountains it became partisan.

Chechens outside the region launched a series of terrorist outrages in Russia including attacks on transport and civilian targets in Moscow. This has led to a stiffening of resolve by the Russian President, Vladimir Putin, to bring an end to the conflict and to exact harsh reprisals against the Chechen people every time they attack Russian targets.

See also: Russia.

Reference

Panico, C. (1995) 'Conflicts in the Caucasus: Russia's War in Chechnya', *Conflict Studies*, no. 281, London: RISCT.

Further Reading

Hoffman, S. (1998) *World Disorders: Troubled Peace in the Post Cold War Era*, London: Rowman & Littlefield.

Children

One of the most horrific aspects of terrorism is the use of children as combatants, in some cases as a result of being kidnapped. They can be used to carry equipment, serve as human mine detectors, undertake suicide missions, carry supplies, and act as messengers (Hansen, 2001). They tend to suffer high casualties, and later turn to crime as they have known no other life. Some Palestinians exhort their children on the love of holy war (Human Rights Watch, 2001).

Some children grow up to be terrorists as their parents are terrorists and often die brutal deaths as terrorists.

Child soldiers have fought as paramilitaries in **Algeria**, **Colombia**, **East Timor**, **India**, Indonesia, Mexico and Yugoslavia. They have been a part of the government armed forces of Burundi, Chad, Eritrea, Ethiopia, **Iran**, **Iraq**, **Israel**, Myanmar and Uganda.

As members of armed opposition groups children have fought in the Congo, **Lebanon**, **Pakistan**, Papua New Guinea, **Peru**, **Philippines**, **Russia**, **Rwanda**, Solomon Islands, **Turkey** and Uzbekistan.

See also: Environmental Influences.

References

Hansen, B. (2001) 'Children in Crisis', *Congressional Quarterly Researcher*, vol. 11, no. 2, pp. 657–680.

Human Rights Watch (2001) *Children's Rights – Human Rights Developments*, London and New York: Human Rights Watch, World Report.

China

The People's Republic of China defines itself, as a socialist state under the people's democratic dictatorship led by the working class and based on the alliance of workers and peasants. The power struggle within the Communist Party, which followed the death of Mao in 1976, was accompanied by various manifestations of opposition to the government, although organised groups were largely confined to those seeking full observance of human rights in China. Externally, the regime in Beijing is faced with no serious threat except from the Taiwanese nationalists who were driven to their island home of Taiwan (formerly Formosa) when the Communists came to power under the leadership of Mao Tse-Tung and Chou en-Lai in 1949. The Kuomintang regime in Taiwan claims it is the legitimate government of the whole of China.

In 1981 the Communist Party issued directives insisting that literature and art must conform to official policy and calling for a total ban on unofficial publications and organisations. These directives were aimed at such organisations as the Chinese Revolutionary Party formed in 1982, and advocating the establishment of a multi-party parliamentary democracy in China; and the Human Rights Alliance, which in 1979 published a manifesto calling for a constitutionally-guaranteed right to criticise state and party leaders, representation of non-communist parties in the National People's Congress, and freedom to change one's work and to travel abroad. The Society of Light has been less successful than the Alliance in that since its inception in 1978 most of its leaders have been arrested. It complained that wages have not kept pace with prices, and has called for 'the fifth modernisation' – democracy, to complement the four modernisation's of agriculture, industry, national defence, and science and technology advocated by the Communist party in 1975. The Society's leader Wei Jingsheng was jailed for eight years in 1980 for 'counter-revolutionary' activities. Dissident activity was reported in Tibet. In 1987 monks marched through Lhasa demanding reform and a dozen were killed. In 1988 following riots during a religious festival thirty monks were killed in a monastery (Brogan, 1989).

Regulations on state secrets adopted in 1951 were reissued in 1980. State secrets are defined as secret information on all aspects of political, economic and military affairs – divulgence of which is considered a treasonable offence.

As the country has opened its doors to the world; the authorities still fear an uprising in Tibet or Xinjiang. The regaining of Taiwan by whatever means, into the fold of the motherland remains an aspiration to be fulfilled in the future.

See also: Guerrilla Warfare in History.

References

Brogan, P.(1989) *World Conflicts: Why and Where they are Happening*, London: Bloomsbury Publishing.
Dally, P. (1986) 'Terrorism and East-West Tension: Peking Blames the USA and Israel', *Asian Outlook*, vol. 21, no. 7, pp. 18–21.

Chinese Revolution 1926–49 (Maoist Thoughts)

China was a rural society led by a corrupt and incompetent regime. The revolutionaries had to wait until they had a large military and political system of their own, equal to the task of meeting the sizeable incumbent forces in open conflict. Revolutionary power was arranged in terms of dictatorship of the proletariat, and the key revolutionary acts were still taking place in the cities. Peasant unrest was merely to create a climate of uncertainty and chronic instability in the cities, which could find the inspiration, and the freedom of manoeuvre to act. Mao Tse-Tung believed that the countryside had to surround the towns. He realised that sieges were not based upon swift assaults but a slow and painstaking process of erosion. He realised the Chinese Communists might be compelled to fight a long-term, defensive struggle, but realised that dynamic elements could transform it into an offensive war. Ultimately, and as it turned out, crucially, he wished to make the most of an army of badly trained, badly equipped and parochially minded peasants. Mao always believed that **guerrilla warfare** was a weapon that a nation inferior in arms and military equipment could employ against a more powerful aggressor. Guerrilla warfare was suited to a peasant society for technical reasons. All such warfare he believed had to have a political goal. Mao believed that the immediate task was of a military nature and the end game was military success. Thus the Red Army was the logical extension of the most basic social and economic apparatus of the mass of the people. Mao always stressed the need for the closest identification between the Communist Party and the army and the hopes of the rural masses. However, for Mao Tse-Tung any armed force divorced from central control could never become an effective revolutionary body. Mao always subordinated purely military considerations to the fundamental long-term demands of the peasant masses amongst which he had chosen to operate. He was constantly utilising appropriate ideological, economic, coercive organisational, patriotic, tactical and strategic options.

Civil War

Defined as 'war between belligerent factions seeking by organised violence to acquire a monopoly of force and political power in a state', civil war is a type of conflict feared by most countries. It is by definition divisive and by its nature requires the channelling of energies and resources inwards to the detriment of trade, state development and international relations. It is extremely destructive, not just in the physical sense, but also more importantly in the moral, creating deep divisions within society, which may take generations to repair. It invariably creates a political vacuum as rival centres of authority emerge, and this invites foreign interference, which may be difficult to shake off once the war is over. In short, civil war threatens the independence of the state and tears its fabric apart.

Civil war occurs with the development of armed hostilities between two or more sections of society, both possessed of political organisations and claiming the right to rule the society, or in the case of one of the parties, the right to independent status. A civil war is distinguished from a rebellion by such claims to political power on the part of the insurrectionary party, and distinguished from a revolution by the approximate balance of forces on each side, though a revolution can precede, accompany or follow a civil war.

It is hard objectively to determine the boundary between the wanton destruction and death caused by terrorists, the guerrilla war (sometimes called low-intensity conflict) pursued by young national liberation movements, and the civil war fought by mature, stronger, national liberation movements. Yet in each of these cases the user of military capabilities as a tool or potential tool of violence is not a state. From this, non-traditional violence may be most simply defined as violence between any two international actors, at least one of which is usually a non-state actor, or receiving external support. Distinctions between war and peace have been blurred; civil wars, revolutionary wars, liberation wars, religious and ideological revolts and terrorism may all affect and be affected by the international system. Since 1945 state authority has been challenged more often from inside the state than from outside the state.

Civil wars rarely lack international dimensions, either because one or another of the parties involved in the war receives support from external sources or because an external actor is vitally concerned with the outcome of the war. During the twentieth century ideology, economics, power and religion have internationalised virtually every civil war.

Civil wars occupy a curious place in any typology of wars and violence. On one hand they are quite often violent. Because of their inordinate violence civil wars have been condemned as needless and senseless destroyers of life and property. On the other hand, civil wars have been defended as the last recourse of action against corrupt, outdated or unyielding social systems and governments.

The world is divided into a number of 'states', geographical entities containing persons ruled by a recognised form of central authority which enjoys at least a degree of independent decision-making – and each contains within its boundaries the seeds of conflict. The population is unlikely to be completely homogeneous, particularly if the borders of the state reflect the arbitrary decisions of outside powers (as is the case with so many ex-colonial members of the **Third World**) or result from a history of expansion by conquest in the search for security.

This means that there will always be groups within the state who do not owe natural allegiance to the central authority, preferring the traditions and beliefs of their own ethnic, tribal or religious backgrounds and this may lead to accusations of their disloyalty, as well as government-sponsored attempts to persuade or force them into conformity.

Similar divisions may result from an uneven spread of wealth or power within the state. Some areas may be starved of resources, growing resentful of the development of other, more favoured regions; others may hold a monopoly of a scarce resource and be loath to share their advantages with the rest of society unless they are given a corresponding monopoly of political power.

In some states these divisions may be controlled by a strong central government which exercises its power by means of accepted forms of democracy or effective totalitarian repression, but even then the potential for internal conflict remains. In extreme cases it may be manifested in the creation of an entirely new state through the secession of the disaffected areas. In 1971, for example, Bangladesh seceded from West **Pakistan**, with aid from **India** after years of being treated as a 'poor relation' by the central authorities in Islamabad. However, the more common result is civil war.

Civil wars have affected many states, but they have increased in both frequency and importance since 1945. In part this is due to the simple fact, that since that date the number of independent states in existence, and therefore susceptible to civil war, has more than tripled in the aftermath of European decolonisation, but there is more to it than that. The division of major parts of the world into two rival ideological camps has pitted communism against capitalism in even the most sophisticated states, deepening already existing political divides, sometimes to the point of violence.

Improved communications have shown people that other groups have attained a level of economic or political development that contrasts sharply to their own, leading to a questioning of government policies and a drift towards conflict. Such groups may, of course, be exploited by outside powers but whatever the background, civil war has developed with ever-increasing frequency.

Many of the more intractable and long-lasting of the conflicts that have taken place since 1945 bear the hallmarks of civil war, even though they are not normally described as such. The Vietnam War was fought mainly by members of the same Vietnamese culture, and until the intervention of the **USA** and North Vietnamese forces the combatants came from within the same state. In Northern **Ireland**, too, the 'troubles of the 1970s' often seemed a species of civil war, with the British Army almost an outside force.

Looking in more detail at the specific causes of civil wars since 1945, it is clear that the ideological clash between communism and capitalism has had a dramatic impact. It has been the direct cause of two of the most significant civil wars of the period, albeit with different results. In **China** the offensive launched by the communists under Mao Tse-Tung in 1946 was designed to destroy the Western-orientated government of Chiang Kai-Shek. Although the resultant war had its origins in the political chaos that had beset China since the overthrow of the Manchu dynasty in 1911, the fighting of 1946–49 was firmly based upon opposing political views. In the end the communists prevailed. A similar clash of ideologies fuelled the civil war in Greece between 1945 and 1949, with the communist-led Democratic Army fighting the Nationalist government, but in this case it was the Nationalists who won, not least because of Western commitment to their cause.

The fact that events in Greece almost led to a more general confrontation between the rival camps of East and West undoubtedly muted the degree of direct support offered by the superpowers to factions in subsequent civil wars, but this did not mean that ideology had ceased to play an important role, merely that the superpowers have been more circumspect, preferring subversion to open battle and using proxies to provide the necessary aid. Events in Angola in 1975 illustrate the point with the communist MPLA receiving arms, advisers and equipment from the Cubans rather than the Russians in their struggle to defeat the South African-backed and CIA funded forces of FNLA and UNITA.

In many cases, it is still local issues, which cause civil wars, centred upon purely internal differences. In Nigeria, for example, the civil war of 1967–70 had its origins among the Ibo tribe of the eastern provinces, who felt that the federal government in Lagos was actively discriminating against them.

A similar pattern of events occurred in Chad after 1968, when the tribes of the northern and eastern provinces, convinced that their rivals from the south and west were enjoying a monopoly of political power, revolted under the banner of Frolinat (the National Liberation Front of Chad) and initiated a civil war which has yet to be completely resolved. In Sudan a civil war took place from the moment of independence in 1956 until a partial reconciliation in 1972 between the Christian and animist inhabitants of the south and the Muslim-dominated government in Khartoum, while the Lebanese Civil War of 1975–76 had its roots in the inevitable clash between the Maronite Christians of the governing elite and the disaffected Muslim majority.

If the causes of civil wars are many and varied, the results are often predictable. Although the superpowers may be deterred from offering direct support, it is one of the characteristics of the post-1945 period that few civil wars have remained self-contained. In an interdependent world, beset by problems of ideological and resource rivalry, too much is at stake to prevent outside interference and this can often be decisive in terms of the outcome or longevity of internal squabbles. The civil war in North Yemen was sustained by the fact that **Egypt** supported the republicans while **Saudi Arabia** backed the monarchists; in Lebanon the rivalries of 1975–76 have been fuelled by Syrian and Israeli intervention, in Chad it was the French and Libyans who offered aid.

In each of these cases, intervening states stood to make substantial gains from the victory of their chosen allies. In Chad, the French committed troops to protect their valuable stake in the mineral resources of the country. This makes a peaceful or lasting solution extremely difficult to achieve. Local issues disappear beneath more global pressures and the degree of violence increases as more sophisticated weapons and even troops are made available, and the fighting drags on, achieving either stalemate (as in North Yemen and Sudan), or eventual victory for the faction which enjoys the most effective outside support (as in Greece, Nigeria and Angola). This pattern will continue.

In any civil war there are political, economic and personal incentives for violence. Civil wars are not just about incompatible identity, ancient hatreds or opportunities. Some violence may have rationality and rational decisions of the contesting sides are made, even when many believe it is pointless to carry on. There is the role of key leaders and personal interests in continuing the war, problems of decision-making, and the inability of belligerents to assess military progress and the efficacy of continued combat.

Ongoing civil wars, unresolved internal disputes and areas of major internal unrest at the time of writing (February 2003) include those in **Algeria**, Angola, Cyprus, Georgia, Indonesia, **Kashmir**, **Peru**, **Philippines**, and Zaire.

Reference

King, C. (1997) 'Ending Civil Wars', London: International Institute for Strategic Studies, *Adelphi Papers*, no. 308.

Further Reading

Bell, J. Bowyer (1985) 'Terrorism and the Eruption of Wars' in Merari, A. (Ed) *On Terrorism and Combating Terrorism*, Frederick, MD: University Publications of America.

Jamieson, A. (1996) 'Political Corruption in Western Europe: Judiciary and Executive', in *Conflict*, London: RISCT, no. 288.

Zartman, W. (ed.) (1995) *Elusive Peace: Negotiating an End to Civil Wars*, Washington, DC: Brookings Institute.

Coercion

This does not need violence, but does require skilled judgement of the way in which the terrorists'

message is to be conveyed to those for whom it is intended without so frightening them that they offer support to anti-terrorist measures.

They claim their actions are morally worthy and their ends are morally justified. Opposing philosophical views exist on the issue. The morality of Kant was that regardless of what others threaten to do, ones own responsibility is to ensure that one does not kill any innocent person.

Arendt believed violence to be an individual or anti-political use of force, whereas what a state employed was power. Terrorists have to be ingenious and use surprise, and they cannot use predictable tactic and methods. They are contemptuous of any negotiations to end violence. Full blooded state terrorism is a great evil and the psychological roots of state terrorism are very widespread and very deep. Terrorist acts of **hostage taking** have a requirement that the use of force has a reasonable chance of success and that the act is properly motivated. Hostages are seized around the world to change the status quo.

Ultimately terrorism is a tactic used to gain control of situations or to fix a shift in the power balance (private or public). It is a short-cut to power or authority, a resort of the relatively powerless or of those unable to justify their uses of power to a public. Terrorism has been compared to rape in that both involve planned or systematic manipulation. Terror, panic and heightened fear makes us vulnerable to manipulation. Women successfully terrorised and others socialised by them, comply with men's demands (Frey and Morris, 1991).

References

Frey, R. and Morris, C. (ed.) (1991) *Violence, Terrorism and Justice*, Cambridge: Cambridge University Press.

Cold War, The

The Cold War was obviously a major factor in post-war guerrilla struggles, as in Greece or Vietnam. A major factor why such wars attained the levels of violence that they did, was that the guerrillas had Communist sponsors with common frontiers that could provide sanctuary and sustained military and economic aid. After Vietnam, the **Soviet Union** propped up beleaguered regimes in power, such as **Afghanistan**, **Angola**, Ethiopia, and to a lesser extent Nicaragua, to which aid could be delivered with reasonable ease. The last occasion on which the Soviet Union could turn local military reputation to widespread political influence was the conflict in Vietnam, Laos and Cambodia. Fears about the intervention of **China** and escalation to nuclear confrontation with the Soviet Union, were constraints on American leaders.

In Afghanistan and Angola, both the **USA** and USSR through their many forces made serious efforts to achieve military victory, yet world peace was never threatened.

The end of the Cold war witnessed the criminalisation of **guerrilla warfare**. In Angola, Bolivia and Cambodia guerrillas largely financed themselves through smuggled diamonds, smuggled cocaine, and smuggled gems and hardwood, which are moved from insurgent bases via corrupt local authorities and criminal middlemen. Such change can turn guerrilla leaders into warlords, intent on maintaining armed forces to protect trafficking.

International affairs have been fragmented by the collapse of the Soviet Union. A proliferation of small arms in the world market mainly from USSR and Warsaw Pact Forces allowed *ad hoc* guerrilla forces to arm themselves quickly and cheaply and adopt a credible military nature. In Afghanistan such arms proliferation has permitted age-old chronic tribal rivalries to degenerate into a frenzy of violence. Great powers have shown a lack of interest in trying to stop these guerrilla wars, due to the collapse of Communism and the crumbling of bloc international politics. Blocs and nation states have a diminished role in the super-national, globalised world of today.

See also: Afghanistan; Soviet Union.

References

Dallin, A. and Breslauer, G. W. (ed.) (1970) *Political Communist Systems*, Stanford, CA: Stanford University Press.

Goren, R. (1984) *The Soviet Union and Terrorism*, London: Allen & Unwin.

Colombia

This is one of the worst countries in the world in terms of guerrilla and terrorist infiltration. It is a struggle against the government, which seeks to take over power in order to change not the regime but the system – it has provoked fear, panic, uncertainty, and weakened the economic infrastructure in the country.

The terrorists' procedures are flexible and they can adopt to every situation, assuming diverse forms depending on the opponent. The terrorists have made themselves appear to be victims of official repression.

The groups call on terrorism as an arm to cause war, anguish and anxiety in communities. They also take power through armed struggle; and wish to destabilise the state and cause a collapse of the system. Military action of the terrorist groups is based on the ambush of regular troops, which are part of the tactical and administrative movements. They and their command installations are basically migrant in order not to become targets. Recruitment is done by knowing those who relate to them among the masses of unemployed and by providing for them and their families in the zones where the terrorists exercise their influence.

The international community is worried by the growth of drug related terrorism (**narcoterrorism**) and in this regard in recent years, the Colombian government has had to take action against terrorism through the co-ordinated efforts of international intelligence. What the Colombians have found hard to achieve are the development of economic efforts in order to create the conditions which will overcome inequalities among the people that constitute a vulnerable situation enabling terrorists from all backgrounds to act. With international help the forces of order have specialised units, equipped, instructed and trained and capable of confronting terrorist activity. For years the Colombian terrorists have operated with significant advantages – knowledge of the population, knowledge of terrorism, mobility and numerical superiority at a particular point of action.

See also: FARC; Narco-Terrorism.

Reference

Buckwalter, J. R. (ed.) *International Terrorism: The Decade Ahead*, Chicago: Office of International Criminal Justice, The University of Illinois.

Further Reading

Lee, R. W. (1989) 'Narco-terrorism – the Colombian Case', *Terrorism*, vol. 12, no. 6, pp. 435–7.

Commercial Interests and Security

In the counter-terrorism effort, the role of international commerce from enhancing trade to economic boycotts has to be considered. Western nations for two or three decades have tried to curtail commerce undertaken with states that support international terrorism – **Cuba**, **Iran**, **Iraq**, **Libya**, North Korea, Sudan, and **Syria**. For example the American containment policy towards Iran was designed to force Iran to reform, to revise its rejectionist stance on regional issues, and change its behaviour internationally. The **USA** had allowed millions of dollars to be used to finance efforts to undermine the Iranian regime. **Europe**, particularly Britain, France, Germany and Italy is far more dependent on Gulf and Libyan oil than the USA. Nevertheless, there were inconsistencies in American policy and their exports to Iran were quite substantial. Iran has proved the weakness of unilateral sanctions, in that it and other cultures faced with such measures can become more reasonably self-sufficient through forced changes in circumstances.

Sudan, conversely, is a different story. In the 1980s it received much assistance in terms of bilateral and multilateral aid but this declined in the 1990s and the economy collapsed. The Sudanese refused to end their isolation from the international community due to fanaticism and radicalism in the country.

As the cases of Iran and Sudan show, symbolic sanctions and sporadic dialogue are inadequate.

The global community has to be seen to collaborate and participate in collective economic and political sanctions against states opposing terrorism.

See also: Businesses Targeted by Terrorists.

Reference

Feiler, G. (1993) 'Counter Terrorism and Commercial Interests: Do They Conflict?' *Terrorism and Political Violence*, vol. 10, no. 2, pp. 15–22.

Further Reading

Adams, J. (1986) *The Financing of Terror*, London: New English Library.

Conflict Management and Conflict Resolution

Solving violent and protracted ethnic conflict is very hard if not impossible. It is perhaps easier to manage tensions and rivalries rather than solving the problem. As a result more realistic policies can be adopted.

Crises involving Ugandan Asians (expulsion), Bulgarian Turks (forced assimilation), Kurds (repression) and Hutus (genocide), Tamils in Sri Lanka (racial repression), Palestinians (self-determination), Greek/Turkish Cypriots (tensions over land), Ulster (Protestant/Catholic tensions over whether Northern **Ireland** should be British or Irish) have been stretching the minds of conflict solvers and trouble shooters for, in some cases, generations. Such 'peace-keepers' or managers can do no more than reduce physical violence.

Societies are polarised by militarism and ethnocentrism. Moreover, there is geographical separation because people are forced to leave mixed areas under threat or intimidation i.e. Cyprus, Northern Ireland, Palestine, Sri Lanka. Leaders and followers then become very bigoted and narrow-minded, and unwilling or unable to explore alternatives. Their perceived 'causes' then become 'sacred cows'.

Peace-keeping operations provide a period of relative calm and order to allow an effective search for any negotiated settlement.

In the stages of conflict within a crisis there are five key stages and terrorism can feature in many of them.

First, there is a peaceful stable situation with a high degree of social stability and regime legitimacy. Second, there is a situation causing political tension in which there are growing levels of systemic strain and increasing social and political cleavages often along factional lines. This is sufficient to bring about a political crisis.

In the third stage there is a violent political conflict, with the erosion of a government's political legitimacy and a rising acceptance of factional politics. The next stage is low-intensity conflict with open hostility and armed conflict among factional groups plus regime repression and insurgency. It is hardly surprising that a humanitarian crisis results, Finally, there is a high-intensity conflict with organised combat between rival groups, massive killings and a displacement of sections of the civilian population.

The above can all afflict democratic nations, as can 'democide' which is the intentional killing of people by governments, including the killing of them with weapons, or caused by military action. Democracies rarely commit violence against each other. The more democratic a regime the less its foreign violence, and the more democratic a regime, the less its democide.

Democracy is a method of non-violence and the less democratic a state, the more severe is its domestic violence and also its proneness for foreign violence.

Many observers see direct response as a key to emergency management. Anti-terrorist programmes have to be comprehensive and include programmes to prepare for, mitigate the effects of, and recover from the destruction, as well as react to the immediate crises caused by the violence.

Any terrorist threat can be somewhat unpredictable with tremendous variability in possible intensity. Policies and programmes designed to address the threat of terrorism have to be comprehensive. The nature of the terrorist problem has changed with violence becoming more destructive on a mega-scale. Emergency managers have a key role to play and are concerned with minimising threats to and loss of life and property. Such changes show that governments in democratic nations are having to find an appropriate link between the nature of the hazard that the violence presents and the policy options chosen. A clearly focused set of programmes of counter-terrorism or a broader focus of policies and programmes that terrorist violence might engender are at the behest of government and emergency managers.

See also: Crisis Management.

References

De Bono, E. (1985) *Conflicts: A Better Way to Resolve Them*, London: Penguin.
Ryan, S. (1990) 'Conflict Management and Conflict Resolution', *Terrorism and Political Violence*, vol. 2, no. 1, pp. 55–70.

Further Reading

Cohen, S. P. and Arnone, H. C. (1988) 'Conflict Resolution as the Alternative to Terrorism', *Journal of Social Issues*, vol. 44, no. 2, pp. 175–189.
Jongman, A. and Schmid, A. (1999) 'Trends in Contemporary Conflicts and Human Rights Violations', *Terrorism and Political Violence*, vol. 11 no. 3, pp. 119–150.

Counter-insurgency

Counter-insurgency is the term for measures taken by governments against insurgents or those people who take part in an uprising against incumbent governments, usually in the form of an armed insurrection.

Good government is the best method to avoid insurgency, and effective counter-insurgency must involve political action by civilians as well as military action by soldiers. Soldiers have to act in a political context and civilians, for their own safety, have to accept military rule. There are a wide range of political situations in which insurgency occurs, or may occur, depending on the nature of the arena chosen (urban or rural), and the status of the territory in which it occurs (a province, a dependent territory, a protectorate or a friendly state), as well as on the political order of the state that is combating the insurgency (liberal democracy, authoritarian government or dictatorship).

The main lesson of counter-insurgency is the importance of maintaining the primacy of civilian government. In the case of insurgency in a colonial territory, the best results have been achieved where the colonial government has had the option open to it of handing over power in the medium term to an elected civilian government that can command popular support and has been prepared to embrace this opportunity. Counter-insurgency forces operating in a friendly state are always liable to be regarded by the local inhabitants as anti-national, if not indeed as an occupying force. The perceptions and attitudes of the opposition have to be understood.

Success in counter-insurgency depends on certain conditions being met: planning is an essential prerequisite, and lack of planning has led to more serious trouble than any other omission. A government confronted for the first time with an armed insurgency threat tends to give a panic response.

The first response to an armed threat should be through the police and not the armed forces.

The history of counter-insurgency in the twentieth century has shown a natural tendency to develop in parallel with developments in the concept of insurgency itself. From 1945 up to the mid-1960s, the main theatre of insurgency was the countryside. Emphasis was given to **guerrilla warfare**, which as a development of partisan warfare was well understood to be dependent on an infrastructure of civilian support for motivation, the supply of food and other material resources, and the provision of disguise. In Malaya, for example, psychological warfare was aimed primarily at the small number of active terrorists with the aim of encouraging them to surrender. The combined effects of isolation, fear and hunger led many to do so, once they knew that they could surrender in safety.

After 1967, counter-insurgency was to evolve into the 'justification' for what was later known as the 'national security state' in the 1970s and 1980s. The 'national security state' was typically a Latin American military government obsessed with the overall objective of permanently eliminating foreign 'subversion' by the imprisonment, torture and execution of political opponents, many of whom had no connection with any form of insurgent activity. Fuelled by inter-service rivalry, such military establishments built up vast intelligence organisations whose functions had little enough to do with real intelligence – the gathering and evaluation of information. Four steps can be discerned in the nature of any counter-terrorist intelligence. First, *direction* – the determination of intelligence requirements, preparation of a collection plan, insurance of orders and requests to information collection agencies, and a continuous check on the productivity of collection agencies. The second step is *collection* – the systematic procurement and selection of information relevant to a specific intelligence problem. Third, *processing* is the step whereby 'information' becomes 'intelligence' through evaluation, analysis, integration and interpretation. Fourth, there is *dissemination* – the conveyance of intelligence in suitable form (oral, graphic or written) to agencies which need it.

Counter-terror forces need to be aware of the type and nature of the terrorist operation, its relationship to the revolutionary process, its organisation, ideology, type of propaganda, tactics, weapons, targets, audience and **media** coverage.

Projections can be made in relation to the purpose, reason or cause of the planned event, the nature of the situation, groups or individuals involved, the number of persons expected, locations affected, the time and duration of the event or situation, the potential for disorder, the effect upon the law enforcement agency, the wider significance of the event or situation and the evolving patterns and trends.

Counter-intelligence functions are needed to strengthen the counter-insurgency operation, and to combat the surprise effects of terrorism, which can be used to: create a situation for which police and security authorities are unprepared; force security authorities into hurried or ill-considered actions; dislocate or disperse security forces; allow deployment of terrorist elements in unexpected strength; allow assault from an unexpected direction; facilitate exploitation of unexpected timings; capitalise on the use of unexpected tactics.

See also: Insurgency; Third World Insurgency.

Reference

Bucket, I. F. W. (1985) *Armed Forces and Modern Counter-Insurgency*, New York: St Martin's Press.

Further Reading

Charters, D. and Tugwell, M. A. (eds) (1989) *Armies in Low Intensity Conflict: A Comparative Analysis*, London: Brassey's.

Hocking, Jenny (1988) 'Counter-Terrorism as Counter-Insurgency: The British Experience', *Social Justice*, vol. 15 (spring), pp. 83–97.

Counter/Anti-Terrorism

Counter-Terrorism

Terrorism is a direct threat to democracies around the world and to people's **human rights** – in other words, it is a global war crime and has to be treated as such by the global counter-terrorist forces (intelligence, military and police). If terrorism produces public reactions and moulds opinion or a change of opinion on a certain action or an issue then counter-terrorism policy must be equal to the task and respond in kind. There was little will in democracies to fight back with force, until the events of **September 11**. Consistency is needed in any anti-terrorist policy and governments can then be assured of public support. The public support around the world soon wanes if governments invoke concessions to protect their own countries to get hostages back or to bargain with extortionists. Terrorism ultimately is a human problem as it can produce victims, refugees and homeless or displaced people.

Military support to the police is a tenet of counter-terrorism. Surveillance of suspects and groups is allowed under certain conditions in many democracies, as long as it does not become the norm.

Many democracies are now reappraising extradition treaties to tighten up the legal phraseology and to broaden the scope without it must be stated, affecting asylum rights of the persecuted.

Terrorist threats have to be seen around the world as fair, and the spin-offs can be of judicial and political value. Snatches of suspects involved in **kidnapping** and hijacking have occurred. Covert actions have been undertaken by Americans and Israelis against Arabs and Palestinians.

Counter-terrorism skills are interchangeable among democracies especially between the **USA** and Western European countries and these have mushroomed post-September 11.

Military strikes have taken place i.e. President Clinton's authorisation of attacks on terror bases in Sudan and **Afghanistan** in response to the embassy bombings in **East Africa** in 1998 and include the use of commando forces trained for direct action. Perhaps controversially, states may authorise the assassination of terrorists.

If military measures are not taken, political and economic **sanctions** are often implemented. The breaking off of diplomatic relations, expulsion of diplomats for example, Libyans from the **United Kingdom** in 1984 after the siege at the Libyan People's Bureau in St James's Square, London.

Much needed supplies: food, fuel, medicines, engineering spare parts can be halted to try and bring terrorist states in order such as **Cuba**, **Iraq**, **Libya** and **Syria**. Nevertheless, effectiveness can be varied and the states' economies continue to operate quite effectively. Sanctions can be problematic in that they can cause more harm to innocent parties than to governments.

Any counter-terrorism operation must have the will of, and be shaped by, political leadership.

In recent years it has become a sophisticated operation as well as big business. International agencies co-ordinate the actions of states in tracking and apprehending suspected terrorists, as does **Europol** in Europe. National governments have investigative agencies such as the **FBI** and CIA to break through the wall of secrecy around terrorist operations. Many private companies have expanded the business of providing security services, including anti-terrorist equipment and forces, to companies and individuals doing business internationally (Goldstein, 1999).

Counter-insurgency, used in combating **guerrilla warfare** often includes programmes to 'win the hearts and minds' of rural populations so that they stop sheltering the guerrillas.

References

Clutterbuck, R. (1994) *Terrorism in an Unstable World*, New York: Routledge.

Cotler, I. (1998) 'Towards a Counter-Terrorism Law and Policy', *Terrorism and Political Violence*, vol. 10, no. 2, pp. 1–14.

Goldstein, J. S. (1999) *International Relations*, Harlow: Longman.

Livingstone, N. C. and Arnold, T. E. (eds) (1986) *Fighting Back: Winning the War against Terrorism*, Lexington, MA: Lexington Books.

Lodge, J. (1991) *Counter-terrorism in Europe: Implications for 1992: Frontier Problems and the Single Market*, London: Research Institute for Study of Terrorism.

Reinares, F. (ed.) (2001) *European democracies against Terrorism*, Aldgate: Dartmouth.

Further Reading

Dewar, M. (1995) *Weapons and Equipment of Counter-Terrorism*, London: Arms & Armour Press.

Dobson, C. and Payne, R. (1982) *Counter-attack: The West's Battle against the Terrorists*, New York: Facts on File.

Kozlow, C. (1997/8) *Jane's Counter-terrorism*, Jane's Information Group.

Leeman, R. W. (1991) *Rhetoric of Terrorism and Counter-Terrorism*, Westport, CT: Greenwood Press

Lesser, I. O. (ed.) (1999) *Countering the New Terrorism*, Santa Monica, CA: Rand Corporation.

Livingstone, N. C. (1982) *The War against Terrorism*, Lexington, MA: Lexington Books.

Lodge, J. (ed.) (1981) *Terrorism: A Challenge to the State*, New York: St Martin's Press.

Morris, E. and Hoe, A. (1987) *Terrorism, Threat and Response*, Basingstoke: Macmillan Press.

Netanyahu, B. (1995) *Fighting Terrorism: How Democracies Can Defeat Domestic and International Terrorism*, New York: Avon.

Pillar, P. R. (2001) 'Lessons and Futures' in *Terrorism and US Foreign Policy*, Washington, DC: Brookings Institute Press.

Smith, G. Davidson (1990) *Combating Terrorism*, New York: Routledge.

Trivalio, G. M. (2000) 'Terrorism, International Law and the Use of Military Force', *Wisconsin International Law Journal*, vol. 18, no. 1, pp. 145–191.

Waugh, W. L. (1982) *How Nations Respond to Terrorism*, Salisbury, NC: Documentary Publications.

Government Response to Terrorism

General conclusions on effective government response can be drawn from selective experience. Concessionary policies and failure to extradite terrorists are associated with an increase in terrorist activity. The establishment of a tough policy following a period of softness appears to require consistent actions applied over a period of time. A period of soft, concessionary policies may result in the establishment of a terrorism infrastructure. Isolated policy events, regardless of events and regardless of intensity, have no impact when they run counter to general policy implementation. A constantly applied, increasingly tough policy toward incident management is associated with significant decreases in all serious events. Ultimately, the failure to adopt and implement a tough, consistent incident management policy during a specific period of time can be associated with increases in terrorist activity.

Policy Responses to Terrorism

When one speaks of the 'policy response' to terrorism, then one is thinking of a complex and broad set of challenges for the policy-maker and for the country. Terrorism is but one feature of a much larger and more threatening pattern of low-level conflict. There are a number of measures which can be taken in response to terrorism: detecting, capturing and prosecuting terrorists; and avoiding terrorist acts by counter-measures such as physical security of facilities, personal security of targeted officials, and behaving in ways that make the person or place difficult to target. The costs of committing terrorism have to be seen to be high, and direct retaliation against the terrorist or terrorists must be undertaken, assuming one knows precisely who and where they are. Terrorists and would-be terrorists have to be persuaded to seek non-violent means to achieve their goals or redress their grievances; this is a tough aspect of terrorist incident management.

Working to mitigate the underlying causes of terrorism is hard. Where the issues concern social justice, lack of participation, lack of social or economic opportunity, or grievances of this type, the need and the opportunity exist to do something constructive about the complaints of people who would resort to terrorism. Much terrorist activity stems from actual or perceived problems of social justice. The practice of terrorism by states raises questions about when, where and how to use force, which are not necessarily raised by terrorist acts committed by small non-state groups or individuals.

Gaps exist in the laws of many Western nations – criminal statutes need updating; the law needs to influence activities like training and equipping terrorists abroad. Authority has to be used to pay rewards for information about international terrorist acts that might result in saving lives or obtaining the release of hostages. Changes of national laws are needed in order to implement fully international agreements such as the Montreal Convention against aircraft sabotage, and the **United Nations** Convention against taking hostages.

In changing laws and practices to deal with terrorism, the West has to be seen not to damage institutions and must protect the rights of citizens. Response to the problem must not destroy the fabric of society.

International co-operation is good in some respects and poor in others. The Western democracies work well together, particularly within the framework of NATO or the Summit Seven, the so-called Bonn Declaration Group Despite the growing pattern of terrorism which affects almost all countries, many have not seen the need actively to enter into either bilateral discussion of the issues or to take decisive stands in international forums. There is a need with respect to the laws of many countries for greater concordance of laws on the prosecution, extradition and punishment of terrorist acts. The Western community is concerned that differences of law do not provide unintended safe havens.

Differences of views among states as to what is an act of terrorism can cause obvious problems. Some states want to exclude terrorism of the Left. Some wish to make a specific exemption respecting wars of national liberation, which gives problems in contexts such as enforcement of the Helsinki Declaration. The West has always had a problem with the ambivalent terms of terrorism, and perhaps a lack of clarity as democrats as to what terrorism is and what its dangers are for the West.

The public have a need of a better understanding of how serious is the new challenge posed by state-sponsored terrorism.

The number of active terrorist groups, their target range, their capabilities, their causes and world events all change on a daily basis. World events very much influence terrorist activities. Through the media the coverage of terrorism is more extensive now than ever before in human history – more pervasive, more vivid, more emotional and more massively powerful in its impact on people and events. Mass communications have accelerated the post-war revolutionary tide by rapidly transferring information from one society to another. Total **media** silence will not stop the terrorist.

From the economic and business point of view there are some preventive measures to reduce the risks of terrorist attacks. Prevention can result from trying to stop loss or injury to employees and other assets; terrorist success can be limited by prior planning, and there needs to be communication with employees in the event of a serious problem. Multinational businesses have to find out about a country, its people and problems, whether it is already established there or is considering investment.

Any successful response for combating terrorism requires the West to study intelligence capabilities, the conditions and limitations under which force will be employed in response to terrorism, and public attitudes to the problem.

See also: Western Europe.

Reference

Sloan, S., Kearney, R. and Wise, C. (1976) 'Learning about Terrorism: Analysis, Simulations and Future Directions', in *Terrorism – An International Journal*, vol. 1, nos. 3/4, pp. 315–329.

Further Reading

Sloan, S. and Schultz, R. (eds.) (1980) *Responding to the Terrorist Threat: Prevention and Control.* New York: Pergamon.

Counter-Terrorism Laws

Any counter-terrorism policy has to take into account the increasing lethality of terrorism, the growing fanaticism including religions, fundamentalists and suicidal forces, and ultimately weapons of mass destruction.

Terrorists have become more sophisticated in terms of transnational communication and transportation networks. As September 11 showed, open and advanced technological societies can be vulnerable, leading to possible mega-terrorist incidents. Many of the weapons used by terrorists are getting smaller and harder to detect. Pariah or rogue states will always be there and perhaps only too keen to deliver sophisticated equipment to groups and individuals.

In any democracy one has to balance tightened security against infringement of civil liberties. This leads into the question of rights – human rights – which the terrorist will be quick to exploit. A basic premise of international law on terrorism is that it is a crime against humanity and terrorists are therefore the enemies of humanity. International jurisdiction must feature in any national counter-terrorism policy. Here, the creation of the International Criminal Court in 2001 is germane to the future development of policy. Extradition laws have to be universally and rigorously applied.

Every citizen in every country in the world is entitled to life, liberty and security. This is especially pertinent in the international globalised community in which we live. Nations must not become terrorist havens. Terrorists have to be dealt with under the democratic process of law. National and international commitments have to be found not to allow terrorist intimidation to block conflict resolution, to universalise extradition procedures, and to stop all financial support for terrorist organisations.

In building up initiatives leading to a counter-terrorism policy there has to be an international understanding and support for such a policy linked to human rights issues. More countries will be expected to sign up to the existing International Conventions on Terrorism. Ultimately, each nation's citizens have to be aware of the formulation, application and implementation of such a policy, as they are the key recipients of rights and dignity.

Preventive Action

Any preventive action in the fight against terrorism has to achieve five objectives: to make it harder for terrorists to act in the first place; to stop terrorist actions at inception and to disrupt others; to reduce friendly casualties while inflicting costs on the terrorists infiltrating and curtailing the actions of terrorist groups; arouse resistance in public opinion and educate them about the evils of terrorism.

These measures are in direct response to the terrorists laying down the challenge that they are all powerful; their opponents are weak, brutal, corrupt and inept; the tide of history is with them; and only by meeting their demands will their problem be solved (Bailey, 1995).

At all times police and military efficiency has to be superior to that of the terrorists, who although not usually well-trained are fanatics and zealots who will risk and sacrifice their lives for their beliefs. Since terrorists replicate and intensify normal criminal actions, successful anti-criminal tactics can be adapted to subdue them.

Because of its importance, terrorism is an effective instrument for mobilising public opinion and can be used to generate support for a wide range of policies.

The media play a part in mobilising public attitudes toward terrorism and generating pressure on governmental policy-makers to eliminate the terrorist threat. The problem of terrorism can be confronted, contained and defeated in specific instances; but the phenomena itself can never be completely eradicated.

Definitional problems do not help preventive action against terrorism. Terrorism wears many hats. Persons who answer a question or a charge by levelling a counter charge deepen the problem of definitions.

Without a basic definition one is not sure if terrorism is a threat to national stability or the criminal justice system. There are ambiguities about the morality of terrorism and the meaning of related terms: terror, coercion, force and violence.

Many people are concerned whether special laws in protection of a liberal democracy against violence of a political or terroristic nature are ever justifiable as a matter of principle. Liberal democracies can defend their existence and their values, even if this involves some temporary limitation of rights, but many observers are worried if this becomes carte blanche.

Citizens in democratic nations want special measures to be clear and precise and safe-guards provided to prevent their improper introduction or exercise. Special laws should be distinct from ordinary powers. Special powers have been built up over many years and after many reviews, debates in Parliament and battles in the courts. Catalogues of measures have expanded but the forms of scrutiny and safeguards have also been augmented. There has been a real attempt to respect the rule of law (Walker, 1996).

Earlier Prevention of Terrorism Acts in the late 1970s and 1980s were criticised by civil liberty groups as they severely undermined principles of natural justice and the rule of law in the eyes of many people in Britain (Scorer *et al.*, 1985). Furthermore they had violated international standards on human rights – standards accepted by the British government itself.

References

Bailey, W. G. (ed.) (1995) *Encyclopaedia of Police Science*, New York and London: Garland Publishers.

Burton, A. M. (1975) *Urban Terrorism: Theory, Practice and Response*, New York: Free Press.

Scorer, C., Spenser, S. and Hewitt, P. (1985) *National Council of Civil Liberties and the New Prevention of Terrorism Act: The Case for Appeal*, London: Yale Press.

Walker, C. (1996) 'Anti-Terrorism Laws for the Future', *New Law Journal*, vol. 146 (26 April), pp. 586–588.

Further Reading

Hacker, F. J. (1976) *Crusaders, Criminals, Crazies: Terror and Terrorism in Our Time*, New York: Newton.

Counter-Terrorist Laws in Individual Countries

It is because terrorists, by definition, deliberately conspire to carry out acts of violence, that violate the basic rights of humans, that their deeds are counted as crimes decoding to the judicial codes of all societies under the rule of law. The notions of crime, implies the moral responsibility of individuals for their actions and hence for any violation of the legal code (Berwick, 1996).

Concepts of legal justice, criminality, civil rights and obligation are central to the fabric of any civilised society. The liberal democratic state has an obligation to use criminal justice and law enforcement powers to protect its citizens and to uphold the law against such threats. Terrorists will do their utmost to stop this, while states have to carry out this fundamental responsibility.

France

The French government has wide ranging and strong powers to deal with terrorism. The French Parliament can be given authority to act by decree for a defined period on specified issues such as collecting information on anyone who might be a political threat to the security of the state. The powers of anti-terrorism laws have also been extended on widening the definition of offences, possession of weapons and assisting an illegal entrant.

Germany

The country has no special law on terrorism but the penal code covers terrorism and extremist groups. A special anti-terrorism unit has a huge database and computerised intelligence. Police co-ordination has been tightened up to hunt down extreme right-wing terrorists who have been hounding immigrant minorities over the past decade.

Italy

In the mid-1970s a measure was brought in to give the police increased powers of arrest and search, but the measure was to some extent weakened by the absence of co-ordination between the various police forces and other security agencies such as the intelligence services. The Red Brigade were defeated by public opinion and the political parties turning against the terrorists. There was an internal crisis of morale and solidarity; and in the 1980s a law came into effect giving incentives to convicted terrorists to turn state's evidence.

Spain

To combat the rapid rise of the Basque separatist group, ETA, an anti-terrorism decree law was passed in the 1970s to give police greater power to detain suspects and to accelerate terrorist trials. A new criminal code was created in 1996, to increase prison terms for those causing the death of a person, severe injury or kidnapping or supplying arms and fundraising for terrorist groups. They have also introduced legislation to provide political reforms to reduce the underlying causes of terrorism stemming from the Basque conflict.

United Kingdom

The *Prevention of Terrorism Act* was introduced in 1974 by a Labour government in response to the Birmingham pub bombings (in which 21 people were killed) and increasing IRA attacks on mainland United Kingdom at the time.

Over the next decade or so, new powers such as greater powers to arrest and detain terrorist suspects were seen by the police as core powers for dealing with the threat of IRA terrorism. Longer detention was necessary because terrorists hide their identities and are trained to resist questioning. The power of exclusion and the issue of no right of appeal by terrorists are based on practical security considerations. Such orders cover those who would more than likely be involved in terrorist activities.

The European Court of Human Rights has criticised some of the measures in the Act, especially the extension of the period for which an individual can be held for questioning.

Public opinion believes the *Prevention of Terrorism Act* is necessary, but only if there is a threat of major terrorism on the mainland.

The major points from the *Prevention of Terrorism Act* are: the Act should apply throughout the UK; terrorism should be defined as 'the use of serious violence against persons or property, or the threat to use such violence, to intimidate or coerce a government, the public or any section of the public, in order to promote political, social or ideological

objectives' (Para 5.23); there should be new offences of membership of a terrorist organisation (Paras 6.11 and 6.13); the power to proscribe terrorist organisations should be retained and extended to cover foreign as well as domestic terrorist organisations.

Arrest for any terrorist offence will carry with it the right to detention for 48 hours for questioning. Powers to stop, question and search. Such powers should be continued subject to the Secretary of State's approval.

The power to examine people at ports should remain in force substantially (Para 10.56).

The arrest and prosecution of those who conspire here to commit terrorist acts abroad (Para 12.40).

The power to order forfeiture of funds should be extended to all terrorist offences (Para 13.24).

Where a terrorist gives evidence against a fellow terrorist, he should be entitled to receive a statutory discount of between one-third and two-thirds on the sentence which the court would otherwise have imposed.

Additional powers and offences for use in the case of a new terrorist emergency should be the subject of primary legislation when the emergency arises. There should be public discussion of possible new powers and offences in advance of the emergency (Berwick, 1996).

One of the main difficulties in formulating an anti-terrorism policy is the inherent contradiction between the need for a consistent long-term approach and the necessity of dealing with individual situations on their own terms as they arise (Long, 1995). As the law in many democratic nations is trying to make clear anti-terrorism policy has to include a number of general principles, covering a wide span of policy issues in order to maintain an overall policy direction.

The Prevention of Terrorism Act, 1999 updated legislation that was over two decades old. Terrorism was defined as the use or threat for the purpose of advancing a political, religious or ideological cause, of action, which involves serious violence, endangers life or causes a risk to health and safety of citizens. The Act is a protective device for the public, and puts an end to summary exclusions and extradition procedures (Whittaker, 2002). Extra powers were given to the police to stop and search, after approval by the Home Secretary. It was easier to change and arrest a terrorist subject, and measures for this were enshrined in law.

In 2001 the Anti-Terrorism, Crime and Security Act became law which was to amend the Terrorism Act 2000: to make further provision about terrorism and security; to provide for the freezing of assets; to amend or extend the criminal law and powers for preventing crime and enforcing that law; to make provision about the control of pathogens and toxins; to provide for the retention of communications data; and to provide for inclusion in the Treaty on European Union.

The idea of this Act was to plug loopholes on earlier measures and tighten the noose around international terrorist activities. Significantly criminal law was to be amended and extended to defeat international terrorism.

United States

Recent events have shown that Americans are no longer immune from major terrorist attacks within their own borders. No federal law existed explicitly dealing with terrorism. Post the Oklahoma bombing in 1995 it was proposed that the FBI be given more powers to monitor and infiltrate extremist groups including their financial records and phone-tapping powers. Streamlined procedures were sought to deport aliens and designate certain groups as terrorists. The proposed anti-Terrorism Bill was subjected to many amendments and issues of guns and explosives were removed from the proposed legislation.

The FBI has the reputation of being highly professional and effective in the counter-terrorism role when it is given a proper remit – but there are severe restrictions on how it can collect evidence about potential extremists.

References

Berwick, Rt Hon Lord Lloyd of (1996) *Inquiry into Legislation Against Terrorism*, vol. II, London: HMSO.

Long, D. E. (1995) *The Anatomy of Terrorism*, London: Free Press.

Whittaker, D. J. (2002) *Terrorism: Understanding the Global Threat*, Harlow and London: Pearson Education.

Crime and Security Act 2001

This measure was passed in direct response to the events and repercussions of September 11. Some parts of the Act i.e. Part 4 or detention without trial are controversial, and it has been suggested that such draconian anti-terrorist laws have an impact on human rights.

Some provisions were uncontentious: further powers to forfeit terrorist property (Part 1); governing freezing orders (Part 2); controls over WMD (Part 6); improvements in aviation security (Part 9).

Other measures are contentious such as failing to disclose to the police any information which may be of material assistance to the terrorist.

Another range of measures were included which were unconfined to terrorism: the government arguing that wide-ranging measures were needed to render the detection of terrorists more probable. This perhaps set the pattern for future criminal justice measures being introduced for use against terrorism. The Act in response to such a terrible event as September 11 is perhaps seen as having few democratic ideals; but in the name of enhancing the reach of investigation techniques and to placate people's fears about reduced freedoms post-September 11.

Anti-Terrorism Act 2001

Police in the United Kingdom have arrested more than 300 people as terrorist suspects since September 11, but only three have been convicted of any offence under the Terrorism Act. Only about forty persons have been charged with offences under the Act. Not until 2003 was there a proven link connection with Islamic extremist terrorism or links to the Al Qaeda network. The majority of these charges have come from North Africa.

The UK's first Al Qaeda trial finished in Leicester in April 2003 resulting in the sentencing of two Algerian illegal immigrants for eleven years each for financing Islamic terrorism. They were convicted of raising hundreds of thousands of pounds through credit card counterfeiting, spreading Osama Bin Laden's propaganda and seeking recruits for global jihad.

Anti-Terrorism Act 2001 – Criticisms

The Anti-Terrorism and Crime and Security Act 2001 have been subjected to much criticism in spite of the worldwide revulsion at the events of September 11 which brought about its creation.

There was a doubt as to the effectiveness of the measures. Many observers were worried that far reaching legislation had been hurried through Parliament. There was perceived to be a breach of sound constitutional principles with regard to major legislative changes. Ultimately people voiced negative comments about the effect or violation of civil liberties and human rights in relation to the due process of the law.

A sizeable body of opinion believe that it is far from clear that even a single terrorist will be thwarted that could not have been prevented under the pre-existing laws, which were widely acknowledged to be very extensive as they stood.

References

Anti-Terrorism, Crime and Security Act 2001: Chapter 24, London: HMSO.

Scorer, C., Spenser, S. and Hewitt, P. (1985) *National Council of Civil Liberties and New Prevention of Terrorism Act: The Case for Appeal*, London: Yale Press.

Terrorism Act 2000: Chapter 11, London: HMSO.

Walker, C. (1996) 'Anti-Terrorism Laws for the Future', *New Law Journal*, vol. 146 (26 April), pp. 586–588.

Further Reading

Berwick, Rt Hon Lord Lloyd of (1996) *Inquiry into Legislation Against Terrorism*, vol. II, London: HMSO.

Fenwick, H. (2002) 'Legislation: The Anti-Terrorism Crime and Security Act 2001: A Proportionate Response to September 11?', *The Modern Law Review*, vol. 65, no. 5 (September).

Long, D. E. (1990) *The Anatomy of Terrorism*, London: Free Press.

Payne, S. (2002) *Britain's New Anti-Terrorist Legal Framework*, London: RUSI Journal (June), pp. 44–51.

Whittaker, D. J. (2002) *Terrorism: Understanding the Global Threat*, Harlow and London: Pearson Education.

International Co-operation

The essential pre-requisites for an insurgency or terrorist campaign are exploiting a cause; confronting a strong but preferably weak opponent; seizing a strategic opportunity when the political environment was favourable and relying on outside support from state and non-state actors (Williams, 2002). Al Qaeda does enjoy real legitimacy potential from the global Muslim communities; and terrorist groups only need relatively few highly committed killers to be lethal. The trend is clear; fewer terrorist incidents but more casualties.

As many observers have noted, especially since September 11, terrorism can never be eradicated, but can only be contained or deterred. Currently the phase of the war against terrorism is an American war with support from its allies in a secondary role. The greatest threat, perhaps since the Second World War, comes from militant Islam or rogue states armed with weapons of mass destruction. Such states act as 'force multipliers' for contemporary terrorist groups, supplying them with cash, arms, explosives and encouragement.

Mutual suspicions and rivalries remain between some intelligence agencies. There is public and political resistance to the introduction of a European Union (EU) identity card system (Latter, 1991). Differing national legal systems can cause problems regarding extradition. Mega-terrorism is developing and state sponsorship of terrorism is likely to become widespread.

Positive trends can provide pointers for the future. There is increasing, although as yet limited, worldwide co-operation to counter-terrorism. Within the European Union there are improved levels of counter-terrorists co-operation and technological developments including better protection for and on civilian aircraft and at airports (Latter, 1991).

Since September 11 in particular, there has been a very rapid expansion by the democracies to co-operate at government level and promote links between respective counter-terrorist agencies. Border controls have to be strengthened in Eastern Europe and countries of the former Soviet Union.

Europol and Interpol should continue to promote contact between heads of police and to standardise attitudes towards the prosecution and punishment of terrorists. The public and governments and law enforcement officers have to be educated about terrorism. Sanctions and the use of force have to be used to discourage state sponsorship of terrorism. Access to weapons of mass destruction (WMD) has to be prevented. These measures can only be implemented fully by international co-operation between governments. To get every state in the world to agree that terrorism is unacceptable remains an essential but distant goal.

See also: State Sponsorship; Weapons.

References

Latter, R. (1991) 'Terrorism in the 1990s', *Wilton Park Papers*, no. 44 (August), London: HMSO.

Williams, G. Lee (2002) *Can Terrorism be Defeated?*, Keynote address at TUCETU/AC (UK) Annual Conference, Stoke Rochford, Grantham, England, 9 February.

Simulation

Through the use of simulations, individuals and groups can be trained to respond effectively to terrorist attacks. An act of terrorism is like a theatrical performance. The terrorists write the scenario, from which they, the hostages and the responding forces improvise the action. The members of the media prepare the reviews and the public is the audience. Today terrorists use a global stage to dramatise their causes and with mass communications they play to a mass audience. They can strike anywhere at any time. Acts of terrorism are characterised by high drama and uncertainty. However, common behaviour patterns assist the authorities in responding to terrorist acts. Careful planning can produce a highly realistic exercise in crisis management and effective procedures for evaluation. The resulting simulations integrate the skills and considerations of the military and the law with social-science and improvisational theatre techniques. Participants learn under pressure how to resolve the crises and acts of violence surrounding an act of terrorism.

Society often chooses to insulate itself from acts of violence that it witnesses. Even when individuals grudgingly recognise that they may be potential targets, the temptation remains to avoid thinking the unthinkable. If individuals accept the possibility that they are vulnerable, the realisation can provoke anxiety in an already pressured society. The concern over the threat has come to influence policy-making and its implementation.

There needs to be a set of integrated programmes in which specialists can combine their different skills to respond effectively to the alliances formed by the new terrorists. Simulation has partly met this need. It is an approach that not only provides training, but also can be used to evaluate fully the forces designated to deal with a threat. Programmes that emphasise formal procedural checklists often break down under the stress of actual events. Simulation avoids that danger. At the same time it provides means by which police and policy-makers can test existing plans, revise them, or develop new measures based on training that generates the pressures occurring in actual incidents.

The development of a simulation combines the analysis and application of terrorist tactics and strategies with an exercise in imagination. In the formulation and execution of the exercises – from the development of the plot (the scenario) to the writing of the script (the operations order), and the subsequent reviews (the evaluation) – a mixture of different approaches are used. The line between the terrorist 'play' and the actual terrorist event is deliberately blurred in a successful exercise.

In building a scenario, several elements have to be considered: the selection of the type of incident and target, the selection of hostages, the motivation and ideological factors behind the incident, the selection or recruitment of the terrorists and the organisational framework. The operational phase includes the means of infiltration and breaching security; securing the hostages; the communications function and the development of potential alternative conclusions.

In writing scripts or operations orders for the simulations, adjustments have to be made to meet the various requirements created by the imaginary local conditions under which the simulation exercises are carried out.

Operations orders adhere to the format employed by the military in planning for small-unit exercises. The writing of operations orders by the would-be terrorists assists them in physically preparing for the assault. It prepares them for a simulation by helping them to assume their individual and collective roles. The recruitment of the terrorists takes place without the knowledge or co-operation of those representing the law.

In initiating a simulation care has to be taken to reconcile the need for surprise and realism with adequate safety measures. The likely emotional and intellectual responses of the participants have to be assessed.

In simulations, while the victims await their uncertain fate, the responding police forces and military units attempt to override a reactive, emotive response with administrative techniques and related tactical measures to manage the siege. The initial shock and disorientation created by an assault are replaced by attempts by the responding forces to develop a series of counter-measures at the start of a protracted siege. The responses of the individual hostages differ as a result of their different personalities; but a simulation experience enables the victims not only to evaluate responses under stress, but also to appreciate how others feel when they face the barrel of a terrorist's gun. Some simulations end in stalemate and many are 'resolved' by the resort to force. Routines to deal with each of these situations have to be established by the responding units.

Command posts in simulations are microcosms of critical tension areas. The patterns observed in them are experienced by policy-makers who have to prepare for a potential crisis, and by those who may have to deal with an actual incident in the execution of everyday responsibilities. Confronted with changing threats, simulations are one means by which authorities can learn to deal with terrorism.

See also: Intelligence roles; Intelligence on terrorism.

References

Gilboa, E. (1981) 'The Use of Simulation in Combating Terrorism', *Terrorism*, vol. 5, no. 3, pp. 265–280.
Sloan, S. (1981) *Simulating Terrorism*, Norman, OK: University of Oklahoma Press.

Crime

Civil Disorders

Civil disorders are a form of collective violence interfering with the peace, security and normal functioning of the community. They are public in character even though like institutional disorders they may take place in a restricted setting. Although occasionally they begin with surprising suddenness and develop with alarming speed and intensity, mass disorders are always outgrowths of their particular social context. Civil disorders can develop out of legitimate expression of protest, lawfully organised and conducted. Many are symptomatic of deep-seated tensions in community relationships, and when a precipitating event occurs, these tensions erupt into violence. The immediate, official response to disorder must restore order and permit the normal functioning of the community. Only a long-range strategy can remove the root causes of disorder and ensure that it will not recur when emergency constraints have been lifted.

Disorders and terrorism have common characteristics and specific differences. Both are forms of extraordinary violence that disrupt the civil peace; both originate in some form of social excitement, discontent and unrest and both can engender massive fear in the community. Disorders and terrorism constitute in varying forms and degree, violent attacks upon the established order of society. Nevertheless, the focus, direction, application and purpose of terrorism are different.

Civil disorders are manifestations of exuberance, discontent or disapproval on the part of a substantial segment of a community. They do not necessarily have political overtones. In many cases disorders are haphazard events rather than systematically staged and directed expressions of social or political violence.

Acts of extraordinary violence, such as terrorism, are the work of a comparatively small number of malcontents or dissidents who, their rhetoric notwithstanding, threaten the security of the entire community. Acts of terrorism are planned in advance, although their execution may be a matter of sudden opportunity. To be effective, terrorism requires a calculated manipulation of the community to which its message is addressed. In the case of civil disorders, the terror generated is incidental and spontaneous, though not always unexpected. In the case of terrorism, the fear is deliberate; it is the very purpose of violent activity. Civil disorders, and the fear and disruption incidental to them, are ripe for exploitation by the same dissidents responsible for acts of terrorism. When such exploitation takes place, the purpose is the same; the disruption of normal political and social life. Whatever the immediate or ulterior objective of the terrorist, their prospects for success depend to a large extent upon the involvement of the community in their purposes. Terrorism without an audience is an exercise in futility. In this respect, terrorism is as much a collective phenomenon as the mass disorder.

The nature of American society, unlike European society, has enabled it to absorb a great deal of undifferentiated violence without real damage to its political structure or the prospect of a true revolution.

Less organised forms of urban rioting precede or complement outbreaks of organised terror or **guerrilla warfare** in urban and rural areas. Such breakdowns in public security tend to be preceded or complemented by the development of a parallel or underground movement in direct competition with the threatened regime.

Stages in collective violence range from primitive communal brawls or gang fights, to reactionary violence, which is actively political, with a conservative desire to return social conditions to some previously achieved state, and finally to modern types of violence, which grew from confrontations between authorities and politically sophisticated groups.

See also: Organised Crime.

Reference

Zinam, O. (1978) 'Terrorism and Violence in the Light of a Theory of Discontent and Frustration' in Livingston, M. H. (ed.) *International Terrorism in the Contemporary World*, Westport, CT: Greenwood Press, pp. 240–265.

Further Reading

Jamieson, A. (1996) *Political Corruption in Western Europe: Judiciary and Executive in Conflict*, London: RISCT, no. 288.

Monti, D. J. (1980) 'The Relation Between Terrorism and Domestic Civil Disorders', *Terrorism*, vol. 4, pp. 123–142.

Crisis Management

A terrorist action is generally well organised and part of its plan will be to catch the target unprepared. This surprise may prevent the target from taking effective action so that it therefore has to accept the only alternative of complete and prompt compliance with all of the terrorists' demands.

The term crisis management means a planned efficient response to a crisis, that is, any event that significantly disrupts the operations of the organisation. In this ease, crises are categorised as actions directed against the executives of the organisation and perpetrated by terrorists.

Crisis management plans furnish guidance and a list of resources which facilitate a co-ordinated and effective response to terrorists' actions against business. A crisis has to be anticipated against threats of **kidnapping**, ambush, assassination, harassment and extortion.

To counter these events, plans have to contain organisations' and businesses' stated policy with regard to crisis management. This will include whether or not to pay ransom, designations of responsibility, executives covered by the plan and criteria for the implementation of the plan. Crisis management teams have to include those individuals with authority to implement and carry out policies and procedures in the crisis management plan, i.e. decision-makers or those in direct communication with the decision-making authority. A typical team for crisis management has to include a co-ordinator or security director, an assistant to the co-ordinator, legal counsel, and negotiators, special analysts and consultants.

The purpose of the crisis management centre is to serve as the focal point for directing a co-ordinated, planned response during a crisis situation. The centre has to be located within the particular organisation. Management centres have all the equipment, documents and supplies needed during a crisis. Plans give precise instructions concerning who does what, when, how and by what authority. Once a businessman has been kidnapped, threat has to be verified, and there has to be proof that an executive actually has been abducted. Verification of the threat is not always a simple matter of locating and confronting a supposedly abducted executive. An attempted extortion could be based on the fact that the extortionist knows the executive would be hard to locate. Criteria for a crisis management programme have to be based on past experience of extortion threats, and the current terrorist or extremist activity in the area.

The threat is a coercive tool of an extortioner, the validity of the threat and who is doing the threatening are questions threat analysis seeks to answer. Threat analysis of terrorist activities has both long-range and immediate applications. Such analysis, based on pre-event information, is a long-range, constantly updated process that provides a current threat profile of the corporation, key facilities and key personnel. It provides a barometer of the seriousness of the threat.

Threat analysis has to verify the validity of the threat – does it in fact exist? Is the threat as serious as the creators of the threat would have the organisation believe? Is the threat delivered by an individual or group that presupposes that a response will be a specification? Is the threat from a terrorist group, or from a criminal group posing as terrorists?

Any demands of the terrorist, whether they take the form of threats of physical actions, or the holding of a hostage, have to be communicated by oral or written messages. Verification of the level of threat in a hostage situation can often be obtained from the victim if he is allowed a rudimentary form of communication. Case history files have to be maintained, storing available information of previous events by category. Liaison with other

individuals or organisations is a support to threat analysis because it allows different perspectives to be obtained about specific crises. Propaganda analysis is important to crisis management. The majority of ransom demands come from persons who have a full-time commitment to terrorist activity. In a kidnap situation, negotiations are most successful when the negotiators have a clear understanding of the level of threat and the personality of those who are threatening.

The purpose of threat analysis is to turn any form of threat into a manageable problem that can be analysed and neutralised by the crisis management team. The crisis management process involves pre-planning, threat perception, threat verification, threat analysis and threat response. However, no two negotiating situations are alike. Kidnapping can be defined as extortion with abduction; and extortion is often used as the encompassing term for threats and attacks. Perpetrators of extortion include the professional criminal, the psychotic or mentally disturbed and the terrorist.

The objectives of **hostage negotiation** plans are to save lives. The professional criminal will normally take a hostage as a shield or as someone he can bargain for his getaway, and he is more apt to view his situation rationally, as a clear exchange of the hostage for his freedom. Conversely, a mentally disturbed hostage-taker can have any number of motives for his act, thus negotiating with this type can be far trickier than with the professional criminal. The mentally disturbed individual tends to be irrational and unpredictable. Taking a hostage may be for him a way of acting out a fantasy or to feel power, or it may be part of a suicide plan.

Terrorists are different from criminals or the mentally disturbed. There are criminals and psychotics in the ranks of terrorist organisations, but that does not alter the basic premise. A terrorist seldom acts alone, he is part of a group; even though there may be a leader of the terrorist group, the group code of conduct will influence him since his motives will be dominated by the objectives of the group. Several individuals have to be worn down to save the hostages, and efforts at establishing contact and rapport have to be aimed at more than one person.

The terrorists will be indoctrinated with revolutionary political ideology, and have a sense of the total 'justice' of their cause. For the hostage negotiator, this means the terrorists' negotiators may be immune to many of the psychological techniques employed against the mentally disturbed or the criminal. However, like the professional criminal, terrorists are rational in their views of alternatives; life and freedom in exchange for hostages is usually a prime negotiable demand.

As with hostage negotiations, no two negotiating situations with terrorists will be alike. Demands will differ, strategic objectives of the terrorists will vary and terrorist negotiators will come to the negotiations with different sets of skills. Any trick leaving the terrorists empty-handed could have disastrous consequences, especially in a kidnap situation. Terrorists do not normally kidnap somebody to kill him because once he is dead, they have lost their bargaining lever. Terrorists will execute their captive without hesitation if they believe their just cause has been slighted.

Terrorists may enter negotiations with demands that differ from the original extortion threat, or there may be additional demands. Terrorists' demands and objectives fall into several categories: to obtain ransom money in exchange for the safe return of a kidnapped executive or a member of his family; medical supplies in exchange for their captive; public recognition of the terrorist organisation; release of fellow terrorists jailed by the authorities; protest at national politics or policies or those of the organisation; and to embarrass the target organisation. Terrorist demands can be presented as non-negotiable, specifying that all demands are to be met in full within a specified time period; or the consequences will be a prompt carrying out of the threat if demands are not met. Depending on what information is available to them, negotiators can ask for proof that the victim is still alive and for the exact time and place of the executive's release and for time to study the demands. Negotiations can be effectively concluded only when reasonable guarantees can be given as to when and where the executive will be released; and when there is agreement that acceptance of the terrorists' conditions means no future extortion threats against the organisation.

Given the special nature of a crisis it is mandatory that it can be analysed and the resources employed to cope with it reviewed. It can be defined as a situation in which there is an uncertain outcome; as a period of tension and time pressure in which decisions must be made; and as a situation involving threats to personnel or to the organisation.

A crisis calls for innovation, and in a very real sense a crisis must be treated as a crime to ensure all relevant information to the case is collected, preserved and evaluated.

Clues about a terrorist group's propensity to violence can be revealed by the types and number of the weapons they carry or have stockpiled. The terrorists' degree of discipline is also shown by the way they handle weapons and how they respond to orders or the mere presence of certain individuals. Outright statements or unconscious slips by the terrorists could reveal a strategy of trying to force the organisation out of the host country, or of wanting the organisation to remain so that the terrorists could extract an annual extortion tax to help fund activities. Thus the keys to successful negotiations are a clearly defined strategy, knowledge of the opponent, experience as a negotiator, and careful preparation.

The end of the **Cold War** was a relief to many, but it had to be remembered that the USSR had strong nuclear, biological and chemical warfare capabilities. There were strong enough temptations for rogue states to become increasingly involved in a black market for these new weapons which had become more easily available. Moreover many of the weapon storage facilities were poorly guarded and defended.

The **Gulf War** and its repercussions highlighted other problems namely the growth of religious-based fundamentalist international terrorism. Such people have a common hatred globally of all things 'American', and have targeted US interests worldwide.

Globalisation has changed the way most terrorists operate. Transnational groups have arisen which cannot be controlled by governments and instant global communication has become possible. Controllers of such groups have global power and can run multiple independent cells from a single place. Globally funds can be transferred and banking conducted electronically with encrypted digital communication. Crisis management involves means to identify, acquire and plan resources needed to overcome a terrorist threat. This now has to work in conjunction with consequence management to try to curtail damage, loss and hardship resulting from emergencies.

Management of the rapidly growing **cyber-terror** potential is a new problem. A single individual with a single strike on a computer can disrupt the world's financial markets, cause chaos in public safety, deplete the health services and destroy telecommunication networks.

Information warfare is relatively cheap to wage and can offer a big return in investment for resources for poor adversaries. Computer hackers are satisfied with just breaking into a system, but over the past decade hackers have developed who are able to totally destroy networks or systems. What the public demand from sound crisis management, is a full assurance of public health and safety.

The rapid rise of the internet makes it very difficult to adopt an effective crisis management scenario. The Net explains how to manufacture nuclear bombs for instance, which makes it easy for terrorists to construct the same.

See also: Extortion; Negotiations.

References

Cohen, S. P. and Arrone, H. C. (1988) 'Conflict Resolution as the Alternative to Terrorism', *Journal of Social Issues*, vol. 44, no. 2 (Summer), pp. 175–189.

Ryan, S. (1990) 'Conflict Management and Conflict Resolution, Terrorism and Political Violence', vol. 2, no. 1, pp. 54–71.

Crisis Management of Disasters

The course and outcomes of crisis management appear to be heavily influenced by political forces and considerations. Crises are part and parcel of the political process.

A very short act of political terrorism makes for one of the strongest cases supporting information intake during crises. Information overload characterises the very first stage of crisis response and subsequently may give rise to moments, indeed, periods, of information shortage.

In a disaster while centralisation of decision making does occur, in a terrorist event lower-level, frontline personnel will usually be affected. Given the degree of surprise and/or the constraints of time, they need to take initial steps in coping with the crisis more or less autonomously, as a matter of direct response.

Disaster recovery plans are vital; for example after the IRA bombings in the city of London in the early-1990s. A plan is essential for all businesses. Communication with staff clients and shareholders needs to be maintained at the earliest possible opportunity. Everyone needs to know what is expected of them at all stages. Supplies of equipment and services need to know how best they can help. Everyone needs to know that a disaster has occurred, but they also have to know that you are coping with it. A review of a disaster recovery plan should take place after every terrorist incident to ensure that plans are not vulnerable.

People caught up in a terrorist incident – obviously a very traumatic event – invariably experience a range of upsetting symptoms. These include intrusive thoughts or visions, vivid dreams, loss of interest in everyday life, an inability to express or feel love, and inability to sleep or concentrate, or just a general sense of depression or anxiety. The sufferers often conceal such issues.

Victims of disasters such as terrorism outrage experience common features. Both experience an unpredictable disruption of their lives, they are in a helpless position, as bargaining occurs between government and local authorities and terrorists, they experience grief and a loss of freedom and threats to their bodily integrity, and, ultimately their life. Centres have been created to deal with victims of hostage situations. They also specialise in the treatment of individuals who have experienced torture.

The concept of post-traumatic stress disorder has a long history, and is classed among the anxiety disorders. Yet the diagnostic signs and symptoms required for the diagnoses include many features usually associated with depression. Markedly diminished interest in activities, detachment from others, constructed affect, guilt, impairment of memory and concentration, sleep difficulties and re-current thoughts of death.

The victims of terrorism share all the psychological elements characteristic of man-made disasters, and share the same experience, psychologically, namely post-traumatic stress disorder. The disaster victim and the hostage share much in common.

Reference

Thackrah, J. R. (1996) *Crisis Management of Disasters*, unpublished MS at National Police Library, Bramshill, Hampshire, England.

Further Reading

Crelinsten, R. (1999) 'Television and Terrorism Implications for Crisis Management and Policy-Making', *Terrorism and Political Violence*, vol. 9, no. 4 (winter), pp. 8–32.

Littlejohn, R. F. (1986) 'When the Crisis is Terrorism', *Security Management*, vol. 35, no. 8 (August), pp. 38–41.

Waugh, William L. (1982) *International Terrorism: How Nations Respond to Terrorism*. Salisbury, NC: Documentary Publications.

Cuba

Since 1961 the Republic of Cuba has had a Government which has been designated as Communist under Dr Fidel Castro, the First Secretary of the Cuban Communist Party, receiving the 'fraternal friendship, aid and co-operation of the **Soviet Union** and other socialist countries'.

Political opposition to the Castro regime has found most of its support among Cuban refugees, several hundred thousand of whom have settled in the **United States**. Some of these refugees have joined a group called Omega Seven, which is an underground paramilitary wing of the Cuban Nationalist Movement, an above-ground anti-Castro movement based in Miami and Union City in Florida. According to the **FBI** it is the most dangerous terrorist group in the USA. Over the past decade many other anti-Castro refugees from Cuba have made their homes in Florida and undergone clandestine training in guerrilla warfare

and the use of sophisticated weapons, even though the latter is a contravention of American law.

In 1961 the newly formed Cuban National Revolutionary Council was involved in an attempt made by a force of Cuban exiles to land in the 'Bay of Pigs' area on the north Cuban coast. This was repulsed by the Cuban army and militia with heavy losses. At the same time Cuban forces also suppressed the activities of anti-Castro guerrillas inside Cuba. A similar attempt at landing exiles to overthrow the Castro regime was made by another group, Cubans United, in 1981 but this was frustrated by a tropical storm. The Alpha 66 Group also tried in 1970 and 1981 to land members in Cuba, but the Cubans caught many members. The United Revolutionary Organisation Co-ordination, founded in Chile in 1975 by an anti-Communist Cuban has the objective of trying to undermine all links between Cuba and other American states.

In 1980 the Inter-American Human Rights Commission of the Organisation of American States (from which Cuba has been excluded since 1962) claimed that Cuba ill-treated political prisoners, of whom there were over one thousand, some held without trial. The United States, and in particular the administration of President Ronald Reagan (1981–89) believe that the Cuban government gives direct support to communist insurgents in many Central and South American states – especially Chile, Costa Rica, El Salvador, Honduras and Peru.

Hard currency dollars are desperately needed in Cuba, and sadly but inevitably narco-terrorism thrives, perhaps even instigated and supported by Raoul and Castro. The Cuban authorities have alleged that there are plots by the CIA to penetrate, inflame and undermine Cuba. In the 1920s there were cases of narco-terrorism involving the commander of Cuban forces in Angola and a brigadier at the Ministry of the Interior.

See also: Guevara.

References

Enders, T. (1982) *Cuban Support for Terrorism and Insurgency in the Western Hemisphere*, US Department of State Bulletin (August), pp. 73–5.

Fontaine, R. W. (1988) *Terrorism: The Cuban Connection*, New York: Crane Russak.

Further Reading

Hudson, R. A. (1987) 'Castro's America Department: Systemising Insurgencies in Latin America', *Terrorism*, vol. 9, no. 2, pp. 125–168.

Cults

Cults began to become commonplace in the 1960s coinciding with the growth of a variety of alternative and experimental lifestyles. Religion, indeed, has re-emerged in contemporary times as a powerful inspiration for conflict, as shown by the rise of Islamic fundamentalism.

In the 1980s, 104 individuals who were members of, or associated with, the Christian Identity Movement were indicted for terrorism or terrorist-related offences in the **USA**. This movement originated in England in the 18th century and was known as Anglo-Israelism – based on the premise that Christ was of Aryan origin and the ten lost tribes of Israel migrated to **Europe** and Britain. The settling of America by British colonists was the fulfilment of a directive by God to create a Promised Land. It was strongly racist.

Identity groups in general had been preparing to fight and prevail in the final conflict on earth for many years, and did not turn to terrorism until the early-1980s. Identity ideology justified the use of terrorism as a prelude to war – the Armageddon that would establish Christ's kingdom on earth. In 1988 some members were charged with conspiracy to overthrow the American government, but they were acquitted. The Identity extremists chose to build popular support by creating permanent survivalist corps, which could easily be located and observed by the **FBI**. It was easy to find the written communications and tape telephone calls. The FBI was able to infiltrate some extremist groups and persuade other members to testify against their former comrades.

The siege at Waco, Texas between the Branch Davidian cult and the FBI led to the deaths of over 100 persons in April 1993 including 24 British, and David Koresh (formerly Vernon Howell) became their Messiah, and died with them in the siege; but whether by the fire caused when the FBI stormed the building using CS Gas or by collective suicide will never be known.

The incident brought to an end 35 years of tenure at Waco by the Branch Davidians. This cult was devoted to a liberal interpretation of the Bible who follow the tenets of the Seventh Day Adventist Church (a strongly Protestant group who believe Christ's coming is imminent and they observe Saturday instead of Sunday as their Sabbath).

The Branch Davidians were an example of a doomsday cult. Revenge for the Waco siege was wrought against Oklahoma two years later.

The Militia Movement attracted many people including non-whites and others who did not share Identity goals but who served as 'useful fools' in a mass resistance to gain control. The militia's Identity leaders sought out sympathisers from the ranks who could be recruited into terror cells.

In 1995, the **Oklahoma Bombing** split the Militia Movement, bringing it underneath greater public scrutiny. Timothy McVeigh, a Militia member was found guilty of the atrocity and executed in 2001.

Militias, however, still exist in over half of the states in America, and since 1995 numerous incidents purporting to come from their ranks have occurred: bombs, train derailments, attacks on abortion clinics, and events on 19 April each year (the anniversary of the Waco Siege and Oklahoma bombing).

In Canada, the Order of the Solar Temple has been active – the movement was founded in Switzerland in the late 1970s and in Canada in 1984. Nearly 50 members died in Switzerland in 1994 when firebombs exploded in two villages. They embraced a variety of doctrines including Christianity, New Age beliefs, the occult, and science fiction and practised Druid-style worship. They believed in an imminent apocalypse and therefore stockpiled arms and built nuclear bomb-proof bunkers. Money was obtained by deception from gullible wealthy professionals. They attacked targets in Quebec province, suicides occurred, and one could surmise there was sympathy with Quebec Separatists.

In the former Soviet bloc, cults have arisen again with the collapse of Communism, the most significant in terms of violence being a doomsday cult, the White Brotherhood in the Ukraine.

Terrorists and insurgent groups have contacts and some common interests with their opponents which make a peaceful resolution of conflict possible. Cults by contrast have aims and beliefs so fantastic and unrealisable that they may not even be comprehensible to outsiders, let alone form the basis for negotiation. They have no rational objective and can come into harsh conflict with a society that they view sinful, lost and fore-doomed to extinction. Only a small group of unorthodox religious groups represent any danger to society, however, these can wreak havoc out of all proportion to their size or importance.

Cults often harbour fantastic and unrealisable aims, which may not even form the basis of negotiation. Cults can appear suddenly and long established groups can take a radical turn under a new leadership. They can adopt a persecution complex and once a decision has been taken they recognise few of the limits on violence which even some of the most fanatical of terrorist groups observe. Irrational cults wish to make the apocalypse a self-fulfilling prophecy.

Doomsday cults have single charismatic leaders, and are cohesive religious groups with communal-style living and organisation. They have sexual and physical control of members and stockpile weapons, ammunition and explosive materials. Above all they believe in the impending end of the world and have a persecution complex maintaining that central government is against them.

These cults are also known as millennial religious cults and include Christian white supremacists, messianic Jews, Islamic Fundamentalists and radical **Sikhs**. They are all characterised by religious zealotry and in destroying entire classes of enemies.

A new horror was perpetrated in March 1995 by the Aum Shinrikyo (Supreme Truth) cult. The nerve gas Sarin was released in a Tokyo subway station, killing 12 people and injuring over 5,000. The Aum Shinrikyo cult took credit for this attack; but over the previous six years they had been involved in a series of unsolved kidnappings of Japanese children, who were forced to study the teachings of Shinrikyo which included the technical preparation of the nerve gas Sarin (which the cult believed would be a primary weapon in the final

world war). The discovery of the lethal poison caused panic and fear throughout Japan. As a weapon of terror, nerve gas causes great fear, as a single droplet can kill.

See also: Cults; Millennial Violence; Oklahoma Bombing 1995.

References

Brackett, D. W. (1996) *Holy Terror: Armageddon in Tokyo*, New York: Weatherhill.
Hubback, A. (1997) *Apocalypse When? The Global Threat of Religious Cults*, London: RISCT, No. 300.

Further Reading

Kaplan, D. E. and Marshall, A. (1996) *The Cult at the End of the World*, New York: Crown Publishers.
Lifton, R. J. (1999) 'Destroying the World to Save It: Aum Shinrikyo', *Apocalyptic Violence and the New Global Terrorism*, New York: Henry Holt.
Watanabe, M. (1998) 'Religion and Violence in Japan Today: A Chronological and Doctrinal Analysis of the Aum Shinrikyo', *Terrorism and Political Violence*, vol. 10, pp. 80–100.

Cyber-crimes

The phrase 'cyber-space' was first used in 1982 in science fiction. Six years later the World Wide Web (www) was created to assist computer software engineers, and scientists were soon using the 'Web' to monitor research. Its use in crime was not far behind. These developments had occurred two decades after the Internet had been formed – a loosely linked system of computers using telephone lines as a means of communication. The military in the **USA** in the 1960s were keen to ensure that by using computers they could ensure continued communications in the event of a nuclear attack. Today the Internet is filled with a vast array of information – a 'computer encyclopaedia'.

Criminality grew apace with the growth of computers. 'Hackers' became prolific. These people have a desire to learn how computer systems work, how to get into them undetected and how to find their security weakness. In the 1970s the word meant one adept and clever in programming. In the following decade it meant a person adept at 'cracking' new systems undetected. Nowadays it is applied to anyone accused of a crime involving technology.

'Crackers' are malicious hackers. They utilise systems to vandalise, plant viruses and worms, delete files or simply cause technological havoc. Cyber-espionage exists between countries as well as companies, so it poses a threat to national security.

It is frightening to realise that anyone with a computer and a modem connecting it to a telephone line can commit a computer crime (crimes committed with a computer, crimes occurring in cyber-space and crimes committed against a computer). 'Phone phreaks' explore the cyber-world through a telephone line and can break into voice mail and email accounts – they particularly like long-distance access codes. A money-launderer (one who makes illegally acquired or 'dirty' money look legal and clean) using computers is able to carry out this crime more quickly and efficiently. It would only take a few hackers to close down the USA.

Many of the crimes, which take place in the real world, occur in cyber-space. This includes cyber-sex: stalking, sexual harassment, rape, child abduction and child pornography. Many paedophiles are very clever in their corrupting use of the computer. Frustratingly, many computer crimes are untraceable. For example, remailers are email forwarding sites that 'resend' electronic mail from pseudonymous addresses, making it untraceable. Encryption and anonymous re-mailers can give criminals, terrorists, child abductors and perverts, and bombers free reign.

See also: Cyber-terrorism; Technology.

References

de Angelis, G. (2000) *Cyber-Crimes*, London: Chelsea House.

Kozlow, C. (1998) *Jane's Counter-terrorism*, London: Jane's Information Group.

Further Reading

Cooper, J. (1999) 'New Skills for Cyber Diplomats', *The World Today*, vol. 55, no. 3 (March), pp. 20–22.

Cyber-terrorism

Cyber-terrorism has been described as the crime of the future involving the usage of crime and computers. It threatens the safety of millions of people across the globe; especially the vulnerability of military computer networks to casual hackers. Indeed, this form of terrorism could be more devastating than biological or chemical warfare.

Cyber-terrorists have a political motivation for their crimes. All computers, especially government ones, contain information which other terrorists might need. In 1991 during the Gulf War, the Pentagon computer was 'entered' and secret material about the Patriot missile was read.

The FBI's homepage (fbi.gov) believe key areas requiring protection to be telecommunications; electrical systems; gas and oil production; banking and finance; water supply systems; emergency services and government services (de Angelis, 2000).

In 1997 'crackers' broke into the Pentagon computer network and downloaded classified files. Terrorists can use viruses and other 'cyber-critters', as a means to shut down important computer systems. This is more serious than 'cyber-graffiti' or other pranks undertaken by most hackers. In the worst case scenario some viruses may attack system files causing irreparable damage to the computer's hard drive.

In 1992 the Michelangelo virus was created. This was a form of 'logic bomb' and resulted in over 10,000 computers worldwide not starting up (the start up section of the disk being affected). Nowadays, anti-virus software can detect Michelangelo. Technological capability combined with political instability can create an especially explosive mix. Political and economic instability in the former communist states of Eastern Europe and the Soviet Union means that talented computer professionals are tempted to sell their skills to the highest bidder, even to international terrorists.

References

de Angelis, G. (2000) *Cyber Crimes*, PA: Chelsea House Publishers,

Stern, J. (1999) *The Ultimate Terrorists*, Cambridge, MA. and London: Harvard University Press.

D

Dagestan

Dagestan is a constituent republic of the Russian Federation lying between **Chechnya** and the Black Sea. In late-1999 a wave of massive terrorist bombings of apartments for civilians and military personnel followed Muslim rebel incursions into Chechnya from Dagestan. Russian federal forces repulsed the incursionists. Dagestan is one of the homes of the Lezgin who are mostly **Sunni** Muslims influenced by the Afghan **Al Jihad** – they are also based in Azerbaijan and their goal, like the Pushtuns in **Afghanistan** and **Pakistan**, is to unify their homeland into one independent Lezgin state. Apart from Dagestan, it has to be remembered that the Chechen conflict had spilt over into neighbouring Ingushetia and North Ossetia. Chechens had also made incursions into Dagestan to try to capture key targets such as power stations.

1999 was a high point from the point of view of Afghan Arabs in Dagestan who were battling against Russian troops in pursuit of their aim of turning Dagestan into an independent Islamic state.

Reference

Panico, C, (1995) 'Conflicts in the Caucusus: Russia's War in Chechnya', Research Institute for the Study of Conflict and Terrorism, no. 281 (July).

Data Sources

With regard to the criminality of terrorism, there are a number of sources which can be used. Court proceedings leading to the trial of terrorists are an under used but potentially rich source. Local newspapers give ample coverage to court proceedings, but initially one would use first-hand police records and court proceedings, which provide a narrative account of incidents. Psychiatrists and psychologists have shown that interviews with terrorists in prison are also a valuable source if convicted terrorists are willing to talk. However, in this context the interview situation can be seen as more of an interrogation, perhaps even combined with the threat of torture. Therefore on moral grounds this information is often unusable. Interviews in the real-life environment in which terrorists operate perhaps yield more genuine information but are difficult to obtain. Even more useful are the writings of ex-terrorists who have stayed underground and who keep equal distance from former colleagues and adversaries. Some insight into the style of terrorists can be gleaned.

Memoirs of former terrorists are easier to obtain as a data source, but one has to be aware of the degree to which reminiscences are useful and of the element of self-justification. Terrorists are neither born as terrorists nor are condemned to stay terrorists for the rest of their lives. Some become adherents of violence or become statesmen. Most importantly, memoirs can tell us something about when and why terrorists gave up terrorism or switched to another tactic. The study of post-terrorist careers of terrorists can even yield policy results.

Memoirs are personal histories, often more informed but also more biased than other accounts. Indeed the study of past terrorist organisations and movements can increase our understanding of contemporary terrorism. On regime or state terror of a repressive nature, there is very little systematic material. The only sources of information on state repression are reports and documents issued by Amnesty International. Their reports form an account of state terrorism and violations of human rights in more than two-thirds of all the countries forming the **United Nations**. While the overlap between state terrorism and **genocide** is only partial, persecution and genocide are social warning indicators which can be made relevant to the study of state terrorism.

For research on terrorism to become cumulative there has to be some uniformity in collected data. Problems exist in getting access to data collected by a variety of government agencies. Data is needed on a wide range of issues, all of which can be classed as worthwhile. Data from public opinion surveys for various countries over time, using comparable incidents in order to assess public attitudes and reactions is invaluable. Data about non-negotiation techniques, terrorist demands and the target of demands, concessions and their relationship to non-violent solutions of incidents and to future demands and concession policies is all of use. Furthermore, data on terrorist victim selection patterns and threat perceptions in audiences sharing victim characteristics, data on counter-measures taken by governments against insurgent terrorism and on counter-measures taken by populations against regime terrorism can help to build up patterns on the terrorist way of life.

Social scientists, who are the principal users of the databases have to decide whether terrorism is a function of larger ambitions and aims, thereby making it a dependent variable; they have to distinguish types of violence and injury perpetrated against persons and places, in order to help establish some qualitative measures of terrorism and counter-terrorism, and to provide empirical assistance to the efforts to develop international legal measures to combat the terror of guerrillas and counter-terror of the state.

The collection of data on terrorism can be based on both subjectivity and objectivity. Systems for data collection were developed initially in the **United States. Definitions** have to be used to establish a basis for the facts and theories have a place in deciding the relevant aspects. If a data collector is

interested in terror he will concentrate on the data relating to terrorism, **guerrilla warfare** and political violence. A data collector alone accepts or rejects the material which he uses. It has to be remembered that the data obtained is only as good as the reliability of its source. For example, the media is used as a popular source for building up data on terrorism and yet one is only too well aware, in democracies at least, of their political proclivities.

The gathering of data for analysis started in the early-1960s in the United States, the primary source of comparative political violence being the Index of the *New York Times*. The only problem was deciding whether an entry under 'bombings' or 'assassinations' could be classed as terrorism. The early databases in the United States tended to cover four main manifestations of terrorism: political assaults against persons and things; political assassinations and executions; political **hostage taking** and **kidnapping**; and hijacking of aircraft. The data was not very specific and was uneven for many countries.

Chronologies of incidents are the more common form of data collections. Sometimes they are based on the type of incident and are global in scope, such as in the case of hijacking data. Nevertheless, they more commonly concentrate on incidents of certain terrorist movements or cover the domestic events within a nation. The national framework for data collection is still most widespread in countries like Germany, the **United Kingdom**, the Netherlands and the United States.

Apart from country-based chronologies there are also a number of incident-type-based chronologies, both national and international. The United States for example, produces a list of hijacking attempts worldwide, and the first data to cover international conflicts was based on the Palestinian problem and published in 1977. The Rand Corporation chronology has been the prototype for most other chronologies of incidents, and was developed by a think-tank, RAND in California for the State Department and the Department of Defence, and concentrated primarily on international terrorism. The RAND chronology covers all incidents of terror with international repercussions – incidents in which terrorists went abroad to strike their targets, selected victims or targets that had connections with a foreign state, or created international incidents by attacking airline passengers, personnel and equipment. Their first public report was issued in 1975 and thousands have been produced since that time. RAND has looked into such research areas as the potential for nuclear action, hostage survival chances, the profile of a typical hijacker and a typical terrorist. Using statistical methods, these quantitative studies led to findings which apparently have had influence on the American government's anti-terrorist policies. For instance, most members of a kidnapping team will escape death or capture whether or not they successfully seize hostages; and more terrorists have died during assaults by security forces than from cold execution for deviance by other terrorists. RAND and other organisations have used chronologies to analyse trends in terrorism, yet due to the flexible definition of terrorism it is questionable whether overall assessments are possible.

A chronology similar to RAND was developed at the University of Oklahoma using a data collection based on clear-cut incidents of kidnappings, armed attacks involving hostage taking, hijackings and assassinations. From their data they came to the conclusion that when confronted with a situation involving terrorist demands, few nation states show any evidence of constant and coherent response strategies, and that terrorists do not usually comply with time limits they have imposed on various authorities for meeting their demands.

Another company, Risks International, produced an Executive Risk Assessment in which the database covers incidents within the United States as well as abroad, and the information is derived from the foreign and English-language press, American and foreign government and police reports. The data is grouped by the type of activity; the categories used are kidnapping, hijacking, assassination, maiming, attack against facilities, and bombing.

The most ambitious publicly accessible data-gathering effort was undertaken by the Central Intelligence Agency (CIA). The data system ITERATE – International Terrorism: Attributes of Terrorist Events – covers a wide range of attributes, including the educational level of members of the terrorist group, the rank of hostages involved, the demands, the attitudes of the groups to life and death, the type of negotiator, the

negotiating behaviour of the terrorist, the reliability of warnings and the organisations claiming or denying responsibility for an incident.

Such data can be used for studying global diffusion patterns of transnational terrorism over time; for terrorist trends analysis; to improve hostage negotiation techniques; to compare terrorist campaigns; to evaluate policies for use in crisis management; to evaluate possibilities for deterrence of terrorism; and to evaluate the effects of publicity on terrorist behaviour.

Policy considerations in general over the past decade appear to be playing a bigger role than scientific criteria in determining the inclusion or exclusion of incidents of political protest and violence. A largely American source which was internationally accessible to researchers was the Clandestine Tactics and Technology Data Service of the International Association of Chiefs of Police's Bureau of Operations and Research which distributed documents to selected applicants relating to analyses on terrorist groups' activities, tactics and counter-measures. Microfiches of terrorist incidents were compiled by the US National Criminal Justice Reference Service. The results of the work of Congressional committees on terrorism to which national and foreign experts were invited as well as representatives of various government agencies, and the numerous statistics and chronologies on all aspects of insurgent terrorism so gleaned are held at the Library of Congress – one of the best libraries in the world for the study of terrorism literature. The terrorist events in the early 1970s brought an international awareness of the need for the study of terrorism. National and international bodies and study groups were created, generally being integrated into existing bureaucracies. The US Office of Combating Terrorism was formed within the State Department while the United Nations formed an *ad hoc* committee to study the question of international terrorism. There are also many monitoring and operative agencies usually linked to policy-making bodies.

See also: Threat Assessment Guidelines.

References

Jorgman, A. J. (1992) 'Trends in International and

Domestic Terrorism in Western Europe 1968–1988', *Terrorism and Political Violence Special Issue: Western Responses to Terrorism*, pp. 26–53.

— (2001) 'Dimensions of Contemporary Conflicts and Human Rights Violations', *Terrorism and Political Violence*, vol. 13, no. 2 (Summer), pp. 173–177.

Jorgman, A. J. and Schmid, A. (1999) 'Trends in Contemporary Conflicts and Human Rights Violations', *Terrorism and Political Violence*, vol. 11, no. 3, pp. 119–150.

Schmid, A. P. and Jorgman, A. J. (1997) 'Violent Conflicts and Human Rights Violations in the mid-1990s', *Terrorism and Political Violence*, vol. 9, no. 4 (Winter), pp. 166–192.

Sproat, P. A. (1997) 'Can the State Commit Acts of Terrorism? An Opinion and Some Qualitative Replies to a Questionnaire', *Terrorism and Political Violence*, vol. 9, no. 4, pp. 117–150.

Death Squads

Death squad terrorism has traditionally been associated with Latin America. It often occurs after a revolutionary terrorist campaign when rulers perceive that normal governmental actions will not thwart the terrorist movement. Embarrassingly for many governments, death squads tend to come from official security forces (White, 2003).

In cases where the government is supporting death squad activity, it is referred to as political repression. But when squads operate outside government channels they are simply terrorists.

References

Livingstone, N. C. (1983/4) 'Death Squads', *World Affairs*, vol. 146, no. 3, pp. 239–48.

White J. R. (2003) *Terrorism and Introduction Update of 4th edition*, Belmont, CA: Wadsworth/Thomson Learning.

Further Reading

Amnesty International Reports (1997–2000), London: Amnesty International Publications.

Krane, D. A. and Mason, T. D. (1989) 'The Political Economy of Death Squads: Toward a

Theory of the Impact of State-Sanctioned Terror', *International Studies Quarterly*, vol. 33, no. 2, pp. 175–198.

Sluka, J. A. (ed.) (1999) *Death Squad: The Anthropology of State Terror*, Philadelphia, PA: University of Pennsylvania Press.

Debray, Regis

b. 1941

Regis Debray was a French revolutionary theorist who was active in the urban guerrilla activity in South America in the 1960s. He believed that intellectuals were invaluable to the success of any revolutionary cause – but that when they took part in such activity that had a bad conscience. The struggle against oppressions was his overriding concern and approached the status of a fight for a sacred cause.

He regarded the urban working class (not excluding the Communist Parties) as an essentially conservative element. In the view of Fidel Castro, the **Cuban** leader, the city was the grave of the guerrilla, and Debray was even more outspoken. Life in towns was for him tantamount to an 'objective betrayal', for in his view the mountain proletarianises, the bourgeoisie and peasant elements, whereas the city embourgeoises the proletarians. Living conditions in the towns were fundamentally different from those prevailing in the countryside. Even the best comrades were corrupted in the cities and affected by alien patterns of thought. Debray's arrest shortly after the death of Che Guevara highlighted the ultimate failure of rural guerrilla practice in South America.

To Debray the guerrilla *foco* or nucleus was composed of foreign career revolutionaries and selected indigenous participants. Jungle and mountain reconnaissance amidst maximum secrecy helped to adapt guerrillas to the environment. This allowed for small training operations against the regime.

The guerrilla base would now be established with regional guerrilla and urban squads, which would increase in numbers from natural evolution. The people's army would then go on the offensive. Regional and urban groups would keep government forces tied down, and the mobile force would attack selected targets. A general strike would then precede a conventional offensive on the capital.

In 1970 Debray sought refuge in Chile, where he became involved in writing about political matters. From the mid-1980s to the mid-1990s he held a number of official posts in the office of the late President Mitterrand of France.

Reference

Debray, R. (1967) *Revolution in the Revolution?* Westport, CT: Greenwood.

Further Reading

Radu, M. and Tismaneanu, V. (1990) *Latin American Revolutionaries: Groups, Goals, Methods*, Washington, DC: Pergamon-Brassey's.

Decolonisation

Decolonisation is a change in sovereignty in which a state recognises the independence of a segment of people formerly under its rule and their right to government formed according to procedures determined by them. The colonial powers had been unable in many cases to destroy or weaken the subject people, who, in many instances took up arms against their former masters. In countries such as **India**, Vietnam, Zimbabwe, and **Angola**, the critical development was the organisation of powerful nationalist political movements to secure freedom. Technological development in the economically weaker regions tended to create urban cultures, new bureaucracy and higher levels of education which stimulated the rise of demands by the colonial subjects.

In 1989–90 the ending of the **Cold War** witnessed the colonies of Eastern Europe released from their ideological/colonial masters, the **Soviet Union**, which had treated these countries almost as colonies since 1945 (Krieger, 1993). Protest became widespread and sometimes revolutionary in its objectives, and both dissidents and authorities were restrained in their use of violence.

See also: Guerrilla Warfare; Soviet Union.

Reference

Krieger, J. (ed.) (1993) *The Oxford Companion to the Politics of the World*, Oxford: OUP.

Further Reading

Ate, B. E. (1988) 'Terrorism in the Context of Decolonisation' in H. Kochler (ed.) *Terrorism and National Liberation*, Frankfurt: Verlag Peter Lang, pp. 79–86.

Definitions

Terrorism manifests itself through distinctive deployment of a variety of criminal acts calculated to harm human life, property and other interests. The ultimate test is the examination of the differing circumstances and events which terrorism is designed to classify. Definitions become standards by which each set of circumstances is judged. In the following set of definitions terrorism is defined solely in terms of its ultimate objectives, rather than in terms of ideology and manner of action. It is easier to identify that which is not terror than attempt to label exactly that which is terror.

The following range of definitions and issues illustrates the difficulty faced by people, groups and organisations who seek to solve the problem of terrorism in the contemporary world.

'Terror can strike without any preliminary provocation; its victims are innocent even from the point of view of the prosecutor.' (Arendt, 1951)

'An action of violence is labelled terrorist when its psychological effects are out of proportion to its purely physical result.' (Aron, 1966)

'Terrorism may be described as a strategy of violence designed to inspire terror within a particular segment of a given society.' (Bassiouni, 1981)

'a strategy of violence designed to promote desired outcomes by instilling fear in the public at large ...' (Bassiouni, 1981 in Reich, 1990)

'International terrorism is politically and socially

motivated violence.' (Bite, 1975)

'Terrorism is a method of action by which an agent tends to produce terror to impose his domination on the state in order to transform it.

Political terror is the planned use of violence or threat of violence against an individual or social group in order to eradicate resistance to the aims of the terrorist.' (Chisholm, 1948)

'Terrorism is the recourse of a minority or even of a single dissident frustrated by the inability to make society shift in a desired direction by what that society regards as "legitimate" means.' (Clutter-buck, 1977)

'Terrorism is the use or threat of violence against small numbers to put large numbers in fear or as stated by an ancient Chinese philosopher: kill one, frighten 10,000.' (Clutterbuck, 1986)

'One man's terrorist is another's holy warrior.'
'One man's heretic and unbeliever is another man's fighter for the true faith'. (Cooley, 2000)

'Terrorism is part of a revolutionary strategy; it is manifested in acts of socially and politically unacceptable violence. Terrorism's attractiveness and significance for revolutionary organizations are due to a combination of economy, facility and high psychological and political effectiveness.' (Crenshaw Hutchinson, 1972)

'The systematic components of a definition of revolutionary terrorism are a systematic and purposeful method used by a revolutionary orga-nisation, it is manifested in a series of individual acts of extraordinary and intolerable violence, a constant pattern of symbolic or representative selection, and is deliberately intended to create a psychological effect on specific groups of people.' (Crenshaw Hutchinson, 1978)

'What distinguishes terrorism from both vandalism and non-political crime, is the motivated violence for political ends.' (Crozier, 1974)

'There is an element of arbitrariness both in the decision-makers ability to disregard any binding legal norms and in the calculability of the application of terror as perceived by the citizen.' (Dallin and Breslauer, 1970)

'Terrorism is the language of being noticed.' (Don DeLillo, 1992)

'the recurrent use or threatened use of politically motivated and clandestinely organised violence, by a group whose aim is to influence a psychological target in order to make it believe in a way which the group desires.' (Drake, 1998)

'The peculiarity of the horror of terrorism is what people remember.' (Fairbairn, 1974)

'International terrorism embodies an act which is essentially politically motivated, and it transcends national boundaries.' (Fearey, 1976)

'In the West, terrorism is distinguished from guerrilla warfare in that the latter term refers to paramilitary combat carried out against regular military forces. However, almost all guerrilla movements make use of terrorism at one or another stage of their development, and some rely on it.' (Francis, 1981)

'Terror is violence used to create fear, but it is also aimed at creating fear in order that the fear, in turn will lead somebody else.' (Fromkin, 1975)

'Terrorism is a subset of coercive diplomacy when violence or its threatened use is present to induce the opponent to revise his calculations and agree to a mutually acceptable termination of the conflict.' (George, 1991)

'Terrorism is an anxiety-inspiring method of repeated violent action, employed by (semi) clan-destine individuals, groups, or state actors, for idiosyncratic, criminal or political reasons.' (Schmid and Jongman, 1988 quoted in Guelke, 1998)

'Terroristic actions are demonstrative, spectacular and theatrical, and the victims are mere pawns in the terroristic game.' (Hacker, 1981)

'the use of violence against civilians, by opposition

forces either within a domestic context or internationally.' (Halliday, 2001)

'Terrorism consists of planned acts of violence employed for explicitly political purposes directed against an established state or organizational power; and involving a relatively small number of conspirators.' (Hamilton, 1978)

'Terrorism is a method of combat in the struggle between social groups and forces rather than individuals, and it may take place in any social order.' (Hardman, 1936)

'Terrorism can certainly be a strategy and not merely a tactic, or incidental event ... terrorism is chosen for definite purposes and is the chief means to advance political ends.' (Harmon, 2000)

'Terrorism relies for its effects not so much on any general unpredictability, but rather on its specific unexpectedness as well as on the eruption of violence into environments normally free from it.'

'Non-governmental terrorism is the considered and systematic use of widespread offensive violence, murder and destruction aimed at governmental employees and the general population as well as public and private property, to force individuals, groups, communities, economic entities and governments to modify or change their actual proposed behaviour and policies so as to concede to the terrorists' political demands.' (Herman and van der Laan Bouma, 1981)

'By terrorism, one means a series of intentional acts of direct, psychological violence, which at indeterminable points but nevertheless systematically, with the aim of psychic effect, are conducted within the framework of a political strategy.' (Hess, 1981)

'Terrorism is the use or threat of extraordinary political violence to induce fear, anxiety or alarm in a target audience wider than the immediate symbolic victims. Terrorism is violence for political effect as opposed to military impact.' (Heyman, 1980)

'Terrorism is political violence in or against true democracies.' (Heyman, 1998)

'Terrorism is ineluctably about power.' (Hoffman, 1998)

'The definition of someone who is a terrorist is purely a labelling device.' (Horowitz, 1973)

'The selective use of fear, subjugation and intimidation to disrupt the normal operations of a society.' (Horowitz, 1977)

'Individual terror is a system of modern revolutionary violence aimed at leading personalities in the government or the Establishment.' (Iviansky, 1977)

'The threat of violence, individual acts of violence or a campaign of violence designed primarily to instil fear – to terrorise – may be called terrorism.' (Jenkins, 1975)

'Terrorism is used to create fear and alarm to gain attention.' (Jenkins, 1977)

'One man's terrorist is everyone's terrorist. All terrorist acts are crimes and many also would be violations of the rules of war, if a state of war existed.' (Jenkins, 1978)

'The definition of the terrorist act is provided by us, the witnesses – the ones terrified – and not by the party committing the act.' (Juergensmeyer, 2000)

'Terror is the use of force in a context which differentiates the victim of the violence employed from the target of the action.' (Kaplan, 1981)

'Terrorism may be defined as systematic and organised violence against non-resisting persons to create fear in them for the purpose of retaining or gaining governmental authority.' (Karanovic, 1978)

'Terrorism always involves violence or the threat of violence.' (Laqueur, 1987)

'Terrorism is an atmosphere of despair.' (Leiden and Schmidt, 1968)

'Terrorism can be used to create an atmosphere of despair or fear, to shake the faith of ordinary citizens in their government and its representatives.' (Leiser, 1986)

'Terrorism is seen as the resort to violence for political ends by unauthorized, non-governmental actors in breach of accepted codes of behaviour.' (Lodge, 1982)

'The basis of terror tactics is the threat; and terrorism is a form of guerrilla warfare. The basic tactic for guerrilla warfare is to hit and run and hide, hit, run, hide. Guerrillas conceal themselves in mountains or rural areas; and terror tactics are employed in urban areas as well.' (Mallin, 1971)

'The use or threat of use of anxiety, induced by extra-normal violence for political purposes by an individual or group, whether acting for or in opposition to established governmental authority.' (Mickolus, 1978)

'The use or threat of use, of anxiety-inducing extra-normal violence for political purposes by any individual or group.' (Mickolus, 1980)

'Transnational terrorism is carried out by autonomous non-state actors, whether or not they enjoy some degree of support from sympathetic states. International terrorism is carried out by individuals or groups controlled by a sovereign state.' (Milbank, 1976)

'An act of political violence, but terrorism escapes definition when it becomes embellished with value-ladened political meaning.' (Miller, 1980)

'Events involving relatively highly organised and planned activities on the part of small but cohesive groups are the chief characteristics of terrorism.' (Morrison et al., 1972)

'Terrorism is the systematic use of intimidation for political ends.' (Moss, 1971)

'Politics by violence and propaganda by the deed are the hallmarks of terror.' (Neale, 1973)

'Terrorism is the deliberate and systematic assault on civilians to inspire fear for political ends.' (Netanyahu, 1995)

'Terrorism involves the intentional use of violence or the threat of violence by the precipitator against an instrumental target in order to communicate to a primary target a threat of future violence.' (Paust, 1977)

'Terrorism is every method of political struggle that fulfils three conditions – namely the involvement of the extreme use of violence against innocent people, and is not a legitimate method of struggle.' (Pontara, 1979)

'The use of terrorist violence is based on the assumption that the intended victim is unreasonable and incapable of seeing the viewpoint of the terrorist.' (Qureshi, 1976)

'Premeditated, politically motivated violence perpetrated against non-combatant targets by subnational groups or clandestine state agents, normally intended to influence an audience.' (US State Department in Reich, 1990)

'Sociologically, terror is a person or thing or practice that causes intense fear or suffering, whose aim is to intimidate, subjugate, especially as a political weapon or policy. Politically, its main function is to intimidate and disorganise the government through fear, and through this political changes can be achieved.' (Roucek, 1962)

'Politically motivated behaviour of a non-state group without electoral prospects in a democratic context which aims by means of violent acts against persons and or property to coerce people in order to obtain its will thereby.' (Schwind, 1978)

'Terrorist acts are severe bouts of violence directed at non-combatants by the contending sides of a political struggle.' (Sederberg, 1981)

'Political terrorism is the threat and or use of extra-normal forms of political violence in varying degrees with the objective of achieving political objectives and goals.' (Shultz, 1978)

'The distinctive question of morality cloaks any consideration of terrorism.' (Silke, 1996)

'Terrorism as an element in the process of violent change can be defined as the use of physical violence. It is a complementary tactic to both guerrilla and conventional warfare. Terrorism differs from guerrilla warfare in as much as its purpose is to influence the opponent and any third parties rather than annihilate him. The purpose of the act, not the nature of the act itself is the essential characteristic which distinguishes terrorism.' (Silverman and Jackson, 1970)

'Terrorism is a state of intense fear which threatens the most fundamental human drive – the will to survive intact.' (Silverstein, 1977)

'Terrorism is neither senseless nor random: it is a highly purposeful act committed by deadly serious people with big payoffs in mind.' (Simon, 2001)

'Two facets are incorporated in terrorism – a state of fear or anxiety within an individual or group, and the tool that induces the state of fear.' (Singh, 1977)

'Terrorism involves both the use and the threat of violence.' (Smith, 1977)

'The process of terrorism consists of the act or threat of violence, the emotional reactions to such an act or threat and the social effects resultant from the acts and reactions.' (Stohl, 1981)

'Terrorism is one of the most emotive and subjective words in the English language. It is a value judgement in itself.' (Taylor, 1993)

'Terrorism is politically motivated violence directed against non combatant or symbolic targets which is designed to communicate a message to a broader audience.' (Louise Richardson, 2000 in Taylor and Horgan, 2000)

'It is pejorative. Even terrorists do not admit to being terrorists anymore.' (Louise Richardson, 2000 in Taylor and Horgan, 2000)

'Terrorism is an abstract phenomenon of which there can be no real essence which can be discovered and described.' (Thackrah, 1987a)

'Terrorism is an organised system of extreme and violent intimidation to create instability within democracies. International terrorists seek to launch indiscriminate and unpredictable attacks on groups (police, army, multinationals or nations) to change the politico-economic balance of the world.' (Thackrah, 1987b);

'Political terrorism is the systematic use of violence for political ends directed against outsiders in a political conflict. Its increase can be seen in terms of four factors – arms, mobility, communication (publicity) and money.' (Tromp, 1979)

'Terrorism is a method of action by which an agent tends to produce terror in order to impose his domination.' (Waciorsky, 1939)

'Terrorism is a method of action by which an agent tends to produce terror in order to impose his domination.' (Waciorsky, 1939)

'A process of terror is the act or threat of violence, the emotional reaction and the social effects; whereas the system of terror may be defined to include certain states of war as well as certain political communities.' (Walter, 1964)

'Any attempt at defining terrorism will be predicated on the assumption that some classes of political violence are justifiable whereas others are not.' (Wardlaw, 1989)

'Political terrorism can be defined as a strategy, a method by which an organised group or party tries to get attention for its aims, or force concessions toward its goals, through the systematic use of deliberate violence.' (Watson, 1976)

'Violence, in order to be terrorism, must be political.' (Weisband and Roguly, 1976)

'A general intention of terrorism is to force the hands of authority.' (Whittaker, 2001)

'Terrorism is a tool to be employed, a means of reaching a goal, for many types of political actions ...' (Wieviorka, 1993)

'Terrorism is the most amoral of organised violence.' (Wilkinson, 1973)

'Terrorism is the coercively intimidatory weapon of revolutionary movements.' (Wilkinson, 1974)

'Political terrorism can be defined as coercive intimidation, and is one of the oldest techniques of psychological warfare.' (Wilkinson, 1977)

'Terrorism is the systematic use of coercive intimidation, usually to service political ends. It is used to create a climate of fear ...' (Wilkinson, 2000)

'Religious terrorism assumes a transcendental dimension, and its perpetrators are consequently unconstrained by the political, moral or practical constraints that may affect other terrorists.' (Hoffman, 2001 quoted in Williams, 2002)

'Terrorist strategy aims not to defeat the forces of the incumbent regime militarily, but to bring about the moral alienation of the masses from the government until its isolation has become total and irreversible.' (Wolf, 1976)

'The apex of violence is terrorism.' (Zinam, 1978)

All these authors of definitions of terrorism have tried to contribute toward the understanding of a complex subject, and their definitions are the result of varied academic backgrounds and attitudes to research on terrorism. The concepts of terror and terrorism are vague and much abused, and their relation to other forms of political violence and to criminality is often ambiguous. It is the interplay of subjective factors and responses within terror and terrorism that makes them difficult concepts for social scientists to define.

See also: Definitions: Issues and Problems.

References

Alexander, Y. and Finger, S. M. (eds) (1977) *Terrorism: Interdisciplinary Perspectives*, New York: John Jay Press.

Arendt, H. (1951) *The Origins of Totalitarianism*, New York: Harcourt Brace, Jovanovich Inc.

Aron, R. (1966) *Peace and War*, London: Weidenfeld and Nicholson.

Badey, T. J. (1998) 'Defining International Terrorism: A Pragmatic Approach', *Terrorism and Political Violence*, vol. 10, no. 1, pp. 90–107.

Bassiouni, M. Ch (1981) 'Terrorism, Law Enforcement and the Mass Media: Perspectives, Problems, Proposals', *The Journal of Criminal Law and Criminology*, vol. 72, no. 1, pp. 1–51, New York.

Bite, V. (1975) 'International Terrorism', *Foreign Affairs Division, Library of Congress. Appendix of US Congress, Senate Committee on the Judiciary. Subcommittee to Investigate the Administration of the International Security Act and Other Internal Security Laws*, Part IV, May 14, Washington, DC: GPO.

Brown, D. J. and Merrill, R. (1993) *Violent Persuasions: The Politics and Imagery of Terrorism*, Seattle: Bay Press.

Chisholm, A. J. (1948) *The Function of Terror and Violence in Revolution*, Washington, DC: Georgetown University (MA Thesis).

Clutterbuck, R. (1977) *Guerrillas and Terrorists*, London: Faber and Faber.

— (ed.) (1986) *The Future of Political Violence*, London: Macmillan, RUSI.

Cooley J. K. (2000) *Unholy Wars: Afghanistan, America and International Terrorism*, London and Sterling, VA: Pluto Press.

Cooper, H. H. A. (2001) 'The Problem of Definition Revisited', *American Behavioural Scientist*, vol. 44, pp. 881–893.

Crenshaw Hutchinson, M. (1972) 'The Concept of Revolutionary Terrorism', *Journal of Conflict Resolution*, vol. 16, no. 3, pp. 383–396.

— (1978) *Revolutionary Terrorism: The FLN in Algeria*

1954–1962, Stanford, CA: Hoover Institution Press.

— (1981a) 'The Causes of Terrorism', *Comparative Politics*, Chicago.

— (1981b) *Revolutionary Terrorism: The FLN in Algeria 1954–1962*, Stanford, CA: Hoover Institution.

Crozier, B. (1974) *A Theory of Conflict*, London: Hamish Macmillan.

Dallin, A. and Breslauer, G. W. (eds) (1970) *Political Terror in Communist Systems*, Stanford, CA: Stanford University Press.

DeLillo, Don (1992) *Mao II*, New York: Penguin.

Drake C. J. M. (1998) *Terrorists' Target Selection*, New York: St Martin's Press.

Fairburn, G. (1974) *Revolutionary Guerrilla Warfare: The Countryside Version*, London: Penguin.

Fearey, R. A. (1976) *Remarks made 19 February 1976 as US Co-ordinator for Combating Terrorism*, quoted in Wolf (1981).

Francis, S. T. (1981) *The Soviet Strategy of Terror*, Washington, DC: Heritage Foundation, pp. 683–698.

Fromkin, D. (1975) 'The Strategy of Terrorism', *Foreign Affairs*, vol. 53, no. 4, Washington, DC.

George, A. (1991) *Western State Terrorism*, New York: Routledge, Chapman and Hall

Guelke, A. (1998) *The Age of Terrorism and the International Political System*, London and New York: I. B. Taurus Publishers.

Hacker, F. J. (1981) 'Contagion and Attraction of Terror and Terrorism' in Alexander, Y. and Gleason, J. M. (eds) (1981) *Behavioural and Quantitative Perspectives on Terrorism*, New York: Pergamon Press, pp. 73–85.

Halliday, F. (2001) *The World at 2000: Perils and Promises*, Basingstoke: Palgrave.

Hamilton, L. C. (1978) *Ecology of Terrorism: A Historical and Statistical Study*, Boulder, CO: University of Colorado.

Hardman, J. B. S. (1936) 'Terrorism' in *Encyclopaedia of Social Sciences*, vol. 14, New York: Macmillan.

Harmon, C. C. (2000) *Terrorism Today*, London and Portland, OR: Frank Cass.

Herman, V. and van der Laan Bouma, R. (1981) 'Nationalists without a Nation: South Moluccan Terrorism in the Netherlands' in Lodge (ed.) (1981) *Terrorism: A Challenge to the State*, Oxford: Martin Robertson 1981, pp. 119–146.

Hess, H. (1981) 'Terrorismus und Terrorismus – Diskurs', *Tijdschrift voor Criminologie*, no. 4, Amsterdam.

Heyman, E. S. (1980) 'Monitoring the Diffusion of Transnational Terrorism', in Sloan, S. and Schultz, R. H. (eds) *Responding to the Terrorist Threat Prevention and Control*, New York: Pergamon.

Heyman, P. B. (1998) *Terrorism and America: A Commonsense Strategy for a Democratic Society*, Cambridge, MA and London: The MIT Press.

Hoffman, B. (1998) *Inside Terrorism*, London: Victor Gollancz.

Horowitz, I. L. (1973) 'Political Terrorism and State Power', *Journal of Political and Military Sociology*, vol. 1, Los Angeles, pp. 147–157.

— (1977) 'Can Democracy cope with Terrorism', *Civil Liberties Review*, May–June, pp. 29–37.

Iviansky, Z. (1977) 'The Terrorist Revolution: Roots of Modern Terrorism', *Journal of Strategic Studies*, vol. 10, no. 4, pp. 127–149.

Jenkins, B. M. (1975) 'International Terrorism: A New Mode of Conflict', *California Seminar on Arms Control and Foreign Policy*, Los Angeles: Crescent Publications.

— (1977) 'Combating International Terrorism: The Role of Congress', Santa Monica: Rand.

— (1978) 'The Study of Terrorism: Definitional Problems' in Alexander and Gleason (eds) (1981) *Behavioural and Quantitative Perspectives on Terrorism*, New York: Pergamon Press, pp. 3–10.

Juergensmeyer, M. (2000) *Terror in the Mind of God: The Global Rise of Religious Violence*, Berkeley, CA, Los Angeles and London: University of California Press.

Kaplan, A. (1981) 'The Psychodynamics of Terrorism' in Alexander and Gleason (eds) (1981) *Behavioural and Quantitative Perspectives on Terrorism*, New York: Pergamon Press, pp. 35–50.

Karanovic, M. (1978) 'Pojam Terorizma' (The Concept of Terrorism), *Jugoslovenska Revija za Krimilogiju i Krivicnofravo*, no. 14, Belgrade.

Laqueur, W. (1987) *The Age of Terrorism*, Boston: Little and Brown.

Leiden, C. and Schmidt, K. M. (1968) *The Politics of Violence*, Englewood Cliffs: Prentice Hall.

Leiser, B. M. (1977) 'Terrorism, Guerrilla Warfare and International Morality', *Journal of International Studies*, vol. 12, Stanford.

Lodge, J. (ed.) (1982) *Terrorism: A Challenge to the State*, Oxford: Martin Robertson.

Mallin, J. (1971) *Terror and Urban Guerrillas*, Florida: University of Miami Press.

Mickolus, E. (1978) 'Trends in Transitional Terrorism' in Livingston, M. H. (ed.) *International Terrorism in the Contemporary World*, Westport, CT: Greenwood Press.

— (1980) *Transnational Terrorism: A Chronology of Events 1968–1979*, London: Aldwych.

Milbank, D. L. (1976) *Research Study: International and Transnational Terrorism*, Washington, DC: CIA Political Research Dept.

Miller, A. H. (1980) *Terrorism and Hostage Negotiations*, Boulder, CO: Westview Press.

Morrison, D. G. *et al.* (1972) *Black Africa: A Comparative Handbook*, New York: The Free Press.

Moss, R. (1971) *Urban Guerrillas: The New Face of Political Violence*, London: Temple Smith.

Neale, W. D. (1973) 'Terror – Oldest Weapon in the Arsenal', *Army* (August), Washington, DC.

Netanyahu, B. (ed.) (1995) *Terrorism: How the West Can Win*, London: Weidenfeld and Nicholson.

Paust, J. J. (1977) 'A Definitional Focus' in Alexander, Y. and Finger, S. M. (eds) *Terrorism: Interdisciplinary Perspectives*, New York: John Jay Press and McGraw Hill Book Co., pp. 18–29.

Pontara, G. (1979) 'Violenza e Terrorismo: Il problema della Definizione e della Giustificazione' in Bonanate, L. (ed.) *Dimensioni del Terrorismo Politico*, Milan: Franco Angeli Editore.

Qureshi, S. (1976) 'Political Violence in the South Asia Subcontinent' in Alexander, Y. (ed.) *Terrorism. International, National, Regional and Global Perspectives*, New York: Praeger, pp. 151–193.

Reich, W. (ed) (1990) *Origins of Terrorism: Psychologies, Ideologies, Theologies and States of Mind*, New York: Cambridge University Press.

Roucek, J. S. (1980) 'Terrorism in its Sociological Aspects', *Sociologia Internationalis*, vol. 18, pp. 1–2, 97–110.

Schmid, A. P. (1993) 'The Response Problem as a Definition Problem' in Schmid, A. and Crelinsten, R. D. *Western Response to Terrorism*, London: Frank Cass.

Schmid, A. P. and Jongman, A. J. (1988) *Political Terrorism: A New Guide to Actors, Authors, Concepts, Databases, Theories and Literature*, Amsterdam: North Holland Publishing.

Schmitt (1986) 'Enemies of Mankind', in Netanyahu, B. (ed.) *Terrorism: How the West Can Win*, New York: Farrar, Strauss, Giroux, pp. 155–156.

Schwind, H. D. (1978) 'Zur Entwicklung des Terrorismus' in Schwind (ed.) *Ursachen des Terrorismus der Bundesrepublik*, Berlin: Walter de Gruyter.

Sederberg, P. C. (1981) 'Defining Terrorism' (unpublished paper).

Shultz, R. (1980) 'Conceptualising Political Terrorism: A Typology', in Buckley, A. D. and Olson, D. D. (eds) *International Terrorism: Current Research and Future Directions*, Wayne, NJ: Avery pp. 9–18.

Silke, A. (1996) 'Terrorism and the Blind Man's Elephant', *Terrorism and Political Violence*, vol. 8, no. 3 (autumn).

Silverman, J. M. and Jackson, P. M. (1970) 'Terror in Insurgency Warfare', *Military Review*, vol. 50, Fort Leavenworth, KS: October, pp. 61–67.

Silverstein, M. E. (1977) 'Medical Rescue as an Anti-Terrorist Measure: A Strategists' Cookbook' in Crelinsten, R. D. (ed.) *Research Strategies for the Study of International Political Terrorism*, Montreal: International Center for Comparative Criminology.

Simon, J. D. (2001) *The Terrorist Trap: America's Experience with Terrorism*, 2nd edition, Bloomington, IN: Indiana University Press.

Singh, B. (1977) 'An Overview' in Alexander, Y. and Finger, S. M. (eds) *Terrorism: Interdisciplinary Perspectives*, New York: John Jay Press and Maidenhead: McGraw Hill Book Co., pp. 5–17.

Smith, W. H. (1977) 'International Terrorism: A Political Analysis' in *The Year Book of World Affairs 1977*, vol. 31, London: Stevens.

Stohl, M. (1981) 'The Three Worlds of Terror', *TVI Journal*, vol. 3, no. 6, July pp. 4–11.

Taylor, M. and Horgan, J. (eds) (2000) *The Future of Terrorism*. London and Portland, OR: Frank Cass.

Taylor, P. (1993) *States of Terror*, London: BBC Books.

Thackrah, J. R. (1987a) 'Terrorism: A Definitional Problem' in Wilkinson, P. and Stewart, A. M. (1987) *Contemporary Research on Terrorism*, Aberdeen: Aberdeen University Press, pp. 24–41.

— (1987b) 'Terrorism: A Definitional Problem' in *Royal United Services Institute and Brassey's Defence Yearbook*, London and New York: Brassey's Defence Publishers, pp. 181–204.

Tromp, H. W. (1979) 'Terrorism and Political Violence', Brussels: AFK/VVK (unpublished Paper).

Waciorsky, J. (1939) *La Terrorisme Politique*, Paris: A Pedone, as quoted in Crenshaw Hutchinson, M. (1972) 'The Concept of Revolutionary Terrorism', *Journal of Conflict Resolution*, vol. 16, no. 3, pp. 383–396.

Walter, E. V. (1964) 'Violence and the Process of Terror', *American Sociological Review*, vol. 29, no. 2 pp. 248–257.

Wardlaw, G. (1989) *Political Terrorism: Theory, Tactics and Counter Measures*, Cambridge: Cambridge University Press.

Watson, F. M. (1976) *Political Terrorism: The Threat and the Response*, Washington, DC: Robert B. Luce.

Weisband, E. and Roguly, D. (1976) 'Palestinian Terrorism: Violence, Verbal Strategy and Legitimacy' in Alexander, Y., Carlton, D. and Wilkinson, P. (eds) (1978) *Terrorism Theory and Practice*, New York: Praeger, Westview Special Studies in National and International Terrorism.

Whittaker, D. J. (ed.) (2001) *The Terrorism Reader* (2nd edn), London: Routledge.

Wieviorka, M. (1993) *The Making of Terrorism*, Chicago, IL: University of Chicago Press.

Wilkinson, P. (1973) 'Three Questions on Terrorism', *Government and Opposition*, vol. 8, no. 3, pp. 290–312.

— (1974) *Political Terrorism*, London: Macmillan.

— (1976) 'Terrorism versus Liberal Democracy: The Problem of Response', *Conflict Studies*, no. 76, London: RISCT.

— (1977) *Terrorism and the Liberal State*, London: Macmillan Education Ltd.

— (2000) *Terrorism versus Democracy: the Liberal State Response*, London and Portland, OR: Frank Cass.

Williams, P. L. (2002) *Al Qaeda: Brotherhood of Terror*, London and Harlow: Pearson.

Wolf, J. B. (ed.) (1989) *Antiterrorist Initiatives*, New York: Plenum Press, pp. 240–265

Zinam, O. (1978) 'Terrorism and Violence in the Light of a Theory of Discontent and Frustration', in Livingston, M. H. (ed.) *International Terrorism in the Contemporary World*, Westport, CT: Greenwood Press.

Political Terrorism – Definition

The paradox of having the definition judged rather too narrow or too broad might be linked to the problem of whether terrorism is a unitary concept. It can occur in war and insurgency contests and where popular support for the struggle is virtually absent. Terrorist acts are means of communication.

Typologies of Terrorism: Some of the common bases for classification include actor, victim, cause, environment, means, political orientation, motivation, demand, purpose, and target.

Terrorism as Surrogate Warfare: Terrorism is often treated as a form of international war, or rather, as its substitute. Terrorism is characterised by dramatic actions staged by clandestine groups aimed at prominent targets whose connection to the professed conflict remains obscure.

Conflict stems from two main factors – concepts in some historical past and on-going attempts to undo them and modern revolution and counter-revolution.

Terrorism is still in search of a theory.

Further Reading

Badey, T. J. (1998) 'Defining International Terrorism: A Pragmatic Approach', *Terrorism and Political Violence*, vol. 10, no. 1, pp. 90–107.

Brown, D. J. and Merrill, R. (1993) *Violent Persuasions: The Politics and Imagery of Terrorism*, Seattle: Bay Press.

Cooper, H. H. A. (2001) 'The Problem of Definition Revisited', *American Behavioural Scientist*, vol. 44, pp. 881–893.

DeLillo, Don (1990) *Mao II*, New York: Penguin.

George, A., Hall, D. and Simons, W. R. (1988) *The Limits of Coercive Diplomacy*, Boston, MA: Little, Brown and Co.

Reich, W. (ed.) (1990) *Origins of Terrorism*, Cambridge: Cambridge University Press.

Schmid, A. P. and Jongman, A. J. (1988) *Political Terrorism: A New Guide to Actors, Authors, Concepts, Databases, Theories and Literature*, Amsterdam: North Holland Publishing.

Silke, A. (1996) 'Terrorism and the Blind Man's Elephant', *Terrorism and Political Violence*, vol. 8, no. 3 (autumn), pp. 12–28.

Wieviorka, M. (1993) *The Making of Terrorism*, Chicago, IL: University of Chicago Press.

Wilkinson, P. and Steward, A. M. (eds) *Contemporary*

Research on Terrorism, Aberdeen: Aberdeen University Press.

Defining International Terrorism

In international terrorism, threats are often parts of the pattern of violence – but they do not replace the use of violence. The actual use of violence is often a prerequisite for terrorism. While all terrorists are criminals not all criminals are terrorists even if they commit exactly the same acts.

Any United Nations measure needs a common agreement on the basic premises and the global community still has to accept that terrorism can be distinguished from other types of violence through repetition, motivation, intent, actors and effect.

Issues and Problems

Regarding the concept of terrorism, the emotive nature of the subject matter, the term's derogatory thrust and the political discourse are all major contributory factors to its complexity. Although there is hardly a definition which does not contain the word violence, the concept, rather than being considered as a technique of applying violence which in principle can be used by anyone in all sorts of conflict situations, is linked to certain actors only for certain types of conflicts. Often the well-worn phrase 'one man's terrorist is another man's patriot' is used, proving that the concept has been subjected to a double standard, and an 'in-group, out-group' distinction.

In spite of the spread of terrorist incidents throughout the world, terrorism has neither a precise definition nor one which is widely acceptable. Like many political terms it is pejorative. Some governments are prone to label as terrorism all violent acts committed by their political opponents, while anti-government extremists claim to be the victims of government terror. The imprecise nature of the term means that it can be applied to almost any set of fear-producing actions to serve a variety of purposes. More generally it can apply to similar acts of violence – kidnappings and hijackings – which are not intended by the perpetrators to be terror-producing. Political sociologists argue that no definition can, in principle, be reached because the very process of definition is in itself part of the wider contestation of ideologies or political objectives. Definitions support the argument that the perspectives change according to when and where the terrorist act takes place. The question of the definition of terrorism is central to an understanding of the phenomenon and to the success of any rational measures directed against it. To many observers almost any act of violence may be included under the rubric of terrorism. Others would not label as terrorism violent acts carried out within a revolutionary context which a number of people would recognise as terroristic. Confusion can arise over a seeming similarity of behaviour when a violent act is carried out by a politically motivated individual, a criminal or the mentally unbalanced.

Terrorism is also a moral problem, and attempts at definition are based on the assumption that some classes of political violence are justifiable whereas others are not. For instance, students of terrorism find some difficulty in labelling an event as terrorist without making a moral judgement about the act. Governments and lawyers and politicians find themselves unable to take such a detached view. Violence has been defined in terms of force, coercive power, authority and legitimacy. One of the problems of implementing criminal sanctions occurs in the case of acts of terrorism that produce a terror outcome by threats of violence, without actual physical injury to any human or non-human targets. A generally accepted definition of terrorism requires an element of terror and coercive purpose. All terrorist acts involve violence or the threat of violence, often coupled with specific demands.

The word terrorism is often used with qualifying terms – 'often', 'mainly', 'generally' and 'usually'. These qualifiers allow for the injection of personal views in deciding whether a particular act is or is not 'terrorist'. Conversely, defining terrorism by focusing on the nature of the act rather than on the identity of the perpetrators, or the nature of their cause makes a substantial degree of objectivity possible. The Central Intelligence Agency distinguishes between transnational terrorism or terrorism carried out by basically autonomous non-state actors, whether or not they enjoy some degree of support from sympathetic states, and international terrorism, which is terrorism carried out by individuals or groups controlled by a sovereign state. So far the General Assembly of the United Nations has been unable to agree on a standard definition, and if the time ever comes when there is general agreement that international terrorism must be curbed, any definition adopted will have to be couched in universal, and not pro-Western terms. International terrorism can be distinguished from purely domestic terror/violence by the presence of an international jurisdictional element. Transnational terrorism, a term often used erroneously as a synonym for international terrorism, can be considered a sub-classification with specific reference to non-state or non-political actors.

Although specially constituted UN committees have continually condemned acts of international terrorism in principle, they have exempted from their definition of such acts those activities which derive from the inalienable right to self-determination and independence of all peoples under colonial and racist regimes, and in particular the struggle of national liberation movements in accordance with the purposes and principles of the Charter and the relevant resolutions of the organs of the United Nations.

In the absence of an international definition, the West has tended to go it alone as a community and to act as a group against terrorism. Governments in both East and West often use the word terrorist to describe their opponents, even when these opponents have not used violence. Guerrilla groups refuse to let themselves be seen by governments as terrorists and will prefer to call themselves guerrillas. While it is easier for governments than for terrorists to legitimate their activities, terrorists often strive for legitimacy. Governments are often seen as having substantial resources, and as rational beings whose actions serve a longer goal, while individuals have little social claim and are typified by meagre resources and limited modes of violence coupled with an irrational drive and a deranged mind.

Terrorism, by definition, is an act that seeks to influence a population significantly larger than the immediate target. The quality of the public's understanding, and its response to terrorism of all varieties is highly significant. One of the prime purposes of terrorist activity is to put a grievance on the public agenda. Terrorism is a strategy whereby violence is used to produce certain effects upon a group of people. With special reference to political sub-state terrorism, this strategy is one of four 'ideal type' strategies whereby a group out of power can effect violent social change, the other three being the *coup d'état*, insurrection and guerrilla warfare.

Many of the definitional problems plaguing analysts of terrorism can be found in the scientific and ideological discourse on violence. Terrorism has been defined in terms of violation, violation of the corporal integrity of the state, violation of territorial or special integrity, of moral and legal decency, of rules and expectations and even as violations of self esteem, dignity and autonomy. It has been defined in terms of force, coercive power, authority, legitimacy, behaviour, motives, intentions, antecedents and consequences. In relation to the differing perceptions of violence, terrorism can be seen as an easily recognised and undesirable activity, subjectively determined and shaped by social and political considerations.

Terrorism can be committed for several purposes. Individual acts of terrorism may aim at wringing specific concessions such as the payment of a ransom or release of prisoners. Terrorism may seek the deliberate provocation of repression, hoping to induce the government to self-destruct. It may be used to enforce obedience and co-operation and as in the Irish troubles, it is frequently meant to punish. Terrorists often declare the victim of their attack is somehow guilty.

No one desires to have the appellation terrorist applied to his activity. Terms such as 'freedom fighter' or 'liberator' are attempts to mitigate what is in fact an ugly profession. A fine line can be encountered between terror and terrorism, with attempts to legalise or justify the former being made while proscribing the latter. Terror practiced by a government in office appears as law enforcement and is directed against the opposition, while terrorism, on the other hand, implies open defiance of law and is a means whereby an opposition aims to demoralise government authority. While the terrorist group makes no presence at legality, legitimate government must at least formally adhere to law. A definitional struggle has thus arisen between those who claim an exception at law for certain manifestly harmful forms of conduct and those who will not admit it.

The difficulty that surrounds accurate definitions of terrorism presents itself again in dealing with typologies. It can be viewed in three ways: terrorism committed or taking effect outside the territory of a state of which the alleged offender is a national; terrorism intended to damage the interests of a state or an international inter-governmental organisation; and terrorism committed neither by nor against a member of the armed forces of a state in the course of military hostilities.

The International Chiefs of Police see terrorism as a purposeful human activity primarily directed toward the creation of a general climate of fear designed to influence, in ways desired by the protagonist, other human beings and, through them, some course of events. If the word 'political' is inserted between the words 'human' and 'activity' one avoids mixing terrorism with gangland intimidation or similar acts. In describing an act of terrorism there must be a terror outcome, or else the process could hardly be labelled as terrorism. The judicial dividing line between fear and intense fear is very small. Terrorism can occur at an instant and by one act. Definitional approaches which relate merely to acts of violence, the threat or use of violence, repressive acts, and similar categorisations are incomplete and unhelpful in terms of meaning and effective guidance for decision. These types of approach ignore the critical need for a focus upon the use of intense fear or anxiety for coercion of a primary target into behaviour or attitudinal patterns sought in connection with a demanded power outcome. Terrorism's success is measured not only by the ability to topple the social order but also to loosen that order in symbolic terms; by weakening the law-making capacities of elected officials and casting doubt on the concept of rights in society and the obligations of the state.

There is a popular belief which terrorists perhaps wish to hold of their actions that violent or lawless acts, from skyjacking and indiscriminate bombing to ritualistic murder and politically inspired kidnappings, assassinations and the destruction of property, are simple manifestations of man's basic aggressive and destructive nature.

Terrorism is not a universal phenomenon, but it is a historical one, emerging only at particular times and associated with particular developments in people's consciousness. Terror can be seen as a counter value campaign, depending on the target attacked, and a guerrilla campaign can be judged in terms of what is being defended. To a large number of observers terror is by definition political. Changes sought by terrorists short of total revolution, have to be achieved within a given political context, i.e. the government institutes reforms, the government falls, or alternatively the government represses the terrorists.

Although terror is in part political violence, not all political violence is in fact terrorism. Vague generalised definitions can mean that the scope of the analysis is too broad and so the findings may be meaningless. Too narrow a definition means there is little opportunity for comparative analysis which can show patterns common to a variety of acts of terrorism. Vague generalised definitions can mean that the scope of the analysis is too broad and so the findings may be meaningless.

A terrorist campaign that causes a significant level of fear among the target population may achieve its aims. Not all the violence espoused by terrorists is mindless. In some instances terrorism is potentially more effective especially from a cost-benefit strategy than conventional or guerrilla warfare. Unlike other forms of warfare, the goal of terrorism is not to destroy the opposing side but instead to break its will and force it to capitulate. The response to an act of terror or guerrilla activity can vary greatly depending on the danger of repetition and the degree of identification with the victim. If the observed identification is not with the victim but with the target of terroristic coercion, it is unlikely to be terror or guerrilla activity, and if the identification of the observer is with the terrorist himself, it might even be euphoria.

Definitions of terrorism have to be studied within the overall subject matter of terrorism and related to its history, philosophy, psychology, sociology, politics, statistics, language and law. In the field of terrorism there is no agreement about any single definition; but there is considerable agreement about the elements which definitions should contain. Open-mindedness and objectivity can be some help in the problem of definition.

Terrorism is a purposeful human political activity directed to the creation of a climate of fear and designed to influence, in ways desired by the protagonist, other human beings and through them, some course of events. It is an unacceptable challenge to the principles on which organised society rests.

While no definitions of terrorism can be agreed upon by theorists (sometimes referred to as terrorologists) most people have a firm conception of what it is.

It has many guises and forms – repression, deception, racism, sexual exploitation, regulations, control of information, surveillance, the invasion of privacy, the suppression of personal liberties and the corruption of ideals. The vexing questions surrounding the morality of terrorism centre less on its political goals as the emancipation of oppressed peoples, the end of colonial rule, the collapse of an authoritarian regime, the survival of people marked for destruction; and more on its means and the strategies, conditions, and losses associated with violent political behaviour.

The social conditions that precipitate the terrorist act sway public opinion nowadays as much as in the past.

Deadly violence against states perceived as 'democratic' may be less acceptable, say, than the violent rebellion of colonised or oppressed peoples in nations where free expression and dissent are prohibited. The intended (or even accidental) victims of the attack may alter public opinion i.e., the murder of an innocent child in Northern Ireland would most probably elicit outrage, that of a desperate politician such as President Ceaucescu in Romania, in 1989, a sense of relief (Brown and Merrill, 1993).

Misconceptions

The literature on terrorism provides key generalisations about the topic such as: 'surrogate warfare', 'pathological', 'a weapon of the weak', 'liberal democracies are prone to terrorism', 'a reaction to violence by the state'.

International interdependence has sparked the growth in international terrorism.

Such generalisations and vague explanations perhaps lead one to the conclusion that this causes so many differing definitions about the subject and why international counter-terror legislators have a problem defining the problem. Definitions tend to be from a Western perspective. In the Third World rural guerrillas can be seen as terrorists. Defiance of central government is commonplace in the Third World where the capacity of a state to maintain law and order is more a function of the level of economic development in the society than it is a reflection of the type of political system. Where there is a lot of violence taking place it is difficult to isolate particular incidents as acts of terrorism and to distinguish it from other forms of violence. The experience of people suffering terrorism is far removed from the context of the Western use of the term 'terrorism'.

The conclusion bipolarity in 1989 ended some conflicts and led to a de-escalation of others but it created new sources of instability in the world which are likely to generate violence across national frontiers. New definitions about what is terrorism come into play and vague generalisations multiply.

Terrorism cannot always be stopped by a state's draconian measure. The context in which a campaign of terrorism is likely to end is if it proves impossible even for the participants to establish its relevance to the political ends used to justify it. Times of uncertainty tend to arise at different times in different societies as a result of domestic developments – and they can add to the problem of ending terrorism. The absence of any international agreement on the meaning of self-determination means judgements on political violence are vague, and also is one of the reasons for the perhaps simplistic maxim, 'one man's terrorist is another man's freedom fighter'. Instability in the New World Order post Cold War and uncertainty about the future make the outcomes of the use of political violence uncertain and even more disagreement about the term 'terrorism'.

As the world becomes globalised and polycentric there are going to be many interpretations of the term 'terrorism'. To some observers it is easier to pontificate on specific terrorism campaigns than to talk in general terms about the topic. Potential motives from the consequences of the actions will also increase (Guelke, 1998).

As President Bush said post-September 11, a war on terrorism is open ended; and for generations others have said that terrorism can never be defeated. The age of terrorism can last aeons.

Definitional experts may in future express increasing doubts about the judgemental use of the term 'terrorism' and 'terrorists'.

See also: Morality; UK (Northern Ireland).

References

Brown, D. J. and Merrill, R. (1993) *Violent persuasions: The Politics and Imagery of Terrorism*, Seattle, WA: Bay Press.

Guelke, A. (1998) *The Age of Terrorism and the International Political System*, London and New York: I. B. Taurus.

Laqueur, W. (1977) *Terrorism*, London: Weidenfeld and Nicholson.

McCauley, C. (ed.) (1991) *Terrorism and Public Policy*, London: Frank Cass.

McGurn, W. (1990) *Terrorist or Freedom Fighter? The Cost of Confusion*, London: Institute for European Defence and Strategy.

Shafritz, J. M. *et al.* (1991) *Almanac of Modern Terrorism*, New York: Facts on File.

Further Reading

Parry, Albert (1976) *Terrorism from Robespierre to Arafat*, New York: Vanguard Press.

Vetter, H. J. and Perlstein, G. R. (1991) *Perspectives on Terrorism*, Belmont, CA: Wadsworth Thomson Learning.

Democracy and Violence

There has been a long link between democracy and terrorism dating back to the Reign of Terror during the French Revolution (1789–99), which ironically, aimed to make France fit for democracy. Many anti-colonial terrorists fighting for independence from their European masters in the mid-twentieth century claimed to be democrats. Violent conflict can occur even in the most stable and successful democracies. The leaders and financiers of terrorist groups from around the world have often found sanctuary in democracies. The courts in democratic nations have argued in some extradition cases that some alleged crimes were political in nature and therefore the person

under scrutiny should be given sanctuary. Asylum has on occasions been claimed by individuals who believe they are targets of political persecution in their homelands – and this has proven not to be the case by some Algerians in the **UK**. It is ironic that elections, so vital in democratic societies, are linked to violence, and have on occasions sparked **civil war**.

Further Reading

Schmid, A. P. and Jongman, A. J. (1988) *Political Terrorism*, New York: North-Holland.

Wilkinson, P. (2002) *Terrorism versus Democracy: The Liberal State Response*, London and Portland, OR: Frank Cass.

Destabilisation, Exploitation and Collapse in Democratic Societies

Security, intelligence and the rule of law are bulwarks of pluralist societies. The **army** and **police**, and the intelligence services and judiciary are a slender barrier against crime, political violence, chaos and civil war.

Agitational propaganda can lead to street disorder, intimidation and terrorism. Subversion and propaganda and direct action can lead to an erosion of confidence and can create insecurity.

Intimidation is aimed to induce the majority to opt out; and to deter collaborators, informers, journalists, teachers and employers. The law can be made unworkable by the intimidation of witnesses, juries, police and officials (Clutterbuck, 1986). A climate of collapse may develop when government, police and judiciary seem to lose the will and the ability to enforce the law. Terrorists get a sense of impunity; and rural groups take the law into their own hands. The rabble clutches in desperation at whatever offers the best hope of restoring order. Terrorists aim to undermine civil rights whether they are minority rights, but not to kidnap or kill, or majority rights which provide tranquillity and the right to live.

Protest movements have a genuine and legitimate purpose but political activists may join with different aims. Sympathetic issues can be developed and exploited; and a broad base can give the police no option but to react. Clashes can be provoked to get people involved in the struggle. Confrontation breeds comradeship and commitment. The **media** can have their appetite for action and drama exploited. Emotive pictures can be stage-managed especially for TV; and this can arouse public fear of a collapse of order. An exploitation of opportunity by violent activists can occur.

Anti-police riots can exploit grievances to create an explosive situation; and build up hatred between deprived groups and the police. A tiny spark can cause an explosion of discontent and activists are ready with an organisation to exploit such a situation.

See also: Army-Police Co-operation; Intelligence Roles.

Reference

Clutterbuck, R. (ed.) (1986) *The Future of Political Violence*, London: Macmillan.

Developments *see* History of Terrorism

Diplomacy

The law of diplomacy is repeatedly violated through acts of terrorism. Because states care so much about diplomatic sanctity (immunity), the diplomats make a tempting target for terrorists, and because terrorists do not enjoy the benefits of diplomatic law (as states do) they are willing to break diplomatic rules. If any diplomat is attacked, so is the state from which the diplomat is accredited.

Terrorists' actions are seldom traceable to governments. **International law** (enforced through reciprocity or collective response) is of limited use in stopping terrorist attacks on diplomats. Incidents involving the misuse of the diplomatic 'bag' for carrying weapons or documents of use to terrorists have declined in recent years.

Can a state therefore specifically commit acts of terrorism?

Definitions of state terrorism can be very useful around the world in trying to understand the phenomena of terrorism from many different perspectives.

There are serious shortcomings more so in that the definition can be too vague, as a result of the inclusion of specific words. It can be too broad in that almost any act of war or any law could be included. They can also be too narrow in that all acts committed in warfare are excluded, as are all legal acts; all acts committed abroad or at home or all actions of a particular type of regime.

Basically the acts of a state have to be labelled as acts of terrorism by the same criteria that cover the acts of non-state actors. The states legal acts of violence at home are generally considered as non-terrorist. Any organisation can become the state. Moreover, the state can maintain unlimited authority over all areas of life.

Further Reading

Freedman, L., Hill, C., Roberts, A., Vincent, R. J., Wilkinson, P. and Windsor, P. (1986) *Terrorism and the International Order*, London: Routledge and Kegan Paul.

Herz, M. F. (ed.) (1982) *Diplomats and Terrorists: What Works, What Doesn't: A Symposium*, Washington, DC: Institute for the Study of Diplomacy, Georgetown University.

Dynamics of Terrorism *see* Terror and Terrorism

Dynamite Terrorism

Irish revolutionaries undertook dynamite terrorism in the last quarter of the nineteenth century. It was important and indeed perhaps politically and psychologically necessary for them to endow dynamite's power with the broadest theoretical and philosophical meanings. Super-explosives were interpreted to represent 'power to the people' for use against the state. The state used raw power and violence against the people – so they should do likewise in return. Super-explosives represented scientific power. To some terrorists it seemed proper for science to enable man to unleash the forces of nature against the state. They believed that the highest form of revolutionary terror should utilise the most advanced science and technology of the time.

Super-explosive terror represented a moral form of power because it elevated violence above the level of common criminality. Conventional weapons might have been easier to use, but they aroused conventional prejudices and lacked grandeur. Super-explosives were claimed to constitute a humane form of power. Since the state was the chief source of inhumanity and immorality, according to some terrorists, the quicker it was destroyed the better for humanity – even though some people were killed or harmed in the process.

Last, super-explosives were seen to impart a mystical, magical kind of power – useful at least to charm the audience and perhaps to create an apocalyptic breakthrough to a new millennium.

The threat potential and tactical applications of dynamite were often greatly exaggerated by both terrorists and defenders.

Reference

Crenshaw, M. (1990) 'The Logic of Terrorism: Terrorist Behaviour as a Product of Strategic Choice' in Reich, W. (ed.) *Origins of Terrorism: Psychologies, Ideologies, Theologies, States of Mind*, New York: Cambridge University Press and Woodrow Wilson International Center for Scholars.

E

East African Embassy Bombings

These occurred on 7 August 1998 at the US Embassies in Nairobi, Kenya and Dar Es Salaam, Tanzania. The Americans indicted **Osama Bin Laden** and fourteen others for the attack. Since early-1998 he had been 'planning to terrorise the enemies of God' by bombing. This was certainly achieved in that year by the **Al Qaeda** members. A truck bomb exploded in Kenya killing 213 people and injuring over 4,500, while in Tanzania 11 were killed and 85 injured (Mylroie, 2001).

The Americans made retaliatory strikes on the El Shifa Pharmaceutical Plant in Khartoum, Jordan (which the **USA** believed had the capability to manufacture VX Nerve Gas). Raids were also made on Bin Laden's positions in **Afghanistan** but some bombs fell in **Pakistan**. There was no proof of state-sponsorship but links could be established with Bin Laden's threats and the crisis over weapons inspection in **Iraq** and the on-the-ground preparations for bombing loose networks of Muslim extremists had come together in a very effective manner, and proved that any US interests anywhere in the world could be targeted. Basically the role of states is usurped by shadowy entities (Mylroie, 2001).

Reference

Mylroie, L. (2001) *Study of Revenge: The First World Trade Center Attack and Saddam Hussein's War against America*, Washington, DC: The AEI Press.

East Timor

Following the April 1974 revolution in Portugal, several political groups manoeuvred for power in the small Portuguese colony of East Timor. After a short **civil war**, the left-wing Frente Revolucionária Timorense de Libertação e Independência (FRETILIN) proclaimed independence on 28 November 1975.

On 7 December, East Timor was invaded by Indonesian troops who expelled Fretilin from the capital, Dili. Guerrilla fighting continued, even though East Timor was formally annexed by Indonesia on 14 August 1976, and Fretilin was able to survive repeated Indonesian offensives. Negotiations took place between FRETILIN and the Indonesian authorities in March 1983, but fighting was renewed in August 1983, following the ambush of a group of Indonesian soldiers.

Casualty figures on both sides are unknown. Indonesia has long claimed that resistance to its occupation is insignificant while the East Timorese claim that a 'hot' war is under way between Indonesian regulars and Fretilin guerrillas.

Indonesia consistently feared that a successful independent government in a small state in the midst of its far-flung island territory would set an example for parts of the country beset by secessionist rumblings.

Indonesia's denial of strong resistance from the East Timorese was challenged by photos and tape recordings smuggled out by guerrillas, which showed that the ceasefire took place in 1983. Fretilin forces were organised into companies and operated in ten military zones in the central and eastern districts. There is evidence that the most wanted of the guerrillas were still fighting. There were new names in the leadership, including veterans from the first phase of the war, who rejoined the guerrillas after having surrendered to the Indonesians in 1979. Indonesian activity was focused in the east, where the strategy since 1983 was to build a cordon across the island to contain the guerrillas.

In 1986 Fretilin sought closer ties with the Timor Democratic Union (UDT), and formed a co-ordinating body, the National Convergence.

Throughout the 1990s Indonesian occupation and repression continued in East Timor. It was internal disorder in the country that forced the leaders to change their attitude to East Timor. Indonesia was determined to hold the stand at all costs due to its mineral reserves especially the oil and natural gas in Timorese territorial waters. Change began in 1998 with a new regime in Indonesia, but it was not until 2002 after elections that full independence came to the area.

Reference

Carey, P. (1996) 'East Timor: Third World Colonialism and the Struggle for National Identity', *Conflict Studies*, no. 293/294, (October/November), London: RISCT.

Eco-Terrorism

Environmental militants have made 'eco-terrorism' a growing concern in many Western democracies in the last two decades. Eco-terrorists are groups and individuals that commit terrorist acts related to ecological and environmental issues. The Earth Liberation Group made their presence felt with a variety of attacks including damage at an American ski resort in 1996 which caused $12 million damage, in order to protest at the destruction of a forest habit that was the home of the lynx.

In the case of radical ecology, the borderline between environmentalism and terrorism is crossed once it is believed that the salvation of the planet depends on the destruction of civilisation. The history of radical eco-terrorism goes back to 1980

when a group of militants in the USA decided that drastic action was needed in view of the imminent destruction of nature. They have advocated the destruction of dams in environmentally sensitive areas or the opposing of their building. Bridges, transmission lines and towers and electrical power transformers have been dynamited and logging equipment destroyed (Laqueur, 2001). In some areas environmentalism became a 'fashion' enticing the trendy and the militant; which in some ways diluted the eco-terrorists' central aim of saving nature by destroying industrial civilisation.

References

Hamilton, L. C. (1978) *Ecology of Terrorism: A Historical and Statistical Study*, Boulder, CO: University of Colorado.
Laqueur, W. (2001) *The New Terrorism: Fanaticism and the Arms of Mass Destruction*, London: Phoenix Press.
Simon, J. D. (1994) *The Terrorist Trap: America's Experience with Terrorism*, Bloomington, IN: Indiana University Press.

Further Reading

Savage, J. A. (1986) 'Radical Environmentalists: Sabotage in the Name of Ecology', *Business and Society Review* (summer), pp. 35–37.

Efficacy of Terrorism

To some people and nations terrorism works. Terrorism without efficacy would be only an expression of some destructive pathology. By definition terrorism works when the target of terrorism acts in such a manner that it either loses public support for its political position or it lessens its own political capabilities. Terrorism is the strategy of the weak. If those wanting to weaken a hated political authority were strong, they would not use terrorism as their main strategy because successful terrorism depends entirely upon the actions of the target. The target, in effect, has control of the situation. If those wanting to weaken a hated political authority are strong, they will use strategies for which the outcome is more within their own control. If successful terrorism depends on the target's action, then to explain successful terrorism one has to study the behaviour of the target and not the behaviour of the terrorists.

Targets can take responses that will weaken their political authority and give credence to the terrorist – namely, over-reaction, power deflation, failed repression of moderates, appeasement of moderates, and massive intimidation. Key variables can explain each of the five responses – the target's perception of self, of the terrorists and the relative capabilities between self and terrorists.

Over-reaction by a target, whether subject to regime or insurgent terrorism, is a familiar pattern of behaviour. The loss of public support is inevitable – and the target is seen to have acted to transform a country's political situation to a military one. If the target over-reacts with ostentatious protective measures, it magnifies the political stature and threat of the terrorists. Over-reactions can result in the target lessening its own capabilities. Counter-terrorism can be very expensive in money, attention, equipment and labour. Over-reaction usually entails ever-greater costs. When **insurgents** are the target, regime terrorism denotes that it is the regime that is weak. The regime then uses terrorism to provoke the opposition to over-react, to use formidable state measures so as to reduce its popular support, or to deplete the force capabilities of the insurgents. Over-reaction is made more likely when the target sees itself as powerful and able to inflict a lesson upon so unworthy a foe.

A target that is incapable of responding to terror will find public support decreases and its capabilities and confidence to fight terrorism will recede. If either a regime or insurgent group cannot protect its people, then it will lose legitimacy. The same result occurs when terrorists can choose the timing and victims of their strikes without hindrance, and then successfully collect ransom, release prisoners, have manifestos read or printed in the media, destroy symbols of state authority or injure or kill victims. Since the function of political authorities centres on protecting people and controlling the policy-making process, those authorities who fail in these tasks lose their legitimacy as authorities. The more failures, the more their power deflates. Terrorists are serious, dedicated fighters who

skilfully match the target's action with spectacular reaction. The terrorists create situations where options for actions all have greater costs than benefits. The first difficulty may be identifying and finding the terrorists. Usually the anti-terrorist service is hampered by a public which gives the terrorists sanctuary and anonymity.

The terrorists' target chooses to attack not only the terrorists but the moderate, non-violent opposition as well. If the target is a regime, it can ban political parties, institute censorship, increase surveillance, arrest and incarcerate protectors and even kill moderates as an example to others of the costs of opposition. If the target is an insurgent group, it can kidnap, bomb, and assassinate the moderates, both in the regime and in the non-violent opposition to the regime. Moderates conclude that moderation is untenable and to protect themselves from the target they go to the side of the original terrorists, usually as the lesser of two evils.

Vigorous political reforms, which appease moderates, alienate the avid supporters of the old order. These supporters can move into the camp of the irreconcilable opposition. In the 1980s, for example, when Prime Minister Pierre Trudeau made major reforms on behalf of French Canadians on the issue of language and political appointments, a substantial number of English-speaking Canadians considered these actions as nothing more than outright appeasement of the Front de Libération du Québec (FLQ). Concessions seemed to be a reward for planting bombs and blowing up Canadians. Reforms remove the injustices that stimulated the terrorism in the first place. Removing grievances will not end terrorism, but it isolates the radical and habitual terrorists from the mass of the people who do not like the risks of disorder and violence, especially if they bear them for no apparent cause.

While the causes of terrorism, that is of the terrorist's behaviour, are largely sociological, the success or failure of terrorism, which is determined by the target's behaviour is largely dependent on psychological factors. Terrorists must know or manipulate the target's psychological perceptions to induce it to act in the way it is predisposed to act. Successful terrorism changes the relative capability of the contestants. The target is weakened and the terrorist strengthened. Political strategies are always dependent upon relative capabilities. A large moderate, non-violent opposition movement in tandem with a terrorist movement forces the target to deal with the issues behind the opposition. Repression radicalises and militarises the moderates. The only other option is to appease the moderates via reforms. Targets who usually avoid using strategies of violence are forced to reform, while targets that like violence will not be moved to reform by non-violent protests.

Reference

White, J. R. (1998) *Terrorism: An Introduction*, London: Wadsworth Publishing.

Further Reading

Crenshaw, M. (ed.) (1995) *Terrorism in Context*, University Park: Pennsylvania State University Press.

Smylie, Robert F. (1988) 'Terrorism: Probing the Dynamics', *Christian Society*, vol. 78 (May–June), pp. 6–36.

Egypt

The Arab Republic of Egypt is a 'democratic and socialist state' with a limited system of party pluralism. The franchise was restricted in 1978, specifying that the right to belong to political parties and engage in political activities did not apply to those who had been involved in political corruption before the 1952 revolution or to those convicted of political offences who had subjected the national unity or social peace to danger.

The Muslim Brotherhood has been the most powerful opposition group against the regime, and its Islamic fundamentalism has been supported by many small militant groups intent upon destroying the state's leadership, one of them being responsible for the death of President Sadat in 1981. Communist and other left-wing groups have been involved in acts of violence protesting against the Camp David Agreements with Israel of 1978. Some former politicians and military personnel had called for the abandonment of Egypt's pro-Western

policies and a return to close relations with the **Soviet Union**.

In its sixty years of existence, the Muslim Brotherhood has had a chequered history of banning and rehabilitation at the hands of many governments. For example, the Wafdist government legalised the Brotherhood in 1951; the Neguib government ordered its dissolution in 1954 and then restored it a few months later. President Neguib was then deposed by Nasser in late 1954 after it was alleged that he had been involved in a conspiracy by the Brotherhood. Many members of the Brotherhood were condemned to death or imprisoned. In 1964 an amnesty was declared and many Brotherhood members were released. In order to counter the influence of communists, a number of Brotherhood members were appointed to official posts and some played a leading role in anti-government plots. Others were accused of plotting to assassinate Nasser – and death sentences or imprisonment resulted.

In the late 1960s, the Brotherhood was revived in Egypt and President Sadat from 1970 gradually came to regard it as a natural ally against the Nasserite socialists and communists. Sadat's pro-Western policies led to renewed opposition by all Islamic fundamentalist organisations, including the Brotherhood, who harshly criticised the President's policies and offered a detailed political alternative based on Islamic Law. Considerable support came from the universities and its influence was further strengthened by the social disruption caused by the increasing westernisation of Arab countries, the growing strength of the Arabs through oil wealth and later the Islamic revolution in Iran.

After Sadat's assassination in 1981, hundreds of Islamic fundamentalists were arrested and suspected Brotherhood sympathisers purged from the armed forces. Over the last three to four years, security clampdowns on Islamic fundamentalists have tended to be concentrated on an array of smaller groupings rather than on the Brotherhood in particular. The government appears to have adopted a policy of encouraging the Brotherhood as a moderate alternative to the more extreme fundamentalist groups.

Another strong fundamentalist group is the Repentance and Holy Flight, which is sizeable, highly organised and spread horizontally and vertically throughout Egyptian society. Their goal is to topple Egypt's present social order and to establish an Islamic order. There are up to 5,000 active members and about 300 of these are professionally trained, heavily armed and financed by a foreign power.

The Egyptian Communist Party, although illegal maintained close relations with other pro-Soviet Communist parties and has posed a security threat to Egyptian governments in periods when the latter have pursued a Western-aligned foreign policy.

In 1986 dissident servicemen on National Service caused considerable violence and panic in Cairo in which over 100 deaths were reported. The current leader, President Mubarak, has many dissident elements opposed to him.

In 1989 the Egyptian leader proposed arranging an Israeli-Palestinian dialogue with no prior conditions. It condemned Iraqi action in Kuwait in 1990, but there was opposition to the war against Iraq. An Anti-Terrorism law was passed in the early-1990s in response to the increasing violence from Islamic fundamentalists. However by the mid-1990s increasing attempts were made against the lives of foreign tourists culminating in the deaths of over 60 tourists near Luxor in November 1997, killed by a group of fundamentalists. The action was aimed at curtailing tourism – one of the mainstays of the Egyptian economy.

Reference

Hourani, A. (1997) *A History of the Arab People's*, Cambridge, MA: Belknap Press.

Further Reading

Ezeldin, A. G. (1987) 'Terrorism and Political Violence: An Egyptian Perspective', *Studies in Terrorism*, Chicago, IL: Office of International Criminal Justice.

Reeve, S. (1999) *The New Jackal: Ramzi Yousef, Osama Bin Laden and the Future of Terrorism*, Boston, MA: Northeastern University Press.

El Salvador

The root of the social conflict which led to the outbreak of open **civil war** in El Salvador in 1979 went back over a hundred years. Between 1879 and 1882 three successful land reforms abolished collective ownership of the land from which the peasants scraped a subsistence living, and substituted a free market in land and labour. The result was the emergence of an economy based upon the export of coffee, and an extremely unequal pattern of land ownership. It made possible the creation of a powerful landed elite usually known as 'the fourteen families', which controlled a densely settled peasantry. Many confrontations occurred between the peasantry and the elite.

Between 1961 and October 1979, El Salvador was ruled by the army dominated Partido de Conciliaçion Nacional (PNC). There was a growth in the urban working class, and growing pressure on densely settled land. There was a dramatic increase in the number of landless peasants, from 12 per cent of the population in 1961 to 65 per cent by 1981.

There was a growth in political mobilisation and electoral competition. The 1970s started with the army asserting that it was not prepared to lose power through the ballot box, and this process of radicalisation continued throughout the decade. The Union Nacional Opositora (UNO) was founded in 1972, uniting the social-democratic Movimiento Nacional Revolucionario (MNR) founded in 1968 and the Union Nacional Democratica, a front for the banned Partido Comunista Salvadoreño (PCS) – against the military. In the 1977 elections fraud kept UNO out of power yet again, and substantial elements of the democratic opposition responded to the increasing repression and the blocking of all democratic change by deciding to take up arms against the regime. The relative complexity of the guerrilla alliance that emerged was explained by the diverse political origins of the various groups, and by the different stages at which they joined the armed struggle.

The communist PCS had been involved briefly in an unsuccessful guerrilla campaign during the early 1960s, from which it had drawn the lesson that it would be more profitable to pursue its goals through electoral alliances. But in 1970, a group led by Salvador Cayetano Carpio broke away from the RCS to form the first of the guerrilla groups, which emerged in 1972 as the Fuerzas Populares de Liberación – Farabundo Marti (FPL-FM), operating from a base in the North West (Marti) had been a leading member of the PCS, who had been executed during the 1932 uprising.

Radicalised urban supporters of the Christian Democrat PDC, disillusioned by the events of 1972, formed the Egercito Revolucionario Popular (ERP), which though initially committed to a Guevarist strategy of revolution carried out by a small guerrilla elite, subsequently adopted the aim of a mass insurrection. A dissident faction of the ERP formed the Fuerzas Armadas de la Resistencia Nacional (FARN) during the mid 1970s, and became increasingly committed to the creation of a broad opposition alliance. FARN quickly got involved with a series of lucrative kidnappings.

Yet another group emerged in 1979, the Partido Revolucionario de los Trabajadores Centro-Americanos, founded in 1975 and making its existence as a fighting force known in 1979. The army of guerrilla organisations was completed in 1980 when the PCS abandoned its stubborn faith in the electoral process and opted for armed struggle.

By the late 1970s the ruling military had continued to pursue its policy of repression, but also introduced a number of limited reforms. These contributed to a gathering crisis and provoked the development of a number of extreme right-wing political and paramilitary groups, determined to resist change. Under General Carlos Romero, the hardline right-wing military leader, and former head of a paramilitary rural security network, right-wing death squads such as the Union Guerrera Banca extended their operations, and the poor human rights record in El Salvador deteriorated.

A reformist coup led to a brief political honeymoon, but the security forces soon decided to block all reform. Reformers were driven out and replaced by individuals prepared to collaborate with the hard-line approach of the armed forces.

By 1980 the civil war was well underway. The unarmed opposition groups had been progressively radicalised by the brutal repression of peaceful political activities. The Archbishop of San Salvador, Oscar Romero, was murdered in his cathedral, and even his funeral was a violent incident resulting in many deaths. Faced with these outrages, the MNR and the Christian Democrats joined with other opposition groups linked to student and trade union organisations to form the Frente Democratico Revolucionario (FDR).

The PCS issued a joint communiqué with FPL and FARN in 1980, calling for an armed popular revolution. Guerrilla groups united on a permanent basis on 21 October with the formation of the Frente Farabundo Marti de Liberacion Nacional (FMLN). The group FDR pledged support to armed struggle when six of its leaders were assassinated later that year during severe repression that followed a series of general strikes it had organised.

Fighting increased, and allegations of direct Cuban and Nicaraguan backing for the FDR-FMLN led to a rapid increase in US military assistance to El Salvador. Bombing and sabotage increased and electricity supplies were badly affected.

Allegations were widespread that army units were massacring innocent peasants whom they suspected of sympathising with the guerrillas. While USA backing for the El Salvador government prevented the FDR-FMLN from successfully launching the all-out offensive which brought the Sandinistas victory in Nicaragua in 1979, the government forces were unable to prevent guerrillas from consolidating control of many areas, especially in the north and north-east.

Casualties of the war and murder campaigns of right-wing death squads mounted, and a systematic FDR-FMLN campaign of economic sabotage hit El Salvador severely – especially the attacks on bridges.

In spite of American assistance, the El Salvador army was unable to seize the strategic initiative and continued to react to guerrilla activities by launching large, clumsy and generally unsuccessful search and destroy operations which did little damage to guerrillas, but alienated peasant support. The army kept reoccupying previously-held guerrilla territory but with little effect on long-term progress in the war. On several other occasions, guerrilla units inflicted heavy casualties on government troops.

Napoleon Duarte – a long time UNO supporter – emerged as President in 1983. This improved the national image of El Salvador, and the US Reagan administration was able to counter criticism of its

Central American policy and continue the supply of equipment to the regime. President Duarte, backed by Washington, opened peace negotiations with the FDR-FMLN in 1984, but the depth of conflict made any permanent solution to the crisis unlikely.

By the mid-1980s, the guerrillas began to admit that power-sharing with the government and the initiation of reform from within was their only real hope of exerting political influence (Ellis, 1995). In 1993 the group which had mounted the major insurgency in 1980, the Frente de Farabundo Marti Liberacion Nacional (FMLN) disarmed itself and prepared for elections.

Reference

Ellis, J. (1995) *From the Barrel of a Gun*, London: Greenhill Books and Mechanicsburg, PA: Stackpole Books.

Further Reading

McClintock, M. (1985) *The American Connection*, vol. 1, State Terror and Popular Resistance in El Salvador, Oxford: Zed Press.

Entebbe Raid 1976

In June 1976 an Air France aircraft carrying 257 people, including 12 crew members, from Tel Aviv to Paris, was hijacked out of Athens by seven members of the Popular Front for the Liberation of Palestine (PFLP). Nationals from Britain, Canada, Cyprus, France, Greece, **Japan**, Jordan, **Lebanon**, New Zealand, and the **United States**, had boarded at Athens.

The plane landed in Benghazi for refuelling, and later flew to Entebbe in Uganda. The German leader of the hijackers announced that the hijackers were the Che **Guevara** Brigade of the PFLP. At Entebbe, the hijackers were provided with additional weapons by the Ugandans, who also guarded the hostages. Three additional terrorists joined the original seven here.

The release was demanded of 53 terrorists imprisoned in French, Israeli, Kenyan, Swiss, and German jails. The hijackers demanded that Air France bring these 'freedom fighters' to Entebbe

Airport to be exchanged with the hostages and the aircraft. None of the governments gave in to the demands. On 30 June, three days after the hijack, 47 elderly women, sick persons and children were released. The Israeli Cabinet then announced it was willing to negotiate for the release of some of the prisoners in return for the hostages. On 1 July the terrorists released 100 more hostages and it was learned from this group that a selection had taken place; the non-Jewish hostages were separated from the Israelis or persons of dual nationality. A day later, the terrorists increased their demands, adding five million dollars in compensation for the return of the Air France plane. The Israelis also learned from the tapped telephone of Wadi Haddad (the PFLP's planner of terrorist operations), in Somalia, that he had ordered the deaths of the Jewish hostages regardless of the response of the Israelis.

As a result of this message, planning began for 'Operation Thunderbolt', a daring rescue of the hostages. The plan called for flying several C130 Hercules transport planes 2,500 miles to Entebbe from Tel Aviv, securing the release of the hostages and returning to **Israel**. The Israelis claimed that no other nations were involved in the rescue operation, although many reports held that the Kenyans allowed the planes to refuel in Nairobi, and it was noted that the Israelis were allowed to treat the wounded there with a medical team of 33 doctors.

Because of superior intelligence, which many believed was derived from questioning the released hostages, overhead photography and Israeli agents on the scene in Entebbe, the Israeli mission was a success. Flying low to avoid hostile radar, the planes landed at a deserted section of the airfield. A black Mercedes led the first group of commandos who raced to the airport lounge where the hostages were being held. A second group set off bombs in another section of the field, creating a diversion. They later destroyed 11 MIGS of the Uganda air force so that their planes would not be attacked while returning to Israel. A third group secured the airfield entrance gate, holding off a squad of Ugandan soldiers. In the gun battle, the terrorists were taken by surprise and did not have a chance to shoot any of the hostages before they were all killed. A few hostages were killed or wounded when they stood up in the crossfire. The operation lasted 53 minutes, and all the planes returned successfully to Israel, with a stopover in Nairobi.

Reports conflicted regarding casualties. Israeli authorities believed seven of the terrorists were killed and three who were not present at the airfield escaped. Eleven other Israelis, civilian and military, were wounded. The Israelis believed 20 Ugandan soldiers were killed. Idi Amin, the Ugandan leader, later admitted that 20 Ugandan soldiers were killed.

Several governments condemned the Israeli action in press statements and during a United Nations debate. Amin later telephoned the Israelis to add his own congratulations, to request weapons and military spare parts and to announce that he had broken relations with the Palestinian terrorists. Idi Amin was ignored by the Israelis.

Amin was reported to have engaged in a widespread purge of individuals connected with the guarding of Entebbe airport, with some claims that 245 were killed by Amin's troops as punishment. Among those killed was Dora Bloch, an Israeli-British citizen who was left behind in a Ugandan hospital where she had been taken after choking on some meat at the airport lounge. It is believed she was strangled in hospital on the direct orders of Amin.

The identity of the terrorists was difficult to ascertain – although it is believed the initial leader was Wilfrid Bose, an associate of **Carlos** closely aided by high-ranking members of the military branch of the Popular Front for the Liberation of Palestine. It was learned that the terrorists had flown on Singapore Airlines to Athens from Kuwait and had taken their weapons on board the plane because they stayed in the Athens transit lounge, where they were not subjected to searches. Amin, who unsuccessfully demanded several million dollars in compensation, returned the Air France plane. The whole episode buoyed the Israelis' spirits and aided the domestic popularity of their government.

Reference

Maoz, Z. (1981) 'The Decision to Raid Entebbe: Decision Analysis Applied to Crisis Behaviour', *Journal of Conflict Resolution*, vol. 25, no. 4, pp. 677–707.

Further Reading

Akinsanya, A. A. (1982) 'The Entebbe Mission: A Case of Aggression?', *Journal of African Studies*, vol. 9 (summer), pp. 46–57.

Boyle, F. A. (1983) 'The Entebbe Hostage Crisis' in H. H. Han (ed.) *Terrorism, Political Violence and World Order*, Lanham, MD: University Press of America, pp. 559–602.

Stevenson, W. and Uri, D. (1976) *Ninety Minutes at Entebbe*, New York: Bantam Books.

Environmental Influences in the Growth of Terrorism

Terrorism, an age-less phenomenon, has begun to exhibit a new energy and a new dimension.

The new energy is the emergence of a second generation of antagonists in protracted conflicts, whose unusual psychological experience and life-long rage have altered the focus and calibre of political violence in the Middle East. The new dimension is religious extremism, which has moved into a second, more ominous phase in the region since the 1979 Iranian revolution. It is no longer exclusively Islamic.

New trends were visible in **Lebanon**, where the years of civil strife were increasingly being played out in car bombings, kidnappings, and other indiscriminate violence.

The spate of attacks on Israeli troops and settlers on the West Bank are the work not of trained **Palestine Liberation Organisation** cadres, but of local youth who had grown up under years of Israeli occupation and who were acting on their own initiative.

At least four factors come together to produce terrorists among a generation that has known nothing but bloodshed and enmity. Psychologists call this is the 'rejuvenation' of violence.

(1) An environment of conflict makes it difficult for normal educational, familial, and environmental exposure to suppress instincts of aggression in children. Instead, those instincts go unchecked or are further encouraged by the violence.

(2) Those who grow up in conflict consider violence

a justifiable means of expression, not a last resort as their parents view it. They define justice and power differently from their parents, often by the calibre of a gun.

(3) The sense of being a victim is conditioned, since the second generation feels it is blameless for the conflict's outbreak. And a victim has special rights in the fight for survival.

(4) The normal dynamic of adolescence – the moulding of an independent identity through rebellion against authority – becomes closely associated with the political situation. Carrying a gun or being inducted into a militia is often a rite of manhood.

See also: Children.

Ethics

Ideological issues come to the fore. The Left have concerns about the effects on target audiences and wish to attract and appeal to sympathisers. They wish to coerce and intimidate defectors, rurals and the authorities. Selective targeting is popular in order to avoid indiscriminate slaughter.

The Right aim to undermine public confidence, spread violence and force firm and repressive government. Indiscriminate slaughter in the past was popular, but over the past few years this has changed. They are national socialist rather than conservative and overlap and sometimes co-operate with the Left.

Islamic religious fundamentalists see it as their duty to kill those who block the spread of Islam. Religious fervour can stifle conscience or compassion; and there is little concern with the effects of outside opinion.

Nationalists such as the PLO and IRA arouse supporters, provoke government repression, intimidate defectors, rivals, police, witnesses, juries and gain publicity for a cause (local and international) and have some concern for the public image on the international stage. They see themselves as soldiers with no guilt feelings and the killing is often cold and impersonal.

It is virtually impossible to get an agreed code of conduct in international relations on an international basis. Nevertheless, various agreements on

the laws of war do establish important principles on the question of terrorism including the immunity of civilians from direct attack. Confusion existed in international organisations on how to view national liberation struggles and whether they are a legitimate means for dispossessed people to pursue.

Ethics and the rule of law on the issue of the phenomena of terrorism point to the importance of avoiding, wherever possible a resort to violence and of focussing on the laws of war as they affect the targeting of civilians, the proper treatment of prisoners, of challenging fanatics and stopping the self-defeating destructiveness of terrorist action.

On codes of ethics, terrorists either claim indifference or exemption to them. Yet terrorism is the antithesis of the rule of law and a basic threat to **human rights**. Terrorists refuse to recognise the legitimate legality of the courts.

Terrorism can be defined as a kind of revolution crime analogous to a war crime. Terrorists and their propagandists have nothing but contempt for conventional morality and legal norms; and they defiantly reject constraints; and the crimes committed by them are regarded as the execution of a higher revolutionary justice. They see their acts as heroic, and the civilised world see them as cowardly and barbaric.

See also: Freedom Fighters.

References

Roberts, A. (1989) 'Ethics, Terrorism and Counter-Terrorism', *Terrorism and Political Violence*, vol. 1, no. 1 (January), pp. 48–69.

Wilkinson, P. (1989) 'Ethical Defences of Terrorism: Defending the Indefensible', *Terrorism and Political Violence*, vol. 1, no. 1, pp. 7–20.

Further Reading

Adams, R. (1989) 'Ethics, Terrorism and Counter-Terrorism', *Terrorism and Political Violence*, vol. 1, no.1 (January), pp. 48–69.

Goertzel, T. (1988) 'The Ethics of Terrorism and Revolution', *Terrorism*, vol. 11, no. 1, pp. 1–12.

Hoffman, B. (1989) 'The Contrasting Ethical Foundations of Terrorism in the 1980's', *Terrorism* and Political Violence, vol. 1, no. 3 (July), pp. 361–377.

Schmid, A. P. (1989) 'Terrorism and the Media: The Ethics of Publicity', *Terrorism and Political Violence*, vol. 1, no. 4 (October), pp. 539–565.

Zoppo, C. (1982) 'The Moral Factor in Interstate Politics and International Terrorism', in Rapoport, D. C. and Alexander, Y. (eds) *The Rationalisation of Terrorism*, Frederick, MD: University Publications of America, pp. 136–153.

Ethnic Cleansing and Conflicts

Basically, ethnic cleansing is the removal of members of an ethnic community from a particular country. It can be a government policy or the government can ignore the issue of ethnic cleansing. The practice infers racial superiority and historical justice (Combs and Slann, 2002). In the 1990s in the former Yugoslavia Croatians removed Serbs from the eastern part of the country, and both Serbs and Croats attempted to rid Bosnia of Muslims. In the African states of Rwanda and Burundi Hutus murdered over half a million Tutsi people.

Ethnic conflicts, especially when linked with territorial disputes, are very difficult to resolve because of psychological biases. For example, it is hard to explain why people's loyalties are sometimes to their ethnic group and sometimes to a multi-ethnic nation.

Ethnic groups share ancestral, language, cultural or religious ties, and a common identity. Ethnic groups form the basis for nationalist sentiments. Territorial control is closely tied to the aspirations of ethnic groups for statehood. State borders can deviate from the location of ethnic communities (Goldstein, 1999).

Other ethnic groups lack any home state, such as Kurds – they share a culture and aspire to create a state Kurdistan, but they are distributed across four nations – **Iraq**, **Iran**, **Syria** and **Turkey**, all of which are hostile to a Kurdish state. When ethnic populations are minorities in territories controlled by rural ethnic groups they may be driven from their land or terminated.

Ethno-centralism or in-group bias is the tendency to see one's own group very favourably.

Based on such an in-group bias, ethno-centralism can bring about intolerance and dehumanisation of an out-group such as in Bosnian and Rwandan **genocide**. Dehumanisation can lead to the stripping of human rights.

These conflicts are hard to resolve because a person inflamed with hatred of an enemy is willing to lose value in absolute terms in order to deprive the enemy of value as well. Therefore such conflicts drag on without resolution for generations.

See also: Genocide; Rwanda.

References

Combs, C. C. and Slann, M. (2002) *Encyclopaedia of Terrorism*, New York: Facts on File Inc.

Corrodo, R. R. and Evans, R. (1988) 'Ideological Terrorism in Western Europe', in M. Stohl (ed.) *The Politics of Terrorism*, New York: Marcel Dekker, pp. 373–444.

Goldstein, J. S. (1999) *International Relations* (3rd edn), Harlow, Essex: Longman.

Harff, B. (1986) 'Genocide as State Terror' in M. Stohl and G. A. Lopez (eds), *Government Violence and Repression*, Westport, CT: Greenwood Press pp. 165–68.

Further Reading

Carment, D., James, P. and Puchala, D. (eds) (1998) *Peace in the Midst of War: Preventing and Managing International Ethnic Conflicts*, Columbia: University of South Carolina Press.

Dutter, L. E. (1987) 'Ethno-Political Activity and the Psychology of Terrorism', *Terrorism*, vol. 10, no. 3, pp. 145–163.

European Union (EU)

The European Convention on the Suppression of Terrorism signed in 1978 was the first agreement reached by members of the European community in reaction to the rise of terrorism.

This measure was adopted by the Council's Committee of Ministers at deputy level in 1976, formally concluded in 1977 and came into force in 1978.

The aim of the Convention was to facilitate the extradition and prosecution of perpetrators of terrorist acts even though such acts might be politically motivated and be excluded from extradition arrangements.

Act 1. Covered extradition and which offences could not be regarded as political.
Act 2. Covered other offences that were not seen as political.
Act 3. Looked at the provisions of extradition treaties.
Act 8. Stated that contracting states shall afford one another the widest measure of mutual assistance in criminal matters.
Act 13. Stated that states could refuse extradition in respect of any political offence.
Acts 14–16. Covered opt out clauses and details of other signatures, ratifications and declarations.

The European Commission being a federation of European democratic governments has always believed that terrorism threatens human rights and fundamental freedoms. Terrorism exploits legal loopholes arising from geographical limits of investigations, and has extensive logistical and financial support. Given that there are no borders within the EU and that the right of free movements of people is guaranteed new measures in the fight against terrorism must be taken. The EU has become aware over the past few years of the need to draw up legislative proposals to combat terrorism and to strengthen police and judicial co-operation.

In September 2001 the European Parliament adopted a resolution concerning the role of the EU in combating terrorism, calling on the Council to adopt a framework decision to abolish formal extradition procedures, to adopt the principle of mutual recognition of decisions on criminal matters in particular establishing minimum rules at European levels relating to the constituent elements and penalties in the field of terrorism.

The **United Kingdom** legislation, *Terrorism Act 2000*, is the largest piece of terrorist legislation in the EU member states. Terrorism is defined as meaning:

'the use or threat of action where the use or threat is designed to influence the government or to intimidate the public or a section of the public'; and 'the use or threat is made for the purpose of advancing a political, religious or ideological cause'. That action includes among others 'serious violence against a person', 'serious damage to property' or 'creating a serious risk to the health or safety of the public or a section of the public'.

(European Communities Commission, 2001)

The EU is keen to adopt a framework decision for the approximation of the sub-structure laws of the member states, to ensure that terrorist offences will be punished by effective, proportionate and dissuasive criminal penalties. It will facilitate police and judicial co-operation, as common definitions of offences should overcome the obstacles of double criminality.

In EU terms terrorist offences can be defined as offences internationally committed by an individual or group against one or more countries, their institutions or people with the aim of intimidating them and seriously altering or destroying the political, economic or social structures of a country. To a far greater extent than ordinary offences, terrorist acts usually damage the physical or psychological integrity of individuals or groups, their property or their freedom.

The EU is aware that the important work performed by international organisations in particular the **United Nations** (UN) and the Council of Europe (CE) has to be complemented with a new and closer approximation in the EU.

The actions of the EU over **Chechnya** in 2000 made the world aware that it has a key role in speaking out against terrorism. In April 2000 as the new Chechen guerrilla war raged on in the foothills of the **Caucasus**, the EU states, after some prevarication suspended the voting rights of **Russia** in the Council of Europe. The members placed democracy and human rights to Russia above new trading or financial concessions in the IMF and other world financial institutions (Cooley, 2001).

The EU has been working with united pressure to target terrorist finances, and imposing financial sanctions over different national jurisdictions i.e. on the Milosevic regime in Serbia in 1999. However, the power of the EU is not helped by the fact that the security of Europe is the responsibility of many different organisations (Halliday, 2002).

Within the EU anti-Muslim prejudice and assertions have become quite common; and many measures are set up against the background of rising Islamic fundamentalism. In recent years Britain has supported its fellow EU member states in terms of extradition, the freeing of assets, and the liaison with other anti-terrorist investigation teams across Europe. However, the United Kingdom will only agree to extradite suspects to the **USA** if the Americans will provide an assurance that no execution will follow.

Immediately after the events of **September 11** the EU put into action an arrangement for partnership with the USA covering police and judicial co-operation. On the diplomatic front efforts were made to improve and co-ordinate European security and defence policies to freeze terrorists assets. Humanitarian aid was offered to **Afghanistan**; measures were brought in to improve security at airports and economic and financial measures included in particular a strengthening of laws relating to money-laundering. With the ever-present threat of weapons of mass destruction being developed by certain states, the EU enacted measures to counter bio-terrorist threats.

One of the former alleged 'rogue' states, **Libya**, has been keen to improve economic relations with Europe, and in order to try to get economic sanctions lifted has been co-operating with the West over the **Lockerbie** trial including offers of compensation to the victim's relatives.

The EU is mindful of its democratic ideals and has brought in safeguards for anti-terrorist legislation. Anti-terrorist policy has to be under the control of civil authorities; all anti-terrorist operations have to be within the law; and any special powers authorised should only be for a limited period. Problems can still arise in that each state is proud of its own national laws and perhaps popularly mistrustful of their neighbours' political and legal systems. EU members naturally get upset if they feel that a neighbouring state is shielding terrorists they wish to have extradited. Nations like to see, if possible, the police role separate from the military, in internal security against terrorism. **Europol** and **Interpol** are there to assist if necessary.

Over three-quarters of the member states of the EU have agreed to be signatories of the 1977 Convention on the Suppression of Terrorism (Wilkinson, 2002). A high number of terrorist attacks still occur in the EU and the Interior Ministers meet regularly to discuss practical multi-lateral co-operation including such measures as the transportation of nuclear fuel.

Members of the European Union struggled with obtaining security without frontiers. Their work led to the Schengen Agreement signed in 1990 by France, Germany and the Benelux countries to open frontiers; and was a path-finder for the single European Act which came into force on 1 January 1993. This Act opened the internal frontiers of Europe (similar to the USA) but the differences in languages, legal systems and attitudes would remain. There is a free movement of persons, goods, capital and services. The external frontiers of the EU were made tighter. The main sources of threat are indigenous terrorists operating across frontiers i.e. the IRA and ETA terrorists with pan-European or wider aims; international terrorists; and single-issue groups such as environmentalists and animal rights activists. Illegal immigrants could try to come in large numbers; international drug traffickers and other smugglers can pursue their aims, and other international criminal gangs i.e. **Mafia** and Triads are taking advantage.

Dilemmas in this move to a united Europe are considerable. Easy entry can occur across the Mediterranean coast, and there, terrorists can merge easily among the immigrant population. Safe houses can be provided by sympathisers in any EU country. The difficulty is how to control without eroding civil liberty.

Within the judicial system of Europe action has been taken against terrorists with varying degrees of success. On the issue of detection and arrest anti-terrorist special squads have used varying methods i.e. supergrass informants in Northern **Ireland**; requiring proof of identity at the scene of a crime (France); and telephone tapping and apartment block searches occur throughout the EU.

On detention and arrest, ten days are allowed before charge in Spain and seven days in the UK. There is a 'Right to Silence' and taping of interrogation (audio and video) and there can be a delay caused by intimidation of witnesses and jurors. Trials of suspected terrorists can be heard by judges and assessors as in France and the Netherlands; by a single judge as occurs in Northern Ireland; and by banning lawyers who disrupt trials or who have assisted terrorist activities as in Germany.

On the issue of goods, effective spot checks have been needed to detect guns, explosives and drugs (abroad police co-operation in this area has been improved). Illegal money can easily be transferred to terrorist organisations – this was reorganised at an early stage after 1992 with the monitoring and recording of electronic money transactions. The police have required access to bank accounts and power to seize funds pending investigations. Much has been achieved in this area, but judicial safeguards have to be built into the system. 'Shell Companies' or those with falsified accounts have attracted police attention, to stop criminals obtaining illegal funds. Drug seizures have taken place at border crossings and police and customs have the power to conduct spot checks. Assets illegally acquired have to be forfeited.

With all these measures, civil liberties have to be safeguarded and there have to be the means to prevent or detect abuse. Police computers are being used to automatically record breaches. Every spot check has to be recorded, identifying the police officer and the person checked. Identity cards (ID cards) have been a tendentious issue. The British, Dutch and Irish have no ID cards, most other countries do. Germany was one of the first countries to adopt a machine-recordable system of ID cards, and these increasingly have been developed to activate police national computers. Furthermore, machine readable Euro-passports and visas have been developed. Harmonisation of ID, passport and visa systems have developed in a progressive way. A growing need has been seen for anti-impersonation data such as digital fingerprints.

Over the last five years problems have arisen over temporary immigrants and terrorist asylum seekers: the arrests of people of North African origin in the UK has been a cause of concern i.e. Algerians arrested in London and Manchester in January 2003 accused of manufacturing the deadly poison ricin which is obtained from the seeds of castor-oil plants.

Bilateral co-operation on intelligence matters developed slowly until September 11, since when various measures have been put into place – jealousies and rivalries have been set aside. National police and intelligence computers have been linked. On policy matters, good bilateral co-operation and hot pursuit arrangements have been agreed i.e. regarding the **Channel Tunnel**, French and British officers are working in each other's countries near the tunnel.

National armies are being developed by member nations, in the area of anti-terrorist commanders. Joint training and liaison has been developed and there has been an exchange of specialist equipment and techniques. Key personnel in each country have been used for operations where appropriate.

Two of the most important conventions have been adopted in the last five years. In December 1997 the Convention for the Suppression of Terrorist Bombings provided that any person commits an offence if that person unlawfully or intentionally delivers, places, discharges or detonates an explosive or other lethal device in, into or against a place of public use, a state or government facility, a public transport system or an infrastructure facility with the intent to cause extensive destruction and major economic loss.

In December 1999 the Convention for the Suppression of Financing Terrorism stated that it was an offence to provide or collect funds, directly or indirectly, unlawfully or intentionally, with the intent to use such funds or knowing that they will be used to commit any act included within the scope of earlier Conventions (EC Commission, 2001).

See also: United Kingdom: Northern Ireland.

References

Cooley, J. K. (2001) *Unholy Wars: Afghanistan, America and International Terrorism*, London: Pluto Press.

Day, A. J. (1986) *Treaties and Alliances of the World*, Harlow: Longman.

European Community Commission – Proposal for a Council: Framework on Combating the Terrorism, Brussels, September 2001.

Halliday, F. (2002) *Two Hours That Shook the World*

September 11, 2001: Causes and Consequences, London: Saqi Books.

Wilkinson, P. (2002) Terrorism versus Democracy: The Liberal State Response, London and Portland, OR: Frank Cass.

Further Reading

Lodge, J. (1988a) 'The European Community and Terrorism' in H. H. Tucker (ed.) Combating the Terrorists, New York: Facts on File, pp. 45–74.

Lodge, J. (1988b) 'The European Community and Terrorism: From Principles to Concerted Action' in J. Lodge (ed.) The Threat of Terrorism, Brighton: Wheatsheaf Books, pp. 229–264.

Europol

A European Police Force (Europol) was established as a result of the Maastricht Treaty in 1992. Many types of crimes are covered in its remit, but terrorism was not added to Europol's list until 1998: it helps to facilitate the exchange of information about terrorist crime; it facilitates and participates in common analytical projects in relation to terrorism; it undertakes detached research projects into aspects of terrorist criminality; and creates and facilitates access to various central reference documents of relevance in combating terrorism. In fighting terrorism, joint investigation teams or task forces are co-operating between European Union member states and Europol. Facilitating better international co-operation is vital in fighting the war against terrorism (Taylor and Horgan, 2000).

Reference

Taylor, M. and Horgan, J. (eds) (2000) The Future of Terrorism, London: Frank Cass.

Extortion

Product extortion has increased rapidly in **Western Europe** and the **United States** since the 1970s. There is generally a high yield and low-risk provided the extortioner is not too greedy and has secured the means of receiving payment.

There are a number of dilemmas for any company subjected to extortion. Commercially and managerially it can be seen to be cheaper to pay and hush up and get rid of the problem quickly. Morally the company must maintain a publicly defensive position, and avoid failure to warn the public of possible risks, and failing to recall or destroy suspect stock. Possibly there can be long-term implications for the corporate image. Legally there is liability for failure to warn of a known risk, and there is a public policy of responsibility not to reward or encourage crime. The dilemma for the police is that they have the responsibility to protect the public from risk even though the threat may be a hoax. Publicity can inflict huge losses on the target company, but the police have the responsibility to make arrests and to prevent or deter future crime. So far mainly small-time criminals have been involved, but this could easily escalate to include criminal gangs and political groups.

The cost of product contamination and extortion can be enormous. In 1982 in the United States the pharmaceutical company Tylanol suffered a $500 million loss in profits; in Britain in 1984 the Mars confectionery company suffered a loss of sales of £15 million, a loss of profits of £2.5 million and had to destroy 3,000 tons of stock. A few months later, a confectionery company in **Japan** suffered a 43 per cent loss of sales in the first month after contamination of their product, followed by a disastrous fall in share prices. Extortionists threatened to contaminate beer and lager produced by the Heineken Company in 1984 and demanded £500,000. Supermarket chains throughout the world have occasionally suffered at the hands of extortionists.

In 1986 Tamil guerrillas alleged that potassium cyanide had been put in exported Sri Lankan tea. In 1989, minute traces of cyanide were discovered in Chilean grapes. Such people often work with limited resources, but are driven by the lure of money. They are keen to try and damage the export trade of a particular country or embarrass a government by placing poison or other substances in food or pharmaceutical products. The threat can result in significant financial losses for businesses as their products cannot be distributed (Simon, 1994).

See also: Businesses Targeted by Terrorists.

Reference

Simon, J. D. (1994) *The Terrorist Trap: America's Experience with Terrorism*, Bloomington: Indiana University Press.

Further Reading

Council of Europe. European Committee on Crime Problems (1986) *Extortions under Terrorist Threats*, Strasbourg: Council of Europe.

F

Fanon, Frantz

b. 1925; d. 1961

Frantz Fanon was born in Martinique and served in the French army during the Second World War. In 1954 he joined the Algerian Liberation Movement, after training as a psychiatrist. He edited the Group's newspaper and rapidly became a revolutionary theorist of some standing, and an exponent of terrorism. He was a prolific author on such subjects – his most widely read work being *The Wretched of the Earth*.

Fanon argued that violence directed against oppressors made native populations fearless and restored their self-respect. He argued that when people had taken part in national liberation struggles they would allow no one to set themselves up as 'liberators'.

He was a supreme advocate of violence to achieve one's end, and insisted on maintaining this view as the colonial system was a function of violence. Armed struggle was vital and liberation could only be achieved by force. Fanon was hostile to all aspects of imperialism, colonisation and Fascism.

Developing countries have used terrorism as the last resort to repudiate the core's economic, military and political dictatorship. Fanon firmly believed that peasants were capable of leading a violent revolution.

He believed that the intelligentsia and bourgeoisie played a part in the structures of terrorism, as they organised the 'confiscation' of natural resources from the **Third World**. He argued that

Imperialists had used the lumpen-proletariat against the natural liberation struggle. These were the amorphous social groups below the proletariat consisting of criminals and tramps.

Reference

Fanon, F. (1983) *The Wretched of the Earth*, London: Pelican Books.

Further Reading

Sonnleitner, M. (1987) 'Of Logic and Liberation – Fanon on Terrorism', *Journal of Black Studies*, vol. 17, no. 3 (March), pp. 287–304.

FARC

The Revolutionary Armed Force of Colombia (FARC) led by Manuel Marulanda and Jacobo Arenas started in 1964. These rural-based guerrilla movements were opposed by large landowners who organised armed and paid 'self-defence' groups. They conducted their activities in the 1970s; but in 1980 they reached an agreement which led to a ceasefire between them and to the adoption of political, social and economic reforms. In 1991 the government met with FARC and other guerrilla groups to discuss demobilisation of guerrillas, the subordination of the armed forces to civilian authority and the dismantling of paramilitary groups. Guerrilla fighters were encouraged to reintegrate into areas where they could exert political influence. The peace process, however, foundered about the time that many groups were involved with the burgeoning drugs trade: the most powerful being the Medellin Cartel, a drug trafficking ring headed by Pablo Escobar. He was killed in a police shoot out in late-1992. The Cali Cartel, an even more powerful ring, became active. FARC and other groups stepped up their activities against the government and opposition and attacked industrial, police and military facilities. Due to the actions of the drug cartels aid to **Colombia** was suspended and access was blocked to foreign financial sources. Since 1997 one million Colombians have been displaced from their homes in areas of conflict, mainly due to the activity of paramilitary groups. In 1998 between 40 and 80 soldiers died in confrontations with the FARC the worst loses in a long guerrilla campaign. It is estimated that guerrilla groups obtained an annual net income of $750 million, substantially more than that earned by coffee (the countries major export).

In February 2003 the group shot down a helicopter over the jungle. Its occupants were reported to be CIA operatives – two were killed and three possibly kidnapped. In September 2003 a group of tourists were taken hostage near a lost city in the jungle.

See also: Colombia.

Reference

TVI Report Profiles, 'Revolutionary Armed Forces of Colombia (FARC)', *TVI Report*, vol. 9, no. 1, pp. 5–7.

Fatwa

A fatwa is religious legitimacy for an act of self-martyrdom. **Osama Bin Laden** proclaimed in a fatwa against the **USA** in February 1998 that the 'world was at war'. He claimed that his acts were defensive since it was America who declared war on Muslims by its 'crimes and sins' committed in the Middle East. The USA in his view deserved to be targeted because it was the 'biggest terrorist in the world'.

The Western world first became aware of the meaning of fatwa in 1989, Salman Rushdie, a

Pakistan born author wrote a controversial novel *The Satanic Verses*, which the Ayatollah Khomeini denounced as blasphemous for its depiction of the life of the Prophet Mohammed. **Iran** condemned Rushdie to death in 1989 – he went into hiding in Britain – and offered a $1 million bounty for his assassination – the bounty was increased to $3 million several years later. Riots erupted in many Muslim countries over the publication of the book and a number of bookshops were bombed. When Rushdie tried to have his death sentence lifted by renouncing *The Satanic Verses* and claiming he had now converted to Islam, it had little effect on the Islamic extremists. The prevailing view in the Muslim world, was that if Rushdie was indeed now a Muslim, then he should prepare to die like a good Muslim (Simon, 1994).

The Sunni extremists who bombed the **World Trade Center**, New York, in 1993 obtained a fatwa from Sheikh Omar before planning their attack. The Islamic decrees issued by **Al Qaeda** illuminates the motivation of such martyrs to kill and their supreme indifference to death. The force of a fatwa depends entirely upon who pronounces it. In Islamic law an attack on an enemy has to be preceded by an Islamic decree. The role of a fatwa is to justify Al Qaeda's actions. When a recruit is inducted he agrees to pursue Al Qaeda's agenda and execute any order provided a fatwa justifying the action is cited.

Further Reading

Simon, J. D. (1994) *The Terrorist Trap: America's Experience with Terrorism*, Bloomington, IN: Indiana University Press.

Fear *see* Psychology of Terrorism: Fear

Federal Bureau of Investigation (FBI)

Founded as the Bureau of Investigation in 1908 it became the **FBI** in 1935. It was prominent in the campaign against organised crime in the 1930s and also against the anti-Communist activities of Joseph

McCarthy in the 1950s. It carries out investigations into possible breaches of federal law, especially those relating to national security.

The FBI only recently has started to collect data on terrorism in the USA. In 1993 in the New York area due to an informant being placed in a group of radical Islamic Fundamentalists, a bombing and assassination campaign was stopped.

Understandably the FBI has been reluctant (at least prior to **September 11**) to share information. Strict rules govern the FBI's ability to investigate potential (as distinct from known) terrorists. They may not be able to investigate millennium **cults** or white supremacist organisations unless a crime is about to be committed. Local police agencies have to adhere to their guidelines. Nevertheless the FBI has primary jurisdiction over the investigation of politically inspired terrorism occurring in the USA. The criminality of political terrorist activities falls into two broad categories: violent attacks designed to make a political statement; and illegal activities intended to gain whatever is necessary to allow the group to continue operating. The European presence of the FBI at **Lockerbie** in 1988 was very helpful, but as the FBI is a domestic law enforcement agency, the Scottish police were the lead investigative agency.

The FBI provides one of the most authoritative, official explanations of what is the new terrorism. The Terrorism Research Analytical Center (TRAC) of the National Security Division of the FBI prepares annual reports on Terrorism. The report in 1994 in the wake of the **World Trade Center** bombing characterised the new terrorism as International Radical Terrorism (Mylroie, 2001).

The Joint Terrorist Task Force is an FBI led organisation. It was formed in 1980 to pool the resources of the FBI and the New York Police Department. The Force was involved in trying to solve the first terrorist attack on the World Trade Center in 1993. The Force played a major part in tracking down Sheikh Omar who was charged and given a life sentence for the attempt to blow up the Trade Center. In the weeks after the attack they began to uncover evidence of how **Osama Bin Laden** had started plotting against the USA.

Ramzi Yousef one of the masterminds behind the plot to bomb the World Trade Center attack was eventually tracked down to a hotel in Islamabad in 1995.

See also: Cults; Millennial Violence.

Reference

Mylroie, L. (2001) *Study of Revenge: The First World Trade Center Attack and Saddam Hussein's War against America*, Washington, DC: The AEI Press.

Further Reading

Sessions, W. S. (1990) 'The FBI's Mission in Countering Terrorism', *Terrorism*, vol. 13, no. 1, pp. 1–6.

Webster, W. H. (1987) 'International Terrorism: The FBI's Response', *International Business Lawyer*, vol. 15, no. 2 (February), pp. 54–58.

Finance

The direct costs of terrorism are the economic damage due to bombings, armed assaults, arson and sabotage, the amount of ransom paid in hostage situations, currency losses due to thefts and extortion payments. One also has to take into account the flight of foreign capital from nations experiencing terrorist campaigns, as well as decisions not to invest in those countries in the first place. The opportunity costs for hostages, and opportunities lost while a given corporation consolidates its losses after an attack should also be included. The costs of security measures taken to prevent attacks is also high and must include the costs of metal detectors, sky-marshals, bodyguards, security training for corporation people and embassy staffs, as well as more intangible costs, such as randomly re-routing airline flights, ships, motorcades and home to office travel to evade attacks. Another intangible cost is the personal anxiety faced by victims and possible victims of attacks, as well as whatever anxieties are faced by the terrorists themselves. Finally, one can include the costs of all academic and governmental research on terrorism, as well as the costs of policy staffs assigned to develop national responses to terrorism.

Strategically, terrorist groups aspire to control the apparatus of state. As far as can be determined, no campaign of terrorism by itself has ever led to the fall of a government, although the independence of **Algeria** and **Israel** can be attributed in part to pressure on colonial authorities by the sustained attacks by the National Liberation Front and the Irgun respectively.

At a tactical level, terrorists have sought changes in the length of prison sentences, elimination of torture, or the outright release of specified political prisoners including members of their own groups. Money ransoms and extortion payments frequently occur.

Combating Terrorism Financing

Post-**September 11** the international armoury of responses to countering terrorist funding has been broadened by the **United Nations**' development of extended sanctions regimes against terrorism in general and **Al Qaeda** in particular; and by the provision of technical assistance to countries. Since September 11 over 160 countries and institutions have taken concrete action to freeze terrorist assets, and $112 million has been frozen worldwide. The **United Kingdom** has frozen the assets of over 100 organisations and over 200 individuals. In response to UN Security Resolutions particularly those targeting Al Qaeda and the Taliban, the UK froze a total of $100 million of terrorist assets (House of Commons, N. Ireland Affairs Committee 2001–02).

Terrorism comes with a price. The American authorities have put the cost of the planning and staging of the September 11 attacks at around $200,000. In the UK the City of London bomb in 1993 caused over £1 billion worth of damage to property yet cost only £3,000 to mount. Since the attacks in America, international action has been taken in an attempt to stop terrorist finances. Sanctions have been put in place to cut off money flows to individual terrorists and organisations. Standards have been adopted to stop the financing of terrorism and technical resources have been put in place to help countries develop the measures and infrastructure necessary to root out the financing of terrorism.

Under the powers of a Financial Action Task Force countries are required to criminalise the financing of terrorism, to freeze and confiscate terrorist assets and to impose anti-money laundering requirements. The IMF has been involved in a programme of anti-money laundering and countering terrorist finances.

Many countries including the UK and European countries have co-ordinated their own action across governments regarding terrorist finance to build up a wider common understanding amongst departments based on assessment material and wider circulation; enhanced and more efficient information flows and broader international understanding and action.

The Anti Terrorism, Crime and Security Act, 2000 enables the authorities to seize terrorist cash, to freeze funds at the start of an investigation, to monitor accounts which may be used to facilitate terrorism, and the Treasury can freeze the assets of foreign individuals and groups if they pose a threat to the UK economy. Persons working in financial institutions can report if there are grounds to suspect that funds are destined for terrorism.

Multilaterally information is being shared in detecting terrorist funding before such funds can reach terrorist networks. In depth intelligence can be developed on the nexus between terrorist groups and organised crime in the raising and moving of terrorist funds. There is a need to maintain the promotion of broader multilateral mutual understanding of legal and administrative requirements in acting against terrorist financing.

The campaign against terrorist financing is a long-term and complex endeavour that requires commitment and resilience from the international community.

Globally there are about 100 terrorist budgets with about $20 million being an average deposit. Robberies usually take place at banks or arms depots. **Kidnapping** and ransom can involve families, firms and governments. **Extortion** can be by threat of death, injury, kidnap and damage. Protection money including bogus security companies can involve small businesses, buses, taxis, and hotels. Monopolies can be enforced by intimidation such as taxis. Racketeering is widespread, for example tax and social security frauds, clubs and gaming machines. Money and arms, comes from supporting governments and foreign communities. Investments can be huge, for example the PLO has excess of £6 billion (Clutterbuck, 1990).

See also: Aviation Security; Maritime Security.

References

Clutterbuck, R. (1990) *Terrorism, Drugs and Crime in Europe after 1992*, London: Routledge.
House of Commons, N. Ireland Affairs Committee, *The Financing of Terrorism in Northern Ireland*, Fourth Report of Session 2001–02, vol. II, Minutes of Evidence and Appendices.

Further Reading

Adams, J. (1987) 'The Financing of Terror', *TVI Report*, vol. 7, no. 3, pp. 30–35.
Henderson, H. (2001) *Global Terrorism: The Complete Reference Guide*, New York: Checkmark Books.
Mullins, W. C. (1997) *Sourcebook on Domestic and International Terrorism: An Analysis of Issues, Organisations, Tactics and Responses* (2nd edn), Springfield, Illinois: Thomas.
Pilgrim, M. K. (1982) 'Financing International Terrorism', *International Security Review*, vol. 7, no. 1 (spring), pp. 47–68.

Foreign policy

Foreign policy and terrorism issues are inextricably linked in many countries' agendas, and can dominate proceedings. For example the hostage crisis involving Americans in the embassy in Teheran, **Iran** in 1979–80 remained at the forefront of American foreign policy during the latter period of Jimmy Carter's Presidency. Four years later, the US withdrawal from **Lebanon** was seen as a victory for terrorists at the expense of American foreign policy goals. Under President Regan terrorism rose to the top of the foreign policy agenda of the **USA** due to high profile incidents in the Middle East and Europe due to the coverage that terrorism was given in the **media**. A military solution to the various problems of terrorism was seen as increasingly important in foreign policy formulations (Simon, 1994).

Terrorists are happy if they can create a crisis atmosphere in foreign policy. The policy to be adopted towards hostage takers and the victims is one example. Terrorism remains an elusive threat for practitioners of foreign policy (Simon, 1994).

In the last decade since the end of the **Cold War**, the G8 nations – the group of eight largest industrialised nations have shared a common concern about terrorism, so they may co-operate to effectively pressure any state providing sanctuary to terrorists. Acting together these nations can bring powerful economic threats or diplomatic measures against any sanctuary state that supports political violence.

Factors such as different foreign policy commitments and ties can limit concerted action against terrorism. France and Italy have ties with **Libya** and **Syria** to a greater degree than the USA, **UK**, Germany, Canada and **Japan** (Heymann, 1998). In 1997, French defiance of a ban on certain transactions with Iran had to be accepted by the USA who has too many beneficial relationships with its closet allies and could not risk rupturing them over the issue co-operating in using sanctions against particular nations offering sanctuary to particular terrorist groups (Heymann, 1998).

Increasingly since the 1950s terrorism was used to promote the ideas and objectives of radical ideologies, while governance by terror continued on the Left and Right of the political spectrum. During the Cold War both super-powers carried their rivalry into the **Third World** political arena where **insurgency** and **counter-insurgency** attracted outside interest. By adopting such methods opportunities were available to promote their interests and influence which were not available through more traditional channels.

See also: Teheran Embassy Seige.

References

Heymann, P. B. (1998) *Terrorism and America. A Commonsense Strategy for a Democratic Society*, Cambridge, MA: and London: The MIT Press.
Simon, J. D. (1994) *The Terrorist Trap: America's Experience with Terrorism*, Bloomington, IN: Indiana University Press.

Further Reading

Marks, E. (1984) 'The Implications of Political

Terrorism for the Management of Foreign Policy and the Protection of Diplomacy' in Han, H. H. (ed.) *Terrorism, Political Violence and World Order*, Lanham, MD: University Press of America, pp. 203–218.

Schlagheck, D. M. (1990) 'The Superpowers, Foreign Policy and Terrorism' in Kegley, C. W. (ed.) *International Terrorism: Characteristics, Causes, Controls*, New York: St Martin's Press, pp. 170–77.

Wardlaw, G. (1988) 'Terror as an Instrument of Foreign Policy' in Rapoport, D. C. (ed.) *Inside Terrorist Organisations*, New York: Columbia University Press, pp. 237–259.

Freedom Fighters

In historical terms freedom fighters, unlike terrorists, were bound by certain rules of behaviour which form the cornerstone of ethical behaviour. These draw a distinction between soldiers and small **children**, between repressive authorities and helpless women, between governmental agents and ordinary citizens, between a military outpost and a house. Thus a terrorist kills civilians while a fighter for freedom saves lives and fights on at the risk of his own life until liberty wins the day.

Nevertheless, since the Second World War these distinctions have changed. Freedom fighters or national liberation movements have all, or nearly all, practiced or continue to practice pure terrorism – that is acts of violence in which innocent members of the public are the sufferers, whether deliberately or through callous disregard for the risks of death or injury on the part of the perpetrators.

A reason that freedom fighters make efforts to present themselves effectively as terrorists is that freedom fighters have generally not achieved government recognition and response.

Terrorists constantly portray themselves as *bone fide* (freedom) fighters if not soldiers, who are entitled to treatment as POWs and should not be treated as common criminals.

See also: Ethics.

References

Merari, A. (1997) 'Terrorism as a Strategy of Insurgency', *Terrorism and Political Violence*, vol. 5, no. 4 (Winter), pp. 213–257.

McGurn, W. (1987) *Terrorist or Freedom Fighter? The Cost of Confusion*, London: Alliance Publishers Ltd.

O'Neill, B. (1990) *Insurgency and Terror*, London and Washington: Brassey's.

G

Gadaffi, Colonel Muammar

b. 1942

Colonel Gadaffi has maintained himself in power for over thirty years, longer than most leaders in the Arab world. Although he is considered by some to be the arch-proponent of international terrorism, his position has become increasingly insecure, and indeed after the American air raid in April 1986, Gadaffi failed to appear in public for several months. He has carried his interpretation of Islamic law to unprecedented lengths in flouting diplomatic conventions, for example by ordering his diplomats to shoot Libyan demonstrators in the streets of London from inside the Libyan Embassy in 1984. The only crime of these demonstrators was that they were anti-Gadaffi.

To many millions of people throughout the world, Gadaffi is a direct sponsor of Islamic fundamentalist terrorism. Diplomatic privilege has been abused through the use of the diplomatic bag to smuggle weapons with which to kill anti-Gadaffi Libyans in European countries. Because of its involvement in world affairs and its liberal traditions Europe will always attract exiles. Unscrupulous states such as **Libya** under Gadaffi and **Iran** under the Ayatollah Khomeini seek them out, so that European states will continue to suffer from political conflicts and disputes to which they are not a party. Gadaffi has provided supplies of weapons, usually obtained originally from the **Soviet Union**, to Irish republicans.

In 1980 Gadaffi sent his hit squads to seven different countries. They carried out fourteen separate attacks abroad against Libyan exiles in 1980 alone, murdering eleven people.

Since he came to power Gadaffi has concentrated on killing Libyan exiles opposed to his regime, destabilising the governments of neighbouring Arab countries and supporting violence, particularly by funding and arming small, violent groups which might otherwise be unable to survive. However, although he has castigated the West and his Arab enemies and made much of his support for revolutionary movements including support for more than thirty terrorist groups in the past, from the Red Brigades to the IRA and **Abu Nidal**, none of his protégés has ever been wholly dependent on him for survival. Support for Nidal, however, does represent a new and radical step for Gadaffi. His global ambitions have been fuelled by his oil wealth, and as the cash supply increased, so he began to influence small terrorist groups more for political ambitions than as a dedicated terrorists' patron.

Gadaffi's relations with Palestine have been mercurial, which has led him to become one of the least popular of the backers of the **Palestine Liberation Organisation** (PLO). While the recruiting of terrorists has fallen off in recent years, there are still training camps in Libya, although Gadaffi owes the Soviet Union considerable cash sums for arms. During the 1980s Gadaffi has supplied almost no money to terrorist groups and his global ambitions have had to be contained within budgetary constraints. Nevertheless Gadaffi has become the bogeyman of international terrorism, despite others who arguably could be considered more supportive of terrorist groups, such as Khomeini or Abu Nidal.

Gadaffi is credited with ordering the murder of Moussa al Sadr, the founder of Amal (Hope), the minority Shi'ite group in the Lebanon, who disappeared in mysterious circumstances on a visit to Libya in 1978. This was as a result of a quarrel between Moussa and Gadaffi over the Palestinians, whose presence in **Lebanon** was resented by the Shi'ites but supported by Gadaffi. Gadaffi was a proven source of money supplied to the IRA from abroad, in a cargo aboard a ship, the *Claudia*, which contained weapons and explosives.

Gadaffi consulted with Abu Nidal, a PLO rebel and renegade controlling bands of 'hit men' who travel the world to kill their victims, and has worked closely with the transnational terrorist, **Carlos**, especially in support for the raid on **OPEC** headquarters in Vienna. He intervened in the outcome of a series of hijackings, allowing the hijackers to land in Libya, make their deals and then disappear into the terrorist underground. Gadaffi has backed anti-government groups in many countries and has threatened to support urban terror groups of a number of countries if their governments do not fall in with his wishes. The **United States** above all is most concerned about the possibility of Gadaffi-inspired terrorism, and this has accounted for their acts against Libya in the Gulf of Sirte in August 1981 and March 1986, and for the bombing raid on Tripoli in April 1986. The April 1986 raid raised arguments on the subject of what the West can do about international terrorism. Since 1988 Gadaffi's relations with the West in terms of terrorism were dominated by the **Lockerbie** affair.

Colonel Gadaffi has mellowed considerably in his attitude to the West; and has condemned incidents of international terrorism over the past few years, most notably **September 11**.

A Libyan colonel and statesman who led a revolt in 1969 that overthrew the Libyan monarchy and in 1970 became chairman of the Revolutionary Command Council. His Arab nationalist and socialist policies have led to a reorganisation of Libyan society and an active foreign policy.

See also: Abu Nidal; Libya; Lockerbie.

Reference

Blundy, D. and Lycett, A. (1987) *Gadaffi and the Libyan Revolution*, Boston, MA: Little, Brown and Co.

Generalisations and Difficulties *see* Definitions: Misconceptions

Generational Terrorism *see* Environmental Influences

Genocide

Genocide is the systematic elimination of a group of people who have been designated by another community or by a government to be destroyed. It is a form of state terrorism and often follows a government propaganda effort both to dehumanise and to demoralise the victims. It does not occur where governments protect the rights of all their citizens (Combs, 2003).

War crimes are violations of laws in wartime. In the 1990s for the first time since the Second World War, the **UN** Security Council authorised an international war crimes tribunal directed against war crimes in the former Yugoslavia and for those who committed genocide in **Rwanda**. The tribunals are based in the Netherlands, but have been hampered by a lack of funding and lack of power to physically arrest suspects who enjoyed the sanctity of Serbia and Croatia. The aggressor has not been conquered and its leaders not been arrested (unlike Nuremberg in 1945) (Goldstein, 1999).

War crimes can include the mistreatment of prisoners of war and the unnecessary targeting of individuals.

See also: Ethnic Conflicts; Rwanda.

References

Combs, C. C. (2003) *Terrorism in the 21st Century*, New Jersey: Prentice Hall.
Goldstein, J. S. (1999) *International Relations* (3rd edn), Harlow, Essex: Longman.

Further Reading

Green, L. C. (1983) 'Is there an International Criminal Law?', *Alberta Law Review,* vol. 21, no. 2, (spring), pp. 251–261.

Kressel, N. J. (1996) *The Global Rise of Genocide and Terror,* USA: Perseus Books.

Globalisation

The world is a global village, a small international community and what affects one society directly or indirectly affects another society. Local terrorism is an offshoot of global terrorism 'which can be described as the use of violence by a dissident group or nation to avenge against the actions of a core state in peripheral or semi-peripheral country or conjugal nation allied to the core country in order to achieve a stated mission' (Onwudiwe, 2001; 123). Iraq's use of scud missiles against **Israel** in 1990 showed Iraq's dissatisfaction with the **USA**, and **China** punishing Taiwan for its close military links with the USA. In 1999 terrorists bombed the American embassies in **East Africa** to express anger with the USA, and yet hundreds of Africans were killed. In turn the Americans attacked missile sites in **Afghanistan** and a pharmaceutical plant in Sudan in direct retaliation for the attacks in East Africa.

Osama Bin Laden started his intercontinental terrorist 'crusade' in 1996 against the USA for championing the Christian-Zionist conspiracy against Muslims as he claimed. He views the American presence in **Saudi Arabia** as a military occupation of sacred land, and wishes to restore **Islam** to its traditional glory (Onwudiwe, 2001). His actions have led to a persistent fear of global terrorism and ultimately mega-terrorism. Offender or rogue states are clamouring to have nuclear capabilities and this in turn provides horrendous realisation to the proliferation of global terrorism. Such a situation can make global terrorism real in the minds of those who can analyse terrorist activity around the world.

Global terrorism is the subversion of traditional ways of war because it does not care about the sovereignty of either its enemies or allies who shelter them. It causes victims to take measures that in the name of legitimate defence, violate knowingly the sovereignty of those states accused of encouraging terror (Hoffman, 2002).

Terrorism is a global phenomenon that reinforces the enemy – the State – at the same time as it tries to destroy it. States that are targets have no interest in applying the laws of war to their fight against terrorists, and have every interest in treating terrorists as outlaws and pariahs.

Globalisation is changing the context in which terrorists operate. A transnational group that cannot be controlled by governments, either individually or collectively, increasingly affects even so called domestic terrorism. Information Technology (IT) has removed the ability of countries to isolate themselves. Networks are possible with the advent of public access to the Internet, the ability to transfer funds and conduct banking electronically, the international arms market, encrypted digital communications technology and the emergence of 'stateless terrorism'. Controllers have a global reach and can run multiple independent cells from a single location with no interaction between the cells.

Terrorism and guerrilla activity may lead to governmental interactions and more interdependency in the system. Governments have acted together to train anti-guerrilla and anti-terrorist units. Governments have acted through the **United Nations** and the Organisation of American States to outlaw or provide for co-operation against certain acts i.e. treaties prohibiting offences against diplomats.

The growing gap between the rich and the poor in many regions and worldwide and the persistence of extreme poverty among over a billion people, has helped to create a climate that is ripe for fundamentalism and extremism. The horror of the events of **September 11** has caused people everywhere to contemplate the root causes of the disaster. Terrorists had struck at the heart of the global economy by targeting the **World Trade Center**.

International travel and tourism plummeted in the wake of the terrorist attack and the global economy was in a dangerously precarious state. The events in New York came at a time of global public unease about globalisation as experienced by the strength of the anti-globalisation movement.

The events furthermore were reminders that the ecological instability of today's world is matched by instability in human affairs that must be urgently addressed. To many global observers, building a more sustainable and secure world based on human values and mutual support is urgent. Many societies are struggling with the difficult transition from traditional rural societies to more modern, urban middle-class ones. The absence of democratic political representation and the concentration of economic and political power in a few hands has created a fundamental instability in many nations: most notably terrorism and drug trafficking (French, 2002).

International mechanisms have to address issues raised by groups that use physical force to secure national or religious ends where other forms of political action are not available. A global legal framework for terrorism will be hard to achieve – it depends on stopping injustice and securing the legitimacy of international order (Taylor and Horgan, 2000).

Most of the proscribed terrorist groups on the US Department of State Counter-terrorism list come from non-Western countries. Terrorism has shown up in the lack of enforcement and policy implementation in the international system.

See also: Political Sub-State Violence; Political Violence.

References

French, H. (2002) *Reshaping Global Governance in State of the World 2002*, London: Earthscan Publications.

Hoffman, S. (2002) 'Clash of Globalisation', *Foreign Affairs*, vol. 81, no. 4, (July/August).

Onwudiwe, I. D. (2001) *The Globalisation of Terrorism*, Aldershot: Ashgate Publishing.

Taylor, M. and Horgan, J. (eds) (2000) *The Future of Terrorism*, London: Frank Cass.

Further Reading

Campbell, K. M. (2002) 'Globalisation's First War?', *The Washington Quarterly*, vol. 25, no. 1, (winter), pp. 7–14.

Mackinlay, J. (2002) *Globalisation and Insurgency*, London: International Institute for Strategic Studies, Adelphi Papers no. 352.

Maniscalco, P. M. and Christen, H. T. (2002) *Understanding Terrorism and Managing the Consequences*, London: Pearson Education and Upper Saddle River, NJ: Prentice Hall.

Government Responses to Terrorism *see* Counter/Anti-Terrorism

Government Support

Governments perhaps inadvertently or inattentively can give in to the terrorist and in so doing make their country seem an easy place for terrorists to operate. They can give in to terrorist demands and fail to ratify or be slow to ratify treaties to **counter-terrorism**. Others refuse to extradite on legal technicalities and deals can be done by governments who allow terrorists to live in their country in return for a promise of no attacks on their citizens.

Support can be given by states within international organisations; and groups can be permitted to open offices on local soil, for example, the **PLO** opened many offices in the 1970s and 1980s in Western Europe. Hijackings can often take place regularly to countries where the perpetrators know they will be given safe haven – **Cuba** and Somalia are two examples of 'popular' destinations in the past. Some countries have refused to allow rescue squads to rescue hostage victims on their territory. Others, particularly in the Middle East have been active in training terrorists. Covert financial contributions have been provided to 'offices' or 'undercover' or 'umbrella' terrorist organisations in these countries. False document utilisation especially passports and visa's are common occurrences, and the misuse of the diplomatic bag has regularly taken place.

In Central America and some African nations government personnel have become increasingly involved in activity that is not compatible with their status. Under this criterion, diplomats can be asked to leave accredited countries if their actions are not conducive to their status. In 'rogue' states and countries formerly part of the Soviet empire, nuclear scientists and arms manufacture experts have often 'changed sides' on payment of financial inducements to work with terrorist organisations.

See also: State Sponsorship; 'Terrorist States'.

Group Origins and Dynamics *see* Terror and Terrorism

Guerrilla Warfare in History

The term 'guerrilla' was originally used to describe military operations carried out by irregulars against the rear of an enemy army or by local inhabitants against an occupying force. Tactics are based on enemy harassment, cutting off communications and carrying out surprise attacks.

Primitive people in general had an aversion to open fighting; for example, Jiftah and David in the Bible. The Maccabean revolt in 166 BC made use of guerrilla tactics in the early phase, but guerrilla units played only a minor role in the Jewish war against the Romans. The Romans made use of guerrilla warfare as an invasion battle attempt to wear down the enemy, to attack small detachments in ambush by day and larger units by night.

Few guerrilla acts took place in the Middle Ages because of the development of new tactics; great emphasis was placed on cavalry and the use of missile weapons. The Hundred Years War was originally a dynastic conflict between Britain and France, but guerrilla tactics soon developed. Peasant revolts spread throughout Europe between the fourteenth and seventeenth centuries; and the Balkans became the main banditry area from the fifteenth to the late eighteenth century. Partisan warfare played a notable part in the American War of Independence – it was not a crucial factor between defeat or victory, but did have a delayed influence on military thinking.

In post-Napoleonic Europe, guerrilla warfare developed in the south and east of the Continent. The Carlist Wars (1830) showed that guerrilla tradition had become deeply rooted in Spain, while the Greek War of Independence (1820), genocidal in character, was essentially a series of uncoordinated operations by irregular troops. Polish insurrections in 1793, 1831 and 1863 were a blend of regular and guerrilla war. During the period of Italian unification, the elements of political propaganda and indoctrination foreshadowed guerrilla wars of a later age.

The Spanish War against the French in the early nineteenth century first produced a solely guerrilla war; and South America was the area where guerrilla warfare occurred on a vast scale. Guerrilla warfare was the high road to political and economic power, and yesterday's brigand could be tomorrow's government minister. In South America, and indeed in many other parts of the Third World, guerrilla warfare has taken many forms – wars of national liberation, the struggles of landless peasants and small farmers against large landowners, and fighting between local chieftains for political power.

Guerrillas have been active in the periods of Imperialist expansion by European colonial powers, and indeed in three wars in the nineteenth century, guerrilla warfare played some role; in the American Civil War 1861–65, the Franco-Prussian War of 1870 and the Boer War 1899–1902 – the latter being a three-year war of attrition.

The demarcation between guerrilla warfare and banditry has been unclear. Most guerrilla movements have included members of semi respectable professions – such as smuggling and poaching. Guerrillas and bandits have lived off the land, with horses and food provided by the local population, without having to pay for them, i.e. during the guerrilla phase of Chinese Communism, recruits were drawn from robber bands.

Guerrilla warfare has been successful only if the enemy army was not large enough to occupy the whole territory. The essential element of success in guerrilla warfare is surprise, followed by retreat before the opponent could recover. A partisan unit had no lines of supply and communication and success depended on surprise. Their actions had purely strategic significance and the contribution to warfare was to weaken the enemy without making a special contribution to any major battle, i.e. in the Russian Civil War 1918–19, and in the fight against the Germans in Yugoslavia in the Second World War.

Essential differences were evident in the nineteenth and twentieth centuries between guerrilla warfare on the fringes of European colonial empires, which were long drawn-out affairs in which success was neither sought nor achieved, and revolutionary uprisings in West European capitals which could only prove victorious by rapid and decisive action. In the First World War guerrilla operations were restricted to two theatres – **Saudi Arabia** and **East Africa**, under the leadership of Lawrence and Vorbeck. To both men, guerrilla doctrine became an exact science if pursued properly. If the enemy could be encouraged to stay in harmless places in large numbers, the enemy could be permanently weakened. Warfare could be adapted to local conditions, human and geographical.

Lenin maintained that guerrilla warfare should be waged by worker combatants. Trotsky maintained that guerrilla warfare was the true peasant form of war. The secret services attached importance to the role of the guerrilla in the **Soviet Union** between the two world wars; guerrilla groups formed just one aspect of intelligence and sabotage work behind the enemy lines. In Macedonia in the Balkans from 1910 to 1912 separatist activity was undertaken by many disparate groups; in Mexico in the revolution in the decade after 1910, bandits gave support but provided no political leadership. Resistance in Mexico was regional and wanting in organisational ability and necessary minimum political sophistication.

By the end of the Second World War, guerrillas were faced with changing circumstances. Due to a shift in public opinion, the chief powers in the world could not act with the same degree of ferocity as on past occasions. The development of modern weapons favoured the guerrillas more than those operating against them. There were difficulties in combating guerrillas in populated areas. Europe's decline after 1945 led to deep economic and political unrest and revolutionary situations the world over. The Second World War had been the guerrillas' opportunity – and the political impact of partisan activity had been far greater than its military contribution. The relation between communist and non-communist partisan units always had been strained. The Warsaw Uprising of 1944 was the chief urban insurrection of the Second

World War, while in France resistance was dogged by betrayal. For the Communists in the **Cold War** 1945–50, guerrilla activity proved excellent cadre training, a school for the mobilisation of the masses and a tool for the seizure of power. In **China**, Mao Tse-Tung argued that guerrilla operations by themselves could not win a war, nevertheless the Communists achieved victory in 1949 and instigated a new social and political order after a fifteen-year guerrilla war.

Vietnam proved to be longest of the guerrilla wars (1954–73), and provoked a deep moral crisis in the Western world, especially the United States. The Vietcong stressed political propaganda and indoctrination, while the Communists were enthusiastic, determined and dedicated.

Three stages in the development of guerrilla warfare occurred in the post-Second World War period – first, to the end of the Malayan insurgency, the lull in Indo-China and the defeat of such groups as the Huks in the **Philippines** and **Mau Mau** in Kenya; second, in the 1960s the scene of operations shifted to Vietnam and Latin America, and third from the late 1960s urban terrorists replaced rural guerrillas. The main problems facing guerrillas have been the necessity to establish rural bases, in which many have failed, and the internal splits between nationalists, pro-Moscow Communists, Trotskyites and Maoists. Lessons were learnt – for example, from the Cuban revolution. Popular forces can win a war against the army; it is not necessary to wait until all conditions for making a revolution exist – insurrection can create them, and ultimately, as Latin America showed, the countryside is the main area for armed fighting.

Counter-insurgency theorists agree that guerrilla warfare is cheap, but the fight against it is costly. It is a form of warfare by which the strategically weaker side assumes the tactical offensive in selected forms, times and places – it is a weapon of the weak, and usually only decisive when the anti-guerrilla side puts a low value on defeating the guerrillas and does not commit full resources to the struggle.

In connection with guerrilla activity, some important assertions can be made. The geographical milieu is important, for example the bases. Guerrilla wars generally occur in areas in which such wars have occurred before. There is a negative correlation between guerrilla war and the degree of economic development. It has undergone profound changes and can never be seen as apolitical. Peasants have formed the traditional mass basis of guerrilla movements and motives are generally manifold for joining the guerrillas. Guerrillas are very dependent on the terrain, the size and density of the population, and the political constellation. During the 1970s and 1980s urban terrorism has been more frequent than rural guerrilla warfare, and guerrilla movements have become increasingly beset by internal strife in their own ranks or between rival movements. Guerrilla warfare is perhaps on the decline because colonialism and liberal democracy are also on the decline.

See also: Counter-Insurgency; Debray; Fanon; Guevara; Marighella; Revolutions; Third World.

References

Asprey, R. B. (1975) *War in the Shadows: The Guerrilla in History*, London: Macdonald and Jane's.

Clutterbuck, R. L. (1977) *Guerrillas and Terrorists*, London: Faber and Faber.

— (1990) *Terrorism and Guerrilla Warfare: Forecasts and Remedies*, New York: Routledge.

Fairburn, G. (1974) *Revolutionary Guerrilla Warfare: The Countryside Version*, London: Penguin.

Further Reading

Chaliand, G. (ed.) (1982) *Guerrilla Strategies: Revolutionary Warfare and Counterinsurgency: An Historical Anthology from the Long March to Afghanistan*, Berkeley, CA: University of California Press.

Dewar, M. (1992) *War in the Streets. The Story of Urban Combat from Calais to Khafji, Newton Abbot*, Devon: David and Charles.

Griffiths, S. B. (ed.) (1989) *Mao Tse-Tung on Guerrilla Warfare*, Washington DC: US Marine Corp Department of the Navy.

Mao Tse-Tung (1963) *Selected Military Writings of Mao Tse-Tung* (2nd edn), Beijing: Foreign Languages Press.

White, J. B. (1996) 'Irregular Warfare: A Different Kind of Threat', *American Intelligence Journal*, vol. 17, pp. 57–63.

Wickham-Crowley, T. P. (1992) *Guerrillas and Revolution in Latin America: A Comparative Study of Insurgents and Regimes since 1956*, Princeton, NJ: Princeton University Press.

Guevara, Dr Ernesto 'Che'

b. 1928; d. 1967

Che Guevara was an Argentinian revolutionary and guerrilla fighter. He was the right-hand man of Fidel Castro in the guerrilla campaign against the Cuban Batista regime in **Cuba**. He analysed the theory and practices of guerrilla warfare in his book *Guerrilla Warfare*, published after his death, which introduced basic modifications into hitherto accepted Marxist-Leninist theories. He disappeared from Cuba in March 1965 in order to organise guerrilla wars in other Latin American countries. In December 1966 he launched a guerrilla campaign in Bolivia, where in October 1967 he lost his life when he was captured by Bolivian government forces. Following his death, 'Che' became the legendary hero of a growing cult among left-wing students and other young radicals in the Western world.

Guevara believed that popular forces can win a war against the army; an insurrection can create all the conditions for making a revolution, and the main area for armed fighting was the countryside. After initial scepticism, he came to believe that the conditions for armed struggle existed everywhere in Latin America. Democratic governments had to be compelled by guerrillas into using inherently dictatorial powers. Guerrillas had to be morally superior to their enemies and to be social reformers. To Guevara the stages of guerrilla warfare moved from a small guerrilla force being hunted by superior enemy forces to becoming a popular army (Laqueur, 1998: 327–36), overrunning government forces and seizing big cities.

Guerrilla leaders would learn the art of warfare in the practice of war itself.

See also: Debray; Fanon; Guerrilla Warfare in History; Marighella.

References

Guevara, C. (1969) *Guerrilla Warfare*, Harmondsworth, Penguin.
Laqueur, W. (1998) *Guerrilla Warfare: A Historical and Critical Study*, NJ: Transaction Publishers.

Further Reading

Guevara, C. (1978) 'Guerrilla Warfare: A Method', in W. Laqueur (ed.) *The Guerrilla Reader: A Historical Anthology*, London: Wildwood House.

Gulf War

The United States of America, as soon as the **Cold War** ended, began to face a new threat of Islamic militancy and this was confirmed by the Gulf conflict. The missiles of Saddam Hussein highlighted the vulnerability of Israel and the self-confidence of the PLO was undermined as Yasser **Arafat** had ruled with Saddam. The very fact that America had sent its troops to Kuwait during the Gulf War was deemed hostile to Islam, and a Christian plot versus the Islamic faith (Halliday, 2002).

In **Iraq** the USA never finished off the Gulf War and Hussein's hold on power and his support for international terrorism has been relentlessly pursued. A large contingent of US military forces in close proximity to the most holy Islamic sites was anathema to many Arabs. Moreover, the scare that Saddam Hussein gave the world with his threat to unleash weapons of mass destruction during the 1991 Gulf War is a lesson not lost on tomorrow's terrorists.

The aftermath of the Gulf War contributed to a new surge in arms sales and transfers in the Middle East and elsewhere. Whenever there is an abundance of weapons in unstable regions the risk of some of the weapons being acquired by terrorists or state sponsors of terrorist's increases.

The War brought into the open the issue of biological agents and warfare. Terrorists have seen the fear, anxiety and reaction generated by threatening to unleash biological and chemical agents – and it is alleged Saddam Hussein has stockpiled such agents. The West feared an Iraqi sponsored terror campaign, including **hijacking** and bombings. The irony of the Gulf War was that it was probably the safest time to travel abroad, since security at all airports and airlines was at its highest point; although on the day of the Iraqi invasion of Kuwait (2 August 1990) a British Airways flight had been seized at Kuwait airport en route to Malaysia, and its passengers held as hostages and human shields against allied bombing raids of Iraq.

From the Gulf War onwards the **media** played a significant role with respect to the public's concerns that terrorists might unleash weapons of mass destruction. Events on the media kept the world well informed of the implications of the war on terrorism (Simon, 1994).

Oil was at the core of the Gulf War and has been at the heart of terrorist–guerrilla activity in the Middle East in terms of vital resources to the global economy.

Terrorism continued apace during the Gulf War in other parts of the world – Germany, Jordan, **Lebanon**, **Philippines**, **Saudi Arabia** and **Turkey** – with quite a few incidents involving American nationals. Terrorist groups took advantage of the situation in the Gulf to perpetuate their violence. During this time the IRA attacked in London – a bomb at Victoria Station and an attempt to destroy 10 Downing Street with a missile (at the time a Cabinet meeting was taking place).

During the Gulf War, Saddam Hussein made threats to terrorise the world that were nullified by worldwide security and intelligence, and moreover, he had no organised central command of terror networks.

The actions of Saddam Hussein showed how unprepared the USA was against terrorism within its borders (Simon, 1994).

References

Halliday, F. (2002) *Two Hours that Shook the World*

September 11, 2001 – Causes and Consequences, London: Saqi Books.

Simon, J. D. (1994) *The Terrorist Trap: America's Experience with Terrorism,* Bloomington, IN: Indiana University Press.

Hamas (Harakat Al-Muqawama Al-Islamiyya)

A movement of Islamist resistance in Gaza and the West Bank which grew up in the 1990s in response to the armed interventions by the Israeli's against Palestinian military attempts to achieve statehood. It is a **Sunni** Palestinian group with roots in the **Afghanistan jihad**.

One of the founders was Abdullah Azzam who worked in the **United States** in the 1980s recruiting for the holy war and raising funds for Hamas. He was killed by a car bomb in 1987.

Hamas were prepared to kill Palestinian clerics considered to be co-operating with the Israeli occupation authorities in the West Bank and Gaza. This intensified after the intifada began in 1987 (Cooley, 2001).

In view of what Hamas has violently undertaken it is perhaps surprising that it was initially a charitable or teaching organisation. In the early-1990s the special target of Hamas was the peace which the **PLO** leader and Palestinian Authority President Yasser **Arafat**, sought with **Israel** under the Oslo Accords in 1993 (Cooley, 2001).

To some observers Hamas can be described as both a religious group and a separatist group. Insofar as it is an Islamic group (desiring to set up an Islamic Palestinian state) it can be seen as a religious terrorist group, but it is also separatist because it advocates Palestinian autonomy from Israeli control.

Their favourite method of attack is **suicide** car bombing on 'soft' and military targets and individual suicide attacks. Hamas, works round family ties and some of its operations in **Lebanon** have been partially aimed at gaining freedom of imprisoned family members. The worry for counter-terrorists is that suicide bombers are not likely to be deterred by security measures which only threaten their lives once they have carried out an attack.

Hamas has sought to mobilise Palestinians and Arab governments against the Accord by provoking the Israelis into breaking the Accord and into further military repression. Many Hamas supporters believed in a worldwide **Zionist** and Jewish hostility to **Islam**. In turn right-wing Israelis see the Islamic threat as everywhere masterminded by Hamas (Halliday, 2002). Hamas did create a demoralised feeling of helplessness in Israel after each suicide bombing. Israel has been unable to wipe out Hamas. More worryingly, **Al Qaeda** has forged ties with Hamas and Palestinian jihad, as many Palestinians went to Afghanistan and rose to positions in the organisation. Members of Hamas have experimented with the deadly poison, ricin. There is the notion in Hamas and other extreme Islamic groups of them representing primitivism against modernism (Reeve, 1999). The idea of primitive nomadic peoples burning out the corruption associated with city life has been a regular theme of the sociology of Islamic societies for generations. Hamas has developed the largest network of all militant Islamic organisations.

References

Cooley, J. K. (2001) *Unholy Wars: Afghanistan, America*

and *International Terrorism* (2nd edn), London: Pluto Press.

Halliday, F. (2002) *Two Hours That Shook the World September 11, 2001: Causes and Consequences*, London: Saqi Books.

Reeve, S. (1999) *The New Jackals: Ramzi Yousef, Osama Bin Laden and the Future of Terrorism*, London: Andre Deutsch.

Further Reading

Israeli, R. (1990) 'The Charter of Allah: The Platform of the Islamic Resistance Movement (Hamas)' in Y. Alexander and A. H. Foxman (eds) *The 1988–1989 Annual of Terrorism*. Dordrecht: Martinus Nijhoff, pp. 99–134.

Nusse, A. (1999) Muslim Palestine: The Ideology of Hamas, London: Harwood Academic Publications.

Hijacking

The first hijacking occurred in **Peru** in the 1930s; they became more frequent in the late 1960s and early 1970s when the world was made aware of their terror impact on innocent civilians through worldwide media access.

Two Conventions were created to address this problem. The Tokyo Convention (1963) on Offences and Certain Other Acts Committed on Board Aircraft covered the question of jurisdiction over hijacking whilst an aircraft was in flight. The Hague Convention (1970) for the Suppression of Unlawful Seizure of Aircraft made hijackers subject to extradition to either the country of registry of the aircraft, the country where the aircraft with hijackers on board landed or the country whose citizens charter a plane without chartering the crew. In 1978 the Bonn Economic Summit Declaration stated that all flights should cease to countries that refuse to extradite hijackers or did not return such aircraft. In this regard what deters terrorists today is that fewer and fewer countries listen to terrorist demands.

New difficulties of negotiation for the authorities were created by the hijacking of the passenger ship Achille Lauro, as the ship was moving and was not effectively detained.

Until recent times, the type of person seen as a hijacker was poor, young and badly educated. The events of **September 11** showed that they could be well educated and professional with a high degree of knowledge on information technology.

Other types of hijacking also have occurred. For example, in 1984 an Israeli bus was hijacked by Arabs from the Gaza strip – it was stormed by Israeli forces and hostages released. In 1975, in the Netherlands, Moluccan terrorists near the town of Beilen seized a train and passengers were held hostage for three weeks. Two years later another train was seized at Assen in the Netherlands and 50 hostages were held also for three weeks. In the USA and South Africa, thefts at knifepoint or gunpoint (carjackings) have become fairly common.

Historically high profile air hijackings have occurred. In September 1970 three airbuses were hijacked by the Popular Front for the Liberation of Palestine. Two were taken to Dawson's Field in Jordan and one to Cairo. Terrorists failed to take an El Al plane. The passengers were freed and the planes blown up. The incident led to the expulsion of the **Palestine Liberation Organisation** from Jordan.

Such incidents show that the purpose of hijacking is not to wantonly kill or otherwise harm innocent persons, but to use passengers as pawns in pursuit of publicity and the extraction of concessions from governments perceived as hostile by the hijackers.

Air piracy has become a synonym for hijacking. Both hijackers and pirates make use of spaces that lie outside the jurisdiction and control of states. Hijackers have in general political motivation for their action while the motive for piracy can be seen as personal enrichment.

References

Griset, P. L. and Mahan, S. (2003) *Terrorism in Perspective*, Thousand Oaks, CA, London and New Delhi: Sage Publications.

Guelke, A. (1998) *The Age of Terrorism and the International Political System*, London and New York: IB Taurus Publishers.

Wardlaw, G. (1989) (2nd edn) *Political Terrorism: Theory, Tactics and Counter-Measures*, Cambridge,

New York and Melbourne, Sydney: Cambridge
University Press.

Wilkinson, P. (2002) *Terrorism versus Democracy: The
Liberal State Response*, London and Portland, OR:
Frank Cass.

Further Reading

Harmon, C. C. (2000) *Terrorism Today*, London and
Portland, OR: Frank Cass.

Hoffman, B. (1998) *Inside Terrorism*, London: Victor
Gollancz.

History of Terrorism

Terrorism has always engendered violent emotions
and greatly divergent opinions and images. At the
end of the last century, the popular image of the
terrorist was that of a bomb-throwing alien
anarchist, dishevelled, with a black beard and a
smile, fanatic, immoral and sinister. His present-day
image is very similar. Those practicing terror have
certain beliefs in common – they can be on the Left
or Right, nationalist or internationalist, but in
many respects their mental make up is similar.

There is widespread belief that terrorism is a
new and unprecedented phenomenon, one of the
most important and dangerous facing mankind
today. Since it is a response to injustice, the only
means of reducing the likelihood of terrorism is a
reduction of grievances, stresses and frustration.
Terrorists are fanatical believers and terrorism can
occur anywhere.

Terrorism was first used as a word during the
French Revolution as a synonym for a reign of
terror, and later developed to mean the systematic
use of terror. Many varieties have appeared
throughout history: peasant wars, labour disputes
and brigandage accompanied by systematic terror,
general wars, **civil wars**, wars of national liberation, and resistance movements against foreign
occupiers. Terrorism was often a subordinate
strategy in many of these cases. Terrorism has
emerged from political protest and revolts, social
uprisings and religious protest movements. One of
the early examples of a terrorism movement was
the Sicarii, a highly organised religious sect
consisting of men of lower orders active in the

Zealot struggle in Palestine around 70 AD. They
attacked targets in daylight, using a short sword.
Messianic hope and political terrorism were the
prominent features of the **Assassins** sect, an
offshoot of the Ismailis who appeared in the
eleventh century and were suppressed by the
Mongols in the thirteenth century. Secret societies
like the Thugs in India did not wish to terrorise the
government or population, but rather the individual. Political assassinations of leading statesmen
were relatively infrequent between the sixteenth
and eighteenth centuries in the age of absolutism,
once the religious conflicts had lost some of their
acuteness. Monarchs, whatever their personal
differences, had no thought of killing one another.
Systematic terrorism began in the late nineteenth
century and there were several distinct categories
from the very beginning.

The Russian revolutionaries fought an autocratic
government from 1878 to 1881, and again in the
early twentieth century. Radical nationalist groups,
such as the Irish, Macedonians, Serbs and Armenians used terrorist methods in their struggle for
autonomy or national independence. Last, there
was the anarchist 'propaganda by the deed' during
the 1890s in France, Italy, Spain and the **United
States**.

The three waves of Russian terror were the
Narodnaya Volya between 1878 and 1881, and
their notable successes included the head of the
Tsarist political police and Tsar Alexander II. The
second wave of terror was sponsored by the Social
Revolutionary Party, and their victims between
1902 and 1911 included two ministers of the
interior, a Grand Duke and some provincial
governors. Finally, the third small wave occurred
after the Bolshevik coup in 1917.

The achievements of Irish terrorism have been
less striking, but it has continued on and off over a
much longer period. Armenian terrorism against
Turkish oppression began in the 1890s and has
continued at varying levels until the present day –
with church dignitaries, political leaders and
Turkish diplomats being the popular targets.
Another revolutionary organisation directed
against the Turks was the Macedonian IMRO,
which started out as an underground civilian
propagandist society and turned into a military
movement, preparing for systematic terror and a

mass insurrection. Polish socialists and some Indian groups, particularly in Bengal, developed anarchist traditions which were to continue well after independence had been achieved.

The high tide of terrorism in **Western Europe** was the anarchist 'propaganda of the deed' in the 1890s, in which bomb-throwing by individuals coincided with a turn in anarchist propaganda favouring violence. The expected international conspiracy never existed. However, there were many attacks on the lives of leading statesmen in Europe and the United States until the First World War.

There were no systematic terrorist campaigns before 1945 in Central and Western Europe, although they did exist on the fringes of Europe in **Russia**, the Balkans and in Spain. Labour disputes in the USA were more violent than in Europe almost from their beginning. Up to the First World War, terrorism was considered to be a left-wing phenomenon, even though the highly individualistic character of terrorism did not quite fit the ideological pattern.

After 1918, terrorist operations were mainly sponsored by right-wing and national separatist groups. Sometimes these groups were right-wing and separatist, as in the case of the Croatian Ustashi. The Croatians wanted independence and had no compunction about accepting support from any quarter. The Romanian 'Iron Guard' was a budding Fascist movement which resorted to violence. Assassinations were few but spectacular, such as those of Liebknecht and Luxemburg (both German Communists), in 1919 and of the British commander-in-chief of the Egyptian army in 1924.

Individual terrorism played a minor role in the European resistance movement during the Second World War – a few high-ranking Nazis notably Heydrich, the governor of the Czech protectorate, were killed.

For many years after the war, it was chiefly in the urban regions such as mandated Palestine (1945–47), and later in Cyprus (1955–58) and Aden (1964–67) that the terrorist strategy prevailed. Urban terror was overshadowed by large-scale guerrilla wars.

Urban terrorism was regarded at best as a supplementary form of warfare, at worst as a dangerous aberration. It was only in the mid-1960s that urban terrorism came into its own as a result of the defeat of rural guerrillas in Latin America, and following the emergence of urban terrorist groups in Europe, North America and **Japan**.

Terrorism has always been justified as a means of resisting despotism, and as such its origins can be traced back to antiquity. Plato and Aristotle believed tyranny to be the worst form of government. Tyrants never worked alone, they could not function without assistants, and thus it was necessary to attack the system on a broad front. The proponents of armed insurrection rather than of individual terror, such as Blanqui and Baboeuf, nevertheless influenced later terrorists through their advocacy of violence, scant regard for human life and belief that a few determined people could make a revolution. Occasional terrorist acts were perpetrated by the Carboneria in Italy, but these did not amount to a systematic campaign.

The idea of an alliance between the revolutionary avant-garde and the criminal underworld was a feature of nineteenth-century terrorist movements, i.e. the Narodnaya Volya in Russia, and among American and West German New Left militants of the 1960s. The Russian revolutionary Bakunin was a great enthusiast for merciless destruction, especially of members of the Church, the world of business, the bureaucracy and army, the secret police and even royalty. Thus, for Bakunin there was an irrepressible need for total revolution, and for institutions, social structures, civilisation and morality to be destroyed root and branch. The revolution in Russia developed in stages, starting with sporadic acts of armed defence in resisting arrest and as a reaction against individual police officers who had maltreated arrested revolutionaries – and ending with total revolution and paralysis of the state. Russian revolutionaries believed that terrorist operations were far more effective in promoting the revolution, if only because of the tremendous publicity they received – very much in contrast to illegal propaganda and organisational work, which had no visible effect. Some Russians believed that terrorism was not only effective, but humanitarian. It cost fewer victims than a mass struggle, and was the application of modern science to the revolutionary struggle.

By the last decade of the nineteenth century there were active terrorist operations in Spain, Italy, France, **India**, the USA, Poland and among stateless groups such as the Armenians. Despite their approval in principle of a direct bomb-throwing approach, both Marx and Engels condemned the foolishness of conspiracies, denounced the purposeless 'propaganda by deed' and dissociated themselves from individual actions. Communists have shown ambiguity in their approach to terrorism. It might be rejected in principle, but on certain occasions the practice of terrorism has not been ruled out.

In history, terrorism has been practiced as much by right-wing and nationalist groups as by left-wing groups. Terrorism in India had a strong religious base; the Clan-na-Gael in America stood for bloodless terrorism directed against buildings; whilst in Northern **Ireland** in the 1880s the Invincibles practiced individual terror such as the Phoenix Park murder of a British minister. Some Irish groups were keener on gimmicks – such as spraying the House of Commons with osmic gas, and collecting money to purchase poisoned stilettos, Lucifer matches and other unlikely weapons.

Assassinations of political opponents carried out in pre-1914 Russia are also examples of terrorism as carried out by the extreme right. The Fascists under Mussolini in Italy tended to intimidate opponents rather than eliminate individual enemy leaders, the Nazis showed the tremendous use which could be made of political violence to maximise publicity in the mass media. The composition of right-wing terrorist groups varied greatly from country to country, ranging from criminal elements to young idealists. Terror carried out by individuals was infrequent; instead there was terror of incitement – of speech, and of the written word.

Generally in the inter-war years, the decision by a group to adopt a terrorist strategy was taken on the basis of a detailed political analysis. An initial sense of grievance and frustration would later be supported by ideological rationalisation – ranging from a systematic strategy to imprecise doctrines.

See also: Assassins; Terror and Terrorism.

Terrorism in the 1960s

By the late 1960s the signs in the global community were that violence was gaining ground. Broad historical changes, ideological changes and technological changes were occurring. The world was living under a nuclear stalemate created by the super-powers and it was becoming more attractive for groups to use low-risk, potentially high-yield and very effective methods of struggle such as terrorism. European colonialism had ended, leaving a host of newly independent nations to grapple with unfamiliar problems. Restless minorities in many of these countries were no longer restrained by European-style police and military forces. Disputes arose with neighbouring states over boundaries that had often been established arbitrarily by colonial administrations. Guerrilla uprisings and low-intensity warfare often included terrorist activity. A growing emphasis on human rights led Western democracies to place high value on the life of a single citizen. Democracies proved to be susceptible to hostage taking threats. Terrorists found kidnapping could bring concessions unattainable by other means.

Several key religious and political changes also occurred during the late 1960s. Guerrilla warfare became increasingly urbanised, and indeed urban terrorism came into its own mainly as a result of the defeat of the rural guerrillas in Latin America. Islamic fundamentalism growing out of the reaction against Westernisation and modernity provided a breeding ground for Shi'ite terrorism. The Vietnam War radicalised large numbers of young people in developed nations throughout the world, and taking up the cause of inequality between first and third world nations, they became more committed to Marxist-Leninist ideals, created underground cells and took up terrorism.

The growth of mass communications, especially television, and the importance of the media, was seized upon by terrorists as a propaganda tool. By 1970 air travel had come of age, and this helped to provide rapid movement for terrorists between target nations and countries that provided safe havens. The number of hijackings also increased; in 1969 alone there were 33 successful hijackings of American planes bound for Cuba. Weapons also improved and by the start of the 1970s it was clear that, for example, modern rapid fire submachine guns fitting easily into briefcases could be a major weapon in the armoury of the terrorist.

1968 was the year which witnessed the big upsurge in terrorism with a number of events uniting in that year in its favour. Members of the Popular Front for the Liberation of Palestine (PFLP) seized an El Al airliner and forced it to fly to Algeria – launching a campaign of air piracy that has since become the hallmark of terrorism. In Germany the Baader-Meinhof gang began to gain prominence through a series of arson attacks. In Egypt, Yasser Arafat was appointed leader of the Palestine Liberation Organisation. Across the world in the Americas, two important events occurred. In the United States Martin Luther King was assassinated, unleashing a spate of domestic violence by groups such as the Black Panthers and Weathermen. In Mexico City marches culminated in protests at the Olympic Games in 1968, aiding growth of a terrorist movement with Cuban and Soviet connections. Cubans gave more or less indiscriminate support to Latin American guerrilla movements and terrorist movements. Doctrinally, the Cubans should have assisted only rural guerrillas but they also supported urban terrorism, especially after the collapse of most Latin American rural guerrilla movements. The first widespread terrorist training centres were established in North Korea in 1968–69; since then former trainees have been traced to and in some cases apprehended in Latin America (Mexico, Brazil, Bolivia, Colombia and other countries), to the Middle East (in the PFLP), Asia (Sri Lanka, Malaya, Indonesia) and Africa.

Most of the terrorist groups of the 1960s were left-wing in orientation or used left-wing phraseology in their appeals and manifestos. Right-wing terrorist groups operated in Turkey, Italy and Guatemala, in Argentina and Brazil, but their impact was felt on the domestic scene only. Foreign powers began to intervene directly or discreetly, and provide help to terrorist movements. It was only in the 1960s that this new form of warfare by proxy really came into its own, thus opening entirely new possibilities for terrorism. Operations in third countries became far more frequent; in past ages it had been the rule that Russian terrorists would limit their attacks to Russia, and the Irish to

Ireland or the United Kingdom. In the 1960s, on the other hand, Palestinians operated in Paraguay or France, Japanese terrorists in Kuwait, Israel and the Netherlands, and Germans in Sweden or Uganda. This new multinational terrorism was bound to create confusion about the identity of the attackers and the purpose of their actions.

While political violence became intellectually respectable in the 1960s in some circles, the ability of the authorities to counteract terrorism was more restricted than in the past. Up to the Second World War, terrorists who had been apprehended by the authorities faced in many cases long prison terms. With the dawning of the permissive age, it became far less risky to engage in terrorism, except in a few less enlightened countries. Where terrorism would have been dangerous, it was rare. If the judiciary was reluctant to impose draconian penalties on its own citizens, the foreign terrorist could expect to get away with light sentences if his case reached trial at all, for his imprisonment would have exposed the host country to retaliation, to fresh terrorist attacks, to the seizing of hostages and to blackmail.

Like the Palestinians, the Latin Americans realised that the mass media, domestic and foreign, were of paramount importance; on various occasions they seized radio and television stations and broadcast their propaganda. They were the first to engage in the systematic kidnapping of foreign diplomats and businessmen, correctly assuming that such operations would both embarrass the local government and attract worldwide publicity.

Manifestations of urban terrorism were reported from many parts of the globe, excepting always the Communist countries and other effective dictatorships. By the late-1960s the achievements of the small terrorist groups which had evolved from the much broader New Left Movement in Europe, Japan and the United States were few and far between. The small New Left groups withered away or were absorbed in the new international terrorism. This was also to expand at a far greater rate than the Latin American and the nationalist-separatist movements. Wide publicity for terrorist acts contributed to the growing international status of the Palestine Liberation Organisation. Democratic societies were compelled to divert some resources to defence against terrorist attacks but these were minute measured by any standards. It was not until the 1970s that there was the internationalisation of terrorist violence, which in the 1960s had been centred on mainly domestic problems within Latin America, Europe and the Middle East.

Origin of Terrorist Groups 1950–1990

A violent group can emerge from a peaceful campaign of social protest. Groups can be attracted to a cultural, religious or ethnic minority, demanding independence. People in exile can help in the formation of groups. The urban guerrilla group can appear – usually left-wing, and right-wing groups (some with anti-Semitic ideals) can emerge to challenge them. There are of course, the traditional groups – anti-Colonial and rural guerrilla.

Colonial groups include EOKA (the National Organisation of Cypriot Struggle – formed in 1955 to drive British occupying forces from Cyprus) or the IRA in its early years; ethnic, religious, cultural minorities such as ETA and the Black Panthers, left-wing ideological minorities such as the RAF; right-wing ideological minorities such as the New Order; double minority such as the Red Brigade and FLN; and exiles portrayed by South Moluccans and Japanese Red Army; and urban guerrillas such as the Montoreros and Tupamaros.

Terrorist Developments 1982–2002

Two decades ago, terrorist motives were associated with nationalism and separatism and leaned toward revolutionary and Cold War ideological zeal. Now there is greater complexity, diversity and unpredictability. State sponsors are more secretive and economical with the truth. Single issue fanatics such as suicide bombers can commit terrible attacks with great persistence. Religion, extremism and hatred have made the motives of terrorists more complex.

Increasingly intelligence has served to support strands of counter-terrorist activity, but they are facing huge difficulties, for example the absence of state sponsorship which makes them more unpredictable and controllable, the hybrid character (partly political and partly criminal); and enormous killing power.

Today Italian, Turkish and Russian Mafia, Colombian and Mexican cartels, Japanese yakuzas and Chinese triads control financial and 'military' assets of a clearly strategic nature; and participate in the most murderous forms of terrorism. They are trafficking in drugs, computer chips, humans, toxic wastes and nuclear materials and are based in many cities in the Third World and metropolises in Europe. The joint presence of gangsters, terrorists and drug traffickers trading in human beings, arms and illegal substances is a lethal combination. Environmental issues have also come to the fore and anti-nuclear groups have even blown up trains transporting nuclear fuel in Germany to make their point in a terrifying way, and in the USA tried to poison water reservoirs.

Gangster-terrorism is becoming more prevalent as on the island of Corsica where over 500 bomb attacks in 1996 for example, were said to involve terrorism 25 per cent of the time and gangsterism the rest of the time.

Four types of terrorism have emerged which are unique to the present time. First, mass casualty terrorism – the successful destruction of the World Trade Center in 2001 following the relative failure of the attack in 1993. Second, state-sponsored chemical or biological weapons – where a rogue state for example, North Korea, might help a terrorist group. Third, small scale chemical or biological attacks and lastly super-terrorism: the use of chemical or biological agents to cause a huge death tolls numbering hundred and thousands of deaths.

Terrorism can pose different levels of challenge, varying in scope and scale. They can be ambiguous and throw nations off balance which resulted on September 11. Nevertheless the cycle of terror can be ended due to the organisation behind it imploding – the Baader-Meinhof gang in Germany – or intelligence resulting in the arrest and conviction of the main actors (the Medellin drug cartel in Colombia) – political initiatives render terror activities inappropriate such as the Provisional IRA.

Force alone has never ended a terrorist campaign. Revenge is understandable, but history has proved it to be rarely effective.

The arena of terrorism is taking place in two worlds. The globalised world is made up of relatively stable systems adapting the tolerant values of multicultural pluralism. The other world is one of traditional rivalries where national or religious myths flourish and where force dominates the political life. In this arena of fragmentary states, chaos and genocide the new forms of terror are born which the globalised world finds it hard to challenge and overcome. Moreover this globalised world is dominated by the United States and as a result has been able to defend a traditional role of national sovereignty that has emphasised its ability to shape events without paying too much attention to the opinion of others. In any war against terrorism who is the enemy? Indeed, what is the new terrorism? Nations view this latter question from very different perspectives – ranging from strategic, highly dramatic attacks to recruiting new operatives.

In the era of new terrorism, the democratic nations of the world are aware of the need to maintain the role of international law, humanitarian responses, protection for human rights and the protocols of war.

See also: Mafia; Narco-Terrorism.

References

Granville, B. (2001) 'Shaken', *The World Today* vol. 57, no. 10 (October).

Griset, P. L. and Mahan, S. (2003) *Terrorism in Perspective*, London and New Delhi: Sage Publications.

Klare, M. T. (1996) 'Redefining Security: The New Global Schisms', *Current History* vol. 95, no. 589 (November), pp. 353–8.

Lodge, J. (ed.) (1982) *Terrorism: A Challenge to the State*, Oxford: Martin Robertson.

Further Reading

Bulmer-Thomas, V. (2001) 'Targeting Terrorism', *The World Today*, vol. 57, no.10 (October), pp. 8–10.

Garden, T. (2001) 'Weapons of Mass Destruction', *The World Today*, vol. 57, no. 10 (October), pp. 4–6.

Grosscup, B. (1998) *The Newest Explosives of Terrorism: Latest Sites of Terrorism in the 1990s and Beyond*, Far Hills, NJ: New Horizon Press.

Hasham, M. (2001) 'New Century, New War', *The World Today*, vol. 57, no. 10 (October), pp. 12–13.

Jones, D. M. and Smith, M. L. R. (2001) 'Franchising Terror', *The World Today*, vol. 57, no. 10 (October), pp. 10–12.

Sweitzer, G. E. and Dorsch, C. C. (1998) *Super-Terrorism: Assassins, Mobsters and Weapons of Mass Destruction*, New York: Plenum Trade.

21st Century

Terrorism has developed rapidly evolving forms through the use of technology and as a result is often one step ahead of the law. Information technology can be used as a means to an end, whereas terrorists can target information technology systems as the end itself.

Armageddon-style terrorism will be recognisable by a global network that enables events to be directed with anonymity. They will utilise technology's maximum potential for operational and administrative purposes. They will use satellite phones and sophisticated encryption devices and will purchase protected technology and substances from rogue states.

Nerd-style terrorism is the mutation of the passive resistance of the 1960s. Unlike the Armageddonists who are religiously motivated the Nerds are ideologically founded seeking symbolic disruptive action on a large scale. They can use computer viruses and logic bombs to attack information and control systems which are ideologically flawed; such as banking systems, money markets and air traffic control centres; or the power and water networks of large metropolitan networks.

Ultimately cyber-terrorism is a result of the Internet, not just computer technology. The worry is that several Internet sites provide data on Semtex for example.

Conventional counter-terror efforts have recognised the value of technology and the benefits of networks comprising members of law enforcement, military and intelligent agencies. The big challenge in facing up to the challenge of terrorism in the new millennium is that the world is shrinking (Lynch, 1999).

References

Chaliand, G. (1987) *Terrorism from Popular Struggle to Media Spectacle*, London: Saqi Books.

Gurr, T. R. (1989) 'Political Terrorism: Historical Antecedents and Contemporary Trends' in Gurr, T. R. (ed.) (1989) *Violence in America* vol. 2: Protest, Rebellion, Reform, Newbury Park, CA: Sage Publications, pp. 201–230.

Howard, L. (ed.) (1992) *Terrorism: Roots, Impact, Response*, New York: Praeger.

Lynch, L. (1999) 'Terrorism and Technology' in *New Millennium*, Platypus Magazine, no. 65 (December).

Taylor, E. (1998) *Lethal Mists: An Introduction to the Natural and Military Sciences of Chemical, Biological Warfare and Terrorism*, Commack, New York: Nova Science.

Further Reading

Bell, D. H. (1987) 'Comment: The Origins of Modern Terrorism', *Terrorism*, vol. 9, no. 3, pp. 307–11.

Ivianski, Z. (1987) 'The Terrorist Revolution – Roots of Modern Terrorism', *Journal of Strategic Studies*, vol. 10, no. 4 (December), pp. 127–149.

O'Sullivan, N. (1986) *Terrorism, Ideology and Revolution*, Brighton: Wheatsheaf Books.

Hizbullah

Hizbullah, or the Party of God, was formed in 1982 in Baalbek and is considered the largest radical movement in **Lebanon**, although its strength cannot be accurately judged because it has no official structure or membership list. Any **Shi'ite** state which adheres to Islamic tenets is, in theory, a member of Hizbullah. The movement, which was started by militant local clerics, is aided by the Iranian Revolutionary Guard, which had deployed in Lebanon's eastern Bekaa Valley after the Israeli invasion.

By the mid-1980s Hizbullah had infiltrated Beirut. At first, it did not publicise its presence, but gradually militant posters and the return to conservative Islamic dress by Shi'ite women revealed the strength of Hizbullah. At this time the group had at least three offices in West Beirut.

Hizbullah addresses its message to the downtrodden, opting for religion, freedom and dignity over humiliation and constant submission to the **USA** and its allies. The movement is loyal to Ayatollah Khomeini and has listed three goals in Lebanon: first, to expel the US, France and the influence of any imperialist power from the country, and the expulsion of Israel 'as a prelude to its final obliteration from existence' and the liberation of 'venerable Jerusalem'; second, the submission of the Christian Phalange Party, and trial of its members for crimes against Muslims and Christians; and third, to give people the opportunity to determine their faith (although Hizbullah has an overriding commitment to the rule of Islam).

Hizbullah has become the umbrella cover for a host of smaller factions including Islamic Amal, the Hussein Suicide Squad, Dawah (the Lebanese branch of the Iraq-based al-Dawah al-Islamia), and other smaller movements.

See also: Iran; Lebanon.

References

Kramer, M. (1990) 'The Moral Logic of Hizbullah' in W. Reich (ed.) *Origins of Terrorism*, Cambridge: Cambridge University Press, pp. 131–160.

TVI Profile Report (1990) Hizbullah (Party of God), *TVI Report*, vol. 9, no. 3, pp. 1–6.

Further Reading

Jaber, H. (1997) *Hizbullah: Born with a Vengeance*, London: Fourth Estate.

Homeland Security *see* September 11: Homeland Security

Hostage Negotiation

This often devolves down to a policy debate on whether deterrence deters, and to a 'no ransom' versus negotiation argument.

On the general question of deterrence, those who demand prisoners' freedom focus adverse publicity on the government. Those who demand ransoms put targets in a bad light. Many attacks are made in retaliation for governmental moves against terrorist organisations. Groups may engage in

kidnapping to publicise an overall ideology. Some kidnappers hope to disrupt society's expectation of security and order. Terrorists hope to provoke government repression against themselves. A hostage may be of some value to those who have seized him. An incident may represent an individual's personal affirmation of solidarity with the norms of a terrorist group. Many observers believe that if a tough policy stopped terrorist incidents, terrorists would engage in other types of violent action that did not involve hostages.

The 'no ransom' position is centred on certain basic approaches. Terrorists are all the same – with a leftist ideology, and employ the same tactics. Due to their links, there is perhaps the creation of a terrorist international – with the same funding sources, worldwide meetings and joint operations. While capitulation encourages others, in isolated incidents the opposite is true. The temptation to kidnap diplomats can be removed by denying rewards. The 'no ransom' view maintains that it is morally wrong to give in to the demands of groups engaging in terrorist acts. Governments have responsibility to protect political prisoners; and ultimately a stated policy cannot countenance giving in to terrorist demands.

The flexible response position is perhaps more complex. Primarily, terrorists are not all the same and do not react in the same way in hostage situations. They differ in ideology and purpose in the choice of terrorism, differ in tactics, and do not have the same views on the sanctity of life, and rarely double-cross bargainers. Links between groups do not lead to a commonality of tactics, strategy, and agreed perceptions of motivations. Rarely do terrorists attend relevant international meetings. Some groups, notably the **Palestine Liberation Organisation** (PLO), are split on the sanctity of life, tactics and strategy. Many terrorist groups fight primary terrorist groups – and nation states have many links – including trade and communications. Examination of the site of incidents provides clues on how to conduct negotiations. The contagion hypothesis rests on shaky evidence. Governments have a moral duty to protect nationals. Terrorists care about what happens to them after an incident. Ultimately, granting asylum is a time-honoured practice, and the politics of desperation is the last refuge of the weak.

See also: Hostage Taking; Kidnapping.

Hostage Taking

In recent years hostage taking has become a favourite tactic of political terrorists, largely because of the intense publicity surrounding such terrorist situations where hostages are involved. Hostage taking has also burgeoned as a tactic of mentally unstable and criminal individuals. Because of its high profile and the attendant publicity, and the extreme actions which governments have been prompted to take as a consequence of hostage situations, they exemplify many of the policy issues surrounding anti-terrorist operations.

Three broad groups of hostage-takers exist:

(1) *The mentally ill hostage-taker.* Primarily because of the high media exposure given to hostage and siege situations, it has become increasingly apparent to mentally unstable individuals that taking someone hostage guarantees individual recognition by the news media, the opportunity to exercise power and to put the police into a defensive posture. For those with suicidal tendencies a hostage or barricade situation is often seen as a spectacularly successful method of bringing about one's demise. It is important for the negotiators who communicate with the hostage-taker to try to understand that individual's world. The individuals involved are people with limited personal power who feel their problems occur because they are being persecuted by the world or significant segments of it. Their feelings of frustration, helplessness and lack of worth may overwhelm them so that they feel they must strike back by taking power and control over someone or some organisation that symbolises their problems.

(2) *The criminal hostage-taker.* Criminals take hostages usually as a last resort. Sometimes the police response to a crime in progress may be sufficiently rapid that the offender is trapped with what appears to him to be no alternative but to take a hostage in an attempt to bargain his way out of custody. While criminals are generally rational when committing a crime, they obviously do not want to be arrested and

may display somewhat less than their usual reason when the police corner them.

(3) *The social, political, ethnic or 'religious crusade' hostage-taker.* Such a hostage-taker is generally a member of a group, which can be defined as terrorist, and will have a strong sense of commitment to or belief in a particular idea or cause. Terrorist groups are usually small, but extremely dedicated, even to the point of dying for the furtherance of their beliefs and ideas. Whatever the goal of their particular movement, professional terrorists have usually studied revolutionary tactics and effective methods of promoting and broadcasting the basis for their ideology or cause. Terrorist groups are most difficult to deal with because of their total commitment. Although rational, they often enter a situation with set demands and identified limits as to what they are willing to do in the furtherance of their cause. Frequently members of these groups are committed to the extent that they will kill or die if necessary. Although situations involving terrorists are complicated by their determination, extensive planning, and ability to exert power effectively, experience has shown that alternatives to the original demands can often be worked out, frequently ones which concede little in political terms.

Since hostage and siege situations are a major form of terrorist activity (not necessarily in terms of frequency, but certainly in terms of impact), security forces around the world over the past decade have been developing special negotiating procedures to cope with these situations in order to prevent the killing of innocent hostages or the granting of significant political concessions to the terrorists. The leaders in this field have been the British and the Dutch in dealing with political terrorists, and the New York City Police Department in dealing with criminal hostage-takers. The development of hostage negotiation techniques is an evolving process, with new approaches becoming necessary as new types of hostage situations emerge or as hostage-takers become aware of negotiating techniques and seek to minimise their effects. Terrorists do change their tactics in response

to information about what factors swing the balance of the negotiating situation in favour of the authorities.

Hostage taking incidents have risen in the world over the past two decades, which has always attracted instant **media** coverage. The events of **September 11** were triggered by suicide hostage-takers in the four planes hijacked in the USA. The terrorist extremist is well trained and disciplined fighting to establish an independent state and such an event can remain in the headlines for days, weeks or years. The ideological zealot is one who is ready to sacrifice his or her life for a cause; as has been seen in the Middle East.

The outcome of such events can be to rescue hostages, kill hostage-takers, the surrender or flight, or suicide of the hostage-takers.

Social impacts of such events can also be widespread – a new type of criminal behaviour is promoted; new legislation is enacted; there is a heightened public and private security awareness; police specialised units are created and international co-operation is improved.

Their demands are for the release of prisoners, the payment of a ransom and publication of a manifesto. The police can respond by giving in to demands, sit out 'the crisis', attempt a rescue mission or negotiate (the latter requiring high quality trained negotiators).

People can copy hostage-takers, particularly those who have participated in high-profile events. Tighter security measures will continue to predominate strategies to defeat hostage-takers. Even this state of affairs cannot overcome fear, which can result from prolonged media exposure to hostage taking and violent behaviour. This fear was long lasting in the case of the New York **World Trade Center** bombing in 1993 and the Federal Building in **Oklahoma** in 1995.

The basic concepts of hostage taking include selecting and training hostage negotiators, securing the co-operation of the media, identifying all hostages and hostage-takers, but above all, issuing a precise chain of command.

Information about hostage-takers must include demographic characteristics, emotional conditions and special requirements such as police officers being held hostage. Detailed information must be ascertained about the hostage site including self-observation postures and food availability (Poland, 1998).

The negotiator must be able to 'deal' with the hostage-taker who controls the hostages and makes the decisions. The hostage negotiator must adopt a positive self-image and have sound verbal skills. Differences in perception, anger or frustration and hostility have to be acknowledged by both negotiator and hostage-taker. The greatest enemy of a hostage is de-moralisation by inactivity and contemplating the worst possible things that hostage-takers may do.

In recent years a new generation of hostage-takers has appeared – namely young people who have grown up in an atmosphere of violence and terrorism, whether it be in Northern **Ireland**, **Lebanon** or Sri Lanka. Such people view violence as the only legitimate way to address their grievances – they are characterised as having a sense of hopelessness being young, poor and with limited education. They are hostile to Western values in society.

A real threat exists that hostage-takers could capture an intact nuclear weapon, which would create an international crisis.

The misuse of biological agents such as bacteria, viruses, fungi and protozoa, could also create great fear as mass casualties can occur and whole countries taken hostage. Such agents are silent killers and can be used to extort large sums of money to undermine a country's economy but above all to inhibit the development of natural resources. In the future more sophisticated hostage taking techniques can be anticipated from future criminal, terrorist and psychotic hostage-takers.

For each hostage rescue mission, detailed information is needed to try to ensure maximum success. The terrorists have to be studied in detail – how many are involved? What weapons are they armed with? Their initial demands; their description and background; which group do they represent and their operational history; and what outside support can they access.

Regarding the hostages, one has to know how many are involved; where they are located; their physical and psychological condition and their names and particulars.

If an aircraft is involved, one needs to know the internal layout, fuel, range, speed and flight duration; the situation inside the plane in particular with regard to food and water.

If a building is taken over detailed street maps and engineering plans are required; telephone numbers; lists of people who work in the building and detailed plans of adjacent buildings – the safe ending of the Iranian Embassy in London in 1980 proved the value of having this information.

See also: Hostage Negotiation; Kidnapping; Psychology of Terrorism; Stockholm Syndrome.

References

Miller, A. H. (1980) *Terrorism and Hostage Negotiations*, Boulder, CO: Westview Press.
Poland, J. M. (1998) *Understanding Terrorism: Groups, Strategies and Responses*, Upper Saddle River, NJ: Prentice Hall.

Further Reading

Antokol, N. and Mayer, N. (1990) *No One is Neutral: Political Hostage Taking in the Modern World*, Medina, OH: Alpha.
Cooper, H. H. A. (1980) *The Hostage Takers*, Boulder, CO: Paladin Press.
Coughlin, C. (1992) *Hostage: The Complete Story of the Lebanon Captives*, London: Little, Brown and Co.
Taillon, J. P. de B. (2002) *Hijacking and Hostages: Government Responses to Terrorism*, Westport, CT and London: Praeger.

Human Rights

In recent years the human rights issue has become more prominent in international relations. International human rights are no longer binding on the **USA** and it has been very negative in its attitude to the **International Criminal Court** set up in 2002. Post **September 11** the Americans have ignored reports of abusive treatment of detainees in **Afghanistan** and **Cuba**. Human rights issues have also played a role in US policy concerning **China**, **Iran**, **Iraq** and **North Korea** (Booth and Dunne, 2002). Although the USA and China had agreed a most favoured

nation trade agreement there was much controversy in America over human rights and repression in China during the 1980s and 1990s
especially in Tibet and Xinjiang (Cooley, 2002).
With regard to **Chechnya**, most countries in the
West found themselves at odds with **Russia** over
human rights violations in Chechnya. The Russians consistently referred to the Chechen fighters
as terrorists. Yet the Russians themselves were to
complain to the West about human rights
violations of the Serbs in the Balkans; while the
West pursued Milosevic his attitude and hatred of
Croats, Bosnians and Muslim/Albanians. **Algeria**
justified its repression of Islamic militants on anti-
terrorist grounds whereas other nations saw widespread human rights abuse in that country (Booth
and Dunne, 2002). With regard to Northern
Ireland, many people in America and Russia
saw the policy of the British government –
especially towards the IRA in the 1960s, 1970s
and 1980s as human rights abuse.

Public opinion in many democratic nations
perhaps comes to the view that terrorists who take
part in war crimes do not deserve any protection
by the democratic organs of the state. Homeland
security is a policy first used in the USA to secure
the country against terrorist threats, and is now
being considered in other countries. To some
observers it can be used to control day-to-day
lives. The rapid growth of transnational terrorism
has resulted in nations re-empowering themselves
by tightening immigration controls. In such a
situation an abuse of human rights – deliberately
or accidentally – is bound to occur, as people
perceive a sense of increasing insecurity. Many
observers have argued that the war against
terrorism will lack legitimacy unless the powerful
nations undertake to reduce global inequalities
and end extreme poverty. Yet the events post
September 11 have seen a commitment to a
universal code of human rights to be a long time
in the making. There is scepticism about the
validity of unequal human rights – and many are
concerned by the pressure of external sanctions on
Iraqi civilians and the threat of air strikes if non-
compliance with Western demands occurs (Booth
and Dunne, 2002).

Terrorism seriously jeopardises human rights,
threatens democracy and aims to undermine
pluralistic civil society and destabilise democratic
governments. Terrorist acts can never be excused or
justified by citing motives such as human rights.
The fight against terrorism implies long-term
measures with a view to preventing the causes of
terrorism, by promoting societal cohesion and a
multi-cultural and inter-religious dialogue (Council
of Europe, *Guidelines on Human Rights and the Fight
against Terrorism*, 2002). States have an obligation to
respect in their fight against terrorism the international instruments for the protection of human
rights. The penalties incurred by a person accused
of terrorist activities have to be provided for by law
and a person deprived of his/her liberty for
terrorist activities must in all circumstances be
treated with due respect for human dignity. All
requests for asylum have to be dealt with on an
individual basis; and extradition has to be seen as
an essential procedure for effective international
co-operation in the fight against terrorism.

Courts of human rights argue that states may
never act in breach of international law or in
breach of international humanitarian law.

The European Court of Human Rights argues
that a basic definition of terrorism is any offence
committed by an individual or groups resorting to
violence being motivated by separatism, extreme
ideological concepts and fanaticism – all intending
to create a climate of terror.

A terrorist act in their view is one which
seriously intimidates a population, destabilises or
destroys the fundamental structures of society;
compels a government or international organisation to do or not do a specific act; **kidnapping**;
attacks on a person; the seizure of planes or ships;
the manufacture, possession or supply of weapons,
explosives and the release of dangerous substances.
The directing of a terrorist group and a structured
group (one not randomly formed for the immediate commission of a terrorist act) is also
considered an offence. On the issue of legal
proceedings, a person accused of terrorist activities
has the right to a fair hearing, within a reasonable
time, by an independent impartial tribunal
established by law.

See also: Children; Rights.

References

Booth, K. and Dunne, T. (eds) (2002) *Worlds in Collision: Terror and the Future Global Order*, Basingstoke and New York: Palgrave Macmillan.

Cooley, J. K. (2002) *Unholy Wars: Afghanistan, America and International Terrorism*, London: Pluto Press.

Further Reading

Guidelines on Human Rights and the Fight against Terrorism, (2002), Strasbourg: Council of Europe Publishing.

Kupperman, R. H. (1985) 'On Terror and Civil Liberties', *Harvard International Review*, vol. 7 (May/June), pp. 16–17.

Quigley, J. (1988) 'Government Vigilantes at large: The Danger to Human Rights from Kidnapping of Suspected Terrorist', *Human Rights Quarterly*, no. 10 (May), pp. 193–213.

India

In terms of terrorism and political violence in recent times in India, the world thinks of the Sikhs and their demands for an independent state, especially after the Golden Temple incident in June 1984 and the assassination of Mrs Gandhi in October that year. Nevertheless, there are other illegal movements, many of which are separatist, and mainly represent communities or are extreme left-wing. There is also a profusion of legally existing political parties, both at national and at state level. Divisions of existing parties, defections from these parties and formations of new parties have been frequent.

Hindu movements are well-established in origin. The All Assam People's Struggle Council was set up to oppose the inclusion of aliens, or Muslims who had fled from East **Pakistan** in 1971, when that territory seceded from Pakistan and became Bangladesh. Many atrocities have been committed against Bengalis and three massacres were reported in 1985. The All Assam Students Group actively campaigns against Bengali immigrants in Assam. On a broader scale many Hindus have been attracted by the paramilitary nature of the National Union of Selfless Servers. It is a communal group functioning as a secret society offshoot of the Hindu Jan Sangh sect that provoked street violence with Muslims. It is estimated to have up to ten million members. Less paramilitary but equally extremist is the left-wing Hindu group known as Ananda Marg. It wishes to establish global unity on the basis of a new social economic theory, and regularly uses suicide as a way of expression. It has been active in

Australia against Indian diplomats. The political wing of this movement is the Universal Proutist Revolutionary Party. The word Proutist is derived from the 'progressive utility" theory developed by one of its members, P. R. Sarkar.

The most well-known of the left-wing movements are the Naxalites who originated from an armed revolutionary campaign launched in North Bengal in 1965. This extreme faction of the Communist Party of India (Marxist-Leninist) was formed as a result of disagreements over operational strategy for the spread of communism in rural India. The Naxalites were committed to Maoist principles of people's liberation warfare. In the 1970s some members led by Satya Singh rejected revolutionary Marxism and support parliamentary democracy. Nevertheless, extremists continue to carry out attacks in over half of India's provinces, with membership numbers of around 15,000. The Naxalites support the upholding of both armed struggle and all other forms of struggle complementary to it. The other chief Left-wing movement is the Dalit Panthers, who appeared in the late 1960s as an organisation of young militant untouchables which took its inspiration from the Black Panthers in the **USA**. They have been active in encouraging conversions of Harijans to **Islam**, as a means of escaping from the caste system.

In addition to the **Sikh** and Kashmiri separatists, other separatist groups are active in other parts of India. In Manipur the People's Liberation Army is active. It is a Maoist organisation operating mainly in Manipur, but advocating independence from the whole north-eastern region of India. Support comes from tribes who have rejected

Hinduism as a faith identified with the cultural domination of New Delhi. Like the People's Liberation Army, the People's Revolutionary Party of Kungleipak (PREPAK) has been active in the state of Manipur, whose secession from the Union of India it seeks.

In Mizoram, and in particular in the Mizo Hills district in southern Assam, the Mizo National Front is active, as well as around the borders of Bangladesh. The Naga separatist movement has had a history of armed and non-violent resistance to the incorporation of Nagaland in the Union of India, of which that territory became a constituent state in 1972. In recent years factional groups have been formed which have reduced its effectiveness.

Also in North East India in Tripura, one finds armed extremists campaigning for an independent Tripura. The radical, cultural and social organisation of Tripura Hill Youth has links with the Mizo National Front in terms of weaponry, training and logistical support.

In 1987, India intervened in the conflict in Sri Lanka, pressing for a ceasefire and an agreement between Tamils and Sinhalese by sending in troops. After suffering many casualties they withdrew in 1990, Rajiv Gandhi was assassinated by the Tamil Liberation movement in May 1991.

Throughout the 1990s tensions mounted with Pakistan who had increased its support for the Kashmir Independence Movement. Violence occurred during elections in various parts of the country. In 1992 numerous acts of violence took place at the instigation of Hindu fundamentalists against the Islamic population in the northern cities of Bombay and Ayodhya. Violence continued to simmer among the religious communities. The exploding of an atomic device by India in May 1998 caused upset and outrage provoking a similar action by Pakistan a few weeks later. The tense nature of relations between the two countries has continued to the present day.

See also: Sikhs.

Reference

Qureshi, S. (1976) 'Political Violence in the South Asia Subcontinent' in Alexander, Y. (ed.) *Terror-ism: International; National; Regional and Global Perspectives*, New York: Praeger, pp. 151–193.

Further Reading

Leof, M. J. (1987) 'The Punjab Crisis' in W. Laqueur (ed.) *The Terrorism Reader*, New York: Meridian.

Mulgannon, T. (1988) 'The Sikhs of Punjab', *TVI Report*, vol. 6, no. 2.

Tiwari, S. C. (ed.) (1990) *Terrorism in India*, New Delhi: South Asia.

Indoctrination see Psychology of Terrorism: Indoctrination

Insurgency

In its most general sense insurgency is a struggle between a non-ruling group and the ruling authorities, in which the former consciously employs political resources (organisational skills, propaganda or demonstrations or both) and instruments of violence to establish legitimacy for some aspect of the political system which the ruling authorities consider illegitimate.

Legitimacy and illegitimacy refer to the public perception of whether existing aspects of politics are moral or immoral. Insurgents seek through violent means to separate themselves from existing arrangements and to establish a separate political community.

Dissidents can grant legitimacy to the regime but reject individuals in power. This is exemplified by coups in which insurgents seize the key to decision-making offices without changing the regime of their predecessors. Basically, it is a crisis about political legitimacy.

Six types of insurgent movements have been isolated from the general theories of **political violence**. Secessionist insurgents reject the existing political community of which they are credibly a part and seek to constitute an independent organisation. Revolutionary insurgents seek to impose a new regime based on egalitarian values and centrally controlled structures to activate the people and change the social structure. Restorational insurgent movements wish to displace the regime and the values and structures they champion are identified with a recent political order. Reactionary insurgents seek to change the regime by reconstituting a past political order, but their vision relates to an idealised golden age of the distant past in which religious values and authoritarian structures were predominant – i.e. the Ayatollah in **Iran** seeks to recreate the seventh-century Islamic society, as perceived by **Shi'ite** Muslims. Conservative insurgents seek to maintain the existing regime in the face of pressures on the authorities to change it, as exemplified by Protestant organisations in Ulster who wish to retain the regime in Northern **Ireland** which they see as threatened by the Irish Republican Army. Reformist insurgents such as the Kurds in Iraq have attempted to obtain more political, social and economic benefits without necessarily rejecting the political community, regime or authorities.

Insurgent movements use both political resources and instruments of violence against the ruling authorities in order to accomplish their objectives. Organisation can be of two types – conspiratorial, where small elite groups carry out and threaten violent acts, or internal warfare where insurgent elites attempt to mobilise large segments of the population on behalf of their cause. Internal warfare cases are widespread and include Vietnamese, Cambodian, Chinese, Algerian and Portuguese colonial conflicts. Ample cases of conspiratorial insurgencies exist, such as those led by the Bolsheviks in Tsarist Russia, the Red Army in **Japan**, the Red Brigades in Italy and the Muslim Brotherhood in **Egypt**.

Insurgents need to maximise the effectiveness of political techniques and violence. Popular support can be divided into two categories – active and passive. Passive support includes those who merely sympathise with the aims and activities of the insurgents, and active includes individuals who are willing to risk personal sacrifices on behalf of the insurgents. Active supporters are individuals who provide insurgents with supplies, intelligence information, shelter, concealment, liaison agents and carry out acts of disobedience or protest which bring severe punishment by the government. Insurgents seek to gain support and recruits by charismatic attraction, esoteric or private appeals, public

appeals, terrorism, the provocation of government **counter-terrorism** and a demonstration of potency. The latter includes meeting the needs of the people through social services and a governing apparatus and obtaining the military initiative.

Insurgency can be seen as more of a political phenomenon than a military one. The analysis of an insurgent organisation involves scope, complexity and cohesion, and assessing whether the government is providing services and channels for expressive protest. 'Scope' refers to the number of people who either play key roles in the movement or provide active support. If there is a need to supplement membership an insurgent organisation will increase its activity and demands and through the efforts of its political cadres penetrate hamlets, villages and cities, especially in areas in which neither the government nor insurgents have firm control. In many cases insurgents have established parallel hierarchies to compete with government institutions. What can occur is the penetration of the existing official administrative structures by subversive agents, or the creation of autonomous insurgent structures to take over full administrative responsibility when military-political conditions are deemed appropriate. For greater support, new branches can be created, such as youth groups, peasant organisations, workers' groups and women's organisations.

Insurgents engaged in a lengthy armed struggle can diversify their military organisation by creating logistics units, terrorist networks and guerrilla forces with the last mentioned divided between full-time and part-time fighters. Full-time guerrillas can operate from secure bases attack government military units and installations on a continual basis and constitute a nucleus for a regularised force in the event that the movement gets involved in mobile conventional warfare. Part-time guerrillas stay in their communities and provide a number of invaluable services – collecting intelligence, storing supplies and protecting political organisers. For the individual, participation can yield material benefits if the organisation has the resources, and it can generate psychological satisfaction by virtue of the new sense of identity that stems from the perception that one is engaged in common endeavour.

To achieve unity, insurgent movements stress

common attitudes, sanctions and organisational schemes. Organisational formats are important in the establishment of cohesion – control by politicians, independent political and military commands and control by the military. Rival movements can still continue to exist and operate and as a result insurgents may attempt to co-ordinate activity by creating a unified command for a particular operation, by arriving at a division of labour among various groups or by establishing a unified command for all operations.

The most publicised aspect of insurgent strategy is its frequent stress on external support as yet another means to offset the government's advantages. Moral support is the least costly and risky for a donor, for all it involves is public acknowledgment that the insurgent movement is just and admirable. Political support advances a step further as the donor nation supports the strategic goal of the insurgent movement in the international arena. Material assistance is more concrete and risky for an outside power, and includes money, weapons, ammunition, medical supplies, food, training and perhaps the provision of military advisers, fire support or combat units. It is valuable as the insurgents can increase the scale and intensity of violence, since such a development necessitates greater logistical support.

In terms of conceptual sophistication, insurgent strategies range from the carefully articulated to the chaotic.

Insurgents who adhere to a Leninist strategy believe that a small, tightly knit, disciplined and highly organised conspiratorial group that has obtained support from major disconnected social groups, such as the military and working class, provides the most effective means for achieving the goal of the movement. The Leninist approach assumes a government that is alienated from its population, hence one which will surrender when confronted by low-level terrorism, subversion of the military and the police and the final seizure of radio stations, government offices and other state institutions.

The most elaborate insurgent strategy is expounded by Maoist theoreticians who ascribe great significance to popular support, extensive organisational efforts and the environment as resources necessary for a prolonged conflict with an enemy

perceived as being in a superior position prior to hostilities. The Maoist approach unfolds in distinct steps, each of which is designed to achieve part of the goal and is dependent on the outcome of the step before it. These stages of political organisation are terrorism, **guerrilla warfare** and mobile conventional warfare. Initially the insurgents stress esoteric and exoteric appeals as well as the social services and mutual help aspects associated with demonstrations of potency. Guerrilla warfare is a 'social' stage – the earliest part of this stage is characterised by armed resistance carried out by small bands operating in rural areas where terrain is rugged and government control weak. **Civil war**, the final stage of a Maoist-type insurgency, involves regularisation of guerrilla forces and mobile-conventional warfare. Maoist insurgent strategy emphasise three inter-related elements; popular support, organisation and the environment. Environmental characteristics are important in the Maoist strategy. However, external support has an ambiguous place in the framework of Maoist strategy. Although self-reliance is the overriding consideration, in practice, moral, political, material and sanctuary support have played a key role, especially in offsetting similar assistance to the government.

In recent decades insurgents have found the urban terrorist model to be attractive. Emphasis is placed on popular support and erosion of the enemy's will to resist, rather than on defeating the enemy in classical military engagements. Unlike the Maoist example, the focus of conflict during initial phases is in the cities rather than the countryside, because of the assumption that the increased size and socio-economic differentiation of urban centres makes them vulnerable to terrorism and sabotage. For an urban strategy to be successful it would seem the regime would already have to be on the brink of collapse.

Within the general rubric of insurgency, terrorism emerges as but one means of achieving political ends. As a decisive strategic technique there is little to undermine its efficacy. However, insurgents do have political and military weaknesses, and the prolonged use of insurgent activities is normally counter-productive, in that it galvanises governments to greater efforts and outrages the previously apathetic public.

See also: Chinese Revolution; Counter-insurgency; Guerrilla Warfare in History.

References

Merari, A. (1993) 'Terrorism as a Strategy of Insurgency', *Terrorism and Political Violence*, vol. 5, no. 4 (winter), pp. 213–251.

Nayak, S. G. (2001) 'Intensity and Impact Analysis of Insurgency/Extremism', *The Police Journal*, vol. 74, pp. 316–329.

O'Neill, B. (1990) *Insurgency and Terrorism*, London: Brassey's.

Silverman, J. M. and Jackson, P. M. (1970) 'Terror in Insurgency Warfare', *Military Review*, vol. 50.

Further Reading

Laqueur, W. (1976) *Guerrilla: A Historical and Critical Study*, Boston, MA: Little, Brown and Co.

— (1987) *The Age of Terrorism*, Boston, MA: Little, Brown and Co.

Liddell Hart, B. H. (1954) *Strategy: The Indirect Approach*, London: Faber.

O'Neill, B. E. (ed.) (1980) 'Insurgency: A Framework for Analysis' in B. E. O'Neill (ed.) *Insurgency in the Modern World*, Boulder, CO: Westview Press.

— (1984) 'Insurgency: The Context of Terrorism' in H. H. Han (ed.) *Terrorism, Political Violence and World Order*, Lanham, MD: University Press of America.

Intelligence Roles

Generalised measures are never sufficient to stop terrorists, even though they may be very effective in drying up the potential bases of popular support for the terrorist movement. Authorities have to be prepared for the attacks and campaigns of varying duration and intensity launched by numerically tiny groups which may entirely lack popular sympathy or support.

Widespread support is rare, and groups are usually based on a structure of cells or 'firing groups' of about six persons. They exercise a degree of operational independence and initiative and are obsessively concerned with the security of their organisation and lines of communication. This cell structure is designed to enhance secrecy, mobility and flexibility while at the same time facilitating tight overall central control by the terrorist directorate. Paramilitary command structures and discipline are fostered to ensure unswerving obedience to the leadership; offenders against the terrorist code are ruthlessly punished, often by death. Experienced terrorists develop sophisticated cover against detection and infiltration. They are adept at hiding in the anonymity of the urban landscape and at swiftly changing their bases of operations. Terrorists are constantly engaged in training new 'hit men', bomb-makers, small-arms specialists and assassins. In a protracted and carefully planned campaign certain individuals and cells in the terrorist movement will be strategically placed as 'sleepers', to be actuated later in the struggle as and when required.

The terrorists' small numbers and anonymity make them an extraordinarily difficult quarry for the police in modern cities, while the ready availability of light, portable arms and materials required for home-made bombs makes it difficult to track down terrorist lines of supply. Once the key members of a cell have been identified it is generally practicable to round up other members. On the basis of information gleaned from interrogating a relatively small number of key terrorist operatives it is possible to spread the net more effectively around the whole organisation.

A crucial requirement for defeating any political terrorist campaign therefore must be the development of high-quality intelligence, for unless the security authorities are fortunate enough to capture a terrorist red-handed at the scene of the crime; it is only by sifting through comprehensive and accurate intelligence data that the police have any hope of locating the terrorists. Government and security chiefs need to know a great deal about groups and individuals that are seeking rewards by terrorism, about their aims, political motivations and alignments, leadership, individual members, logistic and financial resources and organisational structures.

The greatest weakness of modern liberal states in the field of internal defence is a reluctance or inability to see subversion as a problem until it is too late. The primary objective of an efficient intelligence service must be to prevent any insurgency or terrorism developing beyond the conceptual stage. A high-quality intelligence service is required long before the insurgency erupts. It is vital that such a service should have a national responsibility, and be firmly under the control of the civil authorities and hence democratically accountable. In a liberal democratic state the most appropriate body for the tasks of intelligence-gathering collation, analysis and co-ordination is the police Special Branch or its equivalent. It is normally the case in a liberal state that the police service enjoys at least some public co-operation. The routine police tasks of law enforcement and combating crime at every level of the community give the police service an unrivalled bank of background information from which contact information can be developed.

The development of a reliable, high-quality intelligence service is not easily accomplished. There are serious pitfalls. The police may lose the confidence and co-operation of certain key sections of the population. This is especially probable where the police have been controlled, administered and staffed predominantly by one ethnic or religious group and are regarded as partisan by rival groups. In such conditions it often becomes impossible for the police to carry out law enforcement functions let alone develop high standards of criminal investigation and intelligence work. In extreme cases, as in Northern **Ireland** in 1969, when the police system was faced with almost total breakdown, another agency, the army, has to be brought in to provide the intelligence system as well as exercising the major constabulary function. **Army-Police co-operation** has proved to be fairly effective since that time.

The breakdown of normal policing due to political and communal conflict is a rare occurrence in liberal states. Police and intelligence services are costly to establish and maintain and their breakdown creates grave internal dangers. Armed forces are even more expensive and no liberal state can view with equanimity the diversion of large numbers of expensive military personnel, some with very sophisticated technical training, from their vital external defence role and into what are essentially internal police functions. It is certain that Britain's small, professional, all-volunteer army

cannot afford the manpower, time or special training required for such tasks.

If the state is faced with the breakdown of civil policing and the total collapse of law and order either nationally or in a particular region, the army has an absolutely crucial though unenviable role as a weapon of last resort. It has the duty to restore order in such cases. The tasks of intelligence in an incipient civil or inter-communal war are onerous in the extreme, and the routine work of gathering and building up contact information consumes reserves of time, training and manpower that an army can ill afford. A recurrent problem for the police forces of liberal states is the difficulty of co-ordinating and gathering intelligence on a nation-wide basis. This has particularly adverse effects on anti-terrorist operations.

Crucial preconditions exist for effective co-ordination of intelligence at national level. The continuing confidence and co-operation of political leaders and the general public must be maintained. It is vital that such agencies are seen to operate within the law and that constitutional safeguards against the abuse of their powers should be seen to be effective. There has to be constant and close liaison and co-operation with the military and state security services in intelligence matters. Access to the very latest technologies of intelligence-gathering, communications and surveillance is essential. A most important need is for centralised intelligence data computerisation which can provide information swiftly for all levels of the security forces. Among the fundamental intelligence needs is the requirement for closer international co-operation among allied states in the exchange of information about terrorist movements and activities, about the involvement of hostile states and transnational or foreign revolutionary movements, and other relevant data for combating political violence.

See also: Data Sources.

Intelligence on Terrorism

Intelligence generally has a good record in warning of terrorist attacks, but in the case of the **Bali** and Mombasa bombings in 2002, it appears a breakdown in communications occurred.

MI5 was accused by a British Parliamentary Intelligence and Security Committee of misjudgement in failing to warn travellers of the threat posed by terrorists in Indonesia before the Bali bombing. At the same time the British government was accused of ignoring intelligence warnings pointing to the Bali bombing and the attack on **Israel** tourists in Mombassa, Kenya in 2002. The **United States** had warned both Britain and Australia about the possibility of attacks but it appeared only Australia heeded the prior warning of the atrocity.

See also: Data Sources; Threat Assessment Guidelines.

References

Betts, R. K. (2002) 'Fixing Intelligence', *Foreign Affairs*, vol. 81 (January–February), pp. 43–59.

Cimbala, S. J. (ed.) (1987) *Intelligence and Intelligence Policy in a Democratic Society*, Dobbs Ferry, NY: Transnational Publishers.

Martin, G. (2003) *Understanding Terrorism: Challenges, Perspectiives and Issues*, London: Sage.

Robertson, K. G. (1987) 'Intelligence Terrorism and Civil Liberties', in P. Wilkinson and A. M. Stewart (eds) *Contemporary Research on Terrorism*, Aberdeen: Aberdeen University Press, pp. 549–570.

International Community *see* Counter/Anti-Terrorism

International Criminal Court

In 1997–98 the **United Nations** made moves to establish an International Criminal Court to deal with war crimes, **genocide** and crimes against humanity. This court is able to try individuals rather than merely states for crimes. The events in former Yugoslavia and **Rwanda** created an international awareness for an international court to try individuals, such as former President Milosovic of Serbia for acts of terror. The need to solve the issue of responsibility for the **Lockerbie** tragedy in 1988 showed there was a need for an international tribunal (Combs, 2003). However, the

ICC initially was not given authority to consider crimes of terrorism. The issue was viewed as 'too politically difficult' to be included in the Courts' jurisdiction.

This court will eventually replace the International Criminal Tribunals for the former Yugoslavia and Rwanda, and will be a permanent body that will eventually try individuals for crimes against humanity throughout the world. The International Court of Justice (sometimes called the World Court) rules in disputes between governments, and cannot prosecute individuals.

By 2003, seventy-six states had ratified the treaty setting up the ICC and a further 139 said they may ratify in the future. The **USA** has refused to become involved, arguing that their soldiers may be the subject of politically motivated or frivolous prosecutions. Other countries such as **China** and **India** have not signed the treaty; while others such as **Russia** and **Iran** have signed but remain dubious. There are growing accusations levied against the court that it is geographically unrepresentative and Western dominated. The absence of the USA and **Japan** make the funding of the court more expensive for others; and Germany, France and the **UK** will be the largest contributors.

References

Combs, C. C. (2003) *Terrorism in the 21st Century*, 3rd edition, Upper Saddle River, NJ: Prentice Hall.

International Law

Contemporary principles of international law permit a state to intervene or interpose on humanitarian principles to prevent another state or persons within a state from committing a gross act of persecution or barbarism.

There have been infrequent instances of intervention or interposition for humanitarian purposes due to the decentralised nature of the contemporary international system and the mistreatment of foreign individuals does not adversely affect the intervening state except in a community sense. Intervention may ultimately operate against the interests of the persecuted individuals unless it is backed up by continuing control measures (Thackrah, 1993: 27).

International law implies a general obligation of a state not to permit its territory to be used in such a way as to endanger the legally protected interests of other states. Foreigners can expect protection from the host state. In the event the host state fails to provide such protection, they can expect their natural government to seek redress on their behalf.

Terrorism is intimidation by means of a demonstration of the impotence of the innocent to secure protection by the authorities, however much in theory they are bound to provide it. As soon as it became possible to achieve a like affect by way of international violence, terrorism became international. War does not invest terrorism with any legality, nor can it divest terrorism of criminality.

It is the absence of any international legal consensus regarding the nature and prevention of terrorism that causes governments faced with a serious terrorist threat to resort to extra-legal counter-measures. Terrorists cannot shut down a healthy society, but government over-reaction can. The contemporary terrorist is seen as a surrogate of a patron state utilising terrorism as an extension of its foreign policy. 'Phantom Warfare' can describe the surrogate nature of much of today's terrorism where it is often difficult to identify the patron state. It describes the 'hit and run' or 'hit and die' tactics employed by most terrorist groups – and new approaches under international law have to be devised to deal with it.

Terrorists provide few lucrative targets for conventional military attack. The goal of any retaliatory operations is to force a hostile government into abandoning its use or support of terrorism.

Terrorism and terrorist acts are not only a challenge, but also a twofold threat to the law of a state: a direct threat in that they jeopardise the life and physical integrity of individuals; and an indirect threat in that in combating terrorist acts, the aggressed state runs the risk of departing from the law, possibly under the influence of public opinion. Terrorism threatens the law of each individual state and also the law of the international community.

International law cannot provide a direct answer to most questions raised by terrorism simply because it is not applicable outside armed conflicts. However, such law unconditionally prohibits terrorist acts and provides for their repression. Under the law, armed conflicts of an international character include national liberation wars, i.e. armed conflicts in which people are trying to secure self-determination. If a terrorist takes part in a genuine national liberation war he has to carry arms openly and comply with the rules of international humanitarian law, which strictly prohibits any terrorist act.

In peacetime, terrorist acts must and can generally be dealt with under the domestic law of states, for international humanitarian law is not applicable outside armed conflicts. Terrorist acts are forbidden, but to those who do not observe this prohibition, international humanitarian law grants a minimum of humane treatment, but at the same time allows, and in most cases, obliges states to punish them for their acts. For the benefit of combatants, i.e. members of the armed forces, the law imposes certain restrictions on the terrorist acts, which the enemy may direct at them.

In internal armed conflicts captured terrorists, whether civilians or military agents, benefit from the same fundamental guarantees as all other persons who do not or no longer take a direct part in the hostilities. In international armed conflicts, if a member of the armed forces commits terrorist acts, and if these constitute war crimes, he may and must be punished for his war crimes by the power or state on which he depends. If he has fallen into the power of the enemy, he has prisoner of war status, but may and must be punished by the detaining power for his war crimes. If he failed to comply properly with his fundamental obligation to distinguish himself from the civilian population while engaged in an attack or in a military operation preparatory to an attack, he forfeits his right to be a prisoner of war, but must be granted equivalent treatment. This means that he may be punished not only for his war crimes but also for his mere participation in the hostilities. If the armed forces of one party to the conflict commit terrorist acts, one could maintain that they do not qualify as armed forces, and consequently their members are not entitled to prisoner of war status. If the persons who have committed terrorist acts are civilians, their own party may and must punish them for their participation in the hostilities and for their terrorist acts. If they have fallen into the power of the enemy they are protected civilians, but they may be punished for participation in hostilities and for their terrorist attacks.

Terrorist acts, in so far as they are grave breaches of the conventions become universal crimes under the jurisdiction of all parties to these instruments. Each party is under an obligation to enact the necessary legislation to extend its criminal jurisdiction to any person who has committed a grave breach, regardless of the nationality of the perpetrator, the victim or the scene of the crime. Linked to this issue is extradition and its resultant complexities.

Extradition is part of the process of criminal justice – the acquisition of custody of the accused for trial, or where the person has escaped from prison, for completion of his sentence.

The extradition process is generally spelled out in bilateral treaties, supplemented by statutes or provisions in codes of criminal procedure. The ultimate decision about whether an accused person should be surrendered is a matter for the government of the country concerned, but the actual determination of whether a valid claim for surrender has been made by the requesting state is a matter for the courts, so that the factor of a strict or moderate interpretation of a given treaty may advance or inhibit the grant of extradition.

In connection with the extradition of terrorists, policy considerations can be a substantial bar. Even where a treaty exists and diplomatic relations obtain between parties, extradition may be denied on the ostensible grounds that the charge against the accused is political in nature, or that extradition formalities have not been complied with, or that the accused is being tried in the requested state, whereas the real grounds for the denial of extradition may lie in daily relations between the requested state and other countries with which it desires to be on cordial terms.

Policy considerations also include economic considerations, ranging from concern for the protection of air transport franchises and other trade advantages in a given geographical region, to maintaining a bargaining position in regard to foreign economic, technical and military assistance. The extradition process is fraught with opportu-nities for carelessness or genuine error in the paperwork and in communications between the requesting and requested states – and Britain has experienced such problems many times in claiming the return of suspected terrorists from the **United States** and the Republic of **Ireland**.

In terms of treaties for the control of international terrorists, governments have to decide whether in contemplating the apprehension of offenders 'ex-tradition' is the term that is wanted, or whether the concern is for 'lawful return', and whether, in supplying an alternative to apprehension, 'submit to prosecution' is recognised as being a concept that is open to widely varying interpretations, reflecting particularist moral principles, legal precepts, poli-tical practices and other considerations.

Extradition is the prerogative of the requested state and in the absence of a bilateral treaty between the requesting and the requested state, there is no international legal duty to extradite. Even where there is an applicable extradition treaty, the scope of the duty to extradite may be narrow. Extradition may be requested only for offences listed in the treaty, and the political offence exception may determine whether the alleged offender will be returned to the requesting state or granted asylum by the requested state.

Traditional international legal measures have lacked established procedures for international co-operation in preventing and punishing violations of diplomatic inviolability. States that are parties to anti-terrorist conventions have an international obligation to prosecute the offender, whether prosecution follows lawful return or takes place in the state where the offender was found.

Thus, extradition is a difficult and complex process – differences in criminal codes procedures and judicial traditions have to be taken into account, and so far only a small minority of terrorist suspects have been successfully extradited.

See also: Counter/Anti-Terrorism; Definitions; International Criminal Court; Organised Crime; Rights.

References

Evans, A. E. and Murphy, J. F. (eds) (1978) *Legal*

Aspects of International Terrorism, Lexington, MA: Heath.

Greenwood, C. (2002) 'International Law and the War Against Terrorism', *International Affairs*, vol. 78, no. 2, pp. 301–317.

Roberts, A. (2002) 'Counter-Terrorism, Armed Force and the Laws of War', *Survival*, vol. 44, pp. 7–32.

Suter, K. (1984) *An International Law of Guerrilla Warfare: The Global Politics of Law Making*, New York: St Martins Press.

Thackrah, J. R. (1993) 'The Relationship Between International Law and International Terrorism', unpublished MS at National Police Library, Bramshill, Hampshire.

Further Reading

Alexander, Y. and Nanes, A. (eds) (1986) *Legislative Responses to Terrorism*, Dordrecht: M. Nijhoff.

Freedman, L., Hull, C., Roberts, A., Vincent, R., Wilkinson, F. and Windsor, P. (1988) *Terrorism and International Order*, London: Routledge.

Feith, D. J. (1987) 'The Law of War: The Terrorists are Rolled Back', *Atlantic Community Quarterly*, vol. 25, pp. 210–212.

Friedlander, R. A. (1993) *Terrorism: Documents of International Law and Local Control*, vol. 1–6, New York: Oceana Publications.

Gearty, C. A. and Kimbrell, J. A. (1996) *Terrorism and the Rule of Law*, Oxford: OUP.

Higgins, R. (1997) *Terrorism and International Law*, New York: Routledge.

Lambert, J. T. (1990) *Terrorists and Hostages in International Law*, Cambridge: Grotius.

Reisman, M. and Antoniou, C. T. (1994) *The Laws of War: A Comprehensive Collection of Primary Documents on International Law Governing Armed Conflict*, New York: Vintage Books.

Information Terrorism *see* Technology

Interpol

The International Criminal Police Organisation (Interpol) was set up in 1923 to provide a means of international co-operation in the prevention of

crime; but it was not until January 1987 that an anti-terrorism unit came into existence.

Preventive efforts address the aspect of increased sophistication and progressive development on the part of the terrorist. The organisation has worked on developing detection and screening capabilities emphasising prevention. From the late 1980s, Interpol has looked in detail at how to combat the work of surrogate terrorists – these are part of state-sponsored actions whereby individuals of another ethnic or natural background conduct terrorist activities.

The greatest worry for Interpol is that terrorist groups can call upon support at any given time. Widespread dissemination of information useful to law enforcement personnel in several different countries regarding terrorists and terrorist activities is the hallmark of Interpol's terrorist policy. Its existing global communications network and universal structure is a potential tool in the struggle against international terrorism – and the more information passed around – photographs, modus operandi, information about explosives, the more the problem of such terrorism can be alleviated (Buckwalter, 1989).

See also: Terror and Terrorism

References

Buckwalter, J. R. (ed.) (1989) *International Terrorism: The Decade Ahead*, Chicago: Office of International Criminal Justice, University of Illinois.

Further Reading

Bossard, Andre (1988) 'Interpol and Law Enforcement Response to Transnational Crime', *Police Studies*, vol. 11, no. 4 (winter), pp. 117–182.

Fooner, M. (1989) 'Interpol: Issues' in *World Crime and International Criminal Justice*, New York: Plenum Press.

Iran

The Islamic Republic of Iran is ruled by a Council of Revolution consisting of (**Shi'ite**) Islamic spiritual leaders following the fundamentalist guidelines of Ayatollah Khomeini. In general, political parties and other organisations enjoy freedom as long as they do not 'infringe the principles of independence, freedom, national unity and the bases of the Islamic Republic'. The Ayatollah has many political enemies ranging from supporters of the late Shah, overthrown in 1979, and liberal politicians, to non-fundamentalist Muslim groups and militant members of ethnic minorities, in particular Arabs, Azerbaijanis, Baluchis, Kurds and Turkomans. Suppression is undertaken by the Revolutionary Guards (Pasdaran) who are directly responsible to the Council of the Revolution. Guerrilla activity against the government has increased in recent years, and it is estimated that nearly 10,000 executions have taken place since the Ayatollah came to power in 1979.

As a result of the large groups of regional minorities in the country there are many separatist groups. The Arab Political and Cultural Organisation is based in Khuzestan province in the south-western part of the country, and they resent the influx of Iranians attracted by the oil finds in the region. In spite of the Ayatollah granting limited autonomy to the region clashes with the government have occurred regularly. Many deaths and bomb explosions have occurred in Korramshahr, and throughout their dispute other Iranian opposition movements, especially the Kurds, have supported the Khuzestan Arabs. Closely associated with the Organisation has been Black Wednesday, an Arab rebel force that has engaged in many acts of sabotage in the oil-rich province of Khuzestan.

In London, six Iranian Arabs calling themselves the Group of the Martyr seized the Iranian Embassy in April 1980, taking 26 hostages and demanding that in return for their release, 91 Arabs imprisoned in Iran should be set free. After the six had killed two of the hostages, members of the British Special Air Service penetrated the Embassy, killing five of the Arabs and seizing the sixth, who was sentenced to life imprisonment in January 1981.

In another area of Iran the Azerbaijan Autonomist Movement gains members from the nearly ten million Azerbaijanis who form the largest ethnic group in Iran. They were mainly Shi'ite Muslims who acknowledge Ayatollah Shariatmadari, who rejected the leadership of Ayatollah Khomeini and the involvement of the clergy in the running of the country. The movement boycotted the referendum to approve the Constitution in 1979, and within weeks, as a result of house arrests of some of the Movement's members, a rebellion broke out in Tabriz, the chief city in Azerbaijan. Although the Ayatollah Shariatmadari reduced his violent activities in this region, he remained under close suspicion of wishing to kill the Ayatollah Khomeini.

In Iran's south-eastern province of Baluchistan the Baluchis who are Sunni Muslims form the majority of the population, while the minority Sistans who are Shi'ites enjoy a higher standard of living. Baluchi demands for limited autonomy within Iran and economic concessions have been largely ignored. Many incidents have taken place between the two groups, which are both opposed by the government. Baluchi separatists have intensified their guerrilla activities.

The two chief Kurdish movements demanding autonomy for Kurdistan on the frontier between Iran and **Iraq** are the Kurdish Democratic Party of Iran and the Kurdish Sunni Muslim Movement. Both believe in seeking a social revolution in Iran and stress that only armed struggle would bring about the overthrow of the Ayatollah's regime. Many believe that the current **Gulf War** between Iran and Iraq, and in particular the regular Iranian offensives against Iraq were, in fact, manoeuvres to encircle the Kurds.

In north-eastern **Iran** after the revolution in 1979 the predominantly **Sunni** Muslim Turkomans called for concessions involving the redistribution of land owned by supporters of the former Shah, the right to set up their own police force, the official recognition of their language and representation in the local revolutionary committees dominated by Shi'ite Muslims. None of these demands has been met and the Revolutionary Guards actively seek to suppress the autonomists.

Left-wing movements have for many years been dominated by the Tudeh, the outlawed Iranian Communist Party. Other groups do exist. The Forqan group claims responsibility for the assassination of a minor Ayatollah and an army general, in its role as a major Marxist underground organisation. The National Democratic Front, an offshoot of the Union of National Front Forces is, like the Union, an essentially secular anti-regime movement. It has consistently resented the Ayatollah's attempt to establish a religious dictatorship. The People's Sacrificers is a nationalist Marxist group on the far left whose support is drawn from young students and the radical wing of the intelligentsia.

Although the theoreticians of the Fedayeen differ sharply over tactics they all condemn what they consider to be capitalist and imperialist exploitation, and seek to build a radical socialist state in Iran. Its members are intensely ideological and have a fifteen-year history of **guerrilla warfare**. In 1980 the Fedayeen splintered into three factions, including the Fedayeen guerrillas (Cherikha), the Aqaliyyat minority and the Aksariyyat majority. While the guerrilla and minority splinters have sought to pursue their radical goals independently, the majority group has revealed a willingness to compromise.

A more extreme group are the Iranian People's Strugglers, a party based on the major principle of *towhid*, a divinely integrated classless society, a society with total equity. In this ideal society there will be an end to the exploitation of man by man. Consistently, the group have attacked the rule of the religious leaders on the right whom they see as repressive, reactionary and revolutionary dilettantes. By the early 1980s they were viewed as a major armed force fighting the Ayatollah's regime. Many of their 100,000 guerrillas, out of a reputed membership of 400,000, were trained by the Palestine Liberation Organisation. The Peykar and Union of Communists are both small pro-Chinese formations that have actively opposed the Khomeini regime.

Monarchist groups had obvious motivations, with the country totally dominated by the Ayatollah Khomeini in the 1980s. The government, in announcing that plots have been uncovered, have generally stated that those involved were army officers and other members of the armed forces intent upon restoring the monarchy. The Armed Movement for the Liberation of Iran was led by a niece of the late Shah. In May 1981 some members of the Pars Group were arrested in connection with an alleged plot to restore the monarchy, with the authorities accusing the Group of having links with Dr Shapour Bakhtiar, the leader of the National Resistance Movement, then living in France, and with certain members of the late Shah's family.

Externally based movements developed either during the latter stages of the Shah's rule or after the Ayatollah came to power. The National Front opposed both leaders. However, the National Council of Resistance for Liberty and Independence initially supported the Ayatollah, then, due to a disagreement over the powers of the government, the leader of the Council ex-President Bani-Sadr attacked the rule of the Islamic Republican Party for worsening the condition of the country. The National Resistance Movement was led by Dr. Bakhtiar, the Shah's last Prime Minister, who had the task of implementing a programme of liberalisation, including the dissolution of the Shah's secret police, and the granting of a greater role to the Muslim religious leaders in drafting legislation. The Ayatollah considered Bakhtiar's government to be a betrayal, and Bakhtiar was forced to flee to France to continue his opposition.

The main religious minorities in Iran are the Bahais, Christians, Jews and Zoroastrians. The last three of these groups are officially recognised in the Constitution whereas the Bahais are not, and they have been subjected to considerable repression since the 1979 revolution, before which they had held many senior posts under the Shah.

Iran still continues to be on America's list of 'the axis of evil' countries. Iranian agents have been widely active and over eighty dissidents have been killed in Europe. The xenophobic nature of the government has appealed to many terrorists and there are numerous terrorist training camps set up in the country covering all types of violence. **Hizbullah** is actively supported by Iran. The Pasdaran, a so-called 'cultural' group with the government, supports the military, controls the secret police and has all its own divisions of power – soldiers, fighters, officers and commandants. This command structure also controls Iran's nuclear programme.

Pasdaran agents have recruited parties and agents for worldwide operations in **Algeria**, the **Philippines** and Sudan. Whilst the **USA** has remained distant from Iran many West European nations have close ties for business purposes. The main worry is the usage to which the country's nuclear programme may be put. Yet

138 Iraq

animosity exists to the West in spite of recent diplomatic meetings and Iran–Iraq relations remain tense.

See also: Kurdish Insurgency; Shi'ites; Teheran Embassy Siege.

References

Sick, G. (1985) *All Fell Down: America's Tragic Encounter with Iran*, New York: Random House.
Venter, Al (1997) 'Iran still Exporting Terrorism to Spread its Islamic Vision', *Jane's Intelligence Review,* vol. 9, no. 11.

Further Reading

Kostiner, T. (1988) 'War, Terror, Revolution: The Iran–Iraq Conflict' in Rubin, B. (ed.) *Politics of Terrorism*, Lanham, MD: University Press of America.
Timmerman, K. R. (1987) 'Iran and International Terror: Trying to Export the Islamic Revolution', *Journal of Defence and Diplomacy*, vol. 5, no. 1, pp. 21–24.

Iraq

Under its 1968 Constitution, Iraq is a popular democratic and sovereign state with **Islam** as its state religion and an economy based on socialism, dominated by the Ba'ath Arab Socialist Party. Although the Iraqis allow a Kurdish Legislative Council with limited powers to pass legislation for the Kurdish region on social, cultural and economic development as well as on health, education and labour matters, the Council has not been supported by the majority of Kurds, whose ultimate aim is full autonomy or even complete independence for Kurdistan. The Democratic Party of Kurdistan was founded in 1946 by Mustapha Barzani who for over thirty years led the struggle for autonomy of the Kurds in Iraq. The struggle came to a temporary end in 1975 after the Shah had ceased to support the Kurds and had concluded a treaty with the Iraqis. However, two years later, after Barzani's death in exile, the Party resumed the armed struggle against Iraqi govern-

ment forces. An offshoot is the Kurdish Socialist Party, while the Patriotic Union of Kurdistan is in conflict with the Democratic Party over ideological issues.

The Iraqi Communist Party has had a chequered history. It was a legalised party when it entered the National Front government in 1973. With its pro-Moscow orientation, it occasionally criticised the regime on both domestic and foreign policy grounds including its handling of the Kurdish insurgency, with which some elements of the party have been associated. In May 1978, the government executed 21 Communists for engaging in political activities within the armed forces, and by the early 1980s members of the Communist Party had either fled the country or moved to the Kurdish areas.

The predominantly **Sunni** Muslim regime has encountered strong opposition from militant elements of the **Shi'ite** Muslim community; Shi'ite Muslims constitute over half of Iraq's population. They are in sympathy with and supported by the regime of Iran and have formed their own Dawah Party. The Ba'ath Party, Arab socialists, were actively opposed by dissident Ba'athists supported by the Syrian government. The National Democratic Patriotic Front consists of a coalition of eight opposition parties to try and bring down the government led by Saddam Hussein who came to power in 1978. On similar lines, the Supreme Council of the Islamic Revolution, formed in 1982, aims to provide a focal point for Iraqi Shi'ite opposition to the prosecution of the war with Iran; and wished Hussein's government to be overthrown and replaced by an Islamic republic led by a theologian on the Iranian model.

Involvement of a growing nature in international terrorism has for a long time been levelled against Iraq.

Iraqi intelligence was closely involved in the 1993 **World Trade Center** bombing, but this was not obvious until the trial of the participants a few years after the attack. Iraq has been behind repeated incidents of terrorism against the USA over the past decade or so. Terrorist attacks have continued undiminished and, as the administration has warned, are likely to become unconventional. It appears that Iraq is allied with Muslim extremists in carrying out acts of terrorism. Saddam Hussein ended **United Nations** weapons inspections, but left world opinion strongly suspicious of his ability to build unconventional armaments. The Iraq leader was seen as the single greatest terrorist threat to the USA. Basically he sought revenge for the **Gulf War** even as he also seemed to think his terrorism undermined the anti-Iraq coalition (Mylroie, 2001). The Fatah Revolutionary Council (FRC) also known as the **Abu Nidal** Organisation, quickly became an instrument of Iraqi policy.

The Americans and British (with support from Polish, Spanish and Australian forces) called the Coalition and invaded Iraq in mid-March 2003; most of the country was occupied by early May 2003. However, the efforts to win a lasting peace are being hampered by regular attacks on the coalition forces by Saddam Hussein loyalists and Islamic extremists. In late July 2003 members of the American military leadership for the first time admitted that they could be involved in a guerrilla war. The American and British administrators in Iraq are finding the process of bringing normality and creating a civilian government acceptable to all political groups hard to achieve. Even creating a remodelled police force is proving difficult. Saddam Hussein remains at large and it is not known definitely if he is alive or dead. However, in late July, his two sons Uday and Qusay were killed during a gunfight with American forces in Mosul. Weapons of mass destruction have not been found which was the cause of a pre-war split in the international community with China, France, Germany and Russia being opposed to military action. Differences are currently being resolved between these countries and members of the Coalition.

The potential for war with Iraq in the wake of the failed attempt to capture **Osama Bin Laden** polarised Western opinion. The hawks believed the American campaign to eliminate the terrorist threat must also end unfinished business in Iraq dating back to the Gulf War. The hawks maintain that the West failed to act early and strongly enough against **Al Qaeda** and the regime that harboured it. The war versus terrorism should include striking at other centres of Islamic terror that are in south-west Asia and Africa. Hostile states have to be challenged, as they support terrorism and seek to acquire weapons of mass destruction – and many

observers include **Iran** and **Syria**, who despite criticism of the **September 11** attacks and Bin Laden and the Taliban, support terrorism. The Iraqis' sole aim was to develop weapons of mass destruction and to challenge the West with impunity.

Those who argued against a war with Iraq believed it could destabilise the Islamic world and boost recruitment to Al Qaeda and other terrorist groups. By concentrating troops in the cities, Iraq could force the US and its allies to attack major centres of population, which would increase Iraqi civilian and Allied casualties. War should not have occurred, the doves maintain, as the UN Security Council had not sanctioned it. Iraqi land forces are probably weaker than in the first Gulf War. Furthermore many Allied soldiers feel that the cause was not just as the attack occurred without the backing of the UN. Several governments could fall, notably Saudi Arabia, Jordan, and possibly Egypt. Others opposed to action argued it was about the USA securing its oil supplies; and to possibly break OPEC's control of supply and price. A pre-emptive strike is illegal under international law.

Saddam Hussein refused offers to go into exile to spare his country another Gulf War. During 2002–03 co-operation with the UN weapons inspection team led by Hans Blix was limited; and the procedure for destroying missiles and other materials was a deliberate slow process.

The Allies in favour of war believed that the liberation of Iraq would lead to the spread of democracy in the Middle East, and ultimately to resolving the Israeli–Palestinian conflict.

The Arab league members had difficulty in achieving co-ordinated action to stop the invasion of Iraq. Few of the leaders of the Arab league countries believe Saddam Hussein wished to avoid war.

See also: Gulf War; Iran; Kurdish Insurgency; Shi'ites; World Trade Center 1993.

References

Mylroie, L. (2001) *Study of Revenge: The First World Trade Center Attack and Saddam Hussein's War against America*, Washington, DC: The AEI Press.

Van Bruinessen, M. (1988) 'Between Guerrilla War
  and Political Murder: The Workers Party of
  Kurdistan', *Middle East Report*, vol. 18, no. 4
  (July/August), pp. 40–46.
Viotti, P. R. (1980) 'Iraq: The Kurdish Rebellion' in
  O'Neill, B. E., Heaton, W. R. and Alberts, D. J.
  (eds) *Insurgency in the Modern World*, Boulder, CO:
  Westview Press, pp. 191–212.

Ireland

Until the end of the sixteenth century Ulster was
the centre of the most intransigent resistance to
English rule. Radical change was brought by the
Reformation, the defeat in 1603 of the anti-English
rebellion led by the chiefs of O'Neill and
O'Donnell and the union in 1605 of England and
Scotland. In 1608 the plantation of Ulster began
with Protestant settlers from the Scottish lowlands
and England, expelling the native Catholic and
Gaelic-speaking people to the poorer lands of the
south and west. The old Gaelic order of Ireland
had been crushed and Ulster became, in effect, a
British province. Catholic emancipation and the
growth of militant Irish nationalism saw religion
restored in the late nineteenth century as the
dominant and divisive factor in Ulster affairs. In
1914, with the passage of the third Home Rule Bill,
the Orange Unionist Protestant Ascendancy of
Ulster, with the active support of many leading
members of the Conservative opposition at Westminster, threatened armed rebellion. After the First
World War, following the victory of the nationalist
Sinn Fein Party in 1918 and the subsequent
guerrilla war against the British power, the Ulster
Unionists in 1920 reluctantly accepted the provisions of the Government of Ireland Act. Under this
measure, which superseded the Home Rule Act of
1914 Ireland was to have two parliaments subordinate to Westminster – one in Belfast for six of
Ulster's nine counties, and one in Dublin for the
remaining 26 counties of Ireland. Thus the
government of Northern Ireland, now a federal
province of the United Kingdom, came into being
against a background of **civil war** and sectarian
disorder. This government was to last until 1972
when Stormont was suspended. The rest of Ireland

– the Irish Free State – was accorded dominion
status, but in 1949 it was declared a republic.

Political movements have abounded in Ireland
for most of this century, and have been mostly
radical and militaristic. Sinn Fein was the original
Irish nationalist party, which took over the effective
leadership of the Irish nationalist movement from
the Irish Parliamentary Party after the death of
Parnell in 1891. An open split in the movement
occurred in 1921 when the republican wing led by
de Valera refused to accept the Anglo-Irish Treaty
of 1921 and precipitated the Civil War of 1922–23.
De Valera soon returned to parliamentary politics
and the label of Sinn Fein was taken over by the
dissident rump of intransigents.

The Irish Republican Army (IRA) is the name of
the military instrument of Sinn Fein. It has the
distinction of being the longest-lived organisation in
history, exhibiting a remarkable continuity in both
goal and method. The roots of violence in Ireland
are tangled and deep, which perhaps explains the
extraordinary tenacity of the IRA. It had its origins
in the National Volunteer Force and became the
Irish Republican Army in 1924. Its influence
subsequently waned and it was declared illegal by
the Irish government in 1939. After a period of pro-
German activity during the War, calm returned.
However, from 1956 to 1962, the IRA conducted a
bombing campaign in Northern **Ireland**, but the
authorities were able to confine this action to the
border areas. In the mid 1960s, the Marxist wing of
the IRA was recreated – and from the outset was
more concerned with exploiting social issues than
with taking part in the armed struggle which
emerged from the communal violence of the mid
and late 1960s in Northern Ireland. After the
breakaway of the Provisional IRA in 1969, the
rump of the IRA became known as the Official
IRA, whose political wing was the Official Sinn
Fein, which in Northern Ireland was known as the
Republican Clubs. The Officials argued that class
politics should supersede sectarian issues, and that
the violence practiced by the Provisionals merely
entrenched reactionary attitudes. Some Officials
still continued with violence, and indeed a violent
clash between the two wings of the IRA occurred in
1975.

The Provisionals soon came to be seen as a
direct-action organisation intent upon launching a

guerrilla campaign and making Northern Ireland ungovernable by forcing the British Government to withdraw its armed forces and relinquish all responsibility for the province. Politically, the Provisionals have operated through the Provisional Sinn Fein, legal in both the north and south of Ireland, but declared a proscribed organisation in mainland Britain under the Prevention of Terrorism (Temporary Provisions) Bill enacted in 1974. The Provisionals, or Provos, are militarily organised with both a women's section involved in gathering information, planting fire-bombs and providing shelter in safe houses, and a youth wing which gather intelligence, act as lookouts and transport weapons. They have resorted to sniping, bombing, the use of rocket launchers, letter bombs and parcel bombs. Their action provoked 'Bloody Sunday' in 1972, when 13 persons were killed by British soldiers; and internment without trial of suspects, which remained in force for four years in spite of a civil disobedience campaign called by Roman Catholic opposition parties in Ulster.

Over the past fifteen years the Provisional IRA (PIRA) has been involved in a concerted plan of bombing in mainland Britain, and despite some ceasefires, it has achieved worldwide notoriety and revulsion, notably the deaths of 18 British soldiers at Warrenpoint in 1979. It has received weapons from abroad, especially the United States. The most conspicuous operation carried out by PIRA members in the Republic was in August 1979, with the murder of Earl Mountbatten of Burma by a bomb placed on his fishing boat. In England, their most conspicuous act was the bombing of a public house in Birmingham in 1974 in which 21 persons were killed and 120 injured.

During the early 1980s it was clear that public support for the PIRA among the Roman Catholic section of Northern Ireland's population was increasing, mainly at the expense of traditional Catholic parties. Many Provisionals undertook hunger strikes in 1980–81 to try to obtain special treatment and ultimately political prisoner status. The most notable was Bobbie Sands who died in prison in May 1981, a month after being elected a Member of Parliament.

More extreme than the Provisionals is the Irish National Liberation Army (INLA), the political wing of the Irish Republican Socialist Party, created in 1974 with the aim of conducting armed warfare to compel the British to a military withdrawal from Northern Ireland, which would then unite with the South. This new socialist republic would then withdraw from the European Economic Community. Notable attacks have included the deaths of Airey Neave, a Conservative politician, in 1979, of 11 soldiers and six civilians at a pub near Londonderry in 1981, bombs in London parks in 1982, five persons killed outside Harrods store in London in 1983, and a bomb at the Grand Hotel, Brighton, also killing five people during the Conservative Party Conference in 1984.

On the Protestant side, radical and extreme groups have played an active role in fomenting discord. Prime among these is the Ulster Volunteer Force, a group of militant Protestant Loyalists whose origins go back to 1912. It is a military body dedicated to upholding the constitution of Ulster by force of arms if necessary. The potential membership of the UVF has always been more important than its actions. The Ulster Defence Association (UDA) has been regarded as the strongest of various extreme Protestant paramilitary organisations set up in response to the violent activities of the Provisionals. In spite of being in difficulties through the development of factions, it was the UDA, which manned the Protestants' barricades of 1972. They made explosives and planted bombs in hotels and IRA meeting places. It also had strong links with Scotland. The Protestant equivalent of INLA was the Ulster Freedom Fighters, a militant paramilitary Protestant organisation loosely composed of violent elements anxious to take the law into their own hands. Members carried out assassinations on a widespread scale.

Terrorism has little effect on the domestic political structure of **United Kingdom** or Ireland – for example, it is not an election issue in either country but it has resulted in policy changes oriented toward suppressing the IRA. Equally as important as the effects of terrorism on formal power structures and government policies is its impact on popular attitudes and on participation. Among the Protestants of the North, terrorism has only stiffened pre-existing attitudes of resistance to any compromise that hints of a drift toward Irish unity – as exemplified by the polarised reactions across the political divide to the Anglo-Irish

Agreement in 1985. Among the IRA's potential Catholic constituency, there seems to be every indication that although terrorism did spark a brief Peace Movement, which expressed a strong revulsion for violence, over the past decade a residual amount of support for the IRA remains constant. Terrorism has general and diffuse consequences for the long-term prospects for democracy and stability, and in particular it affects the quality of life, patterns of political socialisation and political culture. In Northern Ireland there has been resilience in the social order – life goes on, despite high levels of violence.

It appears that the British will stay in Northern Ireland until the British population tires of violence or until Protestants agree to a united Ireland. The lesson that violence pays has been seen by extremists, and discord has been fomented by the presence of the British army. Power sharing in the mid 1970s was achieved only in Londonderry, with a balance of Protestants and Catholics.

The Troops Out Movement of the mid-1970s was more successful. Since direct rule in 1972 the security forces have succeeded in eroding the terrorist movements by measures which have been within the existing legal framework, and the conviction of proven terrorists cannot be taken for granted in a community intimidated by terrorism. After eighteen years of trouble, no clear solutions to Ulster's political problems have been found, any more than to the problems of security.

The full recognition of Northern Ireland as an Anglo-Irish dilemma came in 1985 with the signing of the controversial Anglo-Irish Agreement between Britain and the Irish Republic. It seeks to establish a framework within which nationalists will be able to join with unionists in a devolved local executive. By encouraging the development of constitutional nationalism, both London and Dublin hope to erode support for physical force republicanism. Bitterly complaining that they were never consulted, nor even kept informed about the discussions leading up to the Agreement, unionists have rejected it as an act of treachery. Two possibilities can occur. The first is that a majority of unionists will eventually grudgingly accept the Agreement; the second, that there will be a continued and irreversible alienation of the Protestant community and the refusal of the unionist leaders to co-operate in any way with a British government which, in their eyes, has effectively destroyed the Union. The dilemma is how to handle the unionists and react constructively to their antagonism to the sharing of responsibility, which is now proposed.

In 1998 Ireland and the UK disagreed over the British government's refusal to investigate members of the RUC accused of shooting at terrorist suspects before attempting to arrest them. The following year the Irish government succeeded in persuading the British to review the Ulster Defence Regiment's links with Protestant paramilitaries. Both governments agreed in 1996 to exclude Sinn Fein representatives from any peace negotiations, as they believed IRA behaviour, which in February 1996 had ended the two-year bombings in mainland UK, had made no contributions to peace. Over the past few years Bertie Ahern, the Irish Prime Minister, and Tony Blair have repeatedly tried to get peace talks restarted after direct rule had to be imposed in Northern Ireland due to the crucial and controversial issue of IRA arms decommissioning.

See also: United Kingdom (Northern Ireland).

References

Bell, J. B. (1990) *IRA: Tactics and Targets*, Dublin: Dufour Poolberg Press.

Messenger, C. (1990) *Northern Ireland: The Troubles*, New York: Gallery Books.

Further Reading

Alexander, Y. and O'Day, A. (eds) (1984) *Terrorism in Ireland*, New York: St Martin's Press.

Kearney, R. (1997) *Post Nationalist Ireland*, London: Routledge.

O'Brien, B. and Alexander, Y. (1994) *Dimensions of Irish Terrorism*, Aldershot: Dartmouth.

O'Brien, B. (1999) *The Long War: The IRA and Sinn Fein*, Dublin: The O'Brien Press.

Smith, M. I. R. (1994) *Fighting for Ireland? The Military Struggle of the Irish Republican Movement*, London: Routledge.

Islam

The essential creed of Islam (Submission to God), which originated in Arabia in the 7th century is that there is one God, Allah, and Muhammad is his prophet. The *Koran* is the basis of Islamic belief and practice and the source of a complex legal and social system. Five fundamental duties are incumbent upon the individual Muslim – expression of belief in one God and prophet; observance of five daily prayer times; fasting during Ramadan; payment of a charity tax; and to go on a pilgrimage to Mecca (hajj). Islam shares some beliefs with Judaism and Christianity and accepts the Books of Moses and the Gospels of Jesus as part of the same divine scripture expressed in the *Koran.*

The purpose of terrorism, whether national or international, is to murder political enemies, deter potential foes and destabilise society. Many of the more dramatic and violent incidents of recent decades have been perpetrated either in the Middle East or elsewhere by groups involved in the domestic and inter-state conflicts in that region. Groups such as the **Palestine Liberation Organisation** (PLO) and most of its constituent factions are defined by their opponents and victims as terrorist bodies, and therefore any act of warfare or violence conducted in their name must be 'terrorist' by definition.

Sympathisers with their cause would regard Middle East groups as fighting a war of national liberation and therefore, the PLO, say, would not be regarded as a terrorist group.

Terrorism has been a prominent feature of politics of the Middle East, and large-scale atrocities have been committed in pursuit of some political, religious or other ideological goal. Both terrorism and movements for fundamentalist Islamic reform have frequently appeared in times of political, social or economic crisis. They represent no new or modern phenomenon. In any kind of man-made upheaval or natural disaster, men turned to Islam and to the mosque which served as the fortress of the most conservative, reactionary and xenophobic elements of society, and at the same time, as the custodian of the only true vision of a just society, which offered hope and guidance

to the poor, the disenfranchised and the disillusioned.

The recent Islamic revival has enhanced the political significance of Islam to an extent rarely witnessed in modern times. There is strong anti-Western sentiment in many Muslim countries and various attempts have been made in countries such as **Iran**, **Pakistan** and the Sudan to re-impose strict Islamic law. Another feature has been the intensification of the traditional enmity between the various Muslim sectarian forces' and in particular between the two main groups, the Sunnis and Shias.

Islam has never been simply a spiritual community. Instead, from its rise in the seventh century it developed as a religious and political movement; the belief that Islam embraces faith and politics is rooted in its bible, the *Koran*, and the example or custom (Sunna) of Muhammad, its founder and prophet. This belief has been reflected in Islamic doctrine, history and politics. It was from a seventh-century revolt that the major division in Islam between **Sunni** and Shi'ite emerged. The belief that participants in that revolt were martyrs to injustice has provided Shia Islam with its major theme – the battle of the forces of good (Shia) against the forces of evil (anti-Shia). Their goal is to establish righteous rule and social justice through martyrdom and protest under the political leadership of the imam, and this is the fundamental political and legal difference between the majority Sunni stream of Islam and the minority Shi'ite denomination. There are about 800 million Sunni Muslims in the world, who are in the majority in all Islamic countries except Iran, **Iraq**, **Lebanon** and Bahrein.

In contrast to the Sunnis, Shi'ites believe that both the spiritual and temporal leadership of the Muslim world were vested by divine command in the descendants of Ali (a seventh-century caliph), and that successive leaders were to appoint their successors by divine inspiration. For Sunnis, success and power were signs of a faithful community and the validation of Islam, its beliefs and claims. For Shi'ites, history was the struggle of a righteous few in protest and opposition against the forces of evil in order to realise its messianic hope and promise – the establishment of the righteous rule of the imam.

A common theme inspires the modern '**assassins**'. They, and the Muslim fundamentalists in

Iran, decry the ungodliness and corruption of most contemporary societies. For them, man's only hope of salvation lies in making society conform strictly to the word of God as revealed in the authoritative sources of faith.

The fundamentalist revolution in Iran owes its legitimacy to its secular success in over-throwing the regime of the Shah and replacing it with Ayatollah Khomeini's version of an Islamic theocracy. This is based upon a blend of radical Shi'ism, anti-Westernism, leftist radicalism and religious extremism.

Terrorism has its place among the means employed by extremist Muslim fundamentalist factions. For the terrorist, the enemy or target is the 'non-Muslim', the 'unbeliever', the 'infidel'.

The success of Khomeini's revolution in Iran provoked a resurgence of Islamic militancy. In various Middle Eastern countries, such as **Libya**, **Iraq** and **Syria**, the consolidation of power by autocratic military rulers bent on total domination at home and abroad has produced the phenomenon of state terrorism. The Islamic groups have been successful, but only where support for the existing regime was already crumbling. To date, the powerful autocratic military rulers of the Middle East have, in practice, largely been able to suppress these groups when they appeared to present a serious threat.

Islam and the West

Conflicts between the West and **Islam** focus less on territory than on broader inter-civilisation issues such as weapons proliferation, human rights and democracy, control of oil, migration, Islamic terrorism and Western intervention. Most of the states seen in Western eyes and classified as terrorist states are Muslim states – **Iraq**, **Syria**, **Libya** and the Sudan. In turn Muslim states are very radical when it comes to condemning terrorist acts against the West.

Historically, terrorism is the weapon of the weak that is, of those who do not possess conventional military power (Huntington, 1996). In the past terrorists could only inflict limited violence, killing a few people here or destroying a facility there. Massive military forces were required to do massive

violence. The events of **September 11**, however, showed that a few terrorists could produce massive violence and destruction.

Separately, terrorism and nuclear weapons are the weapons of the non-Western weak. If and when they are combined, the non-Western weak will be strong, hence the global fear over weapons of mass destruction

There are two mainstreams of fundamentalism: Sunni and Shia. Sunni's is a moderate mainstream religion (Mecca based). The fundamentalist Muslim Brotherhood has pan-Arab links with strong minorities in **Egypt** and Syria, which are opposed to the government (Clutterbuck, 1990).

Shi'ite is a puritanical sect that rejects materialism and appeals to the poor. Their aim is to expel all Western influence from Islam and the world. Fundamentalists have a duty to kill any that block the spread of Islam. There is a Shia majority in **Iran** and Iraq with large minorities in Bahrain and **Lebanon**.

Iran is their spiritual base with the deep rooted influences of the mullahs. The **cult** is of blood and martyrdom and suicide bombs and seizure of hostages. The **Soviet Union** and now Russia feared the spread of Islamic fundamentalism to the southern republics (formerly Soviet and now shakily independent). **Afghanistan** has already been a concern for infiltration by Shia fundamentalists.

Islamic fundamentalists are able to penetrate the political systems of other countries in the name of Islam. As fundamentalists they are more successful than many other sects and religious groups in achieving their aim. It is the youngest of the three major non-theistic religions and growing the fastest in terms of believers compared with Jews or other Christian Churches. Some observers would describe it as a protest movement with strong links in the Third World. Islam is a total civilisation, and a religion of practical commandments covering all aspects of life. In some ways it is a political religion with an orientation to collectivist issues. It encourages an overhaul of the entire social system to conform to its ideals. This leads into the existence of an explicit doctrine of fighting for the faith what to some is described as a 'holy war'; which occupies a prominent place in the thoughts of Muslims.

Fundamentalism has had peaks and troughs and is associated with failure, humiliation and backwardness, which many contemporary Muslims are trying to overcome.

The first Muslim cleric to be prosecuted in the British criminal courts over the contents of his preachings was convicted in February 2003 of soliciting the murder of Hindus, Jews and Americans. Abdullah El-Faisal, an associate of Abu Hamza, the extremist cleric ousted from the Finsbury Park mosque in January 2003, was also found guilty of stirring up racial hatred in a series of sermons against non-Muslims. He was sentenced to 15 years imprisonment. El-Faisal was linked to some members of **Al Qaeda**.

See also: Assassins; Egypt; Iran; Palestine Liberation Organisation; Religious Terrorism; Shi'ites.

References

Clutterbuck, R. L. (1990) *Terrorism and Guerrilla Warfare: Forecasts and Remedies*, New York: Routledge.

Donohue, J. T. and Esposito, J. L. (eds) (1982) *Islam in Transition: Muslim Perspective*, New York: OUP.

Esposito, J. L. (2000) *The Oxford History of Islam*, Oxford: OUP.

Hourani, A. (1997) *A History of the Arab Peoples*, Cambridge, MA: Belknap Press.

Huntingdon, S. P. (1996) *The Clash of Civilisations and the Remaking of World Order*, London: Touchstone Books.

Israeli, R. (1994) 'Muslim Fundamentalists as Social Revolutionaries', *Terrorism and Political Violence*, vol. 6, no. 4 (winter), pp. 462–475.

— (1997) 'Islamikaze and their Significance', *Terrorism and Political Violence*, vol. 9, no. 3 (autumn), pp. 96–121.

Jaber, Hala (1997) *Hizbullah: Born With a Vengeance*, New York: Columbia University Press.

Jansen, G. H. (1981) *Militant Islam*, London: Pan Books.

Johnson, J. T. and Kelsay, J. (eds) (1990) *Cross, Crescent and Sword: The Justification and Limitation of War in Western and Islamic Tradition*, Westport, CT: Greenwood Press.

Further Reading

Ahmed, Akbar (1998) 'World Without Honour? Islam and the West', *The World Today* (October), pp. 246–266.

Ben-Dor, G. (1996) 'Uniqueness of Islamic Fundamentalism', *Terrorism and Political Violence, Special Issue on Religious Radicalism in Greater Middle East*, vol. 8, no. 2, pp. 239–252.

Harman, C. C. (2000) *Terrorism Today*, London: Frank Cass Publishers

Horrie, C. and Chippindale, P. (1993) *What is Islam?*, London: Virgin Books.

O'Ballance, Edgar (1997) *Islamic Fundamentalist Terrorism 1979–1995: The Iranian Connection*, New York: New York University Press.

Taheri, A. (1987) *Holy Terror: The Inside Story of Islamic Terrorism*, London: Hutchinson.

Wright, R. (2001) *Sacred Rage: The Wrath of Militant Islam*, New York: Simon and Schuster.

Israel

In May 1948 the state of Israel was proclaimed. This act immediately led to the first of four wars between Israel and varying numbers of her Arab neighbours. Israel's most consistent ally throughout its existence as a modern state has been the **United States**. Israel was soon transformed into an expansionist power in control of areas housing thousands of Palestinians.

Israel through the wars with other Arab states gained territory; Golan Heights, east Jerusalem, Gaza and parts of the West Bank. Despite **United Nations** resolutions calling on Israel to withdraw from the occupied territories, Israel refused claiming a need for 'secure borders' in order to resist Arab threats to its existence.

In 1977 Menachem Begin came to power and he rejected any negotiation with the **Palestine Liberation Organisation** (PLO); but was persuaded by the USA to agree to an agreement with **Egypt** (the Camp David Agreement) leading to peace between the two countries and the return of Sinai to Egypt.

World attention was soon shifted to the plight of the Palestinians and the PLO gained sympathy and allies.

In 1982 the murder of Palestinians in refugee camps in the Israeli-controlled areas of **Lebanon** fermented some dissent in Israel. Mass protest demonstrations also occurred on the Palestinian side. General strikes and civil protests marked the beginning of the intifada. Successive territorial apprehensions have incorporated some two million Arabs into the present territory of Israel.

At the time of the **Gulf War** in 1990, **Iraq** launched several missile attacks against Israel to try to force it to enter the war. Israel did not join the conflict leaving defence to Patriot and anti-missile units manned by American troops. After the Gulf War, a 'land for peace' proposal was suggested by the USA and supported by the Arabs but rejected by Israel; nevertheless the Israeli government began transferring immigrants to new settlements on the West Bank. The Arabs demanded that resettlement cease in order for the peace talks to continue. The Oslo Accords foresaw the installation of a limited autonomy system for Palestinians in the Gaza strip and the city of Jericho.

From the mid-1990s there was a growing division in Israeli society regarding the peace process – but the predominance of conservatives in Israeli politics has hindered negotiations with the Palestinians. Open war has been declared on the homes of the suicide bombers who have increased their attacks against Israel, and in 2003 the situation appears bleak with no sign of an agreement between the two nations.

Further Reading

Ben-Rafael, E. (1987) 'Israel–Palestine: A Guerrilla Conflict' in *International Politics*, Westport, CT: Greenwood Press.

Katz, S. M. (1990) *Guards without Frontiers: Israel's Counter-Terrorist Forces*, London: Arms and Armour Press.

J

Jabril, Ahmed

b. 1938

Jabril was the leader for the Popular Front for the Liberation of Palestine General Command, one of the more extreme Palestinian terrorist groups which provided support for the most rejectionist that is, the most vehemently opposed to the Israeli-Palestine peace process and dialogue. Jabril's base was mainly in **Syria**.

In 1988 a year after the introduction of the intifada Israel mounted a massive raid on Jabril's headquarters outside Beirut, to show it was not intimidated by the intifada.

There was much rivalry between Jabril and Yasser **Arafat** as Jabril was supported by Syria which was determined to control all the groups in the **Lebanon** including Arafat's. He carried on the war with Israel by using suicide bombers; as he was very bitter and hateful toward Arafat after he had formerly recognised Israel's right to exist and renounced terrorism in December 1988.

See also: Arafat.

Japan

Since the debacle of defeat in 1945, Japan has emerged, thanks to American help, as one of the most economically strong and democratic nations in Asia. Although the Liberal Democratic Party has held power for the past three decades, there has been much opposition, and acts of politically motivated violence have been carried out by both extreme right- and left-wing groups. Although there are many right-wing organisations, membership of each of them is small, and generally they advocate totalitarian government as the best solution to overcome corruption, exploitation and unequal treaties with foreign powers. Extreme left-wing groups have extended operations to targets outside Japan, particularly in terms of hijacking to which until the late 1970s the Japanese government meekly acceded. Since then tougher approaches have been adopted to hijacking. Left-wing groups take part in violent clashes and ideological feuds with each other on regular occasions.

The most well-known of the radical groups is the United Red Army (Rengo Shekigun), although in recent years its activities have decreased. This terrorist group was established among disillusioned students who saw in the Paris student riots in May 1968 their blueprint for bringing about world revolution. The group has been noted for its violent clashes, the extremism of the original female leader, Fusako Shigenobu, and the number of radical leftists who have been killed in internal clashes.

In spite of these problems, and the success of the security forces against them, the United Red Army has declared that it will continue to fight for the materialisation of a people's republic of Japan by uniting and joining forces with the oppressed people, comrades and friends in confrontation with Japanese imperialism. During early operations it stressed the need to fight against **Zionism**, and later affirmed the need for a revolution in Japan and its solidarity with the Japanese people in their struggle against the monarchy, and criticised Japan's economic exploitation of South Korea. Its major operations have included, for example, the **hijacking** of Japanese airliners over South Korea (1970), Dubai (1973) and Bombay (1977), resulting in deaths of innocents and of some of the terrorists. Oil refineries were attacked in Singapore in 1974, the French embassy in The Hague was occupied in 1974 and the US consulate and Swedish embassy seized in Malaysia in 1975. The most notorious incident was a massacre at Lod airport, Tel Aviv, **Israel** in May 1972, when three terrorists opened fire in the departure and arrivals lounge, killing 26 persons (mainly Roman Catholics from Puerto Rico) and wounding 78 others. Of the three gunmen, one was killed by police, one committed suicide and the other, Kozo Okamoto, was captured, tried and sentenced to life imprisonment but with the onset of insanity was released in 1985. In 1982 Shigenobu admitted that the United Red Army had abandoned terrorism because it had failed to win international support. This was perhaps surprising in view of the links (admittedly tenuous) with the Basque separatist organisation ETA, the Red Army Faction (Baader-Meinhof Group) in Germany, and with the Popular Front for the Liberation of Palestine (PFLP).

Other extreme left-wing groups have had limited success. The East Asia Anti-Japanese Armed Front, formed in 1976, fights for the rights of the Ainu, who were the original inhabitants of the most northerly of Japan's four main islands, Hokkaido. The Front claims to fight for the rights of the Okinawan, Korean, Taiwanese Buraku (social outcasts) and other Asian peoples. They have also attacked offices of large business companies such as Mitsui and Mitsubishi who are accused of exploiting underdeveloped Asian nations. In 1974 the Front tried to assassinate Emperor Hirohito, for which two terrorists received the death penalty.

The Fourth Trotskyist International (Japanese section), along with other radical groups played a leading role from the early 1970s in actively opposing the construction and opening of a new international airport at Narita near Tokyo. Demonstrations by local farmers, left-wing student groups and environmentalists led to several years' delay in the completion of the airport. Attacks on its communications and other installations continued until well after the opening in May 1978.

The National Federation of Students' Organisations contains some Marxist breakaway groups, one of whom the Middle-Core Faction, opposed the security treaty concluded between the **United States** and Japan. A breakaway splinter group is the Revolutionary Marxist Faction. The Okinawa Liberation League has expressed opposition to the rule of the Imperial family over Okinawa in the Ryukyu Islands and its use as a military and oil storage base.

Until the Aum Shinrikyo attack on the Tokyo underground rail network in 1995, the country remained quiet despite the seemingly endemic political corruption. From 1997 the economy of Japan has been in somewhat of a crisis. The **cult** intended to kill many thousands of people. The 1995 poison gas attack in the Tokyo subway was carried out in haste and did not represent the cult's full potential. They had amassed hundreds of tons of chemicals used in the production of sarin.

At the time of the Tokyo attack Aum Shinrikyo had 50,000 members, 30,000 of whom were Russians. It had assets worth $1.4 billion and offices in Bonn, New York and Moscow as well as several Japanese cities.

The subway attack involved disseminating a chemical agent in an enclosed space. This method and the use of food are probably the easiest ways to use weapons of mass destruction and are likely to remain the most common forms of terrorism involving these weapons.

References

Angel, R. C. (1990) 'Japanese Terrorists and Japanese Countermeasures' in Rubin, B. (ed.) *The Politics of Counter-Terrorism*, Lanham, MD: University Publications of America, pp. 31–60.

Farrell, W. R. (1990) *Blood and Rage: The Story of the Japanese Red Army*, Lexington, MD: Lexington Books.

Jihad

Jihad literally means 'striving' and is often translated as 'holy war'. Maintaining the purity of religious existence is thought to be a matter of jihad. The Muslim concept of struggle – jihad – has been employed for centuries in Islamic theories of both personal salvation and political redemption. To the Ayatollahs in **Iran**, the notion of fighting was basic to human existence and on a par with religious commitment. Moderate observers believe that the jihad has social and economic dimensions, as well as the more widely known political and military (Jurgensmeyer, 2000).

In **Egypt**, 'al Gihud' as it is known there, has managed to infiltrate its armed and teaching cells into many levels of society. In 1981 along with another Islamic group Gamaa al Islamiya, they assassinated the countries President, Anwar Sadat at a military parade. This caused distrust between civilians and the military and led to a renewed period of Islamic terrorist activity in the 1980s and 1990s including the targeting of tourists at Luxor in 1997 (Cooley, 2002).

The Arabic term jihad is equivalent to 'self-control' and 'self-exertion' to undertake a variety of activities in furtherance of the will of God. Since **Islam** addresses the individual Muslim directly, there is a strong sense of obligation to comply with what is believed to be Sharia, regardless of the policy of the state and this can be jihad. The proponents of jihad as an aggressive war are more likely to be supported by the majority of Muslims in a world where military force and self-help prevail over the rule of law in international relations. After **September 11**, in repeating an open call to jihad issued by the Taliban and its supporters, some Islamic nations acted out of interest, others out of principle, but most out of a combination of both. Muslim leaders who distanced themselves from **Osama Bin Laden** believe the notion of jihad is best understood in terms of spiritual rather than physical struggle (Booth and Dunne, 2002). Jihad confuses religion with a love of death and this perhaps accounts for its unacceptability in many parts of the non-Islamic world. Bin Laden's alliance and the World Islamic Front for the Jihad against Jews and Crusaders and in his view jihad is an attack on **globalisation**.

References

Booth, K. and Dunne, T. (eds) (2002) *Worlds in Collision: Terror and the Future of Global Order*, New York and Basingstoke, Palgrave Macmillan.

Cooley, J. K. (2002) *Unholy Wars: Afghanistan, America and International Terrorism*, London: Pluto Press.

Jurgensmeyer, M. (2000) *Terror in the Mind of God: The Global Rise of Religious Violence*, Berkeley and London: University of California Press.

Further Reading

Halliday, F. (2002) *Two Hours that Shook the World. September 11, 2001: Causes and Consequences*, London: Saqi Books.

Just War Theory

A terrorist will claim a right to redress grievances as a reason for a war on society. Contrary to the unworthy and morally debilitating notion that 'anything goes', once a conflict has began our own ethical code has imposed limits on individual and collective behaviour. In considering complicity most people think about the merits for and against the particular case of hijacking, **hostage taking** or assassination for which the terrorist is responsible. Most terrorists, however, ignore constraints. Terrorists argue that they fight the way they do and conduct harassment campaigns, because they do not have the means at the enemy's disposal – a police force, an army and an intelligence apparatus. The terrorist demands that we recognise the righteousness of his cause, but he denies the principle that gives the righteousness meaning. He denies any such limits and therein lays the terror he seeks to engender. A terrorist often attempts to draw a distinction between himself (a guerrilla or **freedom fighter**) and his opponents (terrorists). A terrorist makes moral claims for his struggle. However, freedom fighters do not blow up buses containing non-combatants and do not assassinate innocent people or hijack and hold hostage innocents. These innocent victims are deemed by the terrorist to be the best way to advance some particular cause. Terrorists never address the emotive issues of violence, and always look at the question of those whom they oppose. Ordinary people form their own judgement from what the terrorists do rather than their reasons for doing it. Terrorists are those who terrorise and by contrast innocent civilians do not board planes, meet in restaurants or travel to work worried that they will be terrorised by their own democratically elected leaders.

The arbitrary selection of victims, is what inspires the terror. Much depends on the distinction between legitimate and non-legitimate targets. The recognition of limits is what distinguishes liberal democratic society and forms the basis of all law whether international, civil or moral. In the case of terrorism, the line crossed is the prohibition against targeting innocent lives.

In the terrorists display of viciousness and hatred they say that discrimination was never an issue. They choose to attack weak and defenceless civilians.

Terrorists believe that everyone who is not an ally is an enemy, and as such, a potential threat. Their acts can be committed illegally or individually in the course of a regular war. This is the terrorists' policy and he counts on the terror for impact and the only principle is one of expediency. Who believes a terrorist cause is just when their behaviour is unjust? Both the means and the ends employed are unjust; and they have a complete disregard of any limits to their behaviour.

References

Donelan, M. (1987) 'Terrorism: Who is a Legitimate Target?', *Review of International Studies*, vol. 13, pp. 229–233.

Dugard, J. (1982) 'International Terrorism and the Just War' in Rapoport, D. C. and Alexander, Y. (eds) *The Morality of Terrorism*, New York: Pergamon Press.

Walser, M. (1997) *Just and Unjust Wars*, New York: Basic Books.

Further Reading

McGurn, W. (1987) *Terrorists or Freedom Fighter? The Cost of Confusion*, London: Alliance Publishers for the Institute for European Defence and Strategic Studies.

O'Brien, W. V. (1987) 'Counter-Terror Deterrence/Defence and Just War Doctrine', *Theological Studies*, vol. 48 (December), pp. 647–675.

K

Kashmir

Over the past half century tense Hindu-Muslim relations in **India**, including riots in cities like Mumbai and Kolhhata has posed new strains on India-Pakistan relations. The unabated conflict in the disputed territory of Kashmir remains a major threat to regional peace and security. With its Muslim majority, Kashmir rejects Indian authority.

In 1988 the old dispute was revived. Militant Muslim groups wanting secession of Kashmir to Pakistan resorted to 'violence', using weapons bought in from **Pakistan** and **Afghanistan**. There are six major groups of Kashmiri secessionists claiming 45,000 guerrillas in all – some wanting independence some wanting union with Pakistan, some were Islamic fundamentalists and others wanted a democratic state (Brogan, 1992).

The most dangerous are the Jamma and Kashmir Liberation Front, led by Javad Ahmad Mir, which supports independence for Kashmir including that part of the ancient province now occupied by Pakistan and known as Azad Kashmir (Free Kashmir).

Growing ethno-nationalism is fuelling the conflict. The separate Kashmir identity is substantiated on the basis of geographic, linguistic, historical and religious differences. Over 35,000 Kashmiri's have lost their lives in armed encounters since 1989. Any possible solution – a **United Nations** supervised plebiscite, complete independence, regionally guaranteed autonomy or further partition will upset either India or Pakistan and lead to further bouts of terrorism and violence (Malik, 1993).

References

Brogan, P. (1992) *World Conflicts: Why and Where They are Happening*, London: Bloomsbury.

Malik, I. H. (1993) 'The Continuing Conflict in Kashmir: Regional Détente in Jeopardy', *Conflict Studies*, no. 259, London: RISCT.

Khmer Rouge

The Khmer (Cambodian) Liberation Army – dubbed the 'Khmer Rouge' by Cambodian head of state Prince Norodom Sihanouk in the late-1960s, was a peasant-based revolutionary force which established its political authority over all Cambodia in April 1975. Three years later there was a Vietnamese invasion of Kampuchea in December 1978 and a war that flickered on until the mid-1980s.

The split between Vietnamese and Cambodian revolutionaries dates back to 1954, when the new government in Hanoi, North Vietnam, anxious to adhere to the terms of the Geneva Agreements withdrew support from the Cambodian Communist Party and left the state to pursue a neutralist policy under the autocratic Sihanouk. He achieved widespread popularity and the relative prosperity of Cambodia grew. Communists in Cambodia, convinced that the North Vietnamese government in Hanoi had betrayed the revolution, went underground. However, they could achieve little on their own apart from setting up safe base areas on the Maoist pattern and organising occasional guerrilla attacks.

A turning point occurred in 1967, when Sihanouk ordered his new Prime Minister Lon Nol to deal with a peasant uprising in Battambang Province; his ruthless violence quickly alienated substantial elements of the population. A sudden influx of recruits enabled the communists to step up their activities and, as Sihanouk wavered, Lon Nol seized the opportunity to organise a military-backed coup in Phnom Penh (March 1970). Turning to the **USA** for aid, he initiated a campaign of deliberate repression and the war acquired a new and vicious intensity. By 1973, with an estimated 4,000 regular troops and up to 50,000 guerrillas available, the Khmer Rouge was strong enough to exert its control over the northern provinces of the state.

There followed a two-year campaign in which Khmer Rouge guerrilla groups, armed by the North Vietnamese and Chinese, infiltrated government lines, destroyed isolated military outposts and gradually drew a noose around Phnom Penh. The fighting was not one-sided. In late-1973 and early-1974, for example, Lon Nol was able to defeat a major communist offensive against the capital – but by spring 1975, with US support halted by Congress and up to 60 per cent of Cambodia already in Khmer Rouge hands, Lon Nol was isolated and communist victory assured.

By this time the Khmer Rouge had made what seemed to be a smooth transition from guerrilla force to regular army, but its new-found strength was dissipated by the bizarre actions of its leaders, particularly Pol Pot. Basing his policies on the views of Khieu Samphan, who advocated a return to the simplicity and self-sufficiency of rural life, Pol Pot forcibly removed the population of Phnom Penh to the countryside, and introduced a campaign of terror and murder against those who would not contribute to the new utopia. By 1978 the Khmer Rouge had lost much of its military cohesion, and the Vietnamese invasion force found it surprisingly easy to advance as far as the Thai border. Sporadic guerrilla attacks continued into the 1980s, demonstrating the ability of the Khmer Rouge to survive at a basic level as an insurgent force.

Kidnapping

Kidnapping, similar to assassination, has been used for many generations. The rise of gangsterism in the 1920s led to a massive growth of kidnapping for ransom in the **United States**; and there has also been a strong Italian flavour about the growth of kidnapping and gangsterism in many American cities. Italy has the highest incidence of kidnapping in Europe and there are still strong links between the American and Italian **Mafia**.

One of the more dramatic tactics of contemporary terrorists is that of kidnapping. The capture and detention of a prominent person has served numerous ends, including publicity, the release of colleagues being held as political prisoners, and the receipt of substantial funds in ransom payments. Many terrorist groups have relied on the prolonged detention of their kidnap victims, thus enjoying sustained media attention and inducing a state of chronic embarrassment on the part of the governments concerned.

The kidnapping of well known people – whether they are politicians, newspaper editors or the sons or daughters of eminent persons, can provide a series of major media events over a period of several weeks. Although kidnappings may be logistically cumbersome, they can provide more media attention than a single robbery, bombing or assassination. Moreover, the eventual release of a hostage can serve to minimise an adverse public reaction.

The most desirable setting for kidnappings has been the busy street in an urban area. There the prospective kidnappers are able to set up an ambush while attracting minimal attention; and following such an attack, and the immobilisation of the victim's vehicle, a capture and speedy getaway can be easily and unobtrusively accomplished. Other than the victim totally varying his or her movements, only an armed escort or intensive patrols by police and security forces can serve as adequate preventive measures. Occasionally in the course of kidnapping, escape may be precluded. At other times, kidnappers deliberately seek to hold a hostage in public, or at least in a location known to the authorities. The siege that follows is usually the most dramatic of terrorist events. In such situations kidnappers' demands may include calls for ransom or for the release of political prisoners, and these are usually accompanied by a demand for safe passage to a friendly country as well. Sieges of this nature tend to take place in and around diplomatic missions and have occurred with considerable frequency over the past two decades.

The most dramatic form of kidnapping is that which can occur in the context of an airline hijacking. Aside from those who are motivated by personal financial considerations or those with severe personality disorders, the vast majority of skyjackers seek either to obtain the release of certain political prisoners or to express protest against a particular regime. A safe passage to a friendly country has almost always been demanded. Even after the advent of rigorous security procedures hijackers have been able to exploit the crowded and hurried settings of urban airports to their considerable advantage.

Self-appointed avengers can seek retribution through threats or acts of violence. This is typically the case in the kidnapping of foreign businessmen by Latin American terrorists, where exorbitant ransoms are extracted as 'reparations' and murder is justified as 'execution'.

While the tactic of hijacking demands patience on the part of the operatives, and an ability to handle a duration operation, it is kidnapping which is the most demanding, rewarding and lucrative. The operation requires intricate planning, split-second timing, a large support apparatus to sustain the group holding the victim and the ability to remain secure while still communicating demands or negotiating with third parties.

Ransoms paid can be of a size almost beyond comprehension – millions of dollars or pounds can change hands. Once in the terrorists' hands, the money is often spread under various names over banks in Europe and the United States, and has been and will continue to be used to finance more political terrorism. A kidnapping for ransom can be carried out by a group of any size, criminal or political, ranging from large international organisations to a single cell or even, as in the case of children, to a single criminal. The decision to kidnap is based on an assessment of the potential victim's family or firm, whether they are rich enough to find a large ransom and how willing they are likely to be to pay. Other factors are the victim's

vulnerability, his lif
to it, the predicta
attitude to precau
protection at home,
a political kidnappin
and the potential leve
be important; and oth
and the extraction of i
Professionally organised   ...p groups carry out
detailed research into the background of the potential victim.

The terrorists have big advantages in kidnap situations. They have the initiative; they hold the victim and they know where everyone on both sides is based; they are willing to maim their victim, while the authorities' recognise self-imposed restraints; and the terrorists know that most people will pay rather than allow a husband or child or colleague to be killed. The kidnappers' greatest weakness is that time is on the side of the police, whether measured in days or months, and every extra day brings greater chance of detection and may accumulate more evidence for eventual arrest and conviction.

The interests of those involved on the side of the law will often conflict – the victim has interests that conflict in themselves; his family will probably be less willing to sacrifice his life than he is himself; and his negotiators have a duty to balance their obligations to their client and their obligations, legal or moral, as citizens. The victim's firm may well be involved, and if the firm is a subsidiary of an overseas corporation, corporate headquarters may see the problem differently from its representatives on the spot. The police have a dual responsibility to the victim and to society; and the army can in some countries act instead of the police in terrorist operations. Security firms and advisers are often involved; the judiciary and the legislature may both be involved in serious cases, and are concerned with the provisions and operation of the laws under which the battle will be fought. The media forgo sensational news only if they are confident that all their rivals also will forgo it. Ultimately, the government stands over all these agencies and individuals, as it will want to be seen to be firm, and even overseas governments can get involved if the victim or his firm are expatriates.

With regard to the ransom, kidnappers may

paid in hard currency in a foreign country into a number of different bank accounts or possibly dumped in cash for collection by accomplices there.

Most kidnappers, in fact, settle for payment in local currency, but specify that it must be in well-worn notes of low denomination, not with consecutive numbers, to avoid detection. Volunteers will be needed to drop the money, and the negotiator will be in a stronger position than before because the kidnappers will be tense and wish to end the business quickly. The negotiator can thus be firm over his conditions. The better the individual or organisation is prepared, the less likely they are to be selected as targets and the greater their chances of survival.

See also: Aviation Security; Hostage Negotiation.

References

Clutterbuck, R. L. (1978) *Kidnap and Ransom: The Response*, London: Faber and Faber.
— (1981) 'Management of Kidnap Risk' in Wilkinson, P. (ed.) *British Perspectives on Terrorism*, London: Allen and Unwin, pp. 125–138.

Further Reading

Alexander, A. J. (1985) 'An Economic Analysis of Security, Recovery and Compensation in Terrorist Kidnappings' in Jenkins, B. M. (ed.) *Terrorism and Personal Protection*, Stoneham, MD: Butterworth, pp. 176–199.

Kurdish Insurgency

In September 1961, Kurdish demands for autonomy within Iraq led to the outbreak of a **civil war** which continued for almost fourteen years, interrupted by a number of ceasefires and an armistice negotiated in January 1970, under which the **Iraq** government agreed to implement the Kurds' demands. The Kurdish rebels, whose armed forces were known as Peshmerga, controlled the mountains of north-eastern Iraq, where regular government offensives achieved little, although Iraqi bombing raids destroyed many Kurdish villages.

The heaviest fighting occurred after the collapse of the armistice in 1973, with the Kurds adopting a conventional static defence of the area, which they controlled. Nevertheless the Iraqis advanced to within 20 miles of the Kurds' headquarters, which led the Kurds' ally, the Shah of **Iran**, to dispatch a contingent of Iranian troops to man the Kurds' air defences. Iranian backing was suddenly withdrawn in March 1975, however, when the Shah reached agreement with the Iraqi government over a long-standing territorial dispute. The Iranian border was closed to the Kurds and as the Iraqis moved in, the revolt collapsed.

The Iranians provided fresh support to Iraqi Kurdish guerrillas following the opening of the **Gulf War** with Iraq in September 1980. The Iraqi Kurds formed an alliance with anti-government **Shi'ite** fundamentalists and communists and by early-1985 controlled a twenty-mile-deep strip of territory along the Turkish border.

The Iranians experienced their own conflict with Kurdish insurgents, however. Having fought against the Shah, the Iranian Kurds demanded autonomy after his overthrow in 1979. The Ayatollah Khomeini regime sent Revolutionary Guards into the Kurdish region to suppress opposition, and serious fighting broke out, which continued into 1985, with the Kurds forming an alliance with left-wing Mujaheddin guerrillas.

The end of the first Gulf War between Iran and Iraq in 1988 did the Kurds no favours. In 1988 Saddam Hussein launched massive conventional assaults against base areas, planted thousands of mines in the Kurdish areas and sprayed mustard gas on villages (most notably Halabja). The Iraqi leader wanted the destruction of Kurds as a socio-economic entity.

After the second Gulf War (between Iraq and the West) in 1992, Saddam launched another series of concerted offensives against Kurdish guerrillas, but the Allies gave the Kurds a safe haven which the Iraqi military could not penetrate. The Kurdish people still bicker among themselves and this has only allowed for zones of influence to be established for each major Kurdish party rather than genuine power-sharing.

In **Turkey**, despite the hostility of the state, the

guerrillas were able to live in Kurdish villages and strike at random against the Turkish authorities who in the period 1984–93 killed 5,000 Kurds (guerrillas, civilians and security) for the loss of about 2,000 troops. In 2002 in an attempt to influence the **European Union** to accept them into the group, the Turkish authorities agreed to make the Kurdish language official in schools and to treat the Kurdish minority as equal with other minorities in the country (Ellis, 1995).

The defeat of Saddam Hussein's regime in Iraq in April 2003 has given renewed hope to the Kurds – at least in Northern Iraq – that their dreams of a homeland at some time in the future might be a step closer to reality.

See also: Iran; Iraq; Turkey.

Reference

Ellis, J. (1995) *From the Barrel of a Gun*, London: Greenhill Books and Mechanicsburg, PA: Stackpole Books.

Further Reading

Gunter, M. (1994) 'The Changing Kurdish Problem in Turkey', *Conflict Studies*, no. 270 (May), London: RISCT.

L

Language of Terrorists

The statements of terrorists characterise their philosophies and ideologies, which are a frontal attack on liberal values and principles. Terrorism is an instrument or political weapon developed by revolutionaries, and they believe that because states commit acts of terror and violence, it is permissible for terrorists to do the same.

Armed struggle (German terror groups) – a legally justified campaign against the power of the state.

Armed struggle (Marighella) – includes civilian elements and can develop into a peasant struggle.

Gorillas (**Marighella**) – the military in Latin America, in the opinion of guerrillas such as Marighella.

Guerrilheiros (Marighella) – the revolutionaries.

Guerrilla warfare (Marighella) – a technique of mass resistance – a type of complementary struggle, which will not by itself bring final victory. In ordinary warfare and in revolutionary struggle, guerrilla warfare is a supplementary form of combat.

Latifundio (Marighella) – large estate worked by peasants and generally under-exploited.

Mass front (Marighella) – a combat front, an action front going as far as armed action.

Military struggle (Marighella) – conflict within the armed forces which must be combined with working-class and peasant struggle in line with the tactics and strategy of the proletariat.

Outlaw (Marighella) – concerned with his personal advantage and indiscriminately attacks exploiters and exploited.

Resistance (Mao) – is characterised by the quality of spontaneity; it begins of its own accord and then is organised.

Revolutionary army (Guevara) – an army which is welded to the people – the peasants and workers from whom it sprang. An army which is conversant with strategy and ideologically secure. It is invincible.

Revolutionary guerrilla movement (Mao) – is organised and then begins.

Terrorism (Marighella) – a form of mass action without factionalism and without dishonour, which ennobles the spirit.

Urban guerrilla (Marighella) – an armed man who uses other than conventional means for fighting against the military dictatorship, capitalists and imperialists.

Yin-yang (Mao) – a unity of opposites in Maoist theory. Concealed within strength there is weakness and within weakness, strength. It is a weakness of guerrillas that they operate in small groups that can be wiped out in a matter of minutes. But because they do operate in small groups they can move rapidly and secretly into the vulnerable rear of the enemy.

Every terrorist group in a liberal democratic society tries to make maximum use of the freedom of speech and of the **media** that prevails. Only when terrorists have a solid constituency of public support can they hope to become a more effective political force.

References

Marighella, C. (1974) *The Mini-Manual of the Urban Guerrilla*, Vancouver: Pulp Press.

Mao Tse Tung (1954) *Selected Works*, New York: International Publishers.

Lebanon

Since its creation as an independent state in 1943, tensions between Lebanon's various ethnic and religious communities, especially between the Christians and Muslims, have regularly erupted into open hostilities between assorted military groups and factions. Maronite Christian and Muslim interests grew disproportionately, so that by 1975–76 the Lebanese state had collapsed in civil conflict. It had been the only place in the Middle East where a non-Muslim minority was decently tolerated in a Muslim society. However, in the early 1970s Palestinian terrorists had infiltrated into Lebanon in large numbers and almost founded a state within a state, from which they could operate freely against Israel and international targets. The delicate balance of Lebanese democracy had been established by a 'covenant', an unwritten formula that divided power among all the minorities – Christian Maronite, Greek Orthodox, Greek Catholic, Armenian Orthodox, Armenian Catholic, **Sunni** Muslim, **Shi'ite** Muslim and Druze. The President was always a Maronite Catholic, the Premier a Sunni Muslim, the speaker of Parliament a Shi'ite Muslim, the commander-in-chief of the armed forces a Maronite.

The covenant had worked since Lebanon won its freedom in 1943, although there had been a Nasser-inspired **civil war** in 1958, during which American troops had been landed, and another period of fighting started in 1968, caused by Palestinian terrorists.

The left in Lebanon was, and is, Muslim, while the Christians are pro-Western, including the Phalange, a group seeking to preserve the liberal democratic and Christian character of Lebanon. Palestinians became not only an independent establishment, but also a state within a state ruled by the gunmen of Al-Fatah and the Popular Front for the Liberation of Palestine.

The security forces found it difficult to restore law and order, and the army was held out of action, as Muslim leaders feared its largely Christian officer corps would interfere on the side of the Phalangists or other Christian groups. Initially the **Palestine Liberation Organisation** (PLO) remained neutral and the main part of the fighting was left to local groups. Leftist forces were far more numerous and better armed, but arms were easy to buy anywhere in the Middle East and both sides had funds. Palestinians took an increasing hand on the side of the Lebanese leftists, and the Christians were slowly forced back. Fighting was especially fierce in the south, and Israeli forces clashed with Palestinian guerrillas. The Syrians entered the northern part of the country to try to enforce some peace with their Popular Liberation Army (PLA). A series of truces broke down and fighting then occurred between the PLA and the extreme left, and fighting escalated between the Syrians and the Palestinians. The Palestinian refugee camps increased in size, and often became the scene of bitter fighting especially at the hands of the Israelis, who suspected the camps of holding terrorists. A newly created Arab Deterrent Force managed to enforce a ceasefire; however, in the absence of real stability members of Arab countries reduced their contingents, so that it became purely a Syrian force. The **United Nations** (UN) established an Interim Force in Lebanon to assist the Lebanese Government in ensuring the return of its effective authority to the area. Christian forces in southern Lebanon continued to be supported by Israel. In order to eliminate the persistent threat to Israel's northern border areas posed by PLO forces in southern Lebanon, **Israel** launched a full scale invasion in 1982, which resulted in the occupation of most of Lebanon's southern half, and the withdrawal of Syrian forces from Beirut. Palestinian fighters were driven from the south, and then from West Beirut. Phalangist militiamen were held responsible for the massacre of Palestinian inhabitants of two Beirut refugee camps.

Central government authority proved difficult to achieve in Beirut, and Israel insisted that its troops be withdrawn from Lebanon on the basis of a withdrawal of all non-Lebanese Arab forces, coupled with the creation of a demilitarised zone in southern Lebanon. To try to maintain a fragile peace, the United Nations sent in a peace-keeping force composed of US, British, French and Italian troops, but after suicide car bomb attacks against the American and French contingents, the force was finally withdrawn early in 1984. These attacks were instigated by Muslim fundamentalists fired by the Islamic revolution that toppled the Shah in **Iran**, who fought to establish a Shi'ite Muslim state.

Amidst increasing carnage and civil war, which has now lasted intermittently for over two decades from 1995, there has been a progressive weakening of central authority; and to avoid a total stalemate situation, cantonisation of the country was suggested. 8,000 Druze (a pro-Syrian closed community which is an offshoot of the Shi'ites), 10,000 Shi'ites and 10,000 Phalangists and Maronites (Syrian Christians living in Lebanon) want power. Each community is maximising land ownership for its own sect, and each want to gain control of key areas – the port of Beirut, the city itself and the airport. To the Phalange the only hope of stability is the creation of independent mini-states, yet this could lead to intervention.

In any further escalation, the situation will polarise, with each group looking for help from external supporters; for example, the Shi'ites will look to Iran and the Christians to Israel. Yet both **Syria** and Israel are unwilling to send in more men to add to an emotionally charged nationalistic and military situation. In Israel particularly, the war has caused inter-party bickering, a huge increase in the defence budget and also hyper-inflation.

In 1985 the Israeli army withdrew from Lebanon and it insured that the Christian militia had displaced the Muslim from southern Lebanon guaranteeing a 'friendly' civilian population in the ten kilometre security zone they imposed.

Air raids by Israel against **Hizbullah** positions continued in the 1990s and some moderate Lebanese were assassinated. Shi'ite Muslims villages were shelled by the Israelis in retaliation for strikes against northern Israel. The Israelis targeted PLO bases and refugee camps.

Fighting was renewed in 1997 between the Israeli army and the Lebanese guerrillas, but losses were high, prompting talk of a ceasefire but here the difficulty lay with Syria. It was believed Syria wanted the conflict in south Lebanon to continue in order to strengthen its own position in negotiations with Israel to recover the Golan Heights.

At the time of the Israeli advance into Beirut, following the **assassination** of President-elect Gemayel in September 1983, reports began to emerge from Israeli and other sources that armed men had entered the adjoining Chatila and Sabra Palestinian refugee camps in West Beirut in search of PLO guerrillas, and were engaged in wholesale killing of the civilian occupants, including women and children. Confirmation that a large-scale massacre had taken place came on the day after the departure of those responsible, when journalists and relief workers entered the camps to discover a scene of carnage and general devastation. Large numbers of bodies were found, some mutilated, of men, women and children who appeared to have been machine-gunned at close range, many of them while apparently trying to escape. Many houses had been blown up with their occupants still inside and bulldozed into rubble, and there was also a mass grave on the perimeter of one of the camps. Although uncertainty remained as to how many bodies were buried under the rubble in the camps, a commission of enquiry accepted Israeli intelligence estimates of between 700 and 800 dead in the camps as probably the most realistic figure.

As the full extent of the Chatila and Sabra atrocities became clear, a major controversy developed as to the identity of the armed men who had entered the camps and more particularly over the precise role of the Israeli forces who were in military control of the area. On the first point, substantial evidence accumulated to indicate that those directly responsible were Phalangist militiamen (i.e. members of the right-wing Lebanese Christian Movement led by the Gemayel family), whereas initial reports that members of Major Saad Haddad's Christian Forces (based in southern Lebanon) had also been involved remained unsubstantiated. As regards the Israeli role, it became clear that the Israeli forces in the area had facilitated the penetration of the camps. Israeli spokesmen denied any Israeli collusion in or responsibility for the massacre itself and also rejected charges from PLO and other Arab sources that Israeli forces had directly participated in the operation.

From the mid-1980s **hostage taking** escalated in the country. In February 1984 the first Western hostages were seized in Beirut, and three years later in January 1987 the personal envoy to the Archbishop of Canterbury, Terry Waite, was kidnapped and taken hostage. In February 1988 an American Colonel William Higgins serving with the **United Nations** Observer Force was kidnapped. Between September and December 1991 the American and British hostages were released, the last, an American journalist, Terry Anderson held since March 1985 was released in December 1991 – the longest held hostage victim in Lebanon.

In either killing or kidnapping Westerners, the Islamic **Jihad** aimed at ending all Western influence in Lebanon. When a TWA flight was hijacked in 1985, the plane was brought to Beirut and the passengers carried off to Shi'ite strong-holds. They wanted PLO prisoners in Israel to be released. When the USA bombed Libya in April 1986, Lebanese terrorists retaliated by murdering two British and one American hostage, because some of the American planes were based in England.

Although deals with terrorists over hostages were denounced by Western politicians, each country was prepared to deal on occasion if necessary. The American government, in the mid-1980s for example, negotiated with Iran for the release of their hostages – two won their freedom as a result of the delivery of American arms to Iran.

Israel exchanged prisoners with the PLO and the German and French authorities paid ransoms for their citizens. Democratic governments in the West repeatedly warned their citizens to leave Lebanon.

The crisis was brought to an end by hostages being released by degrees – which were part of an elaborate exchange with Israel, which let out its Lebanese and Palestinian prisoners of war in batches. The decision to free the hostages had been taken in Tehran and there were reports that the Iranian government had paid the Hizbullah to let them go. Holding hostages was not profitable, either politically or economically, and the Iranian and Shi'ite leadership admitted as much (Brogan, 1992). There were still the unresolved questions of

the disappearance of Israeli soldier prisoners in Lebanon, some of whom had disappeared.

Hostage taking in Lebanon and elsewhere attracted attention because the lives of ordinary citizens remained at stake. The stories had top priority in the **media** for a longer period than any specific terrorist action. Moreover there was drama in the choice confronting the government between its responsibility to individual citizens and its responsibility to uphold the policies for discoura-ging terrorism. In Lebanon, the locations were kept secret to prevent an armed rescue assault, and to allow kidnappers time to escape (Heymann, 1998).

Iran had succeeded in compelling the Americans and French to leave Lebanon – mainly because no core interest of the Western powers was involved in Lebanon.

References

Brogan, P. (1992) *World Conflicts: Why and Where They are Happening*, London: Bloomsbury.

Heymann, P. B. (1998) *Terrorism and America: A Commonsense Strategy for a Democratic Society*, Cam-bridge, MA and London: The MIT Press.

Jenkins, B. M. and Wright, R. (1987) 'The Kidnappings in the Lebanon', *TVI Report*, vol. 7, no. 4, pp. 2–11.

Further Reading

Fisk, R. (1990) *Pity the Nation: Lebanon at War*, New York: Macmillan.

Norton, A. R. (1984) 'Aspects of Terrorism in Lebanon: The Case of the Shi'ites', *New Outlook*, pp. 19–23.

Sutherland, T. and Sutherland, J. (1996) *At Your Own Risk: An American Chronicle of Crisis and Captivity in the Middle East*, Golden, CO: Fulcrum.

Legislation *see* Counter/Anti-Terrorism

Liberation Theology

For many years there has been an intertwining of liberation theology, politics and violence in Latin America. The theology of liberation is seen as a force for political and social reform. In South and Central America religion and politics have evolved together, taking material and symbolic support from one another. They have both embraced inter-institutional conflict and accommodation (such as 'church/state' relations) as well as more subtle exchanges whereby religious and political orders give legitimacy and moral authority to one another. In Latin America, the zeal to 'convert' the native population of the area gave liberation theology political legitimacy, but also associated it with tyranny and imperialism. Religion and politics have coalesced in meaning. Both have undergone a metamorphosis from individual to collective perspectives. This is true in Latin America where the economic and political contradictions of imperialism have had time to mature. The government's oppression of the people within the state, by selected government bodies (i.e. state terrorism) has given rise to a relatively new type of religious political motivation. To liberation theologists communion with Christ inescapably means a life centred upon commitment of service to others; and in wider terms the uplifting (economic and socio-cultural) of individuals oppressed throughout the world. To these theologists there is a call for the liberating transformation of the history of mankind. In their view the root cause of oppression exists because of the economic, social, political and cultural dependence of some countries upon others, which is an expression of the domination of some classes over others. Only a radical break from the status quo and a profound transformation of the private property system, an access to power of the exploited classes and a social revolution would allow for the change to a new society.

The Western world looks upon this philosophy as provoking violence and terrorism: and the **USA** links such a philosophy with involvement from **Russia** and **Cuba**. Religion, therefore, and politics are inseparable entities in Latin American history, as the theology of liberation is seen in the West as an ideology to foment revolution aided and abetted by the Soviet Union. Clerics will argue that the theology of liberation eventually grew out of the Church's involvement with the working-class poor, both urban and rural, in Latin America. Worker priests found direct involvement with the masses an unsettling experience – and they soon realised that

the Church was alienated from the poor, and began to see religion and the social order through a Marxian lens. Their Church appeared as an agent of pacification and reconciliation in the absence of any effort to change or draw attention to the real situation of the poor and to the structural causes responsible for their plight. The clergy became radicalised by their experience.

The theology of liberation movement found support in Vatican II and the writings of Pope John XXIII. For example, economic growth was viewed as not synonymous with social development: efforts were required to establish conditions promoting the total growth of individuals as persons and assuring a wider distribution of income among all strata of society, especially in Latin America. Not until the 1960s did the Catholic Church ever call for direct action or even passive resistance in political movements attempting to achieve social reform or social justice. The Church has defined social justice as the fair distribution of material and non-material wealth (to include land), and of rewards among all peoples within a society. To the Western eye, these statements contradict the historical non-involvement in secular politics which the Church has traditionally followed.

Although most leaders of the liberation movement espouse a moderate and non-violent strategy for reform, there is considerable support for the use of violence. Bishop Camillo Torres's total conviction to the liberation movement and subsequent guerrilla resistance in **Colombia** led to widespread acceptance of violent revolution as a means to achieve social justice, and the people began to grasp at the reins of their own destiny, namely freedom. Yet to many in the **Third World** the profound basis of liberation theology is rooted in the democratic ideal, aligned with the weak and oppressed, the exploited and the poor. Unlike the strategy of Che **Guevara** to use terrorist tactics such as bombings, robberies, **kidnappings** and assassinations to strike at the heart of the enemy, the liberation movement strives to develop a political infrastructure and mobilisation of the masses through a historical, cultural and religious ideology. Western nations use this linkage to show that liberation theology uses politics as a means to resolve community conflict and uses indiscriminate violence as a political weapon.

See also: Religious Terrorism.

References

Pottenger, J. R. (1982) 'Liberation Theology: Its Methodical Foundations for Violence' in Rapoport, D. C. and Alexander, Y. (eds) *The Morality of Terrorism*, New York: Pergamon Press, pp. 99–126.

Taylor, R. W. (1986) 'Liberation Theology, Politics and Violence in Latin America', paper presented to Terrorism: An International Conference, held 15–17 April 1986 at the University of Aberdeen, pp. 45–54.

Libya

After the overthrow of the pro-Western King, Idris, in 1969, Muammar al-Khaddafi (more commonly known as **Gadaffi**), a Muslim Nasserite and socialist began to expel Western military personnel and impose restrictions on the country's oil industry dealings with the West. He concentrated on economic and social reform and in 1977 Libya became a socialist people's republic. Gadaffi opposed moderate Arab nations and any repprochement with **Israel**. He supported the Polisario Front and **Algeria** in their struggle with Morocco and participated in the **civil war** in Chad.

President Reagan maintained that Libya was linked to world terrorism and the **USA** shot down Libyan fighter planes over the Gulf of Sirte in 1981. In 1986 the Americans imposed an economic embargo on Libya and in April of that year an unsuccessful attempt was made by the USA to kill Gadaffi by bombing Tripoli and Benghazi. Gadaffi initially denied involvement of his country in the **Lockerbie** bombing, and the **United Nations** intensified their trade embargo, which was not fully lifted until after the eventual handing over of the suspects and the trial in 2001.

In the eyes of **Al Qaeda** he made serious errors – having no Islamic credentials; un-Islamic female guards and refusing to back **Iraq** in the **Gulf War**, and handing over the Lockerbie suspects. There is no doubt that Gadaffi's diplomacy has moderated in recent years.

See also: Lockerbie.

References

Blundy, D. and Lycett, A. (1987) *Gadaffi and the Libyan Revolution*, Boston, MA: Little, Brown and Co.

Further Reading

Davis, B. L. (1990) *Gadaffi, Terrorism and the Origin of the US Attacks on Libya*, New York: Praeger.

Sicker, M. (1987) *The Making of a Pariah State: The Adventurist Politics of Muammar Gadaffi*, New York: Praeger.

Lockerbie

In December 1988 a Pan Am jet was destroyed over the town of Lockerbie in Scotland resulting in the deaths of 249 people in the plane and eleven on the ground. Basically the object was to kill the passengers and crew. Initially, there was speculation that the atrocity was an act of revenge for the shooting down by the *USS Vincennes* of an Iranian airliner during the **Iran-Iraq** conflict. Attention, however, soon switched to **Libya** – two Libyan nationals were charged. It was intended as an act of revenge for the bombing of Libya by the **USA** in April 1986. Lockerbie remains the worst terrorist attack in Europe in terms of loss of life. Iran and **Syria** might have been involved in the atrocity, but in the end only Libyan involvement could eventually be proved with reasonable certainty. After months of ground searching following the disaster, a fragment of a circuit-board the size of a fingernail from a bomb placed in a radio cassette was found and matched to an identical board found in the timing mechanism of early bombs (i.e. one seized in Togo in 1986). The Swiss electronics firm that made the bomb admitted they had sold twenty to Libya and two Libyans were eventually charged. A few months before these indictments, a French judge formally accused Libya of directing the bombing of an airliner over Niger in 1989 which killed 171 people (Wilkinson, 2002).

The Lockerbie disaster still causes controversy above all about the number and nature of the warnings received by the intelligence services between the shooting down of the Iran Air Flight 655 and the bombing of Flight 103; and the identities/occupations of all passengers who travelled on the flight or originally planned to travel. A number of CIA operatives were killed in the disaster (Simon, 1994).

Many nations felt dishonoured by the experience, especially the USA, whose national carrier had been attacked (Pan Am) and later went into financial liquidation.

After the trial of the Libyans, acknowledgement of the crime by the perpetrators was still not forthcoming.

Controversy still exists over the idea behind the bombing. Many intelligence analysts believe that it was actually Iran that first approached Ahmed **Jabril**, leader of the Popular Front for the Liberation of Palestine – General Command, to place a bomb aboard the plane, and then turned to the Libyans after several PFLP-GC members were arrested in Germany before the bombing (Simon, 1994).

The authorities were reluctant to admit that a bomb had brought down the aircraft until all the evidence was available; and it was not until a week later that it was admitted that an explosive had wrecked the plane – a Czechoslovakian-made Semtex plastic explosive that could be moulded into any shape. The Americans were also reluctant to initiate immediate retaliatory action in case it jeopardised the outcome of efforts to release the growing number of Western hostages in the **Lebanon**.

The US Presidential Commission into the tragedy reported in 1990 and blamed Pan Am for their lax security at their check-in areas and for not matching baggage with passengers. Most damningly the Federal Aviation Authority and Pan Am were criticised for not releasing to the public information concerning an explicit threat to blow-up Pan Am planes over the Christmas period in 1988 (Simon, 1994). By the time this report was issued the priorities of an impending war with Iraq took precedence over any potential counter-terrorist response for the destruction of Pan Am Flight 103.

The aftermath of Lockerbie showed that people could unite together for emotional and political support. The families had a political agenda they wanted addressed, namely the punishment of those responsible for the murder of loved ones and the implementation of better **aviation security** measures. Even today, questions still remain to be answered. Governments are still trying to combat the threat of aircraft being blown-up in the air, while individuals have to cope with inevitable tragedies of terrorism.

In November 1991 the Scottish Crown Office and the US State Department issued an indictment against two Libyans, Abdel Basset Ali Al Megrahi and Lamen Khalifah Fhimah who they alleged had planted the bomb on Pan Am Flight 103 while working undercover for the Libyan Arab Airlines. Fhimah it was alleged had met up with al Megrahi in December in Malta and brought with them a brown, hard-cover samsonite suitcase used to carry the bomb which was then placed on an Air Malta Flight to Frankfurt and then transferred onto Pan Am Flight 103 for the onward flight to New York via London. The British and American authorities believed they had a cast-iron case.

For many years it was argued that the suspects would not receive a fair trial in a Western country and Libya refused to hand over the suspects and to comply with a Security Council resolution until 1999. The West always maintained that the bombings had been linked to two Libyan intelligence agents acting with official Libyan state sanction and possibly at the behest of Iran as well. Fhimah and Al Megrahi had been on the **FBI** list of 'Ten Most Wanted Fugitives' until their surrender. Eventually Colonel **Gadaffi** agreed to hand over the suspects after agreeing to the trial at a special court convened in the Netherlands under Scottish law with Scottish judges presiding. In January 2001 after a nine month trial the verdicts were announced; Al Megrahi was found guilty of murder and given a life sentence. Fhimah was found not guilty. The USA called for Libya to accept responsibility for the bombing and to pay compensation for the victims. The Libyan leader announced in the autumn of 2002 that he was happy to consider compensation. The acquitted Libyan was given a hero's welcome when he arrived home; while Al Megrahi unsuccessfully launched an appeal and is currently still in prison in Glasgow.

See also: Gadaffi; Libya.

References

Jurgensmeyer, M. (2000) *Terror in the Mind of God: The Global Rise of Religious Violence*, Berkeley, CA and London: University of California Press.

Reeve, S. (2000) *The New Jackals: Ramzi Yousef, Osama Bin Laden and the Future of Terrorism*, London: Andre Deutsch.

Simon, J. D. (1994) *The Terrorist Trap: America's Experience with Terrorism*, Bloomington, IN: Indiana Univeristy Press.

Wilkinson, P. (2002) *Terrorism versus Democracy: The Liberal State Response*, Portland, OR and London: Frank Cass.

Further Reading

Ashton, J. and Ferguson, I. (2001) *Cover Up of Convenience: The Hidden Scandal of Lockerbie*, Edinburgh and London: Mainstream Publishing.

Laqueur, W. (2001) *The New Terrorism: Fanaticism and the Arms of Mass Destruction*, London: Phoenix Press.

Wallace, R. (2001) *Lockerbie: The Story and the Lessons*, Westport, CT: Praeger.

M

Mafia

One of the most active criminal groups in the world is the Mafia. This criminal organisation originated as a secret society in thirteenth century Sicily. By extortion, 'protection' ransom and blackmail, the Mafia formed an immensely powerful organisation, which by the nineteenth and twentieth centuries had become developed in New York assisted by the rapid increase in Italian emigrants.

A potential development in terrorism is that terrorist groups will become more like traditional criminal organisations. There are clear parallels between Mafia-controlled kidnappings of executives for ransom in Italy, long a common form of crime in that country, and the 'politically-inspired' kidnappings of foreign executives in Latin America.

Terrorist tactics are simple but effective from the practitioner's point of view. Bombing, **kidnapping**, assassination, the seizing of facilities and conveyances and maiming are not the monopoly of the terrorist. They are the trade of the criminal, the violently deranged and even the wartime saboteur. The distinctions lie not in the acts themselves, since murder, assassination and execution are all forms of homicide, but in the motivation for the deed, and in the selection of the victims. Carlos **Marighella** points out the distinction between guerrillas and outlaws and he cautions others, like Regis **Debray**, against a group's losing sight of its politics and becoming a mafia.

Many terrorist groups have attracted criminal elements at one time or another. Some originally bona fide politicians later turned to crime; others such as the Mafia were predominantly criminal

from the beginning, but also had political interests. The dividing line between politics and crime was by no means always obvious and clear-cut: criminals were quite often good patriots or instinctive revolutionaries (or reactionaries) and they certainly had useful knowledge to pass on to the terrorists. But they would not accept discipline and their presence caused friction, corruption and eventually demoralisation. The temptation to use the loot from ransom for private gain or to settle personal accounts was overwhelming.

Whatever the ideological reasons for terrorism the nature of it is criminal activity as in many cases it involves murder.

Governments actively condone terrorist acts of violence to keep citizens under control by using terror policies. In turn revolutionary or freedom fighters can adopt different methods of terror to oppose the political establishment. Not only **South Africa** has witnessed this activity, but also many countries in Latin America and rogue states such as **Iraq**, **Iran**, **Libya**, **Syria** and Zaire.

In this era of globalisation, states have the money, technology, information systems, intelligence operations and support that make state terrorism so feared around the world. The events of **September 11** brought home the ultimate in terrorism on the **USA** in its major city.

See also: Crime; Debray; Marighella; Organised Crime.

Reference

Jamieson, A. (2000) *The Anti-Mafia: Italy's Fight*

against Organised Crime, New York: St Martin's Press.

Further Reading

Hoffman, B. (1998) *Inside Terrorism*, New York: Columbia University Press.

Rensselaer, L. (1998) *Smuggling Armageddon*, New York: St Martin's Press.

Marighella, Carlos

b. 1910; d. 1969

Out of the ideals and theories of Che **Guevara**, a new revolutionary philosopher emerged, namely a Brazilian, Carlos Marighella, whose writing has become a gospel for today's **urban guerrillas**. He was an engineer by training, who became a guerrilla fighter at the age of 57 after more than three decades as a Communist party official. According to Marighella the first duty of a revolutionary is to make a revolution, and to engage in both guerrilla and psychological warfare, especially against imperialism and capitalism. He wanted all economic, political or social systems to further the objectives of guerrilla or revolutionary ideology. He provided a set of personal qualities demanded of urban guerrillas; an especially important quality was the ability to live in the urban population.

The advantages of the guerrilla over the enemy were surprise, better knowledge of terrain, greater mobility, and a better information network. Marighella urged that urban guerrillas should take a variety of actions against the authorities, but choose them with care. Possible actions were attacks or raids on banks, radio stations and offices; burglaries of offices and government buildings; occupation of schools, factories and radio stations; ambushing of police, businessmen and army personnel; tactical street fighting and promoting confrontation with police and the army; strike or work interruptions in factories and schools; and liberating prisoners.

Increasingly violent measures included the theft of arms and explosives; attacks against army barracks and police stations; the execution of spies, torturers and police informers; **kidnapping** of police, political figures and businessmen; the sabotage of factories, banks, transport and communications systems, leading to terrorism by bomb attacks and arson; armed propaganda against the **media**; and a war of nerves spreading false rumours among, for example, the police, embassies and international organisations.

To carry out any of these urban guerrilla actions, Marighella advised a number of methods and key factors for success – careful enquiry and analysis of information; observation and reconnaissance, study and timing of routes; mapping; transportation; selection of personnel; firing ability and capacity; rehearsal and execution of the action; withdrawal; removal of the wounded; and the destruction of clues. In Uruguay, for example, the Tupamaros put into practice much of Marighella's advice and with much tactical success, such as in the kidnapping of the British Ambassador, Sir Geoffrey Jackson in Uruguay in September 1971.

Carlos Marighella died in a gun battle in San Paolo, Brazil in November 1969.

See also: Guerrilla Warfare in History.

Reference

Marighella, C. (1985) *Manual of the Urban Guerrilla*, Chapel Hill, NC: Documentary Publications.

Further Reading

Williams, J. W. (1989) 'Carlos Marighella: The Founder of Urban Guerrilla Warfare', *Terrorism*, vol. 12, no. 1, pp. 1–20.

Maritime Security

Although a number of ships have been taken over by terrorists in the past two decades, it is offshore energy terrorism which most concerns the Western nations; although there is a difference in perception between the Western European nations and the **United States**. The motivation for such activity against offshore energy production platforms varies – it may be to raise awareness of pollution, to gain publicity or simply destruction for its own sake, but there is a strong conviction that offshore energy will eventually become a terrorist target and that the preparations by the United States to deter and defend against this threat are woefully inadequate. The American government and industry have tended to give a sceptical hearing to those who call for improved offshore anti-terrorist planning mechanisms and physical safeguards. Often steps are seen as unwarranted in light of the absence of a history of offshore terrorist incidents, and of evidence that an acute threat of such incidents does, in fact, exist.

Certain basic elements enter into the risk-of-terrorist attack education. These are that offshore oil and gas extraction facilities are of national importance, and represent a valuable dollar investment; terrorism is, and is likely to remain, a fact of life; offshore platforms are intrinsically vulnerable to terrorist attack; and terrorists can get the means to stage an attack against a platform.

The proponents of protective measures place the weight of their evidence on the potential consequences of a terrorist incident i.e. loss of life, property, energy, and the threat of pollution. Any legitimate risk analysis has to include a statement on the probability of a terrorist incident. To many, the terrorists' motivation is inherent in the propaganda or extortion value of attacking a platform. Sceptics argue that if terrorists are motivated to draw media publicity, a relatively remote and inaccessible target at sea is a poor choice. Much more accessible, equally lucrative and potentially spectacular targets exist on shore.

All major elements of any domestic country's energy infrastructure such as oil pipelines, refineries, electrical power plants and grids, natural gas processing plants and transmission lines – are readily susceptible to malevolent interference.

The comparative concentration of the North Sea offshore industry has significance apart from its relative economic vulnerability. The more centralised a target, the easier and cheaper it is to protect. In Europe mineral resources, whether underground or undersea, have been viewed as national assets deserving of protection and regulation by the state for the benefit of the nation as a whole. Oil is more of a scarce resource to European than to American countries. Thus there are sound economic grounds to guarantee a heightened degree of European sensitivity regarding offshore energy security. The economic and domestic political impacts of a terrorist disaster in the North Sea would be far greater than in the United States.

As regards West European countries (the **UK**, Norway, Netherlands, Germany) the question of offshore assets and merchant fleets there is close co-operation between industry and government, resulting in contingency planning, training and exercising of plans and clear lines of responsibility and communications. As the value of a barrel of oil or a tanker increases, so does the threat. Thus, economic demands make some assets more attractive targets than others.

It is expensive to protect all assets to the same degree. To determine which assets should receive the greatest attention it is necessary to consider three forces that exert constant pressure on an asset. These are vulnerability, criticality and threat. Each of these forces exerts pressures in varying degrees at various times on the commercial assets of an oil corporation or shipping company; and some of the most valued assets depend on the stockholders' and public's confidence.

Modern skyjacking has been termed by some legal experts to be air piracy. Ships and aircraft have generally been the targets of pirates. The **Achille Lauro** hijacking showed the impact of piracy on the sea. Moreover, in the shipping lanes of the South China Sea, the western Indian Ocean and the Arabian Sea piracy is seen as a large enterprise by wealthy groups and a small-scale endeavour by desperate individuals whose poverty has driven them to this extreme (Combs, 2000).

See also: Oil and Gas Industry.

References

Combs, C. C. (2000) *Terrorism in the 21st Century*, New Jersey: Prentice Hall.

Mueller, G. O. W. and Alder, F. (1985) *Outlaws of the Ocean: The Complete Book of Contemporary Crime on the High Seas*, New York: Hearst Marine Books.

Parritt, B. A. H. (ed.) (1986) *Violence at Sea: A Review of Terrorism, Acts of War and Piracy and Countermeasures to Prevent Terrorism*, Paris: ICC Publishing.

Further Reading

Cassese, A. (1989) *Terrorism, Politics and Law: The Achille Lauro Affair*, Oxford: Policy Press.

MacNair, D. G. (1982) 'The Nature of the Beast: A Solique on Maritime Fraud, Piracy and Terrorism', *Journal of Security Administration*, vol. 1, no. 1, pp. 41–47.

Maimore, E. (1987) 'Maritime Vulnerability and Security', *Terrorism*, vol. 10, no. 3, pp. 233–236.

Marx and Revolutionary Violence

Both Marxist-Leninists and revisionists have tended to interpret Marx for their own purposes. In general, the former have presented a Marx more prone to violence than is actually the case, while the latter have underplayed the importance of revolutionary violence in Marx's theory.

In Marxian thought, violence is never treated as a separate analytical category but integrated into a larger vision of the revolutionary process. The core of the capitalist structure is the class division between the bourgeoisie and the proletariat. The bourgeoisie, through its domination in production, exploits and oppresses the proletariat. Exploitation occurs in the form of expropriation of surplus value. Oppression results when capitalists, in order to maximise surplus value, organise production in a way which requires alienated labour. This denial of opportunity for creative labour is the basic source of revolution in capitalist societies. The economic substructure characterised by class division, exploitation and oppression provides a foundation for a capitalist superstructure which expresses bourgeois domination and sustains it. While the overthrow of the capitalist state is an indispensable condition for workers' liberation, it is not in itself sufficient for socialist transformation. The ultimate ends of revolution require universal liberation from dehumanising modes of capitalist production. If a socialist revolution is to occur, the proletariat will have to achieve a level of conscious behaviour able to maintain an effective revolutionary movement. A socialist revolution has to change the sub-structural economy and provide the foundation for a new way of life. Two major conditions have to be attained prior to a successful socialist revolution – a relatively highly developed capitalist economy and the existence of revolutionary consciousness and organisation within the proletariat.

Marx viewed revolutionary violence as a pre-determined phenomenon which is necessarily a part of the transition from capitalism to socialism. Marx neither condemned violence as a pacifist like Gandhi did, nor did he glorify it like Sorel or **Fanon**. Sorel and Fanon claimed that violence is instrumental in the psychological transformation of the oppressed into 'new men' capable of making a revolution.

Marx made distinctions between political and social revolution. The former altered only aspects of the superstructure, primarily the political institutional framework. Social revolution transformed the substructure, particularly patterns of class domination and the method of production. The essence of revolution could not occur without widespread revolutionary consciousness among proletarians. In such a context violence was inevitable and efficacious.

In Marxist theory violence is not efficacious unless it takes place in the context of developed material conditions. Throughout his life, Karl Marx criticised revolutionaries of the Jacobin (French Revolutionary) tradition who over-emphasised the importance of political will while neglecting the necessity for advanced capitalist development in society and of revolutionary class consciousness in the working class. Marx believed terrorism to be out of step with the larger, impersonal historical process of revolution.

Marx was not opposed to violence in principle. He foresaw it as a necessary ingredient of the complex evolution of events culminating in socialist revolution.

See also: Terror and Terrorism.

Reference

Dinse, J. (1984) 'The Role of Violence in Marx's Theory of Revolution' in Hann, H. H. (ed.) *Terrorism Political Violence and World Order*, Lanham, MD: University Press of America, pp. 59–64.

Mau Mau

The Mau Mau organisation was formed in the 1940s within the framework of the 'legal' Kenya African Union (KAU), but membership was distinguished from that of the KAU by the taking of oaths. While the oath-taking may superficially seem to be of little consequence, it was considered to be sufficiently serious to be declared illegal. All Kikuyu tribesmen discovered or suspected of taking the oath were liable to be imprisoned or detained indefinitely.

The reason for the oath-taking was that the Kikuyu were deeply superstitious, after years of attempting to defend themselves from attacks by both the warlike Masai and Arab slave-traders through the use of magic. Mau Mau leaders therefore contrived awesome oaths designed to cover all contingencies and to ensure that all members would remain both loyal to the move- ment and anti-white. The oath consisted of two parts, the first being a series of magic actions designed to convince the person that he was invoking a supernatural power, and the second the actual taking of the oath in which he would call upon the supernatural powers to support him. By these efforts, the Mau Mau gained some sort of hold, albeit often involuntary, over much of the Kikuyu population.

The Mau Mau soon became divided into two groups, a militant wing and a passive wing. The passive wing was supposed to maintain forces in the field and was made up mostly of people who provided money supplies, shelter, recruits and intelligence information. Only in the capital, Nairobi was any real organisation and direction to be found. The militant wing lived in the Aberdare forests, and consisted of gang members. It purported to be organised into sections of up to 35 men, platoons of up to 100 men and companies of up to 250 men.

Initially orders from the passive wing were related to field operations feasibility, and the supplies of both arms and ammunition were far from abundant. Furthermore, there was little contact between individual Mau Mau groups. They were held together by an awed respect for the unit leaders, the fear of breaking oaths and the possibility of punishment.

It was not until 1951 that the Mau Mau really began to take the offensive with attacks on white farmers. By the time the state of emergency had been declared in October 1952 there were 12,000 guerrillas in the field. Despite arrests of leader figures, including Jomo Kenyatta, the organisation of Mau Mau was so loose that the effects of these arrests were hardly noticeable. Such was the nature of Mau Mau that the administration found it hard to recognise the leaders and this led to the detention of thousands of suspects.

In March 1953, Mau Mau raids took place which proved to be of profound significance. At Naivasha, insurgents stormed the police station, releasing over 170 prisoners. At Lari, insurgents killed 74 people (mostly women and children), wounded 50 more and left 50 people missing, probably dismembered. The Lari massacre did much damage to the prestige of the Mau Mau. Lari had been a settlement forced upon the Kikuyu by the government, yet despite the reluctance of the tribesmen to go, those who accepted the land were considered by the Mau Mau to be traitors and were subsequently killed. The massacre removed support for the Mau Mau both within Kenya and internationally.

'Operation Anvil' in 1954 and the detention of some 20,000 Kikuyu destroyed the Mau Mau hierarchy and its cells in Nairobi, severed lines of communication from the city and isolated the forest groups. As the security forces' measures began to bite, lack of organisation, loss of support and extremely limited supplies of arms and ammunition forced the Mau Mau into isolation, leaving them to fight as loosely-based armed gangs relying upon sabotage and terror as their key weapons.

See also: Third World.

References

Davidson, B. (1981) *The People's Case: A History of Guerrillas in Africa*, Harlow, Essex: Longman.

Lacquer, W. (1997) *Guerrilla Warfare: A Historical and Critical Study*, New Brunswick, NJ: Transaction Publishers.

Media

A free people need a free press; but **terrorism** needs a propaganda platform. So in all Western countries, the news media faces a dilemma: is it possible to keep citizens informed of daily events, including the often graphic tragedy of terrorism, without becoming, to some degree, propagandists for the perpetrators?

The question of whether information is news or propaganda is very important. Even straightforward news stories about terrorism can involve agonising decisions. Do they contribute to the free marketplace of ideas helping people to understand the central issues of their day? Or do they give terrorists a megaphone through which to spread their message of fear to their ultimate target – the public at large? Do the news media provide the oxygen of publicity on which terrorism thrives, and help in the spread of sedition? Does extensive coverage by the media inflate the terrorists' ego to that of folk heroes, or does such coverage produce a sense of outrage – public revulsion against terrorist acts and demands for tougher measures by the government? Does journalism put so much pressure on the government that it acts irresponsibly, or does it provide important information to officials, since in hostile situations reporters can sometimes go where decision-makers in government dare not venture? Many people and organisations consider the media to be hooked on terrorism. To some people in the media terrorism is drama; does the media, in an effort to captivate viewers, cover terrorist incidents whenever possible? Or do they, as they themselves believe, report the facts which are verified, and with total fairness and straightforwardness?

These issues are outlined in question form because there is so much disagreement on which is the correct approach. A broad consensus exists on three points. Television is the terrorist's medium of choice. It is far preferable to print or radio as the outlet with the most immediacy and the most terrifying impact. Television is no longer simply reporting about the story, but has become part of the story. In the never-ending debate about the role of the news media in a free democracy, television is at the centre of an ongoing controversy.

Should a journalist be concerned with getting a one-time scoop or with saving lives? Throughout the debate on the media's role, the call for self-regulation by journalists and not censorship has been common. One of the biggest victories terrorists could ever achieve would be to force democracies to adopt the repressive press restrictions of dictatorships. With the pace of today's technology, satellite television beamed from any part of the world and receivable by viewers anywhere, censorship would not work. In Western Europe to a far greater extent than in North America state-run television networks have worked out fairly high standards of editorial taste and agreements with national security forces to withhold or delay broadcasts in certain cases. In a Western society there are obvious disadvantages of the public's not being accurately informed, or being informed only by government spokesmen.

The Western media is vulnerable to misuse by international terrorists. The fact that terrorism by definition tends to be dramatic and also pictorial through the terrorist acts which take place, makes the media vulnerable.

Nevertheless, if the public are allowed access to all the information, no matter how dramatic or devastating it may be at any given point, they will eventually reach the proper conclusion. Certain standards, concepts and precepts have to be imposed on the media and obeyed. Journalists have to be aware of the role they are playing and the risks for society if the journalist lets himself be used by the terrorists to magnify whatever are their intentions. In the West and indeed in other parts of the world an event is legitimate news and one cannot deny the media's legitimate response.

If events are repetitive enough, such as the spate of hijackings in the late 1960s and early 1970s, terrorists can be faced with diminishing returns, for there were few tangible achievements in this time and even the publicity value of hijacking decreased. The success of a terrorist operation depends almost entirely on the amount of publicity it receives. This was one of the main reasons for the shift from rural guerrilla to urban terror in the 1960s, for in the cities the terrorists could always count on the presence of journalists and TV cameras and consequently a large audience.

It is not the magnitude of the terrorist operation that counts but the publicity; and this rule applies not only to single operations but to whole campaigns. The media have always magnified terrorist exploits quite irrespective of their intrinsic importance. Terrorist groups numbering perhaps a dozen members have been described as armies, their official communiques have been discussed in countless television shows, radio broadcasts, articles and editorials. In a few cases even non-existent groups have been given a great deal of publicity. All modern terrorist groups need publicity; the smaller they are, the more they depend on it, and this has, to a large extent, affected the choice of their targets. Even an apparently illogical or senseless attack becomes more effective if given wide coverage in the media than an operation against a seemingly obvious target which is ignored. These strategies work only in societies which have no censorship.

What terrorists want most of all from the media is publicity, usually free publicity that a group could not normally afford to buy. They want the public to think positively about their cause and their act; and desire legitimacy. In hostage situations, and where sponsors are involved, they want details about any plans for military retaliation. They seek media coverage which causes damage to the enemy.

It goes without saying that the government seek understanding, co-operation, restraint and loyalty from the media; without advancing the causes of the terrorist through giving them a propaganda platform. In hostage situations they want a restrained approach by the media and perhaps even a long period of silence at the height of any **hostage taking** incident. Governments are always grateful for any information provided by media representatives.

What the media wants is to be the first with the story; and to make the story timely, dramatic and as accurate as possible. They want to operate as securely and freely as possible in the society. The media believes terrorists have a right to know.

Current issues which impact on terrorism and the media are a trend to more violent terrorist incidents and to attacks on media personnel and institutions. The media can be wrong-footed by anonymous terrorism where no one claims responsibility and no demands are made. The media has to have trust in the government and vice versa – and this could be supported by a code of voluntary behaviour or guidelines; for example on limiting

information, on police and military movements during rescue operations. It is in the interest of both parties to prevent the cause of terrorism from prevailing and in preserving democracy.

Depictions of terrorist devastation – through journalistic photographs, television, and even in artistic or film recreations – are profoundly powerful. Paradoxically, confronted with the reality of destruction and murder, the public fears or resents the political causes represented through violent acts. The immediate images from **Lockerbie** (1988) and the **World Trade Center** (1993, 2001) bombings will be seared on the minds of many forever.

Terrorists are known for their interest in publicity-seeking and are always trying to explain themselves to TV reporters. The symbol of terrorism brings to mind the image of a swarthy and sinister figure carrying a bomb; the portrayal has been Jewish or Arab. Terrorism is an excellent vehicle for propaganda messages to arouse the public and engineer consent for desired lines of policy. Disinformation occurs because there is an elimination of any sense of history, any understanding of history, particularly when it might be embarrassing. The media's definition of terrorism can be very different from our own, and the term 'terrorism' can be politically manipulated to cover-up what is really happening in countries such as El Salvador, Nicaragua and **Peru**.

Genocide, violence, torture, disappearance and mass extermination of peoples have been met with a range of responses. Depending on our quota of ignorance, racism, xenophobia and homophobia we may claim that the histories are 'political propaganda' or 'exaggerations' 'maybe true but don't have anything to do with us' or 'just the way things are'. Globally, it seems too overwhelming to have to confront these events as having something to do with our own lives. Disappearance, in places such as South America, where dissidents are taken from their homes or off the streets and never seen again, can provide relatives with an agony of not knowing which is worse than acknowledged torture or death.

The mass media rarely make the link between what is happening out there and the policy that is made in the leading parliaments of the world. This is because they are instruments of state policy (Brown and Merrill, 1993).

A number of options could bring governments and media into closer co-operation – joint training exercises, an information response centre, and the promotion of voluntary press coverage guidelines. If terrorism sustains itself, freedoms shrink and a free press is one of the first institutions to go. Censorship in a democracy is very difficult to sustain – ultimately the media cannot be cautioned, leaned on or controlled.

See also: Propaganda; Restraint.

References

Brown, D. J. and Merrill, R. (1993) *Violent Persuasion: The Politics and Imagery of Terrorism*, Seattle, WA: Bay Press.

Carruthers, S. L. (1999) *The Media at War: Communication and Conflict in the Twentieth Century*, New York: St Martin's Press.

Farnen, R. F. (1990) 'Terrorism and the Mass Media: A Systematic Analysis of a Symbiotic Process', *Terrorism*, vol. 13, no. 2, pp. 99–144.

Miller, A. H. (ed.) (1982) *Terrorism: The Media and the Law*, Dobbs Ferry, NY: Transnational Publishers.

Shpiro, S. (2002) 'Conflict Media Strategies and the Politics of Counter-terrorism', *Politics*, vol. 22, no. 2, pp. 76–85.

Tugwell, M. A. (1986) 'Terrorism and Propaganda: Problems and Response', *Conflict Quarterly*, vol. 6, no. 2, (spring), pp. 5–15.

Wilkinson, P. (1990) 'Terrorism and Propaganda' in Alexander, Y. and Latter, R. (eds) *Terrorism and the Media*, New York: Brassey's, pp. 26–34.

Further Reading

Anderson, T. (1993) 'Terrorism and Censorship: The Media in Chains', *Journal of International Affairs*, vol. 47, no. 1, pp. 127–136.

Clutterbuck, R. L. (1981) *Terrorism: The Media and Political Violence*, London: Macmillan.

Herman, E. S. and O'Sullivan, G. (1989) *The Terrorism Industry: The Experts and Institutions that Shape Our View of Terror*, New York: Pantheon.

Nacos, B. L. (1994) *Terrorism and the Media: From the Iran Hostage Crisis to the World Trade Center Bombing*, New York: Columbia University Press.

O'Sullivan, J. (1986) 'Media Publicity Causes Terrorism' in Szumski, B. (ed.) *Terrorism: Opposing Viewpoints*, St Pauls, MN: Greenhaven Press, pp. 75–81.

Paletz, D. L. and Schmid, A. P. (1992) *Terrorism and the Media*, London: Sage Publications.

Perl, R. F. (1997) 'Terrorism, the Media, and the 21st Century: Perspectives, Trends and Options for Policy Makers', *Low Intensity Conflict and Law Enforcement*, vol. 6, no. 2 (autumn), pp. 93–102.

Schmid, A. P. (1989) 'Terrorism and the Media: The Ethics of Publicity', *Terrorism and Political Violence*, vol. 1, no. 4 (October), pp. 539–65.

Slone, M. (2000) 'Responses to Media Coverage of Terrorism', *Journal of Conflict Resolution*, vol. 44, no. 4 (August), pp. 508–522.

Millennial Violence

Millennial thought relies on the static image of '**cults**' as being controlled by very powerful leaders whose 'whims' are eagerly carried out by followers and dismiss the significance of interaction between groups and their opponents. There is the unqualified assumption that specific dates such as 2000 serve as triggers for millennial violence.

Religious-ideological totalism entails an absolute division of humanity into dual categories such as saved/doomed, human/sub-human, godly/demonic.

In the year 2000 contrary to 'popular' expectations around the world, millennialists did not engage in proactive violence; and religiously moderated extremists did not initiate violent conflicts to facilitate the onset of Armageddon or to help fulfil a 'prophecy'. Martyrdom was a possible choice for the extremists when confronted by the police or military, but after the events of Waco, Texas in 1993, this did not occur.

'Apocalyptic' relations have existed, and do exist in Jewish-Christian relations. Cataclysmic apocalyptic relations have always existed between Jews and Muslims, between modernity and the Arab world, between an arrogant and missionary secular West and the wisdom of other cultures.

Reference

Barkun, M. (ed.) (1996) *Millennialism and Violence*, London: Frank Cass.

Further Reading

Kaplan, J. (ed.) (2002) Special Issue on 'Millennial Violence, Past Present and Future', *Terrorism and Political Violence*, vol. 14, no. 1.

Mindset *see* Psychology of Terrorism: Terrorist Mindset

Misconceptions *see* Definitions and Morality

Models of Terrorism

Case study analysis of terrorists and their life patterns has a short history. However, empirical estimates of model parameters have been obtained from data on international terrorism since 1968. Some evidence suggests that the tendency of acts of terrorism to incite further violence is more easily reversed in less democratic, poorer and less well-educated societies. It appears that reversal of a terrorism 'epidemic' is more likely under conditions which facilitate repression rather than reform, and more open societies face particular difficulties in responding to terrorism effectively.

Quantitative empirical studies have consisted of tabulations or attempts to fit models of 'social contagion'. Theoretical formulations have concentrated on issues of definition and typology. Many controversies have been raised on historical, ideological and tactical concerns, but these have not been formally addressed in quantitative social research. The concern that the main effect of terrorism is increased police repression is a common theme among a number of leftist warnings. **Marighella** (1971) argued that terrorism leads to repression, but made this relationship the foundation of terrorist strategy. Hyams (1974) sees liberal reform as the ultimate consequence of terrorism. Terrorism, says Hyams, improves the climate for reform and brings about a more just society. Moss (1972), Clutterbuck (1975) and Laqueur (1978) dispute the claim that terrorism is primarily a weapon of the miserable and oppressed, and they point out that it is often the work of idle elites, particularly students and intelligentsia. Terrorism is much easier and safer in more open societies; and the terrorist faces surprisingly low risks of harsh punishment or even arrest (Wilkinson 1978). Writers from a variety of liberal and conservative perspectives maintain that reform becomes less likely, and repressive reaction more likely in the climate of insecurity and violence produced by a terror campaign. Terrorism is usually unsuccessful in bringing about social changes sought by terrorists and it has a good chance of making those changes far more difficult to attain. The overall message of writers is that society has difficulty in responding to terrorist acts. Whereas authoritarian states opt for straightforward violent situations, states founded upon liberal democratic principles have to find other approaches.

Thus a new model of terrorism, adopted among others by Heyman and Mickolus (1980), considers the view that terrorist incidents may encourage further violence through a process of imitation or diffusion, giving rise to a dynamics of terrorism similar to that observed in the spread of a contagious disease. If terrorism is contagious between countries, then commonalities of culture, circumstances and personnel and the ease of rapid communication make the phenomenon of contagion even more visible within countries.

Chronology data can be useful, especially if it is comprehensive and current. However, the necessary dependence on news service sources for incident reports creates inevitable biases in favour of countries with well-developed and unrestrained news media. Incident counts for less-developed countries or countries with highly restricted information tend to be deflated relative to counts for the more public industrial democracies. **Data** often refers only to incidents of international terrorism in which two or more states were somehow involved. The great majority of terrorist acts are purely domestic in character, but reliable domestic terrorism chronologies are available for very few countries. Much of the literature on terrorism does not distinguish between domestic and international terrorism, or sees the latter primarily as an extension of the domestic struggle.

Contagion terrorism at some point can be reversed, when the cumulative number of incidents begins to decrease, rather than increase the probability of future incidents. Reversals can result from a tendency of terrorism to generate successful repression, which destroys the terrorist organisation or makes rebellion too dangerous; or a tendency for terrorism to generate social reform, which undermines the grievances that produced the terrorism in the first place. Terrorism is least reversible in relatively open and affluent societies, which proves that concerns about the dilemma of the liberal state are well founded. Terrorism seemingly confronts citizens of open societies with a no-win choice between tolerating terrorist violence on the one hand, or accepting loss of basic freedoms and important restraints upon government behaviour on the other. The middle ground can be narrow and dangerous, and whatever the goals of terrorism, by its nature as a means it is likely to have malignant effects. Autocratic, poor and un-educated countries do not seem to suffer from these effects.

The Poisson model of terrorism appears to be the best of the models for analysing the occurrences of terrorist events. It has three bases: the probability that an event of terrorism will occur during a time interval increases with the length of the time interval; the probability is almost negligible that two events of terrorism will occur in a very small time interval (with the exception, of course, of co-ordinated efforts); and generally the incidents of terrorism which occur during one time interval are independent of those which occur in any other time interval. However, with regard to the latter point, it is conceivable that an event of terrorism, if given sufficient publicity, will generate a climate which is conducive to other events of terrorism.

The study of international terrorism has been the domain of the psychologist, political scientist, sociologist and those in the legal profession for many decades. Analytical attempts to study the problem suffer from the lack of hard data.

References

Clutterbuck, R. (1975) *Living with Terrorism*, London: Faber and Faber.

Heyman, E. S. and Mickolus, E. (1980) 'Responding to Terrorism: Basic and Applied Research' in Sloan, S. and Shultz, R. (eds) *Responding to the Terrorist Threat: Prevention and Control*, New York: Praeger.

Hyams, E. (1974) *Terrorists and Terrorism*, New York: St Martins Press.

Laqueur, W. (1978) *The Terrorism Reader*, New York: The New American Library, Inc.

Marighella, C. (1971) 'Mini-Manual of the Urban Guerrilla' in Mallin, J. (ed.) *Terrorism and Urban Guerrillas: A Study of Tactics and Documents*, Coral Gables, FL: University of Miami Press.

Moss, R. (1972) *Counter Terrorism*, London: The Economist Brief Books.

Wilkinson, P. (1978) 'Terrorist Movements' in Alexander Y., Carlton, D. and Wilkinson, P. (eds) *Terrorism, Theory and Practice*, New York: Praeger: Westview Special Studies in National and International Terrorism, pp. 99–117.

Morality

The problem of the limits of the permissible is the central issue in any discussion of both revolutionary and counter-revolutionary violence, or of terror and counter-terror. Someone who embarks on terrorism, like one who clings to power, knows where he begins but never knows how or where to finish. The terrorist dream of a final, redemptive blow, the dream of both state and individual terror is a false dream. Terror flourishes in a step-by-step struggle, whether it is embarked upon as a stage in some overall, long-term strategy, or perceived from the outset as a sole and total weapon.

Another lesson learned from the history of individual terror is the decisive role played by society in its prevention and eradication. Society has to live up to its responsibilities, even when this involves abandoning its tranquil ways and its illusions of safety. The danger of terror has and should continue to alert and awaken society to just this degree of responsibility. The prevention of such a horror cannot be left to the technicians. There can be no substitute for society's own critique, for its own treatment of its ills. It is a moral struggle which has been and will continue to be waged fearlessly.

The means and their realisation must be determined by humble and critical attitudes toward the aims. Aims cannot justify the means. One cannot abandon the balancing of means against ends, but it must be kept free of religious fanaticism and rigid dogmatism. Terror is a fact of life to which one must respond somehow or other. Terror tempts society to violent reprisal because it strikes one as irrationally violent. On the other hand, a violent response caters to the propaganda of terror. Society's violence supports the terrorist's otherwise weak case, or seems to do so for many. Therefore accommodation is sought, which may appear as a sign of the success of the terrorist methods.

Democratic societies have to admit that the terrorist's uncompromising position makes it impossible to treat him or her as other than the enemy – as an outlaw.

Guilt transfer is a very old technique of propaganda more widely used today than ever before. It involves a switch of public attention away from the embarrassing acts of its originator toward the embarrassing acts of the adversary, so that the former may be forgotten or forgiven, while the latter may erode the confidence and legitimacy of the other side. In the campaign to discourage and contain international terrorism, as well as in the East-West struggle, the liberal democracies cannot afford to operate under the handicap of the guilty mind. Contemporary society seems particularly vulnerable on account of its confused attitudes and lack of moral reference points. Part of the answer lies in political leadership and part in a better-informed and more responsible news **media**. The public have to understand the technique and reject fraudulent appeals directed at their consciences.

Terrorism is part of a strategy aimed at establishing world domination and un-restrained by moral considerations, lack of restraint can be due to the role of the permissive society, the psychological failures of terrorists, and also a product of moral choice.

Terrorism can be practised by armed soldiers of an established government, police officers or other agents of purportedly legitimate governments.

Terror may be used for political and moral ends, to terrify those who might commit assorted evils into desisting from such acts.

Nobody can tolerate a society in which anything as important as the deprivation of life is left to the judgement of private persons. Terrorism is difficult to justify on strategic grounds, in the nature of the case.

Terrorists hold that there are no innocent persons and the evils brought about by terrorism are real and present. Social change for the better has to be attainable by voluntary co-operation and not by violence (Frey and Morris, 1991).

References

Frey, R. and Morris, C. (ed.) (1991) *Violence, Terrorism and Justice*, Cambridge: Cambridge University Press.

Harmon, C. C. (2000) *Terrorism Today*, London: Frank Cass.

Khatchadourian, H. (1998) *The Morality of Terrorism*, New York: Peter Lang.

Leiser, B. M. (1977) 'Terrorism, Guerrilla Warfare and International Morality', *Journal of International Studies*.

Further Reading

Becker, J. (1989) 'Is There a Case for Terrorism? The Sacrifice of Strangers', *Encounters* (Jan/Feb), pp. 19–24.

Hoffman, B. (1997) 'Why Terrorists Don't Claim Credit', *Terrorism and Political Violence*, vol. 6, no. 1 (Spring), pp. 1–6.

Rapoport, D. C. and Alexander, Y. (eds) *The Morality of Terrorism: Religious and Secular Justifications*, New York: Pergamon Press.

— (1997) 'To Claim or Not to Claim: That is the Question – Always!', *Terrorism and Political Violence*, vol. 9, no. 4, pp. 10–17.

Misconceptions

The morality of acts of terrorism is a thorny issue. Many see terrorism as violence that the West does not like. Terror is violence, which no moral person can like or approve as innocents get killed. It is trite and almost mythical to argue that either one man's terrorist is another man's freedom fighter or that terrorism is the only way the weak can fight against the strong. Most terrorist groups can grow very quickly. Furthermore we have seen another mis-judged phrase used that terrorists only respond to violence imposed on them by policemen and the military – as seen in IRA thinking.

Both wings of terrorist movements/groups – the Left and Right – are against the status quo (which can be democratic, stable, moderate and abiding by the rule of law). Terrorism moreover is far from being just mindless – it is deliberate and systematic and each action is coldly calculated, for example, the seizure of the Japanese Embassy in Lima, **Peru** in 1996 by the Shining Path group was a calculated attempt to drive a wedge between Peruvians and their Japanese minority of whom President Fujimori is the symbol. The attempt by Chechen separatists to kill hundreds in a theatre near the Kremlin in **Russia** was calculated to bring the Chechen issue to the heart of Russian politics and to try and force the Russian leadership to negotiate.

Terrorists certainly are not ignorant, on the contrary they are well educated, psychologically astute and impressive strategists. Many PLO members have been postgraduates. Many have been trained in religious institutions; others are specialists in science and technology and in making explosives (Harmon, 2000).

It is a myth to believe that all terrorists are male, many are female, especially in the Red Army of **Japan**. In 1987 a North Korean woman planted bombs that destroyed a Korean Air Flight, in an unsuccessful attempt to get the 1988 **Olympic Games** in South Korea can-celled. In Sri Lanka many of the leaders of the **Tamil Tigers** were women. In the Tupamaros, **Sandinistas** and Sendero Luminoso many fe-males have risen through the groups to positions of authority.

See also: Children; Women.

Reference

Harmon, C. C. (2000) *Terrorism Today*, London: Frank Cass.

Motivation

The scope and complexity of the enigma of terrorism is a real problem for the world commu-nity. The terrorist is dedicated to the political goal, which he sees as one of transcendent merit. He seeks attention and publicity for his cause. Terror-ists aim to erode support for the established leadership or undermine the authority of the state by destroying normality, creating uncertainty and polarising the country. They aim to liberate colleagues in foreign jails and desire money to buy arms and finance the organisation. Their action is a measure of deep frustration when there is no legitimate way to redress grievances.

Frustration escalates in its expression, developing from protest, violent demonstrations, disruption, sabotage, robbery, burning, bombing and casual killing, to selective killing and kidnapping. When one level of the escalation fails, terrorists try the next level. Many drop out at each stage of the escalation. Frustration may arise from the success of the society in a democratic form that is perhaps too successful for the extremists.

The most feared terrorists are those with sound organisational skills that are determined to succeed – they have an established order or routine which makes them maximise their chances of success. They require good intelligence, and ability to learn from their mistakes, and careful planning often taking years in the process. Even the naming of their organisations is carefully chosen to show images of self-defence, freedom and liberation and righteous vengeance. Ethno-nationalist terrorist organisations have stated long term goals of self-determination and nationhood. This has proved to be a potent and persuasive rallying cry throughout recent history.

See also: Psychology of Terrorism.

References

Crenshaw, M. (1988) 'Theories of Terrorism: Instrumental and Organisational Approaches' in Rapoport, D. C. (ed.) *Inside Terrorist Organisations*, New York: Columbia University Press, pp. 13–31.
Henderson, H. (1991) *Global Terrorism: The Complete Reference Guide*, Checkmark Books – Facts on File.

Further Reading

Janke, P. (1983) *Guerrilla and Terrorist Organisations: A World Directory and Bibliography*, Brighton: Harvesters Press.

Post, J. M. (1987) 'Group and Organisational Dynamics of Political Terrorism: Implications for Counter-Terrorist Policy' in Wilkinson, P. and Stewart, A. M. (eds) *Contemporary Research on Terrorism*, Aberdeen: Aberdeen University Press.

N

Narcissistic Terrorism

Narcissistic terrorists are loners with a deep sense of alienation, who harbour a grudge and have sought to wage war on society. Usually they have a political view and so their own acts of violence are terroristic. The best example is Theodore Kaczynski the so-called **Unabomber** (Jane's, 1997).

See also: Millennial Violence; Technological Changes; Unabomber.

Reference

Jane's Terrorism: A Global Survey (1977), London: Jane's Information Group.

Narco-Terrorism

Narco-terrorism is a new and sinister aspect of the international terrorist phenomenon because its effects are insidious, persistent and more difficult to identify than are the sporadic, violent outbursts of the armed assailant.

The manufacture and delivery of narcotics is part of the terrorist portfolio for venous reasons. The most obvious is that drugs are a source of revenue to support the general activities of terrorist organisations. Another reason is that the use of drugs in target countries, such as the **United States**, is part of the terrorists' programme to undermine the integrity of their enemies. This is achieved by weakening the moral fibre of society by encouraging widespread addiction and by nurtur-

ing the socially enervating criminal activities that flourish around the drug trade. There is no lack of evidence of connections between the international narcotics trade and terrorist organisations. For example, the **Palestine Liberation Organisation** has been involved in over a hundred operations in the last decade involving drugs, and linking that organisation through Bulgaria, **Cuba** and **Syria** to drug traffic to the USA. Many of these examples include such organised crime networks as the effective distribution mechanisms, and also involve drugs-for-arms transactions.

Narco-terrorism in the USA has been uncovered during investigations of illegal immigration, organised crime, political corruption and Japan's penetration of the American car market. For some years the Sandinista guerrillas were involved in the international drug trade both before and after achieving power in Nicaragua.

The narco-terrorist, connected to drug traffic and employing the method of random killing of innocent bystanders, is a very special hybrid and the latest in a long line of terrorist groups. The Federal Government of the USA has known for quite some time about the narco-terrorist threat to the integrity of the state, but generally has been unable to control the spread of the problem.

The links between terrorist and insurgent groups and traffickers are most substantial in drug source countries, including Burma, **Colombia**, **Peru**, and Thailand. In Colombia, four major insurgent organisations work in collaboration with cocaine traffickers. In 1982 the Revolutionary Armed Force of Colombia (FARC) reportedly obtained over 3.8 million dollars per month by collecting protection tax. Such taxes are used to buy weapons and supplies which are often shipped into Colombia on return drug flights.

Both the terrorist problem and drug problem are international and domestic issues; but governments and the media in many Western countries, notably the United States, treat the drug issue and terrorist problem on separate agendas. Information gathering and dissemination and policy formulation about narco-terrorism and how to confront it are subject to overlapping and competing jurisdictions, especially on the American continent.

Many terrorist groups have been involved in the production or sale of drugs, for example more spectacularly in recent times, **Al Qaeda** despite repeated US claims to the contrary (Gunaratna, 2002).

Narco-terrorism can be classed as a new form of terrorism, starting in the 1970s. All types of ideologically motivated guerrillas and terrorists have been motivated in the production and smuggling of drugs. The Taliban, who are Sunni and extreme **Shi'ite** groups, especially in **Lebanon** have long believed that the production and trade of drugs is acceptable even though under Islamic law the consuming of drugs is forbidden.

Colombia is one of the key centres for narco-terrorism in the world and a combination of cocaine cartels and left-wing terrorist groups repeatedly tried to subvert Colombian elections and to try and destroy successive governments. Medellin almost became known as the narco-terrorist capital of the world. In 1989–90 in the city the cartels took journalists and businessmen hostage to try and prevent the extradition of cartel members to the USA. One of their other aims was to cause public anxiety in order to undermine the government (Hoffman, 1998).

Drug barons can use their own people to commit terrorist attacks as they have unlimited financial resources to buy equipment. Narco-terrorism is based on the pursuit of money and power that drives the drugs barons. Even when such men are captured, extradited or killed, new or rival ones come along to take their place. The police and military in Latin America are no match for narco-trafficking organisations operating transnationally and backed by private armies, advanced weaponry and intelligence systems.

References

Gunaratna, R. (2002) *Inside Al Qaeda's Global Network of Terror*, London: Hurst and Co.

Hoffman, B. (1998) *Inside Terrorism*, London: Victor Gollancz.

Further Reading

Blakesley, C. L. (1992) *Terrorism, Drugs, International Law and the Protection of Human Liberty: A Comparative Study*, Ardsley-on-Hudson: Transnational Books.

Ehrenfeld, R. (1990) *Narco Terrorism*, New York: Basic Books.

Miller, A. H. and Darmask, N. A. (1996) 'The Dual Myths of Narco-terrorism', *Terrorism and Political Violence*, vol. 8, no. 1 (Spring), pp. 144–131.

Steinitz, M. S. (1987) 'Insurgents, Terrorists and the Drug Trade' in Laqueur, W. (ed.) *The Terrorism Reader*, New York: Meridian, pp. 327–336.

National Liberation Movements *see* Third World Insurgency

Negotiations

Many people argue that if one negotiates with terrorists it gives them the power of legitimacy and perhaps encourages them to commit further atrocities to achieve their ends. Worse still in the eyes of many observers, is that terrorists can take hostages and kidnap people to be used as negotiating tools. Terrorists can easily manipulate the situation and use the **media** if possible to further their aims. They can then be seen to be dictating rather than negotiating. At least negotiation envisages compromise.

Counter-terrorist experts perhaps would argue that one should never negotiate except from great strength and to great advantage. They might support the argument of negotiating to please. Hostages merely put others at risk and cause more to be taken. The more hostages there are, the greater might become the terrorists' bargaining position. One can by negotiations make sovereignty and government policy a hostage. No government can accept dictation of policy, but must not be seen to be inflexible.

With regard to a ransom being paid, one has to note that they are set, if they are negotiated, rather than dictated, by what the donor can afford. Terrorists have often seized hostages to secure the release of their own friends imprisoned for previous terrorism.

In any negotiation, terrorists will sometimes raise the right to a fair trial; which will in some cases be exploited by terrorists. Terrorists have no rights.

If terrorists were given legitimacy would they leave behind terror? Negotiation could be a search for legitimacy in the other side. Exclusive legitimacy belonging to one side or the other causes tensions which will not go away.

See also: Crisis Management; Hostage Negotiation.

References

Hughes, M. (1990) 'Terror and Negotiation', *Terrorism and Political Violence*, vol. 2, no. 1, pp. 72–82.
Roukis, G. S. (1983) 'Negotiating with Terrorists' in Montana, P. J. and Roukis, G. S. (eds) *Managing Terrorism*, Westport, CT: Quorum Books, pp. 109–122.
Trager, O. (ed.) (1988) *Fighting Terrorism: Negotiation or Retaliation*, New York: Facts on File.

Further Reading

Connor, M. (1987) *Terrorism: The Solutions*, London: Paladin.
Robertson, K. G. (1987) 'Intelligence, Terrorism and Civil Liberties', *Conflict Quarterly* (spring), pp. 46–56.
Wilkinson, P. (1986) *Terrorism and the Liberal State*, London: Macmillan.

Neo-Nazi Terrorism

German right-wing terrorism has two roots. One is the National Democratic Party (NPD) which is still the strongest force in German right-wing extre-mism, at least in its numbers. The NPD is experiencing a continuing decline. In the last twenty years it has lost 25,000 members. Today it has only 4,000 members. This process of decay fed some small neo-Nazi groups which are the second root for the now existing German right-wing terrorism. Young members of the NPD went into ranks of these neo-Nazi groups and brought into their organisations more militancy. Neo-Nazi groups which became a hotbed for terrorism are the Aktion-gemeinschaft Nationaler Sozialisten and the Deutsche Aktionsgruppen. Two other organisations of German right-wing extremism which went into terrorism later were the Wehrsportgruppe Hoffmann, and the Volkssozialistische Bewegung Deutschland/Partei der Arbeit (vssD/PdA).

Right-wing terrorists are much more ready to use violence than it was believed in the past. Killings happened for the first time in 1980 – the most spectacular being the killing of 12 visitors at the Munich Oktoberfest, and the suicide of the perpetrator. Another killer committed suicide after murdering two Swiss customs officials. Others have blown up American cars, attacked Jewish cemeteries, Jewish restaurants and daubed paint on synagogues. Many Neo-Nazis have been captured and are currently in jail.

The Neo-Nazis failed to obtain support from potential criminals and disaffected young people outside the political arena. The links between the German Neo-Nazis and Middle Eastern terrorists have collapsed. The worldwide publicity given to their links with the PLO and their training in the Al Fatah camps, has deterred even terrorists like Abu Iyad, responsible for the 1972 Munich massacre. Neo-Nazi organisations in Denmark, Belgium, France and the **USA** have had their communications severed by the success of the German security services. Extreme Right terrorism has lost its motivation and no longer represents any real danger in the near future. It has lost its leaders and ideologists for some time to come, and consequently there is no sign of any significant political comeback, as opposed to straightforward crime.

See also: Anti-Semitic Terrorism in Europe.

Nepal

Over the past decade anti-white insurgents and rebels have been increasingly active in the country. Maoist in origin, and stemming from the development of radical social movements, their targets have been the army and military; but they have also taken heart from domestic rivalries within the Nepalese Royal family which led to the gunning down of members in 2000 in a bloody event in the Royal Palace in Kathmandu. With suspected support from like-minded people over the Himalayas in **China** they have effectively stopped the tourist industry and dealt a blow to an already enfeebled economy.

The Maoist movement wields a *de facto* control over most of Nepal, and the government has been unable to contain the threat. The movement stemmed from the genuine grievances of an impoverished low caste, peasant majority, suffering under the rule of a corrupt, high caste urban elite.

Democracy came to Nepal in 1990 with little tangible result and the insurgency began in 1996 and has claimed over 5,000 lives, especially military and police.

The insurgents, uniquely among guerrilla movements, have no state sponsor and are hostile to the Chinese government as they abandoned Maoism. The rebels get their weapons and cash from a Maoist network in northern **India**. The insurgents resort to extortion on a huge scale. Many Nepalese businessmen pay protection money and peasants face endless threats and demands for cash.

New Left

The late 1960s and early 1970s witnessed the rise and decline of the New Left, which became the leading force on the university campuses. There were many thousands of students, and since they were among the most politically active members of society, their radicalisation was bound to have political consequences.

The New Left was of mixed parentage: there was a genuine idealism, and anti-militarism, revulsion against the inequities of modern industrial society, of poverty, hunger and exploitation in the **Third World**. Politically it was not a very innovative movement – its gurus such as Marcuse, were men of an older generation. The ideas they advocated had been floating around for many years – Gramsci, Lukacs, the unorthodox German Marxists of the 1920s, and Reich. Perhaps the only new admixture of any significance was the concept of **Fanon** of the liberating influence of violence. He avowed that violence not only unified the people but that it was a cleansing force, freeing the native from his inferiority complex and from his despair and inaction.

The New Left lasted for three or four years, after which some of its proponents converted to orthodox (Soviet-style) communism, a few turned to anarchism, others to Maoism, situationism and a variety of small sects. In the **USA** the great majority opted out of politics while retaining a vaguely liberal (American-style) orientation. In Western Europe, on the other hand, the process of depoliticisation did not go so far. When the rapid decline in the fortunes of the New Left set in, a few of its members opted for terrorism. Thus, more or less simultaneously, the United Red Army developed in **Japan** out of Zengakuren; the extreme student organisation, the American group Students for a Democratic Society (SDS) gave birth to the Weathermen; and some of the German students of the far Left founded the Rote Armee Fraktion (Baader-Meinhof) and the Second of June Movement. There were smaller groups in Italy (Brigate Rosse) and in England (Angry Brigade).

Reference

'The New Left', *TVI Journal*, vol. 2, no. 10, pp. 3–8.

New Styles *see* Terror and Terrorism

North Atlantic Treaty Organisation (NATO)

This alliance was formed in April 1949 by the **United States**, Canada and the Western European nations. It was designed during the **Cold War** to protect the Western world against possible

Soviet aggression. All member states are bound to protect any member against attack.

In the 1970s and 1980s, left-wing terrorist organisations with only minor success, tried concerted attacks against Western NATO defence interests in Europe. The French-based Action Directe, Italy's Brigate Rosse, the Belgium Communist Combatant Cells, the Irish Republican Army and Germany's Red Army Faction all were actively involved. With the ending of the Cold War in November 1990, they were unable to adapt to changed global ideologies and faded from the scene – apart from the IRA which continued its struggle in Ireland.

NATO airbases around Europe were used increasingly for counter-terrorist operations. In the late-1980s NATO's Sub-Committee on Terrorism argued that murder, **kidnapping**, arson and other acts often linked with terrorism constituted criminal behaviour (Hoffman, 1998). Nevertheless since that time NATO and the G8 states have been deeply divided in their response to state-sponsors of terrorism. To show their genuine opposition to terrorism, many believe a more concerted response should be adopted (Wilkinson, 2002).

In the era of the New World Order, NATO has seen political instability develop in countries of the former **Soviet Union**, especially in **Chechnya** where **guerrilla warfare** appears endemic. NATO's ability to prevent terrorist crime has been hampered by the enormous cuts in the NATO Allies' defence budgets. Moreover, anti-terrorist and internal security duties absorb considerable manpower and involve diverting trained personnel from their primary NATO and external defence roles. Some states find it hard to co-operate in internal security and law and order, partly due to considerable hostility to the US influences in Europe among their constituent populations (Wilkinson, 2002). As far back as 1986, France and Spain, refused permission for US planes to over fly their territories on their way from England to bomb **Libya**.

References

Hoffman, B. (1998) *Inside Terrorism*, London: Victor Gollancz.

Wilkinson, P. (2002) *Terrorism versus Democracy: The*

Liberal State Response, Portland, OR and London: Frank Cass.

Further Reading

Crozier, B. (1986) 'International Terrorism: How NATO Became Impotent', *The American Legion*, vol. 120, no. 6.

Kellen, K. (1985) 'The New Challenge: Euro-terrorism Against NATO', *TVI Journal*, vol. 5, no. 4, pp. 3–5.

O'Ballance, E. (1985) 'NATO and the Enemy Within', *Journal of the Royal United Services Institute for Defence Studies*, vol. 130, no. 2, pp. 45–49.

Simon, J. D. (1994) *The Terrorist Trap: America's Experience with Terrorism*, Bloomington, IN: Indiana University Press.

North Korea

North Korea is on the US State Department's blacklist of seven states which the **USA** say are officially supporting **terrorism** – the others being **Cuba**, **Iraq**, **Iran**, **Libya**, Sudan and **Syria**. However, from about 1993 there have been signs that the North Koreans have taken a step backwards from direct support for terrorist violence or liberation movements (Cooley, 2002).

North Korea has been described as a Stalinist and a 'hermit' state facing desperate economic and political difficulties and fighting for survival therefore not able to engage in major foreign political adventures.

In the early-1990s the North Koreans realised that investment in international terrorism was not productive, while the production of weapons of mass destruction was far more promising. They eventually realised it was impractical to pursue international terrorism and engage in building long-range missiles and nuclear bombs.

Their worst atrocity was in 1987 when a bomb was planted on a South Korean airliner that exploded in flight killing 115 people. In 1968 the US naval intelligence ship the *Pueblo* was seized after it had strayed into their waters. The crew were tortured and held hostage for a year, and only released after admitting to spying.

North Korea regularly gave sanctuary to

Japanese Red Army members after they had committed atrocities within **Japan**.

What has worried the global community has been North Korea's willingness to aid in the proliferation of nuclear capacity in other countries. The situation is not helped by the fact that few countries have diplomatic engagement with North Korea. In his State of the Union address to Congress in January 2002 President Bush cited North Korea, Iran and Iraq as the 'axis of evil', implying that such countries might become targets for military attack and coercive diplomacy. States such as North Korea know that the USA can only be held at bay by deterrence and weapons of mass destruction are the only means by which they can deter America.

Reference

Cooley, J. K. (2002) *Unholy Wars: Afghanistan, America and International Terrorism*, London: Pluto Press.

Further Reading

Bermudez, J. S. (1990) *Terrorism: The North Korean Connection*, New York: Crane, Russak.

Kim, J. T. (1988) 'North Korean Terrorism: Trends, Characteristics and Deterence', *Terrorism*, vol. 11, no. 4, pp. 309–322.

Northern Ireland *see* UK: Northern Ireland

Nuclear Terrorism

The possibility that terrorists might test fissionable material or nuclear weapons, attack nuclear facilities, use radioactive material to contaminate or create alarming nuclear hoaxes, has drawn increasing attention from government, the news **media** and the public.

The rapid growth of the civilian nuclear industry, increasing traffic in plutonium-enriched uranium and radioactive waste material, the spread of nuclear technology both in the **United States** and other Western nations, have all increased the opportunities for terrorists to engage in some type of nuclear action. To many observers the increased

public concern with the potential terrorist threat to nuclear programmes and the virtual guarantee of widespread publicity may increase the possibilities that terrorists will attempt such actions.

The possibilities for action by nuclear terrorists can encompass the creation of potentially alarming hoaxes, acts of low-level symbolic sabotage, the occupation or seizure of nuclear facilities, acts of serious sabotage aimed at causing widespread casualties and damage, thefts of nuclear material or weapons, armed attacks on nuclear weapons storage sites, the dispersal of radioactive contaminants, the manufacture of homemade nuclear weapons and the detonation or threatened detonation of such devices.

Potential perpetrators are diverse, ranging from common criminals, disgruntled guerrillas, employees, ex-guerrillas and political extremists among whom there may be anarchists, leftists, racists, rightists, separatists, or simply authentic lunatics. Motives may be personal or collective. Objectives may include, but are not limited to, seeking publicity, sabotage, extortion, causing widespread damage and casualties or possibly discrediting the nuclear industry by demonstrating that current security measures are inadequate. To date a few nuclear hoaxes and a handful of incidents involving contamination with radioactive material or sabotage of nuclear facilities represent the range of practical experience in nuclear terrorism.

The primary attraction for terrorists in 'going nuclear' is not necessarily the fact that nuclear weapons would enable terrorists to cause mass casualties, but rather the fact that almost any terrorist action associated with the words 'atomic' or 'nuclear' automatically generates fear in the mind of the public. Terror is violence for effect and is theatre; nuclear power, whether in the form of peaceful energy or weapons, is the most potent and to many people the most sinister force known to mankind.

Terrorists may try to take advantage of the fear that the word 'nuclear' generates without taking risks or making the investment necessary to steal plutonium and build a working atom bomb. A well publicised hoax could be as alarming as actual possession of a real weapon, provided people have no way of knowing that it is a hoax. A well publicised terrorist attack on a civilian nuclear facility, even if the terrorists failed in their intended mission, could be almost as alarming to the world as a terrorist success. Thus anything nuclear could, in the terrorists' plan, be little more than a dramatic backdrop or prop that guarantees them worldwide attention. The public may be comforted to know that nuclear terrorism is the least likely threat.

Among the possible employers of nuclear terrorism are anti-nuclear extremists whose primary objective would be to halt all nuclear programmes. The spread of nuclear technology and growth in numbers of nuclear facilities throughout the world will increase the opportunities for some type of nuclear action by terrorists. Terrorists do not have to build a nuclear bomb and indeed may not be interested in or capable of doing so. Within their resources and technical proficiency, they may carry out actions on nuclear targets that will give them almost as much publicity and leverage at less risk to themselves and with less risk of alienation or retaliation. Any incidents involving nuclear material or facilities are certain to receive extensive media coverage.

At some time in the future, the number of low-level nuclear incidents might then decline, possibly because alarm generated by these incidents conceivably might suffice to bring about the abandonment of nuclear power as a safe source of energy. The nuclear terrorism of the future can be seen, from a political and psychological viewpoint in the same light, as dynamite terrorism in the last century. Super-explosives were useful for attracting attention to demands whilst simultaneously publicising the identity and ideals of the perpetrators. They were deployed to avenge unjust acts, and were justified as an instrument for self-defence whereby the weak could prevent further exploitation and oppression by the state.

Nuclear power may appeal to terrorists who crave attention for their demands, or who wish to wreak vengeful punishment against specific targets. It is hard to imagine nuclear devices being advocated for defence of the interests of the workers.

Nuclear terror constitutes the greatest threat to democracy in the future because, more than any other extant form of struggle, it represents a serious attempt to establish a political system by which a tiny minority can rule a vast majority. The principal object in obtaining a nuclear weapon would be to blackmail the leaders of a society into meeting demands and to threaten the lives and effectiveness of the principal authorities concerned in dealing with terrorist activity, for example, the government and the police.

There have been very few actions directed against nuclear facilities and no nuclear installations have been attacked, seized or sabotaged in a way that caused the release of radioactivity. No nuclear weapons have been stolen. No special nuclear materials have been diverted or taken by force from installations or while in transit; and no radioactive matter has been maliciously dispersed so that public safety was endangered.

Nuclear terror seems more attractive as a threat than as an action. Once in possession of a nuclear device it seems terrorists could demand anything. The idea of nuclear blackmail has some weaknesses notably the ability to turn the capacity for destruction into commensurate political gains.

Even with a nuclear device, terrorists could not make impossible demands. They probably could not permanently alter national policy or compel other changes in national behaviour; to do so would require at least the maintenance of the threat and it is unclear how long this could be done without discovery or betrayal.

The probability of nuclear terrorism remains in the final analysis a matter of speculation; and many people believe that when the next nuclear bomb is used, it will be by terrorists and not by a national government. Terrorists emulate states. If a nuclear device becomes a widely perceived symbol of state power, terrorists may be more inclined to go nuclear or at least to try to attack or seize nuclear reactors. Terrorists could also try to obtain nuclear material for the clandestine fabrication of a nuclear explosive or to spread radioactivity, or they could try to steal a nuclear weapon which they could threaten to detonate if demands were not met. Alternatively they could fabricate alarming nuclear hoaxes intended to cause public panic.

In recent years the possibility of nuclear terrorism has become both a source of dread and an ally for the supporters of nuclear disarmament and the opponents of nuclear energy. To possess nuclear weapons illegally would be to possess a potential for great wealth, through extortion, ransom or sale to a competitive market. Recourse by terrorists to nuclear terrorism would depend on their access to nuclear weapons, inclinations to nuclear violence, insensitivity to conventional weapons and a degree of co-operation between terrorist groups.

The long-term results of nuclear terrorism might well be a strengthening of opposition to the use of nuclear energy and a serious loss of confidence in the government. The threat exists due to the growth of the nuclear popover industry and its vulnerability to theft or attack by small groups. Moreover, it could become a reality because of the increasing international flow of information about high technology. From current international relations theory, it is impossible to predict the likely threat in the future from nuclear terrorism.

The possible proliferation of nuclear terrorism has been linked to the long lasting legacy of the Cold War and the stockpiles in the former Soviet Union.

No one knows the exact quantities of nuclear materials produced because security at the facilities was deficient. Russian criminal organisations can have an interest in such materials and in other nuclear facilities and can buy or steal nuclear materials. Much corruption exists in the country and border controls are weak.

Nuclear terrorism is likely to increase due to: the rise in sophistication of nuclear terrorism; state support for terrorist groups; the storing and developing of nuclear weapons and black and grey markets in nuclear equipment and materials.

Only international policy to stem the proliferation of such weapons across the board will bring success in stopping terrorism (Taylor and Horgan, 2000).

See also: Dynamite Terrorism; Technology; Terror and Terrorism; Threats.

References

Beres, L. R. (1990) 'Responding to the Threat of Nuclear Terrorism' in Kegley, C. W. (ed.) *International Terrorism: Characteristics, Causes, Controls*, New York: St Martin's Press, pp. 228–240.

Taylor, M. and Horgan, J. (eds) (2000) *The Future of Terrorism*, London: Frank Cass.

Further Reading

Buck, K. A. (1989) 'Super-terrorism – Biological, Chemical and Nuclear', *Terrorism*, vol. 12, no. 6, pp. 433–34.

Lee, R. W. (1998) *Smuggling Armageddon: The Nuclear Black Market in the Former Soviet Union and Europe*, New York: St Martin's Press.

Sterling, Claire (1987) 'Responses to Terrorist Grievances: Another Perspective' in Leventhal, P. and Alexander, Y. (eds) *Preventing Nuclear Terrorism*, Lexington, MA: Lexington Books, pp. 78–88.

Oil and Gas Industry Security

The industry is a tempting target for the terrorist seeking **media** publicity or financial gain. In oil/gas exploration where the likelihood of success is felt to be sufficiently high then the presence of terrorists or guerrilla groups will not necessarily deter the company from conducting the exploration. In **Algeria** the Armed Islamic group has been targeting foreigners who have been employed by the oil and gas industry.

If any of the industries employees are kidnapped terrorists have quickly realised that the foreign company sees itself as morally responsible for its local work force and will pay for their release (Jane's Information, 1997). If the ransoms are small the government will make no attempt to apprehend the kidnappers and the oil company in order to retain its good relationship with the government will not press the issue (Jane's Information, 1997).

Terrorists have cut supply lines to remote drilling rigs for example in **Colombia**, and this has delayed production especially if pipe lines are fractured by explosives. Liquefied natural gas plants have been attacked in **Pakistan** and Indonesia. In 1994 the IRA failed in their attempt to destroy a British Gas complex in Warrington, Cheshire and in Louisiana, **USA**, in 1992 a local militant group ruptured a gas pipe line. In 1995, in Germany, environmental militants attacked petrol stations belonging to Shell as part of the 'Brent Spar' protest.

Terrorists are aware that delays while drilling cost money and closing a rig by threat of force places them in a position to extract payments from the company.

The world is still so dependent on oil that the industry will press on regardless with production whatever the risks within manageable proportions.

In April 2003 one of the worst fears of the industry was realised when a hundred oil workers were held hostage aboard offshore installations off the coast of Nigeria by striking Nigerian workers complaining about redundancies and unfair dismissal of Nigerian staff. The hostages included over twenty Americans and over thirty British personnel.

References

Jane's Terrorism: A Global Survey (1997), London: Jane's Information Group.

Stephens, M. M. (1979) 'The Oil and Gas Industries: A Political Target of Terrorists' in Kupperman, R. H. and Trent, D. M. (eds) *Terrorism, Threat, Reality and Response*, Stanford, CA: Hoover Institution Press, 1979.

Further Reading

Breemer, J. S. (1983) 'Offshore Energy Terrorism: Perspectives on a Problem', *Terrorism*, vol. 6, no. 3, pp. 455–468.

Jenkins, B. M. (1988) 'Potential Threats to Offshore Platforms', *TVI Report*, vol. 8, no. 2, pp. 1–10.

Oklahoma Bombing 1995

In April 1995 the Alfred P. Murrah Federal Building in Oklahoma City was bombed by home-grown American extremists Timothy McVeigh (later executed) and Terry Nichols using a 4,800 lb bomb made of ammonium nitrate fertiliser and fuel oil.

At that time it was the worst terrorist attack ever on American soil, causing damage to 300 buildings and the total destruction of thirty. Among 168 dead were 19 children and eight federal agents. The event made a deep psychological impact on the nation. McVeigh had parked a truck loaded with explosives in front of the building and detonated the bomb: Nichols helped McVeigh make the bomb and place it in the truck. They had both served in the army and had attended meetings of the Michigan Militia, one of several anti-government right-wing militia groups in the country. They were upset by the federal raid on the Branch Davidian sect at Waco, Texas in 1993 – and Oklahoma occurred on the second anniversary of that raid.

Much fear and anger was evoked by the bombing and it was seen by many as an act of deliberately exaggerated violence. The picture of the mangled bodies of an infant, carried by a rescue worker portrayed the righteous anger of many over what appeared to be a hideous and senseless act. It magnified the horror far beyond the numbers immediately affected by the blast. The terrorist's message was sent by the **media**.

In the militia's view this building housed the regional offices of the Federal Bureau of Alcohol, Tobacco and Firearms, from which agents were sent to Waco to enforce firearm laws in the confrontation that led to the stand-off at Branch Davidian headquarters.

The attack raised the possibility of a sustained campaign of violence on American soil with each incident outweighing the other in intensity. Oklahoma demonstrated what a massive explosion could do in a densely populated area using easily obtained materials. The bombing was an example of 'new terrorism' which was becoming effective in the 1990s (Jurgensmeyer, 2000).

See also: Cults.

Reference

Jurgensmeyer, M. (2000) *Terror in the Mind of God:* *Global Rise of Religious Violence*, Berkeley and London: University of California Press.

Further Reading

Hamm, M. S. (1997) *Apocalypse in Oklahoma: Waco and Ruby Ridge Revenged*, Boston, MA: Northeastern University Press.

Jones, S. and Israel, P. (1998) *Others Unknown: The Oklahoma City Bombing Conspiracy*, New York: Public Affairs.

Serrano, R. A. (1998) *One of Ours: Timothy McVeigh and the Oklahoma City Bombing*, New York: Norton.

Simon, J. D. (1994) *The Terrorist Trap: America's Experience with Terrorism*, Bloomington, IN: Indiana University Press.

Olympic Games Attacks

On 5 September 1972, eight members of **Black September** led by Abu Iyad broke into the Israeli quarters at the Olympic Games village in Munich, killing two Israeli athletes and taking nine others hostage. They demanded the release of 236 guerrillas in Israeli jails including Kozo Okamoto (captured during the Lod Airport Massacre), the release of Andreas Baader and Ulrike Meinhof of the Red Army Faction, and safe passage to a foreign country. After a shoot-out with police, the hostages were killed as were five of the terrorists and a German policeman. The three surviving terrorists, two of whom were wounded, were released after the hijacking of a Lufthansa jet in October 1972.

The police were unsuccessful in plans to trick the terrorists, which included a suggestion to poison food sent to them. The terrorists further demanded to be flown to Cairo with their hostages and called for a swap of hostages for the prisoners in **Israel** when the plane touched down. The German Chancellor was urged by Israel not to meet the demands of the terrorists, although the Israelis were willing to give the group safe passage if their athletes were released.

The terrorists then agreed to leave the building with their hostages and were taken by helicopter to a nearby military airport to board a Lufthansa jet; police had initially been on board the jet disguised as the plane's crew, but had been ordered off at the last minute. Three terrorists were then killed, after killing a policeman during the exchange of shots, and a further two terrorists threw a grenade into the helicopter before they were shot. The grenade exploded, killing all the hostages. Some terrorists were captured.

In the aftermath, the Games, which had been allowed to continue during the negotiations, were postponed for one day while a remembrance service was held for the Israeli athletes. The dead terrorists were flown to **Libya** and a heroes' funeral. Three Israeli government officials were fired as a result of poor security arrangements; and Germany later toughened immigration and registration restrictions on Palestinian students and workers. The **Palestine Liberation Organisation** stated that it was not responsible for the attack and that their own objective was only to pressure Israel to release detained guerrillas from Israeli jails.

In February 1973 a Palestinian, Abu Daoud, who later figured prominently in a 1977 extradition squabble between Israel, West Germany and France, was arrested by Jordanian police and questioned. Despite Daoud's protestations of innocence, many observers believed Daoud was a major organiser of the attack – and certainly his passport contained a valid German visa. No German national or Arab resident in Germany took part in the operation. The terrorists themselves were based in Beirut, Damascus, Tripoli and Tunis, received tacit support from these governments, and made use of terrorist training facilities.

In late October, Black September hijacked a Lufthansa flight flying from Damascus to Frankfurt and successfully obtained the release of the three remaining terrorists. The Israelis retaliated by raiding refugee camps in **Lebanon** in February 1973, killing 31 people. They later shot down a Libyan airliner that had over flown Israeli air space, killing all 107 on board. Israeli officials blamed **Egypt**, **Syria** and Lebanon for being behind the Olympic attack, and the Egyptians in particular were the prime party blamed. Israel believed Egypt had the power and influence to stop these groups instead of actively encouraging them.

At the 1996 Summer Olympics in the USA a pipe-bomb exploded at the Centennial Olympic Park in Atlanta on 27 July killing one person and injuring 112. A guard who warned of the explosion by reporting a suspicious package sued various **media** organisations who claimed he was a suspect. The bomb was eventually linked to an anti-abortion terrorist, Eric Robert Rudolph, who is still at large (Bolz *et al.*, 2002).

Olympic Games are tempting targets for any extremist group, especially due to the worldwide media interest, and the fact that up to five billion people can be watching video and television coverage of the events.

See also: Black June and Black September.

Reference

Bolz, F., Dudonis, K. J. and Schulz, D. P. (2002) *Counter-terrorism Handbook* (2nd edn), Boca Raton, FL: CRC Press.

OPEC Siege, Vienna 1975

In December 1975, six members of the Arm of the Arab Revolution, believed to be a cover term for the PFLP, attacked a ministerial meeting of the Organisation of Petroleum Exporting Countries (OPEC) in Vienna, seizing 70 hostages, including 11 oil ministers. In the attack and subsequent shoot-out with police, three people were killed and eight injured, including one of the terrorists. The group was led by the notorious Venezuelan terrorist Ilyich Ramirez Sanchez (known as **Carlos**)

In an initial attack, the group members ran up the stairs toward the meeting hall where the OPEC conference was in session – killing an Austrian security guard, a security officer with the Iraqi delegation and a Libyan economist.

The terrorists rounded up their hostages and barricaded themselves in the conference roof, where they discovered that they held 11 ministers – from **Algeria**, Ecuador, Gabon, Indonesia, **Iran**, **Iraq**, Kuwait, **Libya**, Nigeria, **Saudi Arabia** and Venezuela. At the start of the siege the hostages were separated into four groups. Libyans, Algerians, Iraqis, Kuwaitis and Palestinian OPEC employees were considered friends. Neutrals included citizens of Gabon, Nigeria, Indonesia,

Venezuela and Ecuador. Austrians were placed by themselves and the rest were considered to be enemies. The terrorists demanded the broadcasting of their political manifesto by Austrian radio and television, and a bus to take them to the airport.

Despite surrounding the building with troops, the Austrian government soon gave in to the terrorists' demands for a flight out of the country. The plane flew to Tripoli, where hostages from Saudi Arabia, Iran, the United Arab Emirates, Qatar, Algeria and Libya were released.

An especially large ransom was demanded from Saudi Arabia and Iran for the release of their oil ministers. These countries had been two of the most important participants in the OPEC meeting, and were in disagreement with the Rejection Front of the Palestinian movement. The ransom sum was estimated at five million dollars, of which Carlos, Habash and Haddad recouped two million dollars. The remaining hostages were finally released in Algiers.

See also: Carlos.

Organised Crime

Organised crime can occur at three levels: the local organised criminal group, the nationwide criminal organisation and criminal associations as loose confederations of internationally operating groups.

The economic effects of organised crime proceeds can create a climate of violence which can discourage foreign investment and lead to domestic capital going overseas.

A characteristic of terrorism is that the psychological effect of terrorist violence is out of proportion to the actual amount of violence. There is an unprovoked and unpredictable application of violence against humans. Such acts are criminal, but also political in that they undermine the stability of a political regime and can affect the distribution of power in society.

The structure of terrorist crimes includes the perpetrator (with or without other actors behind him), a direct victim and the target for the terrorist message or demand. The perpetrators include the ideologues and organisers who work out the strategy and make plans, the operational staff

who undertake the reconnaissance, determine targets, method and weapon to be used, and finally there are the people who execute the terrorist act, but know little about the organisation.

Terrorist violence is targeted at public opinion to win over to the side of the terrorists' grievance or cause the authorities from whom concessions or the release of a 'political' prisoner is requested, and those who identify with the victim as they belong to the same group and fear to be the next victim.

The similarities between terrorism and organised crime are that both sets of members act purposefully. Both use intimidation and produce victims. Similar tactics include **kidnapping** and extortion. They both operate secretly and both are criminalised by the ruling regime, and are opposed to the state. Once in the group it is difficult to leave. Both extort and steal money to finance their dubious and 'shady' activities.

Differences, nevertheless, can be perceived between the organisations. Terrorist groups, especially those on the political left, usually are ideologically highly motivated while organised crime groups are generally not.

In court terrorists often admit to their activities but do not see them as crimes, while organised crime groups down play their involvement. Terrorist groups strive for an increased political following, while criminal groups do not bother. The line between victims and motive is far closer with organised crime than it is with terrorist groups. Terrorists have a wider audience. Internecine rivalry is more common in criminal groups than with terrorists.

Organised crime feeds political conflict including conflicts waged by terrorist tactics. Transnational crimes pose problems in relation to countermeasures. Reaction time and bureaucracy can be slow when many frontiers are involved. Differing legal systems and traditions can be a minefield and the issue of sovereignty is guarded jealously by some states.

See also: Crime; Mafia.

References

Dishman, C. (2001) 'Terrorism, Crime and Transformation', *Studies in Conflict and Terrorism*, vol. 24, no. 3, pp. 43–58.

Findlay, M. (1986) 'Organised Crime as Terrorism', *Australian Quarterly*, vol. 58, no. 3 (spring), pp. 286–396.

Schmid, A. P. (1996) 'The Links between Transnational Organised Crime and Terrorist Crimes', *Transnational Organised Crime*, vol. 2, no. 4 (winter), pp. 40–82.

Sterling, C. (1990) *The Mafia*, London: Hamish Hamilton.

Further Reading

Georges-Abeyie, D. E. (1980) 'Political Crime and Terrorism: Toward an Understanding' in Newman, G. R. (ed.) (1980) *Crime and Deviance*, Beverley Hills, CA: Sage, pp. 313–332.

Patrick, J., Ryan, I. and George, E. (1997) *Understanding Organised Crime in a Global Perspective: A Reader*, London: Sage.

Raine, L. P. and Cilluffo, F. J. (eds) (1994) *Global Organised Crime: The New Empire of Evil*, Washington DC: Center for Strategic and International Studies.

Osama Bin Laden

b. 1957

Osama Bin Laden was born in **Saudi Arabia** in 1957 to a father who was Yemeni and a mother who was Syrian. His father amassed a fortune and became a billionaire. Osama was raised as a strict Islamist in Saudi Arabia and studied at Abdul Ariz University in Jeddah in Saudi Arabia where he gained a degree in Civil Engineering and was introduced to Islamic politics.

He is seen as a hero to radical Muslim youth throughout the Middle East and Africa. He has a simple philosophy – it does not worry him what the United States thinks nor does, what concerns him is to please Allah at all times.

At the time of the Soviet occupation of **Afghanistan** in the early-1980s he travelled widely in Afghanistan and **Pakistan** raising fire armed support for the Mujaheddin. From 1986 Bin Laden constructed his own camps and trained his own fighters and participated in the **civil war** in Afghanistan.

Increasing needs for documentation of members of his organisation led to the creation of **Al Qaeda** (the 'base'). After the Iraqi invasion of Kuwait, Bin Laden was horrified at the increasing pro-Western stance of the Saudi government and he set about creating an anti-Saudi Arabian resistance movement. He was soon forced to leave the country for Pakistan and then went back to Afghanistan and after threats to his life travelled to Sudan in 1991. He was now in a very Islamist environment and was able to set up 'front' companies in Sudan masquerading as engineering companies but in effect raising money for his Al Qaeda group. He became involved in several terrorist operations in Yemen, Saudi Arabia and **Egypt** as well as the 1997 bombing of the **World Trade Center** in New York, **USA**. Talks were held with some elements in the Iranian government and members of **Hizbullah**. He put huge amounts of money into the Sudanese economy through his own business dealings and helped to turn Sudan into a pan-Islamic state. He also worked closely with exiled Egyptian Islamists in Sudan.

Bin Laden and the Sudanese government were concerned about the situation in Somalia which descended into chaos in 1991 after the overthrow of a relatively stable military leader. He then flew 3,000 Arab fighters from Yemen to support militia groups in Somalia and also bought land for training groups in Somalia.

Bin Laden fell foul of the new Sudanese government and was expelled from the country in 1996. However, he did revisit for business reasons.

The Saudi's tried to kill him, his Saudi citizenship was withdrawn and members of his family denounced him. Sudan was put under pressure to make Bin Laden leave and he then relocated to Afghanistan in 1997. He continued his extreme rhetoric of hatred towards the West and the USA in particular. An umbrella framework – the International Islamic Front for **Jihad** Against Jews and Crusaders – which Bin Laden set up in 1998 co-ordinates many groups across the world. More attempts were made on his life; the **UN** imposed sanctions on Afghanistan in December 2000 to try to force them to hand over Bin Laden but without success. Nevertheless, over 150 Al Qaeda members have been arrested in over thirty countries since 1998. Then came the *annus horribilis* of 2001 imposed by Al Qaeda on the world community, with the destruction of the twin towers of the **World Trade Center** on **September 11**. The US government produced compelling evidence of Al Qaeda's involvement in this 'day of infamy' and this led President Bush to announce before US Congress on 20 September 2001 a 'global war against terrorism'. Because Afghanistan refused to immediately hand over Bin Laden and other Al Qaeda members to the Americans, an Allied force occupied the country in 2001–2 and the Taliban regime soon fled. In September 2003, a message was broadcast on Al Jazeera TV by Osama Bin Laden. It is believed he is now in Pakistan near the Afghan border.

Many of Bin Laden's foot soldiers are in the affluent cities of Western Europe, and Al Qaeda has never been infiltrated by Western networks: they will always vow to kill Americans and their Allies. The more people Al Qaeda kill, the better their members feel in Paradise – their religious propaganda is very strong. Many members have lived Westernised lives but when they attend universities or radical Islamist mosques they become aware of the prejudice towards North Africans and Arabs. At least two London mosques were hotbeds of extreme opinion and had links with Osama Bin Laden. A number of the operatives had been trained in Afghanistan to blow up transport facilities, and worked with false identities and travelled on false papers.

The Russians who monitored Al Qaeda very closely warned the West of a possible aerial attack on the G8 summit meeting in Genoa, Italy in June 2001. As a result of the threat Genoa became almost a fortress with anti-globalisation protestors held at bay, and the political leaders met on a boat. Anti-aircraft guns were brought in to ring fence the summit venue. A threat was made to launch a suicide truck bomb against the US embassy in Paris in 2001; the Belgians arrested the suicide bomber and explosives were found in the Arab quarter of Brussels.

In London radical voices in one or two of the mosques talk about a **jihad** against the enemy.

Three years earlier it was believed by intelligence sources in America that Bin Laden wanted to create a Hiroshima-style catastrophe using uranium and links with suppliers in Sudan and Afghanistan. It is interesting to note that on September 11 the fourth plane in the attack was supposedly heading for a nuclear power station as it would be able to penetrate reinforced concrete. However, it crashed in a field in Pennsylvania due to the heroic efforts of the passengers who tried to overpower the crew. All nuclear power stations at least in the West, were checked on the orders of the International Atomic Energy Agency to prevent radioactivity in the event of such an attack.

Bin Laden wishes to see civil liberties, freedom of speech and democracy come under threat in these doctrines.

See also: Al Jazeera; Al Jihad; Al Qaeda; September 11.

References

Alexander, Y. and Swetnam, M. S. (2001) *Osama Bin Laden's Al Qaeda: Profile of a Terrorist Network*, Ardsley, NY: Transnational Publishers.
'The Hunt for Al Qaeda One Year on', *Guardian*, 4 September 2002.
Lesch, A. M. (2002) 'Osama Bin Laden's Business in Sudan', *Current History*, vol. 101, no. 655 (May), pp. 203–209.
O'Ballance, E. (1999) *Osama Bin Laden and his Al Qaeda Organisation*, Intersec (February).

Further Reading

Bergen, P. L. (2001) *Holy War Inc: Inside the Secret World of Osama Bin Laden*, New York: Free Press.
Bodansky, Y. (1999) *Bin Laden: The Man Who Declared War on America*, Rocklin, CA: Forum.
Jacquard, R. (2002) *In the Name of Osama Bin Laden*, Durham, NC: Duke University Press.
Ranstorp, M. (1998) 'Interpreting the Broader Context and Meaning of Bin Laden's Fatwa', *Studies in Conflict and Terrorism*, vol. 21, pp. 321–330.
Voll, J. O. (2001) 'Bin Laden And the New Age of Global Terrorism', *Middle East Policy*, vol. VIII, no. 4 (December), pp. 1–4.

P

Pakistan

The Islamic Republic of Pakistan is ruled by the Pakistan People's Party. Since independence in 1947 it has suffered numerous political crises: with civilian governments replacing military and vice versa and martial law having to be imposed on certain occasions.

In 1971 after a **civil war**, East Pakistan broke away from West Pakistan and formed Bangladesh. Zulfiqar Ali Bhutto was a popular civilian ruler in the 1970s but he was ousted by General Zia-ul Haq, arrested and sentenced to death on a charge of murdering an opposition political leader. Islamicisation was accelerated in all spheres of political and social life and many political opponents were harassed and detained. Zia himself was killed in a mysterious air crash in 1988 and Bhutto's daughter Benazir became the head of state for two periods in the late-1980s and 1990s. **Kashmir** remained a problem in relation to India; and Pakistan was opposed to the Soviet intervention in **Afghanistan** in December 1979. It supported the Mujaheddin, Afghan resistance groups based in Pakistan, and allowed the **USA** to use Pakistan territory to supply arms to the rebel groups. In the first **Gulf War**, in spite of the pro-**Iraq** tendencies of the population, troops were sent to **Saudi Arabia** to offer limited support.

Islamicisation continued in the 1980s and 1990s coupled in recent years with evidence of attacks on the minority Christian population by religious extremists. The country has been periodically shaken by inter-ethnic violence in particular between the Sindhi's and the Muhajirs (former Indian refugees).

Pakistan began to develop its nuclear weapon construction project to the alarm of many Western countries, and this came to a head in 1998 when both Pakistan and **India** tested nuclear devices within weeks of each other. Political and ethnic violence in the mid-1990s tainted Bhutto's efforts to bring democracy and equal rights to the country.

Islamic fundamentalist parties have grown in influence. The Islamic Democratic Revolution Party hope that their threat of an Islamic revolution in Pakistan on the pattern of the Iranian revolution will force the government to effect peaceful constitutional changes. Many of its leaders have been detained under house arrest. The Jamiat-i-Jalaba is a rigidly orthodox right-wing Islamic fundamentalist organisation strongly opposed to the emancipation of women and to liberal and Western influences in education. A similar party, the Jamiat-i-Ulema-i-Islam, is a fundamentalist party which advocates a constitution in accordance with Islamic teachings.

Separatist and minority movements are common. In Baluchistan, a tribal area in south-west Pakistan, there has been an intermittent guerrilla war over the last two decades – with as many as 25,000 guerrillas under arms. Even the ending of the Sadari system, i.e. the rule of tribal chiefs with private armies and the power to administer justice and raise taxes, has not curbed the hostility felt by Baluchis to the strong controls imposed by the Pakistan government. Both the Baluchistan Liberation Front and the Baluchi Students' Organisation stand for the creation of an independent state of Baluchistan.

There is also a claim for an independent Pathanistan – a claim for separate nationhood which was first made in 1946 by political leaders of what was then the Indian North-West Frontier province, who strongly objected to a British proposal to group the province with the Punjab. Pathans number over three million and have their own distinctive culture, language, legal code, traditions and calendar, and distinctive natural skills and ambitions. For many years the Afghan and Pakistani governments have disputed the control of Pathanistan. The issue of statehood appears no nearer solution.

Since the **September 11** attacks, Pakistan has been fearful of **Al Qaeda** operatives on their soil and of Islamic radicals acting in violent response to the American led operation in neighbouring Afghanistan. Growing tension with India exists since both countries test fired nuclear devices in May 1999 and there is the ongoing war over the disputed territory of Kashmir.

Two Islamic 'terrorist' groups currently exist: Harakat ul-Mujahedin. It is a **Sunni** group originally established to fight in Afghanistan against the Soviet forces. It is now linked to Al Qaeda and seeks Kashmir's accession to Pakistan. The group was suspected of several bombings in 2002 including one that killed 11 French engineers in May. It has many armed followers from Bosnia and **Chechnya** to **Egypt** and the **Philippines**. It is a distinct threat to Westerners in Pakistan.

Lashkar e Toiba or The Army of the Pure wants an end to India's sovereignty over Kashmir. It also wants the restoration of Islamic rule in India. It was accused of the bombing of the Indian Parliament building and accepted responsibility for a number of armed attacks in Indian Kashmir, perhaps with the backing of Pakistani intelligence. The group is banned in Pakistan (its leader may be in custody) but is still operational.

See also: India; Kashmir.

Reference

Sadullah, A. M. (1986) *Terrorism: A Political Weapon. Pakistan Horizon*, vol. 39, no. 4, pp. 91–97.

Palestine Liberation Organisation (PLO)

The PLO is a 'government-in-exile', dedicated to the aim of establishing an independent Palestinian state in territory now under Israeli control. Formed in 1964 after a sixteen-year period in which resistance to **Israel** had been fragmented and largely ineffective, the PLO was designed to co-ordinate and command the nationalist movement.

Politically the organisation has achieved much – since 1964 over a hundred states have recognised the PLO as the official voice of the Palestine people, and since 1974 it has enjoyed observer status at the **United Nations** – but in military terms the PLO has failed to have a decisive impact.

There has been a lack of consensus about the most effective use of military force. The first chairman of the PLO, Ahmed Shugairy, favoured the creation of an 'army-in-exile', organised along conventional lines and allied to the armies of the other Arab states intent on the physical destruction of Israel. As the 1948 war had already shown, this was a questionable approach, implying a dependence upon ineffective non-Palestinian forces and an acceptance of PLO subordination in military terms. As early as 1965, Yasser Arafat's Al-Fatah group mounted selective 'hit and run' raids into Israel, indicating the potential for guerrilla warfare, and after the crushing failure of the conventional war approach in June 1967 (the Six Day War) this became the favoured strategy. Yasser **Arafat** was elected chairman of the PLO in February 1969, but he could not unite the movement behind a single approach. Already Georges Habash had declared his preference for terrorism, founding the Popular Front for the Liberation of Palestine (PFLP) in 1968, and this triggered the creation of a number of splinter groups, each one progressively more extreme.

But even if coherence had been achieved, success would probably have remained elusive, for despite the existence of a large, predominantly pro-PLO refugee population, within which guerrillas could be raised, trained and supported, the Palestinians have lacked the benefits of unassailable 'safe bases'. In the early 1960s this may not have been an acute problem since refugee camps in the Gaza Strip, the

West Bank and the Golan Heights forced the PLO to withdraw deeper into **Egypt**, Jordan and **Syria**. This lessened the impact of the guerrillas as they had to travel so much further through hostile terrain to reach their targets in Israel (a factor which contributed to the growing preference for international terrorism), but more importantly it created intolerable strains between the Palestinians and their host nations. As 'front line' Arab states suffered the effects of Israeli retaliatory raids in response to guerrilla attacks and faced the emergence of PLO controlled enclaves inside their own territory, the Palestinians lost significant support. In 1970 King Hussein of Jordan forcibly ousted the PLO from its bases east of the Jordan river, while both Egypt and Syria imposed close controls upon the Palestinians within their boundaries. A PLO move to bases in South Lebanon enabled the guerrillas to regain a degree of effectiveness, but the subsequent **civil war** there (1975–76), followed by an Israeli invasion in 1982 and its continuing repercussions weakened them still further.

The result was an undermining of PLO independence, particularly in the aftermath of Arafat's enforced withdrawal from Beirut in 1982, the humiliation of defeat, coupled with the effects of both Israeli and international counters to guerrilla and terrorist activity, drove a deep wedge into the Palestinian movement. A virtual civil war between Arafat's supporters and a Syrian-controlled faction led by Abu Musa in northern **Lebanon** in late 1983 reinforced this division, leaving the PLO militarily a spent force. Arafat survived, exploiting the political strengths of the PLO, but the Syrians assumed the power to dictate Palestinian strategy destroying the military initiative of the PLO and subordinating its aspirations to those of a wider Arab world.

As a result of initiatives towards peace proposed by President Reagan and the Arab League in 1982–83, serious differences were generated within the PLO itself. Syria claimed that five PLO groups specifically rejected the proposal for a Palestinian-Jordanian federation on the grounds that it ran counter to the PLO's commitment to a fully independent Palestinian state. The five PLO factions were the Popular Front for the Liberation of Palestine (PFLP) led by Dr Georges Habash; the Popular Front for the Liberation of Palestine –

General Command (PFLP-GC) led by Ahmed **Jabril**; the Democratic Front for the Liberation of Palestine (DFLP), formerly known as the Popular Democratic Front for the Liberation of Palestine, led by Nayef Hawatmeh; the Popular Struggle Front (PSF) led by Bahjat Abu Gharbuyya and Dr Samir Ghosheh; and the Palestine Liberation Front (PLF) led by Abul Abbas. However, the PFLP, the DFLP and the PLF all denied Syria's claim and reaffirmed their commitment to the unity of the Palestinian cause. Moreover the chairman of the Palestine National Council (the Palestinian parliament-in-exile), Mr Khaled Fahoun, said that although differences existed within the PLO on the federation proposal, these did not amount to a split and in no way represented a challenge to Mr Arafat's leadership.

Following the December 1983 evacuation from Tripoli (Lebanon) by Al-Fatah forces loyal to Mr Yasser Arafat, the leader of Al-Fatah and chairman of the PLO, the existing split within the PLO was widened when Arafat met President Mubarak of Egypt (this constituted the first official high-level contact between the PLO and the Egyptian regime since the conclusion of Egypt's peace treaty with Israel in March 1979).

An agreement between Al-Fatah and the Democratic Alliance (a grouping of four smaller PLO factions which had expressed varying degrees of sympathy for the anti-Arafat rebels) was concluded in June 1984 after a series of meetings in Aden and Algiers. This agreement was denounced by the National Alliance (composed of rebel Fatah members and three other PLO factions based in Damascus).

The four organisations grouped together by the mid-1980s, and known as the Democratic Alliance, were the Popular Front for the Liberation of Palestine (PFLP), the Democratic Front for the Liberation of Palestine (DFLP), the Palestine Liberation Front (PLF), and also the Palestine Communist Party. Those grouped within the National Alliance were the Popular Front for the Liberation of Palestine – General Command (PFLPGC); Al-Saiqa; the (Palestinian) Popular Struggle Front (PSF), and the Al-Fatah rebels.

Palestinian operations retained a terroristic aspect throughout the 1980s and 1990s. Even after Arafat's renunciation of terrorism in December

1988 splinter groups such as the PLF continued to commit terrorist violence. Over the past decade in particular, **Hizbullah** inspired attacks on Israeli occupation forces and civilians have become a much greater military threat than PLO incursions from southern Lebanon had ever been. Fundamentalist guerrillas have continually tried to undermine **Israel**.

The PLO has striven for, and in many ways succeeded in gaining international respectability. Agreement was reached between Israel and the PLO for Palestinian autonomy in the Gaza strip and Jericho and for on-going discussions about Palestinian self-rule throughout the West Bank. At the same time the Intifada has taken hold.

Intifada (meaning shuddering) is the term given to large-scale Palestinian disturbances in the West Bank and Gaza between 1987 and the establishment of a Palestinian authority under peace accords with the PLO in September 1993. The movement arose among alienated predominately youthful Palestinian refugees, 80 per cent of who were under 34 years of age. To counter this urban terrorism in the West Bank and Gaza the Israeli's adopted a hard line, militaristic approach.

During this period hard line Islamic groups emerged such as **Hamas** (Zeal) – which challenged Arafat's leadership of the Palestinian cause. This contributed to the revival of the Intifada in 2000. The sustained campaign of strikes and civil disturbances within the Palestinian territories attracted worldwide sympathy. Intifada activists could well condemn the area to years of mutually destructive guerrilla attrition involving Israeli settlers who remain adamant about staying in the Palestinian areas.

It was the PLO, however, who persuaded the Israelis to compromise with Palestinian moderates rather than a capitulation to fundamentalist zealots (Ellis, 1995). There is still a mixture of peoples and groups – Hamas and Islamic **Jihad** terrorists, Israeli settlers, Intifada activists, ongoing tensions in Lebanon and Muslim fundamentalism which could lead to guerrilla attrition in the long term.

Terrorism has been justified in parts of the occupied territories as realism. Politics is seen as a struggle for power and military power is essential for the promotion of the states' national interest. Moral considerations should not affect the conduct of foreign policy as human nature is wicked. Over the decades, the Palestinian problem has moved to being a human rather than a political problem. The Palestinians have increasingly refused to remain quiescent in the face of Israeli terror and occupation, and they have tried to rid themselves of their sense of inferiority and powerlessness in order to reawaken their national consciousness. They are desperate to convince the world that no settlement of the Arab–Israeli conflict is possible without PLO participation. They have shown the world that the PLO is the sole spokesman for the Palestinian people and have preserved the Palestinian State in the West Bank and Gaza.

In the PLO context the revolutionary terrorist justifies terrorism by saying that it is a response to state or official terrorism as practised by Israel. Terrorism is used to advertise its grievances. Violence and terror are justified on the grounds that the ends sought are moral and legitimate. Yet the Palestinians have never established a state using these methods, but they have achieved some objectives using such tactics.

See also: Al Aqsa Martyrs Brigade; Arafat; Asbat Al-Ansar.

References

Ellis, J. (1995) *From the Barrel of a Gun*, London: Greenhill Books and Mechanicsburg, PA: Stackpole Books.

Inbari, P. (1995) *The Palestinians Between Terrorism and Statehood*, Brighton, Sussex: Academic Press.

Livingstone, N. C. and Halevy, D. (1990) *Inside the PLO: Covert Units, Secret Funds and the War against Israel and the United States*, New York: William Morrow.

Usher, G. (1995) *Palestine in Crisis: The Struggle for Peace and Political Independence after Oslo*, East Haven, CT: Pluto Press.

Weisband, E. and Roguly, D. (1976) 'Palestinian Terrorism: Violence, Verbal Strategy and Legitimacy' in Alexander, Y. (ed.) *International Terrorism*, New York: Praeger.

Yodfat, A. and Yuval, A. O. (1981) *PLO: Strategy and Tactics*, London: Croom Helm.

Further Reading

Gowers, A. and Walker, T. (1990) *Behind the Myth: Yasser Arafat and the Palestinian Revolution*, London: W. H. Allen.

Peru

The Republic of Peru has alternated between military and democratic rule throughout its history. Military regimes have generally predominated, increasing the numbers of political prisoners, expropriating newspapers considered to be danger-ously destabilising, and dismissing workers at random. In 1981 the civilian government elected in 1980 passed an anti-terrorist law, largely in response to the terrorist activities of the Maoist Sendero Luminoso guerrilla movement, which provided for prison sentences of up to twenty years for those convicted of terrorism. Subsequent governments have frequently declared states of emergency in areas of guerrilla activity (notably Ayacucho department in the south), and the Peruvian army has been regularly deployed in the struggle against the insurgents.

Outside Peru the group which is often in the news is the Sendero Luminoso or Shining Path, which is a Maoist movement founded during a period of student unrest in the 1970s. It broke away from other leftist groups and went underground with plans to organise the peasantry. Bombings and bank robberies becoming a regular occurrence in the early 1980s. Thousands of attacks have been carried out in the course of waging a people's war from the countryside in order to carry it eventually into the cities. The group aims to pursue total war until the government is overthrown. There are four stages of activity acts of sabotage designed to draw attention to the existence of the Shining Path, attacks on business premises and banks to obtain funds; actions against police posts in remote areas with the aim of seizing weapons; and ultimately the seizure of power.

In September 1992 the founder and leader of the Shining Path guerrilla group Abimael Guzman was arrested. This dealt a severe blow to the group's chances of seizing power in Peru. Never-theless the war which had begun in 1979 had cost

30,000 lives and done almost irreparable damage to the economy and security of the country. Much of the country was under a state of emergency. Political violence continued after his arrest, as the group remained structurally intact with a strong military organisation. In many ways this forced the Peruvian government to depend on the military which appears less professional in its activities. In 1993 Shining Path made an offer of peace to the government and it declared at the end of the decade that it still maintained this offer.

A Red Sendero leadership still exists (the Black Sendero leaders are in prison) whilst guerrilla finances are generated within their rural base areas mainly from taxes on the widespread cultivation and trafficking of the coca plant.

References

Ellis, J. (1995) *From the Barrel of a Gun*, London: Greenhill Books and Mechanicsburg, PA: Stack-pole Books.

Strong, S. (1993) 'Shining Path: A Case Study in Ideological Terrorism', *Conflict Studies 260*, Lon-don: RISCT.

Further Reading

Tarazona-Sevillano, G. (1990) 'Sendero Luminoso and the Threat of Narco-Terrorism', *Washington Papers no.144*, New York: Praeger.

Philippines

In August 1946, peasant rebels, many of whom were former members of the wartime communist-led anti-Japanese guerrilla movement were fighting against landowners supported by the Philippine security forces and their own private armies. They were joined by a group of communists opposed to the newly independent regime of President Manuel Roxas, and by 1950 the Hukbong Managpalaya ng Bayan (People's Liberation Army – known simply as the Huks) led by Luis Taruc, was engaged in battalion-sized operations against government forces.

Huk successes were countered increasingly successfully after the appointment of Ramon

Magsaysay in September 1950 as secretary for national defence. Magsaysay reorganised the armed forces and promoted a number of reforms in order to undermine peasant support for the Huks. The rebels were isolated and ruthlessly hunted down, and by 1954 the back of the rebellion had been broken.

A succession of presidents, under the control of American economic interests and the Filipino landowning class, did little to help the peasant majority or to curb disorder and political violence. In 1965, President Macapagal (Liberal Party) was defeated by President Ferdinand Marcos of the Nationalist Party.

For two decades until 1986 the Philippines were ruled by Marcos, who wielded ever-increasing and wide-ranging executive powers. The two main guerrilla groups, though not constituting an immediate threat to the regime, engaged almost the full strength of the country's armed forces, are the Moro National Liberation Front (MNLF), which is Muslim autonomist or secessionist, and the New People's Army, which is Maoist.

The Moro National Liberation Front is an Islamic nationalist movement in rebellion against the government, with the particular objective of achieving independence or autonomy for the Muslim population of the Philippines within the area of Mindanao island in the southern part of the country. It has a factionalised political wing with separate groups allegedly supported by **Egypt**, **Libya**, and **Saudi Arabia** while the military branch is the Bangsa Moro Army. The guerrilla war has already resulted in the deaths of more than 60,000 people. By February 1974 the Moros were strong enough to capture a city for several days, but by 1975 Moro guerrilla activity had begun to decline and Marcos opened negotiations with the MNLF in order to end the war. Although Marcos's diplomatic offensive resulted in the withdrawal of Libyan support for the rebels, the Moros fought on, though their chances of gaining a separate Muslim state continued to decline as Christian settlers began to form a majority in many areas of the south. The MNLF split into several factions and many Moro guerrillas took advantage of government amnesty offers in order to surrender.

The Front stopped establishing control over territory after it realised that the army's tactic of burning down a whole village or destroying a whole island dominated by the Front was causing the people too much hardship. The guerrillas began to attack the enemy in isolated incidents, and the army maintains that this is a result of reduced firepower. The chain of command has weakened, and quite often local commanders act on their own initiative. Because supply lines can no longer be maintained as a result of the government patrols, a cottage industry of weapon manufacture has developed. The Moros continue to demand an end to the reported repression and mass extermination of Muslims in the southern Philippines and to take prompt measures to provide protection and security for the Muslim minority and to resettle the thousands of refugees in their homes. Basically, the Front is in a state of stalemate because it has never established a military capability.

Since 1969 the military branch of the Maoist Communist party has been the New People's Army (NPA), formerly the People's Liberation Army. It is particularly active in Luzon province, with several thousand guerrillas and a large support base among the population. By 1971 the NPA had some 2,000 men under arms, but as the Philippines' security forces became more professional during the mid 1970s the NPA suffered a series of reverses, and was forced to reorganise.

By the mid-1980s, the NPA was operating in alliance with the MNLF as far south as Mindanao, where it became firmly entrenched, remaining seemingly unbowed by the political changes. The struggle is organised into at least 30 strategic guerrilla fronts, each with its own party structure, militia and political machinery.

In 1987 a new constitution was approved. Autonomy was granted to the Mindanao and Cordillera regions thus paving the way for a truce with guerrilla groups operating in those areas. Conflict in the Muslim held areas in Mindanao grew during the 1990s as a 20,000 strong Moro Liberation Front considered that the government was not respecting conditions set out in the 1987 constitution. In 1993 the government tightened their links with Muslim secessionists and the guerrillas in northern Luzon. By the late-1990s two thirds of the people were living below the poverty line.

In September 1996 the government and the Muslim guerrillas signed a peace agreement. Nur

Misuari, leader of the Moro National Liberation Front, became governor of Mindanao. The armed wing of the Communist party, the New People's Army, continued to operate in cities and rural towns.

Abu-Sayyaf is the Muslim terrorist and **kidnapping** group linked to **Al Qaeda**, and has been involved with the Moro Islamic Liberation Front to win self rule for the Muslim majority area in the southern Philippines. In March 2003 they bombed Davao city airport on Mindanao Island and at least twenty people were killed and 115 injured. Abu Sayyaf's stronghold is the island of Jolo nearby.

They number a few hundred active fighters but have over 1,000 followers, who were impressed by the group seizing foreign tourists for ransom payments in 2000 and 2001. Their external aid can be described as largely self-financing through ransom and extortion and active support is provided by Islamic extremists in the Middle East and South Asia.

Reference

Mulgannon, T. (1989) 'Inside the Philippines: A View from the Countryside', *TVI Report*, vol. 8, no. 3, pp. 10–14.

Further Reading

Wainstein, E. S. (1985) 'Muslim Rebels in the Philippines', *TVI Report*, vol. 6, no. 2, pp. 11–13.
Zwick, J. (1984) 'Militarism and Repression in the Philippines' in Stohl, M. and Lopez, G. A. (eds) *State as Terrorist*, Westport, CT: Greenwood Press.

Phraseology *see* Language of Terrorists

PLO *see* Palestine Liberation Organisation

Police and Response to Terrorism

Police Response in the UK

In the 1960s the police were confronted with an escalation of a phenomenon, the violent expressing of politically motivated unrest, at unprecedented levels. In the **United Kingdom** it is the function of the police to investigate terrorist crimes and bring the perpetrators to justice.

From the late-1960s the policing of the problem of terrorism was seen to be associated with London, which reflected the national and international importance of the city, the fact that it is the capital, the seat of government and the largest centre of population. It plays host to hundreds of foreign diplomats, other VIP's gatherings of world leaders for every conceivable purpose and is the centre of world finance. The policing of terrorism in the London City and metropolitan area is the responsibility of several branches of the Metropolitan Police – the Anti-Terrorist Squad, the Special Branch and the Royal and Diplomatic Protection Branch. Other groups such as the Special Patrol Group and the Paramilitary Intervention Squad become involved on an 'as required' basis. At grass roots level all police may find themselves performing duties associated with actual or suspected terrorists' incidents.

The terrorist threat was first evaluated in 1968 when there was a revolt against authority, signifying political and social unrest, not just in Britain but across Europe. A year later there were demonstrations which became violent, including the throwing of petrol bombs.

In 1970 explosives were blamed on the Angry Brigade – a group of political activists whose ideological belief was anarchistic. The Bomb Squad was formed at that time and in 1971 it was upgraded to include Flying Squad and Special Branch men and ex-Army explosive experts. This period marked a turning point in the governments' determination to undertake serious measures to combat terrorism. Countermeasures were effective in spite of the police response being made in the face of considerable other demands on manpower resources. The response has centred on the Special Branch and Anti-Terrorist Branch.

In 1988 the Metropolitan Police assumed responsibility for the policing of Heathrow Airport – a change derived from the threat that terrorists posed. Military deployment was a further measure of the impact of politically motivated terrorists on the British way of life.

The threat of terrorism has created a sense of unity where a degree of rivalry would normally exist between forces. This was welcome news in the late-1970s and early-1980s when terrorist attacks began to concentrate on specific targets rather than on earlier indiscriminate attacks. Terrorism is a unique contravention of the laws of society and in Britain it has consolidated itself as a problem requiring its own police response. In the case of a terrorist incident the event usually comes to police attention by way of prior information and/or intelligence or by an occurrence (bombing, shooting).

To react to a terrorist incident requires a response from the police counter-terrorism structure according to a preconceived plan. Prevention is better than cure, but the problem of preventing is made difficult by the very nature of the terrorist psyche and by a motivation quite different from that of the usual law breaker.

Covert pro-active policing in countering terrorism is highly skilled, dangerous and demanding. The impact of terrorism on the issue of police manpower has thrown up the issues of shortages and spiralling costs. The police have always had to have the ability to adapt to terrorist variations.

Emergency legislation over the last two or three decades has placed the police in a difficult position. The intention of the government is clear: to overcome the terrorist problem and to maintain public approval for government policies. To achieve this, the government relies upon the police to use the legislation provided to defeat the terrorists. **Counter-terrorism** legislation has not only provided the police with far greater powers than they previously wielded it has enabled a hybrid version of many of these powers to become part of the normal police powers. The question of arms for police in an anti-terrorist situation was a difficult issue for the British people – with a history of unarmed police protecting them – to accept.

For example there is concern over the use of the Heckler and Koch MPSK sub-machine gun. The arms that the terrorists carry aggravate the nature of their crimes and entitle the police to at least comparable firepower to defend themselves – and law and social tradition only allow operational deployment of elements of the military only in extreme emergency. The overt use of firearms by

police as an actual part of the counter-terrorist strategy became evident with the creation of the paramilitary Intervention Squad (D11) in the mid-1970s.

In the 1970s the concept of Military Aid to the Civil Power (MACP) was incorporated in an armoury of government responses. To facilitate the conduct of major counter-terrorism or other civil contingency operation a crisis centre known by the acronym Cabinet Office Briefing Room was devised. The centre was equipped to enable ministers to be constantly in touch with police and military leaders anywhere in the country during crises. This enabled almost instantaneous decision making at the highest level of government. Such a facility was particularly necessary in terrorist situations where foreign governments are involved. It enables the government of the day to exercise closer and more direct influence over the conduct of major incidents and insure the primacy of the civil authority.

Realisation by the police of the value of good intelligence resources has led to the creation of the Criminal Intelligence squad (C11) at Scotland Yard.

On the international police scene, terrorism has facilitated a wide interchange of experience and technological expertise generally. The police in the UK have gained much influence from the **USA**; particularly in relation to countering the IRA threat. The UK police now have international recognition as counter-terrorist authorities.

In Northern Ireland the nature of policing in the province reflected the society itself. In its struggle to come to terms with the social dichotomy, the Royal Ulster Constabulary (RUC) has been moulded by the extremes of social circumstances. It was the model developed to police the British colonies an armed instrument of the authorities. Allegations of sectarian influence permeated every aspect of RUC development and activity. The problem has remained one of over-whelming Protestant membership of the force (over 80 per cent). This was one of the reasons which led after years of debate to the RUC being disbanded and replaced by the blander sounding Police Service of Northern Ireland, to appeal to people across the community to join the police. Heavy casualties were suffered by the RUC but its critics always maintained that it had regressed to being a military force rather than a civil force. The RUC in the 1980s responded to huge staff increases and technological development by becoming a powerful weapon in an attempt to enforce law and order in a situation where each group in a divided society had different perceptions of what law and order meant. Attempts by the RUC to take the middle of the road continually encountered the bipolarity of Northern Ireland society. The emotive issue of armed police has been thrust to the forefront by the need for adequate protection from terrorists.

Hope is the main saviour for peace in Northern Ireland. Violence is no longer so widespread and anarchic and the terrorist tactics of both the IRA and extreme Protestant loyalists have in general become more targeted on participants not on innocent observers.

Police Response in Europe

Unlike the Anglo-American community-operated police, the European police forces were always government-orientated structures that emerged from the military. This is not only evident in a term such as 'gendarmerie', which dates back to a military rural unit of the eighteenth century, but also in uniforms, armament and training. Many European police officers were discharged army veterans and this left its mark on the tactical and structural development of the police.

Police response to terrorism is twofold – terrorism has to be dealt with at the tactical level, both preventive and reactive, and it demands an investigative and intelligence approach. In both the patrol and the criminal investigation departments, hierarchical bureaucracies exist which have an inbred reluctance towards change and reforms.

Specialised tactical police response teams have been developed in Germany (GSG9, Grenzschutz-gruppe 9); the USA (SWAT, Special Weapons and Tactics, and CIRT, Critical Incident Response Team); France (GIGN, Groupe d'Intervention Gendarmerie Nationale); Austria (the Cobra); and Spain (the GEO). These have some basic tactics in common – the men are police officers with training and prior experience as officers of the law, coming from regular patrol or investigation work. Their missions, their use of force, and their employment of firearms are subject to the same legal safeguards as normal police actions. Trained specialists always function as a team where tasks and responsibilities are divided, making it easier for a member of the team to concentrate on and fulfil his appointed task.

Speed, not haste, which is essential to any counter-terrorist operation, results from this team approach. The key to success is a system of mutual 'overwatch', in which every team member is covered by one or two of his partners so that a real need to use one's guns in self-defence seldom arises. Over the years many incidents have proven that even hardcore criminals and terrorists are likely to give up when faced by a swift-moving police response team barring all exits. Experience in the West has shown that the use of such teams has lowered a department's use of deadly force in arrest situations.

In 1971 Germany provided a turning point in the history of criminal investigation. The Bundes-skriminalamt, the federal investigative office, was remodelled to become a central agency to guide, control and co-ordinate the work of the various state investigative offices, the Landerkriminalamter. It had quickly emerged that an effective counter-terrorist campaign cannot be run without a centralised intelligence-gathering and evaluation network. To many people the build-up of any such computer network will be on a confrontation course with the restraints and safeguards embodied in the constitution of any democratic society. Despite this, there has been a tendency to neglect conventional detective work in favour of the highly technicalised systems such as databases and computer terminals.

Terrorists generally choose their targets with great care to detail, and an awareness of their symbolic value. Few victims are chosen at random. Schleyer and Moro were kidnapped although they were both guarded by a detail of policemen; the terrorists took possible resistance into account and used more firepower. Throughout recent years, airport security has been considerably increased, but this has not deterred attackers willing to pay the price, as witnessed at Rome and Vienna airports in 1985.

Special units do have a deterrent effect to some degree, and most of the groups currently existing worldwide have a healthy respect for such units as the GSG9, the SAS, Delta Force, the Israeli Jamam or the French GIGN. These teams cannot guard every airport, every embassy or politician. The terrorists recognise the reactive character of the tactical response units and plan accordingly – to create the damage before the police can rush in the specialised counter-terrorist teams. Conversely many people in the democratic countries are aware that much time is lost every year in highly visible 'deterrent' guard duties, at road-blocks and similar routine police jobs.

Although international terrorism has demonstrated repeatedly that there is no neutral ground anywhere and that in the long run no country is immune, there has been very little effective international co-operation between the democratic nations apart from political pronouncements, the establishment of isolated measures and international declarations. Tactical response groups have been in the forefront of informal co-operation, but certain directives of their respective agencies and governments restrict them.

See also: Counter/Anti-Terrorism; Trevi Group.

References

Bryett, K. (1987) 'The Effects of Political Terrorism on the Police of Great Britain and Northern Ireland since 1969', PhD dissertation. Aberdeen: University of Aberdeen.

Gregory, F. E. C. (1986) 'Policing the Democratic State: How Much Force', *Conflict Studies*, no. 194, London: Centre for Security and Conflict Studies.

Thackrah, J. R. (1985) 'Reactions to Terrorism and Riots', in J. R. Thackrah (ed.) *Contemporary Policing: An Examination of Society in the 1980s*, pp. 145–160, London: Sphere.

— (1993) *The Police and the Response to Terrorism within the UK and Ireland*, Unpublished MS at National Police Library, Bramshill, Hampshire.

Further Reading

Bailey, W. G. (ed.) (1986) *Encyclopaedia of the Police Service*, New York/London: Garland Publishers.

Levinson, D. (ed.) (2002) *Encyclopaedia of Crime and Punishment*, vol. 4, London: Sage.

Thackrah, J. R. (1982) 'Army-Police Co-operation: A General Assessment', *Police and Society Papers* (October), pp. 10–11.

— (1983) 'Army–Police Collaboration against Terrorism', *Police Journal* (Jan–Mar), pp. 41–52.

Williams, H. (1986) *Terrorism and the Local Police*, vol. 8, no. 4, pp. 345–350.

Political Sub-State Violence

Sub-State violence is directed against a state (whether or not that state practices terror) from within the state.

Violence at sub-state level has a particular relevance to those groups which have definable political objectives and can be called 'rational rebels'. The problem facing political leaders and contemporary states is that one man's terrorist is another man's freedom fighter. Sub-state violence and its particular problems are inseparable from the operation of the state and the international system generally, and raise questions about the nature and morality of government as well as of those who take violent actions against established governments. There must be a good prospect of an end in view and a chance for the cause to succeed before blood will be shed.

Newly formed small terrorist groups usually find it easier with each passing year to obtain at least minimal means for taking life. Well-established terrorist groups find it easier to obtain supplies of conventional weaponry, often of a sophisticated level. A terrorist group may well decide that concentration on the ownership of a nuclear bomb is not the most expeditious means of inflicting mass destruction. Advanced democracies are much more vulnerable than in the nineteenth century. With or without terrorists, some communities may become ungovernable because of largely non-violent conflicts of interests. Those states with democratic constitutional frameworks are greatly at risk from both terrorism and non-violent conflict, and some may decide on authoritarian solutions. Even advanced states without ballot-box democracy face strains due to the delicate balance of the inter-relationship between different parts of a modern

advanced economy. Advances in modern communication, allow small groups to internationalise
their activities with ease. There is a strong
relationship between improvements in technology
and the growth of international terrorism. Many
observers believe it is only a matter of time before a
terrorist group obtains weapons of mass destruction, if they have the wish and strong determination
to do so. Terrorists are often more interested in
drawing attention to their cause than in the mass
destruction of life for its own sake, without
reference to geography or nationality. Some
terrorists can be driven to radical innovation by
continuing failure to achieve success by previous
methods.

Restraint by terrorists in their use of violence
can be broken down as a result of a cumulative
series of random events, or by a deep yearning by
terrorist leaders to pursue uncontrolled escalation
of the struggle. In the post-colonial era, it has
proved impossible for states to pursue policies that
can remove many of the conditions and the
grievances, real or imagined, that motivate
terrorists. It is inevitable that terrorism will grow
in conditions in which many governments face
increasing difficulty in governing effectively with
broad consent.

The line separating wars between states and
conflicts between sub-national actors is hard to
determine. State-sponsored terrorism can increase
without becoming widespread. State-sponsored
groups are unlikely to wish to threaten the use of
weapons of mass destruction at any early date, and
most non-sponsored groups have difficulties in
doing so. Most sovereign states do not feel
sufficiently threatened to sacrifice their narrow
interests for the collective good. *Ad hoc* deals in
international agreements to cover events such as
hijacking may be attainable. Some sovereign states
will sponsor terrorist groups, but there are limits
beyond which states find it imprudent to progress.
Sponsorship, in this context, will mainly originate in
Third World countries. Ingenuity and sophistication will be the hallmarks of future political sub-
state violence.

See also: Political Violence.

Reference

Carlton, D. and Schaerf, C. (1981) (eds) *Contemporary Terrorism Studies in Sub-State Violence*, London:
Macmillan.

Political Terrorism

Political terrorism is generally defined as the
systematic use or threat of violence to secure
political goals. It is a sustained policy involving the
waging of organised terror either on the part of the
state, a movement or faction, or by a small group of
individuals. It is different from political terror,
which occurs in isolated acts and also in the form of
extreme, indiscriminate and arbitrary mass violence. Such terror is neither systematic nor
organised and is often difficult to control.

Political terrorism can be divided into three
types: revolutionary terror, sub-revolutionary terror
and repressive terror.

Revolutionary terror can be defined as the use of
systematic tactics of terrorist violence with the
objective of bringing about political revolution. It
has four main attributes: first, it is always
conducted by a group, and is not an individual
phenomenon, even though groups may be very
small; second, both the revolution and the use of
terror to promote it are always justified by some
revolutionary ideology or programme; third, there
exist leaders capable of mobilising people for
terrorism; fourth, alternative institutional structures
are created because a revolutionary movement
must change the political system and therefore must
develop its own policy-making bodies.

Revolutionary terror is part of a revolutionary
strategy, it is manifested in acts of socially and
politically unacceptable violence, and there is a
pattern of symbolic or representative selection of
the victims or objects of acts of terrorism. The
revolutionary movement deliberately intends these
actions to create a psychological effect on specific
groups and thereby to change their political
behaviour and attitudes.

Sub-types of revolutionary terror exist – organisations of pure terror, in which terror is the
exclusive weapon; revolutionary and national

liberationist parties and movements in which terror is employed as an auxiliary weapon; guerrilla terrorism and short-term terrorism in the course of a revolutionary rising; the revolutionary Reign of Terror; propaganda of the deed, when this form of terror is motivated by long-term revolutionary objectives; and international terrorism motivated by revolutionary objectives.

Sub-revolutionary terrorism is terror used for political motives other than revolution or government repression. Whereas revolutionary terrorism seeks total change, sub-revolutionary terrorism is aimed at more limited goals such as forcing the government to change its policy on some issue, warning or punishing specific public officials, or retaliating against government actions seen as reprehensible by the terrorists.

Repressive terrorism is the systematic use of terroristic acts of violence for the purpose of suppressing, putting down, quelling or restraining certain groups, individuals, or forms of behaviour deemed to be undesirable by the oppressor. Repressive terror relies heavily on the services of specialised agencies whose members are trained to torture, murder, and deceive. The terror apparatus is deployed against specific opposition groups and can be later directed against much wider groups, for example ethnic or religious minorities.

Political terrorism is thus the systematic use of murder and destruction, and the threat of murder and destruction, in order to terrorise individuals, groups, communities or governments into conceding to the terrorists' political demands. Terror is often employed within the political context and this makes it different from some other violent acts.

See also: Terror and Terrorism

References

Egendorf, L. (2000) *Terrorism: Opposing Viewpoints*, San Diego, CA: Greenhaven Press.

Schmid, A. P. (1983) *Political Terrorism: A Research Guide to Concepts*, Theories, Data Bases and Literature, Amsterdam: North-Holland.

Wardlaw, G. (1982) *Political Terrorism*, Cambridge: Cambridge University Press.

Wolf, J. B. (1976) 'Controlling Political Terrorism in a Free Society', *Orbis*, vol. 19, no. 34.

Further Reading

Bjorgo, T. (ed.) (1995) *Terror from the Extreme Right*, London: Frank Cass.

Merkl, P. H. and Weinberg, L. (eds) (1993) *Encounters with the Contemporary Radical Right*, Boulder, CO: Westview Press.

Watson, F. M. (1976) *Political Terrorism: The Threat and the Response*, Washington, DC: Robert B. Luce.

Wilkinson, P. (1973) 'Three Questions on Terrorism', *Government and Opposition*, vol. 8, no. 3.

— (1974) *Political Terrorism*, London: Macmillan.

Political Violence

Political violence is either the deliberate infliction or threat of infliction of physical injury or damage for political ends, or it is violence which occurs unintentionally in the course of severe political conflicts. Political violence is particularly difficult to classify and analyse because it frequently involves the interaction and effects of the actions of many persons and collectives, with widely different motivations and attitudes. Most political violence serves both instrumental and expressive functions simultaneously. Almost invariably, the 'price' of relaying a message of terror to a 'target audience' is the death, injury or dispossession of victims whose rights and liberties have been arbitrarily curtailed by the perpetrators of violence.

Political violence is often measured by its scale and intensity. By scale is meant the total numbers of persons involved, the physical extent of their area of operation, the political stakes involved in the conflict and the significance of the level of violence in the international system. Major indicators of its intensity would be the duration of the violence, the number of casualties caused and the amount of firepower and weaponry employed. Most violent states, movements or groups employ violence simultaneously at several different levels for their political ends. For example, terrorist violence is a thread running through modern war, revolution and internal political struggles in the contemporary history of many countries. In many regimes concurrent traditions of *inter-communal*; *remonstrative*; *praetorian* (used to coerce changes in government leadership and policy), and *repressive* violence have wrought endemic instability. The most serious threats of violence facing liberal states internally are those which directly endanger the survival and stability of the liberal constitution itself, and those which indirectly and cumulatively undermine the state's authority and support through major defiance of law and order, and by endangering the lives of citizens to the point where confidence in the authorities is eroded. In reasonably secure and well-established liberal democracies these really dangerous levels of internal political violence are likely to occur only if there is mass disaffection among large sectors of the population, combined with large-scale popular support for a resort to violence in defiance of the state.

Some of the most frequent contributory causes of internal political violence constantly recurring in the recorded history of political conflict include ethnic conflicts, hatreds, discrimination and oppression; religious and ideological conflicts, hatreds, discrimination and oppression; perceived political inequalities, infringements of rights, injustice or oppression and lack of adequate channels for peaceful communication of protests or grievances and demands; the existence of a tradition of violence, disaffection, or popular turbulence. Other contributory causes are the availability of revolutionary leadership equipped with a potentially attractive ideology; weakness and ineptness of the government, police and judicial groups; erosion of confidence in the regime, its values and institutions afflicting all levels of the population including the government, and deep divisions within governing elites and leadership groups.

In strict terms, where a majority is subjected to tyrannical or despotic rule by a minority, the minority is imposing its sovereignty by violence and therefore can be legitimately opposed by force of just rebellion or resistance by the majority. By definition such a purely coercive regime cannot be a lawful democratic state and therefore majority opposition to it cannot be regarded as seditious or violent according to liberal democratic principles. In two situations a *prima-facie* case can be made for a morally justifiable resort to political violence by a minority within a liberal democratic state. There is the situation of the minority whose basic rights and liberties are denied or taken away by arbitrary action of the government or its agencies. The

second situation arises when one minority is attacked by another minority and does not receive adequate protection from the state and its forces of law and order. In such circumstances the attacked minority community may have little alternative but to resort to violence in order to defend itself.

Many variables exist in the study of political violence. Scale is of primary consideration – at first sight this may not appear to be a variable in itself, but any particular set of events being studied will need to be placed on a scale relative to previous acts of political violence. The number of people and the size of the group behind the violence is important whether it be an individual, small group, members of a social class, an institution, domestic state, foreign state, or group of states. The power and legitimacy of the individual or group have to be borne in mind. Targets of violence can vary from a person, object or symbol, to a foreign state or a group of states. A variety of means can be used; the threat or use of loud noise, fists, sticks, Molotov cocktails, rifles, bombs, the deprivation of freedom of movement, direct injury or killing. Intentions can be wide-ranging – to gain publicity, deter attack, prevent an action, physically destroy a symbol (either person or object), change the policy of the institution or government, replace government personnel, change the social, economic or political system, or destroy the state and cause international war. The effects can be felt by spectators, targets opponents, and the domestic and international system. Timescales can vary; incidents may be single, sporadic, frequent or continuous. Political violence can reflect precedents which are historical or contemporary, or it can take a new direction. The cost depends on the economics of damage – this is not central to typologising but is an important measurement of scale from the point of view of perpetration and target. The state and security forces can often respond by illegal or legal means, changes in law, detention, death penalties and **genocide**. Nevertheless, the respondent to violence may be another group in society, especially if they are the target, or feel threatened. Similarly, if the perpetrator of political violence is the state, the respondents may be various groups within society, who can emigrate, riot, or plant bombs.

There are numerous scenarios for the origin of violent groups, which have developed over the past fifteen years. Violent groups can emerge from a previously unopposed campaign of government violence, or violence by another organised group or community. The American government in the 1960s responded to civil rights marches with violence, from this developed the Black city riots of the 1960s, and the 1968 Democratic Convention violence from which emerged the Black Panthers and Weathermen. At the same period in Northern **Ireland**, from the Northern Ireland Civil Rights Association (NICRA) marches and Protestant violence, the Ulster Defence Association, Ulster Defence Force and Provisional IRA emerged. There are also scenarios where small, violent groups such as some of those supporting animal rights, have emerged from a single-issue campaign without being provoked by a violent response by anybody.

Second, there can be the appearance or reappearance of a group attracted to a cultural, religious or ethnic minority, demanding independence, autonomy, respect for religious practices or simply to be allowed to indulge in activities declared illegal by the state, i.e. ETA, the Corsicans and the Shi'ites. New patterns of behaviour have emerged with Islamic fundamentalism.

Auxiliary groups have been created by exile movements such as the Palestinians.

The appearance of the urban guerrilla has led to a new set of tactics being adopted by already existing groups, who wish to change the nature of various regimes in Latin America or in response to a takeover of a regime by military coup. This is a genuinely revolutionary scenario and involves professional revolutionaries, i.e. the Montoneros and Tupamaros. Some groups are facing military regimes and responding to violence by those regimes, and others are facing regimes which are democratic but corrupt.

Groups have appeared in response to immigration of new ethnic groups, usually with anti-Semitic overtones, i.e. FANE in France.

Both right- and left-wing organisations have appeared to counter changes of government seen as resulting in a revolutionary path, or to challenge a government imposed by conquest, i.e. the Mujaheddin in **Afghanistan**.

More recently groups have been formed to settle scores with the opponents of particular regimes,

particularly within the Palestinian movement, or at the behest of the Iranian and Libyan regimes.

Traditional anti-colonial scenarios are numerous; because of the defeat of the occupying power or examples of liberation close at hand, a population would often take to violence after years of subservience.

Finally, groups may be formed in attempts to create continent-wide insurrection, like Action Directe.

Once a group exists, possible scenarios of development can occur.

First, splitting is the most frequent cause of development in a group, arising from the perception by some of its members that violence has become counter-productive. Violence has successfully publicised the cause, but it is now time to adopt peaceful tactics. Foreign sponsors may make unreasonable demands – the Sino-Soviet split led to the appearance of Maoists. Similar splits among state supporters of the Palestinian cause have produced similar effects in the movement. There can be genuine ideological differences of emphasis, i.e. among the IRA, Basques and Palestinians. Right-wing groups can split around individuals, new factions can take members away with them, and regional splitting can develop.

A second means of development is amalgamation – where groups may begin operating in restricted geographical areas, as in Italy, and later amalgamate, even with groups on other continents. Some groups may dwindle numerically to the point where they have to join other groups to continue operating.

Third, there is the 'generational' change. Many European groups began with symbolic attacks on property, and the first generation leadership was older and more idealistic than its successors. It was more sophisticated about its use of violence and when this could be counter-productive. The arrest of the first generation results in the leadership passing to a more hard-nosed group that favours hijacking and **kidnapping**. In turn, a third generation arises that is much more cold-blooded and engaged in more killing – this can result from a perception by activists, as in Italy, that the government responds more to kidnapping and killing than to symbolic bombing.

Turning to exile as a source of violent action, the Jews were themselves the first exiles who used violence to try to return home. In the process they in turn have exiled the Palestinians. Exile groups have frequently become mercenaries – either for other groups or for governments who wish to cause problems for other groups. As a result, they frequently split.

Where there is a double minority, the demands made by one group or social category threaten the position of another group – especially where religion or race are the root of their disagreement. Violence can frequently be used by one minority to pre-empt or discredit a relatively peaceful campaign of protest. It then produces counter-violence from small groups that emerge from the peaceful campaign, who may also use violence against the government and security forces.

With reference to the development of urban guerrilla groups, many groups have taken this route, but without the success that their rural or colonial counterparts have achieved. None has moved successfully from pinprick attacks to the use of large units. Towns and provinces have been overrun for short periods, but only in Nicaragua has there been any lasting success.

There are five main scenarios why a group may collapse. There may be total victory, in which the terrorists become the government and the armed forces – as in rural anti-colonial sectors; partial victory, where the government makes sufficient concessions to split the insurgents; partial defeat: the government makes sufficient concessions to satisfy the insurgents' constituency, but not the insurgents themselves, and the insurgency collapses as the insurgents are killed or captured one by one. In a situation of total defeat, there are no concessions and potential support can be alienated by the violence. Finally, the government may respond with state terror and arbitrary violence, which terrorises the population into submission. Loss of foreign sponsorship can mean that with no easy source of money or weapons the group will move back to logistical operations and lose the initiative. Scenarios also occur where the state sets out to wear down the insurgents and new issues arise to arouse the popular imagination. Most of the campaigns of political violence that began twenty years ago continue today. The US Weathermen,

Tupamaros and Montoneros are the most notable casualties. European, African, Asian and Central American campaigns have proved more durable.

Defence of one's country provides one of the most basic justifications of political violence, similar to the defence of one's country against external attack. When the British government announced in the mid-1970s that it would not negotiate with terrorists in future, this amounted to a policy of criminalising political violence and playing down the notion that Northern Ireland was in a state of **civil war** that urgently required a political solution (Guelke, 1998).

Basic values can be thwarted and eroded and violence can take over the human mind. There appears to be a growing tolerance for violence, pitilessness toward victims, and sometimes sheer pleasure in killing. Political violence involving a huge number of casualties has become more commonly an aspect of state control in recent decades. There is a strong record of anti-elite action by radical groups seeking political changes as we saw in the events culminating in **September 11**. US forces overseas have experienced political violence over two decades (Booth and Dunne, 2002).

Political terror continues in many parts of the world including in countries that maintain support from Western democracies. September 11 showed the horrifying vulnerability of highly developed states to asymmetric paramilitary action, and the inevitable reaction is to seek to maintain control with greater vigour and expanded military force. The events of September 11 could have set in train over the longer term, a cycle, or perhaps a spiral, of violence between elites and radical anti-elite groups. To many observers political violence and terrorism will only cease to be linked if there is a fundamental attempt to address the issue of global inequalities and mass poverty (Rogers in Booth and Dunne, 2002).

See also: Political Sub-State Violence.

References

Arendt, H. (1951) *The Origins of Totalitarianism*, New York: Harcourt, Brace, Jovanovich Inc.

Aron, R. (1966) *Peace and War*, London: Weidenfeld and Nicholson.

Booth, K. and Dunne, T. (eds) (2002) *Worlds on Collision: Terror and the Future of Global Order*, Basingstoke and New York: Palgrave Macmillan.

Carlton, D. and Schaerf, C. (eds) (1981) *Contemporary Terror Studies in Sub-State Violence*, London: Macmillan.

Cline, R. S. and Alexander, Y. (eds) (1986) *Terrorism as State-Sponsored Covert Warfare*, Virginia: Hero Books.

Clutterbuck, R. (ed.) (1986) *The Future of Political Violence*, London: Macmillan, RUSI.

Guelke, A. (1998) *The Age of Terrorism and the International Political System*, London and New York: I. B. Tauris Pub.

Rogers, P. (2002) 'Political Violence and Global Order' in Booth, K. and Dunne, T. (eds) *Worlds in Collision: Terror and the Future of Global Order*, Basingstoke: Palgrave Macmillan, pp. 215–226.

Schechterman, B. and Slann, M. (eds) (1998) *Violence and Terrorism*, Guilford, CT: Dushkin, McGraw Hill.

White, J. R. (1974) *Political Violence*, Tallahassee, Florida: Institute for Intergovernmental Research.

Further Reading

Crenshaw, M. (1983) *Terrorism, Legitimacy and Power: The Consequences of Political Violence*, Middletown, CT: Wesleyan University Press.

Crozier, B. (1974a) *A Theory of Conflict*, London: Hamish Hamilton.

— (1974b) 'Aid for Terrorism', *Annual of Power and Conflict 1973–74. A Survey of Political Violence and International Influence*, London: RISCT

Frey, R. and Morris, C. (eds) (1991) *Violence, Terrorism and Justice*, Cambridge: Cambridge University Press.

Han, H. H. (1984) *Terrorism, Political Violence and World Order*, Lanham, MD: University Press of America.

Hoffman, S. (1998) *World Disorders: Troubled Peace in the Post-Cold War Era*, London: Rowman and Littlefield Publishers.

Leiden, C. and Schmitt, K. M. (1968) *The Politics of Violence*, Englewood Cliffs, NJ: Prentice Hall.

Preventive Action *see* Counter/Anti-Terrorism

Propaganda

Propaganda can be defined as any information, ideas doctrines or special appeals disseminated to influence the opinion, emotions, attitudes or behaviour of any specified group in order to benefit the sponsor either directly or indirectly.

Propaganda and **terrorism** are identical insofar as they both seek to influence a mass audience in a way that is intended to benefit the sponsor. The aim of terror is to induce fear and uncertainty, while propaganda can and does serve every imaginable purpose from religion to politics and commerce. Terror might be seen as a subspecies of propaganda. The political objectives of propaganda can only be reached by a complex psychological-military process in which propaganda and violence play a key role. Successful terrorism depends on effective propaganda about terrorist operations. The true revolutionary believes that crimes committed for the cause are just and argues that he or she is answerable only to the revolutionary leadership, or to some higher authority such as God or history. The dissemination of revolutionary propaganda requires a circle of true believers with the object being one of total, unquestioning loyalty. This creates a need for totalitarian state propaganda, which can only exist within a tightly disciplined organisation.

Although terrorists regard the regime, its institutions, and its agents as evil enemies to be destroyed without mercy, they see the general public as an audience whose allegiance is required. The purpose of all revolutionary activity is conversion. Elimination is reserved for symbolic or vengeance targets, those who threaten the movement, and those who refuse conversion. True believers, who are in fact dedicated to extreme objectives are seen and heard by the public arguing for reasonable objectives within the existing norms. Their real agenda is hidden behind tactical reasonableness. Over many terrorists' campaigns this century, some consistent attitudes to the public have emerged.

Terrorists blame the consequences of all violence

on the regime they are opposing. All that the police and military do is presented in the worst possible light, and casualties are made into martyrs. Terrorist violence is often blamed on the authorities too, as in El Salvador. Terrorists also use the ploy that the violence they use is a reluctant but inevitable response to violence by the state.

The term 'long war' is used frequently, as a terror campaign is often seen as a full-scale revolution with victory ultimately assured. For the regime to win, the authorities have to eliminate every last terrorist and extinguish the cultural and spiritual inspiration. This is often an impossible demand. The IRA and Latin American terrorists, particularly the Shining Path in **Peru**, have used this technique.

Spurious arguments are used to protect terrorists from the full force of public wrath. Murder is justified by reference to injustices, i.e. the Iranians speak of a war by the impoverished and deprived against the **USA**, **Israel** and all enemies of Islam. Television appearances by terrorist leaders and spokesmen provide occasions for justification; and Yasser **Arafat** justified the role of Palestinians in the terrorist field when he addressed the **United Nations** in 1974.

Whether terror is itself a theme in propaganda is hard to measure, because propaganda is slow and unacknowledged. Journalists who decide to report from direct contact with terrorist groups have no alternative in this dangerous situation but to bias their reporting, i.e. Western journalists in **Lebanon**. Terror isolates the police and other security force members because the judiciary, bureaucracy and general public fear to commit themselves to the fight. Violent campaigns hope to deflect government responses until it is too late to reverse the shift of popular allegiance from regime to terrorist. Terrorist campaigns never seem to fail – for their whole reason for existing seems not to be for the solution of a social problem to be bound up in the struggle, which becomes an end in itself.

If terrorists promote a 'just cause', this can help in the recruitment of alienated youth, the creation of networks of survival in urban environments and opportunities for exploiting the weaknesses, divisions and confusions already present in NATO. Anti-NATO terrorists could tempt mainstream

peace movements into a supportive or at least ambivalent position in relation to terrorism.

With regard to counter-propaganda against the terrorists and the possible infusion of a psychological component – this can fail under the weight of public opinion being uneasy at any form of propaganda. If the subject were handled effectively, then an informed public might agree that in a choice of evils terrorism was worse than government publicity to help control it. Counter-propaganda has to work within the accepted norms of publicity or public relations. To a large extent government contact with the public on terrorism issues is through the media. Media coverage of terrorism can be closely linked to propaganda. Terrorism directed at the democracies is a direct attack on democracy itself, because by its very nature it proclaims that elected governments and their laws are subordinate to demands backed by violence or the threat of violence. The West perhaps has an ambivalent attitude towards terrorism. Moulded by Soviet propaganda, the West now seems generally to believe that the use of force and of deliberate counter-propaganda to defend democracy is illegitimate in the wake of the inevitable victory by 'progressive' forces.

See also: Media; Restraint.

Reference

Hoffman, B. (1998) *Inside Terrorism*, New York: Columbia University Press.

Further Reading

Laqueur, W. (1977) *Terrorism*, Boston, MA: Little, Brown and Co.
— (1987) *The Age of Terrorism*, Boston, MA: Little, Brown and Co.

Psychology

Many theories regard the terrorist as a peculiar personality with clearly identifiable character traits. A cross-section of rural and urban terrorist guerrilla groups shows that they are composed largely of single men aged 22 to 24 who have some university education. The women terrorists, except for those in the Baader Meinhof and Red Army Faction in Germany, and an occasional leading figure in the Irish Republican Army, Japanese Red Army and Popular Front for the Liberation of Palestine, are preoccupied with support rather than operational roles. Terrorists come in general from affluent, urban middle-class families, many of whom enjoy considerable social prestige. Like their fathers, many of the older terrorists have been trained for the professions and may have practiced these occupations before their commitment to a terrorist life. Whether they turned to terrorism as university students or later, most were provided with an anarchistic or Marxist world view and recruited into terrorist operations while at university.

A terrorist is a person engaged in politics who makes little distinction or differentiation between tactics and strategy on the one hand and principles on the other. Terrorists possess a self-fulfilling image of their own role in life, and plan with varying degrees of success their actions involving murder, destruction and other activities against society. They are always 'death-seekers', and generally take part in killing from patricidal impulses, directed against anyone in authority. Terrorists believe that the act of violence will encourage the uncommitted public to withdraw support from a regime or institution and make wider revolutionary acts possible by weakening the resolve of the opposition. Terrorists can direct their activities against the leadership of the opposition or against the symbols and agencies of the establishment.

Many terrorists are zealots who seek aggressive confrontations with authority in the name of social justice. Over the last two decades three character traits have become apparent: terrorists' handling of their own emotions is disturbed, which shows itself in fear to engage in real commitments. Fear of love leads them to choose violence. Attitude towards authority is disturbed and ambivalent, in the sense that a principally negative attitude to traditional authorities is combined with an uncritical subjection under the new counter-authorities. Most importantly, they have a disturbed relationship with their own identity; and having failed to develop an identity of their own they try to achieve this by the use of violence.

They are unable to be part of the community,

lose the capacity to understand reality and experience aimlessness due to lack of felt authority. To be effective they have to pursue absolute ends, which coalesce into violence.

Driving forces behind terrorism include the assertion of masculinity, or femininity in the case of women, the desire for depersonalisation, that is to get outside or away from oneself, as a result of a chronic lack of self-esteem; the desire for intimacy, and belief in the magic of violence and blood. Terrorists tend to resemble each other, regardless of their cause. Most are individuals for whom terrorism provides profound personal satisfaction, a sense of fulfilment through total dedication to the point of self- sacrifice; and a sense of power through inflicting pain and death upon other humans. Insecurity, risk-seeking behaviour and its associated suicidal intentions are present in varying mixtures in the terrorist. Out of this insecurity, the need for self-realisation and ego inflation arises.

The use of the term 'identification' in terrorism is generally confined to the identification with the aggressor which manifests itself in the positive attitude some hostages show to their captors (as in **Stockholm syndrome**).

The development of a sense of closeness and attachment between hostage and captor was first noticed during a bank robbery in Stockholm and came to be known as the Stockholm syndrome. The attempted robbery became a barricade and hostage situation. During the episode, a young woman hostage allegedly initiated sexual relations with her captor. The motivation was not a response to fear or coercion, but an intimacy that developed from sharing a common fate in a situation of mutual crisis and the protracted dependence of the woman captive on her captor. The relationship persisted after the bank robber's incarceration.

In the United States **FBI** agents have noted that had observers been attuned to the problem of transference earlier, the syndrome would have been called Shade Gap syndrome rather than Stockholm syndrome. Their reference is to a kidnapping that took place in Shade Gap, Pennsylvania, in 1967. When law enforcement officials came upon the kidnapper in a wooded area, he was hurriedly walking to escape pursuit and encirclement. A considerable distance behind him was the kidnap victim straining to keep up. The victim had only to turn round and walk off to freedom.

The most publicised episode of transference by a hostage to captors was in the case of newspaper heiress Patricia Hearst, who not only took a lover from among her captors but also provided them with covering gunfire when they were about to be seized for shoplifting. Patricia Hearst's behaviour was different only in degree from what is commonly observed in hostages under long-term stress. If Patricia Hearst's responses were more extreme, it is also true that the conditions of her captivity were severe, in terms both of deprivation and duration. These factors were probably exacerbated by her age and lack of experience.

The tremendous public interest in acts of **hostage taking** seems to be because most members of the audience identify with the fate of the victim, sharing his suffering in an act of empathy. Not all members of an audience will automatically show compassion for the victim. Some will identify with the terrorist because he represents the awesome power of one who can destroy life at his whim. If the victim is guilty in the eyes of the spectator he may derive pleasure from humiliation and suffering. Depending on the identification, with victim or terrorist, the spectator's attitude may be either empathy or cruelty. The direction of the identification can be determined by factors like class, race, nationality and party. The process of taking sides whenever a polarising act occurs stirs some members of the passive audience so deeply that they emerge as actors of their own, engaging in new polarising acts.

The switch from love for mankind to destruction of human beings is easier for young people, who may find it hard to identify with the older generation or with their nation. Identification, which enables one to empathise with others, is capable of leading to wide-ranging emotions – to anger and aggressiveness towards the source of the misery of the person or group for whom one has love and compassion. The strategy of terrorism of an insurgent nature is to bring about identification processes. In many cases terrorists attack the targets with which people consciously identify. The terrorist in this context uses the identification mechanism to bring home the terror to a target group by stimulating the identification between the instrumental victim and the victims' reference group.

Terrorist psychology is so important and to understand terrorism one must look at the context in which the violence has taken place and the individual who commits the acts. An individual terrorist has been made aware of a wide array of influences, related to family, community and identity. Although they can be distinguished from non-terrorists because of what they do, they are not necessarily mad.

Terrorism exists within society and is never separate from it, while the contexts of conflicts may change, conflict will remain, and terrorist violence will continue to affect our lives.

See also: Psychology of Terrorism; Beliefs of Terrorists and Terrorist Mindset; Targets.

References

Alexander, Y. and Gleason, J. M. (eds) (1981) *Behavioural and Quantitative Perspectives on Terrorism*, New York: Pergamon Press.

Reich, W. (ed.) (1990) *Origins of Terrorism: Psychologies, Ideologies, Theologies, States of Mind*, Cambridge: Cambridge University Press.

Taylor, M. and Quayle, E. (1994) *Terrorist Lives*, London: Brassey's Defence Publishers.

Further Reading

Crenshaw, M. (1986) 'The Psychology of Political Terrorism', in Hermann, M. G. (ed.) *Political Psychology*, San Francisco, CA: Jossey-Bass.

Crozier, B. (1960) *The Rebels*, Boston, MA: Beacon Press.

Kaplan, A. (1981) 'The Psychodynamics of Terrorism', in Alexander, Y. and Gleason, J. M. (eds) (1981) *Behavioural and Quantitative Perspectives on Terrorism*, New York: Pergamon, pp. 35–50.

Prolstein, R. M. (1991) *The Mind of the Political Terrorist*, Wilmington, DE: S. R. Books.

Strentz, T. (1987) 'A Hostage Psychological Guide', *FBI Law Enforcement Bulletin* (November), pp. 1–8.

Taylor, M. (1988) *The Terrorist*, London: Brassey's Defence Publishers.

Psychology of Terrorism

Beliefs of Terrorists

The actions of terrorist organisations are based on a subjective interpretation of reality that differs from the perceptions of the governments and societies they confront. The actions of terrorists are not governed by a consistency and reason that are based on accurate perceptions of reality; one of the aims of terrorist organisations is to convince their audiences to see the world as they do. An important aspect of the struggle between governments and terrorists concerns the **definition** of the conflict. Each side wishes to interpret the issues in terms of its own standards of political legitimacy. Belief systems composed of dominant images, symbols and myths contribute to perceptions (and misperceptions) which determine actions and expectations. The content and origin of terrorist beliefs affect why and how terrorist strategies are adopted, terrorist reactions to government policies, and the outcomes of terrorist challenges.

Systems of beliefs may be derived from numerous sources. The political and social environment in which the terrorist organisation operates comprises one set of origins. In this category can be included general culture variables (history, tradition, literature, religion), which are imparted to individual members of society through socialisation patterns, and formal ideologies, which are acquired in young adulthood and are consciously borrowed.

Sources of beliefs may also be internal. The situation in which terrorists operate is filled with stress and uncertainty, making particular beliefs relevant and satisfying and also persistent and hard to change. Both the mental stress and the ideological commitment inherent in terrorism encourage reliance on a rigid set of beliefs and inhibit flexibility and openness. Terrorists may be rational about convictions that the majority of society sees as deluded.

A significant element in the belief system is the image which can be a mental portrayal of oneself, of another actor, or of the world. Images are frequently stereotypical, falling into preconceived and rigid categories that simplify reality. Dehumanisation and deification of the enemy dominate thinking.

Most leftist revolutionary terrorists see themselves not as aggressors but as victims. Their self-perception is that they are representatives of the oppressed – workers or peasants – who are unable to help themselves. They are the enlightened among the mass of unenlightened; the elect, who unlike the masses recognise dangers. The struggle is an obligation and a duty, not a matter of voluntary choice. Often they think of themselves as morally superior, more sensitive, and more noble. In their self-definition, the term 'terrorist' has become a subjective label applied by the enemy, and as global values have changed in the aftermath of anti-colonial struggles the image of 'freedom fighter' or 'national liberation front' has become a superior legitimising device. Many terrorists define their role as that of sacrificial victim; whether or not this image accords with reality, the notion of being willing to die for a cause is important to the terrorist's self-perception. Revolutionary terrorists often see the enemy as much more powerful than themselves, with many alternatives to choose from; terrorists have no course of action but terrorism, which they see as a response to government oppression, not a free choice on their part.

Two other aspects of terrorists' beliefs about the nature of the conflict are intriguing. The first is the tendency to define the struggle in elaborately legalistic terms. They do not see what they are doing as murder or killing – instead they perform 'executions after trials'. Their victims are usually termed traitors. If they are kidnapped they are held in people's prisons. A second feature of the terrorists' view of struggle is their military imagery and symbolism.

Although terrorists appeal to popular support and often seem to believe that mass revolution is their goal, little attention is devoted to the development of beliefs about the role of popular support. As exemplified by the Basque terrorist organisation, ETA, the inevitability of support is assumed. For terrorists, **victims** among the 'enemy' are not seen as individuals but as representatives of the hostile group. If terrorists admit that innocent victims exist, they may blame the government either for refusing to concede their demands or ignoring warnings. They often refuse to accept responsibility for violence. Any action in the service of the cause can be interpreted as a success.

There can be no failure if all violence brings the desired change nearer.

A significant source for terrorists' beliefs is the political and social environment from which the group springs, and often its historical context. Ideology is a powerful influence – an international factor that cuts across national situations but may be interpreted differently in specific circumstances. The primacy of political ideas in motivating terrorism contributes to the resemblances one finds among terrorist groups from different cultural contexts.

In certain cases terrorism reflects social reality – in nationalistic groups individuals are already socialised into patterns of thinking that can make violence acceptable if it appears feasible and productive: Basque resistance to the Spanish state, Armenian opposition to the Turks, and Irish Catholic bitterness toward the British are integral parts of their respective political cultures.

With regard to ideologies, terrorists are not inventors of these, as they tend to be action-oriented rather than philosophical. The fact that nationalism and national liberation have been the greatest sources of political legitimacy in the post-colonial world has contributed to the growth of terrorism. Both Marxist-Leninism (with variants of Trotskyism, Maoism, Castroism or Guevarism), and Fascism have contributed to terrorist doctrine. Although the individual violence associated with terrorism is not condoned by orthodox Marxists, many contemporary terrorists feel obliged to aid the force of historical progress with violence.

Some commentators have argued that many terrorists are in fact ambivalent about the use of violence. This internal conflict may explain why it is necessary for terrorists to believe that they have no choice and that the enemy bears ultimate responsibility for violence. The structure of the terrorist belief system, portraying an all-powerful authority figures relentlessly hostile to a smaller, powerless victim may reflect early relationships with parents, particularly of sons with fathers. Their beliefs may reflect feelings of inferiority, low self-esteem and helplessness.

To many terrorists the neutralisation of guilt is important. The individual who becomes a terrorist is likely to experience guilt for violent acts, so it is necessary for terrorists to maintain the belief that someone else is responsible and that their actions transcend normal standards of moral behaviour.

Once established, belief systems are resistant to change. For example, terrorists deny that there are innocent victims, despite proof to the contrary. Terrorists tend to believe only information sources they trust. Certain types of images can help terrorists to avoid dealing with the complex values inherent in political decisions. The 'inherent bad faith' model of the enemy indicates that the adversary never acts in good faith.

In hostage seizures, terrorists are involved in making decisions that involve momentous consequences. Not only do they accept personal risk, but the fate of the organisation to which they are passionately committed is at stake.

The importance of the group to terrorism is well established. Tendencies towards cohesion and solidarity, present in all primary groups, lead to the suppression of dissent and the internalisation of group standards and norms. Members have to be totally obedient to group norms and members of terrorist organisations have to accept not only a set of political beliefs but systems of social and psychological regulation.

Despite pressures for cohesion, disagreements exist within terrorist organisations; for example, factionalism has been endemic in the Palestinian groups. Factions of terrorist organisations seem to disagree over the best means to achieve collective ends. Variations in belief systems may account for differences in methods. The circumstances of a terrorist group – isolated from society, under constant threat and danger, lacking reliable information sources and channels – and their reliance on rigid and inflexible beliefs about their relationship to the world suggest that the terrorist's ability to adapt to reality is limited. Equally, terrorists are not capable of correctly anticipating the consequences of their actions. Understanding their belief systems enables governments to predict terrorists' susceptibility to communications. Forcing terrorists to accept the falseness of their beliefs or denying them any way out of a threatening situation may lead to their emotional breakdown and a resolution of a crisis.

Characteristics

The terrorist is basically a sociopath. That is he or she feels no guilt at killing or injuring innocent civilians or members of the security forces. A terrorist profile is difficult to construct, as they differ greatly in their values according to their culture and cause. Many theories regard the terrorist as a peculiar personality with clearly identifiable character traits. A cross-section of rural and urban terrorist guerrilla groups shows that they are composed largely of single men aged 22 to 24 who have some university education. The women terrorists, except for those in the Baader Meinhof and Red Army Faction in Germany, and an occasional leading figure in the Irish Republican Army, Japanese Red Army and Popular Front for the Liberation of Palestine, are preoccupied with support rather than operational roles. Terrorists come in general from affluent, urban middle-class families, many of whom enjoy considerable social prestige. Like their fathers, many of the older terrorists have been trained for the professions and may have practiced these occupations before their commitment to a terrorist life. Whether they turned to terrorism as university students or later, most were provided with an anarchistic or Marxist world view and recruited into terrorist operations while at university. One can only say that they are physically fit, intelligent, received some higher education which they failed to complete and are the offspring of professional middle-class parents.

Terrorists live in a fantasy world, in the early stages they are fighting a fantasy war and ultimately grow to believe in their own propaganda. They have a desire to promote change by the threat or use of violence as a result of frustration that they feel no other way will bring results. Weapons symbolise power, and they fondle weapons with loving care.

Their aim is to draw attention to a cause, to provoke over-reaction by the government in an attempt to undermine public confidence and to promote public fear and an atmosphere of alarm. Public reaction is against the terrorists immediately after an incident. The terrorist carries out activities as a result of frustration, feeling that the best way to communicate the message is with the gun. The terrorist tends to operate in the bounds of normal psychology in the manner of the individual, operating under stress.

Operational terrorists tend to be young, and a reason for this is that we are now experiencing the phenomenon of second generation terrorists. There is a tradition of inducting children into paramilitary structures at an early age, by families who pass on the message that violence is the way to struggle for rights.

Further Reading

Long, D. E. (1990) *The Anatomy of Terrorism*, New York: Free Press.

Potter, D. J. (1987) *Terrorism: Characteristics and General Aspects of Psychological Warfare*, Unpublished MS in the Library, Royal Military Academy, Sandhurst.

Fear

Today any person can become a victim of a terrorist, regardless of his or her innocence or neutrality. Fear is deliberately used as a weapon to achieve social change in a Western society, where other legal means of change are available. The legal systems of a democratic state regard a terrorist as just another criminal; but the terrorist, on command of his superiors, will kill without hatred people in whom he has no personal interest, while claiming to be a patriot and a soldier. The terrorist tries to show that his actions are a response to the denial of basic freedoms.

Gaps between people (persons in positions of power, the establishment and discontented elements) have always existed, and continue to separate management from labour, power elites from students, and the urban areas from the countryside. Much of this discord has existed without serving as a catalyst for terrorist campaigns. The contemporary terrorist has identified these issues, and does not act until he has made a careful and rational analysis of the general conditions and manipulative causes which are latent within his society – as well as of the present and potential strength of his group. The organisation and extension of a terrorist campaign are predicated on a supportive propaganda message to attract and condition people to serve as followers and supporters of an extremist organisation. Terrorists search for people who are hurt by fate or nature, that is those suffering from an inferiority complex, craving power and influence but defeated by unfavourable circumstances.

Today's terrorist tries to influence behaviour by extra-normal means through the use or threat of violence while simultaneously creating an atmosphere of perpetual and escalating terror, conducted by patriots whose only options are the bullet or the bomb. Although the terrorist avoids undertaking any action which might fall beyond the ambit of a real or a contrived popular cause, he is ultimately nothing more than a criminal who tries to exploit any available natural social pathology.

See also: Terror and Terrorism.

Reference

Wolf, J. B. (1981) *Fear of Fear: A Survey of Terrorist Operations and Controls in Open Societies*, New York: Plenum Press.

Indoctrination

Many observers believe that terrorists have to be aware only of political indoctrination. Marighella and Debray believed one could become a good fighter only by learning the art of fighting which involves everything from physical training to the learning of many kinds of job, especially those involving manual skills.

According to Marighella and Debray, the accomplished terrorist has to know something of the mechanics of radio, telephones and electronics, and should be able to make maps and plans. The recruit to the terrorist group had to prove himself in action before being given complete training and there are many examples among the Germans, Palestinians, and Latin Americans of this process. In some Latin American movements, the raw recruit, as an act of good faith, has to kill a policeman or soldier before being fully accepted into the band. A terrorist needs discipline and has to be taught the virtue of obeying orders, but after that the need is more for grounding in intelligence work than in strictly commando-type assault operations. There is a need primarily for small-arms instruction, plenty of range practice and a thorough knowledge of explosives and detonators. Training can be of a low level; but what the recruits lack in this respect they make up for in zeal and cruelty.

Terrorists pay much attention to the use of disguise and in successful groups international figures that have reappeared several times look quite different on each occasion. To use explosive devices requires considerable training, and it is bomb making which divides the professionals from the amateurs. To explode a device demands not only technical ability, but a cool head and a steady hand.

Only by taking part in a raid and by a baptism of fire can a terrorist prove himself. In several groups criminals have been welcomed into the movement for their technical skills, and sometimes for the doctrinal satisfaction the participation of genuine working-class outlaws gives to young middle-class or well-to-do terrorists beset by guilt.

The reason for the primacy attached to the act of killing is that it binds the would-be terrorist irrevocably to the organisation. Up to that moment he or she could back out, but once the candidates have killed they are committed. Those terrorists who wish to quit give the reasons of wishing to lead respectable lives, the hatred of killing, reduced opportunities and fewer targets. They are not necessarily fanatics, but some are irrational or crazy. At different stages they are happy in their calling. Terrorists join a group without considering the fateful step and anxiety sets in when the entry trap closes. There is an extreme penalty for defection, and individuals in the same group often do not trust each other. Tensions are many and very severe with strong emphasis on differences of opinion. Leadership, discipline planning and execution of actions can be very lax. Terrorists are unable to cope with any government's declining to take an initiative on abductions and intimidation, and are sensitive to perceived loss of sympathies, especially if they see their task as consciousness-raising.

Terrorist Mindset

Most terrorists are in their early twenties and it is unsurprising that certain characteristics of a terrorist's mind are often attributed to adolescence and youth. Many terrorists are zealots who seek aggressive confrontations with authority in the name of social justice. Over the last two decades three character traits have become apparent: terrorists' handling of their own emotions is disturbed, which shows itself in fear to engage in real commitments. Fear of love leads them to choose violence. Attitude towards authority is disturbed and ambivalent, in the sense that a principally negative attitude to traditional authorities is combined with an uncritical subjection under the new counter-authorities. Most importantly, they have a disturbed relationship with their own identity; and having failed to develop an identity of their own they try to achieve this by the use of violence.

They are unable to be part of the community, lose the capacity to understand reality and experience aimlessness due to lack of felt authority. To be effective they have to pursue absolute ends, which coalesce into violence. Driving forces behind terrorism include the assertion of masculinity, or femininity in the case of women, the desire for depersonalisation, that is to get outside or away from oneself, as a result of a chronic lack of self-esteem; the desire for intimacy, and belief in the magic of violence and blood. Terrorists tend to resemble each other, regardless of their cause. Most are individuals for whom terrorism provides profound personal satisfaction, a sense of fulfilment through total dedication to the point of self-sacrifice; and a sense of power through inflicting pain and death upon other humans. Insecurity, risk-seeking behaviour and its associated suicidal intentions are present in varying mixtures in the terrorist. Out of this insecurity, the need for self-realisation and ego inflation arises.

Terrorists often over-simplify complex issues to black and white. The groups are intensely intellectualised, inward-looking and politically naive in their theorising. The terrorist lives out a fantasy war convinced that he has broad support from numerous like-minded followers.

Terrorists have many pent-up concerns about an individual's inability to change society. Apart from frustration there is also self-righteousness, as the terrorists believe implicitly in their own rectitude.

Intolerance, dogmatism, authoritarianism and a ruthless treatment of their own people who deviate from the set view are common to terrorist mentality.

Many terrorists seem to feel that a reasonable, if not near-perfect future lies just around the corner, once the present order has been destroyed. This utopianism, coupled with frustration at the slow pace of social change, frequently produces left- and right-wing political extremism. Terrorists are often lonely people who use religious or political ideals to interest political recruits. For many of them, the terrorist group has been their first family.

To assert their own existence terrorist actions are laden with symbolic overtones, involving the choice of captives, locations, weapons and timing.

Many terrorist murders are cold-blooded, but captors who hold hostages for protracted periods tend to develop a kind of bond with them that makes cold-blooded murder less likely.

Terrorists externalise and blame others for the problems of the world. They project their own faults onto others such as the government. The terrorist tends to be inward looking and thus a fantasy war situation tends to develop.

Terrorists are frustrated individuals and have a pent up anger that they are unable to bring about change unless they use violence. Self-righteousness is a common characteristic and they believe totally that they have a right to carry out acts of violence in the name of the cause. Intolerance can result from this situation.

The terrorist seems to believe that a near perfect future lies just around the corner once the present order is destroyed. They are lonely people who suffer from severe mental and emotional short-comings. There is a desire to assert their own group existence to draw attention to himself and his cause. Deviant personalities can thrive and the two types encountered are the angry paranoid and the stimulus seeking psychopath. The terrorist displays limited feelings toward others including his or her own group; and is very task orientated. The willingness to die varies considerably between different cultures.

See also: Beliefs of Terrorists; Hostage Taking; Psychology of Terrorism; Stockholm Syndrome.

Terrorist Types

Counter-terrorist organisations all over the world have to try to understand something of the dynamics of the terrorist personality as it functions within certain roles in the group. Three distinct roles are discernible and frequently emerge in terrorist groups found in democratic nations.

The *leader* is a person of total dedication, a trained theoretician with a strong personality; the *activist-operator is* a person with an anti-social personality, frequently an ex-convict, an opportunist; and the *idealist* is usually the university dropout, the minor functionary, with a life pattern of searching for the truth. The leaders of leftist groups were often female, i.e. Nancy Perry of the Symbionese Liberation Army (SLA) in the USA; Ulrike Meinhof of the Baader-Meinhof in Germany; Fusako Shigenobu of the Rengo Shekigun (Japanese Red Army), and Norma Aristoto of the Montoneros in Argentina were active in the 1980s. They were cynical but dedicated and showed few signs of self-interest. Such leaders saw themselves as unique with superior ability and knowledge.

Whilst a leader can be dedicated, he or she is not nearly as dedicated as paranoid personalities within the group. The paranoid individual refuses to be confused by the facts, unlike the leader, and only his interpretation of events is correct; he is right, and others, unless they totally agree with the leader, are not right. The leader is more single-minded, intelligent and theoretically oriented than most people; is more suspicious and inclined to interpret events selectively, but not to the degree found in true mental illness.

The leader reads people well and appeals to their needs, and uses followers in comfortable, fulfilling roles. Allowance is made for the followers' needs for recognition, achievement and self-fulfilment. Each follower is able to be a self-appointed general.

Police involvement with the leader is infrequent, since the leader is behind the scenes as a policy-developer. Occasionally the leader may venture out with the group to show it how to accomplish a particular task. If apprehended, the leader is bright enough to maintain silence. Should he or she begin to talk, a generally superior attitude and an assured discussion of the 'conspiracy theory of history' will begin to emerge. This is true if the leader thinks the interrogator is a possible convert.

The role of opportunist operator is generally a male role, held by one whose criminal activity predates his political involvement. He has similarities to the anti-social personality, also known as the sociopath or psychopath. Terrorist groups that operate against democracies appear to embrace this person, the muscle of the organisation. Some of the more infamous include Donald DeFreeze of the Symbionese Liberation Army; Greg Adornedo of the Emiliano Zapata Unit (EZU); Andreas Baader and Hans Joachim Klein of the Baader-Meinhof gang, and Akira Niehei of the Japanese Red Army. The opportunist generally is oblivious to the needs of others and unencumbered by the capacity to feel guilt or sympathy. He is usually recruited from the prison population by the leader or the third functionary in the organisation, the idealist. The intelligence of the opportunist varies; the brighter he is, the more of a threat he could pose to the leader. The opportunist could take over the group, therefore, to maintain control if the leader became paranoid. Relationships between leader and opportunist are extremely sensitive – and internecine war is a threat. Given his penchant for aggressive behaviour, his criminal experience and his anti-social orientation, the opportunist is well-suited for the responsibilities of a terrorist group field commander. Without the opportunist a group is radical only in rhetoric and he provides the terror element of the terrorist group. The opportunist is familiar to the police officer. The leader of the group can lure the opportunist into the organisation by making him a compellingly attractive offer. This process can be and has been used by the police to develop the opportunist as an informant defector or informant in place.

The idealist role in the group is the soldier; the idealistic follower who reconnoitres buildings prior to bombings, follows the opportunist into the bank, carries the messages and is generally the cannon fodder for the revolution. His rhetoric is heavy with statements calling for protracted wars of national liberation; but generally there is lack of depth in his rhetoric, and he merely parrots pet phrases. He is the group member most likely to become committed to new ideologies, but is unlikely to become an informant. The extreme idealist or 'true believer' is not a successful person, and his self-concept is poor, for he views his life only as a member of the group.

Suicide bombings have again become a feature of terrorist attacks over the past decade, in particular in Israel and Palestine by Hamas and Hizbullah members against Jewish targets. Attacks have occurred on buses, in shopping areas, on the street and in cars. Such bombings have had a considerable political effect and Israeli society has felt particularly vulnerable. Everyday activity in society can be severely disrupted and great terror is invoked in the people. As with many terrorists, suicide bombers exaggerate their success particularly in terms of recruits to the cause and the consequence of such attacks.

Suicide missions have been carried out throughout history. The medieval assassins specialised in suicide missions and were dreaded. Irish terrorism has been highlighted over the years by characters who wish to starve themselves in prison. The kamikaze attacks by Japanese pilots are still remembered from the Second World War, and indeed, in Japanese cultural tradition, suicide played an essential role. In Sri Lanka the Tamil Tigers committed many suicide attacks against the Singhalese majority to achieve recognition.

In the Islamic world, the suicide bombers are young men from poor families, and especially those living in Palestinian refugee camps (Laqueur, 2001). Many such people believe they are going to paradise and that their families will receive large cash payments if they become martyrs. Such potential martyrs are deeply religious but easily led.

More recent suicide attacks have ranged from the suicide bombing of the USS Cole, a guided missile destroyer which was refuelling at a port in Yemen in October 2000 that killed seventeen sailors, to the World Trade Center and Pentagon attacks on September 11 which killed around 3000 persons. Further suicide bombings at sea cannot be ruled out, and single engine low flying planes or helicopters packed with explosives are also possible. Certainly after the suicide kidnappings of four large commercial aircraft on September 11, anything is possible.

The suicide bomber can defeat any so-called adequate physical security and obviously no national or international law can deal with them.

Martyrdom acts of suicide terrorism in turn provide sect leadership with a continual source of martyrs to assist in enticing others into the ranks. Although many willingly went to their deaths, others were drugged or duped. The suicide bombers in the Middle East believe that as long as Palestinians cannot live with dignity and in peace, Israelis should not expect to either. Even though suicide is forbidden by Islamic law, Muslim clerics have lent their support to martyrdom. Suicide bombers say they are poor and have no equipment and can only combat evil by acts of suicide.

Suicide bombers like other terrorists often gloat over their successes – none more so than one of the early 'missions' when 241 US Marines lost their lives when their barracks was attacked in Beirut in 1983.

Suicide itself is forbidden in the Islamic Faith so the Islamic radical groups do not see themselves as suicide bombers but as martyrs, who are noble victims sacrificing their lives in jihad. To die in the cause of Islam is to die a glorious martyr and to ensure oneself an immediate place in paradise with heavenly delights. These rewards in the after-life are thought to be stressed to recruits in their training.

An Islamic terrorist is identified as a Shahid, a hero. In training it is understood that students gain a fanatical hatred of the West and a perception that the West is responsible for all the woes of the Muslim world. After the death of a bomber the families are believed to be well looked after and given significant financial packages. Suicide bombers initially believe along with Islamists that Western values must be rejected as they lead to moral chaos and threaten Muslim identity and self-esteem. It is not surprising therefore that Islam accepts as natural that Muslims should rule non-Muslim.

Islamikaze is a contemporary view which holds that Muslim fundamentalist suicide bombers are not necessarily suicidal, although there are similarities with the Japanese kamikaze pilots active in the Second World War in motivation, organisation, ideology and execution of their task.

Training camps for foreign Muslims have existed in Pakistan for example. The instructors come from Egypt, Saudi Arabia and Yemen and train personnel in using all types of weapons. Furthermore, instruction includes urban guerrilla combat, sabotage, handling and concocting explosives and mounting car bombs. The trainees are all designated, dispatched and financed by their home Islamic organisations.

The Islamists gather their force, their passion and their deep commitment around charismatic leaders who provide them with sincerity, devotion and scholarly knowledge.

The determination to kill the enemy is the driving force. The plan for killing is prepared by the operator and the person chosen must be ready when sent by the operators. Those who are the Islamikaze are young with few responsibilities in life, not particularly successful in their lives and therefore have poor self-esteem. They are a loose grouping of people.

The number of suicide attacks between 1980 and 2000 rose rapidly – the highest figure being among the Liberation Tigers of Tamil Ealam (LTTE) in Sri Lanka and India (168). Fifty-two suicide missions were undertaken by Hizbullah and pro-Syrian groups in Argentina, Lebanon and Kuwait; twenty-two reported by Hamas in Israel and fifteen by the Kurdistan Workers Party (PKK) in Turkey (Gunaratria in Griset and Mahan, 2003: 221).

Many groups are likely to use suicide bombers to infiltrate target countries and conduct suicide attacks against the infrastructures of Western societies in the future (Griset and Mahan, 2003: 225).

See also: Islam; Pakistan; Psychology of Terrorism: Terrorist Mindset.

References

Griset, P. L. and Mahan, S. (2003) *Terrorism in Perspective*, Thousand Oaks, CA, London and New Delhi: Sage Publications.

Gunaratna, R. (2003) 'Suicide Terrorism A Global Threat' in Griset, P. L. and Mahan, S. *Terrorism in Perspective*, Thousand Oaks, CA, London and New Delhi: Sage Publications.

Laqueur, W. (2001) *The New Terrorism: Fanaticism and the Arms of Mass Destruction*, London: Phoenix Press.

Therapy

In anarchist doctrine, atrocities serve two purposes. They were a means of producing politically favourable reactions in others, and they were ends in themselves, enabling the terrorist to gain self-respect. Different terrorist movements subsequently emphasised one purpose at the expense of the other. The more successful political movements have always stressed terror as a means; most groups, which see terror as expedient, have functioned in colonial areas where the limited goal of the enemy's withdrawal was feasible. Arguments about the effectiveness of atrocities are common within a terrorist movement, causing an original nucleus to split into a proliferation of organisations like Irgun and the Stern Gang in Israel, Al-Fatah, PFLP, IRA Officials and IRA Provisionals. Proliferation usually results from arguments about how far terrorists can expand the scope of atrocities without making the target's will to resist inflexible.

Some terrorist movements have stressed terror as an end in itself. They are less interesting as political forces, but like the psychotic who reflects in an exaggerated way tendencies not usually noticed in ordinary persons, these terrorist movements should be studied because each teaches something about the necessary foundations of terrorist movements everywhere.

Terrorism is a form of conflict, and most people enjoy conflict for its own sake. One can gain therapeutic value from conflict, especially if a cause seems worthy.

Serious conflict embraces a variety of concerns. Most people have good reason to feel ashamed of the joy they feel when conflict seems unfair, irrelevant to any achievable social object and in which the participants are being consumed by their own hate. The difference between a normal person, who enjoys a good fight, and a sadist or masochist, is that the sadist inflicts violence on another person solely as an instrument for pleasure and the masochist uses himself for that purpose.

The satisfaction most people get from fighting is related to feelings of respect they feel for the other party, for themselves, and for a cause; these feelings are usually embodied in conventions which are supposed to regulate the conflict even after victory.

The anarchist terrorist assumes that society is corrupt, and as a member of it, the terrorist is corrupt at least to the extent that one limits oneself by society's conventions. To grasp one's true self, one must break through the boundaries of 'normal' actions, thoughts and feelings. In anarchist terms the greatest atrocity a terrorist could commit would be to murder a colleague for the sole purpose of proving himself free of guilt.

One does not know how deep the belief in terror as personal therapy is in contemporary groups, and what new levels of atrocities against themselves is conceivable even to terrorists. It may be impossible simply to pay lip-service to a set of ideas; people will keep trying to raise the commitment of group members to violence.

Reference

Petrakins, G. (1980) 'Terrorism: Multinational Corporation and the Nation State: The Anarchists Rationale for Terrorism (Pt.2)', *Law and Order*, vol. 28, no. 6, pp. 22–24.

Public Perceptions

The effects of the **media** are different for enemies and supporters of terrorism and mere bystanders. In many societies where there is sustained terrorism by indigenous groups, the public is aware of the political goals and ideology of the terrorists. Terrorism receives extensive media coverage, but the media does not invariably reflect the official perspective.

With regard to public concern, public attention can be short-lived and the political results can fall short of what the terrorist wants. The issue for the public is more the violence than the cause. What is obvious is the greater the terrorism, the greater the concern. The economic costs of terrorism can affect the public – rising insurance, more taxes to pay for damage and lost businesses through terrorist action. In most instances, explicit approval of political violence is low, except in places like Palestine with a long history of 'armed struggle'. Militant nationalism can have a high level of support if the nationalists can win the public over to the view that they have suffered an injustice. More intoler-

ance tends to be shown to revolutionary terrorists whose aim is less clear. Indeed, such action can cause a backlash with increased support for tough law and order measures.

Generally, the hope that terrorism would provoke the authorities into massive indiscriminate repression which would turn the public against the government does not happen (Paletz and Schmid, 1992).

State terrorism to destroy legitimate movements of liberation exists. Gandhi is reported to have said that it is best to resist oppression by violent means than to submit. Can terrorism as a considered method to overcome oppression with as little loss of life as possible be, in contrast, less unjustifiable than state terrorism? Terrorists have their manifestos and carry with them their grievances. They have a disdain for the institutions of civil society and therefore the ideal they suppress is nihilistic.

The public are fascinated by terrorists, so too are the press. In reporting terrorism, journalism incorporates selection and discrimination, they illustrate graphically the fascination with dread, directed by persons who lack concerns and restraints on which a stable society rests (Frey and Morris, 1991).

An area of particular concern to the general public in many countries is when holiday areas are targeted.

Tourism is an important and sensitive industry and any upsurge in terrorism affects the numbers of tourists visiting certain parts of the world i.e. Americans coming to Europe and tourists visiting the Middle East. In Spain in the 1980s and 1990s the Basque separatist organisation ETA targeted beaches and resorts which led to a fall off in **UK** tourists and threatened to disrupt the **Olympic Games** in Barcelona in 1992. Events as far apart in time as Lockerbie and **September 11** attacks on the **World Trade Center** in New York led to a curtailment or decline, at least in the short term, of visitors travelling to the **USA**. At the start of the **Gulf War**, a plane was stranded in Kuwait after making a refuelling stop on a flight from the UK to Malaysia, and crew and passengers held hostage for many weeks in Iraq. Tourists have been killed or injured in **Peru** as a result of attacks by the Shining Path guerrilla group and in **Egypt** by Islamic fundamentalists. Tourists are attacked because they are symbolic of capitalism, they are from wealthier countries and much tourism is state-sponsored.

Holiday homes have been attacked in Wales (by the IRA in league with some members of Welsh extremist organisations) and in Corsica. Even in game parks in Kenya, Zambia and Zimbabwe tourists have been targeted.

Across Europe (in particular Spain) and in parts of the USA and Latin America there are links between terrorism, drug trafficking and crime (both petty and organised). Tour operators obviously work closely with travel agents and the public to avoid such terrorist hotspots. Wider world travel has always carried risks, and both terrorists and tourists alike are aware of this risk.

References

Frey, R. and Morris, C. (1991) *Violence, Terrorism and Justice*, Cambridge: Cambridge University Press.
Paletz, D. L. and Schmid, A. P. (1992) *Terrorism and the Media*, London: Sage Publications.

R

Rabin, Yitzhak

b.1922; d. 1995

Yitzhak Rabin, the Israeli Prime Minister had been closely involved in trying to bring about a permanent peace in the Middle East through the *Oslo Accords* especially with **Egypt** and a resolution of the Palestinian crisis. In November 1995 he was murdered by a Jewish extremist Yigal Amir, who was hostile to the idea of land being given to Palestinians on the West Bank and Jewish settlements being taken down. His replacement was Benjamin Netanyahu a man with hard-line views on the whole peace process (Cooley, 2002).

Rabin had been a soldier, who turned to peace-making later in life and became pragmatic in his approach to the **PLO**. He had been instrumental in expelling over 400 members of **Hamas** to the mountains of south **Lebanon**, which led to a resurgence in both Hamas membership and the development of the Intifada.

Rabin's assassination was seen as the first step in a campaign of mass murder designed to disrupt the peace process. The incident occurred only a year after another ultra-nationalistic Jew, Dr Baruch Goldstein killed 29 and wounded 150 Muslim worshippers at the 'Cave of the Patriarchs' before being beaten to death. These events showed the intense religious fervour involved in the enmity towards secular government in **Israel**, and that in the eyes of the extremists the Oslo peace process was playing into the hands of the Palestinian moderates.

From this time radical elements reasserted themselves in Israeli politics, and the Rabin government was held responsible for the rise in suicide bombings.

Though his **assassin**, Yigal Amir was a loner, Rabin's murder was not committed in a vacuum but against an atmosphere in which the extreme right had incited young militants to commit acts of violence. It had the effect of bringing down the Labour government and carrying the Likud Party to power.

Reference

Cooley, J. K. (2002) *Unholy Wars: Afghanistan, America and International Terrorism*, London: Pluto Press.

Ramzi, Ahmed Yousef

b. 1968

Ahmed Ramzi was the individual most responsible for the bombing of the **World Trade Center** in New York in 1993. He was a Palestinian whose journey to the **USA** in 1993 began in **Iraq**. Yousef was at home with intellectuals, ingenious, urbane and very skilled, acting as his own lawyer at his trial in 1996. His background was somewhat shrouded in mystery due to the various forged documents that he used. At various times he was closely linked with Iraq, **Pakistan**, and the USA.

He had regular documentation purporting to show him to be Abdul Basit from Kuwait, which at the time of the Iraqi invasion of Kuwait was a ploy used by Iraqi authorities to fool the Americans into thinking he came from Kuwait.

He was charged with conspiracy to bomb American aircraft – twelve in total – in January 1995. He also worked under at least a dozen aliases (Mylroie, 2001). He was in favour of a project to kill 250,000 innocent humans by toppling New York's tallest tower onto its twin, even using cyanide gas as a lethal enhancement.

Reference

Mylroie, L. (2001) *Study of Revenge: The First World Trade Center Attack and Saddam Hussein's War against America*, Washington, DC: The AEI Press.

Rebel

Rebels become involved in dissent in order to try and change government institutions, policies or personnel, which also as their objectives and the individuals' means, go beyond democratic values and behaviour by employing illegal activity or tactics which can include civil disobedience, protests, demonstrations, marches, sit-ins and riots (Flood, 1991).

People participate in collective action for a number of reasons. Sympathisers will participate if they receive something in return such as appearing on television. Participation will occur if leaders arise who create organisations to pool resources and it is helped if well-financed outsiders substitute the costs of participation. People will participate if they could be certain that their participation will be reciprocated.

Narrow self-interest is often at the core of a rebel's view.

Reference

Flood, S. (1991) *International Terrorism: Policy Indicators*, Chicago, IL: University of Chicago Office of International Criminal Justice.

Rebellion

Rebellion can be considered as open resistance to the authority and commands of a ruler or government. It can take the form of civil war or revolution if it persists or grows. There is violent opposition by a substantial body of persons against the lawfully constituted authority of a state, in the attempt to overthrow it. A rebellion can succeed in installing in power members of the same class as those whom they replace.

Religion

Some of today's terrorist group's can no longer specifically be considered as secular Marxist organisations with specific nationalist and socialist goals. While calling for socio-economic betterment for their people, their motivation is religious. Although their demands have a political content this is distinctly secondary. Violence in the name of religion has been used since Herod the Great (*c.*73–4 BC), but there has been a recent re-emergence of religious terrorism. Both the Inquisition in the 15th and 16th centuries and Oliver Cromwell (1599–1660) practiced terror in the name of religion. In the West where religious faith has been diluted with materialism, the abolitionists' sanction has largely been lost. This is not the case with certain **Third World** movements, for instance the radical **Shi'ites**. Specific historical events have led to the emergence of the new terrorists.

Iran's fundamentalist Shi'ite revolution is primary among these. Besides **Iran**, the Ayatollah's message inspires Shi'ite communities in **Iraq**, **Lebanon** and elsewhere in the Persian Gulf to lash out against the Western influences that permeate the regimes they perceive as corrupt and oppressive. Syria's quasi-Shi'ite Alawite rulers share a number of values, goals and tactical objectives with Iran.

The main goal of the radical Shi'ite factions in Lebanon was to undermine the relatively pragmatic leaders of Lebanon's Shi'ite community and pave the way for more radical, fundamentalist influence. Displaying the impotence of moderate policies, as compared with effective extremist activism is a means of accomplishing this.

Similar motivations lay behind the seizure of the US embassy in Teheran in 1979 by radical Shi'ites. In February they had toppled the relatively moderate Shah government which was then engaged in close political and economic contacts with the **United States**.

Indian Sikh terrorism is also based on religion. The **Sikhs** are acting in reaction to Hindu repression of their aspirations for autonomy. The assassination of Indira Gandhi, subsequent Sikh-Hindu bloodshed, and threatened international terrorism, share some of the more extreme qualities associated with Shi'ite violence.

Violence motivated by religious beliefs is more difficult to cope with than its secular predecessors for several reasons. Threats to kill hostages are credible. For Islamic fundamentalists, killing of 'non-believers' is not perceived as murder. Threats of self-sacrifice are also believable for the same reason. Religious ideologies are also extremely tough for any intelligence organisation to penetrate. Powerful, absolutist convictions are a barrier to the recruiting of agents, even when access can be arranged, and the rudimentary forms of communication used by such groups are often among the most impregnable.

Retaliation to acts of religious terrorism is extremely difficult. A Libyan or Palestinian guerrilla base may be considered an easy and 'acceptable' target, but a mosque complex or holy shrine would not. In the 1980s in the case of Beirut, virtually the entire community was used to disperse and hide hostages.

The more pragmatic a terrorist, the easier it is to negotiate a solution. At one extreme lie money-motivated **kidnapping** of businessmen in Latin America. A group of professionals has come into being, whose business it is to settle the level of nearly automatic ransoms in such cases. Most are now resolved in this manner. In the middle lie the politically based demands of classic secular organisations that use violence as a tool. The new breed of extremists represents the opposite pole. Their demands are absolute, their hidden motivations obscure, their threshold of violence low.

In **India**, Hindu fundamentalism has led to violent clashes and massacres which have reverberated internationally. In Israel Jewish fundamentalists have used violence to try to upset Arab-Jewish peace negotiations.

Over the past decade there has been an increase in religiously motivated terrorism in countries as far apart as **Algeria** where thousands

have died or been injured to **Japan**, where religious **cults** have utilised gas agents to kill and injure and strike terrible fear into the populace. Nigeria and Indonesia are being torn apart by religious strife between Muslims and Christians. Muslim ideals within the Palestinian organisations are split between the hard line hawks and doves. Palestinian Sunnis flock to **Hamas** and Palestine Islamic **Jihad**. Palestinian Shi'ites support Iranian operatives. Hamas has undertaken a spiritual and political declaration of war on Israel, **Zionism**, allies of Israel and others opposed to creating a religious state throughout Palestine. The white supremacist ultra Protestant Ku Klux Klan has a legacy of violent opposition to Catholicism, Judaism and Black American rights. To many observers, the KKK is more racist than religious (Harmon, 2000).

Religion can produce a visible division between groups i.e. Indians are Hindus and Pakistanis are Muslims; Croats are Roman Catholic, Serbs are Orthodox and Albanians are Muslims.

Religions involve core values, defining what is good and bad and which are held as absolute truth. This situation has helped fundamentalist groups to gain strength and power. Fundamentalists organise their lives and communities around their religious beliefs and many are willing to sacrifice and even die for those beliefs. This is especially the case in Christianity, Islam, Judaism and Hinduism. These movements challenge the values and practices of secular political organisations. Terrible atrocities and wonderful works alike have been created in the name of most of the world's religions.

The rise of Islamic fundamentalism has created many difficulties – they reject Western oriented secular states in favour of governments more explicitly oriented toward Islamic values. These movements reflect anti-Western sentiment.

See also: Islam; Shi'ites; Sikh Extremism.

References

Goldstein, J. S. (1999) *International Relations*, Harlow: Longman.

Harmon, C. C. (2000) *Terrorism Today*, London: Frank Cass.

Further Reading

Rapoport, D. C. and Alexander, Y. (eds) (1982) *The Morality of Terrorism: Religious and Secular Justification*, New York: Pergamon Press.
— (1984) 'Fear and Trembling: Terrorism in Three Religious Traditions', *American Political Science Review*, vol. 78, no. 3, pp. 658–77.
— (1990) 'Religion and Terror: Thugs, Assassins and Zealots' in Kegley, C. W. (ed.) *International Terrorism: Characteristics, Causes, Controls*, New York: St Martin's Press.
Sutherland, C.W. (1987) *Disciples of Destruction: The Religious Origins of War and Terrorism*, Buffalo, New York: Prometheus Press.

Responses *see* Counter/Anti-Terrorism

Restraint

Prevention and perspective are two keys to dealing with terrorism, including political **kidnapping**. A substantial degree of physical security ought to be provided for those who are at particular risk. Western nations have to build up security for their government officials overseas.

Meeting the legitimate aspirations of the world's downtrodden is an important means of long-range prevention, so that small groups do not become sufficiently frustrated to seek satisfaction through unacceptable levels of violence. Nations should also decide on broad guidelines within which **media** and government should respond to terrorist acts.

When incidents arise, media, government, victims, and their relatives become unwitting participants in the drama. Restraint is required of all parties. The media have to cover news developments, but without excesses. For terrorists, media exposure constitutes leverage. Terrorists seek to increase their importance to pressure governments to meet their demands.

Government officials should also show restraint, refraining from a public refusal to negotiate, which puts the government in a diplomatic corner. Negotiations generally occur, regardless; they ought to be conducted out of the public view and at a lower level than by senior government members. It is generally counter-productive for any democratic country to confer status and importance on kidnappers. The correct approach in kidnap situations is patient, behind-the-scenes negotiations.

See also: Counter/Anti-Terrorism; Media; Propaganda.

Revolution

Revolution is a relatively sudden violent and illegal attempt to change the regime of a state or other political organisation, in which large sections of the population are involved as participants. During the French Revolution of 1789, the word revolution became identified with the seizure of key political decision-making positions by some coercive force and the introduction of structural changes in society. These can include changes in the political and social system (the French and Russian Revolutions); changes in the mode of production (the Industrial Revolution, and technological revolution), or in some aspect of social, intellectual or cultural life (scientific and cultural revolutions).

Theories of revolution are concerned not with mere changes of rulers (as in palace revolutions), but with changes of ruling classes, of the methods of rule, and of social institutions, and with the revolutionary passions and actions which lead to these changes and with their consequences. Revolutionary theories like Marxism or Leninism not only advocate revolution, but also try to explain how it comes about. Marx concentrated on the relationship between revolution and economic development and Lenin on the relationship between revolution and under-development. The **New Left** emphasised the links between revolution and over-development.

Modern theorists recognise that the important modern events called revolutions have involved the seizure of political power, usually by soldiers or intellectuals. The most successful revolutions have been those which have achieved their ends while avoiding the violence and social upheaval of later revolutions, and which have concentrated on transformation at the political level, while retaining sufficient social continuity to guarantee stability.

Revolutionary leadership is primarily dependent on situation or context. A situation of crisis – whether political, military, social, economic or psychological – catapults the leaders into prominence and provides them with ready and willing followers. Political crises may consist of inter-elite rivalries or *coups d'état*, riots or rebellions, nationalist movements set in motion by imperialist penetration and control, or widespread governmental corruption and ineptitude. Military crises are represented by defeat in war or army mutiny. Social crises include the disintegration of the prevailing ideology, normal order and social institutions. Economic crises are represented by severe inflation or depression. Psychological crises consist of widespread frustration, alienation and relative deprivation. The greater the intensity and coalescence of various crises, the greater the likelihood and the more rapid the emergence of revolutionary leaders. Situations of uncertainty, unpredictability, anxiety and stress rally the people and mobilise them in a common search for safety and security.

Revolutionary elites are broadly middle-class in origin with substantial representation from the lower class, and have extensive histories of involvement in clandestine or open radical activity. They have a positive attitude towards the nature of man and towards their own countries. Their attitudes towards international society are dualistic, seeing it as divided into unmistakable friends and foes.

Revolutionary elites are typically formed legitimately, and the leaders tend to be drawn from mainstream ethnic and religious groups. The jobs performed by members of elites are inconsistent with their expectations, and despite being well-educated, many leave their vocation and become professional revolutionaries. Members of revolutionary elites are cosmopolitan in many senses, and they travel widely, spending long periods of time in other countries, developing foreign contacts and learning foreign languages. From an early age, members of elites are heavily involved in illegal organisation and agitation. Contrary to expectations, revolutionary leaders tend to have normal family lives.

Revolutionary leaders with divergent ideologies do not vary significantly in their attitudes toward human nature, but do vary in attitudes toward their own countries and toward international society.

Formative years are relatively unimportant as sources of radicalisation. The tranquil or stormy nature of early life is not strongly associated with an individual's emergence as a revolutionary.

Education has in some cases been a source of radicalisation for post-war leaders with stormy beginnings from colonial or neo-colonial countries with nationalist, communist or nationalist/communist ideologies. Foreign travel can have a radicalising influence in many ways; the traveller may witness oppression, exploitation and brutality of unimaginable proportions. He or she may see privation, misery, hunger, disease and death and observe or even personally experience cruelty, torture, imprisonment and exile.

Revolutions all occur under identifiable conditions, whether political, military, economic, social or psychological. Distinctions have to be drawn between revolutions that are systematically thought out, planned, organised and executed by elite groups over relatively long periods of time, and revolutions that explode upon the scene as a consequence of a sharp escalation of insoluble conflicts between major social groups, taking relatively short periods of time. Political, social, economic and religious issues coalesce to produce revolutionary explosions. The sluggish and frequently ill-conceived responses of the established regimes serve only to aggravate the situation and mobilise the masses.

Regional variations are found when revolutionary leaders are set apart by their ethnic backgrounds from the populations of their homelands. Asian and Latin American leaders tend to be from the main ethnic groups: African and European and North American revolutionaries represent a variety of minorities, large and small.

Latin American and Asian revolutionaries belong to the main religions of their respective regions, whereas significant proportions of African, European, and North American leaders represent minority religions. These variations are associated with the more pluralistic character of Africa, Europe and North America. European, North American and Latin American leaders are likely to have been educated in institutions in their home country.

African and Asian revolutionaries are more likely to have travelled to foreign lands than their

Latin American, European and North American counterparts. The type of ideology to which revolutionary elites subscribe varies by region. Asian and Latin American leaders are least varied in their political orientations, combining as they do shades of Marxist and nationalist ideologies. African revolutionaries are only slightly more varied, since their pan-Africanism is nothing more than nationalism on a regional basis. European and North American elites are most diverse subscribing to a spectrum of radical ideologies. These people, and to a lesser extent the African elites, are more likely to incorporate both indigenous and foreign doctrines. Asians and Latin Americans tend to adapt foreign ideologies to local needs.

Much of the ideological radicalism of elites is rooted in their proclaimed belief in various shades of Marxism. The relative diversity of ideologies and attitudes among European and North American elites in contrast to their relative conformity among African, Asian and Latin American leaders is most likely a result of history. Revolutions in the Western world span four centuries; revolutions in the other three regions are post-war phenomena.

See also: New Left; Psychology; Psychology of Terrorism: Terrorist Mindset; Terror and Terrorism; Terrorist Types.

Reference

Calvert, M. (1984) *Revolution*, New York: St Martin's.

Further Reading

O'Neill, B. E. (1990) *Insurgency and Terrorism: Inside Modern Revolutionary Warfare*, New York: Pergamon Press.

Rights

Any terrorist explores the outer limits of wrongdoing. Terrorists not only violate the rights of others by violence, but they do so with the purpose of making everyone's rights insecure. Terrorists seek to destroy the community of understanding and mutual self-restraint upon which the existence of rights depends.

A terrorist group sets out systematically to alienate a population from its government. The group does succeed in creating a general sense of insecurity among the populace and provoking repressive measures, including the round up and detention of those suspected of complicity with the terrorists. The terrorists argue that their rights as citizens and human beings are being violated.

Having a right consists precisely in having the title to command respect for demands that others act or refrain from acting in a particular way towards us, and for our complaints when they fail to do so. Terrorists have undoubtedly through their conduct jeopardized their claims to human rights – as they have murdered, tortured, and in every respect, violated the human dignity of their victims.

Rights are important as they give to each person the capacity to decide how and to what extent that person wants to defend his or her interests. To some people even a terrorist has a right to protest the destruction of that capacity which is at the core of humanity – the capacity for autonomous choice. However, if a terrorist is seen not merely as a common criminal, but as an enemy of rights in general, an argument can be made that he has forfeited his rights. A terrorist can respond that he is not the enemy of rights at all, but the only effective proponent of them against a corrupt and illegitimate regime.

There is a tight connection between the idea of having rights and the idea of being allowed to assert them. A human can be respected not simply by refraining from interfering with his interests; rights can be respected by attending to their holder's assertion of them. Both torture and detention violate the rights of those subjected to them. If the conditions of fear created by an effective terrorist campaign require a repressive government to be established it must be regarded as a violation of rights.

The arguments for denying rights to terrorists rest upon the perception that claims of rights are grounded in a relationship; the relationship between people who have a shared understanding of what they owe to one another as people. Terrorists have forfeited the right to have rights, because they have by word and action made clear their complete rejection of that shared understanding, destroying the relationship of which they now wish to take advantage by making claims of right.

Whilst the terrorist, by his acts and words, has damaged that relationship and has lost the capacity to make some claims he could otherwise have made, he has not and could not destroy the relationship entirely. Because he retains the distinctively human capacity to preserve life or seek death through his unique actions, we continue to have a relationship with him, characterised by a duty to respect him as one who has that capacity.

Revolutions can be peaceful or violent, as can civil protests. Guerrilla wars are small wars; and whether riots are crimes or acts of war or terroristic depends on the intention and degree of organisation of the rioters. Some terrorism is an expression of frustration and can be intended as a punishment or to call attention to a problem. Many analysts believe terrorists are divested of any moral principles and therefore any type of crime is possible.

See also: Human Rights.

Risk Management

The task of risk management is to identify precisely the risks and the probable effects of risks on the personnel and organisation to be protected. The threat of terrorism is a serious risk, and only a thorough programme of risk management ensures that security planning is adequate and properly directed. The price for not having a risk management programme is the uncertainty that can breed fear or over-confidence if the threat is under- or over-estimated. The methodology of systems analysis is a format that is useful in implementing risk management. Generally a programme of risk identification, evaluation and reduction, known as a comprehensive systems risk analysis, is undertaken.

In any analysis the original problem has to be kept in mind, as it will determine the scope and structure for recommendations. Defining the problem will determine the current situation. Information has to be gained from discussions with key executives who are potential victims of kidnapping. Whatever the specific objectives of the analysis it has to define and evaluate all threats and risks relevant to the problem; assess the criticality of all threats and risks; and assess the vulnerability to all threats and risks. All resources internal to the company, such as the security programme and personnel, have to be identified and their present and potential effect on the risk evaluated. External resources, both public and private, such as government agencies, police departments, consultants, private security companies and the media have to be examined to determine if the risk can be controlled by recognisable sources.

Since risks are inherent in nearly every situation, types of risk have to be classified according to relevance. The important categories are *property* (reduction in value, or loss); *liability* (responsibility for loss by others); *personnel* (disability, death, reduced efficiency); *physical* (destruction or damage); *social* (individual or group conduct); *market* (price changes and competition); *pure* (chance of loss but no chance of gain), or *speculative* (chance of gain or loss); *static* (caused by irregular condition always possible); *dynamic* (caused by changing trends); and last, *fundamental* (group losses) or *particular* risk (individual loss).

In the case of the risk of terrorism, one is confronting potential pure economic, social and physical risks to property, of liability or to personnel. Present security strength and policy have to be fully detailed, so that the ability to meet threats and reduce risk can be evaluated. The complete spectrum of risks has to be determined so that they can be evaluated in terms of the degree of exposure and level of current protective systems.

Each risk has to be measured by a number of criteria to determine its impact on the organisation – the probability of occurrence, impact of occurrence, and the ability to predict its occurrence. The results of the measurement determine how the risk is to be handled. The impact of the occurrence is determined by measuring the severity of the possible loss (the effect each risk could have on each activity) in terms of maximum possible loss, maximum probable loss and actual expected loss. The most subjective category of measurement is how far it will be possible to predict the occurrence.

Risk avoidance can be accomplished by permanently neutralising the hazard or eliminating the activity which exposes personnel to risk; or simply by occurrence reduction and risk acceptance, which allows the risk to exist because it cannot be cost-effectively reduced. The last types of risk reduction are of risks spreading over a greater part of the organisation, and the transferral of risk, that is the use of insurance or other means to transfer the liability for the loss to other parties.

The assessment of risks allows for priorities of reduction to be created. In the case of acts of terrorism, which frequently involve the loss of life, risk avoidance, occurrence reduction and risk acceptance as means of risk management, are the most important.

Minimising the risk of becoming a terrorism victim, is something people and businesses have to face. It is never possible to have total immunity; but more and more businesses, nationally and internationally, have in place a top-down framework for risk evaluation and management.

In the evaluation sphere firms are looking at how, why and when factors. Specialist analysis sources are used rather than the **media** and this, of course, costs the companies a large amount of cash and inroads into their profits. If a threat occurs, firms are involved in monitoring the situation (Slone, 2000). A strategy to manage risks is put in place in an increasing way and training programmes are implemented. Risk profiles are always altering and situations can change rapidly. Terrorists like companies to overreact to their tactics and firms have to try and make sure that this does not happen and continue as normal.

See also: Crisis Management; Extortion; Threat Assessment Guidelines; Threats.

References

Stone, M. (2000) 'Terrorism: Threat Assessment and Counter-Measures', *International Security Review* (May/June), pp. 14–16.

Waugh, W. L. Jnr (1990) *Terrorism and Emergency Management: Policy and Administration*, New York: Marcel Dekker.

Further Reading

Buck, G. (1997) *Preparing For Terrorism: An Emergency Services Guide*, Albany, NY: Delmar Publications.

Martz, H. F. and Johnson, M. E. (1987) 'Risk Analysis of Terrorist Attacks', *Risk Analysis*, vol. 7, no. 1, pp. 35–47.

Massa, R. J. (1999) 'Terrorism Comes Calling', *Risk Management*, vol. 46, no. 2, pp. 11–13.

Simon, J. (1984) 'The Future of Political Risk Analysis', *TVI Journal*, vol. 5, no. 2 (autumn), pp. 23–25.

Venzke, B. N. (ed.) (1998) *First Responder Chem-Bio Handbook*, Alexandria, VA: Tempest Publishing.

Waugh, W. L. (1986) 'Integrating the Policy Models of Terrorism and Emergency Management', *Policy Studies Review*, vol. 6, no. 2, (November), pp. 287–301.

— (1989) 'The Structure of Decision Making in the Iran Hostage Rescue Attempt'. Paper presented at the Biannual Meeting of the International Association for Conflict Management, Athens, GA: June 1989.

Roles *see* Psychology and Terrorist Types

Russia

In 1985 Mikhail Gorbachev became Secretary General of the **Soviet Union** and introduced *glasnost* (transparency) and *perestroika* (re-structuring) geared to carrying out transformation in the country. These changes brought out into the open the issue of the autonomy of different ethnic groups and nationalities.

Economic reform came slowly; and after a failed coup the Soviet Communist Party was dissolved. Boris Yeltsin became the president of Russia in 1991. In the same year trouble broke out in the Chechen-Ingush region of Northern Caucasia. Rivalry occurred between Russia and Ukraine over control of nuclear weapons and the navy. Confrontations occurred between communist and nationalist protestors and the militia. Tensions also were witnessed between the President and Parliament and amidst fears of a coup; Yeltsin had to order the taking of Parliament by force in October 1992. After some hesitation in 1993 the Tartars signed a bilateral agreement with Moscow but the Chechens refused to do so, and two guerrilla wars with Russia have occurred and stalemate still exists in 2003.

'Terrorist' attacks in Moscow were blamed on the Chechens and Yeltsin's successor, Vladimir Putin consistently refers to the Chechens as terrorists. The taking of hostages in a Moscow theatre in 2002 was blamed on the Chechens. In the operation to release them over a hundred died due to inhaling gas used by the troops.

In other parts of the old Soviet Union tension is evident between South Ossetia and Georgia, the former wanting to form a republic of its own out of the latter. Stalemate exists in 2003 over South Ossetia's status. Ngorno-Karabakh is another region in turmoil – the strikes of 1988 were one of the first signs of instability due to nationalist demands in the Soviet Union. Armenia supported the Karabakhs (Christian Orthodox) and the Muslims in the area were supported by Azerbaijan. An armistice was signed in 1994 but the creation of Ngorno-Karabakh is still in process due to the difficulty of negotiations with Azerbaijan.

Over a decade after the end of the **Cold War** and the collapse of the Soviet Union, Russia is undergoing a period of rapid social and economic restructuring which has produced sharp divisions within its society and led to an explosion of organised crime.

The Black Market is extensive and people involved include drug dealers, arms traders, racketeers and in some cases corrupt officials. Criminally controlled commercial structures, banks and enterprises have been established and these can easily be accessed by Terrorists (Jane's Information, 1997).

See also: Cold War; Soviet Union.

References

Jane's Terrorism: A Global Survey (1997), London: Jane's Information Group.

Further Reading

Golan, G. (1990) *Gorbachev's 'New Thinking' About Terrorism*, Washington Papers no. 141. New York: Praeger.

Panico, C. (1995) 'Conflicts in the Caucasus:

Russia's War in Chechnya', *Conflict Studies*, no. 281, London: RISCT.

Rwanda

Humanitarian intervention and **genocide** in Rwanda have dominated the headlines in this part of Africa over the past decade.

Refugee abuse, **human rights** abuse, environmental disasters and economic disturbances are inextricably linked to regional peace and security. A **civil war** had bedevilled this **East African** country (a former Belgian colony). Ethnic cleavages between the Hutu and Tutsi were caused by political and social reorganisation engendered by the influence of colonialism (preference for employment in political and military posts was given to the Tutsi's).

The current trouble stems from the assassination of the Rwandan President – a Hutu – in August 1994, who was involved in peace negotiations. Tutsi members with the Rwandan Patriotic Front were blamed. Ethnic clashes rapidly worsened between the Hutu majority and Tutsi-dominated military. The civil war that resulted was an amalgam of many factors – colonial intrusion, fragile democratisation, ethnic diversity, economic decline, regional instability and a lack of interest. Ethnic 'cleansing' occurred with brutal Hutu attacks against Tutsi citizens. Genocide was used as a military and political tool and an abuse of human rights.

Refugees fled into the Congo, Uganda and Burundi and each country was blamed by the Rwandan authorities for aiding the **rebel** forces.

See also: Ethinc Cleansing and Conflict; Genocide.

Reference

O'Halloran, P. J. (1995) 'Humanitarian Intervention and the Genocide in Rwanda', *Conflict Studies*, no. 277 (January), London: RISCT.

Further Reading

Wilkinson, P. (2002) *Terrorism versus Democracy: The Liberal State Response*, London and Portland, OR: Frank Cass.

S

Sanctions

Only the **USA** and Britain have been willing to impose significant economic sanctions on such identified sponsors of international **terrorism** as **Iran**, **Libya** and **Syria**. In the case of the USA a military response is readily available i.e. on Libya after the terrorist bombing of a nightclub in Berlin in 1986, and in April 1993 when cruise missiles were launched in response to an Iraqi effort to assassinate former President George Bush.

The end of the **Cold War** prompted a fresh impetus to the activities of the **United Nations** Security Council to curb international terrorism. Sanctions against Libya for example were the first such case of collective action against a state believed to support terrorism. Since the imposition of sanctions against Libya there have been no allegations of state involvement in terrorist attacks against civil aviation (Gazzini, 1996). In the 1990s the role played by the Security Council in the fight against air piracy did contribute to convincing the states that in the past have been accused of sponsoring terrorist activities, to abandon such criminal policy.

Reference

Gazzini, T. (1996) 'Sanctions Against Terrorism: Legal Obligations of States', *Conflict Studies* (May/June), London: RISCT.

Further reading

Bienen, H. and Gilpin, R. (1980) 'Economic Sanctions as a Response to Terrorism', *Journal of Strategic Studies*, vol. 3, no. 1, pp. 89–98.

Sandinist National Liberation Front (SNLF)

The Front was named after a Nicaraguan patriot, General Augusto Cesur Sandino, who having opposed American rule for six years, was murdered in 1934 by supporters of the Somoza family. He was the great example for Che **Guevara** and Fidel Castro. Carlos Fonseca Amador, who with other leaders was killed by government forces in 1976, formed the liberation movement in 1961 as a pro-Havana group. The year before their deaths, the Sandinists split into three factions, the smallest of which was the **Marx**ist–Leninist GPP. The largest was the extreme Third Party, or Terreristas, which waived its ideological bias to allow the bourgeoisie to join their common front against the Somoza regime. In this way it succeeded in winning a broad spectrum of support from peasants to upper-class intellectuals. The Front displayed a great capacity for survival despite numerous 'eradication' attempts during the later years of the Somoza regime. Despite some setbacks, the groups began to co-ordinate activities and establish operational unity by 1978. Subsequently unity waned to some extent and two Marxist groups entered an anti-Third Party coalition, while a fourth faction, the authentic Sandinist, emerged.

The Third Party dominated the 'junta of national reconstruction' which headed a provisional government installed in July 1979 although the three principal tendencies were equally represented in the SNLF's Joint National Directorate. Elections were held in 1985, which brought success for the Sandinists led by Daniel Ortega. His government has faced difficulties because its policies (revealing a growing pro-Soviet and pro-Cuban trend) not only led to strained relations with the United States but also alienated those sections of the Nicaraguan people who wanted even greater democracy. There has been a threat from armed Somocist' groups (i.e. those identified with the former Somoza regime) operating from bases across Nicaragua's northern border with Honduras and including many former National Guards who had fled the country in 1979. The Ortega government claims that such groups receive support from the **United States** and from neighbouring right-wing regimes.

The insurgencies in **El Salvador**, Guatemala and Nicaragua were spread over many years and took up a large part of American foreign policy thinking. Throughout the arduous roving guerrilla days the Sandinistas were able to gain sanctuary in neighbouring countries such as Costa Rica.

Nicaragua witnessed the first practice of the theory known as low-intensity warfare which had two aspects:

(*a*) The use of proxy forces either to undertake one's own subversion of the existing regime through a guerrilla offensive; or to help eradicate guerrillas by providing aid and advisors for the incumbent military and security forces.

(*b*) The regime could be destabilised through economic attrition by denying aid and trade and encouraging other countries to apply similar **sanctions**.

See also: Guerrilla Warfare in History; Guevara; Third World.

Further reading

Chamoro, E. (1986) 'US Sponsored Contras are Terrorists', in Szumski, B. (ed.) *Terrorism: Opposing Viewpoints*, St Paul, MN: Greenhaven Press, pp. 137–141.

Waldmann, P. (1986) 'Guerrilla Movements in Argentina, Guatemala, Nicaragua and Uruguay'

in Merkl, P. H. (ed.) *Political Violence and Terror*, Berkeley, CA: University of California Press.

Saudi Arabia

For many years Saudi Arabia was one of the closest strategic allies of the **USA** in the Arab world. This was important to the Americans as Saudi was one of the world's chief oil suppliers.

Evidence is now emerging that it has encouraged a hard line puritanical and anti-Western brand of **Islam** (Wahabism). It financed religious schools, the Madrassas, in parts of Asia, Africa and even Europe. These schools taught what was seen as primitive Islam and bred some terrorists that operated in **Afghanistan** and **Pakistan**. Disagreements have led to the Americans removing troops from Saudi territory, and Saudi Arabia has lost its position as the top supplier of oil to the USA.

Saudi Arabia has witnessed some rebellions in parts of the various provinces among some of the young, uneducated and unemployed, most of whom resent the opulence of the Saudi royal family.

In June 1996 an American air force barracks in Dhahran, was bombed by religious militants opposed to the Al-Saud regime. Nineteen persons died and over 300 were wounded. Iran was suspected of involvement (Reeve, 1999). It was a massive 5,000 lb truck bomb which destroyed the entire front of the building. The event occurred at the time when **Osama Bin Laden** moved his operational base from Sudan to Afghanistan. Bin Laden probably provided advice, gained moral support for the attack among other Islamic militants in Saudi Arabia and provided technical support (Hoffman, 1998).

The American military presence on Saudi soil is resented by certain groups in Saudi Arabia. This made the USA vulnerable to terrorist attacks in 1995 and 1996, when American military facilities and personnel suffered casualties in Riyadh and in al-Khobar. This military presence was essential to protecting oil interests in the USA. The events of **September 11** caused dismay in America because among the hijackers of the aircraft that hit US targets were fifteen Saudis. This shattered American confidence in one of the few remaining oil allies in the Gulf. The relationship with Saudi was commercial and was never built on trying to form a deeper understanding of these societies and people. This was the cause of some embarrassment because from 1995–1998 both countries were lending some support to the Taliban in Afghanistan. Only Saudi's can provide the spare capacity needed in case of an oil supply disruption. Bin Laden certainly resented support for the Saudi royal family (Nanay, 2001).

References

Hoffman, B. (1998) *Inside Terrorism*, New York: Columbia University Press.

Nanay, J. (2001) *New Friends, New Enemies and Oil Politics: Causes and Consequences of the September 11 Terrorist Attacks*, Middle East Policy, vol. III, no. 4 (December).

Reeve, S. (2002) 'Is it Goodbye, Saudi Arabia?', *Jane's Foreign Report*, no. 2701, 22 August, Coulsdon, Surrey: Jane's Information Group.

September 11, 2001

The Event

On the morning of September 11, 2001 two hijacked passenger planes were crashed into the North and South Towers of the **World Trade Center** complex in New York, **USA**; and another flew into the south-west section of the Pentagon building (US defence headquarters) in Washington. A fourth aircraft probably bound for a nuclear installation or another target in Washington DC crashed into a field in Pennsylvania. Over 3,000 people from eighty countries lost their lives in the resulting devastation. Nineteen men from various Middle Eastern countries had perpetrated the hijacking.

Blame was soon attached to **Osama Bin Laden** known for plotting earlier attacks against American military and diplomatic targets in Kenya, Uganda and Yemen. The attacks proved there were no limits for the new breed of terrorist, and that airport security was very lax. The mission of terror against the World Trade Center was completed eight years after the initial outrage in 1993, and resulted in insurance claims estimated to be billions of dollars. Sinisterly, it showed up the effectiveness

of terrorist sleepers who go quietly about their business until one day they are called into action.

The North Atlantic Council immediately declared its solidarity with the United States and pledged its support and assistance. There were immediate calls for an international coalition against terrorism.

The 'twin towers' of the World Trade Center in New York were state of the art in world architecture at the time of their planning and creation in the late-1960s and early-1970s. They were built as a tube structure with thirty foot of prefabricated panels forming a strong wall of steel and inside there was a steel core for lifts allowing for open floor space. Steel varied in strength and thickness from tower to tower.

The first attack in February 1993 was supposed to lead to the North Tower falling into the South Tower – but the explosion occurred under the complex, two floors down and six feet from the subterranean walls of the North Tower.

On September 11 each plane weighed over 200 tons and crashed at over 400 mph into each tower causing immense damage and blocking off all escape routes above the 75th floor of the South Tower and the 93rd floor of the North Tower. Aviation fuel spilt into the lift shafts and fires spread throughout the buildings. Each floor covered an acre and smoke under pressure extruded over twenty acres of fire. The designers had considered the results of an impact of an aircraft, but not the effects of fuel. Firemen could do little to save the buildings as kerosene and plastic have a huge potential to destroy.

When steel heats up, it becomes weaker, loses strength and buckles and twists. Fire-proofing had been sprayed on the steel, but blew away from the steel on impact. Supports for the massive open planned floors melted, the explosions blew out windows.

The Achilles heel of the whole structure was the columns which supported the floors. They had weak connections and the trusses of lightweight construction with prefabricated panels over them, were susceptible to fire and lethal to firemen. After only five minutes of fire, the unprotected steel trusses, devoid of fire-retardant, failed at their connections to the main supports. With any one element removed the entire structure would fail.

The South Tower took 53 minutes to burn and collapsed in 11 seconds and the North Tower crashed to the ground thirty minutes later. 500,000 tons of steel travelled about one quarter of a mile and hit the ground at 120 miles per hour. The daring and innovative design of the 'Twin Towers' hastened their own destruction. The design prevented people escaping and the whole building was uniquely vulnerable to a disaster.

Reference

Moore, T. (2000) 'Buildings and Bombs', *Intersec*, vol. 10 (5 May), pp. 166–168.

September 11, Arrests

In February 2003 Mounir el Motassadeq a Moroccan student, was sentenced in Hamburg to fifteen years' jail for his role in the murder of more than 3,000 people. He was the first suspect to be convicted of involvement in the September 11 attacks.

He was a founding member of the Hamburg-based cell that plotted his attacks. He helped to arrange bank transfers and utility payments and later covered up for three would-be suicide pilots when they went to the **USA** to undertake flight training as well as for three associates in charge of the operation.

This sentence was announced a week after three Saudi Arabian members of **Al Qaeda** were jailed by a Moroccan court for ten years for plotting to attack British and American warships in the Straits of Gibraltar in 2001.

Al Qaeda and September 11

The attacks were given the code name 'Operation Holy Tuesday' and were precisely planned at an Al Qaeda meeting in Kuala Lumpur, Malaysia, in January 2000. Here, details were given of how the hijackers should train and hide in the USA and how the attacks should be carried out. A number of terrorists attended, including one who was a key planner in the October 2000 bombing of the *USS Cole* in Yemen; and later some who had been at the meeting travelled to the USA.

The events of September 11 were a turning point in international terrorism, when the **United States** was attacked not by a fellow state, but by a non-state terrorist organisation. Al Qaeda showed what can happen on the downside of globalisation, with the transnational nature of the organisation everywhere across the globe. In November 2002 it admitted responsibility for the attempt to bring down an Israeli charter jet over Kenya with a guided missile, and for the blowing up of an Israeli owned hotel in the Kenyan resort of Mombasa, killing 14 people and injuring a further 300.

Al Qaeda has the ability to penetrate countries with passport fraud and other illegal immigration techniques; and to infect indigenous groups with their terroristic zeal.

On September 11 it exposed fundamental weaknesses of modern Western states, including vulnerable borders, inadequate immigration controls and insufficient anti-terrorism surveillance.

The group serves a psychological and ideological purpose as much as a military and political one and provides a brotherhood of a shared world view. The Muslim world has been and continues to be in turmoil. A majority of the world's refugees are Muslim, which is an indicator of the wars and political upheaval in that part of the globe. Political ideology and religion are a potent combination.

The defeat of Al Qaeda, the end of Bin Laden and the fall of the Taliban should not make us forget that the broad band of terrorism has global networks and financial powers.

What has to be avoided is letting Bin Laden succeed by turning post-September 11 retaliatory measures into a clash between **Islam** and the West.

In January 2003 an Al Qaeda assassination cell was discovered in Naples, Italy. Among items found were photographs including one of the UK Chief of Defence staff, explosives, fuse laced with nitroglycerine and detonators. There were also religious texts, photographs of jihad martyrs, false documents, maps of many European city centres, addresses of global contacts and 100 mobile telephones.

Reference

Charcoal World News, 10 July 2003, 'Al Qaeda called Sept 11 attacks "Operation Holy Tuesday"', a report of the US Commission investigating the September 11 attacks.

International Responses to September 11

The events of that day were seen as an act of war and as an affront to all humanity, and brought a swift response from the international community based round the four tenets of making no concessions to terrorists and striking no deals; bringing terrorists to justice for their crimes; to isolate and apply pressure to states which sponsor terrorism to force a change in behaviour and each country to bolster its counter-terrorist capabilities.

The day after the attacks the **United Nations** Security Council condemned the attacks and reiterated the inherent rights of collective self-defence.

On 21 September, the Organisation of American States invoked the collective self-defence clause of the Inter American Treaty of Reciprocal Assistance (the Rio Treaty) (Keelty, 2002).

On 5 October NATO invoked Article 5 of the founding treaty which stated that an armed attack on one or more of the allies in Europe or North America shall be considered an attack against them all.

Many countries from around the world offered help: 136 countries offered military assistance; 89 countries granted over flight authority for American planes; 76 granted landing rights for US military planes and 23 countries agreed to host American and coalition forces involved in military operations in **Afghanistan**.

The major surprise was a failure of imagination rather than a failure of intelligence. It was never foreseen that large commercial aircraft could be used as supercharged cruise missiles. The attack showed anger and resentment against American dominance and increasing access to the technological fruits of globalisation. September 11 conveyed the essence of one of the ideas of terrorism – the complete transformation of sane human beings into brutal and indiscriminate killers.

Like **guerrilla warfare**, terrorism is a strategy and an idea that cannot be once defeated and forgotten.

Reference

Keelty, M. Commissioner (2002) 'A Changed View for the Australian Federal Police a Year after September 11', *Platypus Magazine*, no. 76 (September).

Afghanistan

The military response to the events of September 11 was code-named *Operation Enduring Freedom*; conducted by American and Allied forces, its objective was to remove the Taliban from power in **Afghanistan**. The other aims were the destruction of the **Al Qaeda** camps in that country and the capture or death of **Osama Bin Laden**. The difficult endgame to this operation was to try and establish a permanent regime that was democratic and stable (Combs, 2003).

Over a year after the Taliban regime collapsed, security across the country is still fragile. In September 2002 an attempt was made to assassinate the new President Hamid Karzai, which in turn came shortly after a devastating bomb blast in Kabul. These incidents occurred despite the presence of the International Security Assistance Force and after efforts to pacify feuding warlords and hunt down the remains of the Al Qaeda and the Taliban.

In July 2002 one of the new vice-presidents Haji Abdul Qadir was shot dead outside his Kabul office; and days earlier a bomb had exploded outside a **UN** guesthouse. A threat to the new regimes stability also comes from a former prime minister, the Islamist mujaheddin warlord Gulbuddin Hekmatyar. Western governments have been trying to build a national army despite the fact that Afghanistan is a nation of feuding ethnic groups.

American intelligence officials claimed in September that Al Qaeda fighters who fled to **Pakistan** were moving back into Afghanistan in small groups. The secret police are also building up power.

Reference

Combs, C. C. (2003) *Terrorism in the 21st Century*, New Jersey: Prentice Hall.

Camp X-Ray

In January 2002 the American military authorities began transferring **Al Qaeda** and Taliban

detainees captured in **Afghanistan** from Kanda-
har and from a US naval vessel stationed in the
Arabian Sea to the US naval base at Guantanamo
Bay, **Cuba**.

This event caused friction between the Americans and their allies since the prisoners, of whom
there were 158 by the end of January, were not
guaranteed prisoner-of-war status under the Geneva Convention of 1949.

The detainees were classed as 'unlawful combatants' or 'battlefield detainees', although the
American officials insisted that the captives were
kept in conditions and circumstances that were
'consistent' with the Geneva Convention. Under
this Convention, the right of captors to interrogate
POWs was severely restricted and POWs had to be
tried by court-martial or civilian courts and not by
military tribunals. Legal observers argued that
under the Convention there was a presumption
that the prisoners had POW status until an
independent 'competent tribunal' could determine
their status. The American military authorities
could not determine the status of Al Qaeda fighters
and were obliged to treat them as POWs until such
a tribunal had issued a ruling.

The release of photographs showing shackled
detainees forced to sit on the floor wearing face
masks and blindfolds only heightened unease
among America's allies. The USA maintained this
measure was adopted only while detainees were in
transit.

Reference

Keesings Contemporary Archives (2002), Washington,
DC: Keesings Worldwide LLC.

Osama Bin Laden

Osama Bin Laden and most of his top-ranking
Arab associates were able to escape from **Afghanistan** in the autumn of 2001 because of a series of
blunders by the US military.

Due to Allied armies being overstretched in the
field, several high profile military operations to
capture Bin Laden and his associates failed. It is
believed he may now be in Pakistan. Large
numbers of **Al Qaeda** fighters were able to return
home to carry on the conflict. The people who

assisted Al Qaeda members escape were keener on
getting the cash for this activity than in helping the
USA conquer the problem.

As shown by the **Bali** bombing a new Al Qaeda
front appears to have opened in South East Asia
especially Indonesia and the **Philippines**. **Pakistan** has been made to pay for the support its
President, Musharraf gave the US in its bombing of
Afghanistan. For instance, seven attacks have been
unleashed on Western and Christian interests since
October 2001. Sixteen people from the USA and
other Western countries have been killed including
eleven French engineers. Al Qaeda funded the
attacks and was responsible for the choice of
Western victims, through the work of a terrorist
cell in Karachi. The intent to destabilise Pakistan is
clear.

Al Qaeda has subcontracted some of its terrorist
activity since September 11. This allows the
network to continue commissioning outrages at a
time of unprecedented and debilitating security.

By December 2002 there was great concern that
Britain could be a target because of its overt
support for the USA and its prominent role in
Afghanistan.

The attack on September 11 instigated a massive
manhunt. Attacks and plots linked to Al Qaeda
have included since: a plot to poison water supplies
in Algeria, which was thwarted; and in China
arrests have occurred among Muslim groups in
Xinjiang linked to international terrorism. In
Egypt, Islamic **Jihad** and Al Gama al Islamiya
are alleged to have links with Bin Laden. In **India**
Al Qaeda fighters are claimed to have joined
militants fighting in Kashmir and in Iraq, Ansar al-
Islam group has been active in Kurdish North with
links to Al Qaeda. In Italy a tunnel was found next
to the American embassy, part of a plot by a group
linked to Al Qaeda and in Kyrgyzstan, two Al
Qaeda suspects were arrested over an alleged plot
to blow up the American embassy. In Morocco,
there was a plot to use a dinghy packed with
explosives in a suicide attack on British and US
warships in Gibraltar but the arrest of some Saudis
linked to Al Qaeda stopped this attack. In
Singapore there were alleged plots to blow up
American and Israeli targets, and to crash a
hijacked plane into the international airport. In
Sweden, a Swede of Tunisian parentage was

arrested trying to board a Ryan Air flight with a loaded gun.

In Tunisia a suicide attack on the resort island of Djerba in March 2002 killed 21 people including 14 Germans when a fuel tanker was detonated near a synagogue. In the UK there have been numerous alerts but no actual attacks. In December 2002 a cargo ship was seized in the English Channel by the Royal Navy. Police believe it was carrying explosives but none were found.

In **Saudi Arabia** a British banker was killed in Riyadh in June 2002 by a booby trapped bomb. The British blamed Al Qaeda, but the Saudi authorities maintained that his death was the result of a feud with alcohol bootleggers.

In South America, Al Qaeda supporters have been arrested on the borders of Argentina, Brazil and Paraguay. It is home to an extensive mainly Lebanese community with a history of sympathy for the **Shi'ite** radical movement, **Hizbullah**.

These global attacks are hardly surprising for in the five years that Al Qaeda was organised by Bin Laden in Afghanistan, around 250,000 personnel from over 70 countries trained there. There were up to 10,000 fully formed members of the organisation.

Since September 11 Al Qaeda's captured men number 1,600 from 95 countries around the world. In the Far East many arrests have taken place and in Europe dozens of arrests have occurred in virtually every country. Most Al Qaeda arrests have taken place in Afghanistan and Pakistan.

In Pakistan, the Gulf area and Oman and Yemen Al Qaeda has played hide and seek with the Allied military and intelligence. American frustration over Bin Laden has led to a desire to attack Saddam Hussein. Allied forces invaded Iraq in March 2003.

The British government announced in February 2003 that it has evidence of Osama Bin Laden's network developing a 'dirty bomb' – a conventional bomb releasing a radioactive cloud. It is alleged in London that a small dirty bomb had been built near Herat in Afghanistan.

Emergency Planning Post-September 11

The events in New York speeded up the British preparations against a similar attack occurring in London. Drill and emergency plans are required by law at oil refineries, chemical plants and other dangerous sites, such as nuclear power stations.

'Dirty bomb' contamination can cause long term disruption, and decontamination equipment has to be made available quickly, such as units and suits.

Since the Tokyo subway attack in 1995 there has been concern that this could happen in the Tube in London; and the disastrous fire on the South Korean underground network in February 2003 has only heightened this concern. The best equipped emergency management teams in Europe are in France, Germany, Spain and the Netherlands, and in order to try to catch up with these countries, the British government is bringing a revised Emergency Planning Bill before Parliament. Many countries are still relying on their civil defence planning from the **Cold War** era, and these include the **United Kingdom**.

Media Strategies and Counter-terrorism

The events of September 11 altered the perceptions of millions of people around the world towards terrorism and radical political violence. In the **UK** millions watched with fascinated horror the events unfold on prime time television from the Iranian embassy siege in London. A billion or more people watched with shock, dismay and outrage the live television coverage of 11 September 2001 terror attacks in New York and Washington (Shpiro, 2002). The international news media had cut across distances, natural boundaries and time differences and brought the horrors of terrorism into almost every house around the world. Digital satellite broadcasting, cellular communications and the internet turned terrorism into a live show.

International terrorism has always sought to achieve a very high media profile for its actions; and indeed, the element of violence in terrorism often seems secondary to that of dominating newspaper headlines and television coverage. One has to be careful to satisfy the public demand for more and more information and providing terrorists with a willing stage for their violent acts.

The digital flow of information enables instantaneous and constant news coverage. The international effort against terrorism requires not only a co-ordinated media strategy among the governments involved but also a global media that is aware of its democratic responsibilities. This can be hard to achieve.

Reference

Shpiro, S. (2002) 'Conflict Media Strategies and the Politics of Counter-terrorism', *Politics*, vol. 22, no. 2, pp. 76–85.

Attacks by Islamic Groups since September 11

These outrages have occurred around the world; and have sparked great fear and a renewed determination to catch the killers. In **Saudi Arabia** in October 2001 a suicide bomber struck a busy shopping area in Al Khubar killing one person and injuring many more. No one claimed responsibility. In India in December 2001 twelve people were killed in a suicide attack on the Indian Parliament building. The perpetrators could have been Kashmiri militants or Islamic radicals upset by American attacks in **Afghanistan** or both. In Pakistan three attacks occurred in March 2002 two Americans and others were killed when a man threw grenades into a church. Two months later a bomber killed eleven French engineers in Karachi and in the same city in June a suicide bomber killed 13 persons at the US consulate. In October 2002 off the Yemeni coast a blast occurred on a French oil tanker, it was blamed on a small boat laden with explosives manned by suicide bombers, colliding with the tanker. The *USS Cole*, an American warship had been attacked in similar fashion in Yemen in October 2000. Both attacks were blamed on **Al Qaeda**. Also in October in Kuwait a US marine was killed while on exercises on Failaka Island. Shots were fired on US forces in the country and both were blamed on Al Qaeda.

An individual example was shown in December 2001 by the so-called 'Shoebomber' Richard Reed. Reed, a British-born convert to Islam and Al Qaeda set out to blow up a Paris to Miami flight in December 2001. A stewardess saw him trying to light his shoes with a match. Each of the soles of his shoes on examination contained about four ounces of Pentarythritol Tetranitrate – PETN, a constituent of the plastic explosive Semtex. This was a sophisticated device virtually impossible to detect by airport security. He was arrested on the plane and charged with attempted murder using a weapon of mass destruction. An indication that he was 'mule' (a person who carries out a terrorist atrocity on behalf of a terrorist organisation) with intensive backing came from a strand of hair and a palm print that were not Reeds. It has been suggested that Al Qaeda members in France and Belgium assisted him. Reed was accused of having been trained at an Al Qaeda camp in **Pakistan** having originally attended the British mosque in south London – known for its radical Islamic teaching. In January 2003 under American law he was sentenced to 180 years in jail and fined \$2 million by a Boston court for his various offences.

Foreign Policy

Non-state individuals and groups play a key role in foreign policy. They affect foreign policy in two ways – exercising indirect influence by lobbying their governments, or interacting directly with foreign actors. Ultimately terrorists threaten our sense of well-being. The proliferation of terrorist groups has reduced the sense of security.

As the world has witnessed in relations between **Russia** and **Chechnya**, the world has become enmeshed in a vicious cycle of terrorism and **counter-terrorism**. When governments fail to respect **human rights** their adversaries are unlikely to do so. Political terrorism and common criminality may merge, for example, profits from international drug trafficking sometimes help purchase weapons for revolutionaries – this is particularly prevalent in Latin America.

As we have seen with September 11, lax immigration procedures and growing numbers of political refugees have brought the USA into the front line of global terrorism. State support for terrorist groups and the propensity of terrorists' effect have contributed to the trend of increasing terrorism. Escalating terrorist violence can make countries ungovernable.

In the Middle East, much terrorist violence is directed against **Israel** by violent Arab-Palestinian groups. The difficulty, however, that terrorists have in striking Israel directly has encouraged them to strike at 'softer' targets especially the interests of Americans and Europeans whom the terrorists accuse of being pro-Israeli (Mansbach, 1992). Terrorism is used to poison the atmosphere and rouse popular passions, hoping to sabotage peace efforts by triggering a spiral of violence and counter violence.

Reference

Mansbach, R. W. (1992) *The Global Puzzle: Issues and Actors in World Politics*, Boston/NY: Houghton Mifflin.

Homeland Security Programme

September 11 was a tactical victory for the terrorists. The Homeland Security Programme was devised to stop a recurrence of such activity.

The Programme has been built up to devise attack tactics in conjunction with designing counter-measures. The drivers of new technology have to be broadened in the public and private sectors. Transnational intelligence needs to be improved and information has to be shared with allies. This is necessary as terrorists themselves are transnational in nature. The Programme's creators realise that the means that terrorists employ are potentially more important than the surveillance of persons, and raises far fewer civil liberties issues i.e. checking on those persons seeking information on the layout of a nuclear power plant is more feasible than putting all Arabs in the **USA** under surveillance.

Protective measures for homeland security covers a wide spectrum of possibilities: vaccines, air defences around the *White House* and nuclear power plants. This has to be paid for by the state.

A major ingredient of the protection effort must be safeguarding information infrastructure that is overwhelmingly in private hands.

Containment of damage from an incident of mass terrorism requires that the public health and agricultural systems establishing capabilities that go beyond protecting against naturally occurring dangers. Getting public opinion to accept the conferring of extraordinary powers on the government can be very difficult and they need reassurance that the measures will be disbanded as soon as possible. This is perhaps unlikely as President Bush enunciated a principle of American policy against catastrophic terrorism which if pursued to the logical conclusion, could establish the absolute destruction of the terrorists as an on-going effort rather than an episodic response to actual attacks. As he stated to a joint session of Congress and the American people on 20 September 2001, 'Either you are with us, or you are with the terrorists'.

The term 'homeland security' was first used in 1997 in the USA, in a report issued by the National Defence Panel. Weapons of mass destruction (WMD) would pose a severe threat to the American homeland and to forces overseas, and this could be compounded by threats to information systems. Basically the term meant the protection of American cities and US government infrastructure.

The first Director of Homeland Defence, Tom Ridge, was appointed in 2002 and was charged with directing a cabinet-level initiative without the support of a department and a corresponding budget. The position involved the co-ordinating of over 42 departments and agencies in an environment where combating terrorism had become an overwhelming priority post-September 11.

In the eyes of many people it is still a difficult term to define. The Quadrennial Defence Team had a go and defined it as 'preventing deterrence and pre-emption of, and defence against aggression targeted at American territory, sovereignty, population and infrastructure as well as the management of the consequences of such aggression and other domestic emergencies, civil disturbances and designated law enforcement efforts'.

Of the many departments charged with the dilemma of dealing with terrorism, none are terrorism specific but instead, terrorism is one of the many items for which they are responsible. September 11 showed comparative weaknesses in America's capacity to compile, collect and communicate information about terrorists and potential terrorist activity (Miller and File, 2001).

The idea of a homeland security post will perhaps be considered in other democratic nations, However, in November 2002 the Prime Minister ruled out a similar unit being established in the UK, although, in March 2003 the Home Office provided new guidance to Britons over possible terrorist attacks. The guidelines covered topics ranging from food stocks to emergency phone numbers. The public were advised not to buy protective clothing and to be alert to unusual and suspicious behaviour in public places.

References

Carter, A. B. (2001/02) 'The Architecture of Government in the Face of Terrorism', *International Security* (winter), vol. 26, no. 3, pp. 5–23.

Miller, M. and File, J. (2001) *Terrorism Fact-book: Our Nation at War*, Illinois: Bollix Books.

Further Reading

Burn, M. (2000) *The Next Wave: Urgently Needed New Steps to Control Warheads and Fissile Material*, Washington, DC and Cambridge, MA: Carnegie Endowment for International Police and Harvard Project on Managing the Atom (April).

Terrorist Possibilities – New Threats

The weapons of modern terrorism have ceased to be purely guns and bombs, but have become the mini-cam, videotape, television and Internet. Much planning and attention to detail has gone into planning terrorist attacks utilising this modern equipment. Modern mega-terrorist leaders such as Bin Laden have adopted management styles to run their organisations, i.e. networked structures. Terrorist teams are carefully selected, they are the professionals. Trained amateurs also play a key role. Al Qaeda has funded many radicals who wish to launch their own attacks; and guidance has also been provided to insurgents, guerrillas and terrorists. The motivation for revenge and destruction is very strong.

Possibilities for future attacks inevitably seem endless ranging from attacking nuclear and chemical plants and striking against shipping to using rocket propelled grenades, and as was demonstrated at Mombasa in 2002 portable surface-to-air missiles. WMD are never far from people's minds. All these possibilities engender even greater fear about terrorism across the world especially in states which value personal freedom and fundamental civil liberties (Hoffman, 2002). Hatred among terrorist extremists towards the **USA** and the unpalatable but realistic fact that the 'war' against

terrorism is never-ending has to be accepted as the norm in future (Hoffman, 2002).

In terms of loss of life and property, the attacks in New York were the most destructive terrorist attack ever. The danger since then is that other groups may try to meet or exceed these atrocities.

There is an increased risk that terrorists may turn to weapons of mass destruction – and may obtain chemical, biological or nuclear or radioactive weapons. The United States did not rush into military action and took steps to comply with **international law**. With regard to the **United Kingdom** in the past, the level of resources put into the defence of the homeland has been set principally to reflect the perceived level of threat rather than through an assessment of the weak points in our society. The events of that day have focussed the UK's capabilities on defending its weak points.

As always the primary responsibility for security in the UK mainland rests with the civil power and armed forces are only used in domestic tasks in support of relevant and legally responsible civil authorities. Existing arrangements post-September 11 would be stretched in the event of a similar attack. The reserves have an increasing role to play.

Armed forces in any country need the capability to take pre-emptive military action to attack terrorist groups before they attack. Forces which can be available at short notice are also necessary.

The scale and horror of the attacks set in train repercussions and consequences whose affects would be felt for years to come. There has been a reorientation in terms of relationships between some of the major countries and blocs of the world. For instance, the development in relations between the USA and **Russia** appear to have altered the terms of the debates on ballistic missile defence and the future of NATO.

To many observers the new world order had after the **Cold War** perhaps allowed or even encouraged the growth of a new form of terrorism which brought with it a new level of threat. No warnings have been given for terrorist attacks attributed to **Al Qaeda**. Another 'surprise' was the apparent willingness of the perpetrators to kill themselves as well as their victims. Modern terrorists are determined to kill large numbers of people and have the world watching. Al Qaeda has certainly represented a major development in terrorism. In future the ability of such groups to operate will depend on the availability of reliable bases and the ability to recruit people prepared to carry out terrorist attacks and sacrifice their lives. The risk of grabbing attention is higher from a range of terrorist organisations or political individuals.

WMD might become the norm in the future, due to improvements against conventional forms; the novelty of using such weapons would lead to huge media coverage which would spread public fear and raise the groups own profile. However, such weapons are less controllable than conventional explosions.

Terrorism cannot be defeated by force. It feeds on the grievances of exploited and dispossessed peoples. Tackling global irregularities and injustices must be part of a long term strategy to starve terrorist groups of their support.

Terrorism can represent an almost military scale threat that is neither categorically domestic nor foreign. Therefore one has to cater for all types of assistance which can be offered. The use of armed forces in dealing with civil emergencies has been well defined but in dealing with a large-scale terrorist attack more needs to be done with clear co-ordinated leadership.

Pre-emptive military action has been suggested across government departments as a way to counter the fanatical groups, but the capability has to be proven and we have to ensure that such action does not lead to operations outside international law. Furthermore, for such action to be effective specialist and highly-trained agile forces need to be made available at short notice.

There is no doubt that the threat from terrorism has become more pressing and more dangerous. The campaign is seen by many observers as military, diplomatic and humanitarian and needs to be pursued legitimately and relentlessly.

Reference

Hoffman, B. (2002) 'Rethinking Terrorism and Counter-terrorism since September 11', *Studies in Conflict and Terrorism*, vol. 25, pp. 303–316.

International Law

Public international law recognises the jurisdiction of the **USA** to try a particular crime such as the perpetrators of **September 11**. International law does not require other states to co-operate to allow the trial to occur. There is no general duty under international law to surrender a defendant to stand trial in another state. Many states would be unwilling to hand over suspects due to the death penalty for certain offences being retained by the United States: in fact, this is Britain's position. Observers around the world question whether anyone accused of perpetrating these crimes could receive a fair trial in the USA.

September 11 showed that a terrorist organisation operating outside the control of any state is capable of causing death and destruction on a scale comparable with that of regular military action by a state. Terrorist acts in the eyes of many states would justify a military response.

On September 11 the USA was the victim of an armed attack but from **Al Qaeda** rather than from a state. The attacks were over long before military response was commenced. Self-defence is lawful in international law, but reprisals if involving the use of armed force, are no longer considered lawful. Proportionality in self-defence is also an important consideration, comparing the number killed in Afghanistan with those killed in the **World Trade Center**. The degree of force employed by the USA was extensive, but, given the scale of the threat, it was not disproportionate.

On the issue of prisoners of war and treatment under the Geneva Convention, the USA agreed to treat Taliban prisoners in accordance with the Convention, but captured Al Qaeda detainees would not be treated in the same way and were sent as 'battlefield detainees' to Guantanamo Naval Base in **Cuba** (Camp Delta). Currently 680 people from 42 countries are held there.

International Order

A great range of states, including **China**, **India**, **Russia**, the main European countries, and North America see Sunni Islamist radicalism as posing a danger of terrorism, separation or both. International worries about **Shi'ite** radicalism are more limited as Shia priorities in the above mentioned countries are relatively insignificant.

In the future, states may become more hostile to terrorism in general, whereas in the past they have sympathised with some forms of terrorist activities. There was a change in relations between the **USA** and Russia in the sense of greater co-operation on counter-terrorist issues – for instance, the Americans were able to use staging posts in the former Soviet states such as Uzbekistan and Turkmenistan for the war against the Taliban. Nevertheless in spite of Western pressure, Russia still pursues a brutal war against **Chechnya** and the Chechens. Russia has remained hostile to the ABM Treaty abrogation by the USA, and to the development of the 'Star War' programme. Russia and China are nervous about a long term American presence in Central Asia. Even before September 11, however, Russia had relented on a previous thorny issue, the eastward expansion of NATO.

Issues in the Middle East appear intractable. Lasting peace between Israel and the Palestinians is further away than ever – to achieve such a peace, a viable Palestinian state is necessary. Muslim and Arab have always felt humiliated by the West, especially with consistent long term backing by the West of the Israeli state. For their part, Muslim and Arab nations have failed to develop their countries, or deal with the poverty and socio-economic problems of their poverty and generally 'catch up' with the West. New radical upheavals can occur in the Muslim world at any time in the future, giving rise to new terrorist movements aimed at the USA and its allies.

US Weakness and Vulnerabilities

The people of America believe that Europeans live in a dream world made possible by American protection. In the months since September 11 there has been a growth in tension among nations that initially felt themselves equally under attack. September 11 divided rather than unified the West. The US military revolution has appeared to be of limited application when fighting a war among the shadows. The more the Pentagon spends on Research and Development making America's forces superior to any other country's army and navy, the more America's enemies will turn to unconventional methods to hurt her.

The attacks of September 11 dented America's prestige and its economy; however, such has been the strength of the American response that the long-term result has been to enhance American credibility, and unite the nation around some powerful themes, with a sense of international purpose. The attacks on **Afghanistan** support this view, but the inability to capture **Osama Bin Laden** or to know definitely where he is, coupled with the war with **Iraq** launched in March 2003, have to some extent undermined their earlier position of strength. Unilateral action by the USA could undermine any sympathy gained post-September 11. In 2003 it appears that Americans are now less reluctant to support military action abroad.

American power grew following the **Cold War** which transformed the European landscape, altered the shape of the international system, led to a reconfiguration of the geography of the world system and changed the ideological ways in which politics was to be conducted. The collapse of the **Soviet Union** eroded the main organised resistance to American power.

Will the cures for international terrorism – travel restrictions, border searches, new immigration procedures and new constraints limiting business efficiency – be more debilitating than the disease of international terrorism itself? Over two years after September 11 it appears attacks inflicted only a glancing blow on the American economy and by association against the process of globalisation. Questions still remain about the effects on the globalised economy in any long running campaign against global terrorism.

Some globalisation era improvements may be among the early casualties of the war on terrorism in order to reduce societal vulnerabilities i.e. streamlining procedures for border crossings, freer immigration policies and 'just-in-time' delivery of international packages (Campbell, 2002).

A sustained national campaign against radical Islamic fundamentalism could have cataclysmic consequences for global growth in the short term and could potentially undermine the process of globalisation. A return to a world of unfettered freedom is unlikely but countries can adapt to heightened security measures and disruptions that war brings. In 2003 the developed industrialised countries are trying to seek a balance between enhanced security and greater prosperity.

References

Campbell, K. M. (2002) 'Globalisations First War?', *Washington Quarterly*, vol. 25, no. 1 (winter), pp. 7–14.

Cox, M. (2002) 'American Power Before and After 11 September: Dizzy with Success?', *International Affairs*, vol. 78, no. 2, pp. 261–276.

Halliday, F. (2001) *The World at 2000: Perils and Promises*, Basingstoke: Palgrave.

Hoffman, B. (2002) 'Rethinking Terrorism and Counter-terrorism since September 11', *Studies in Conflict and Terrorism*, vol. 25, pp. 303–316.

Jenkins, B. M. (2001) 'The Organisation Men: Autonomy of a Terrorist Attack' in Hoge, J. F. Jnr and Rose, G. (eds) *How Did This Happen? Terrorism and the New War*, NY: Public Affairs.

Further Reading

Baxter, J. and Downing, M. (eds) (2001) *The Day That Shook the World: Understanding September 11*, London: BBC Worldwide.

Gormley, D. M. (2002) 'Enriching Expectations: 11 September's Lessons for Missile Defence', *Survival IISS Quarterly*, vol. 44, no. 2 (summer), pp. 19–35.

Keelty, M. Commissioner (2001) 'A Changed View for the Australian Federal Police a Year after September 11', *Platypus Magazine*, no. 76 (September), pp. 2–11.

Latter, R. (2001) 'After 11 September: CBW Threat Looms', *Jane's Intelligence Review* (November), pp. 30–31.

Lewis, B. (1998) 'License to Kill: Osama Bin Laden's Declaration of Jihad', *Foreign Affairs*, vol. 77, no. 6 (Nov/Dec), pp. 14–19.

Lieven, A. (2001) 'The Secret Policemen's Ball: The United States, Russia and the International Order after September 11', *International Affairs*, vol. 78, no. 2, pp. 245–259.

Mansbach, R. W. (1992) *The Global Puzzle: Issues and Actors in World Politics*, Boston/New York: Houghton Mifflin.

Nanay, J. (2001) 'New Friends, New Enemies and Oil Politics: Causes and Consequences of September 11 Terrorist Attacks', *Middle East Policy*, vol. VIII no. 4 (December), pp. 11–19.

State of the World 2002 Progress toward a Sustainable Society, London: Earthscan Publications.

Walt, S. M. (2001/2) 'Beyond Bin Laden: Re-shaping US Foreign Policy', *International Security*, vol. 26, no. 3 (winter), pp. 56–78.

Wedgwood, R. (2001) 'The Law's Response to September 11', *Ethics and International Affairs*, vol. 16, no. 1, pp. 8–13.

Shi'ites

(Shi'ah, meaning sect; sha'a, meaning follow). Shi'ites have always felt alienated from more moderate Arab groups, and in the Arab world, even where they make up the majority of the population as in **Iraq** and Bahrain, the Shi'ites are usually treated and often feared as a lower-class minority. Persecution is at the root of the faith. A thirteenth-century parable explains why the Shi'ites believe in martyrdom, or purification through death. The biggest schism in **Islam** emerged within forty years of its founding by the Prophet Muhammad, whose revelations are recorded in the Islamic holy book, the *Koran*. The schism began as a dispute over leadership of the Islamic empire.

The group that became the Shi'ites felt that the line of leadership should descend through the family of the Prophet's cousin and son-in-law, Ali, who eventually became the Caliph, or God's representative on earth. The single strain of Islam formally split after Ali was murdered in 661 AD, and a new leader was selected from outside the family. Those who broke with the mainstream Sunni sect became known as the Shiat Ali, or followers of Ali – today's Shi'ites.

It was Hussein, Ali's son, who set the tone for the Shi'ite faith. Hussein and a small band of followers set out to defend the rights of the Prophet's family to hold the title of Caliph. To Hussein it was more honourable to die for belief than live with injustice. At the Iraqi town of Karbala, Caliph's army massacred Hussein and his followers. It was a precedent for a tradition that grew in importance with time. Hussein left a legacy of the dignity of ultimate protest, and sowed the seeds of a movement centred on revolt against tyranny and oppression as a duty to, and in the name of, God.

Shi'ites' sense of persecution is fuelled by the fact that Shi'ites live in oil rich nations. The eight major Gulf states – **Saudi Arabia**, Kuwait, **Iran**, Iraq, Bahrain, Oman, Qatar and the United Arab Emirates – have 60 per cent of the world's known oil reserves. The Shi'ites, who make up the largest work force on the oilfields, feel they have not reaped adequate benefits from 'Petrodollars'. Most of these dollars have been used to develop other parts of their home countries under Sunni domination. All the Arab Gulf states have experienced growing threats from Shi'ite extremists, resulting in part from Shi'ite resentment over feelings of exploitation and discrimination by the Sunnis.

Shi'ite hostility towards the West dates back two centuries to Napoleon's conquest of **Egypt**, when France became the first Western power to control a Muslim territory. Western colonisation further entrenched **Sunni** rule, even in countries where Shi'ites were the majority. In the wave of independence in the Arab world after the Second World War Shi'ites have been allowed very few positions of political or military power.

Today the world's largest concentration of Shi'ites is in the Gulf, where they form nearly 75 per cent of the population, mostly in Iran and Iraq. Just over 10 per cent of the world's 832 million Muslims are Shi'ites.

The only major nation to be ruled by Shi'ites since 1502 is Iran. The huge protests of 1979, occurred because many Shi'ites felt Shah Muhammad Reza Pahlavi had sold Iran's soul to the West, particularly the **USA**. The Shah and American influence were banished from Iran.

Iran's experience since its 1979 Islamic revolution has inspired not only the minority extremists, but also the general population of Shi'ites and some Sunnis. Iran has survived the challenges of its seven-year war with Iraq, economic sanctions and political ostracisation by most of the world. Those who have seen themselves as underdogs and victims at the hands of other Muslims and foreign ideologies finally have a base and an advocate – and as in the case of the 1985 Beirut hijack, an example to follow in challenging a superpower.

See also: Hamas; Hizbullah; Iran; Iraq; Islam; Lebanon; Sunni.

References

Horrie, C. and Chippindale, P. (1993) *What is Islam?*, London: Star Books.

Hourani, A. (1997) *A History of the Arab Peoples*, Cambridge, MA: Belknap Press.

Juergensmeyer, M. (2000) *Terror in the Mind of God: The Global Rise of Religious Violence*, Berkeley, CA and London: University of California Press.

Further reading

Cooley, J. K. (2001) *Unholy Wars: Afghanistan, America and International Terrorism*, London and Sterling, Virginia: Pluto Press.

Kramer, M. (1987) 'The Structure of Shi'ite Terrorism' in Kurz, A. (Ed) *Contemporary Trends in World Terrorism*, New York: Praeger, pp. 43–52.

Sikh Extremism

The current campaign of violence by Sikh extremists illustrates the challenge **India** faces in maintaining national unity in the face of efforts at sectionalisation. The pull of ethnic and religious factions has strained the Indian nation since its independence in 1947. The Indian Prime Minister, Rajiv Gandhi, is trying to end the strife which existed between his late mother Indira Gandhi, and the Sikhs. In June 1984 she ordered the Indian Army to invade the holy shrine of the Sikh religion in Amritsar to flush out armed resistance, generating deep resentment and outrage among Sikhs. As a result she was assassinated by her two Sikh bodyguards in New Delhi in October 1984, which led to 2,000 revenge killings of Sikhs by Hindus.

Sikhs have always wanted a greater role in a predominantly Hindu India; in addition some seek greater autonomy for Sikhs, especially in the state of Punjab where many live. Some Sikhs demand an independent state of Khalistan.

Before the formation of the National Council of Khalistan in 1972, a demand for an independent Sikh state (Khalistan) had first been put forward by Dr Jagjit Singh, the general secretary of the Akali

Dal (the Sikh political party). Dr Singh stated in London in December 1971 (a day before war broke out between India and **Pakistan**) that President Yahya Khan of Pakistan had promised his support for the secession of Punjab from India and the establishment of an independent Sikh state, and had allowed the Sikhs to open a broadcasting station in West Pakistan. The Akali Dal's working committee expelled Dr Singh from the party at the very end of 1971 for his anti-national activities, and he did not return to India. His followers formed the National Council of Khalistan, which from its headquarters in the Golden Temple in Amritsar (the central Sikh shrine) issued Khalistan passports, postage stamps and currency notes. Critics of the Khalistan movement were in some cases shot; and fundamentalist sects clashed with those who they considered to be heretical. A youth organisation – the Dal Khalsa – was founded in 1979 under the leadership of Gajendra Singh, and two years later took part in the unsuccessful hijacking of an Indian airliner.

The problems in Amritsar started in April 1982 when fighting broke out between Hindus and Sikhs after several cows' heads had been discovered outside two Hindu temples. Responsibility for the desecration was claimed by the Dal Khalsa, which declared that it would be repeated until its demand for a total ban on smoking and cigarette sales in Amritsar was conceded (the use of tobacco being forbidden to Sikhs). A bomb also exploded in the Temple of the Sikh religious leader, Sant Jarnail Singh Bhindranwale. Sikhs burned down cigarette shops and slaughtered cattle in front of Hindu temples, while in Chandigarh, Hindus invaded a Sikh temple and tore up a copy of the Sikh scriptures. About six hundred people were arrested and as a result of the disturbances the National Council of Khalistan and the Dal Khalsa were banned by the Indian government.

Akali Dal leaders, undeterred, launched a new campaign for an autonomous state of Punjab (similar in status to Kashmir), enlarged to include adjacent Sikh-populated areas, and also in support of various religious demands. Although these demands stopped short of the full independence demanded by the Khalistan movement, secessionists participated in widespread agitation and demonstrations, to which the authorities responded by arresting thousands of Sikh activists. Talks between the Government and Sikh leaders towards the end of 1982 failed to produce any agreement on the Sikhs' political demands, although the Prime Minister, Mrs Gandhi, made concessions to their religious demands by announcing that Amritsar would be declared a holy city, and that the sale of tobacco and liquor would be banned within its walls. Tensions have run high since that time, reaching a pitch at the Golden Temple siege in Amritsar.

If Sikhs were offered a substantial degree of autonomy within the Punjab, other minorities could be expected to demand similar autonomy in other regions. Sikh demands are the thin end of the wedge, and India realises its national unity has to be paramount.

Most Indians oppose the Sikhs' demand for greater influence, believing they already have sufficient power. Sikhs are only two per cent of the population, but they have an influence in government, military and economic spheres far beyond their numbers.

Over the past fifteen years other Sikh groups have become active, and these include Dashmesh (active in Canada, Germany and India) Dal Khalsa (active in Germany, India and Pakistan) and Babbar Khalsa (active in Canada, Germany and India). The Dashmesh has made several regular and bloody attacks against the Hindus. The Dal Khalsa wishes to establish an independent Sikh state called Khalistan and was blamed for the bombing of an Air India plane (Combs, 2003). Babbar Khalsa has desecrated Hindu holy places, and undertakes bombings and assassinations.

See also: India.

Reference

Combs, C. C. (2003) *Terrorism in the 21st Century*, New Jersey: Prentice Hall.

Further Reading

Cloughley, B. (1987) 'The Sikh Extremists: Violence at Home and Abroad', *TVI Report*, vol. 7, no. 2, pp. 33–39.

Mulgrew, I. (1988) *Unholy Terror: The Sikhs and International Terrorism*, Toronto: Key Porter Books.

Wheelock, W. (1988) 'The Sikhs: Religious Militancy, Government Oppression or Politics as Usual', *Conflict*, vol. 8, nos. 2/3, pp. 97–110.

Simulation *see* Terror and Terrorism

Sixties Terrorism *see* History of Terrorism

Sociology of Terrorism

Sociologists define terrorism as the use of covert violence by a group, for political ends. Terrorist movements have mainly consisted of members of the educated middle classes, but there has been terrorism by the desperate and refugees, trade unions and working classes (for example in the **United States** 1880–1910 and Spain 1890–1936). In some cases there has been a link with social dislocation and economic crisis, at other times there has been no such connection. Movements of national liberation and social revolution (or reaction) have turned to terrorism after political action failed. Sociologists have been able to account for mass movements, but for small movements this has proved difficult – thus it is hard to generalise about terrorism. For many terrorists, their perceived historical 'mission' ended with the destruction of the system (or of foreign oppression). Yet terrorist campaigns have continued, and inevitably, some terrorists have become concerned with the seizure of power and more distant perspectives.

Urban terrorists have on the whole been aware of the difficulties facing them and, in theory, urban terrorism and rural guerrilla warfare make parallel attempts to win over sections of the army or start a general insurrection or a people's war. But in practice the emphasis is usually on urban terror, either because the countries concerned are predominantly urbanised, or because the masses do not respond, or because the army is not inclined to co-operate with the terrorists.

All major terrorist movements have had a central command, sometimes professional and at other times rudimentary. The central command of

the terrorist movement has sometimes been located abroad – Switzerland the USA and **Lebanon** have been centres for movements operating elsewhere. Terrorists can move around freely, but the more remote the headquarters from the scene of action, the less complete its knowledge of current events. The larger a terrorist movement, the greater the danger of detection. Urban terrorist campaigns have seldom lasted longer than three to four years.

The success of terrorist operations depends on reliable information about the targets to be attacked and the movements of the victim to be killed or abducted (for example, the Irish Republican Army has built up strong sources of information). The dagger and the pistol were the traditional weapons up to the dawning of the age of dynamite. The bomb clearly was not the all-destroying weapon it had been thought to be, but it had become a symbol, replacing the barricade. Terrorists have the great advantage that, unlike the security forces in a democratic society, they are not compelled to act within the law. The police cannot in theory use illegal means to repress terrorism, and so it becomes more necessary for the police to collect information via informers, and perhaps financially tempting for terrorists to act as informers – for instance, by 1912 the Okhrana (the Russian secret police) had some 26,000 paid agents, most of them part-time informers, and in addition a permanent staff of some 50,000. The most dangerous threat to terrorists is the promise of a reward for information leading to their capture. This weapon has been widely used. Many captured terrorists have behaved with dignity and heroism but quite a few terrorists have broken down during interrogation.

Many terrorist groups have attracted criminal elements at one time or another. Criminal elements have joined the ranks of terrorist groups in times of general unrest when there were sound excuses for looting, as in the Russian revolution of 1905.

Internal dissension has dominated the threats faced by terrorist groups. Most groups came into being as a result of a split between the moderate and the more extreme wing of an organisation, and almost all of them later underwent further fission – such as the Narodnaya Volya in Tsarist **Russia**, and the Irish Fenians. The assassination of leading representatives of the 'system' is the oldest method of terrorist tactic and has been the one most frequently adopted by terrorists – it was first practiced in Persia and much later in nineteenth-century Ireland. Expropriation, for example, bank robbery or, less frequently, robbery of trains carrying large sums of money, has also been popular. **Kidnapping** for political purposes and the extortion of ransoms has been practiced for generations.

Agrarian terror took place in the nineteenth century in Andalusia in southern Spain, in Ireland, in eastern Poland and in north Germany against big landowners, tax collectors or government representatives.

With regard to the **media**, it is not the magnitude of the terrorist operation that counts, but the publicity, and this rule applies to single operations and whole campaigns. Terrorist groups usually hope for a measure of public support. Extreme nationalists operating against foreigners can always count on some sympathy from fellow countrymen and at the very least do not expect to be betrayed by their compatriots. In Latin America, as in pre-revolutionary Russia, there has been much goodwill for what terrorists have done – and in an emergency they have been able to count on the support of intellectuals, churchmen and sections of the middle class to defend them against the harsher forms of government repression.

Since the early nineteenth century conspiratorial links have existed between revolutionary groups in Europe. The Russian terrorists of the 1880s found imitators in many parts of the world, and neighbouring countries have often provided sanctuary for terrorists. Historically, the terrorist groups that have been more successful in attaining their aims have been those with narrow, clearly defined objectives, and those with powerful outside protectors; for example, terrorist groups facing imperial powers no longer able or willing to hold on to their colonies or protectorates. Seen in historical terms, terrorism has been effective only occasionally. It has not succeeded against effective dictatorships, let alone modern totalitarian regimes. In democratic societies or against ineffective authoritarian regimes, it has on occasion been more successful. However, terrorists are driven by thirst for action rather than rational consideration of the consequences, and past failures have not acted as a deterrent.

Apart from the fact that most terrorists belong to the early twenties age group, there are few other features they hold in common. Nationalist separatist groups consist of young people of lower social background than the socialist-revolutionary groups. Political issues in nineteenth-century Russia were clear-cut – there were no constitutional or elementary rights, and no legal redress against the abuse of power. The less clear-cut the nature of the political purpose of terrorism, the greater its appeal to unbalanced persons. Men fighting a cruel tyranny have quite different motives from those rebelling against a democratically elected government.

See also: Dynamite Terrorism; History of Terrorism; Kidnapping; Media.

References

Roucek, J. S. (1962) 'Sociological Elements of a Theory of Terror and Violence', *American Journal of Economics and Sociology*, vol. 21, no. 2.

Walter, E. V. (1964) 'Violence and the Process of Terror', *American Sociological Review*, vol. 29, no. 2, pp. 248–257.

Wieviorka, M. (1993) *The Making of Terrorism*, Chicago, IL: University of Chicago Press.

Further Reading

Gibbs, J. P. (1989) 'Conceptualisation of Terrorism', *American Sociological Review*, vol. 54, no. 3, pp. 329–340.

Horowitz, I. L. (1973) 'Political Terrorism and State Power', *Journal of Political and Military Sociology*, vol. 1, pp. 147–157.

Somalia

The country in the Horn of Africa has been plagued with worsening political and security conditions for many years. The war on terrorism is yet another crisis; and most of the south and centre of the country remains ungoverned.

The Somali Islamic movement has been seen as a possible but not a definitive threat – but its radicalism is there. Somali was one of the countries which the West considered **Al Qaeda** might relocate to from embattled **Afghanistan** in late 2001. Sudan and Yemen were other possibilities. To the extent that the war on terrorism includes winning 'hearts and minds' in the Islamic world, the re-engagement of the West in Somalia's development crisis is seen by some as a necessity. There is still great concern that some Somali businesses are being used by the Al Qaeda.

Further Reading

Menkhaus, K. (2002) 'Somalia; In the Crosshairs of the War on Terrorism', *Current History*, vol. 10, no. 655 (May), pp. 210–220.

South Africa

During the apartheid years violence became endemic in African political life, there are many examples of this in existing political regimes – black, white, coloured and Arab – throughout the African continent. In South Africa, violence had become a fact of life, and the use of terror is part of the apparent norm of political action. The possibility that under certain conditions the original aim of the end of apartheid might become lost sight of and violence unleashed, was not confined to any one race, group or community within the Republic. Terrorism as part of the overall attack on the existing government and social system may also be seen as an outcome of a lack of inhibitions regarding the use both of violence and of the established tactics now known as revolutionary warfare. Terrorism included among the tactics being used to force the surrender of the government and the installation of a progressive, radical, political group. Whether the aim of terrorism in South Africa is perceived as liberation, capitulation, or both, is not necessarily dependent upon the observer's racial origin.

The terror campaign in South Africa was carried out, by its own claim, by the African National Congress (ANC), through its military wing, Umkhonto We Sizwe (MK), or 'Spear of the Nation'. Its stated strategy was to destroy the existing political, economic and social structure of South Africa by means of political subversion and propaganda, and sabotage and terrorism. Such tactics, in effect, amounted to a revolutionary war strategy. The term 'revolutionary war' was widely interpreted as the forcible attempt by politically organised groups to gain control of a country's decision-making structure through unconventional warfare and terrorism, which is integrated with general political and social mobilisation to win over the sympathy of the nation.

1976 was regarded as the time when the ANC managed to put into effect its 'second Umkhonto Campaign' of armed action against South Africa. The independence of Mozambique provided a continuous area for infiltration into South Africa and also opened up Swaziland as an infiltration conduit. Widespread domestic troubles throughout South Africa, epitomised by the unrest in Soweto, succeeded in radicalising many blacks. A large number of radicalised and comparatively well educated young blacks fled from South Africa – many joining the ANC. By the late 1970s, several thousand fugitives were undergoing insurgency training in Angola, **Libya** and Tanzania. Increasing ANC operations caused South Africa to deploy police and military forces in increased strength along South Africa's landward borders.

During the 1970s and early-1980s ten main categories of terrorist activity were developed. The main areas of activity were the sabotage of railroad communications, mainly in urban areas, and of links between black residential areas and the city centre; assassination and attempted assassination aimed at perceived opponents; attacks on industrial installations such as electricity sub-stations and oil refineries; contacts between insurgents and security forces; attacks on administration offices, and pamphlet bombs; attacks on police stations; bomb explosions in city centres or public areas; attacks on military targets, and attacks on the diplomatic offices of Homeland states.

The main attacks occurred in African townships, in central business districts and in the countryside. Most incidents clustered around the urban industrial complexes of Johannesburg and Durban and in other areas of the Transvaal and Natal.

Sabotage included a number of spectacular incidents designed to achieve wide national and international media coverage in order to fulfil the aim of a strategy of armed propaganda. These were the sabotage of oil tanks; rocket attacks on military complexes and a nuclear power station; bombs outside and inside government administration buildings, and car bomb attacks on the South African Air Force HQ and on the Department of Internal Affairs. Attacks on police stations have increased, along with the use of more advanced weapons.

The ANC's armed activity escalated, although its scope and intensity were limited. Unable by its nature to challenge the state's control of power the campaign is characterised by armed propaganda, as one step in a multi-dimensional, multi-phase, protracted 'people's war'.

While the ANC has attempted to increase its participation in mass-based local action and to extend its insurrection-type tactics, it has also developed a stronger inclination towards terrorism, as proclaimed at the Kabwe Conference in 1985, and as manifested in incidents of rural and urban terrorism. Kabwe consciously included South Africa's white farmers as legitimate targets of ANC insurgency. As a result many bomb incidents took place on roads near the borders of Zimbabwe and Botswana.

The mobilisation of the masses in South Africa was a major function of front organisations for the banned African National Congress and the South African Communist Party since 1970, when the explosive power of youth groups was realised. This developed into the politicisation of black and coloured schools and other educational centres. A direct result was school boycotts, and also the burning of classrooms, books and, occasionally, teachers. 'Black consciousness' was also fostered, and groups adopting this philosophy or psychological attitude played a large part in politicising that majority group of the population, especially students at tertiary establishments. The South African Student Organisation (SASO) was formed as a result of the efforts of Steve Biko and others at the University of the North Turfloop in 1969. This was a conscious effort to break away from the all-white National Union of South African Students (NUSAS). Most of the followers of SASO were supporters of the Pan-African Congress. Indians and coloureds were also admitted, giving a new dimension to the concept of 'Black African'.

On the question of township unrest, the waves of rioting which swept across South Africa, the often harsh, repressive response by the state, the severe economic recession and unemployment provided the ANC with a firm basis for action in this field. The five main causes of the unrest in the townships were the crisis of legitimacy and credibility of local authorities, which are unable to live up to black moderates' expectations; grievances over influx control; atrocious physical conditions in many of the townships, and unpopular resettlement policies; a lack of say in political decision-making processes; and real and perceived inequalities in education and facilities.

The ANC attempted not only to exploit and take credit for the unrest, but also, if possible, to control the situation. Indeed, the widespread violence forced the ANC to reformulate its strategy to encompass a more detailed perspective on how insurrection could be put to use in the specific conditions of the South African situation. Because of the power of the South African state, unrest and revolt alone would not overthrow the system, but the ANC contended that such tactics could certainly be used as part of a protracted strategy of revolutionary warfare. Insurrection (mass unrest and revolt) could weaken the state and serve as a radicalising and recruiting agent for the ANC's people's army.

Fuelled by local grievances and popular enmity towards the administration, insurrection and armed action were used in attempts to render the urban black areas ungovernable by destroying local government. To this end there were numerous petrol-bomb, hand-grenade and rifle attacks on policemen and town councillors and their property. The ANC ordered cadres to eliminate all blacks who assisted the white government in administering black townships. The Congress has recently called on township residents to move from the stage of ungovernability to one where independent people's political committees are set up.

The aim of the banned ANC, in informal alliance with the South African Communist Party (SACP), was a closely organised seizure of state power. To this end they visualised a protracted struggle against the incumbents of state power, embracing all forms of struggle, violent and non-violent, in a complete revolutionary warfare strategy. Once state power had been captured, the aim of a future ANC/SACP alliance would be defined as the radical restructuring of South African society on the political basis of majority rule, in a military state, within an economic framework of Marxist socialism. A 'nationalist liberation struggle' was defined by the ANC as its primary strategic objective. Limited reform, such as President Botha tried in the 1980s, fell short of a complete transfer of power to the ANC.

ANC insurgency since 1960 fell into distinct phases with varied repercussions: the early period between 1960 and 1964 proved conclusively that the particular conditions existing in contemporary South Africa made any internal organisation highly vulnerable to state counter-action. Indeed, the experiences of this period and later point to the manifest and intractable problems of attempting to establish 'base areas' or 'liberated zones' inside South Africa, in the face of the state's over-whelming coercive apparatus (administrative, legal, social, police and military). The period between 1964 and 1975 served to demonstrate the problems contained in any attempt to develop insurgency against South Africa from external base areas that were not contiguous with South Africa's northern borders. There were almost insurmountable ob-stacles posed by the geographically intervening zones of buffer states which were actively hostile to the aims and intentions of the ANC. Conversely, the period between 1970 and 1984 showed that given access to facilities in neighbouring states, infiltration and insurgency began to develop actively. This development was attenuated by the conditional, restricted nature of the access provided by black states unwilling to allow the development of large guerrilla bases.

Within the Republic, the important factor of information and misinformation was largely con-trolled by government regulations, which consider-ably limits what can be reported for public consumption. Within this situation the English language **media** was accused of left-wing bias, the Afrikaans press of complicity with the govern-ment, the black and Indian press with much of the misinformation and speculation regarding the origins and motives of terror acts – a position which was exploited quite naturally by cadres of the ANC and SACP and by UDF, AZAPO and other front organisations engaged in subversion in South Africa. This state of affairs was not helped by the

banning of publications and people. The state's response, most other countries believe, should be to make all information freely available, or at least not to impede its propagation. Outside South Africa, the ANC seemed to be regarded in many quarters as worthy of assistance in its fight against the evils of apartheid.

For many people, throughout the years of apartheid, South Africa was not a terrorist state since it legitimated its war against the ANC as a war against terrorism. Those who supported the ANC as freedom fighters did so in order to justify the existence of inalienable rights of the majority black population. To many observers in the developed world, the need to watch closely and if necessary try and influence development in South Africa during apartheid were seen as an example of the global economic struggle for scarce resources.

South Africa and the apartheid struggle showed that whether terrorism was used by liberation fighters or by state officials it was still criminal activity. The release of Nelson Mandela in February 1990, after nearly 30 years in jail, signalled the beginning of the end for apartheid and the birth of multi-party government from the first genuine elections in 1994 with Mandela elected the first President of 'the new' South Africa.

References

Cline, R. and Freeman, D. (1988) *Terrorism: The South African Connection*, New York: Crane Russak.
Richardson, L. D. (1987) 'The Threat to Peace in South Africa', *TVI Report*, vol. 7, no. 4, pp. 29–36.

Further Reading

Johnson, P. and Martin, D. C. (1990) *Apartheid Terrorism: The Destabilisation Report*, Bloomington, IN: Indiana University Press.
Waldmeir, P. (1997) *Anatomy of a Miracle: The End of Apartheid and the Birth of the New South Africa*, London: Penguin.

Soviet Union

There has been dispute among experts about whether and to what extent terrorism is sponsored and controlled by the Soviet Union. Many observers believed that Moscow's strategic thinking called for the manipulation of terrorism as a suitable substitute for traditional warfare, which had become too expensive and is too hazardous to be waged on the battlefield except in special circumstances in close proximity to Soviet borders, as in **Afghanistan**. By overt and covert use of non-military techniques, and by exploiting low-intensity operations around the world, the Soviet Union was able to continue its revolutionary efforts against democratic pluralism in a free world, and expand its own influence into a wider target area.

On the other hand, there are those who were sceptical about direct and indirect Soviet control of terrorist groups. While admitting that Moscow approved of and gave some assistance to what it considers legitimate 'liberation movements', or struggles of people for their independence, proponents of this view argue that the dynamics of modern terrorism are so uncontrollable that the Soviet leaders must be ambivalent about the usefulness of this form of warfare.

Whether or not Moscow controls terrorist and guerrilla warfare operations, the Soviet Union continued to supply massive amounts of arms and money to the revolutionary forces involved. The scope and nature of Soviet involvement in terrorist activity was still obscured in the minds of many observers because it was fundamentally secret or covert, ranging from the sanctioning of violence by propaganda to the supply of funds, training, arms and other operational assistance.

The Soviet role in these activities fluctuated over the years in accordance with Moscow's changing appreciation of its vital interests in different parts of the world. Specific terrorist operations sometimes seemed to be no more than militant behaviour or the coincidental by-product of Soviet propaganda.

It was not always easy to determine whether a particular terrorist action or series of actions in any targeted country is home-grown or Moscow inspired. However, the pattern of Soviet sponsorship of violence in many different regional conflicts became clearer. The Soviet Union's position as an undisputed superpower permitted it to control or strongly influence the foreign policy and international conduct of other socialist countries that subscribed to the Soviet ideological line. In this context, Bulgaria, **Cuba**, Czechoslovakia, Germany and **North Korea**, indirectly supported by **Syria**, South Yemen and Nicaragua, acted as Soviet surrogates in exporting violence.

The broad goals the Soviet Union hoped to achieve from terrorism included influencing developments in neighbouring countries and weakening the political, economic and military infrastructure of the anti-Soviet alliances such as NATO. It wished to stir up trouble for the United States in the highly visible regions of Central America, particularly where such a policy entailed no serious financial burden and is politically low-risk because of the use of surrogate supporting nations like Cuba and Nicaragua. It wished to wage a 'secret war' against individuals considered by the Kremlin as 'mortar enemies' of Communism and the Soviet Union.

See also: Cold War; Russia.

References

Alexander, Y. (1987) 'Some Perspectives on Terrorism and the Soviet Union' in Laqueur, W. (ed.) *The Terrorism Reader*, New York: Methuen, pp. 363–8.

Valenta, J. (1987) 'Terrorism and the USSR', *Terrorism*, vol. 10, no. 1, pp. 59–61.

Further Reading

Goren, R. (1984) *The Soviet Union and Terrorism*, London: Allen and Unwin.

Moley, R. J. (1990) 'The Potential for Terrorism within the Soviet Union' in *21st Century Terrorism*, vol. 13, no. 1, pp. 53–64.

State Sponsorship

State terrorism can be viewed as taking the forms of oppression, repression and terrorism. Oppression is a situation where social and economic privileges are denied to whole classes of people, regardless of whether they oppose the authorities. Repression can be viewed as the use or threat of coercion against opponents or potential opponents in order to prevent or weaken their opposition to the authorities and their policies. Terrorism, in this context, is the use of a deliberate act or threat of violence to create fear or compliant behaviour in the victim.

Every government in the world utilises some form of political repression. Many use repression extensively, for it has proved to be an effective tool to shape the media interest groups, political parties and, through them, the ideas and attitudes of citizens. The tactics and strategies of terrorism have become integral to the foreign policy instruments of the modern state. States and their supporters shrink from labelling their own actions as terrorism, preferring more neutral designations such as 'coercive diplomacy', 'nuclear deterrence' and 'assistance to a friendly state in its pursuit of internal security'.

Repression is a coercive and frequently a secretive style of governing. The more it is used by a government the more that government is revealed as insecure and threatened. Repressive governments cannot induce voluntary compliance and support. Enforcement terrorism is the most extreme form of government repression. Techniques of repression can include arbitrary arrests, press censorship and the outlawing of demonstrations, unions and strikes. Enforcement terrorism covers assassinations and secret arrests, followed by torture, mutilation and perhaps death, can be interpreted as enforcement terrorism. Acts of enforcement terrorism are more severe than acts of repression, and more likely to be deliberately lethal and cruel. Both are designed to force compliance through a climate of fear; both can be employed for reactive or pre-emptive purposes; and both are indicators of illegitimate authority.

All political systems face conflicts over who is to rule and what public policies are to be pursued. Many Latin American nations did not achieve political stability in the nineteenth century; they are now confronted with problems of illegitimate governments trying to promote economic growth and distributive justice, and to handle successfully the challenge of increasing political participation. In **South Africa**, both state and anti-state terror emanate from the unique condition of apartheid and not simply from the disgruntled masses and political extremists.

It is hard to measure the extent to which state violence works to destroy or strengthen people's

visions of their community, their future or their deeply held values; and the extent to which some people perceive that they live in a nation of citizens against the government.

Most of the countries which are considered to be supporters of state-sponsored terrorism always argue that they are innocent and infer that it is a Western tactic which leads to this slanderous accusation.

Syria patronises such Palestinian terrorists as Ahmed **Jabril** and the zealots of **Hamas** and Islamic **Jihad**. The country has supported **Shi'ite** terrorists from **Hizbullah** as part of its campaign in **Lebanon**.

Sudan, a relatively recent player on the international terrorism stage, has allowed foreign militants to operate in the country.

Iraq has worked with Abu Abbas' Palestine Liberation front, and was an early supporter of the **PLO** defector **Abu Nidal**.

Both Iraq, and its neighbour **Iran**, and increasingly more countries in the world, murder their enemies to remind their citizens around the world of their ultimate loyalty to the regime at home. Iranian money and materials have been linked to **Al Qaeda** and Hamas.

In **Afghanistan**, the Taliban or student militia a coalition of Sunni fighters, during its years in power in the late-1990s protected hundreds of trained terrorists, and most notably **Osama Bin Laden**. Drug protection is endemic and linked to international crime, many aspects of which are linked to international terrorism.

North Korea for decades has supported violence of a terroristic nature across the world, and guerrilla style military raids by land and sea against the South. Cash and food reserves are low and they will do anything to obtain more resources. It is still Marxist–Leninist verging on Stalinist. Also a relic from Cold War ideology is **Cuba** which is still active in drug trafficking (Harmon, 2000).

See also: Government Support; 'Terrorist States'.

Reference
Harmon, C. C. (2000) *Terrorism Today*, London: Frank Cass.

Stockholm Syndrome

The use of the term 'identification' in terrorism is generally confined to the identification with the aggressor which manifests itself in the positive attitude some hostages show to their captors (as in 'Stockholm syndrome').

The development of a sense of closeness and attachment between hostage and captor was first noticed during a bank robbery in Stockholm and came to be known as the Stockholm syndrome. The attempted robbery became a barricade and hostage situation. During the episode, a young woman hostage allegedly initiated sexual relations with her captor. The motivation was not a response to fear or coercion, but an intimacy that developed from sharing a common fate in a situation of mutual crisis and the protracted dependence of the woman captive on her captor. The relationship persisted after the bank robber's incarceration.

In the United States **FBI** agents have noted that had observers been attuned to the problem of transference earlier, the syndrome would have been called Shade Gap syndrome rather than Stockholm syndrome. Their reference is to a kidnapping that took place in Shade Gap, Pennsylvania, in 1967, when law enforcement officials came upon the kidnapper in a wooded area, he was hurriedly walking to escape pursuit and encirclement. A considerable distance behind him was the kidnap victim straining to keep up. The victim had only to turn round and walk off to freedom.

The most publicised episode of transference by a hostage to captors was in the case of newspaper heiress Patricia Hearst, who not only took a lover from among her captors but also provided them with covering gunfire when they were about to be seized for shoplifting. Patricia Hearst's behaviour was different only in degree from what is commonly observed in hostages under long-term stress. If Patricia Hearst's responses were more extreme, it is also true that the conditions of her captivity were severe, in terms both of deprivation and duration. These factors were probably exacerbated by her age and lack of experience.

The tremendous public interest in acts of **hostage taking** seems to be because most members of the audience identify with the fate of the victim, sharing his suffering in an act of empathy. Not all members of an audience will automatically show compassion for the victim. Some will identify with the terrorist because he represents the awesome power of one who can destroy life at his whim. If the victim is guilty in the eyes of the spectator he may derive pleasure from humiliation and suffering. Depending on the identification, with victim or terrorist, the spectator's attitude may be either empathy or cruelty. The direction of the identification can be determined by factors like class, race, nationality and party. The process of taking sides whenever a polarising act occurs stirs some members of the passive audience so deeply that they emerge as actors of their own, engaging in new polarising acts.

The switch from love for mankind to destruction of human beings is easier for young people, who may find it hard to identify with the older generation or with their nation. Identification, which enables one to empathise with others, is capable of leading to wide-ranging emotions – to anger and aggressiveness towards the source of the misery of the person or group for whom one has love and compassion. The strategy of terrorism of an insurgent nature is to bring about identification processes. In many cases terrorists attack the targets with which people consciously identify. The terrorist in this context uses the identification mechanism to bring home the terror to a target group by stimulating the identification between the instrumental victim and the victims' reference group.

See also: Hostage Taking; Psychology.

References

Post, J. M. (1990) 'Terrorist Psycho-logic: Terrorist Behaviour as Product of Psychological Forces' in Reich, W. (ed.) *Origins of Terrorism Psychologies, Ideologies, Theologies, States of Mind*, Cambridge: Cambridge University Press, pp. 25–43.

Strentz, T. (1980) 'The Stockholm Syndrome – Law Enforcement Policy and Ego Defences of the Hostage' in Wright, F., Bahn, C. and Rieber, W. (eds) *Forensic Psychology and Psychiatry*, New York Academy of Sciences, pp. 137–150.

—— (1982) 'The Stockholm Syndrome: Law

Enforcement Policy and Hostage Behaviour' in
Ochberg, F. M. and Soskis, D. A. (eds) *Victims of
Terrorism*, Boulder, CO: Westview Press, pp. 149–
164.

Suicide Terrorism

Suicide terrorists are willing to sacrifice their own
lives for the greater good of advancing their
ideological aims. A dozen religious and secular
groups around the world use this most extreme of
terrorists' activities to further ideals, particularly in
the Middle East. The personnel involved in such
activities are motivated by religious/ethnic nationalism. **Women** are becoming more regularly
involved. The perpetrators generally wear specially
designed body suits, some of which were found in
Iraq during the war of 2003. Terrorist suicide
bombers are increasingly targeting sites and people
away from their main operation areas.

The use of suicide bombers causes great fright
and terror among populations affected such as in
Israel and Sri Lanka, especially as they have
attacked seemingly impregnable targets ranging
from highly-guarded government buildings to
barracks.

Al Qaeda changed their format of suicide on
September 11, when passenger aircraft were used
like guided missiles by fanatical psychologically
motivated attackers.

Many suicide bombers would do anything if they
thought it was sanctioned by divine order; as they
would be dying with dignity and honour. They
would be giving to Paradise and their surviving
relatives would be financially looked after for the
rest of their lives.

References

Juergensmeyer, M. (2000) *Terror in the Mind of God:
The Global Rise of Religious Violence*, Berkeley, CA,
London: University of California Press.
Gunaratna, R. (2003) 'Suicide Terrorism: A Global
Threat' in Griset, P. L. and Mahan, S. (eds)
Terrorism in Perspective, Thousand Oaks, CA,
London and New Delhi: Sage Publications, pp.
220–225.

Sunni

Sunni is the orthodox sect of **Islam** and Sunni
Muslims are in the majority in all Islamic countries
except **Iran**. Tension often exists between the
Sunni majority and the **Shi'ite** minority. The
Shi'ites broke away from the mainstream Sunni sect
of Islam in the seventh century in a dispute over
who would inherit spiritual leadership (Henderson,
2002: 142–43). Sunni acknowledge the authority of
the Sunna, the body of traditional Islamic law
accepted by most orthodox Muslims as based on
the words and acts of Mohammed.

In the mid-1980s in **Afghanistan** the seven
political parties which emerged among the Afghan
resistance to the **Soviet Union** occupation were
Sunni and formed a united front, the Islamic Unity
of Afghan Warriors. In neighbouring **Pakistan**, the
population is at least 70 per cent Sunni Muslim.
Iraq although it has always been ruled by Sunnis
has a Shi'ite majority. Of the Kurds, 80 per cent are
Muslim. In the Syrian population the Sunni are the
majority sect, and form 70 per cent of the
population; and Saudi Arabia is overwhelmingly
Sunni Muslim.

Sunni law does not recognise the right of the
faithful to overthrow a bad or unjust ruler, as long
as he nominally upholds the Shari'ah and is
prepared to wage **jihad** if Islam is attacked. In
general, Sunni Islam is a deeply conservative
political creed. The exception is the Mahdi, a
divinely-guided political ruler whom Sunni's believe Allah will deliver to them shortly before the
end of time. **Gadaffi** is widely thought of as the
Sunni Mahdi.

In the **United States** the Black Muslim movement which came to the fore in the 1960s as a
'Black consciousness' movement was reformed in
the 1970s into a fairly orthodox Sunni community
known as the Sunni American Muslim Mission
(Horrie and Chippindale, 1993: 123–24).

The Palestinians are split between Sunni and
Shia and they are deadly rivals – the Sunni's flock
to **Hamas** and Palestine Islamic Jihad and the
Shi'ites support Iranian operatives. In the 1990s
throughout the Muslim world Sunni Muslims have
not been a check on the militant Shi'ites. Sunni's
appear to have produced their own extremists to
count as a leading threat and some of the extremists

are willing to use terrorism for their own politico-religious aspirations and appear to operate in league with Shi'ite Iran (Harmon, 2000: 143). One of the many Sunni financial patrons is **Osama Bin Laden**.

See also: Osama Bin Laden; Shi'ites.

References

Harmon, C. C. (2000) *Terrorism Today*, London: Frank Cass.

Henderson, H. (2002) *Terrorism: The Complete Reference Guide*, New York: Checkmark Books.

Horrie, C. and Chippindale, P. (1993) *What is Islam?*, London: Star Books.

Hourani, A. (1997) *A History of the Arab Peoples*, Cambridge, MA: Belknap Press.

Further Reading

Cooley, J. K. (2001) *Unholy Wars: Afghanistan, America and International Terrorism*, London and Sterling, VA: Pluto Press.

Juergensmeyer, M. (2000) *Terror in the Mind of God: The Global Rise of Religious Violence*, Berkeley, CA and London: University of California Press.

Super-Terrorism

This is a term for the growing sophistication of terrorism in the rapidly advancing technological age at the dawn of the twenty-first century. It embraces biological and chemical agents, the use of plastic explosives and attacks against electronic networks playing vital roles in the economic, security and emergency life of society (Sweitzer and Dorsch, 1998).

There is no doubt that technology helps terrorism thrive and continues to make it a global problem. Many groups are desperate for world revolution and there are fanatics in every country and as noted in the Middle East, willing to die for their cause. Technological terrorism is virtually uncontrollable by any state.

Reference

Sweitzer, G. E. and Dorsch, C. C. (1998) *Super-terrorism: Assassins, Mobsters and Weapons of Mass Destruction*, New York: Plenum Trade.

Further Reading

Laqueur, W. (1999) *The New Terrorism; Fanaticism and the Arms of Mass Destruction*, New York: OUP.

Support for Terrorism

Terrorism has been used by hierarchies and dissidents since the dawn of civilisation. 'Kill one to frighten ten thousand' is an ancient Chinese proverb. The technique has been used by governments, sometimes clandestinely i.e. **death squads**, guerrillas, international terrorists and dissidents, left, right, nationalist, religious and fanatics have all developed increasingly since the Second World War (Clutterbuck, 1990).

On matters of internal support, some terrorists have been supported by popular majority, albeit only on rare occasions; some have been supported by a substantial minority for example the IRA and ETA, and by a small minority such as the Brigate Rosse.

External support can come from foreign governments i.e. Libya and Syria; from foreign communities, for example the Irish Americas, Arabs and Armenians and some by sympathetic groups in target countries.

Short term aims are publicity, political blackmail and ransom. Long term aims are ideological, nationalist and religious change.

Destabilisation can occur which destroys confidence, provokes repression, intimidates collaborators, witnesses, juries, journalists; and makes liberal forms of law unworkable.

Above all, public fear can be created – of collapse, chaos and **civil war**. The public rally to whatever offers the best hope of reforming order – organised revolutionary movement or a military coup.

Reference

Clutterbuck, R. (1990) *Terrorism and Guerrilla Warfare: Forecasts and Remedies*, New York: Routledge.

Surrogate Terrorism

Basically surrogate terrorism is 'guns for hire'. Thousands of men, for example, from the four corners of the Islamic world were taught the skills of irregular warfare in the ranks of the Mujaheddin in **Afghanistan**. After the war with the Soviets drew to a close in 1989 they offered their services to the cause of Islamist radicalism in North Africa, Bosnia, Kashmir, and the Philippines (*Jane's Terrorism*, 1997).

Such terrorists also made pacts and alliances with guerrilla groups and narcotic dealers such as those that operate in Latin America and Asia's so-called 'Golden Triangle' (Burma, Thailand, Laos and Cambodia). Terrorist groups indulge in drug trafficking to raise cash. Drugs in turn bring the terrorist groups into contact with **organised crime**.

Reference

Jane's Terrorism: A Global Survey (1997), London: Jane's Information Group.

Further Reading

Petrakis, G. (1980) 'Terrorism: The Terrorist as a Surrogate Soldier', *Law and Order*, vol. 28, no. 9, pp. 31–38.

Syria

This Arab Republic is a 'socialist popular democracy'; its President is head of the predominant Ba'ath party. The government, the left-wing Arab Socialist Ba'ath party and the armed forces are dominated by members of the minority Alawite sect of the **Shi'ite** Muslim community, yet most of the population are Sunnis. Sunnis demand the recognition of Islam as the state religion. The principal opposition to the regime has come from Muslim extremists within the **Sunni** community, their strongest organisation being the Muslim Brotherhood. Violent actions against the regime have also been carried out by dissident Ba'athists supported by the right-wing historic Ba'ath party of **Iraq**.

The Muslim Brotherhood in Syria shares many objectives with the Shi'ite revolutionaries who came to power in Iran in 1979. The Brotherhood propagates Islamic fundamentalist tenets, and demands free elections, a more liberal economy and an end to Alawite dominance. Christians and other non-Muslims are promised the maintenance of their religious rights. A government satisfactory to the people is promised, but full political rights will be given only to ideologies not contradictory to Islam.

After the assassination of a number of Soviet military advisers and an attempt to kill the President, the Syrian army moved against the Brotherhood in 1979–80. There were violent clashes in many parts of the country, and in 1981–82 it was estimated that 25,000 Syrians had been killed, with Aleppo and Hama the worst affected towns. In addition, in Hama an armed Brotherhood insurrection in early 1982 resulted in the deaths of thousands of civilians.

The National Alliance for the Liberation of Syria was an amalgam of 20 political and religious groups with the aim of consolidating opposition to the Assad regime from within Syria and abroad, and created a constitutional elective system in which freedom of faith, expression and association would be guaranteed. The Alliance worked for the liberation of Palestine and for the long-term objectives of Arab unity. An Arab Communist Organisation has been outlawed for acts of sabotage on foreign buildings in Damascus.

In 1991 Syria recognised **Lebanon** as an independent and separate state; and slowly came round to the view that they would have to negotiate with the Israeli's in order to regain lost land. However, these talks failed on military issues.

In the early-1990s Syria refused to negotiate with **Israel** on a peace process revolving around the return of land taken by Israel in the Yom Kippur War, because of the Israeli's hard line attitudes to the Palestinians. Official negotiations in the mid-1990s failed to make any progress over the issue of Israeli military presence in the Golan Heights region. The Syrians strengthened their relations with Iraq in 1997. Since that time the Syrian government has steadfastly refused to talk peace with Israel until there is some settlement of the Palestine issue.

See also: Shi'ites.

Reference

Bishop, J. and Harmon, K. (1987) 'The Syrian Connection', *TVI Report*, vol. 7, no. 3, pp. 23–25.

Further Reading

Tueller Pritchett, D. (1988) 'The Syrian Strategy of Terrorism', *Conflict Quarterly*, vol. 8, no. 3 (summer), pp. 27–48.

T

Tamil Tigers

Sri Lanka achieved independence from the **United Kingdom** in 1948. The 1948 constitution was modelled upon the Westminster Parliament, and was thought to provide guarantees of the civil rights and cultural identity of the predominantly Hindu Tamil minority community. As in Northern **Ireland**, the dominant majority community, in this case made up of the largely Buddhist Sinhalese, was able to manipulate what was formally a model parliamentary democracy by gerrymandering of elections and by its inbuilt parliamentary majority, in order to deprive the minority of effective political representation.

Although Tamils and Sinhalese had both inhabited the island of Sri Lanka for over two thousand years, the status of Tamils remained uncertain after 1948. An act in that year deprived one million Tamils of Indian origin of Sri Lankan citizenship, and a further act in 1949 excluded them from participation in elections. Sinhalese gradually became the single official language, and anti-Tamil riots became more frequent.

The assassination of Prime Minister Solomon Bandaranaike in September 1959 led to the dissolution of Parliament, and in the subsequent general election his wife became head of government. Official policy continued to favour the Sinhalese language, leading to discrimination against Tamils in higher education and the civil service, the main channels of economic advancement. A severe crisis developed in the economy with a fall in the world market price of tea and rubber.

An insurgency waged in 1971 by the Sinhalese Janatha Vimukti Peramuna (JVP) led to the introduction of a nationwide state of emergency, which lasted until 1977.

Sri Lanka became a Republic in 1972 and this coincided with the uniting of Tamil opposition groups to establish the Tamil United Front (TUF), which called for linguistic and religious equality. A year later they proposed the creation of an independent Tamil state, as they were angered by mounting government attempts to impose Sinhalese cultural and political domination.

The change from non-violent to violent tactics came when young Tamil militants, calling themselves 'Tigers', spearheaded a radicalisation of the TUF, transformed to the Tamil United Liberation Front (TULF). The election of 1977 brought a new Prime Minister to power, Junius Jayawardene and established the TULF as the largest single opposition party. This strengthening of Tamil separatism provoked violent anti-Tamil riots resulting in many deaths, and over 40,000 Tamils (mostly tea plantation workers) were forced from their homes and fled to the safety of refugee camps. The government insisted on the unity of the state of Sri Lanka. The appointment of Jayawardene as President gave greater control to central authority, but while the TULF leadership was prepared to compromise with the government, the younger Tamil militants became more radical.

After the deaths of police in 1978, armed forces

were sent to maintain order in the mainly Tamil north and east of Sri Lanka in what virtually amounted to a military occupation of a hostile country. Although the Tigers were banned, they became increasingly active, blowing up the country's only airliner at the time, and killing more police. A Prevention of Terrorism Act passed by Parliament in 1979, which increased penalties for terrorist offences, only appeared to bring further attacks by separatist guerrillas on police stations and patrols, which provided the rebels with a source of arms and ammunition.

The Sinhalese population reacted violently to the increase in Tamil terrorist activity during local elections in 1981. Anti-Tamil disturbances became communal riots and led to a hardening of the ethnic divide as large numbers of Tamils living in predominantly Sinhalese areas fled to the largely Tamil provinces of the north and east.

The capital, Colombo, suffered particularly badly, and massacres here and elsewhere led to nearly 400 deaths. Support for the Tamil cause grew among large Tamil communities in southern **India** and Malaysia. The overseas Tamils were an important source of financial support for the separatist insurgents operating in large areas of the Tamil provinces, well armed with modern automatic weapons. The tacit support of the Indian central government under both Indira Gandhi and Rajiv Gandhi (although denied), and of the state government of Tamil Nadu in southern India was an important factor in sustaining the Tamil separatist movement. From 1984 boatloads of Tamil guerrillas came to Sri Lanka from the Indian mainland, but had mixed degrees of success.

In the mid-1980s the Sri Lankan government appeared to be losing control of many areas of the country and the continued existence of Sri Lanka as a unitary state is threatened. There were 23 anti-government Tamil groups, and two in particular – the Liberation Tigers of Tamil Ealam (LTTE) and the Tamil Ealam Liberation Organisation (TELO) – have had pitched battles which have left over a hundred members of both groups dead, including the assassinated TELO leader, Sri Savaratenam. A bomb aboard an Air Lanka Tristar at Colombo airport in May 1986 killed 15 people, mostly foreign tourists. This was followed by a bomb in Colombo's main telegraph office, which killed 11

people. A group calling itself the Ealam Revolutionary Organisation of Students (EROS) claimed credit for the second explosion.

During the 1990s the Tamil Tigers continued to wage war against the Sri Lankan army and vice versa, and the most pitiless of racial confrontation with civilian butchery on both sides, continued unabated (Ellis, 1995).

In 1987 an agreement was reached between India and Sri Lanka granting certain autonomy to the Tamil minority, and Tamil was given the status of a national language. An Indian peace-keeping force supervised the new agreement. These accords were rejected by the Tamil Tigers, and the peace-keeping forces left. In 1991, the Tamil Tigers were accused of murdering the Indian President, Rajiv Gandhi, in a suicide mission. In August 1991 a major battle took place at Elephants Pass which led to the deaths of 2,000 guerrillas and 1,700 Sri Lankan soldiers.

Negotiations started again in 1992 with both sides, but **human rights** violations were a stumbling block, and in 1993 the Sri Lankan President was killed by a suicide bomber. Fierce fighting soon erupted again around the port city of Jaffna, and bomb attacks increased in the capital, Colombo and in the tourist areas.

The fighting continued with varied degrees of intensity until new negotiations started.

From peace talks in Thailand in September 2002 the long drawn out war between the Tamil Tigers and the Sri Lankan government appeared finally to have come to an end. The government unbarred one of the world's bloodiest insurgent groups that had perfected the art of suicide bombing and murdered two heads of government. The war which killed over 65,000 people, and had its origins in misguided attempts by earlier governments to promote Sinhalese interests at the expense of Tamil ones especially by discriminating against the Tamil language. In December 2001 the new Sri Lankan government announced that it was willing to hand over the north east of the island to an interim administration controlled by the Liberation Tigers of Tamil Ealam (homeland). 100,000 dispersed persons were able to return to their homes. Despite the peace moves there is still tension in the East, for the East still has large Muslim and Sinhalese minorities.

References

Ellis, J. (1995) *From the Barrel of a Gun*, London: Greenhill Books and Mechanicsburg, PA: Stackpole Books.

'Making Peace with the Tigers', *Economist*, 9 September 2002.

Further Reading

Oberst, R. C. (1988) 'Sri Lanka's Tamil Tigers', *Conflict*, vol. 8, nos. 2/3, pp. 185–202.

Targets

The targeting of terrorist organisations, both state and non-state, left- and right, ethnic and vigilante, shows some similarities as well as dissimilarities. The targets of vigilante terrorism are members of the same group or class as the victim. In vigilante terrorism there is often no target for demands. The warning to the target of terror is the message and the demand is implicit: know your subordinate place. Sometimes there is a target of demands, namely a government, which is considered to be too efficient, forcing vigilantes to take the law in their own hands. The link between targeting and objectives is visible in vigilante terrorism. Terrorism is a cost-effective method of freezing the challenging group into its place. Everyone who challenges the *status quo* is likely to become a possible target of vigilante violence.

The targets of violence of authoritarian state terrorists are the representatives of democratic and socialist parties, intellectuals, liberals, trade unionists and other dissidents. The targets of terror are all the other non-members of the ruling elite, the populace and in particular the actual and potential opponents.

The targets of violence of right-wing terrorism are often non-specific, with bombs being exploded randomly in public places. Specific targets can include left-wing leaders, intellectuals and traitors. The targets of terror are regime opponents and more generally society as a whole. Where there is a target of demands in right-wing terrorism it is often the military which is invited to stage a *coup d'état*. A target of attention is sometimes the government,

sometimes the population as a whole, and sometimes other ultra-right groups abroad. The media and potential sympathisers among the populace also figure as targets of attention. Right-wing targeting is highly random. By making the populace rather than the regime in power the major target, it is unlikely that it can seize power by itself.

Ethnic and nationalist terrorist targets of violence are members of the dominant or alien political authorities, especially the security forces and other tools of the ruling regime. Sometimes members of the dominant ethnic population are targeted; sometimes multinational enterprise personnel are selected. Other foreigners, including tourists, have also been targets. Targets of violence are members of the terrorists' own ethnic group, especially leaders who are either considered to be collaborators with the dominant regime or moderates. The targets of terror can be even broader, to include whoever denies the nationalist or ethnic goals.

Potential as well as actual regime opponents have been targeted, independent of class background of the victims. During the **Cold War**, frequent targets of violence and terror were state workers and rival groups challenging the legitimacy of the regime on ideological class grounds. The targets of terror are the domestic public and the émigré communities abroad. People in the camps can be said to be targets of violence with the remaining population figuring as targets of terror. Since the victimisation of the target of terror can be avoided by compliance and obedience, an important element of terrorism, the arbitrariness and unexpectedness of victimisation, is absent.

For left-wing terrorists the targets of violence are representatives of the state apparatus from ministers to policemen, government employees and military men, diplomats, judges, businessmen (from large multinational corporations), and managers (from firms manufacturing military equipment). Targets of terror are all those who share the victim's characteristics or who strongly identify with the victim. The target of demands for left-wing terrorism can be the media, which are expected to report certain statements, wealthy people and the government. The main targets of demands are the government or foreign governments. Targets of attention are groups or classes for which the terrorists purport to fight – the international proletariat, the poor, and the imprisoned. Depending on the way the actual victims of terrorist violence are linked to the target of terror, the target of demands or the target of attention, different objectives can be aimed at. By activating the interplay between the four target groups, terrorism can create multiple secondary effects which serve a variety of purposes.

Since the international terrorist can be a government, a left- or right-wing non-state actor, or a combination of the two, the targeting is largely the same as for the national terrorist. The hegemonic powers, especially the American government and its citizens abroad have become targets. Diplomats, embassies and airlines are prime targets of violence and terror. NATO officials, soldiers and installations have also become favourite targets. Foreign governments which are seen as supporters of local oppressors, and journalists and media seen as conduits to foreign public opinion are major targets for demands and attention.

Most non-state left-wing terrorism is aimed at tactical objectives such as the liberation of imprisoned colleagues through coercive bargaining following acts of **kidnapping** or **hostage taking**, mere advertising of the movement's existence, targeted at foreign terrorist movements, sympathisers who have not yet joined the movement and the terrorists themselves who need reassurance of their activities by seeing their projected image mirrored in an uncritical press. Acts of terrorism such as kidnappings have also been useful in raising funds for terrorists, in extorting concessions from the target of demands.

See also: Terror and Terrorism; Victims.

References

Donehan, M. (1987) 'Terrorism: Who is a Legitimate Target?', *Review of International Studies*, vol. 13 (July), pp. 229–33.

Veness, D. (1999) 'Low and High Impact Conflict', *Terrorism and Political Violence*, vol. 11, no. 4 (winter), pp. 8–14.

Further reading

Wilkinson, P. (1989) 'Terrorists, Targets and Tactics: New Risks to World Order', *Conflict Studies*, no. 236. London: RISCT.

Technology

Changes

There have been significant changes both in the philosophy and tactics of terror and in the social and political environment in which it operates. Many of the differences are directly or indirectly a consequence of technological change. The most relevant developments have been in the fields of transport, communications (particularly as applied to news gathering and distribution) and weaponry. The emergence of transnational terrorism, involving terrorists of different nationalities planning, training for and executing acts of political terrorism has been greatly facilitated by air travel.

The organisation, orientation and technical sophistication (particularly in the field of satellite technology) of the news media have significant implications for the style and range of terrorist activities to which modern society may be prey. **Media** coverage of a terrorist operation is often the major objective of the perpetrators. The insistence of many news directors that they have a social obligation to present the news 'as it happens', without restriction or censorship, while ignoring its potential consequences, makes it very easy for the terrorists to stage events with guaranteed worldwide audiences. One of the possible social consequences of concentrated populations and technological innovations is that the small bands of extremists and irreconcilables that have always existed may become an increasingly potent force.

Because of technological advances, society now also faces threats of a different order to those that have existed in the past. The most obvious example is the possibility that a terrorist group may gain access to nuclear, biological or biochemical materials. The possession of a very crude nuclear device would give such a group unheard of publicity and negotiating power with unknown effects on public confidence. If only for its dramatic publicity value it is likely that a terrorist group in the future will attempt to penetrate a nuclear facility or divert radioactive material.

The consideration which weighs against the likelihood of a threat to detonate a nuclear device or release a biological agent is the realisation that such an action would almost certainly harm the terrorists' cause. In particular for biological and biochemical materials, the possibility has existed for some time that these could be used in a blackmail situation. They have not been used, probably because terrorists want a lot of frightened people watching rather than a lot of people dead. In 1975, German terrorists stole 54 litre bottles of mustard gas from a military store and threatened to release it in several cities. There may be future situations in which a terrorist group perhaps needing to escalate violence to be taken notice of in a world used to killing and maiming feels compelled to employ extreme measures. Another possibility is that the so-called 'lunatic fringe' of the terrorist movement will employ these special weapons. Whatever the cause, it is clear that the potential for the use of special weapons is present and needs to be considered in national and international policy planning.

Probably the greatest threats posed by technological advances, however, are in the field of conventional weaponry. Until recently, most significant advances in military technology have involved relatively large weapons and weapons guidance systems. As a result of the ability to miniaturise weapons and guidance systems, a completely new range of small, portable, cheap, highly accurate and relatively easy-to-operate weapons has been created. They are mass-produced and stand a much greater chance of falling into the hands of terrorists. Furthermore, since advances in weaponry are so rapid, large numbers of these new weapons will quickly become obsolete and be disposed of via arms dealers and other routes, increasing still further the chances of distribution outside the armed forces. Already earlier generation weapons of this type have found their way into terrorist hands, for example the IRA has used the RPG-7 rocket launcher in Belfast.

In addition to delivery systems, there have also been advances in propellants and explosives. Non-military developments such as digital clocks, day-date watches and long-lasting power cells have further increased the flexibility available to the amateur bomb-makers. There is greater scope for terrorist activities from increased accuracy, destructive power, distance from target and most of all a greater dramatic impact. This suggests that there should be more concern for the side-effects of military technology policy, and certainly steps should be taken to increase security precautions for weaponry. Thus, although the authorities have access to equally sophisticated technology to combat terrorism, its application could be costly in terms of human liberty.

See also: Nuclear Terrorism.

References

Bluhm, L. H. (1987) 'Trust, Terrorism and Technology', *Journal of Business Ethics*, (July), pp. 333–341.

O'Keefe, B. (1987) 'Technology: An Introduction', *Terrorism*, vol. 10, no. 3, pp. 269–70.

Wilkinson, P. (ed.) (1993) *Technology and Terrorism*, London: Frank Cass.

Further Reading

Lynch, L. (1999) 'Terrorism and Technology' in New Millennium, *Platypus Magazine*, no. 65 (December).

Shubik, M. (1998) *Terrorism, Technology and the Socio-Economics of Death*, New Haven, CT: Cowles Foundation, Yale.

Sprinzak, E. (1998) 'The Great Super-Terrorism Scare', *Foreign Policy*, no. 112 (autumn), pp. 110–124.

Information Terrorism

It is perhaps a shock to realise that a personal computer and a telephone connection to an Internet Service provider (ISP) anywhere in the world are enough to cause harm.

Information terrorism is terrorism through the exploration of computerised systems deployed by the target.

Computers and associated systems are as much targets and tools and can range from the bombing of a corrupting facility to a digital attack that can cause physical harm.

Cyber-space offers the opportunity to inflict costly disruptive damage, but without physical and human destruction. Many terrorists have advanced and detailed information technology skills.

In developed countries, rich in all aspects of information technology (IT), much information terrorism can be expected. Information terrorism is likely to be popular with anti-establishment groups who perceive technological resources to be a source of vulnerability to their opponent. A move to information terrorism by one group can be expected to be followed quickly by others; and attacks will become more relevant.

During the siege of the Japanese Embassy in Peru, the Islamic Tupac Amaru Revolutionary Movement (MRTA) used a sophisticated multi-media website to keep sympathisers informed. Other Latin American groups have done similar things – the Mexican Zapatistas, Colombia's Revolutionary Armed Forces and Peru's Shining Path.

Sophisticated destructive devices such as viruses and logic bombs allow terrorists to make information technology a weapon and the target (Jane's Information Group, 1997).

Hacker warfare is easy to undertake merely requiring IT expertise, and access to critical systems, this enables hacker terrorists to cross frontiers and distances with considerable ease. Sinisterly Internet communication may shorten the planning time of groups, which make it impossible for authorities to intervene before attacks occur. This is an obvious challenge to established and authoritative sources of information giving greater powers of disinformation to marginalised groups.

The Internet, has given terrorist organisations advanced and cost effective communication and propaganda instruments. The Net and its specific functions such as electronic mail and the World Wide Web can facilitate malicious activities against connected information networks. With the rapid development of Internet, data piracy has become a crucial issue. If terrorists can understand the operating requirements, they can understand an information-dependent infrastructure (Valeri and Knights, 2000).

Terrorists can exploit opportunities provided by inefficient IT risk management procedures. They can intrude into E-commerce and enhance the net's weaknesses.

Measures have been taken to counter the threat of terrorist operations, but policies have to be developed rapidly and constantly changed and updated due to the dynamic nature of the Internet.

Terrorism has become more media-orientated in the last decade; and terrorist organisations have learnt to manipulate mass communication. Many of the groups – Hamas, Sendero Luminoso, the Tamil Tigers, the Basque's ETA – have created Internet sites. There are more in the Third World due to the decline of terrorism in Europe. Obviously, the websites of anti-regime organisations usually operate from outside the state against which they are working.

Most terrorist sites contain basic information and stress two issues: political prisoners and freedom of expression. To add to the impact of their message they are rich in graphic and visual elements. They pay due 'reverence' to the works of their leaders, founders and ideologists.

Their rhetoric includes the 'there is no alternative' approach to the use of violence and to delegitimise the enemy. The organisation to attract sympathy claims that it is the weapon of the weak. Despite preaching violence, some of the sites claim that they seek peaceful solutions, diplomatic settlements or arrangements reached through international pressure.

They are appealing on a regular basis either to potential supporters or to their enemies or to international public opinion. They actively encourage groups to move to other web pages through links appearing on the site.

Violence, however, can easily be concealed over the Internet. The sites contain extensive information and background, not possible on mass media channels that operate with more limited space. The use of such sites can mobilise people to action.

Ultimately, the Internet is a central venue for free speech. It is hard for governments to respond especially as website addresses change frequently. Some close down and then re-open providing another hazard for those who try to track them.

Tactical and technical contagion has become a factor in the evolution of terrorist tactics. A move to information terrorism by one group can be expected to be followed quickly by others. The information context in which the group is operating will influence the degree to which the group turns to information terrorism. Hackers are anti-establishment figures and their motivations have much in common with the psychology of the social revolutionary terrorist. Terrorist groups working underground, rely on powerful group dynamics as do terrorist groups relying on networked organisational structures and computer-mediated communications.

Targeting critical infrastructure or causing casualties using information-based attacks is not easy. In areas with low dependence on IT the activities of information terrorists are nullified. Terrorists often do not wish to attack their supplies of communications and logistical support. The targets, moreover, can be limited to those inspired by ideological opposition to the use of the Internet by government or corporate interests.

References

Devost, M. G., Houghton, B. K. and Pollard, N. (1997) 'Information Terrorism: Political Violence in the Information Age', *Terrorism and Political Violence*, vol. 9, no. 1 (spring), pp. 72–83.

Jane's Terrorism: A Global Survey (1977), London: Jane's Information Group.

Ramsey, T. (1987) 'The Age of Information Technology', *Terrorism*, vol. 10, no. 3, pp. 265–268.

Valeri, L. and Knights, M. (2000) 'Affecting Trust, Terrorism, Internet and Offensive Information Warfare', *Terrorism and Political Violence*, vol. 12, no. 1, (spring), pp. 15–36.

Further Reading

Arquilla, J. and Romfeldt, D. (1993) 'Cyber-war is Coming', *Comparative Strategy*, vol. 12, no. 2 (summer), pp. 141–165.

Cilluffo, E. and Gergely, C. (1997) 'Information Warfare Strategic Terrorism', *Terrorism and Political Violence*, vol. 9, no. 1 (spring), pp. 84–94.

Denning, D. (1998) *Information Warfare and Security*, Reading: Addison Wesley.

Levin, B. (2002) 'Cyberhate: A Legal and Historical Analysis of Extremists' Use of Computer Networks in America', *American Behavioural Scientist*, vol. 45, no. 6, pp. 958–988.

Post, J. M., Ruby, K. G. and Shaw, E. D. (2000) 'From Car Bombs to Logic Bombs: The Growing Threat from Information Terrorism', *Terrorism and Political Violence*, vol. 12, no. 2 (summer), pp. 97–122.

Stewart, B. L. (1987) 'Information and Communications: An Introduction', *Terrorism*, vol. 10, no. 3, pp. 251–52.

Tsfati, Y. and Weinmann, G. (2002) 'www.terrorism.com: Terror on the Internet', Studies in *Conflict and Terrorism*, vol. 25, no. 5, pp. 317–332.

Zanni, Michele (1999) 'Middle Eastern Terrorism and Net-War', *Studies in Conflict and Terrorism*, vol. 22, pp. 247–256.

Teheran Embassy Siege 1979–81

In November 1979, about 500 radical Muslim students attacked the US Embassy in Teheran, seizing 100 hostages after a two-hour battle in which 14 marine guards lobbed tear gas canisters. The students demanded the extradition of the exiled Shah of **Iran**, who two weeks previously had left Mexico for hospital treatment in the **USA** for cancer. The students claimed they were armed with only ten pistols, although they later said they had mined the embassy grounds and had placed explosive charges throughout the buildings. They threatened to kill the hostages and blow up the embassy compound if the USA attempted a military rescue.

Two days after the siege the Iranian Cabinet resigned, leaving all formal authority in the hands of the Ayatollah Khomeini-led Revolutionary Council. There were up to five different groups of students holding the embassy – members of the fundamentalist Phalange, theological students from Qom (Iran's holy city), students from the University of Teheran, Leftists and Communists. Some of these students may have been trained by the Popular Front for the Liberation of Palestine. Although the students said they were loyal only to Khomeini, many observers suggested that they were leading the handling of the negotiations themselves. Even though the Shah left the US for

Panama after successful surgery, the students said this would not affect the freedom of the hostages, whom they threatened to try as spies.

While the takeover appeared initially to be student-led, the government quickly moved to back the demands of the students. A former foreign minister, Bani Sadr, stated that Iran demanded American recognition that the Shah was a criminal and must be extradited, the return to Iran of the Shah's fortune, and an end to American meddling in Iranian domestic affairs. He announced an oil embargo on the United States at the same time President Carter was announcing that the US would no longer buy Iranian oil.

The American response placed incrementally increasing pressures on Iran, as well as the diplomatic isolation of Teheran. Numerous anti-Iranian protests in the United States underscored widespread support for the President's action – for example, Iranian students in the United States were told that they would face deportation unless they proved that they were enrolled as full-time students and had committed no crimes. Pilot training for the Iranians was cancelled, and the USA ordered all but 35 of 218 Iranian diplomats in the USA to leave within five days. Internationally the US focused on obtaining condemnations of Iran's actions by governments and international organisations. Scores of governments agreed that Iran had violated fundamental international legal norms. The **United Nations** proved impotent, and the UN Secretary-General was refused permission to meet the hostages when he visited Iran.

The Iranian government claimed that the issue was not its holding hostages, but rather the crimes of the Shah and alleged American intelligence collusion with the former regime. Numerous demonstrations in Teheran showed the solidarity of the people behind their government's action. The Iranians subsequently released several hostages, holding only those they claimed were spies. Visits by outsiders to the hostages were also carefully orchestrated as media events by the students. Visitors were not allowed to see all the hostages, leading observers to suggest that some of the hostages had been removed from the embassy grounds. Iran refused to state how many hostages

were being held. Envoys from **Algeria**, France, Sweden and **Syria**, were the first outsiders permitted to visit the hostages.

In January 1980, the Canadian government helped smuggle out of Iran six Americans who had escaped from the embassy during the initial attack. Letters from several hostages, including some who had been accused of being spies, trickled out of the embassy to the hostages' families. In February the Greek Catholic Archbishop Hilarion Capucci (who had been held in an Israeli prison for smuggling arms to Palestinian terrorists in the mid 1970s) visited the hostages. In a flurry of behind-the-scenes negotiations, the US agreed to the sending of a UN panel to Teheran to investigate Iranian complaints against the Shah. This coincided with the Shah's flight from Panama to final asylum in **Egypt**.

In early April the United States broke off diplomatic relations with Iran, imposed an economic embargo banning all exports to Iran except food and medicine, ordered a formal inventory of Iranian financial assets in the US and cancelled all future visas for Iranian travel in the USA. Three weeks after this action, an attempt by US military forces to rescue the hostages failed when three of the eight helicopters assigned to the mission became unavailable due to various mishaps in the desert.

The US Secretary of State Cyrus Vance resigned in protest over the mission. The Iranian students claimed that they would prevent future rescue attempts by moving the hostages out of the embassy to other locations throughout Iran.

In mid-1980 the International Court of Justice unanimously ordered Iran to release the hostages. The situation continued in stalemate for the rest of 1980; it became President Carter's aim to achieve the hostages' release before his term as President ended in January 1981. This was in fact achieved in the same week that he handed over the Presidency to Ronald Reagan. The 444-day ordeal of the hostages was over; and the release was the result of a complex financial deal involving Iranian assets in the **United Kingdom** and the USA, with Algeria acting as the honest broker.

See also: Iran; United States.

References

Moody, S. (1981) *444 Days: The American Hostage Story*, New York: Routledge.

Sick, G. (1985) *All Fell Down: America's Tragic Encounter with Iran*, New York: Random House.

Further Reading

American Hostages in Iran: The Conduct of a Crisis, Council on Foreign Relations (1985), New Haven, CT: Yale University Press.

Miller, A. H. (1982) 'Terrorism and Hostage Taking: Lessons from the Iranian Crisis', *Rutgers Law Journal*, vol. 13, pp. 513–529.

Terror and Terrorism

No consensus exists on the relationship between terrorism and terror. Observers often see terror in a historical context such as in France under Robespierre or **Russia** under Stalin. Some see terrorism as the more organised form of terror, and yet others stress that terror is a state of mind while terrorism refers to organised social activity. The most polarised views are that terror can occur without terrorism, and that terror is the key to terrorism.

The suffix '-ism' that is added to terror is sometimes held to denote its systematic character, either on the theoretical level, where the suffix refers to a political philosophy, or on a practical level, where it refers to a manner of acting or an attitude. Some attribute a doctrinal quality to terrorism, but it is more common to see it as a deliberate manner of acting.

Terror originally referred to a period characterised by political executions, as during the French Revolution from May 1793 to July 1794. Originally conceived as an instrument against monarchist traitors, the Terror of the Committee of Public Safety (of which Robespierre was the most prominent member), soon began to kill Republicans as well. The revolutionary allies on the right of the Jacobins (the Indulgents, under Danton) and on the left (the Hebartists), became victims of the unleashed Terror. Altogether at least 300,000 people were arrested during the Reign of Terror and 17,000 were officially tried and executed, while

many died in prison or without a trial. Those who had originally supported the draconian measures of Robespierre began to fear for their lives and conspired to overthrow him. They could not accuse him of the Terror since they had declared it to be the legitimate form of government, so they accused him of Terrorism, which had an illegal and repulsive flavour. For this Robespierre and his associates were sent to the guillotine on the 9th and 10th Thermidor of the year II (27 and 28 July 1794).

Under the reaction to Robespierre the agents and partisans of the revolutionary tribunals were termed 'terrorists', and this name spread over Europe, appearing in England in 1795. The Jacobin terrorists were labelled anarchists under the directorate; while for the émigrés and their monarchist followers the term 'terrorist' was sometimes used synonymously with 'patriots', or used for all republicans and even for the soldiers who defended the liberty of the republic. By the end of the nineteenth century the term 'terrorist', originally used to describe violence in the name of the revolutionary state and then the reactionary state of the Restoration became associated with anti-state violence under the impact of the Russian terrorists of the 1880s and the anarchists of the 1890s. The twentieth-century experience of state terror notwithstanding, the anti-state sense of the term has become paramount again in the late twentieth century, under the impact of wars of national liberation and the revolutionary aspirations of students and ethnic minorities in the industrialised countries.

Terrorism does not only produce terror; and terror is perhaps not even the main result for the majority of the audience of an act or campaign of terrorism. Psychologists define the psychological condition of terror as extreme fear or anxiety. Though terrorism is a real, not an imaginary danger, it is a vague, incomprehensible, unpredictable and unexpected menace. Terrorism affects the social structure as well as the individual, and may upset the framework of precepts and images that members of society depend on and trust. Uncertainty about what sort of behaviour to expect from others results in disorientation.

Terror is a constituent of many ordinary crimes. An act of terrorism has a purpose similar to general deterrence; the instant victim is less important than the overall effect on a particular group to whom the exemplary act is really addressed. Terrorism, although it has individual victims, is an onslaught upon society itself. Terror is a natural phenomenon, and terrorism is the conscious exploitation of it. Terrorism is coercive, designed to manipulate the will of its victims and its larger audience. The degree of fear is generated by the crime's very nature, by the manner of its perpetration or by its senselessness, wantonness or callous indifference to human life. This terrible fear is the source of the terrorist's power and communicates his challenge to society. Intimidation is based on threat and threats have occasionally to be enforced to remain credible.

An implicit assumption is that the product of terrorism is terror. But who exactly is terrorised? The immediate victim of a terrorist bomb explosion may be dead before he gets a chance to be filled with terror. The potential fellow victims, in a hostage situation where one hostage has been killed to show that the terrorists mean business in their demands, are those most likely to be terror-stricken.

Four levels of response can be induced by terror. First, there is enthusiasm among the adherents of the insurgent movement. Second, the lowest level of negative reaction is fright. Third, the middle level of response is anxiety called forth by fear of the unknown and the unknowable. Last, the most extreme level of response is despair, an intensified form of anxiety. The response to an act of terror can vary greatly, depending on the danger of repetition and the degree of identification with the victim.

See also: Crime; Psychology of Terrorism: Fear; Targets; Victims.

Reference

Hymans, E. (1974) *Terrorists and Terrorism*, New York: St Martin's Press.

Further Reading

Gearty, C. (1992) *Terror*, London: Faber and Faber.
Iviansky, X. (1981) 'Individual Terror: Concept and Typology', *Journal of Contemporary History*, vol. 12, no. 1.

Revolution

War and revolution are intimately related. In ancient Greek mythology, terror (Phobos) and dread (Deimos) were the names given to the twin horses that drew the chariot of Aries (Mars), the god of war.

Revolution is like war in that it involves the convincing use of force. Terror, however, must be distinguished from dread, or fear. Fear is a physical and psychological reaction to the strange, the unexpected, or the hazardous. Fear is a normal reaction to major political changes if they are seen as so significant as to threaten the physical safety of individual citizens.

Terror, on the other hand, is the systematic use of fear in revolutionary circumstances to aid the establishment of a new government. It may be directed towards members of the former elite, other likely power seekers or even towards the mass of population to ensure their compliance. It is not a new phenomenon, being referred to by Thucydides in ancient Greece. In the Roman Empire, governments rose and fell by violence, ultimately with significant political and social consequences.

The term revolution designates such periods of fundamental social change. What makes them possible is the change of governments by force, so that new groups rise to power, and it is the successful use of force that marks out revolution as a concept from all other related concepts, such as revolt, insurgency and insurrection.

The modern use of the concept of terror in revolutionary circumstances derives from the French Revolution of 1789. The Terror is the name given to the period after the most extreme faction, the Jacobins, had obtained power, in which physical violence was used in order to create the basis of a new social order. The most spectacular feature of the Terror was the execution of members of the aristocracy, and terror was seen as a method of rooting out opponents of the regime and eliminating them. The Terror was, in fact, a method of legitimising a minority government and justifying its continued maintenance of its position.

The French Revolution was viewed as the classic example of a great social revolution by later theorists of the revolution and above all by Karl Marx. Marx and Engels ridiculed those who believed in terror as a means to initiate revolution. In Western Europe revolution would, Marx thought, be the product of the progressive development of class consciousness among the proletariat. As a Marxist, Lenin did not see terrorism as having a role in the promotion of revolution, but as a Russian he did see it as having a role in its actual execution once open resistance had begun. He believed the purpose of fighting guerrilla operations must be to destroy the government, police and military machinery. Lenin was merely carrying out the view held centuries earlier by Machiavelli that terror is after all merely a development of fear, and fear is the instrument of government.

In sixteenth-century Russia, Ivan the Terrible employed terror simply to instil fear into the majority of the population regardless of their beliefs or intent. Tsar Nicholas I adapted to Russian conditions the secret police, the classic government instrument of terror in the twentieth century.

The role of the secret police is derived from, though by no means identical with, the role of the police in general. The secret police differ from the regular police, not in their secrecy, but in the use of their powers to keep the government secure. All police forces have certain latitude in the interpretation and application of the laws they nominally apply with rigorous impartiality. The secret police, however, make use of this area of uncertainty to focus pressure on individuals believed to be politically unsympathetic to the regime. The use of informants, a normal part of police work, is extended in these circumstances into the systematic compilation of all information likely to lead to the disclosure of political dissent, and the arrest of suspects is conducted in such a way that if the 'right' people have not been arrested, they will be in any event intimidated into conformity.

Terror used to instil fear can be of two kinds: discriminating, i.e. directed towards target groups and capable of being regulated in intensity according to the perceived needs of the situation, as was practiced in the nineteenth century and indiscriminate terror, as has become common in this century as the last resort of the extremist. After the abortive Russian Revolution of 1905, the lesson for revolutionaries was that good intentions were not enough, the seizure of political power was something that could not be achieved simply by instilling fear into an incumbent government; if anything that was likely to strengthen it in its resolve. What was needed was the precise direction of force towards specific political targets and here, as in any other military operation, surprise and careful planning were crucial. This lesson was the main one which made the Bolshevik seizure of power in Petrograd in 1917 possible, and even then this would not have been possible without the impact of war on the social fabric and the corresponding weakness in all respects of the provisional government.

The Bolshevik ideology gave the use of terror additional dimensions it was a strategy in the class war, seen as an armed conflict, in which the use of force was as natural as it would be in any other circumstances of belligerency. Since the basis of class lay in the relation of individual social groups to the forces of production, the achievement of working-class domination could only be attained by the economic restructuring of society.

Up to the Second World War terror remained a feature primarily of the consolidation phase of great social revolutions. It was once again a feature of consolidation of the Chinese and of the Cuban revolutions, as well as in the consolidation of the power of the Islamic regime in Iran after 1979. On each occasion terror was employed not only against the military as supporters of the old regime, but against prominent members of the former oligarchy.

The development of a technique of guerrilla warfare as a path to revolution was to create an important additional role for terror in the theory of revolution. Mao's theory of the three stages of guerrilla warfare envisages a preliminary stage of preparation, followed by a stage in which a guerrilla movement is established and expands its control over a wider and wider area, and finally, a period in which the guerrilla force transforms itself into a regular army capable of defeating the forces of the government in a series of pitched battles.

Violence is a mere tool in the process of psychological warfare, with victims being random victims, not individuals selected on the grounds of justice, revolutionary or otherwise. Thus, though one must always distinguish between 'terror' as a technique and 'terrorism' as a belief in the value of terror, the two are closely related. Indeed, the historical myths of the efficacy of terror in earlier times and other situations have led to the association of the techniques of terror with several varieties of political thought. Both Marxist and militant Islamic groups have used terrorist methods, and links have developed between revolutionary movements of very different backgrounds, including the Japanese Red Army, the Italian Red Brigades (Brigate Rosse), the PLO, the Basque nationalist movement ETA and the IRA.

In the period since 1945 terror has ceased merely to be a feature of the consolidation stage of revolutions, and even then something which may be invoked only when the challenges appear to be otherwise insuperable. It has become instead a feature of the actual achievement of power itself. Just as the stages of guerrilla warfare itself overlap, so the use of terror has moved backwards into the earlier stages of the revolution. It continues to be used in the actual processes of government. It has been assumed in many circles that its use by governments faced with revolutionary challenges is not only normal but natural, and critics have identified and criticised what has often been called 'the national security state', which typically is a Latin American military dictatorship. The use of terror originates in a decision by the armed forces that the political situation is becoming unmanageable as a result of challenges by either rural or urban guerrillas. It forms an excellent excuse for the military to assume supreme power. For this purpose they create a large but unmanageable security apparatus – because of the secrecy which surrounds all military operations, and the impact on such circumstances of traditional inter-service rivalry. Each individual, isolated in themselves, is left to stand alone before the ruthless and uncontrolled power of the state. Today even a relatively weak government has a huge potential for violence and destruction, not only if it chooses to exercise it, but also if it fails to restrain those whose professional duty it is to use it.

Once a government agrees to bind itself, and particularly if it agrees to limit its own term of office, the impetus to violence is much reduced. Che Guevara consistently maintained, that a revolution could not succeed until the possibilities for peaceful change were seen to be exhausted.

Both in theory and in practice the factor most conducive to the use of terror by the political opposition is its use by government; and conversely if terror is to be avoided, repressive measures on the part of government should be eliminated and a tolerable level of government repression established as soon as possible.

See also: Marx and Revolutionary Violence; Targets; Terror and Terrorism.

References

Gilbert, P. (1995) *Terrorism Security and Nationality*, New York: Routledge.
O'Sullivan, N. (1988) *Terrorism, Ideology and Revolution*, Brighton: Wheatsheaf Books.

Further Reading

Alexander, Y., Carlton, D. and Wilkinson, P. (eds) (1978) *Terrorism Theory and Practice*, New York: Praeger, Westview Special Studies in National and International Terrorism.
Chomsky, N. (1988) *The Culture of Terrorism*, Boston, MA: South End Press.
Laqueur, W. (1977) *Terrorism*, London: Weidenfield and Nicolson.

'Terrorist States'

With increasing frequency, acts of terrorism are being labelled the direct or indirect products of state policies.

A number of governments do assist terrorist organisations, although they do not usually plan or direct specific operations. If efficiently employed, the technological resources and knowledge of a state could dramatically increase the sophistication and effect of terrorist actions against the peculiar vulnerabilities of advanced societies. What to date has been only an irritant to modern society could become a true danger.

It is true that a number of **Third World** states

now unashamedly sponsor terrorist activity with only the flimsiest attempts at denial: **Iran** and Islamic **Jihad**; **Syria** and various groups in **Lebanon**, **Libya** and several 'rejectionist' Palestinian and Egyptian groups. But the true extent of the increase in state-backed terrorism is obscured by propaganda charges and counter-charges. Furthermore several other factors can deceptively magnify the image of burgeoning state terrorism. Many of these are intellectual or semantic in nature.

Violent retaliation by a state against enemies ensconced in the midst of a civilian population inevitably takes a toll of those civilians. Israeli attacks against Palestinian guerrillas in refugee camps, for instance, became 'state terrorism' in the eyes of Palestinian supporters.

Conspicuous support to insurgents who periodically practice internal terrorist activity as a part of their overall programme has also come to be considered state terrorism.

Many Europeans considered the **USA** responsible in the 1980s for fostering sporadic terrorism, because of its support for the Nicaraguan guerrilla movement. **Soviet Union** support of various Palestinian factions, while ostensibly similar, is greatly complicated by a Palestinian propensity to operate internationally.

There is also a political imperative that tends to inflate the intensity of accusations of state terrorism. The desire to 'retaliate' or 'pre-empt' terrorists is unfulfilled if no accessible target can be found. Most terrorists cannot be identified and removed without causing unacceptable civilian casualties.

If a state sponsor of the terrorist group is identified, it can be targeted by a range of diplomatic, economic or military reprisals. As a result, policy-makers bent on combating terrorism follow the human urge to find evidence of state complicity. To do nothing would be politically unacceptable. A guilty state provides one other advantage not normally found among terrorists: it responds more or less rationally to outside pressure to change behaviour; terrorists and their organisations do not.

See also: Government Support; State Sponsorship.

References

Harmon, C. C. (2000) *Terrorism Today*, London: Frank Cass.

Mickolus, E. (1989) 'What Constitutes State Support to Terrorists?', *Terrorism and Political Violence*, vol. 1, no. 3, pp. 287–293.

Probst, P. S. (1989) 'State-sponsored Terrorism: Present and Future Trends', *Terrorism*, vol. 12, no. 2, pp. 131–3.

Wilkins, P. T. (1992) *Terrorism and Collective Responsibility*, London: Routledge.

Further Reading

Crenshaw, M. (1990) 'Is International Terrorism Primarily State-sponsored?' in Kegley, C. W. (ed.) *International Terrorism: Characteristics, Causes*, Controls, New York: St Martin's Press, pp. 163–69.

Russett, B., Starr, H. and Kinsella, D. (2000) *World Politics: The Menu for Choice*, Boston and New York, Bedford: St Martin's Press.

Sproat, P. A. (1997) 'Can the State Commit Acts of Terrorism?, An Opinion and Some Qualitative Replies to a Questionnaire', *Terrorism and Political Violence*, vol. 9, no. 4, pp. 117–150.

Stohl, M. (1988) 'States, Terrorism and State Terrorism: The Role of the Superpowers' in Slater, R. O. and Stohl, M. (ed.) *Current Perspectives on International Terrorism*, London: Macmillan, pp. 155–205.

Stohl, M. and Lopez, G. A. (eds) (1988) *Terrible Beyond Endurance? The Foreign Policy of State Terrorism*, Westport, CT: Greenwood Press.

Tanter, R. (1999) *Rogue Regimes: Terrorism and Proliferation*, New York: St Martin's Press.

Terrorist Types

The criminal terrorist hopes to make a personal gain or profit and is usually willing to negotiate in return for profit and for safe passage. The person has a strong expectation of survival.

The 'crusader' type of terrorist has a 'higher cause' which is usually a blend of religious and political beliefs. This person is seldom willing to negotiate since to do so would be seen as a betrayal of the cause. Survival is of no real interest as death offers a reward in 'afterlife' (Combs, 2003).

The motive of a terrorist, who can be classed as crazy, is clear only to the perpetrator. He is willing to negotiate, but only if the negotiator can understand the motive and offer hope and alternatives. There is a strong survival instinct which is perhaps unrealistic.

The type of terrorist is crucial to the counter terrorist operatives dealing with a hostage situation as they wish to know what type of person is controlling that situation. Most modern terrorists feel themselves to be crusaders.

Mass terror is endemic, authorised, enforced and is repressive and is committed by political leaders. Examples include Idi Amin's rule in Uganda with a target of a general population and coercion organised or unorganised as a tactic.

Random terror can be committed by individuals or groups such as in the case of **Lockerbie** and the destruction of Pan Am Flight 103, and the target can be anyone in the wrong place at the wrong time. Bombs can be placed in public places such as cafés and airports.

Focussed random terror is instigated by members or groups targeting members of the opposition with bombs in specific public places frequented by the opposition.

Revolutionary movements, targeting the government, as in **Colombia**, with attacks on politically attractive targets undertake tactical revolutionary terror.

See also: Psychology.

References

Combs, C. C. (2003) *Terrorism in the 21st Century*, Upper Saddle River, NJ: Prentice Hall.
Shultz, R. (1978) 'Conceptualising Political Terrorism: A Typology', in Buckley, A. D. and Olson, D. D. (eds) *International Terrorism: Current Research and Future Directions*, Wayne, NJ: Avery, pp. 9–18.

Further Reading

Maniscalco, P. M. and Christen, H. J. (2002) *Understanding Terrorism and Managing the Consequences*, Upper Saddle River, NJ: Prentice Hall.

Therapy *see* Psychology

Third World Insurgency

To some observers, insurgency and extremist activities are outcomes of neglect; by governments and decision makers of the socio-economic and political limitations and hopes in areas under their control, and the inability to stop corruption in and improve the efficiency of local administration.

Mass mobilisation can have a leading impact on the government. Insurgents can organise rallies against the authorities and boycott polls. They can actively recruit people into the insurgent group. Insurgents have been known to control the flow of information to insurgents and get support from the press (Nayak, 2001). Control of funds can result in the siphoning of public money, contraband smuggling can occur and the forcible grabbing of land and its redistribution is a regular occurrence.

Insurgents' activity can paralyse the administration and lead to its inability to conduct developmental activities; and they can be compounded by infiltration occurring into government services.

Administrations in developing countries can assist the situation and counter the insurgents by helping to ensure a fair wage structure, solving land disputes, and ensuring the proper utilisation of money at local government level. They can help in the rehabilitation of victims of insurgents and solve the water scarcity/electricity problem in interior locations. In the area of communications they can construct new roads and bridges. It is in the area of counter propaganda where an impact can be made: the banning of insurgents; publicising the wrong doings of insurgents; emphasising the achievements of the government and redressing public grievances. The intensity of insurgent activity in particular the level of organisation, violence and of destruction has to be countered (Nayak, 2001).

To achieve this state of affairs the intensity of security forces activity has to be at a high degree of effectiveness. The level of operations can include an ambush, a raid on insurgent training camps, nullifying insurgent attacks, area domination and mopping up operations. Intelligence has to be seized and insurgents disarmed: arms and ammunitions seized; dumps and explosives recovered.

Insurgents have to be neutralised and apprehended, and the supplier and harbourer arrested. Ultimately, insurgents have to be killed and destroyed.

References

Krieger, J. (ed.) (1993) *Oxford Companion to Politics of the World*, Article by S. Neil MacFarlane.

Mazrui, A. A. (1985) 'The Third World and International Terrorism: Preliminary Reflections', *Third World Quarterly*, vol. 7, no. 2 (April), pp. 348–364.

Nayak Shri Giridhari (2001) 'Intensity and Impact Analysis of Insurgency/Extremism', *The Police Journal*, vol. 74, no. 4, pp. 316–329.

Further Reading

Carey, P. (1996) 'East Timor: Third World Colonialism and the Struggle for National Identity', *Conflict Studies*, no. 293, London: RISCT.

Epstein, D. G. (1986) 'Police, Terrorism and the Third World', *Police Chief*, vol. 52, no. 4, pp. 50–52.

Hammond, A. (1998) 'Terrorism's Roots', *Christian Science Monitor* (October).

Threat Assessment Guidelines

The existence of any group in any country or which could gain access into any country needs to be known by the requisite counter-terrorist agencies. They also need to have an idea about the group's credibility i.e. the ability to carry out an attack has to be assessed and demonstrated. Intent has to be analysed, that is the evidence of demonstrated terrorist activity, threat or action by a group has to be perceived. Has the history of the group demonstrated consistent terroristic activity over time? Targeting strategy has to be appraised. A check has to be kept on current credible information which exists on activity indicative of preparations for specific terrorist operations. Above all security information is vital – in particular the internal politics and security considerations that

impact on the capabilities of the terrorists to carry out their missions.

See also: Data Sources; Intelligence on Terrorism.

Threats

The likeliest sources from which threats of violence may come include criminals; disgruntled or dissident groups or individuals attempting arson or sabotage; demonstrators or rioters motivated by political dissent, industrial conflict or social unrest; ideologically motivated terrorists, indigenous or international left-wing, right-wing, environmentalist and nationalist or religious groups. Domestic state terrorists, overtly or secretly sponsored or condoned by their own governments in their own countries; international state terrorists operating outside their own countries and sponsored by their own or foreign governments can also be sources of violence. Warring factions, whose scale of fighting may range from guerrilla terrorist actions to civil war, and with whose conflicts expatriate organisations and individuals may get involved quite incidentally in promoting violence.

Personal attack and intimidation, especially of diplomats and expatriate executives, are likely to increase. The aims will be to force changes in government policy. Methods of intimidation other than killing or wounding are sometimes used, such as harassment of families or malicious damage to cars and homes. The tactic may be extended to intimidate locally recruited staff, to deter them from working for foreign organisations, or to bribe them into sabotage, betrayal of confidential information or collaboration with intruders or kidnappers.

Kidnapping is a growing form of crime, generally for the extortion of a ransom, although there is sometimes an element of political blackmail, for example for the release of prisoners or publication of a political manifesto.

Hostage seizure in a known location presents a problem totally different from that of a secret hideout because from the start it becomes a siege in which the police can deploy whatever force is necessary, and they hold the initiative. The hostage-takers' aim is almost always to gain publicity, so they will pick a newsworthy target such as an embassy, a computer centre, an oil refinery or a power station. Secondary aims may be to extort political concessions or simply to disrupt a key facility.

Hijacking is just another form of **hostage taking** in which the aircraft, ship, train or coach are treated as 'mobile premises' of a government or corporation. Success against aircraft is likely to encourage more hijacking but it should also have the effect of goading airport authorities to tighten security. As with hostage seizure, the level of hijackings will rise and fall. Extortion by threat to kill, maim or kidnap people can be even more effective than threats against property. Multinational corporations have paid ransoms in the face of threats to their executives to try to save lives at the time, prevent future extortions by threats, and ultimately to protect their own property. The long-term motivation of political terrorists is the furtherance of political and religious objectives. To achieve long-term aims there are often short-term tactics such as **media** seeking, political blackmail, extortion of money, humiliating or discrediting a government or corporation, or coercing it to change its policies. Attacks on property can therefore be both a short- and long-term objective.

Arson and sabotage can be carried out clandestinely by people, who have penetrated or bypassed the processes of staff selection, vetting, identification, control of access or control of visitors, including labour employed by contractors doing work in the building, i.e. by people who are inside, and whose malice is unsuspected.

The growing scale and interdependence of data processing systems, including computers and communications, make manufacturing and service industries and public service establishments more vulnerable to sabotage.

Bombing has for many years been the most prevalent of all kinds of terrorist attack. There has been rapid growth over the years, including the use in recent times of huge explosive charges in trucks and cars, occasionally driven by suicide drivers and directed against embassies, government buildings and multinational corporations. Bombs have been used less by the far left than the far right – religious fanatics, racialists or nationalists such as neo-fascists in Germany and Italy, Islamic fundamentalists, the IRA, and ETA. This type of activity will increase because religious and racialist fundamentalism seems to have a growing appeal, especially to those who believe or are persuaded that they are unfairly deprived, and because growing public familiarity with mass killings by terrorists means that still more outrageous shocks are needed to capture attention on television. The development of smaller, slimmer bombs with more sophisticated remote control for activation and detonation makes letter and parcel bombs more effective and harder to detect.

Hoax bomb calls are highly disruptive, and aim to disrupt a commercial organisation at minimal risk. Telephone warnings, hoax or real, are usually at very short notice.

Blocking access to sites by demonstrations is increasingly attractive to anti-NATO or environmentalist movements in Europe against government and corporate targets. This tactic is used especially against installations connected with defence or the processing and storage of data.

Demonstrations can be used as cover by saboteurs, armed raiders or bombers to gain access to sensitive installations, with or without the connivance of the organisers of the demonstrations. This was alleged in relation to demonstrations in France and Germany in the 1970s and 1980s.

Contamination and disruption of utilities (water, electric power, fuel, drainage, ventilation, heating and cooling) can be an attractive tactic to the more ruthless terrorists who now appear to be emerging, particularly those with the religious or racial convictions which engender a disregard for human life and public opinion – such as terrorists sponsored by Libya and Iran. Many such systems are very vulnerable and access to them is often less effectively protected than access to other more obvious key points.

Long-range weapons, with their improving accuracy and power of penetration of steel and concrete, may well become more fashionable for use by terrorists firing from the windows of buildings overlooking factories and office blocks, especially if they can locate key facilities which are close to outside walls.

Product extortion by threat to pollute food, drink or pharmaceutical products has increased substantially in recent years, largely due to the power of the media. The most lethal case on record, which cost at least seven lives, was the injection of cyanide into Tylenol tablets in the USA in 1982.

During the 1990s, authorities have increasingly realised that threats and hoaxes is a form of disruption which can be used by terrorists. It forces governments to assess the vulnerability of targets, and the costs of reacting can be astronomical. Yet each hoax has to be treated as if it is a genuine attack. The one most feared is the threat of nuclear attack or a dirty bomb (Combs, 2003).

See also: Extortion; Hostage taking; Kidnapping; Nuclear Terrorism; Risk Management; Terror and Terrorism.

References

Combs, C. C. (2003) *Terrorism in the 21st Century*, New Jersey: Prentice Hall.
Lodge, J. (ed.) (1988) *The Threat of Terrorism*, Brighton: Wheatsheaf
Morris, E. and Hoe, A. (1987) *Terrorism: Threat and Response*, Basingstoke: Macmillan.

Further Reading

Shultz, R. H. and Sloan, S. (1980) 'International Terrorism: The Nature of the Threat' in Shultz, R. H. and Sloan, S. (eds) *Responding to the Terrorist Threat*, New York: Pergamon.

Trends

An analysis of terrorism shows there has been a big increase in incidents. During the 1970s, 8,114 terrorist incidents were reported around the world, resulting in 4,798 deaths and 6,902 injuries. During the 1980s the number of incidents increased nearly fourfold to 31,426 with 70,859 deaths and 47,849 injuries. From 1990 to 1996 there were 27,087 incidents causing 51,797 deaths and 58,814 injuries. In the late-1990s the number of international incidents declined, but deaths and injuries continued to increase (Stern, 1999: 6)

Why the ultimate terrorists? Weapons of mass destruction (WMD) are valuable to terrorists seeking divine retribution displaying scientific prowess, killing large numbers of people, invoking dread or retaliation against states. Motivations are changing. The Black Market post-**Cold War** offers weapons, components and knowledge. Chemical and biological weapons proliferate in states sponsoring terrorism. Advances in technology make terrorism with WMD easier to carry out. To terrorists WMD are ideal as they are intimidating and mysterious. WMD terrorists might think they are emulating God or in the case of the Millennium, believe an apocalypse would occur with the dawning of the 'mystical' millennium. Others are interested in WMD to impress their target audiences with high technology. They can force a government to evacuate a city and to engage in a costly clean-up operation, by using radiological agents or anthrax spores. As governments implement more sophisticate security measures, terrorists might find WMD appealing as a way to overcome such counter-measures. Some terrorists pervertedly are drawn to WMD as they wish to kill many people – to commit macroterrorism.

If this occurs the terrorists will issue moral justification and displace the responsibility onto the leader or other members of the group. They will also minimise or ignore the actual suffering of the victims. Yet terrorists have long been capable of more lethal acts of violence than they have actually committed, suggesting that they have not wanted to kill large numbers of people.

Since the collapse of the **Soviet Union** in 1989 there has been a real fear of the threat of loose nukes in the hands of fifteen newly created unstable states that were part of the Soviet empire. There were 132 'suitcase bombs' in the Soviet arsenal but by 2003 only 40 per cent have been located. This has been compounded by corrupt government officials working with organised criminals knowing how to market goods and services.

Some of these states have not signed up to arms control treaties. The case of **Iraq** shows that no single policy will prevent WMD terrorism. Even a combination of preventive war and unprecedented intrusive international inspections has not destroyed Iraq's ability to use these weapons in acts of terrorism around the world.

What is to be done? From all accounts terrorists are more likely to use industrial poisons or chemical or biological agents than nuclear weapons. Political vulnerability will influence government response to terrorists (Stern, 1999).

New technologies have made terrorism more lethal but technology also makes terrorism easier to combat. If acts of terrorism do occur governments have to be prepared to minimise the loss of life, reduce public panic and respond effectively to see that justice is done.

Certain key trends can be predicted. The volume of terrorist incidents, that is, the number occurring annually has increased. It has increased in lethality that is the number of people killed in attacks. A trend has developed towards large-scale indiscriminate terrorist attacks in mundane everyday locations such as airports, offices, shopping malls or subways. A surge in right-wing terrorism has recently developed carried out by militant, conservative fundamentalist groups and individuals. A generational difference has developed between young militants and older leaders in the terrorists operating today. Today's terrorists are more willing to throw a bomb first and then talk later if at all about their grievances.

Conflicts today appear to be less coherent, exhibiting several confusing and shifting alliances. As states use terrorism to engage in irregular warfare against other states, the stakes in the conflict become confused and the rules less clear. Nations must weigh the cost in terms of loss of liberties and freedoms, against the gains achieved in subduing terrorism, recognising that to sacrifice too many liberties may well be to give terrorists the victory they seek: the destruction of democratic systems.

References

Cooper, R. (2000) *The Post Modern State and World Order*, London: Demos and the Foreign Policy Centre.

Laqueur, W. (1996) 'Post-modern Terrorism', *Foreign Affairs*, vol. 75, no. 5 (Sept/Oct), pp. 24–36.

Stern, J. (1999) *Ultimate Terrorists*, Cambridge, MA and London: Harvard University Press.

Further Reading

Jenkins, B. (1989) *The Future Course of Terrorism*, Santa Monica, CA: Rand.

Livingstone, N. C. (1982) 'Taming Terrorism: In Search of a New US Policy', *International Security Review*, vol. 7, no. 1 (spring).

Wilkinson, P. (1992) 'International Terrorism: New Risks in World Order' in Baylis, J. and Rengger, N. J. (eds) *Dilemmas of World Politics*, Oxford: Clarendon Press, pp. 228–60.

New Styles in Terrorism

Since the mid-1980s the characteristics and motivations of terrorists have changed. Terrorists are less active and the number of incidents has declined, but the number of people killed has escalated and the levels of deadly activity are on the increase.

Nuclear smuggling from the former **Soviet Union** has increased, and it has proved difficult to clamp down on fissile material smuggling due to the existence of a variety of routes for moving Black Market fissile material. Over 25 countries are trying to obtain nuclear technology and materials – and some of these countries sponsor and practice terrorism.

Over the past fifteen years much more public knowledge has developed on how to make nuclear weapons and it is now straightforward enough to be within the range of a terrorist organisation.

By 2003 no one country can sort out the problem of nuclear terrorism and no national solutions to this intricate international problem exist.

References

Cameron, G. (1996) 'Nuclear Terrorism: A Real Threat', *Jane's Intelligence Review* (September).

Freedman, L. (ed.) (2002) *Super-terrorism: Policy Responses*, London and Oxford: Blackwell Publishing.

Gurr, N. J. (1998) 'A New Style of Terror', *Low Intensity Conflict and Law Enforcement*, vol. 7, no. 1.

Poland, J. M. (1988) *Understanding Terrorism: Groups, Strategies and Responses*, Upper Saddle River, NJ: Prentice Hall.

Tucker, D. (2001) 'What is New about the New Terrorism and How Dangerous Is It?', *Terrorism and Political Violence*, vol. 13, no. 3 (autumn).

Further Reading

Crederberg, P. C. (1989) *Terrorism: Myths, Illusions, Rhetoric and Reality*, Oxford: Prentice Hall.

Spiers, E. M. (1996) *Chemical Weapons: A Continuing Challenge*, Basingstoke: Macmillan.

Trevi Group

A number of meetings of interior and justice ministers to discuss measures against terrorism resulted from a suggestion by the then British Prime Minister, Harold Wilson, at a meeting of the European Council in Rome in December 1975. The first meeting was held in Luxemburg in June 1976 when a six-point programme was designed, principally to help prevent future terrorist attacks in the European Community. Closer co-operation was agreed on terrorism, radicalism, extremism and violence. There was included provision for the exchange of technical information on the operation of terrorists, and the exchange of police personnel between Community members to acquire greater knowledge of operating methods in different countries. Information on past acts of terrorism was to be pooled and mutual assistance was to be provided in the event of future terrorist action. Agreement was also reached on the desirability of closer collaboration on such matters as nuclear safety and air security. The Community programme would complement the anti-terrorist co-operation, which already takes place within other international organisations such as **Interpol**.

All these issues have been discussed at various times over the subsequent decade. In September 1976 the twelve member states of the Community agreed to an unprecedented sharing of information by their police forces as part of a major new campaign against international terrorism. A new hotline was set up for the instant sharing of intelligence on terrorists' movements, supplies of money, arms and equipment. The ministers agreed to examine more effective extradition measures and to consider the present visa arrangements to make more effective use of exclusion and expulsion procedures. A review of the current security checks at airports and in particular the scanning of diplomatic baggage was ordered.

Most important was the achievement of a belated recognition of the problem by all the members of the Community, and the acceptance that terrorism should be treated as a crime and not, selectively, as the pursuit of international politics.

Trevi states (non-Schengen) are Denmark, Greece, Ireland, Italy, Portugal, Spain and the **United Kingdom**. The Schengen group – Belgium, France, Germany, Luxemburg and the Netherlands – were the first to remove internal borders within the EU. Trevi was divided into working groups: Trevi 1 on terrorism – Trevi II on public order issues – and Trevi III on serious and organised international crime, principally drug trafficking. Trevi '92 was concerned with police and security issues of the free movement of people, including measures to combat the relaxation of intra-EC border control (Lodge, 1991). Trevi lacked a permanent secretariat even though it had an ambitious programme of action.

By 1990 Trevi had succeeded in persuading national police forces to increase their co-operation, considered by some to be an embryonic Europol. Judicial co-operation lagged behind police, customs and administrative co-operation.

Critics of Trevi saw it as being a threat to civil liberty, while supporters viewed it as safe-guarding public security.

Reference

Lodge, J. (1991) 'Frontier Problems and the Single Market', London: Research Institute for the Study of Terrorism, Conflict Studies Paper no. 288.

Turkey

From 1980 the Republic of Turkey was under a period of military rule until democratic elections were held in 1985, which led to a Centre Right administration coming to power. The object of the military was to stop the anarchy caused by terrorist groups of both the right and the left, and to develop the new democratic system. To cleanse the political arena, the military rulers dissolved all political parties, confiscated their property, and it was only prior to the 1985 elections that they gave permission for a few parties to be created. After the military takeover in 1980, the military regime of General Evren sought to dismantle militant organisations of the extreme Left, and also brought many right-wingers to trial in connection with violent attacks on the Left committed before the military takeover. Even though over 45,000 persons were in detention for suspected terrorist activities, many of them belonging to left-wing groups, by the end of 1982 over 7,000 alleged terrorists were still at large. The Turkish government claimed that 662 organisations were operating against Turkey from abroad, of which 286 were described as extreme left-wing, 17 as separatist and 280 as religious extremists. Millions of rounds of ammunition and about a million pistols were seized in the early 1980s.

The Revolutionary Left (Dev-Sol) was the first extreme left-wing group to pledge opposition to the military regime, describing it as fascist and anti-working class. Many people have been assassinated by the Revolutionary Left, most notably Dr Nihat Erim, Prime Minister from 1971 to 1972. Hundreds of its members were arrested by the military and charged with breaches of the Constitution, including murders, bombings and robberies, with the object of setting up a **Marx**ist–Leninist social order. They co-operated closely with the Popular Front for the Liberation of Palestine (PFLP), a group led by Dr Georges Habash, which has provided substantial quantities of weapons, and training facilities.

Another movement, the Revolutionary Way (Dev-Yol) is led by a woman and is based in Paris. Before 1980 this organisation held a dominant position in several small towns and had engaged in numerous acts of violence, in particular against political opponents. Under the military regime large numbers of the organisation's members were arrested and tried.

The Communist Party, which took part in the Turkish national movement between 1918 and 1922, was also purged by the military in the 1980s. The Party was blamed for dividing Turkey by calling for the establishment of a Turkish state in

eastern Anatolia, of an independent socialist state without military bases in Cyprus, and by setting up a national democratic front as an umbrella organisation for all anti-fascist elements.

Various movements of the extreme right were engaged in violent action against the left in the period before the military takeover in 1980. Afterwards, these movements backed the Evren regime in its offensive against the extreme left, but were themselves frequently the subject of trials brought by the authorities for illegal activities carried out before 1980. The National Action Party is an ultra-nationalist party known until 1969 as the Republican Peasant National Party. It stands for the defence of freedom and of the interests of the peasantry, and has promoted the formation of various militant right-wing organisations outside its own party framework, such as the Federation of Turkish Democratic Idealist Associations, the Great Ideal Society and the Grey Wolves. The latter is a militant youth wing of the Action Party and has been involved in killing immigrant workers in European countries. One of the Grey Wolves members was Mehmet Ali **Agca**, who killed a newspaper editor in 1979, and received life imprisonment for his attempt to kill the Pope in 1981.

Islamic fundamentalism has assumed greater importance in Turkey in the last decade. After the **Sunni** and the **Shi'ite** Alevi Muslim sects in Turkey had lived for several centuries in relative peace with each other, a polarisation began in 1970, with the Sunnis favouring conservative policies and the generally under-privileged Alevis left-wing policies. A large amount of mutual destruction has been undertaken. The principal Islamic fundamentalist party opposed to the institutionalisation of the secular state in Turkey has been the National Salvation Party. Islamic fundamentalism has also been propagated by the relatively small Turkish section of the Muslim Brotherhood. These groups wish for the establishment of a state based on the rule of Koranic law.

There are numerous Armenian and Kurdish movements, which have each maintained their own culture and associations. The organisations formed to conduct 'warfare' against the Turkish authorities represent only a minority of Armenians as a whole, and many Armenian organisations condemn those of their fellow countrymen engaged in acts of violence. The Turkish Government consistently refuses to give in to demands made by militant Armenians; the Government also never recognises the existence of a Kurdish minority. A number of Kurdish groups adhere to **Marx**ist–Leninist principles.

Reference

Dodd, C. H. (1986) 'The Containment of Terrorism: Violence in Turkish Politics 1965–80' in N. O'Sullivan (ed.) *Terrorism, Ideology and Revolution*, pp. 132–149, Boulder, CO: Westview Press, pp. 132–149.

U

Unabomber

The Unabomber, Theodore Kaczynski, targeted persons associated with either universities or the airline industry in the **USA**. He killed three and wounded 23 others using home-made bombs sent through the post. His offer to stop his campaign if his 'manifesto' was published, led to a 35,000 word article in the *Washington Post* attacking technology, modernity and the destruction of the environment. He was a man obsessed with publicity, a mathematics lecturer from the University of California in Berkeley. He could be described as a frustrated loner, working from a Montana log cabin. His activities showed terrorism had become accessible to anyone with a grievance (Hoffman, 1998).

He was clumsy in his attacks, as often the wrong people were killed or injured. The point is that he believed in his own bitter frustrated way that revolution was easier than reform, because the system grew the more disastrous the consequences and more and more millions of people would be deprived of dignity and authority.

The Unabomber case showed that individuals in contrast to groups were exceedingly difficult to detect. A similar case occurred in Australia with a letter bomber, Franz Fuchs. The frightening aspect of the Unabomber case is that he had scientific knowledge and what might have happened if weapons of mass destruction had been at his disposal. The bizarre, almost eccentric aspect of the event is that he really believed that sending out letter bombs would bring about the end of industrial civilisation. To many global observers he could be seen as a paranoid schizophrenic or one who was psychologically disturbed (Laqueur, 2001).

See also: Suicide Terrorism.

References

Hoffman, B. (1998) *Inside Terrorism*, London: Victor Gollancz.
Laqueur, W. (2001) *The New Terrorism: Fanaticism and the Arms of Mass Destruction*, London: Phoenix Press.

United Kingdom

England

Until the end of the Second World War, from the British perspective, violent insurrection and **guerrilla warfare** were phenomena experienced by foreigners. All has now changed. Britain has had a vital concern in curbing the spillover of international terrorism from the Middle East and Europe and the internecine strife between groups in the Asian subcontinent into London's international diplomatic and business community. The terrorist campaign in Ireland has been a cancer in the British body politic for over a decade, and Britain also has to help safeguard British persons, property and interests overseas. The fight against terrorism has not been without difficulty from a legal point of view, for instance in comparison between a civil law state like France and a common law state like the United Kingdom. In the UK, where extradition is a judicial procedure, the courts have not in practice utilised their power to challenge conduct by reviewing grounds upon which a decision to deport is made. Britain pioneered a compromise whereby either party to an extradition treaty might in absolute discretion refuse to surrender its own subjects. Unlike France, neither British nor American law recognises a 'political murder' and Britain has made it plain that it is not prepared to negotiate if any government minister is abducted. A number of trends can be discerned over the years: the waxing and waning of nationalism in Scotland and Wales, in comparison with the increasing virulence from Middle Eastern and Asian separatist groups. Tactics can range from the kidnap of industrialists to bomb attacks on government premises. So far, state and government targets have been entirely buildings. There has been a decreasing impact of the ultra-left compared with the growth of nationalist terror and attacks on American interests.

Of all European countries, Britain suffered least from the student revolutions of 1968, due to the weakness of the **New Left**. Furthermore, although the Vietnam War was hotly debated, the issue never led to prolonged riots. Race has provoked continuing violence, and led to clashes in a number of cities. For a brief period, Celtic separatism in Wales and Scotland raised the prospects of violence, but the issue subsided with the debate on devolution, so that no conflict arose.

Movements with extremist factions in them exist on both the Right and the Left. The National Front, formed in 1967, despite divisions and defections, including the formation in 1980 of a New National Front, has remained the major extreme right-wing party in Britain. The British Movement, founded in 1968 by Colin Jordan, is an **anti-Semitic** and anti-immigration movement, which encourages military training and has its own leader guard providing uniforms and special training. Some of its members have been accused of arson attacks, and the possession of arms and ammunition. Column 88, formed in 1970 from remnants of the National Socialist Movement, has members well versed in intelligence work, arms handling and the use of explosives. It has carried out a number of postal bomb attacks and raids on left-wing bookshops and guerrilla training programmes. Contacts have been maintained with active terrorist right-wing groups in Italy and with

Palestinian groups. The little-known SS Wotan 71, a terrorist group first known in 1976, has been active against minorities and left-wing organisations.

Anarchist groups in England have been few in number, but in the case of the Angry Brigade its influence was considerable. It was produced out of the free-thinking ideas which led to the 1968 disturbances in France and the development of Baader-Meinhof terrorism in Germany. In a four-year period until 1971, the Brigade was responsible for 125 bomb and machine gun attacks in the London area. Their most spectacular attack was at the home of the Secretary of State for Employment, Robert Carr, in 1971. However, many of their attacks were symbolic, and the trial of the leaders in 1972 largely eliminated the Brigade, although the title Angry Brigade again was ascribed to two incidents in 1982–83, perpetrated by a woman. Other extreme left-wing groups called for radical industrial reform, union power and an intensification of the industrial struggle. England's nationalist groups are extremely weak and virtually non-existent. An Gof 1980 Movement is a Cornish nationalist group, and the English People's Liberation Army has undertaken isolated bomb attacks.

See also: Anti-Semitic Terrorism in Europe.

References

Macleay, I. and Scott, A. M. (1990) *Britain's Secret War: Tartan Terrorism and the Anglo-American State*, Edinburgh: Mainstream.

Sacopulos, P. J. (1989) 'Terrorism in Britain: Threat, Reality, Response', *Terrorism*, vol. 12, no. 3, pp. 153–166.

Further Reading

Wilkinson, P. (ed.) (1981) *British Perspectives on Terrorism*, London: Allen and Unwin.

—(1988) 'British Policy on Terrorism' in Lodge, J. (ed.) *The Threat of Terrorism*, Brighton: Wheatsheaf Books, pp. 29–56.

Northern Ireland

The province evolved from the island of Ireland in 1922 after a protracted civil war. Six counties in the north-east with mostly Protestant populations remained under British control with a devolved administration in Belfast. The threat to its stability came from the old Republican demand to drive the British out creating an Irish Republic on nationalist principles.

After a brief 'border war' in 1956 the latest conflict erupted in 1969, when a number of people were killed and wounded in riots between Catholics and Protestants. The Catholics demanded equal political rights and better access to housing, schools and social security. The Protestant controlled Northern Irish government responded by sending in their armed police reserve against Catholic demonstrators. The response by the British government was to send in their troops to separate the two sides and take control of police and reserve forces away from the Belfast government. In 1971 the Prime Minister of Northern Ireland opened internment camps and authorised the detention of suspects without trial. Violent protests occurred. On 30 January 1972 British soldiers opened fire on a peaceful protest march in Londonderry (Derry as the Republicans called the city) killing thirteen Catholics and injuring hundreds more, this became known as 'Bloody Sunday'. The Irish Republican Army responded with a wave of assassinations. The current enquiry by the British government in follows numerous controversial examinations of the events but it appears as with the Northern Ireland issue over the past thirty years or so that the issue remains intractable. This is in spite of ceasefires and the intervention of American administrations on a number of occasions. In a referendum, as in 1973, the people of Northern Ireland have voted to remain within the United Kingdom rather than join a united Ireland. In 1998 further negotiations on Northern Ireland ended with another peace formula. Approval of the agreements in a May 1998 referendum reached 70 per cent. Under these agreements, Northern Ireland would have a directly elected legislative assembly with safeguards against domination by one population group. At the same time a referendum held in Ireland won 95 per cent approval ending its territorial claim over the North. The killing of 28 people by a car bomb in Omagh in August 1998 saw the peace process falter, further compounded by bickering over disarmament and the 'decommissioning' of weapons.

A number of options have been considered over the past three decades.

A United Ireland – but the difficulty is British non-compliance unless the majority in the North consent to it; the security forces in Dublin are too small; and the majority of people and politicians do not want it.

A United Mandate Law and Order is inseparable from the administration and it would not be feasible unless all the main communities consented to it.

Integration with the UK would be the reverse of a trend toward devolution that would not be acceptable to Northern Ireland Catholics, Dublin or world opinion. An independent Ulster would lead to the loss of subsidy from UK taxpayers, and a Protestant government with no option but to take a hard line. The IRA would gain internal and external support and civil war could ensue.

Devolved Sectarian government, as between 1922 and 1971, could be reactivated but the British people and Parliament would not provide troops or money.

A revision of borders would further reduce the Catholic minority in Northern Ireland; and in January 2003 it was disclosed that the Conservative government led by Edward Heath had suggested this on sectarian grounds in 1972, but it did not progress beyond discussion stage.

A Condominium (joint sovereignty between London and Dublin) would be resisted by both the IRA and Protestant paramilitaries.

Power sharing (as attempted in 1973–74) would not work effectively as the majority of Unionist politicians and people would not co-operate.

Direct rule from London 'everyone's second choice' would be ineffective but there is no other way until power sharing is accepted. Progress is continuing in reducing violence and restoring police primacy (to satisfy some nationalists the Royal Ulster Constabulary was replaced by the Police Service of Northern Ireland in 2001). The police have worked for years on trying to stem the flow of support to the men of violence, from inside and outside the province and to stem the growth of organised crime.

One of the greatest problems facing paramilitary groups in Northern Ireland has been financing their activities and they have traditionally engaged in criminality to build up their funds. Armed robbery and hijacking are higher in the province than in the rest of the UK. Public sector fraud is widespread and includes benefit fraud, fuel smuggling, alcohol and tobacco smuggling and betting and gambling. Agricultural fraud does occur as suspect farmers have been known to collaborate to spread disease and a network of dealers can facilitate the smuggling of cattle for profit. Intellectual property theft and counterfeit goods are major local problems e.g. music CDs, clothing and computer software.

A steady increase has been observed in the occurrence of counterfeit currency. Counterfeit documents and telephone cards are on the increase including driving licences and letters of authority received by a local bank (House of Commons Finances 2001–02). Extortion has been used to excuse paramilitary control over the community. It has spread in the building trade, fast food outlets, restaurants and licensed premises and car dealerships. Extortion threatens inward investment and increases the cost of doing business. Money-laundering has become a vital activity of all profit generating organised crime operations; and the sums of money involved may be very significant. Traditionally paramilitary organisations from both sides of the community have used legitimate businesses such as taxi firms, pubs and clubs to launder funds. Money lending rackets have regularly been used by paramilitary organisations to raise funds and profits are used to fund prisoner welfare and weapons procurement operations.

In Northern Ireland it is estimated that £18 million is now being raised each year through crime. Fund raising activity has switched from armed robbery to both counterfeiting and smuggling.

Dangers inherent in high-profile armed robberies have pushed the paramilitary into areas such as tobacco and fuel smuggling especially. Smuggling is appealing to terrorists because it provides a cover for their activities. In the autumn of 2001 a shipment of cigarettes seized in Northern Ireland had been bankrolled to the tune of £50,000 by Loyalists who had bought the consignment from the IRA. Fuel laundering is popular as large differences in fuel duty between Northern Ireland and the Irish Republic make it lucrative. Two thirds of 700 petrol stations in the north were involved in the trade in 1994 leading to revenue losses of £100,000 a week.

In order to try and halt the build up of funds in terrorist organisations, the police have aimed to disrupt the dealing in contraband goods as a terrorist support activity. Also disrupting such networks that may allow the movement of terrorist material or personnel; as well as building up further intelligence opportunities. The customs service work closely with the police to track down drug consignments, seize counterfeit goods and infiltrate groups who smuggle tobacco, hydro-carbons, oil and are involved in fraud.

For the IRA 1987 was marked by setbacks: in May 1987 two IRA Active Service Units were ambushed at Loughgall by the SAS, nine people were killed and the police station wrecked. It was the biggest IRA loss since the 1920s. The *Eksund* arms ship was seized off France. The war memorial at Enniskillen was blown up on Remembrance Sunday leaving 11 dead and damage to its own strategy.

In 1988 the SAS achieved further success and shot dead three IRA activists in Gibraltar.

The political momentum was stalled by the onset of the 1990s, an era which lead into the peace process.

From 1990 to 1994 there was an intricate web of political contacts formed with much bridge building in Ireland. Significant change was implied provided the use of arms was ended. The IRA would have to focus on the rights and aspirations of the unionist peoples. The IRA wished to end the Unionist veto and secure an unconditional place for Sinn Fein at the negotiating table. They took South Africa as the role model, where the ANC had refused to give up armed struggle prior to entering talks with the white government.

Republican areas were coming under threat from re-equipped and re-organised loyalist paramilitary groups – this was done in retaliation for IRA killings, placing additional pressure on local IRA leaders and activists.

Political dialogue was occurring. A negotiating process was under way involving both governments and the northern constitutional parties. The hope was that the governments would sign up to the Joint Declaration giving expression to the North and exercise of Irish self determination to convince the IRA to call a halt.

Massive destruction occurred in Belfast city centre in early- 1992 through two IRA bombs and retaliatory killings went on apace. In April widespread damage was done in the City of London by an IRA bomb in retaliation for a Conservative election victory.

It came as a relief when the IRA put forward a peace process through settling relationships within Ireland (North and South) without the British being kicked out. As usual, however, the IRA continued parallel military activity alongside the peace process in the hope of extracting concessions from the British government.

In 1993 the US President, Bill Clinton, became increasingly involved in the Irish political peace process, starting by speaking to both the Republicans and Unionists to try and bring about peace talks.

A complete cessation of military operations occurred on 31 August 1994, when both sides accepted that a solution would only be found as a result of the inclusion of negotiations.

The first year of the agreement brought both optimism and disillusionment. The difficulty was that the IRA now budged from its position that no arms would be handed up prior to an agreed entitlement. Conversely this meant that the IRA would face full and verifiable decommissioning as part of an overall settlement.

It was not surprising therefore, that a return to war was seen as inevitable by the IRA unless visible and progressive political movement could be made. In February 1996 a huge bomb exploded at Canary Wharf in London, but this served in the long-term and strategically to weaken the IRA's negotiating position. In June 1996 a huge bomb wrecked Manchester city centre.

On the other side of the fence, there was an increasing stand off between Orange Order marches and the police at Drumcree over the right of Protestants to march down a Catholic road. At the time of writing this stand off is unresolved.

The Republican movement's moral position had been seriously undermined by the resumed cam-

paign. Nevertheless Tony Blair's victory in 1997 brought politics to the fore again over military campaign. The IRA's complete cessation of military operations was restored and Sinn Fein was promised a role in negotiations if the ceasefire held. Violence still continued in a small way but events were overtaken by the signing of the Good Friday Agreement (O'Brien, 1997).

Support in terms of funds came from various sources, but primarily from the Irish Northern Aid Committee the financial broker for the Provisional IRA's transatlantic fundraising. They had a distorted view of events in Northern Ireland and allegedly reacted to propaganda. Millions of dollars was sent to Northern Ireland in the form of cash, arms and pamphlets, and rallying all Irish-Americans especially in New York and Boston, to their cause.

In 1994 the Loyalists announced a ceasefire in the name of the Combined Loyalist Military Command. The previous year saw for the first time since 1975 murders by Loyalists outnumbering those by Republicans. Simply, the Loyalists wished to oppose moves that might lead towards a united Ireland. New leaders of the movement had a more realistic view of Northern Ireland's place in the Union.

In 1998 the arms decommissioning body issued an arms immunity certificate to the Loyalist Volunteer Force (LVF) allowing it to transport guns for decommissioning.

In the same year the LVF announced that the war was over. The announcement of a complete ceasefire was perceived as being influenced by the fact that the organisation's prisoners had not been included on the list of those eligible for early release under the Belfast Agreement. This was viewed with cynicism in some quarters; that their ceasefire would last only until prisoners were released. The IRA alleged later that it had co-operated with other Loyalist groups involved in attacks on Catholic homes (Bew and Gillespie, 1999). In 1999 the LVF warned of a 'great strain' on its ceasefire if the IRA did not again begin decommissioning.

During the ceasefire years since 1994 both groups appear to have been targeting more individuals under the age of 20. The IRA has been putting more resources into vigilantism and their punishment squads are larger and able to inflict more serious injuries than Loyalist attacks. The IRA take risks and their attacks, as a result, are often witnessed as many occur in public places.

Both groups have different approaches to whom they target and the methods they use. The vigilante campaigns are a form of surrogate terrorism, and in fact, people die as a result of the vigilantism more frequently today than in the pre-ceasefire years. The danger is that paramilitary vigilantism could eventually lead to the collapse of hard won ceasefires (Silke and Taylor, 2000).

The Ulster Defence Association had been established at the start of the current troubles. In September 1971 it announced that it had been created by merging a wide range of Protestant vigilante and paramilitary groups and assumed the motto, 'Law before Violence'. It was working-class and organised on military lines and thirty years ago had a membership of about 50,000.

In January 1986 its political think tank, the New Ulster Political Research Group called for a written constitution and a devolved government based on consensus and shared responsibility.

In the early-1990s it threatened to intensify its campaign to a ferocity never imagined. It was involved in internal feuding within the Ulster Volunteer Force (UVF) and the Combined Loyalist Military Command a combination of the Ulster Volunteer Force, the Ulster Freedom Fighters and the Red Hand Commando (first mentioned in April 1991) (Bew and Gillespie, 1999). On a number of occasions it was alleged that there had been collusion with the security forces. It endorsed the Belfast Agreement saying that it would not lead to a united Ireland. In May 1998 the leaders in the Maze Prison announced 'the war is over' and apologised to all victims of UDA and UVF violence.

The Ulster Freedom Fighters were a violent group attacking both Catholics and Protestants throughout the community. Their actions increased during the 1990s. In May 1999 their leader, Johnny Adair was shot and wounded while on parole from the Maze Prison. He claimed Republicans were responsible but the media suggested Loyalists instigated the attack.

In 1998 they endorsed the Belfast Agreement stating that it would not lead to a united Ireland (Bew and Gillespie, 1999). The Red Hand

Defenders is a new paramilitary group which undertook its first killing in October 1998, and its first bomb attack two months later (Bew and Gillespie, 1999).

The Good Friday Agreement was signed on the 10 April 1998 in spite of last ditch brinkmanship by Sinn Fein and the Ulster Unionists. It gave Nationalists, the SDLP and Sinn Fein guaranteed ministries in the new Northern Ireland Executive Government, and started a structured North–South ministerial co-operation at all levels. Major police reform was promised. All political prisoners would be released within two years. Both governments would remove their 'claims' on Northern Ireland leaving the constitutional future in the hands of the people. Separate referendums would be held in both jurisdictions (North and South).

By late- 1998, however, the Agreement's implementation process stalled as the Unionists held out for a start to IRA decommissioning before they would accede to fully establish the next Executive Government. Over 200 IRA prisoners had been released but without any signs of decommissioning.

In December 1999 the new Executive Government for Northern Ireland was formed and within the month the first meeting of the North and South Ministerial Council occurred (Morrissey and Smyth, 2002). The IRA said it would consider decommissioning if police and judicial reforms occurred as well as British demilitarisation. The Agreement was still seen as a vehicle for lasting peace.

Any agreement to end the types of political violence experienced in Northern Ireland is bound to be difficult. The multi-dimensional, multi-locational nature of political violence is signalled by the status of the casualties – 2,000 civilian deaths, 1,000 members of the security forces and 700 members of paramilitary organisations, prove the complexity of the issues.

The early release of paramilitary prisoners was one part of the Good Friday Agreement that increased anger and disaffections amongst some of the bereaved and injured even though it was clear that concessions to paramilitary prisoners would form part of any agreement (O'Brien, 1997).

The Agreement to end such an intractable conflict could take years before any lasting peace is reached. There are particular aspects of identity, location in terms of class and ease of access to weapons. Individual and collective histories have to be lived with – the past will feature in the peace process. The rift that divided Unionists and Nationalists now increasingly divides those who support the Good Friday Agreement and those who do not. There has been a fall off in Unionist support for the Agreement.

The Continuity Irish Republican Army (Continuity Army Council) are a radical splinter group of up to 100 members created in 1999 as the clandestine armed wing of Republican Sinn Fein which split from Sinn Fein in the mid-1980s. The ultimate aim is to force the British to leave Northern Ireland and to this end has attacked security targets in the province and loyalist paramilitary groups (Griset and Mahan, 2003: 349–50). Funding to some extent is known to come from sympathisers in the USA, and arms and material come from the Balkans. The group is opposed to weapons decommissioning.

The Orange Volunteers are a small group of 20 members which appeared in 1999 from those hard liners opposed to the ceasefire. They attack Catholics in order to prevent a political settlement – but they did observe a ceasefire in 2000 and 2001 (Griset and Mahan, 2003: 357).

The Real IRA is a clandestine armed wing of the 32 county sovereignty movement and was formed in early-1998 as a political pressure group dedicated to removing British forces from Northern Ireland and unifying Ireland. They adopt the usual terrorist tactics of assassinations, bombings and robbery. The 200 plus members are former IRA members who left that organisation following the IRA ceasefire (Griset and Mahan, 2003: 341).

A brief ceasefire was observed after the Omagh bombing, but they resumed attacks in 2001 and also included targets in London such as MI6 Headquarters and the BBC. Weaponry has been obtained from the Balkans and some funding has come from the USA.

Red Hand Defenders are a group of about thirty individuals that can be described as extremist and was formed in 1998 out of Protestant hardliners from loyalist groups observing a ceasefire. They are opposed to a political settlement with Irish Nationalists and attack Catholic civilian interests in Northern Ireland (Griset and Mahan, 2003: 358).

References

Bew, P. and Gillespie, G. (1999) *Northern Ireland: A Chronology of the Troubles 1968–1999*, Dublin: Gill and Macmillan.

Griset, P. L. and Mahan, S. (2003) *Terrorism in Perspective*, Thousand Oaks, CA, London and New Delhi, Sage Publications.

House of Commons, N. Ireland Affairs Committee, *The Financing of Terrorism in Northern Ireland*, Fourth Report of Session 2001–02, vol. II Minutes of Evidence and Appendices.

Morrissey, M. and Smyth, M. (2002) *Northern Ireland after the Good Friday Agreement: Victims, Grievance and Blame*, London: Pluto Press.

O'Brien, B. (1997) *A Pocket History of the IRA*, Dublin: O'Brien Press.

O'Day, A. and Alexander, Y. (eds) (1994) *Dimensions of Irish Terrorism*, New York: G. K. Hall.

Silke, A. and Taylor, M. (2000) 'War Without End: Comparing IRA and Loyalist Vigilantism in Northern Ireland', *The Harvard Journal*, vol. 39, no. 3 (August), pp. 249–266.

Further Reading

Bell, J. B. (1996) *Back to the Future: The Protestants and a United Ireland*, Dublin: Poolberg.

Bew, P. and Gillespie, G. (1996) *The Northern Ireland Peace Process: A Chronology 1993–96*, Dublin: Gill and Macmillan.

Bruce, S. (1992) *The Red Hand: Protestant Paramilitaries in Northern Ireland*, Oxford: OUP.

— (1994) *The Edge of the Union: The Ulster Loyalist Political Vision*, New York: OUP.

—(2001) 'Terrorists and Politics: The Case of Northern Ireland's Loyalist Paramilitaries', *Terrorism and Political Violence*, vol. 13, no. 2, pp. 27–48.

Dillon, M. (1999) *The Dirty War*, New York: Routledge.

Wright, J. (1990) *Terrorist Propaganda: The Red Army Faction and the Provisional IRA 1968–86*, New York: St Martin's Press.

Scotland and Wales

For a brief period in the 1970s Celtic separatism in Wales and Scotland seemed to pose a danger to the unity of the UK, but the separatists were weakened by the long-running debate on devolution and the subsequent referendum in 1981, when by quite sizeable majorities the Scottish and Welsh people voted against devolution.

The most well-known of the nationalist movements in Scotland is the Army of the Provisional Government of Scotland – the Tartan Army. It is an extreme nationalist organisation which describes its aim as being to free Scotland of its British yoke, by revolutionary means. Oil pipelines have been bombed, and there have been conspiracies to rob banks and to break into explosives magazines and military establishments. Many of the original members have been sent to jail.

The Scottish National Liberation Army, with a few active and ardent members, claimed responsibility in 1982 for the manufacture of ten incendiary bombs. One of these was sent to the Queen and another to the Defence Secretary. Less well-known groups include the Army for Freeing Scotland and the Army of the Gael.

The most active of the movements in Wales has been the Welsh Language Society, established in 1962 to protect the Welsh language by extending its use in the media. Some members of the Society gradually began to use violence, destroying cottages owned as second homes by English people and removing English language road signs. The arson attacks were undertaken to show that the sale of such houses resulted in inflated prices and put housing beyond the means of most Welsh people. Two other groups, the Remembrance and the Sons of Glyndwr, have also committed arson attacks against holiday cottages. The Welsh Socialist Republican Movement gave close support to Sinn Fein and the Irish Republican Socialist Party.

In 1979, voters in Scotland and Wales turned down autonomy for their region in a referendum. In 1997 two referenda held in Wales and Scotland approved greater autonomy and an elected assembly for each region.

United Nations and International Terrorism

The performance of the United Nations in combating international **terrorism** is a contro-

versial subject. Some observers claim that far from combating terrorism, the UN has been actively promoting it through its support of wars of national liberation and its formal recognition of the **Palestine Liberation Organisation** (PLO). The UN, like so many bodies, organisations and individuals has for most of its existence been unable to agree on a definition of terrorism.

Some modicum of agreement is sustained, but the countries within the UN do not agree on the following issues. State terrorism comprises the use of terror by governments, including torture, **genocide** and assassination of political enemies abroad by the use of diplomats and other persons enjoying special status by virtue of their governmental functions. Within the definition of terrorism are included acts inflicting terror during 'armed conflict' covered by the law of war, i.e. the massacre of defenceless prisoners of war. In the context of international terrorism by private individuals, the UN defines this as the threat or use of violence by private persons for political ends, where the conduct itself or its political objectives or both are international in scope.

In the wake of the Munich Olympics tragedy in 1972 and at America's behest, a draft convention on international terrorism was agreed. The convention was purposely drawn to be narrow in its coverage. It did not seek to define terrorism or to deal with all acts that might fall within the definition of terrorism. Only unlawful killing, serious bodily harm or **kidnapping** fell within the scope of the convention. Four conditions had to apply before the convention could come into force. The act had to be committed or take effect outside the territory of the state of which the alleged offender was a national. The act had to be committed or take effect outside the state against which the act was directed, unless such acts were knowingly directed against a non-national of that state, i.e. the attack on Israel's Lod Airport in 1972. Acts committed either by or against a member of the armed forces of a state in the course of military hostilities were excluded from coverage. The act had to be intended to damage the interest of or to obtain concessions from a state or an international organisation.

The American purpose in drafting such a convention was to meet the concern of Third

World countries that the **USA** initiative was directed against wars of national liberation, and thereby by allaying this concern to gain as wide an acceptance of the convention as possible. In December 1972 the UN adopted a resolution which, while expressing deep concern over terrorism and inviting states to become parties to existing conventions on international terrorism, focused its primary attention on finding just and peaceful solutions to the underlying causes which give rise to such acts of violence.

A dramatic increase in plane hijacking during the 1960s led to the conclusion of the 1963 Tokyo Convention which, in effect, requires state parties to return a plane and passengers if they have been hijacked. The 1970 Hague Convention provides that state parties must either extradite or prosecute the hijackers; and the 1971 Montreal Convention contains the same requirement with respect to those who engage in any kind of sabotage of aviation such as blowing up planes on the ground. These conventions, especially the latter two, were not widely ratified, especially by certain Arab states that provide sanctuary for the hijackers. An International Conference on Air Law and an Extraordinary Assembly of the International Civil Aviation Organisation (ICAO) in 1973 failed to agree on any other proposals to enhance the security of civil aviation.

During the 1970s and early 1980s, General Assembly resolutions as well as negotiations in the Assembly have helped to induce more states, including some Arab states, to ratify the three ICAO conventions against aircraft hijacking and sabotage. In 1974 the General Assembly adopted by consensus the Convention on the Prevention and Punishment of Crimes against Internationally Protected Persons, including Diplomatic Agents. The convention provides for international co-operation in preventing and punishing attacks against diplomats and other persons enjoying a special status under international law.

In 1979, an International Convention against the Taking of Hostages was adopted by the General Assembly. The Convention requires international co-operation toward the prevention, prosecution and punishment of all acts involving the taking of hostages, except where the act is purely domestic in nature. The Convention seeks to ensure that international acts of hostage taking will be covered either by the Convention itself or by one of the applicable conventions on the laws of war.

In the same year, a resolution was adopted which contains a number of useful provisions regarding possible future measures toward combating international terrorism, in particular the request to the Secretary-General to build up a body of national legislation regarding international terrorism. This information would be useful to states wishing to structure their law and policy so as to combat terrorism effectively while safeguarding fundamental **human rights**.

Measures adopted to date by the UN to combat international terrorism have had a narrow focus. They have covered only a particular type of target or victim (civil aviation and diplomats) or a particular manifestation of international terrorism, such as **hostage taking**. There is now a need for the UN to come to grips with other facets of international terrorism. The so-called war of assassination by states against their enemies abroad is particularly disturbing, threatening international peace and security. The UN has to move more effectively against gross violations of human rights, such as torture, that create an environment in which terrorism may flourish. The justness of one cause does not excuse the use of terrorist methods. Whatever the end, the means cannot legitimately include the exploding of bombs in towns, the taking of hostages, the killing of diplomats, the hijacking of planes or the sending of letter bombs. Ultimately all states have an interest in suppressing such actions. The future stability and peace of the world may depend upon recognition of this fact.

In 1985 the UN Security Council condemned terrorism in all its forms and unanimously adopted Resolution 579 which called for the safe release of all hostages in any incident, condemned hostage taking and called for international co-operation to prosecute hostage takers.

The UN has been at the forefront of trying to see that **international law** against various forms of terrorism must be strengthened, and to strengthen the impact of **sanctions**. The UN has been aware of the real need for action not only against terrorists themselves but also against governments who protect them. Financial sanctions have been employed by the UN against UNITA in Angola, the Taliban in **Afghanistan** and guerrillas within Liberia (Kegley, 1990).

In the aftermath of September 11 the Security Council condemned the attacks, but did not subsequently authorise actions against Afghanistan (Booth and Dunne, 2002). Specialised organisations under the UN aegis have taken appropriate action – the International Atomic Energy Agency, the International Civil Aviation Organisation, and the World Health Organisation – and measures have ranged from tightening security at nuclear facilities and on board planes, to countering deliberate infections.

Over the past decade there have been measures on Marking of Plastic Explosives (1991) and the Suppression of Terrorist Bombing (1999). In 2001– 02 an International Convention on the Suppression of Terrorism was agreed. States agreed to condemn all acts, methods and practices of terrorism and to take effective counter-action against them.

Currently the biggest problem facing the UN is how to counter the financing of terrorism. All states will have to adapt their natural laws so as to bear down heavily upon rogue banks and dubious tax havens. The UN is to work in close co-operation with President Bush's Foreign Terrorist Asset Tracking Center. In 2003 the UN is hoping that an International Covenant for the Suppression of the Financing of Terrorism will be put in place, but the whole measure is very difficult to handle, and many groups such as **Hamas** and **Al Qaeda** have huge finances (Whittaker, 2002). The General Assembly met in October 2001 and showed zeal in the priority to counter-terrorism but great difficulty in getting an agreed meaning of 'terrorism'.

In combating terrorism UN recommendations and decisions provide only a minimum of what is needed, because they are not legally binding on states. States can adopt ambiguous responses and raise many reservations.

Co-ordination and connection between the conventions is limited, and it must be stated that United Nations' deliberations on international terrorism has not been a regular feature of UN activities until recently.

An international convention on the prevention of acts of international terrorism would oblige states to subject terrorist acts to criminal prosecution and judicial punishment or to extradition as might be appropriate; they would have to exchange information on all such actions. Significantly under the convention, states would undertake not to support directly or indirectly, terrorist activities in another state and to ban and suppress organisations involved in them. Even in the closing years of the **Cold War**, both superpowers actively supported such a convention.

Terrorists are aware of differences between soldiers and humanitarian assistance personnel, but both can be targeted by violent groups. Forces deployed as NATO or UN makers of peace or keepers of peace are exposed to terrorism risks even though their mission is one of operations other than war (Harmon, 2000).

Peacekeepers force attacks because terrorism works. Attacks can range from hostage taking to attacks with bombs and to logistical sabotage. Aid workers in particular are 'available' and utterly 'defenceless' against hostage-takers.

See also: Aviation Security; Olympic Games Attacks.

References

Booth, K. and Dunne, T. (eds) (2002) *Worlds in Collision: Terror and the Future of Global Order*, Basingstoke and New York: Palgrave Macmillan.

Harmon, C. C. (2000) *Terrorism Today*, London: Frank Cass.

Kegley, C. W. (ed.) (1990) *International Terrorism Characteristics, Causes, Controls*, New York: St Martin's Press.

Romanov, V. A. (1990) 'The United Nations and the Problem of Combating International Terrorism', *Terrorism and Political Violence*, vol. 2, no. 3.

Whittaker, D. J. (2002) *Terrorism: Understanding the Global Threat*, Harlow and London: Pearson Education.

Further Reading

Finger, S. M. (1990) 'The United Nations and International Terrorism' in Kegley, C. W. (ed.) *International Terrorism Characteristics, Causes, Controls*, New York: St Martin's Press.

United States (USA)

The United States is, and has long been, the primary target of a variety of foreign terrorist organisations. The country itself (as has also long been the case) has remained relatively insulated from these escalations of terrorist violence. Although the USA is the country most frequently targeted by terrorists abroad, it is near the bottom of the list in terms of the number of terrorist attacks within its own borders. Despite the fact that the USA has the highest crime and homicide rates in the industrialised Western world (as well as the greatest number of both legal and illegal weapons in the possession of its citizens), politically motivated crimes are relatively infrequent. The country is not a politically polarised country. Unlike France, Italy or Germany, where a variety of political parties represent the extremes of the ideological spectrum in national politics, the USA has traditionally been a two-party country. The two parties differ little in actual substance from one another. Terrorism is also inhibited because of the country's unparalleled upward economic and social mobility which provides opportunities for social and economic advancement.

In addition, the USA is a politically absorbent society. American politics have been ethnic politics, and immigrants have been readily absorbed by the major political parties and integrated into the American political system. While other Western nations have violent irredentist groups, there are none in the USA except for a Puerto Rican faction.

Three types of terrorist organisation do exist in the USA: ethnic separatist and émigré groups; left-wing radical organisations; and right-wing racist, anti-authority, and extreme survivalist-type groups. Two-thirds of all terrorism in the USA is carried out by ethnic separatist or émigré terrorists. Their causes and grievances often have little or nothing to do with domestic American politics. Of the three types of terrorist organisation in the USA, the ethnic émigré groups have generally shown themselves to be the most persistent and violent. These groups also give rise to 'successor' generations of younger terrorists. Despite the potentially wide appeal of these organisations within their own communities, the narrow focus of their parochial, ethnically centred causes means they have a far smaller political constituency than ideological terrorist groups. Support comes only from other ethnic émigré groups in scattered, tightly knit communities around the country.

Radical leftist groups have existed in one form or another since the late 1960s. They originated in student movements that were organised to protest against United States involvement in the Vietnam War. When the War ended, their influence declined. In recent years, US involvement in Central America, and South Africa's apartheid policy have given new life to left-wing groups such as the Weather Underground, or Weathermen, and the Black Liberation Army (BLA). These issues have led to the foundation of new, more narrowly focused, leftist-leaning groups, including the Revolutionary Armed Task Force, the United Freedom Front and the Armed Resistance Unit.

Right-wing terrorists embrace traits of both ethnic separatist and left-wing terrorists. They are violent and concentrate on specific political issues. Such groups can be divided into specific issue-oriented terrorists and traditional vengeance or 'Date' Groups. In recent years, several racist and reactionary groups have surfaced in the West. These include anti-federalists, anti-Semites, racists, extremists and Christian fundamentalists – such as the Aryan Nations, the Order, the Covenant, the Sword and the Arm of the Lord.

The groups are in decline due to the continuing success achieved by the **FBI** as well as state and local law enforcement agencies in tracking down and arresting wanted and suspected terrorists. Widespread arrests of members of ethnic terrorist organisations such as those in the large Armenian and Cuban exile communities have similarly undermined these two movements. An additional factor is disillusionment and exhaustion among old members and the waning enthusiasm of potential recruits.

Friction in relations between the United States and **Libya** has been cited as increasing the likelihood of Libyan 'hit-squads' being deployed to the USA. Libyan actions so far have been restricted to attacks on Libyan nationals in America and not directed against American targets. Libyan student activity is closely monitored.

Domestic left-wing radicals always have had trouble recruiting new members to their organisations. In the 1980s Jewish extremists associated with the Jewish Defence League (JDL) were active. Initially the group used terrorism to draw attention to itself and its causes, to maintain momentum and perpetuate its image as an 'action-oriented', non-traditional Jewish pressure group. The increase of militant Jewish terrorism represents not only an escalation of violence but a significant change in patterns of targeting, and a dramatic shift in tactics. Middle East targets in the USA were hit, and assassinations as well as bombings carried out. By expanding targets the Jewish extremists tried to appeal to a larger and more diverse constituency.

Right-wing terrorists embody many of the traits typical of both ethnic émigré and left-wing terrorists. The rightists, like the ethnic émigré groups, are more violent than their leftist counterparts, have been able to replenish their ranks with new recruits and, like left-wing terrorists, are motivated in some cases to enlarge their power base by ostensibly taking action against controversial, popular political issues (such as abortion).

The greatest threat to US security has been posed by the **Al Qaeda** organisation which has exposed the vulnerability of American society to mega-terrorist incidents.

The major Al Qaeda action has been directed against the USA. States that have been the victims of tenuously related or unrelated terrorist groups have proved responsive to American requests for help i.e. **India**, **Israel** and **Russia**. More problematically the US needs the assistance of states whose leaders believe that they are not terrorist targets, they can easily redirect terror toward others and their own citizens may sympathise with Al Qaeda. Hawks argue that the war against terrorism must be prosecuted ruthlessly for however long it takes with regular follow up actions if deemed necessary. Doves argue for the retaliation post-**September 11**, but believe even now that the USA should do less in the world on the grounds that if it is less involved, it will be less of a target (Ahmed, 2001–2002). Violent regimes and movements exist around the world, and are linked with terrorist activity. None, however, appear to be linked to Al Qaeda, who wish to challenge the American position in the Arab world. Al Qaeda believes that if the USA left the region they could take power in the Gulf and in **Egypt**.

Most overseas terrorism targeted American citizens during this period, and in the eyes of the government in Washington, represented an attack on the USA. From the President downwards through the various administrations, the view has been that they have an obligation to protect the life and property of their citizens from the tactical and strategic threat posed by terrorism.

The US mission to the **United Nations** has signed formal agreements on matters such as extradition and diplomatic security. Non-binding agreements have been agreed at G7/G8 summits. Economic incentives have included anti-terrorism training and debt reduction. Conflict alleviation has been involved using facilitation and negotiation.

The Americans have adopted a consistent stance against specified and designated state sponsors, including trade bans, confiscation of assets and import/export controls. There have been military strikes, assassination and foreign search and surveillance.

Overseas personnel and operations have included overseas security at embassies, intelligence operations covering infiltration and propaganda. Incident management has ranged from rescue missions and negotiations to negotiation and third party agreement. The pursuing of suspects has led to formal investigation.

In the area of domestic criminal law, immigration procedures have ranged from exclusion and expulsion to special courts and secret evidence. Under the criminal law a hard line has been taken on surveillance (wire taps and information access); increased penalties; the utilisation of the Grand Jury and weapons confiscation.

Non-criminal domestic measures have covered aviation security such as sky marshals and baggage checks; and domestic preparedness (exercises, military aid) and efficient administrative structures.

Some observers argue that too many counter-terrorist measures affect civil liberties which could alienate law abiding groups. Too much repression can strengthen the resolve of terrorists. Friendly nations may reduce counter-terror assistance if they believe the measures are too stifling.

American counter-terrorism policy has focussed on preventing acts of terrorism and defending against such acts should prevention fail. Ongoing national domestic preparedness effort has only just come into the equation in American counter-terrorism programmes. WMD attacks could have catastrophic effects on American society beyond the deaths it might cause.

Consequence management involves measures taken to alleviate damage, loss, hardship or suffering caused by emergencies. Terrorism and tactical violence incidents consume supplies and equipment quickly. In the USA the Federal Response Plan (FRP) defines and outlines federal support procedures and these cover: transport, communications, public works and engineering, fire fighting, health and medical services, urban search and rescue, information and planning, hazardous materials, food and energy.

The Federal Emergency Management Agency (FEMA) manages and co-ordinates federal consequence management response in support of state and local governments in accordance with its statutory authorities. The Agency has to activate the appropriate FRP elements as needed (Maniscalco and Christen, 2002).

In the last few years of the twentieth century a clear pattern emerged. The regions include attacks against US facilities and attacks in which American citizens suffered casualties. Latin America followed by Asia, Africa and Western Europe witnessed over half the attacks. The two main types of event were bombing and kidnapping, and the main targets were American businesses (Combs, 2003).

Terrorists in the modern era of the phenomena have attacked American interests and citizens regularly, as they are tempted by the publicity they receive from the worldwide based US news **media**. Many extremists allegedly mention their hostility to the Jewish influence controlling American news media, financial institutions and government. Many terrorists believe that the USA is hell-bent on global domination. To Muslim activists America and Americanism are collective enemies (Hoffman, 1998).

Until September 11 more Americans had been killed in terrorist atrocities overseas than in the USA. In **Osama Bin Laden's** fatwas to kill Americans there is mention on a regular basis of the need to grab US money and assets (Jurgensmeyer, 2000). The USA is a global trader with many political allies and this is a vested interest, but

America is seen by religious extremists as supporting secular governments. America is also resented because it is the home to many multinational corporations, who are perceived as exploiting the poor and widening the gulf between rich and poor. Materialistic ambitions do not sit comfortably with religious fundamentalist ideals. Islam fears the global domestication of US economy and culture. Modern culture has been embraced by the Americans and after all, the Internet and Web were American creations. In the conflict between secular and religious life around the world, the United States is seen as supporting the secular side. Fear and hatred appears mutual between Islam and the USA. Yet many Muslims, however, have chosen to live in what many Muslims refer to as 'the Great Satan' namely the USA.

Since the end of the **Cold War**, the USA has been seen as the only coherent military power in the world, and has been an easy target to blame by the people who are anti-military or question defence spending (Booth and Dunne, 2002).

America has repeatedly said it does not need allies to win the war against terrorism and in so doing is seen as goading the terrorists into thinking they can go on challenging America to react. This ideal could also make it lose some support from some of its allies. Some observers, perhaps controversially believe that the USA needs to re-examine its role in world politics and that perhaps it was not entirely blameless for what happened on September 11. Other observers believe that post-September 11 it had little chance but to respond in a war mode. President Bush argued that the Muslim world (Arabs) hate the United States because of their democratic freedoms.

On a global basis, American influence is contrary to the interests of various groups that are prepared to use violence. Terrorists can choose to act where American intelligence and prevention are least effective and perhaps where the chance of arrest and punishment are minimised (Heymann, 1998).

The Islamic world has been angry at the USA over the past two years. The war in Afghanistan was seen as a war against Muslims who see themselves as an island of justice, compassion, tolerance, charity and humility in a violent world. There is nothing in the *Koran* that is against modernity – indeed, young Muslims enjoy themselves at American style pop concerts and films, but fear that the American government is against them. There is a perception in the Islamic world and in **Pakistan** in particular that the USA tells the Muslims regularly what to do and Americans only care about Muslims when their own interests and own culture are affected. Clerics are as important as politicians in many parts of the Islamic world. There was bewilderment and anger on how the Americans could attack Afghanistan, based on allegations and not justified under international law. The American phrase in relation to the war on terrorism 'if you are not with us you are against us' causes resentment, and combined with the perception that the USA thinks it is culturally superior, acts as a potent source of anger and violence.

The international organisations, especially the International Monetary Fund (IMF) and its hold over the **Third World** debt on interest, are seen as being influenced by the power of the USA in promoting their global agenda on economics and politics.

Muslims feel they have been humiliated in **Afghanistan** and have had to fight the 'infidel', as they have to a greater or lesser extent in Bosnia, **Chechnya** and Palestine.

There is a feeling that the USA must understand the psychology of the Muslim world. As the Afghan war showed in 2001–02 many will fight against the invader, and many Muslims from other countries were willing to fight and die in Afghanistan in the struggle against injustice. Globally 1.3 billion Muslims want the United States to adopt a fair and just foreign policy.

American governments have maintained that any act of terrorism is a potential threat to its national security. To give in to such acts would place even more Americans at risk. Domestic terrorism has been viewed as a spectrum of criminal activity. Concern has remained as to whether the USA has the intelligence capabilities and resources to monitor international groups planning action on American soil and this came to a head as a result of September 11. After the first **World Trade Center** attack in 1993 and the **Oklahoma bombing**, the Americans became more proactive at the tactical level in countering terrorism in the areas of intelligence, security and diplomacy.

The American administration has named over thirty terrorist groups which are designated as Foreign Terrorist Organisations (FTO). The State Department declares that it is unlawful to provide funds or other material support to a designated FTO. Representatives and members of a FTO can be denied visas or excluded from the USA, and financial institutions have to block funds of designated FTO's and their agents. The groups range from the **Abu Nidal** Organisation (ANO), the Group Islamique Armée (GIA) and **Hamas** to **Hizbullah**, **Al Jihad** and the Real IRA.

References

Ahmed Samina, (2001–2002) 'The United States and Terrorism in South West Asia: September 11 and Beyond', *International Security*, vol. 26, no. 3, Winter 2001–02, pp. 79-93.

Booth, K. and Dunne, T. (eds) (2002) *Worlds in Collision: Terror and the Future of Global Order*, Basingstoke and New York: Palgrave Macmillan.

Combs, C. C. (2003) *Terrorism in the 21st Century*, (3rd edn), New Jersey: Prentice Hall.

Falkenrath, R. A., Newman, R. D. and Thayer, B. A. (2000) *America's Achilles' Heel: Nuclear, Biological and Chemical Terrorism and Covert Attack*, Cambridge, MA: MIT Press.

Heymann, P. B. (1998) *Terrorism and America: A Commonsense Strategy for a Democratic Study*, Cambridge, MA and London: MIT Press.

Hoffman, B. (1998) *Inside Terrorism*, London: Victor Gollancz.

Jurgensmeyer, M. (2000) *Terror in the Mind of God: The Global Rise of Religious Violence*, Berkeley and London: University of California Press.

Kingston, R. C. (1992) 'The American Approach to Combating Terrorism', *Terrorism and Political Violence*, vol. 4, no. 3 (autumn), pp. 102–106.

Kushner, H. H. (1998) *Terrorism in America: A Structured Approach to Understanding the Terrorist Threat*, Springfield. IL: C C Thomas.

Maniscalco, P. M. and Christen, H. T. (2002) *Understanding Terrorism and Managing the Consequences*, London: Pearson Education and Upper Saddle River, NJ: Prentice Hall.

Simon, S. and Benjamin, D. (2000) 'America and

the New Terrorism', *Survival*, vol. 42, no. 1 (spring), pp. 59–75.

Further Reading

Bowman, R. (1994) *When the Eagle Screams: America's Vulnerability to Terrorism*, New York: Birch Lane.
— (1998) 'Truth is, We're Terrorised because We're Hated', *National Catholic Reporter*, vol. 34 (October), p. 17.
Donohue, Laura K. (2001) 'In the Name of National Security: US Counter-Terrorist Measures, 1960–2000', *Terrorism and Political Violence*, vol. 13, no. 3, (autumn), pp. 15–60.
Hewitt, C. (2000) 'The Political Context of Terrorism in America', *Terrorism and Political Violence*, vol. 12, nos. 3–4.
Miller, M. and File, J. (2001) *Terrorism Factbook: Our Nation's At War*, Illinois: Bollix Books.
Nash, J. R. (1988) *The American Response to Terrorism – Terrorism in 20th Century: A Narrative Encyclopaedia from the Anarchists through to Weathermen, to the Unabomber*, New York: M. Evans and Co.
Tucker, D. (1977) *Skirmishes at the Edge of Empire: The United States and International Terrorism*, Westport, CT: Praeger.

Urban Guerrillas

The importance of urban guerrilla theories has often been exaggerated and the actions mostly have been in Latin America. Regis **Debray** placed greater emphasis on developing guerrilla warfare than on building a revolutionary party. The appeal of the urban guerrilla was eminently anti-intellectual. In the early 1970s a cult of action emerged in the course of a revolt against the traditional left. The guerrillas were impatient with the pace of developments. The emphasis was upon action, in Uruguay as a means of uniting the left and in Argentina as a way of overcoming a stalemate in the post-war conflict between Peronist and anti-Peronist forces. In Brazil, **Marighella** at times seemed to advocate action for action's sake. Some practitioners of the new variant of the armed struggle claimed that 'objective' revolutionary conditions already existed and presented themselves as a fuse to trigger the explosion.

Urban guerrilla warfare, it was argued, would act as a catalyst to accelerate social and political processes leading to revolution; it would expose the corrupt and oppressive nature of the regimes being challenged while winning mass support through demonstrating the vulnerability of state forces. Under no circumstances did the theory envisage the guerrillas themselves inflicting a military defeat on their enemy; rather, success depended on the guerrilla nuclei developing into people's armies. Originally the Brazilian and Uruguayan guerrillas looked to a rural campaign, but soon realised that what support there was for armed struggle lay in the major cities. The lack of rural potential obliged the insurgents to initiate their struggle in the cities, but in turn rendered the latter suicidal; once urban repression became overpowering; the rebels lacked the option of a secure retreat into the countryside.

Why did they fail? While it is true that the political context in which a guerrilla organisation attempts to develop is an important determinant of the degree of success, general principles as to the optimal conditions for the launching of urban guerrilla campaigns are elusive.

Where possibilities exist for legal mass activity by the population, the initiation or continuation of warfare is likely to engender extreme guerrilla isolation. Urban guerrillas have yet to prosper against well-equipped authoritarian regimes prepared and able to use draconian methods against them.

The most propitious conditions for the implementation of urban guerrilla strategies are either against a quasi-democratic regime inhibited by legal restrictions and electoral considerations from all-out repression, but sufficiently intolerant of democratic opposition for guerrillas to be able to pose credibly as the only viable popular alternative. Or under an authoritarian military regime lacking political legitimacy, already weakened by mass opposition or crisis of some kind, and preparing to return authority to politicians.

Political conditions can and do change during the course of urban guerrilla campaigns. When their enemy is on the defensive, guerrillas can be flexible and modify tactics and strategies to meet new political circumstances; but they cannot retreat when their enemy is on the offensive.

In a war of infiltration and counter-infiltration,

forces drawing upon state resources have an overwhelming advantage, and little can be done by their opponents to over-turn the situation.

Urban guerrillas can be effective through time only if they establish a significant mass base as a source of recruits, auxiliaries, resources and intelligence data. A high degree of isolation is guaranteed by their adopted strategy for a number of reasons. First, urban **guerrilla warfare** is, at least in its origins, a highly elitist form of struggle, embarked upon by would-be vanguards of the masses. It also reflects contempt for the collective struggles of labour. Isolation is very much a question of class. Worker antipathy to the urban guerrilla is an expression of strong economic sentiment and a reformist rather than revolutionary political stance. Urban guerrilla warfare is a physically isolated form of struggle. Since the urban guerrilla operates in the centre of the enemy territory, he cannot establish liberated zones, unlike his rural counterpart. In South America, there was thus no possibility of organising a substantial social, economic and political support base while fighting a guerrilla war in the cities. With regard to guerrilla actions themselves, there was a marked tendency for military operations that were in some way related to popular demands to constitute a declining aspect of urban guerrilla repertoires as campaigns developed.

When the urban guerrillas reached levels of development where open confrontations with the armed forces became technically feasible, their operations became totally divorced from popular activity.

Though many urban guerrillas started out as political activists who regarded armed struggle as an extension of politics by other means, those guerrilla organisations, which grew soon became dominated by military rather than political criteria. As the urban guerrillas developed militarily, and moved on to higher planes of warfare through a

series of leaps, the political wisdom of specific guerrilla actions tended to take second place to considerations of what was technically feasible.

In many campaigns the urban guerrillas would have been more circumspect over promoting armed confrontation had they appraised the strength and capacities of their opponents more accurately. In South America, militarism, in part a product of the weakness of revolutionary parties in the countries concerned was inherent in the logic of urban guerrilla strategy.

Urban guerrilla theory was a defective guide for action, for it failed to explain clearly how guerrilla action would impel the masses to revolutionary deeds. It merely assumed that efficient military operations would galvanise them. Most of the urban guerrilla formations were weak on revolutionary theory and ideologically vague. The commitment of the urban guerrilla was not the only cement holding the groups together but it was considered the most decisive factor in defining who was a revolutionary.

See also: Debray; Guerrilla Warfare in History; Guevara; Marighella.

Reference

Mallin, J. (1971) *Terror and Urban Guerrillas*, Florida: University of Miami Press.

Marighella, C. (1974) *The Mini-manual of the Urban Guerrilla*, Vancouver: Pulp Press.

Further Reading

Moss, R. (1971a) *Urban Guerrillas: The New Face of Political Violence*, London: Temple Smith.

— (1971b) 'Urban Guerrilla Warfare', *Adelphi Papers*, no. 79, London: International Institute of Strategic Studies.

V

Victims

Terrorism purposely uses fear as a means to attain particular ends. It is by nature coercive, dehumanising, theatre of the absurd and designed to manipulate its victims and, through them, a larger audience. The effects of terrorism on society centre on a democracy's peculiar vulnerability to terrorism.

Looking at the impact of terrorism on individual citizens in countries that have consistently borne the brunt of terrorism, such as Argentina, **Egypt**, El Salvador, **Israel**, Italy, **Lebanon**, Nicaragua, Northern **Ireland**, Spain and **Turkey** one notes a serious erosion in the quality of life. Terrorism is exacting a heavy toll on international diplomacy and on the lifestyles and work habits of political leaders, diplomats and business executives the world over. Concerns for personal safety are affecting a widening circle of people, i.e. air travel is now encumbered by the scanning and frisking procedures for travellers who must endure a serious invasion of privacy. Airports, banks, industrial complexes, private and public institutions and even prisons have been affected by terroristic actions.

The fears generated by terrorism and by the possibility of victimisation in an ever widening arena are raising the social costs of the problem, in addition to the economic costs. It does so by weakening the social and political fabric of affected countries and by diverting scarce economic and criminal justice resources from other vital areas.

There are varied circumstances under which individuals may become victims of terrorist acts and these are as varied as the causes of terrorism. Victims can be chosen selectively or at random. In selective terrorism specific groups, such as police, judges, soldiers or prison personnel are targeted. In randomised terrorism, victims are chosen indiscriminately, a method guaranteed to instil maximum fear among the public.

Regardless of the objectives and format of terrorisation, it involves an unpredictable, powerful force, which threatens the victim with annihilation. The experience is immensely stressful and generates in the victim feelings of total helplessness and powerlessness. Terrorisation denies the victim's ability to control his behaviour. The psychological and physical shock characteristics of any severe trauma follow. Since the choice of victim in many terrorist attacks is determined by chance, victims can neither anticipate nor control the event. The multiple threats, to security, bodily integrity and self-esteem, precipitate in most victims a crisis reaction in which the emotions and behaviour of the threatened person are significantly disrupted. A victim faced with the very real possibility of imminent death finds himself unable to muster the necessary physical and mental resources to rise against the assault on his person.

The first phase of the victim's response to terrorisation is concerned with the immediate situation and its experience. The response is one of shock, disbelief, denial and delusion. It is characterised by a paralysis of action and the denial of sensory impressions. Second, there is paralysis of effect, or 'frozen fright', and, unrealistically, victims expect authorities will rapidly rescue them. If victims are not rescued during this period of initial adaptation, the pressures of the situation and terror combine to overwhelm most victims and produce a state of traumatic psychological infantilism. Individuals lose their ability to function as adults and begin to respond instead with adaptive behaviour first learned in early childhood. The identification of the victim with the aggressor becomes a central theme, which has been termed **Stockholm syndrome**.

Victims of terrorism suffer serious and long-lasting damage to their physical, mental and emotional health. Strategies of successful adaptation to the terrorist experience can bring the crisis situation to quick resolution with a minimum of loss of life or injury: keeping one's anxiety level within tolerable limits to remain alert and functional; maintaining one's self-esteem in spite of dehumanising and degrading experiences; preservation of one's relationships with fellow victims and establishing some link with the terrorists without ingratiation. Once caught up in the crisis situation, one's experiences have to be adjusted to the reality of the situation; one has to learn from the coping behaviour of fellow victims and accept constructive criticism without losing one's sense of self-worth and self-esteem.

Pathological transference is found in individuals held hostage by criminal terrorists. Hostage victims become instrumental victims. They are used and exploited by their captors as leverage to force a third party (the family, police or government) to accede to captors' demands. The behaviour of a terrorist victim during captivity cannot be judged or criticised.

Terrorists often assert in their struggle that there are no innocent victims. Nevertheless, human life has value; commitment to this value binds together terrorist, victim and audience in the three-way relationship that characterises modern terrorism and makes activities like hostage negotiation possible. Where the terrorist's aim is to kill, one has assassination; where the terrorist does not value his own life we have suicide; where he values it less than something else, martyrdom; where he sees himself as a soldier who accepts risks of combat, we have a prisoner of war – but not a hostage. Ultimately, where the target of terrorist blackmail does not value individual human life, there is nothing to negotiate. Thus terrorism is not a problem in totalitarian states, but a country like Lebanon, which is conspicuous for the value placed on life and individual rights, has figured disproportionately in the history of modern terrorism.

Terrorism can exist only when and where retributive violence is limited in scope or space. Whereas revenge is limited in space, it is limitless in time. The endurance of revenge and of movements based on vengeance is a major source of discouragement for those who must plan responses to the phenomenon of terrorism.

Grief and mourning may be very much a part of the experience for victims of terrorists. Hostage victims are isolated by their own feelings of guilt and shame: guilt over whether they perhaps should have resisted at the cost of their lives, and shame at having been taken and used. This makes it harder for victims to share experiences with others.

In terrorist incidents, guilt is most likely to become a problem when some hostages have been released before others, or when persons with military or law-enforcement backgrounds have not resisted the hostage-takers with force. Terrorist leaders fight hard to maintain absolute control over the information given to their members and hostages. There has hardly been any real human relationship between the terrorist and his victim before the act that brought them together – and in the case of random bombings, even during the act. A source of strength for the victim of terrorism lies not merely in the possibilities of escape and of coping with stress, but in the possibility of finding the best in the midst of the worst, in the presence of fear and with the memory and possibility of failure.

Terrorisation is very much related to the effect of stress, particularly trauma-induced stress. Children brought up in conditions of constant violence soon become drawn into the terrorist world; although not all children growing up in turmoil and violence become terrorists. Terrorism appears in waves about once every two decades, or about once in every generation. Over time, the ameliorating and exacerbating conditions for a social group are a product of the social system in which they exist.

People who are badly treated and unjustly punished will seek revenge. Even some whose punishment is appropriate will struggle to wreak vengeance on those who imposed that punishment. Once a terrorist incident has occurred, helping efforts must concentrate on reducing the harm it causes. The situation has to be resolved as quickly as possible with a minimum loss of life. Concern for the victims plays a big role in the planning of these interventions and many other political and situational factors also influence decision-makers.

The victim of terrorism holds a special position among victims of premeditated human violence. He or she often represents the government that the terrorist is challenging when he takes his victim hostage. The value of human life is pre-eminent over all other issues in considering responses to human cruelty. Victimisation by terrorists results from groups perceiving conflicts of vital interests, differences in status or differences in beliefs.

See also: Psychology of Terrorism: Fear; Terror and Terrorism.

References

Flynn, E. E. (1987) 'Victims of Terrorism: Dimensions of the Victim Experience' in Wilkinson, P. and Stewart, A. M. (eds) *Contemporary Research on Terrorism*, Aberdeen: Aberdeen University Press, pp. 337–357.

Ochberg, F. M. (1988) 'The Victims of Terrorism' in Moss, R. H. (ed.) *Coping with Life Crises*, New York: Plenum, pp. 367–384.

Waco Siege *see* Cults

War Crimes *see* Crime; Genocide; Organised
Crimes; Rwanda

War on Terror

The report of the Long Commission in the **United
States** into the suicide attacks on the American
marine barracks in Beirut in 1985, advocated a
military response to terrorism in the future. There
was already a strong body of opinion within the
American government that terrorism had to be
viewed as war. Could the military respond?
Defining terrorism as 'war' placed undue pressure
on the military against an ever changing protagonist – **Shi'ite** terrorists in **Lebanon**, leftist groups
in Europe, revolutionary organisations in Latin
America or transnational suicide bombers. Even
the US military cannot be everywhere at once.

The Commission went on to say that fighting
terrorism was not the same as planning for warfare
against an invader. Terrorists did not pay much
attention to military doctrines and force structure
(Simon, 1994). At least the Commission made
people think about how to plan, organise, educate,
train and defend against terrorism and counter-
terrorism. Terrorism is certainly an alternative to
impractical, destructive and expensive conventional
war. Unlike a war situation, governments can cease
to sponsor terrorism when it no longer serves their
purpose. Extradition from a terrorist situation can
be easier than from a war.

Immediately after **September 11** President
Bush predicted a long war on terrorism around the
world. The resulting war against the Taliban and
Al Qaeda in **Afghanistan** brought a clash
between the post-modern forces of the USA and
its allies with the pre-modern units in Afghanistan.
In the time since the autumn of 2001 it has been
seen as a clash between Islamic radicals and Arab
governments which the USA is trying to influence.
It is clear that America needs the police and
intelligence capabilities of other states to track and
apprehend terrorists.

The war on terrorism will have to be broadened
in some observers' views to cover a larger group of
Islamic radicals and Muslims for whom religious
identity overrides political values. In 1991 George
Bush, senior, said that the then military action
against Iraq would make possible a 'New World
Order, a world where the rule of law not the law of
the jungle would govern the conduct of nations'. In
any war between the civilised world and terrorism,
Islam would be the scapegoat and this greatly
concerns the many millions of law abiding Muslims.
This has made the Arab world suspicious of US
intentions. Many countries in the West have
extensive Muslim communities and an invading
and more violent war on terrorism with growing
numbers of Muslim victims would strain and
possibly break multi-culturalism.

Since **September 11** the American objective
has become one of frustration, demoralising and
beating back at Al Qaeda and its associated groups.
Victory will be a matter of degree and unlikely to
be decisive.

It perhaps has to be accepted that one cannot
conduct a war against terrorists – one can only try

to wipe them out, if one is strong enough. Increasingly there is a loser definition being applied to terrorism to perhaps try to win the war. Even after a war on terrorism with all its endless bloodshed and horrors, there perhaps has to be some negotiation and compromise. Yet there is a willingness of Al Qaeda to continue fighting when all is apparently lost.

The September 11 events with attacks on the symbolic and substantive core of American primacy in the world together with the genocidal ethos of the perpetrators, has provided an American response committed to total victory.

The war against terrorism is to protect the freedoms and tolerant spirit of pluralist societies. There is a need to keep the focus on long-term goals and not be carried away by political expediency and narrow military objectives.

The problem of, and solution to, terrorism has similarities. Terrorism not only threatens the free, secular world but also springs from rejection of democracy/secularism. Societies which breed terrorists have to be radicalised and demoralised.

To many analysts the war against terrorism must not be turned into an ideological battle to serve one's strategic interests.

Nearly everyone will agree that terrorism can be stemmed only through concerted, sustained international effort. As an intractable and recurrent phenomena in world history, terrorism has to be fought with diplomatic, economic, political, military and legal instruments.

Different facets of political violence came together on September 11. First, terrorism or the deliberate killing of innocent civilians for political ends. Second, political suicide or the use of agents who kill themselves for political ends and third the mass destruction, or deliberate killing of thousands of people in a single operation.

Each has had a long history, but the combination and integration of them into the attacks of September 11 and the threat of future attacks by Islamic terrorists has created a new kind of warfare.

Since then, the USA has waged war against Islamic terrorists on two different fronts – the war on the foreign front against Al Qaeda, the Taliban and other radical groups and governments (Iraq for instance) in the region and the war on the domestic front which began with measures against terrorist

cells in the USA. The war against terrorism is characterised by systematic organisation; intense concentration of killing power achieved through the high technology of the time and the ruthless and relentless continuation of the war until the enemy, and its support has been annihilated.

Even in the post-modern era of **globalisation** and multiculturalism, the current Western or post-Western civilisations in the future may not be able to develop the effective means to defend themselves against transnational terrorist networks of global reach.

References

Carr, C. (1996/7) 'Terrorism as Warfare: The Lessons of Military History', *World Policy Journal* (winter), pp. 1–12.

Carter, A., Deutsch, J. and Zelikour, P. (1998) 'Catastrophic Terrorism: Tackling the New Danger', *Foreign Affairs*, vol. 77, no. 6 (Nov–Dec), pp. 80–94.

Kurth, J. (2002) 'The War and the West', *Orbis*, vol. 45, no. 3 (spring), pp. 321–332.

Raufer, X. (1999) 'New World Disorder, New Terrorism: New Threats for Europe and the Western World', *Terrorism and Political Violence*, vol. 11, no. 4 (winter), pp. 30–51.

Simon, J. D. (1994) *The Terrorist Trap: America's Experience with Terrorism*, Bloomington, IN: Indiana University Press.

Williams, Prof. G. L. (2002) *Can Terrorism be Defeated?* TUCETU/Atlantic Council UK. Annual Conference, 9 February.

Further Reading

Booth, K. and Dunne, T. (eds) (2002) *Worlds in Collision: Terror and the Future of Global Order*, Basingstoke and New York: Palgrave Macmillan.

Dobson, C. and Payner, R. (1987) *The Never Ending War*, New York: Facts on File.

Klare, M. T. and Kornbluh, P. (eds) (1988) *Low Intensity Warfare: Counter-insurgency, Pro-insurgency and Anti-Terrorism in the1980s*, New York: Pantheon Books.

Livingstone, N. (1982) *The War against Terrorism*, Lexington, MA: Heath.

Rivers, G. (1986) *The War against Terrorists: How to Win It*, New York: Stein and Day.

Whittaker, D. J. (2002) *Terrorism: Understanding the Global Threat*, Harlow and London: Pearson Education.

Weapons

The nature of the weapons and explosives used in terrorist attacks depends very much on the location and the funding for the operations. Typical sources are purchased from or supplied by a sympathetic state or stolen from military depots. They can be purchased through criminal contacts or modified sporting weapons. Some have been stolen during attacks on security forces personnel i.e. police hijacks in **Ireland**. High quality replica manufacture takes place in some **Third World** countries such as **Afghanistan**. Improvisation can occur as with IRA mortars. Weapons can be obtained by coercion from legitimate sources i.e. mining explosives. Past conflict arms caches built up during the Second World War were utilised during the anti-colonial pro-independence struggles in the 1950s and 1960s.

Weapons have considerable emotional significance for the terrorist, more so than for the average soldier or police officer. The weapon is the symbol of power, and a great psychological boost.

Almost any small arms weapon can be a guerrilla weapon, including sub-machine guns, grenades, pistols, automatic rifles, mortars and rocket launchers.

Dynamite has been used by many groups – IRA, the Shining Path in **Peru**. Plastic explosives have been used by the IRA. Grenades have been used by terrorists such as **Abu Nidal** and **Carlos**, by the Khmer Rouge and the IRA. However, the IRA's most common weapon is the mortar which has been used by them at home and abroad. Sniper rifles have been utilised by the IRA and by individuals such as the 'Washington Sniper' in 2002. Pistols and rifles have been used widely and in the USA for example these can be bought over the counter relatively cheaply.

Such weapons can be obtained legally, or on the black market, or by plain theft. Some weapons can be made in the home as in the USA and experimentation can occur with explosives. These terrorists can be very innovative, and can study the weaponry of counter-terrorist organisations in order to outsmart the anti-terrorist hunters. They can be technically 'on the ball' and flexible in their approach.

The most pressing current threat is that of the individual or small group with simple automatic weapons. Equally frightening is the attack by a group with professional skills and a medium-grade conventional weapon, or a surface-to-air missile (SAM) or heat-seeking missiles (Stingers). They caused the destruction of a French jumbo jet over Niger in 1989 and the loss of two Sri Lankan planes in 1995.

More likely than ever in the coming decades is a highly skilled group with a weapon of mass destruction (WMD).

See also: Bio-terrorism.

References

Barnaby, F. (1997) *Instruments of Terror: Mass Destruction Has Never Been so Easy*, London: Vision.

Dobson, C. and Payne, R. (1982) *The Terrorists, Their Weapons, Leaders and Tactics*, New York: Facts on File.

Further Reading

Cameron, G. (1999) *Nuclear Terrorism: A Threat Assessment for the 20th Century*, Basingstoke: Macmillan.

Falkenrath, R. A., Newman, R. D. and Thayer, B. A. (1998) *America's Achilles Heel: Nuclear, Biological and Chemical Terrorism and Covert Attack*, Cambridge, MA: The MIT Press.

Hurley, J. A. (1999) *Weapons of Mass Destruction: Opposing Viewpoints*, San Diego, CA: Greenhaven Press.

Laqueur, W. (2001) *The New Terrorism: Fanaticism and the Arms of Mass Destruction*, London: Phoenix Press.

Tomkins, T. C. (1986) 'The Terrorist Arsenal Part 1 and Part 2', *TVI Report*, vol. 6, nos. 3/4, pp. 27–33, 51–56.

Western Europe

During the **Cold War**, Western Europe became a region for active terrorist activity due to the democratic nature of the government, their membership of NATO and free movement through the area. Middle East terrorist activity was a major security and political problem for most countries in Western Europe long before Islamic fundamentalism became a global concern. Many of these countries (Germany, Spain, the **United Kingdom**, France, Italy, Greece, Portugal and Belgium) were confronted with a serious indigenous terrorist threat from various separatist and Marxist revolutionary groups. The most active and dangerous of these groups were the Red Army Faction and the Revolutionary Cells in Germany; the Red Brigades in Italy; Action Directe, and the Corsican National Liberation Front in France; the Popular Forces of April 25 in Portugal; the Popular Revolutionary Struggle and the November 17 Group in Greece; the Basque separatist movement (ETAM) in Spain; the Fighting Communist Cells in Belgium and the Irish Republican Army in the UK. On 15 January 1985 the RAF and Action Directe issued a joint statement announcing the formation of a united front to combat NATO imperialism.

The continent was attractive for a number of reasons. It provided these groups with a pool of potential manpower which facilitated the building and maintenance of a logistical infrastructure. As at the present time, large communities of Middle Eastern origin, especially students, live in West European countries and businessmen and tourists have frequently travelled to Western Europe. This makes it easy for Middle Eastern terrorist groups to send in operators who can not only blend into the environment but also receive logistical aid from sympathisers and in-country supporters.

The area offers these groups' geographical proximity and compactness, excellent transport and relatively easy cross-border movement. It is easy to get to Western Europe and move around between countries. Groups can be offered abundant, easy and attractive targets. Middle East terrorists carry out attacks against three targeted sectors: Israeli or Jewish, Western, and Arab or Palestinian. The public-city spotlight is broader and brighter in Western Europe than in most other regions. Groups can be provided with a substitute battleground in which to carry out their inter-Palestinian and inter-Arab feuds. The majority of the attacks carried out by Middle Eastern terrorist groups are aimed at other Arab and Palestinian targets; the authoritarian nature of the Arab regimes at home and tight Israeli security measures make it difficult for these groups to operate within Israel. It is less risky and operationally easier to attack Libyan, Syrian, Iranian, Iraqi and Israeli targets.

The types of targets generally ranged from ambassadors, embassies, consular buildings, airline offices and restaurants, to American military bases, mosques, synagogues, railways, buses and multinational corporations. In some cases the attacks were direct retaliations for terrorist events in the Middle East and aimed to secure the release of Arabs imprisoned in European jails for terrorist crimes in various Western European countries.

Since the end of the Cold War terrorism has revolved around focus-based terrorism or **organised crime** related terrorism. Nationalism, ethnicity and religion will drive international terrorism in Europe – due to the clashes between other civilisations imported by refugees and immigrants. The clash between nationalism and religions has fuelled the fires of violence in Bosnia. Aspects of Islamic terrorism have shown the clarity of the relationship between immigrant communities and political violence.

Terrorism exists within society at all times. The distribution of terrorist events may prove to be a leading indicator of the changing character of international conflict (Taylor and Horgan, 2000).

Citizens or residents of Western European countries have been exceptionally common targets of attack carried out by racist right-wing groups in Austria, Germany, Sweden and elsewhere against Muslim residents in these countries. Increasing attacks over the past decade have also occurred on eastern European refugees in the West.

See also: Counter/Anti-terrorism; Organised Crime.

References

Alexander, Y. and Myers, K. A. (eds) (1982) *Terrorism in Europe*, London: Croom Helm.

Clutterbuck, R. L. (1990) *Terrorism, Drugs and Crime in Europe after 1992*, London: Frank Cass.

Lodge, J. (1989) 'Terrorism and the European Community: Towards 1992', *Terrorism and Political Violence*, vol. 1, no. 1 (January), pp. 28–40.

Schmid, A. P. and Crelinstein, R. D. (1993) *Western Response to Terrorism*, London: Frank Cass.

Shackley, T. G., Oatman, R. L. and Finney, R. A. (1990) 'Euro-terrorism', *Chief Executive*, May, pp. 46–50.

Taylor, M. and Horgan, J. (eds) (2000) *The Future of Terrorism*, London: Frank Cass.

Further Reading

Chalk, P. (1996) *Western European Terrorism and Counter-Terrorism: The Evolving Dynamic*, New York: St Martin's Press.

Horchem, Hans J. (1986) 'Terrorism in Western Europe' in Clutterbuck, R. (ed.) *The Future of Political Violence*, London: Macmillan, pp. 145–158.

Lodge, J. (ed.) (1981) *Terrorism: A Challenge to the State*, Oxford: Martin Robertson.

Mommsen, W. J. and Hirschfield, G. (1982) *Social Protest, Violence and Terror in 19th and 20th Century Europe*, London: Macmillan.

Taylor, M. and Horgan, T. (1999) 'Future Developments of Political Terrorism in Europe', *Terrorism and Political Violence*, vol. 11, no. 4.

Vercher, A. (1992) *Terrorism in Europe: An International Comparative legal Analysis*, Oxford: Clarendon Press.

Wilkinson, P. (ed.) (1981) *British Perspectives on Terrorism*, London: Allen and Unwin.

— (1994) *Terrorism: British Perspectives*, New York: Prentice Hall.

Women

In certain guerrilla and terrorist groups such as the Tupamaros in Uruguay, the Montoneros in Argentina, and some of the Japanese groups, women act as collectors of intelligence, taking part in operations as couriers, nurses and medical personnel, and maintaining safe houses for weapons, funds and supplies.

Leftist groups tend to be an exception, sometimes having female leaders; Leila Khaled and Fusako Shigenobu were leaders of the Popular Front for the Liberation of Palestine and the Japanese Red Army respectively; Norma Aristoto was co-founder of the Montoneros in Argentina; Genoveve Tarat played a key role in ETA and Margerite Cagol in the Italian Red Brigades.

Most female terrorists act in a supportive capacity. They play a useful role because several women living together is perceived as more usual than a group of men. Posing as wives and mothers, female terrorists can enter areas where males cannot go. In the early 1970s women formed a third of the operational personnel of the Baader-Meinhof group in Germany, and have taken part in robberies, burglaries and kidnappings.

Unmarried women terrorists are the rule except in the Tupamaros. Women usually work in a familiar or specific area, with many having an urban background. There is a general lowering of the entry age into operational activity, and some women have been operationally trained and undertake operational leadership roles. Many women have the nomadic lifestyle of the groups and have a desire for action and money.

Women in armed struggle become totally interchangeable with their male comrades in arms. In the revolutionary world, women and men are identical in all their functions to the point of losing or renouncing even their own function as mothers. In the context of subversion, women appear to be forced to renounce their femininity to transform themselves into non-conformist beings. For many women armed subversion was seen as an adventure (Valentini and Neuberger, 1996).

To many women terrorists all individuality in armed bands disappears; one becomes the struggle, the objective, the function and the signal. Women in an armed struggle, arguably lose contact with 'everyday woman' as a result of their militancy. Some women terrorists have argued that they fight for the freedom to be a woman, which they have had to do throughout human history.

During the 1990s, a number of women in Palestinian movements became effective suicide bombers.

Abortion violence has been instigated by pro-choice and feminist groups in the United States and direct action emerged in an effective manner from the mid-1980s. They sought to close abortion facilities by demonstrations, sit-ins and invasions (Griset and Mahan, 2003: 113).

From 1977 until 1983 over twenty incidents of arson and bombing were reported; and there have been fluctuations in the level of violent activity since that period. Between 1991–94, over seventy actual and attempted arson and bombings were recorded. The campaign shifted to direct assaults and murders of physicians and clinic staff. Since the late-1970s to date nearly 250 bombings and arson attacks have been reported, plus five murders and eleven attempted murders. Additionally there have been clinic invasions, kidnapping, hate mail campaigns and bomb threats. Arguably this could be viewed as a form of organised terrorism.

References

Griset, P. L. and Mahan S. (2003) *Terrorism in Perspective*, Thousand Oaks, CA, London and New Delhi: Sage Publications, Inc..

Reif, L. L. (1986) 'Women in Latin American Guerrilla Movements: A Comparative Perspective', *Comparative Politics*, vol. 18, no. 2, pp. 147–170.

Valentini, T. and Neuberger, L. de C. (1996) *Women and Terrorism*, London: Macmillan Press.

Further Reading

Blee, K. (2002) *Inside Organised Racism: Women in the Hate Movement*, Berkeley, CA: University of California Press.

Jenkins, P. (1999) 'Fighting Terrorism as if Women Mattered: Anti-Abortion Violence as Unconstructed Terrorism' in Ferrell, J. and Websdale, N. (eds) *Making Trouble: Cultural Constructions of Crime Deviance and Control*, New York: Aldine de Gruyter.

Khaled, L. (1975) *My People Shall Live: The Autobiography of a Revolutionary*, New York: Bantam Books.

Longrigg, C. (1997) *Mafia Women*, London: Chatto and Windus.

World Affairs since 2001

The events of **September 11** changed everything especially international security, and ushered in asymmetric warfare. Prior to September 11 acts of **terrorism** causing mass outrages were hypothetical. Post-September 11 showed bizarrely that the era of science fiction had become reality. There was a surge of Muslim anger and frustration. The **United States** led economic boom had been precariously poised and globalisation appeared to have stagnated so September 11 was a great shock.

The USA was shocked by its own vulnerability and by the feeling that people hated them across the globe; yet the American people recovered quickly and within a year New York had returned to a degree of normality. By early 2002 it was clear there were going to be huge risks for the USA to spread the war to **Iraq**. The Western aligned Islamic nations remained stable but for how long?

South-East Asia became unstable through **Al Qaeda** threats just like **Afghanistan** and **Pakistan**. By the end of 2002 Indonesian democracy had been undermined by Islamic extremism and there were warnings of Al Qaeda threats in Malaysia, **Philippines**, Singapore and Thailand.

Regarding many **Third World** countries and most of the African continent in particular the events of September 11 forced their issues off the global international affairs agenda. There was a growing and indeed urgent need for greater fairness in sharing the benefits of globalisation and for the West to stop blocking markets to poor countries.

India and **Pakistan** remained tense as nuclear powers and tried to use September 11 as an excuse to pursue 'terrorists' in Kashmir. The global problem of terrorism has remained but how to deal with it effectually has opened a Pandora's Box.

On the Israel/Palestine question, the hawks see the peace process on both sides as dead. Indeed, the status of Jerusalem in the future is a core issue for the whole Middle East. Sadly but perhaps inevitably the malaise in the Muslim world both internally and externally has continued. **Islam** is a multidimensional issue – both domestic and foreign.

In 2003 the **Iraq** issue still holds sway on the world stage. The war ending in April after six weeks was deemed a victory for the USA and UK forces but a worry is that Iraq could break up along racial lines – Arabs, Kurds, Marsh Arabs and **Shi'ites**. Saddam Hussein has held Iraq together and its collapse could create a vacuum which would destabilise its neighbours – **Iran**, **Syria** and **Turkey**. Fighting still occurs in some areas of Iraq and coalition forces are seeking UN involvement to stop the fighting.

In the Israeli/Palestinian impasse it appears that both Sharon and **Arafat** may have to go in order to get any resumption of peace talks. The issue with **North Korea** over that country's recommissioning of a nuclear power plant was a concern to the USA. They had no military option due to consequences for South Korea and **Japan** (within artillery and missile range of North Korea).

In Africa, the events at Mombassa saw a connection with problems in Iraq and the Middle East. American potency appeared to be rallying Muslim support for **Osama Bin Laden** in Africa, especially in Kenya, Nigeria and Somalia.

For the United States, the war against terror continues and if there are not too many attacks on the US homeland then President Bush would be seen as a wartime leader.

A new **Cold War** could develop in this decade – commencing with Iraq, North Korea and the war against terrorism (ranging from the large-scale war versus Al Qaeda to small-scale operations by US troops in the southern Philippines).

See also: September 11: Homeland Security.

World Trade Center Attack 1993

In February 1993 at the World Trade Center in New York, as a result of explosives being smuggled into the building, a vehicle bomb exploded in the underground car park beneath the Center, killing six and injuring 1,000 (Drake, 1998). With their technological awareness Islamic radicals who perpetrated this bomb inspired to topple one of the twin towers on to the other and release simultaneously a deadly cloud of poisonous gas. The Sunni extremists had obtained a fatwa from Sheikh Omar before planning their attack (Hoffman, 1998).

Al Qaeda recruited, trained and financed Ramzi Yousef to bomb one of the World Trade Center towers. He was trained in **Afghanistan** and Palestinian-based.

The attack was on a global symbol of financial and economical activity and proved that the **USA** was as vulnerable to terrorism as any country around the globe. The perpetrators say it was to protest at the American political, economic and military support for **Israel** and the rest of the dictator states in the region.

The bombing raised fundamental questions about dealing with terrorism in an open, democratic society. There were calls for better physical security at large office buildings and tourist facilities. The prevailing view, however, was that if terrorists are allowed to change the way people live or negatively affect a country's national or international interests, they will have achieved a victory. There was little panic after this attack. The groups consisted of young militants who acted on their own initiative and who had established links with one or more of the states sponsoring terrorism but were not under their full control. Nevertheless it must be said that if this bomb had been filled with nuclear material it would have been sufficient to destroy lower Manhattan (Laqueur, 2001).

References

Drake, C. T. M. (1998) *Terrorists' Target Selection*, New York: St Martin's Press.

Hoffman, B. (1998) *Inside Terrorism*, London: Victor Gollancz.

Laqueur, W. (2001) *The New Terrorism: Fanaticism and the Arms of Mass Destruction*, London: Phoenix Press.

Simon, J. D. (1994) *The Terrorist Trap: America's Experience with Terrorism*, Bloomington, IN: Indiana University Press.

Further Reading

Mylroie, L. (2001) *Study of Revenge: The First World*

Trade Center Attack and Saddam Hussein's War against America, Washington, DC: The AEI Press.

Z

Zionism

This is a Jewish nationalist movement which emerged during the nineteenth century on a tide of European nationalism and was formally established in 1897. The Congress defined its political aim as the establishment of a Jewish national home in Palestine. Jewish immigration into Palestine (Aliyah) was encouraged through the Jewish National Fund (founded 1901) and the Jewish Agency for Palestine (1929). Since the formation of the state of Israel in 1948 the Zionist movement has continued to foster Aliyah and support for and interest in Israel.

In the Arab world, Zionism became the personification of Satan, the demonic force out to ruin the self-esteem and way of life of the Arab peoples. This was countered by such a group as the Union for the Land and People of Israel, set up by some extreme nationalist spirit rabbis to promote new settlements and a harsh line toward the Arabs. In 1995 the Israeli Prime Minister Yitzhak **Rabin** was killed by a Jewish religious militant, Yigal Amir, who was convinced he was carrying out the will of God as any martyr of **Hizbullah** or **Hamas**. Rabin through talking peace with the Palestinians, was seen by him as a traitor and his government a threat to the survival of Israel and the Jewish people. It occurred at a time when the extreme right in Israel had invited their young militants to commit acts of violence (Hoffman, 1998).

Israeli inspired terrorism has not come close to the successes and support that was achieved in the years leading to the creation of the state. The Irgun Zvai Leumi (National Military Organisation) was ably led by Menachem Begin. He used daring and dramatic acts of violence (such as the bombing of the *King David Hotel* in Jerusalem in July 1946), to attract international attention to Palestine and highlight the Zionists' grievance against Britain as the mandated power in the region, and their claims for statehood. The British had overwhelming numerical power in Palestine but were unable to destroy the Irgun Zvai Leumi and maintain order in Palestine.

See also: Hamas; Hizbullah; Palestine Liberation Organisation; Rabin.

Reference

Hoffman, B. (1998) *Inside Terrorism*, London: Victor Gollancz.

Further Reading

Bell, J. B. (1996) *Terror Out of Zion: The Fight for Israeli Independence*, New Brunswick, NJ: Transaction Publishers.

FILMS AND DOCUMENTARIES

The following films illustrate different aspects of terrorism and political violence.

100 Years of Terror, Produced by the History Channel, Videocassette Series, A&E Home Video (2000).

Air Force One (Paramount, 1997, 123 mins)
Deals with kidnap situation by terrorists of the US Presidential plane with President, his family and US government advisers aboard.

Betrayed (Metro-Goldwyn-Meyer, 1988, 112 mins)
Right-wing supremacist anti-US government inspired terrorism.

CIA: America's Secret Warriors (Discovery Channel, 1997, 2 vols, 50 mins each)
US role in international terrorism.

Crimson Tide (Hollywood Pictures, 1995, 115 mins)
Story about global nuclear crisis between Russia and USA spawned by terrorists, set in Russian and US submarines.

Four Days in September (Miramax, 1998, 110 mins)
Examines demands inflicted when terrorists kidnap an ambassador.

Killing Fields, The (Warner Bros. 1984, 142 mins)
Depicts state-sponsored terrorism.

Little Drummer Girl, The (Warner Bros. 1984, 130 mins)
Highlights women's role in terrorism.

Michael Collins (Warner Bros. 1996, 132 mins)
History of the Irish Republican Army (IRA).

One Day in September (Columbia Tri-Star, 1999, 91 mins)
Deals with the kidnapping of Israeli athletes at the Munich Olympics in 1972.

One Day in the Life of Ivan Denisovich (Leontes-Norsk Films, 1970, 100 mins)
Life in a Soviet labour camp in the Stalin era.

Salvador (Hemdale 1986)
The account of guerrilla war in Salvador in the 1960s, 1970s and 1980s.

Siege, The (20th Century Fox, 1998, 120 mins)
Threat from military in response to terrorism.

Sum of all Fear, The (Paramount, 2002, 119 mins)
Story of nuclear terrorism and the aftermath of a nuclear detonation on US soil.

The Battle of Algiers (Magna Film, Igor Film, Cabash Films, 1966)
Examines the Algerians' fight against French colonial rule in the 1950s.

World Trade Center: Anatomy of the Collapse, produced Darlow Smithson, Film and TV Videocassette Discovery Communications Inc (2001).

WEBSITES

Organisations

Al Fatah
www.fatah.net

Al Jazeera (Qatar)
www.aljazeera.net

Al Qaeda
see under Osama Bin Laden

Al Qaeda 'Training Manual'
www.usdoj.gov/ag/trainingmanual.htm

Animal Liberation–Animal Liberation Front
Envirolink.org/ALF/orgs/alforg.html

Amnesty International
www.amnesty.org

Army of God
http://www.armyofgod.com

Baader Meinhof
www.baader-meinhof.com

Central Intelligence Agency (CIA)
www.cia.gov/cia/public

CIA World Factbook
http://www.odci.gov/cia/publications/factbook

Co-ordinator for Counter Terrorism Department
of State
www.state.gov/www/global/terrorism

Counter-Terrorism

http://www.counterterrorism.com

US State Dept Office of Counter-Terrorism

www.state.gov/www/global/terrorism/index.html

Crisis Management–Federal Emergency management Agency
www.fema.gov/library/terror.html

Diplomats–links from diplomatic/security viewpoints
http://www.alt.gov/policy/terrorism

East Africa Bombing
http://www.fbi.gov/majcases/eastafrica

Eco-Terrorism
http://www.enviroweb.org/nocompromise/features/supportall.html

Education

Jane's Information Group
www.janes.com

Terrorism Research Centre
http://www.terrorism.com/terrorism/index

Library of Congress
http://lcweb.loc.gov/catalog/

Yahoo: Full coverage service on terrorism
http://fullcoverage.yahoo.com/full_coverage/US/Terrorism

Centre for Study of Terrorism and Political Violence
http://www.st_and.ac.uk/academic/intrel/research/cstpu

International Policy Institute for Counter Terror N Ireland Conflict http://cain.ulst.ac.uk/index.html

RAND Corporation
www.rand.org/publications/RB/RB75

Terrorism: Bibliography covering American Texts
http://www.touson.edu/

Egypt
http://www.ummah.org.uk/ikhuran/index.html

Emergency Response
http://www.emergency.co/cntrterr.html

ETA (Basques) (2001)
http://www.basque-red.net/homei.html

FARC (Colombia) (2002)
http://www.farc-ep.org/pagina_ingles/

Federal Bureau of Investigation (FBI)
www.fbi.gov

Foreign Terrorist Organisations
www.state.gov/www/global/terrorism/terror-org.htm

Globalisation: Global Terrorism
http://www.globalterrorism

Hizbullah (1998, 2002)
http://www.hizbullah

Hamas
www.palestine-info.com/hamas
http://www.hamas.org

Human Rights–International Human Rights Watch
http://www.hrw.org/

Interpol
www.interpol.int

Irish Republican Army (IRA) (1998)
http://www.sinnfein.org

Japan (1998)
http://Aum-Shinrikyo.com/enlish
http://www.geocities.com/comlb/JRA.html

Kurdish Workers (1998 & 2002)
http://www.pkk.org

Media
http://dir.yahoo.com/News_and_Media/News papers/Web_Directory

http://fullcoverage.yahoo.com/Full_Coverage/US/Terrorism/

Moslem Brotherhood Movement
http://www.ummah.net/ikhwan

Oklahoma (Bombing) Counter-terrorism
http://www.escape.com/warning/dogpound.html

Osama Bin Laden (linked under Al Qaeda)
http://www.ict.org.il/default.htm

Palestine: Islamic Jihad
http://www.jihadislamic.com/

Peru: Shining Path Group
http://wwwcsrp.org/index.html
(1998, 2002)
 http://www.blythe.org/peru-pep

Popular Front Liberation Palestine
http://members. tripod.com/-freepalestine

Tamil Tigers (1998, 2002)
http://www.eelam.com

Terrorism–Defined at a variety of different sources
http://www.be.pl.lib.md.us/www.ict.org.ill/articles/define.html

Terrorism–Democracy and Technology
http://www.heroes.net

Terrorism–Group Profiles
http://www.ict.org.il/

Terrorism–International Conventions
http://www.state.gov/www/global/terrorism/980817-terror-conv.html

Terrorism Research Center, USA
http://www.terrorism.com/welcome.html

Terrorism - Security Issues: US Commission on National Security in 21st Century
www.ceip.org.npp

Terrorism in USA
http://www.fbi.gov/publish/terror/terroris.html

US Dept of US Army and Homeland Defence
http://hidsbccom.army.mil

Unabomber
www.time.com/time/reports/unabomber/manifesto_toc.html

United Nations
www.un.org

USA State Department
http://www.state.gov/www/global/human-rights/
index.html

US Dept. Homeland Security
www.whitehouse.gov/homeland

Weapons of Mass Destruction (WMD)
http://wchd.neobright.net

TERRORISM – A HISTORICAL TIMELINE

1st century AD	The Zealot Sect founded
11th century AD	Assassin movement active against Islamic faith and Crusaders
14th to 15th centuries AD	Christian led pogroms of Jews in Central Europe.
19th century AD	Russian revolutionaries became first anti-state dissidents
1848	Communist manifesto published
1865	Ku Klux Klan founded in Tennessee, USA
20th century AD	Revolutionaries commonly resorted to terrorism to overthrow existing governments.
1915	Ottoman Turks committed genocide against its American population
1916	Easter Rising in Ireland by Irish republicans to try to end British rule
1930s and 1940s	Political purges and terror in Soviet Union and Holocaust in Germany
1941–1975	Struggle of communists in French Indo-China to win power – especially Vietnam
1961–1996	Guatemalan civil war including state sponsored massacres and death squads
October 1967	Che Guevara's death in Bolivia – a hero for the far Left
June 1969	Carlos Marighella completed his *Mini-Manual of the Urban Guerrilla*
September 1972	Members of Black September kidnapped Israeli athletes at the Olympic village in Munich and later all were killed in the rescue attempt
1975–1979	Khmer Rouge government in Cambodia committed acts of genocide against its own people
December 1975	Carlos the Jackal seized hostages at the OPEC meeting in Vienna and fled to Algeria.
October 1977	West German commandos attacked an airport at Mogadishu in Somalia to rescue hostages after a Lufthansa plane had been hijacked by the Red Army Faction
March 1978	Former Italian Prime Minister Aldo Moro kidnapped in Rome and later murdered by the Red Brigade
April 1980	An attempt to rescue American hostages held in the US Embassy in Tehran, Iran since 1979 was aborted when rescue aircraft had mechanical problems
1990s	The end of the Cold War spelt the end for hard Left movements across Europe and their sponsorship for terrorism ended
1992–2000	Thousands killed in Algeria in fighting between Islamic extremists and the government.
1992	Bosnia Herzegovina declared independence from Yugoslavia.

	Bosnian Serbs refused to accept and this led to widespread civil war in Yugoslavia	September 11, 2001	World Trade Center attack in New York by Islamic extremists. Nearly 3,000 people from 80 countries killed
1994	Rwanda genocide between Hutu and Tutsi tribes began after Rwandan President murdered	February 2002	Religious fighting between Hindu and Moslem mobs in India
March 1995	Aum Shinrikyo cult released Sarin nerve gas into Tokyo underground	June 2002	Homeland Security measures enacted in USA to combat terrorism
April 1995	Bombing of Federal building in Oklahoma City by right-wing American extremists	2002–2003	Hamas and Al Aqsa Islamic extremist inspired attacks against Israel within Israel increase in ferocity with hundreds of casualties.
2001–2002	Use of suicidal 'human bombs' developed during Palestinian intifada		

Index